A COMPARATIVE LAW ANALYSIS OF NO-FAULT
COMPREHENSIVE COMPENSATION FUNDS

A COMPARATIVE LAW ANALYSIS OF NO-FAULT COMPREHENSIVE COMPENSATION FUNDS

International Best Practice and Contemporary Applications

Kim Watts

Cambridge – Antwerp – Chicago

Intersentia Ltd
8 Wellington Mews
Wellington Street | Cambridge
CB1 1HW | United Kingdom
Tel: +44 1223 736 170
Email: mail@intersentia.co.uk
www.intersentia.com | www.intersentia.co.uk

Distribution for the UK and
Rest of the World (incl. Eastern Europe)
NBN International
1 Deltic Avenue, Rooksley
Milton Keynes MK13 8LD
United Kingdom
Tel: +44 1752 202 301 | Fax: +44 1752 202 331
Email: orders@nbninternational.com

Distribution for Europe
Lefebvre Sarrut Belgium NV
Hoogstraat 139/6
1000 Brussels
Belgium
Tel: +32 (0)2 548 07 13
Email: mail@intersentia.be

Distribution for the USA and Canada
Independent Publishers Group
Order Department
814 North Franklin Street
Chicago, IL 60610
USA
Tel: +1 800 888 4741 (toll free) | Fax: +1 312 337 5985
Email: orders@ipgbook.com

A Comparative Law Analysis of No-Fault Comprehensive Compensation Funds.
International Best Practice and Contemporary Applications
© Kim Watts 2023

The author has asserted the right under the Copyright, Designs and Patents Act 1988,
to be identified as author of this work.

No part of this book may be reproduced, stored in a retrieval system, or transmitted, in any form, or
by any means, without prior written permission from Intersentia, or as expressly permitted by law or
under the terms agreed with the appropriate reprographic rights organisation. Enquiries concerning
reproduction which may not be covered by the above should be addressed to Intersentia at the
address above.

Artwork on cover: © 'Solidarity' by Vanessa van Gasselt

ISBN 978-1-83970-298-3
D/2023/7849/5
NUR 820

British Library Cataloguing in Publication Data. A catalogue record for this book is available from
the British Library.

ACKNOWLEDGEMENTS

I would like to thank Professor Thierry Vansweevelt and Professor Britt Weyts, both of the University of Antwerp. They created the opportunity for the research that underpins this book to take place, and selected me to undertake it. I am very grateful for their guidance and support, especially during the upheaval of the COVID-19 pandemic. I would also like to thank Professor Bernard Dubuisson (Université Catholique de Louvain), Professor Jonas Knetsch (Université Paris 1 Panthéon-Sorbonne), Professor Daniel Gardner (Université Laval) and Professor Rianka Rijnhout (Universiteit Utrecht) for their helpful critiques and insights.

I would like to especially thank the staff of the Accident Compensation Corporation, the Manitoba Public Insurance Corporation, the Société de l'assurance automobile du Québec and the Transport Accident Commission. Their cooperation and generosity of time was extremely helpful, and has enhanced the relevance and impact of the research conclusions.

Essential to any comparative law research effort of this size are insights, comments and critiques from knowledgeable experts. It would be impossible to list all those who have provided helpful comments and suggestions, but I would like to especially acknowledge the input of: Dr Wannes Buelens, Dr Simon Connell, Warren Forster, Dr Andrew Fronsko, Professor Genevieve Grant, Dr Sonia Macleod, Professor Geoff McLay, Dr Tina Popa, Associate Professor Māmari Stephens and Associate Professor Stephen Winter. Also essential are the insights, comments and critiques of one's colleagues – so I would like to thank my University of Antwerp colleagues too, especially Larissa Vanhooff.

The strongest critiques of one's work are usually from those closest to you. I thank my husband Regan for his cheerfully blunt views on my research, and his ongoing support and guidance.

Finally, I would like to dedicate this work to the memories of Sir Owen Woodhouse and Professor Patrick Atiyah QC. Their eloquent and perfectly clear writing on the subject of no-fault compensation is something that I have strived to emulate – but of course, could never replicate.

Intersentia

CONTENTS

Acknowledgements. v
List of Cases xiii
List of Legislation and Regulations. xvii

Chapter 1. Introduction 1

1. Overview 1
2. Key Questions Addressed in this Book 3
3. The International Landscape of Compensation Funds 4
   3.1. General Overview 5
   3.2. Focus: No-Fault Comprehensive Compensation Funds. 11
4. General Legal Definition of Compensation Funds 15
5. Specific Definition of a No-Fault Comprehensive Compensation Fund 16
6. Further Comments on Compensation Theory. 20
7. A Note on Methodology 22

**Chapter 2. Analysis of Core Problems in the Classification of
Compensation Funds** 27

1. Introduction 27
2. The Distinction between Social Security Schemes and No-Fault
   Comprehensive Compensation Funds. 27
3. The Distinction between Insurance and Compensation Funds as
   a Redress Solution. 30
4. The Relationship and Distinction between the Concepts of 'No-Fault'
   and '*Ex Gratia*'. 33
5. Should Historical Abuse Compensation Schemes be Included within
   the Definition of a Compensation Fund? 36
   5.1. How have Historical Abuse Schemes been Addressed by
        Other Legal Scholars? 37
   5.2. The Purpose of Payments in a Historic Abuse Scheme: Symbolic
        or Compensatory? 41
   5.3. Do Any Existing Historical Abuse Compensation Funds Fit
        within this Definition?. 44
   5.4. What Further Information is Needed to Better Study this Field?. 46
   5.5. Are Research Findings about No-Fault Comprehensive Funds
        Applicable to Historical Abuse Funds? 47

Contents

6. Can Such Varied Compensation Funds and Legal Traditions be
   Effectively Compared? 48
7. Conclusions 50

**Chapter 3. Review of Existing No-Fault Comprehensive Compensation
Funds** 53

1. Introduction 53
2. New Zealand's Accident Compensation Corporation (ACC) 53
   2.1. The Background to the ACC Scheme 54
   2.2. Legislative Structures and Relevant Doctrines. 57
        2.2.1. *Davies v New Zealand Police* 63
        2.2.2. *McGougan v DePuy International Limited*. 63
        2.2.3. *Accident Compensation Corporation v Calver
               (Estate of Trevarthen)* 65
        2.2.4. The Status Quo: Consistent Inconsistency. 66
   2.3. The Scope of the ACC Scheme. 68
   2.4. The Effect of the ACC Scheme 73
   2.5. Comparison with Other Compensation Fund Structures 78
3. Australia: Victoria's Transport Accident Commission (TAC) 81
   3.1. The Background to the TAC. 82
   3.2. Legislative Structures and Relevant Legal Doctrines 84
   3.3. The Scope of the TAC Scheme 86
   3.4. The Effect of the TAC Scheme 89
   3.5. Comparison with Other Australian Compensation Funds
        and Schemes 92
        3.5.1. Summary 92
        3.5.2. Traffic Accident Compensation. 92
        3.5.3. Worker Injury and Work-Related Disease
               Compensation 97
        3.5.4. Medical Injury. 99
   3.6. The TAC in the Context of the National Injury Insurance
        Scheme Roll-Out 100
4. Canada: No-Fault Comprehensive Compensation Funds for
   Transport Injury in Québec and Manitoba. 103
   4.1. The Background to the Société De L'assurance Automobile
        Du Québec (SAAQ) and Manitoba Public Insurance (MPI) 105
   4.2. Legislative Structures and Relevant Legal Doctrines 108
   4.3. The Scope of the SAAQ and MPI 112
   4.4. The Effect of the SAAQ and MPI and their Roles
        in Context 116
   4.5. Comparison of the SAAQ and MPI with Traffic Injury Schemes in
        Saskatchewan and Ontario 119

viii

Intersentia

4.6.	Reform Efforts Toward Comprehensive No-Fault in British Columbia and Alberta		121

4.6. Reform Efforts Toward Comprehensive No-Fault in British
Columbia and Alberta 121
4.7. Comparison with the Canadian No-Fault Comprehensive
Worker Compensation Landscape. 123
4.8. Comparison with the Wider Canadian Compensation
Landscape 126
4.8.1. Québec Vaccine Injury Compensation Program and the
Impending Federal Vaccine Injury Support Program 126
4.8.2. Wider Canadian Compensation Landscape 127
5. Comparison and Analysis of Selected Compensation Funds by
Purpose 128
5.1. Complete Departure in Purpose 130
5.2. Partial Revolution in Purpose 132
6. Comparison and Analysis of Selected Compensation Funds by
Function. 133
6.1. Traffic-Related Injury. 134
6.1.1. E-Scooters 136
6.1.2. Automated Vehicles 140
6.1.3. Out-of-Jurisdiction Drivers. 145
6.2. Medical and Pharmaceutical 146
6.3. Employment Injury 148
6.4. General Injury Risks 149
6.4.1. What is an Eligible Form of Harm? 150
6.4.2. What is the Right Way to Extend or Limit the Scope
of Eligibility? 151
6.4.3. Why are Economic Losses not Included, as these are
also a General Injury Risk? 152
6.4.4. Should Anybody have Limits Placed on their Ability
to Recover Compensation? 153
7. Principled Comparison with the French and Belgian Approach. 153
7.1. The French and Belgian Compensation Fund Landscape 155
7.2. Overview of the Belgian and French Medical Injury
Funds 156
7.3. Functional and Purposive Comparison of Medical
Injury Compensation. 157
7.4. Overview of French and Belgian Guarantee Funds for
Automobile and Terrorism Victims. 161
7.5. Functional and Purposive Comparison of General Risks
Compensation. 163
7.6. Problem: Does 'Solidarity' Mean the Same Thing as 'Community
Responsibility'?. 164

Contents

8. Principled Comparison with the Nordic Approach.................... 168
    8.1. Overview of the Nordic Compensation Funds for Medical
        and Pharmaceutical Injury 169
    8.2. Functional and Purposive Comparison of General Risks
        Compensation in the Nordic Countries 170
    8.3. Functional and Purposive Comparison of Medical Injury
        Compensation in the Nordic Countries 171
9. Conclusions 175

Chapter 4. Key Pillars 179

1. Introduction 179
2. Establishment: Key Philosophical Steps and Challenges............... 180
3. Operations: Paying Compensation to Claimants.................... 188
4. Establishment and Administration: Quantum and Purpose of
   Compensation.. 198
    4.1. Theoretical Underpinnings................................... 198
    4.2. Structuring of Compensation................................ 201
    4.3. Conclusions on Quantum and Purpose 214
5. Operations: Resolving Disputes about Claims Effectively 215
    5.1. Overview of Dispute Resolution Process for Each Fund 216
        5.1.1. ACC Dispute Resolution 216
        5.1.2. TAC Dispute Resolution 221
        5.1.3. SAAQ and MPI Dispute Resolution.................... 223
    5.2. Survey of Funds and Analysis............................... 226
    5.3. Conclusions on Dispute Resolution.......................... 235
6. Administration: Funding and Sustainability......................... 236
    6.1. New Zealand's ACC Scheme................................ 238
    6.2. Victoria's TAC.. 257
    6.3. Québec's SAAQ... 263
    6.4. Manitoba's MPI... 268
    6.5. Conclusions on Funding and Sustainability.................... 273
        6.5.1. Fully-Funded 273
        6.5.2. Publicly Underwritten and Operating at a Low
            Capitalisation Rate 274
        6.5.3. Reliance on Levies and Investment Income 275
        6.5.4. Supervision of Levy-Setting and Independent
            Investment Management 276
        6.5.5. Reinsurance 276
        6.5.6. Injury Prevention and Rehabilitation.................... 277
        6.5.7. Limited Scope for Financial Reform 278

x

Intersentia

Contents

| | 6.5.8. | Full Compensation for Limited Categories | 278 |

| | 6.5.9. | Financial Interaction with Other Health and Support Structures | 279 |

7. Subrogation, Public Tort Liability and/or Reimbursement. 279
8. Conclusions 294

Chapter 5. Human Rights, Access to Justice and Dispute Resolution 299

1. Introduction 299
2. The Four Funds' Relationship with Human Rights Legislation and Case Law 302
    2.1. Australia. 303
        2.1.1. Historical and Contemporary Context 303
        2.1.2. The Intersection with Issues Relevant to No-Fault Comprehensive Compensation Funds. 305
        2.1.3. The Intersection with Other Compensation Funds 314
    2.2. New Zealand 318
        2.2.1. Historical and Contemporary Context 318
        2.2.2. The Intersection with Issues Relevant to No-Fault Comprehensive Compensation Funds. 320
    2.3. Canada 338
        2.3.1. Historical and Contemporary Context 339
        2.3.2. The Intersection with Issues Relevant to No-Fault Comprehensive Compensation Funds. 341
        2.3.3. The Intersection with Other Compensation Funds 350
    2.4. Europe: A Simple Structural and Analytical Comparison 355
        2.4.1. The Intersection between European Human Rights Frameworks and Private Law Generally 357
        2.4.2. Access to Justice Rights: The Right to a Fair Trial and an Effective Remedy 358
    2.5. Conclusions of Legislation and Case Law Comparative Exercise 368
3. The No-Fault Comprehensive Compensation Fund and Access to Justice. 370
    3.1. Defining Access to Justice 370
    3.2. The No-Fault Comprehensive Compensation Fund as an Enhancer of Access to Justice 372
    3.3. The No-Fault Comprehensive Compensation Fund as a Barrier to Access to Justice 375
4. Conclusion. 380

Intersentia

xi

Contents

Chapter 6. Compensation Fund Goals and Practical Applications 383

1.   Introduction 383
2.   Realistic Legal Goals for Existing No-Fault Comprehensive
     Compensation Funds 388
     2.1.   Improved Coherency of Purpose and Legislative Design 390
            2.1.1.   New Zealand's ACC 391
            2.1.2.   Victoria's TAC 395
            2.1.3.   Québec's SAAQ 397
            2.1.4.   Manitoba's MPI 398
            2.1.5.   Conclusions on Improved Coherency and Legislative
                     Design 399
     2.2.   Improvements to Financial Mechanisms and Supervision 400
     2.3.   Better Compensation for Specific Categories of Claimants 403
     2.4.   Effective Use of Subrogation 406
     2.5.   Compulsory Legislative Reviews and Planning Mechanisms 409
     2.6.   Direct Legislative Consideration of Human Rights Law
            Intersections and Better Access to Legal Information 412
3.   New Applications of Big No-Fault Compensation Funds 415
     3.1.   Artificial Intelligence Applications 416
            3.1.1.   Automated Vehicle Applications: Possibilities
                     and Problems 418
            3.1.2.   Healthcare Applications: Possibilities and Problems 422
     3.2.   A Comprehensive No-Fault Compensation Fund for COVID-19
            Vaccine Damage 426
4.   Conclusions on Goals and Practical Applications 436

Chapter 7. Conclusions 441

1.   Introduction 441
2.   Research Question 1 442
3.   Research Question 2 447
4.   Research Question 3 449
5.   Goals for Further Research 451

Bibliography 453
Index 485

xii   Intersentia

LIST OF CASES

AUSTRALIA (VICTORIA)

Dawson v Transport Accident Commission [2010] VCAT 644 . . . . .310–311, 313
Kracke v Mental Health Review Board [2009] VCAT 646 .311, 313
Lavrick v Lease Auto Pty Ltd [2002] FCA 599 308
Primary Health Care Ltd v Giakalis [2013] VSCA 75 307
Rekatsinas v Transport Accident Commission [2010] VCAT 967 . . . . .311, 313
Shafton v Victoria [2016] VCAT 971 312
Swannell & Transport Accident Commission v Farmer [1998] VSCA 104 . . . . .308, 313
Sweedman v Transport Accident Commission [2006] HCA 8 . . . . 91, 114,
129, 308, 351
Tanska v Transport Accident Commission [2000] VSC 56 88
Transport Accident Commission v Katanas [2017] HCA 32 .87, 395
Transport Accident Commission v Lanson [2001] VSCA 84; [2001] 3 VR 250 . . . . . .309, 313
Transport Accident Commission v Lease Auto Pty Ltd [2002] FCAFC 430 308
Wilson v Nattrass [1995] VicSC 233, (1995) 21 MVR 41 . . . . .307, 313

AUSTRALIA (OTHER)

Attorney-General (Cth); Ex rel Mckinlay v Commonwealth (1975) HCA 53 303
Coco v The Queen [1994] HCA 15 305
Ha v New South Wales [1997] HCA 34 262
Plaintiff S157/2002 v Commonwealth of Australia [2003] HCA 476 306
Public Service Association of South Australia v Federated Clerks' Union of
    Australia & others (1991) 173 CLR 132 305
Rodway v R [1990] HCA 19 306
TRG v The Board of Trustees of the Brisbane Grammar School (2019) QSC 157 46

CANADA (MANITOBA)

Lejins v Manitoba Public Insurance Corporation 2004 MBCA 171 346
Manitoba Public Insurance Corporation v Paul [1985] 4 WWR 714 348
McMillan v Rural Municipality of Thompson [1996] 6 WWR 563 342
McMillan v Thompson (Rural Municipality) (1997) 144 DLR (4th) 53 . . . . .108, 342
Mitchell v Rahman [2002] MBCA 19 118
Troller v Manitoba Public Insurance Corporation 2019 MBQB 157 349

List of Cases

CANADA (QUÉBEC)

Beauchamp v Procureure générale du Québec 2017 QCCS 5184 342
Bouliane v Commission scolaire de Charlesbourg (1984) CS 323 119
City of Westmount v Rossy [2012] SCC 136 117–118
Downer v Procureure générale du Québec et Société de l'assurance
    automobile du Québec 2019 QCCS 1280............................117–118, 345
Downer v Procureure générale du Québec et Société de l'assurance
    automobile du Québec (CA) 2019 QCCA 1893 ....117–118, 345
Fédération des employées et employés de services publics inc v
    Béliveau St-Jacques [1996] 2 SCR 345 353–354
Godbout v Pagé et al 2017 SCC 18; [2017] 1 SCR 283 ....31, 107, 116–118,
    129, 342
J.A. v Société de l'assurance automobile du Québec 2010 QCCA 1328........ 115, 151–152,
    343–344, 354, 397
Lapierre v Attorney General (Quebec) (1985) 1 SCR 241 126
Lepage v Québec (Société de l'assurance automobile) 2015 QCCS 1606............... 347
Lepage v Société de l'assurance automobile du Québec 2019 QCCS 1195 347
Lepage v Société de l'assurance automobile du Québec 2019 QCCA 1981............. 347
Roy v Québec (Société de l'assurance automobile) 2016 QCCS 3920 345

CANADA (OTHER)

British Columbia v Imperial Tobacco Canada Ltd [2005] SCC 49 352
Campisi v Ontario 2017 ONSC 2884.. 351
Campisi v Ontario (Attorney General) 2018 ONCA 869........................... 351
Christie v British Columbia (Attorney General) 2005 BCCA 631.................... 340
Daley v Economical Mutual Insurance Company (2005) 206 OAC 33 (CA)........... 352
Hernandez v Palmer (1992) CarswellOnt 65 ....352, 354
Medwid v Ontario (Minister of Labour) (1988) CarswellOnt 937 352–354
Morrow v Zhang 2009 ABCA 215 352
Moxham v Canada [1998] 2 FC 441 350
Nordquist v Gurniak 2003 SCC 59... 114
Trial Lawyers Association of British Columbia v British Columbia (Attorney
    General) 2014 SCC 59.. 339
Whitbread v Walley [1988] BCJ No. 733 (CA)................................... 352

NEW ZEALAND

Accident Compensation Corporation v Ambros [2007] NZCA 304 45
Accident Compensation Corporation v Calver (Estate of Trevarthen)
    [2021] NZCA 211 ....65, 131
Accident Compensation Corporation v Ng [2018] NZHC 2848 174
Adlam v Accident Compensation Corporation [2017] NZCA 457 174
Alderson v Accident Compensation Corporatioin [2009] NZHRRT 33 336
Allenby v H [2012] NZSC 33.. 74

xiv

Intersentia

List of Cases

Calver v Accident Compensation Corporation (Estate of Trevarthen)
  [2019] NZHC 1581 ....65, 129
Crawford v Accident Compensation Corporation [2019] NZACC 77 158
Crockett v Accident Compensation Corporation [2018] NZACC 11 329
Davies v New Zealand Police [2009] NZSC 47 ....63, 74, 214
Freeborn v Accident Rehabilitation and Compensation Insurance
  Corporation [1998] NZHC 194 331
Hardie v Accident Compensation Corporation [2002] NZACC 256 330
Harrild v Director of Proceedings [2003] 3 NZLR 289 332
Heads v Attorney-General [2015] NZHRRT 12 335–337
J v Accident Compensation Corporation [2017] NZCA 441 378
L v Robinson [2000] 3 NZLR 499 74
McGougan v DePuy International Limited [2016] NZHC 2511 .... 63–65, 77, 144, 284
McGougan v DePuy International Limited [2018] NZCA 91 .... 63–65, 77, 144, 392
P v Attorney-General [2010] NZHC 959 ....74, 185
Pou v British American Tobacco (New Zealand) Limited [2006]
  1 NZLR 661 74
Quake Outcasts v Minister of Canterbury Earthquake Recovery
  [2017] NZCA 332 79
Queenstown Lakes District Council v Palmer [1998] NZCA 190 74
Sinclair v Accident Compensation Corporation [2015] NZACC 231 331
Telford v Accident Compensation Corporation [2016] NZACC 25 329–330
Trevethick v Ministry of Health [2008] NZCA 397 .... 171, 320–321, 338
van Soest v Residual Health Management Unit and Ramstead [1999]
  NZCA 206 74
Vivash v Accident Compensation Corporation [2020] NZHRRT 16 ....333–334, 337
Wikeepa v Accident Rehabilitation and Commpensation Insurance
  Corporation [1998] NZAR 402 217
Williams v Accident Compensation Corporation [2017] NZHRRT 26 ....333–334, 337

OTHER

Allen and others v Depuy International Ltd (2015) EWHC 926 64
Ashingdane v United Kingdom (1985) (Application no. 8225/78) 362
Bellet v France (1995) (Application no. 23805/94) 365
Boxus v Région wallonne C-128/09, ECLI:EU:C:2011:667 359
DEB Deutsche Energiehandels- und Beratungsgesellschaft mbH v
  Bundesrepublik Deutschland C-279/09, ECLI:EU:C:2010:811 359
Döry v Sweden (2002) (Application no. 28394/95) 362, 366
Erdinç Kurt and Others v Turkey (2017) (Application no. 50772/11) 359
Fayed v United Kingdom (1990) (Application no. 17101/90) 365
Ferrazzini v Italy (2001) (Application no. 44759/98) 363
Fexler v Sweden (2011) (Application no. 36801/06) 362
Filip v Waterloo (City) (1992) 98 DLR (4th) 534 352
Göç v Turkey (2002) (Application no. 36590/97) 360
Golder v United Kingdom (1975) (Application no. 4451/70) 363
Hill v Chief Constable of West Yorkshire [1989] AC 53 363

List of Cases

J, R (on the application of) v London Borough of Enfield [2002] EWHC 432
(Admin). 310
Jurica v Croatia (2017) (Application no. 30376/13). 359
König v Germany (1978) (Application no. 6232/73) 363
Lithgow & Others v United Kingdom (1986) (Application no. 9006/80). 363
Lundevall v Sweden (2002) (Application no. 38629/97) 362
McElhinney v Ireland (2001) (Application no. 31253/96). 365
Miller v Sweden (2005) (Application no. 55853/00) 362
Nagy v Hungary (2017) (Application no. 56665/09) 364
*N.W, L.W and C.W. v Sanofi Pasteur MSD SNC, Caisse primaire
d'assurance maladie des Hauts-de-Seine & Carpimko* C-621/15,
ECLI:EU:C:2017:484 432
O'Keeffe v Ireland (2014) (Application no. 35810/09) 357
Osman v Ferguson [1992] EWCA Civ 8 . . . . .363–364, 368
R v London Borough of Enfield, Ex Parte Bernard [2002] EWHC 2282
(Admin). 310
Roche v United Kingdom (2005) (Application no. 32555/96). 363
Rogers v Faught (2002) 212 DLR (4th) 366. 352
Salomonsson v Sweden (2002) (Application no. 38978/97). 366
Schuler-Zgraggen v Switzerland (1993) (Application no. 14518/89) 362
Trade Agency Ltd v Seramico Investments Ltd C-619/10, ECLI:EU:C:2012:531 359
Unibet (London) Ltd and Unibet (International) Ltd v Justitiekanslern C-432/05,
ECLI:EU:C:2007:163 359
Vasileva v Bulgaria (2016) (Application no. 23796/10). 359
Vereniging Milieudefensie et al v Royal Dutch Shell plc C/09/571932,
ECLI:NL:RBDHA:2021:5337 22
Volker und Markus Schecke GbR and Hartmut Eifert v Land Hessen Joined
cases C-92/09 and C-93/09, ECLI:EU:C:2010:662 367
Z & Others v United Kingdom (2001) (Application no. 29392/95) 364, 368
Zumtobel v Austria (1993) (Application no. 12235/86). 368

LIST OF LEGISLATION AND REGULATIONS

AUSTRALIA (VICTORIA)

Accident Compensation Act 1985
Charter of Human Rights and Responsibilities Bill 2006
Charter of Human Rights and Responsibilities Act 2006
Compensation Legislation Amendment Act 2018
Limitation of Actions Amendment (Child Abuse) Act 2015
Transport Accident Act 1986
Transport Accident Amendment Act 2016

AUSTRALIA (OTHER)

Motor Accident Injuries Bill 2019 (Australian Capital Territory)
Motor Accident Injuries Act 2019 (Australian Capital Territory)
Motor Accidents (Liabilities and Compensation) Act 1973 (Tasmania)
Motor Vehicle (Catastrophic Injuries) Act 2016 (Western Australia)
Motor Vehicle (Catastrophic Injuries) Regulations 2016 (Western Australia)
National Disability Insurance Scheme Act 2013 (Commonwealth)
National Injury Insurance Scheme Act 2016 (Queensland)
National Redress Scheme for Institutional Child Sexual Abuse Act 2018
    (Commonwealth)
Territory Insurance Office (Sale) Act 2014 (Northern Territory)

CANADA (MANITOBA)

Highway Traffic Act, C.C.S.M. c. H60
The Manitoba Public Insurance Corporation Act, C.C.S.M. c. P215

CANADA (QUÉBEC)

Act respecting Héma-Québec and the biovigilance committee 2013, c. 11, s. 16.
Act respecting industrial accidents and occupational diseases, CQLR c. A-3.001
Act respecting the Société de l'assurance automobile du Québec 1990, c. 19, s. 1.
Automobile Insurance Act, CQLR c. A-25

List of Legislation and Regulations

Autonomous Bus and Minibus Pilot Project, CQLR c. C-24.2, r. 37.01
Charter of Human Rights and Freedoms, CQLR c. C-12
Highway Safety Code, CQLR, c. C-24.2
Projet pilote relatif aux trottinettes électriques en location libre-service, C-24.2, r. 39.1.3

CANADA (OTHER)

Attorney General Statutes (Vehicle Insurance) Amendment Act 2020 (British Columbia)
Council Directive 2004/80/EC of 29 April 2004 relating to compensation to crime victims
European Convention on the Compensation of Victims of Violent Crimes 1983
European Parliament resolution of 20 October 2020 with recommendations to the
    Commission on a civil liability regime for artificial intelligence (2020/2014(INL))
Government Employees Compensation Act 1985 (R.S.C., 1985, c. G-5) (Federal)
The Automobile Accident Insurance Act, RSS 1978, c. A-35 (Saskatchewan)

NEW ZEALAND

Accident Compensation Act 1972
Accident Compensation Act 1982
Accident Compensation Act 2001
Accident Compensation Amendment Bill (49-1) 2018
Accident Compensation (Motor Vehicle Account Levies) Regulations 2019
Accident Insurance Bill (203-1) 1999
Accident Insurance Act 1998
Accident Rehabilitation and Compensation Insurance Act 1992
Code of ACC Claimants' Rights 2002
Crown Entities Act 2004
Fair Trading Act 1986
Health and Safety at Work Act 2015
Injury Prevention, Rehabilitation, and Compensation Bill (90-3) 2001
Injury Prevention, Rehabilitation and Compensation Act 2001
New Zealand Bill of Rights Act 1990
Royal Commission of Inquiry into Historical Abuse in State Care and in the Care of Faith-
    based Institutions Order 2018
Social Security Act 2018
Victims of Crime Reform Bill (319-1) 2011
Workers' Compensation for Accidents Act 1900

CHAPTER 1

INTRODUCTION

1. OVERVIEW

This book begins with some broad normative philosophical questions about the function and purpose of compensation and liability law. How should societies effectively and efficiently compensate for damage and loss? Legal, social and financial systems in different jurisdictions use a variety of tools to remedy an unexpected loss due to injury or other misfortune. Tort law damages are the classic common and civil law (private law) tool; contracts of insurance (another private law tool) and social security protections (a public law tool) may supplement or replace tort law damages (or the loss falling on the victim's own pocket) depending upon the circumstances.

Despite the best efforts of actuarial and economic experts, it is challenging to predict or pre-emptively design a compensation system that is suitable for every type of misfortune. What remedy is there for individuals who cannot (or cannot easily) access compensation for their loss via existing compensation systems, such as insurance or the courts system? Can legal experts such as judges, legislators and policymakers design a fair and efficient way to provide speedy compensation to a wider range of victims? What is the distinction between misfortune caused by a discrete event of damage and misfortune caused by an ongoing condition or circumstance? Further, in an increasingly 'supranational' and highly digitised world, facing global compensation challenges, can we (and should we) harmonise how compensation is managed in different jurisdictions? There are injuries and misfortune caused by human actions, and increasingly, injuries caused by automated and technology actions. The world is also dealing with a global pandemic that requires a global vaccination programme, which will inevitably result in some injured individuals. We may be coming to a point where we need to consider whether, and in what circumstances, there is in fact a right to be compensated for some kinds of misfortune. However, such a right potentially conflicts with other rights that are often classified as fundamental, such as the right to access justice via the courts.

Alternative compensation systems, such as no-fault compensation funds, have been utilised in different ways in the past century by a variety of jurisdictions to try and answer these general questions, and to solve broader social risk problems. The mid-twentieth century (a generally prosperous era for Western societies) was a time where the concept of no-fault compensation funds and a quest for wider social security supports received much legislative interest. In contrast, the late twentieth century and early twenty-first century saw a political and ideological shift back towards private allocation of loss in many jurisdictions.[1] But compensation funds and alternative access to justice structures are growing in popularity again, as dissatisfaction emerges with existing systems of loss allocation, protection for human rights and socio-economic rights, and support for different types of misfortune. Compensation funds in different jurisdictions have varying functions and objectives. However, a handful of jurisdictions have taken compensation funds' use to their most extreme manifestation – a single publicly-managed structure that provides a near or complete replacement for tort law remedies. These funds feature streamlined quasi-insurance claims management and accessibility for clients – as well as reduced access to the courts in the event of disputes.

To date, there has not been a comparative law analysis of the most comprehensive and publicly-managed types of no-fault compensation funds with one another, along with an application of the relevant research conclusions from such an analysis to the wider landscape. Furthermore, despite the organic growth of compensation funds as a popular alternative compensation mechanism in multiple jurisdictions, there is no comprehensive body of comparative law jurisprudence and debate that analyses and refines all recent developments. It would not be possible for this book to meet that comprehensive need, but it is possible for this study to address the gap in relation to no-fault *comprehensive* compensation funds in particular.

Fortunately, there have recently been some significant leaps forward by other legal scholars with regard to redress schemes and compensation funds generally, particularly in relation to personal injury and medical incidents.[2]

---

[1] This was most clearly espoused in the common law world by the late lawyer and legal philosopher Patrick Atiyah. Although he once favoured publicly administered no-fault compensation systems, Atiyah later concluded that first-party insurance in most cases (and no-fault compensation in the case of motor accidents) was a better solution due to the apparent impending collapse of the welfare state, and because the concept of the state or society compensating for misfortune generally had fallen out of favour. See PS Atiyah, *The Damages Lottery* (Hart Publishing 1997). However the position has changed in the context of a post-Great Financial Crisis world in the 2010s with growing inequality, instability in Western ideals of democracy and a blurring of lines about the causes and effects of misfortune. Atiyah's predictions on this point in *The Damages Lottery* (an otherwise fascinating and vitally important work), now read rather like Francis Fukuyama's now outdated and naïve views that Western society had achieved a pinnacle of development in the post-Cold War era – Francis Fukuyama, *The End of History and the Last Man* (Free Press 1992).

[2] Jonas Knetsch, *Le Droit de La Responsabilité et Les Fonds d'indemnisation : Analyse En Droits Français et Allemand* (LGDJ 2013) <https://docassas.u-paris2.fr/nuxeo/site/esupversions/f60b2840-bda3-453e-8626-788d7c4de001>; Sonia Macleod and Christopher Hodges, *Redress Schemes for Personal Injuries* (Hart Publishing 2017); Matti Urho, 'Compensation for Drug-Related Injuries' (2018) 4 *European Review of Private Law* 467; Warren Forster,

Chapter 1. Introduction

However there remains an urgent need for more work in this area.[3] There is also a need to understand how compensation funds impact or can be reconciled with fundamental human rights concepts, especially if legislatures choose to create more no-fault comprehensive compensation funds that redirect or restrict access to the courts.[4] There is also unresolved conflict between legal scholars about how compensation funds should work in tandem with (or as a replacement for) insurance and social security.

This book makes a significant contribution to the comparative law landscape of compensation funds in general, identifying the key characteristics and principles of the world's most comprehensive no-fault compensation funds that are managed by public authorities and their relevance to the general field of compensation funds. This book also advances the law by analysing the interaction between no-fault comprehensive compensation funds and human rights principles. This book's analysis also considers these funds' contemporary application to multi-jurisdiction risk problems. Finally, this book proposes a number of legal goals for the best future development of no-fault comprehensive compensation funds.

2. KEY QUESTIONS ADDRESSED IN THIS BOOK

The analyses in this book therefore aim to answer the following three questions:

a. What are the key characteristics of no-fault comprehensive compensation funds and the key pillars, common to multiple jurisdictions, for the successful establishment, administration, operation and further development of no-fault comprehensive compensation funds?
b. What is the interaction between comprehensive no-fault compensation funds and human rights law, principles of access to justice and practical dispute resolution issues?

Tom Barraclough and Tiho Mijatov, 'Solving the Problem: Causation, Transparency and Access to Justice in New Zealand's Personal Injury System' (2017) New Zealand Law Foundation Research Reports p 10; Tiho Mijatov, Tom Barraclough and Warren Forster, 'The Idea of Access to Justice: Reflections on New Zealand's Accident Compensation (or Personal Injury) System' (2016) 33 *Windsor Yearbook of Access to Justice* 197.

[3] A recently published update to one of the key common law compensation law texts openly acknowledges that the development of compensation law theory needs reinvigoration: 'It is deeply regrettable that scholarly interest in … compensation has waned, to the great impoverishment of public debate, which now tends to be dominated by interest groups and partisan politics.' Peter Cane and James Goudkamp, *Atiyah's Accidents, Compensation and the Law* (9th edn, Cambridge University Press 2018) xx.

[4] Thierry Vansweevelt and others, 'Comparative Analysis of Compensation Funds' in Thierry Vansweevelt and Britt Weyts (eds), *Compensation Funds in Comparative Perspective* (Intersentia 2020).

Intersentia

3

c. How can no-fault comprehensive compensation funds be used to address contemporary legal problems common to multiple jurisdictions?

This book aims to develop a substantial and detailed comparative law analysis of the world's most comprehensive no-fault compensation fund systems. Where necessary and methodologically appropriate, there is a comparative assessment of the research conclusions with other frameworks, such as functionally relevant non-comprehensive compensation funds in relevant civil European jurisdictions. The comprehensive no-fault compensation funds that will be analysed in detail exist in New Zealand, the Australian state of Victoria, and the Canadian provinces of Québec and Manitoba. These jurisdictions have all developed and are actively using very big compensation funds in novel ways that cross the borders of social insurance, private insurance, tort liability, public law and human rights law. By looking at the different systems we can see indeed that there is a reflexive relationship between concepts of liability, insurance and dispute resolution.[5] No-fault 'liability', something of a misnomer, is usually a key feature of a compensation fund,[6] and the decision to choose a no-fault system or a different fault model is also particularly revealing of a society's loss allocation preferences. A comparative law analysis of no-fault comprehensive compensation funds enables the identification of the 'Key Pillars' of these expansive and truly revolutionary compensation funds that are applicable to multiple jurisdictions. This kind of comparative law analysis also enables conclusions to be drawn about the future development of very big compensation funds.

3. THE INTERNATIONAL LANDSCAPE OF COMPENSATION FUNDS

This section sets out an overview about what is currently known about compensation funds in general and no-fault comprehensive compensation funds in particular. We can begin with a general overview, and then discuss no-fault comprehensive compensation funds specifically.

This approach has been used to present briefly the general landscape of compensation funds, and to highlight the special nature of no-fault

---

[5] Erik S Knutsen, 'A Reflexive Approach to Accident Law Reform' in Eoin Quill and Raymond J Friel (eds), *Damages and Compensation Culture: Comparative Perspectives* (Bloomsbury Publishing 2016).

[6] Ken Oliphant, 'Landmarks of No-Fault in the Common law', *Shifts in Compensation between Private and Public Systems (Tort and Insurance Law Vol. 22)* (Springer 2007) <http://link.springer.com/10.1007/978-3-211-71554-3_3>.

comprehensive compensation funds within the wider field. Because of its overlap with other legal structures of redress and compensation, 'compensation funds' is a field that remains frustratingly unrefined. One of the goals of this book is to provide greater clarity of definition in relation to no-fault comprehensive compensation funds in particular, as a sub-category of the rather nebulous 'compensation funds and redress schemes' field. Therefore, this detailed overview sets the scene of a fluctuating landscape, before helping to define it and then beginning to study it.

3.1. GENERAL OVERVIEW

Internationally, there is a rapidly growing mosaic of compensation funds of different shapes and sizes. Compensation funds are created by different jurisdictions and international actors to address the perceived inability of existing judicial, insurance and/or social security frameworks to adequately compensate (either partially or fully) a class of individuals that have suffered loss in different circumstances.[7] Compensation funds have been created in different jurisdictions to compensate victims of misfortune which has had a pecuniary and/or non-pecuniary impact on individuals. A basic definition is:

> 'an alternative compensation scheme in the form of capital meant for the compensation of victims whose damage is the consequence of certain circumstances, described by law. Eligibility is not connected with potential contributions paid by the victim, nor with the extent of the risk'.[8]

These funds operate in areas ('functions') including general personal injury and loss,[9] motor accident injury,[10] medical treatment injury[11] (including

---

[7]   Willem H van Boom and Michael Faure, 'Introducing "Shifts in Compensation Between Private and Public Systems"' in Willem H van Boom and Michael Faure (eds), *Shifts in Compensation between Private and Public Systems (Tort and Insurance Law Vol. 22)* (Springer 2007) 13; Larissa Vanhooff, Thierry Vansweevelt and Britt Weyts, 'So Many Funds, so Many Alternatives: Compensation Funds as a Solution for Liability Issues in Belgium, the Netherlands and the United Kingdom' (2016) 8 *European Journal of Commercial Contract Law* 41, 41.

[8]   Vanhooff, Vansweevelt and Weyts (n 7) 42; Knetsch (n 2) 499.

[9]   Such as the scheme administered by New Zealand's Accident Compensation Corporation.

[10]   Such as the comprehensive compulsory and non-compulsory publicly administered schemes in New Zealand, Victoria, Québec, Manitoba and Saskatchewan. More limited funds relating to the compensation of individuals for losses caused by the actions of unidentified or untraceable drivers exist in many jurisdictions.

[11]   Such as New Zealand and Nordic countries' comprehensive no-fault cover for treatment injuries, and the more limited no-fault compensation available for medical injury in France and Belgium.

pharmaceutical injury[12] and birth-related injuries[13]), cause-limited disability (including workers' dust disease injuries[14]), and criminal injury (including terrorism[15] and historical harms[16]). Where worker injury compensation schemes are managed by a single public authority and claims paid out of a single pot, that can be categorised as a compensation fund too.[17] Funds for economic losses flowing from natural disasters or uninsurable natural disaster losses also exist.[18]

---

[12] New Zealand and Nordic countries again. In the wake of the COVID-19 pandemic and vaccination campaign, Canada announced that it would establish a federal Vaccine Injury Support Program – see 'Call for Applications: Vaccine Injury Support Program – Canada.Ca' <https://www.canada.ca/en/public-health/services/funding-opportunities/grant-contribution-funding-opportunities/call-applications-vaccine-injury-support-program.html>. Ireland has used compensation funds and *ex gratia* schemes widely to compensate for medical and pharmaceutical injuries widely yet erratically. For example, the Hepatitis C and HIV Compensation Tribunal, the Surgical Symphysiotomy Ex Gratia Payment Scheme, the Lourdes Hospital Redress Scheme. It is likely that more compensation fund systems will be created in the future: for example there is a yet-to-be-enacted government proposal for an *ex gratia* vaccine injury scheme. An *ex gratia* compensation fund was established to compensate some victims of a major cervical cancer screening error; however, an expert group chaired by a judge recommended a tribunal mechanism that will still require most affected women to prove negligence in order to access compensation. See Charles Meenan J, 'Report on an Alternative System for Dealing With Claims Arising From CervicalCheck' (Department of Health, Ireland 2018) <https://www.gov.ie/en/collection/4ed476-judge-meenan-report-on-an-alternative-system-for-dealing-with-claims/>; Gabriel Scally, 'Scoping Inquiry into the CervicalCheck Screening Programme Supplementary Report' (June 2019) <http://scallyreview.ie/wp-content/uploads/2019/06/Supplementary-Report-Final-Master-190607.pdf>; Fiach Kelly, 'CervicalCheck Compensation Scheme Set to Cost up to €15m', *The Irish Times* (4 January 2019) <https://www.irishtimes.com/news/ireland/irish-news/cervicalcheck-compensation-scheme-set-to-cost-up-to-15m-1.3747226>.

[13] Japan and the US states of Florida and Virginia both operate no-fault compensation funds for birth-related defects.

[14] Such as the UK's Diffuse Mesothelioma Payment Scheme and the Dutch and Belgian asbestos funds.

[15] Most notably, France's *Fonds de garantie des victimes des actes de terrorisme et d'autres infractions*, and the similar fund that exists in Belgium. The United States' September 11th Victim Compensation Fund is another high-profile example. It is a uniquely expansive programme in an otherwise tort-focused jurisdiction.

[16] Including Ireland's Residential Institutions Redress Board and the Magdalen Laundries Scheme.

[17] Such as in Canada, where all worker compensation funds in each province are administered by a single public authority. However this is often where there is a shift over to a system that is considered to be fully enmeshed in the social security/social insurance system – as is the case in France, Belgium and Germany, for example.

[18] A well-known example is the Belgian disaster fund. See Larissa Vanhooff, 'Compensation Funds in Belgium' in Thierry Vansweevelt and Britt Weyts (eds), *Compensation Funds in Comparative Perspective* (Intersentia 2020). A useful recent comparison (from a law and economics perspective) of all types of disaster compensation in Belgium, France, Germany and the Netherlands can be found in Veronique Bruggeman and Michael Faure, 'Compensation for Victims of Disasters in Belgium, France, Germany and the Netherlands' (WRR 2018) <https://www.wrr.nl/binaries/wrr/documenten/working-papers/2018/10/10/wp30-compensation-for-victims-of-disasters-in-belgium-france-germany-and-the-netherlands/WRR+WP+30+Compensation+for+victims+of+disasters.pdf>.

Compensation funds are not just a domestic private law tool. At an international law level, compensation funds have been used successfully in the context of international oil pollution incidents[19] and unlawful military invasion and occupation.[20] There have been academic and civil society proposals for multilateral compensation funds to deal with issues as varied as vaccine injury[21] and climate change-related loss.[22] The world's largest no-fault compensation fund was recently established for COVID-19 vaccine injuries suffered by individuals in the 92 low- and middle-income countries covered by the COVAX scheme.[23] Although this fund was conceived and coordinated at the public international law level, it is administered locally and replaces ordinary domestic liability routes for victims.

The basic starting point in virtually all legal systems is that loss should fall where it lies (*casum sentit dominus*,[24] but other principles have equivalence[25]). However, it is also now universally recognised that there may be a good reason to shift loss by instead creating a liability to make or entitlement to receive compensation.[26] Compensation funds typically seek to eliminate or minimise the traditional tort

---

[19]   The International Oil Pollution Funds, established by the 1971 International Convention on the Establishment of an International Fund for Compensation for Oil Pollution and by the 1992 Fund Convention.

[20]   The United Nations Compensation Commission, a subsidiary of the UN Security Council, was established in 1991 to pay compensation for loss and damage to individuals, corporations, governments and international organisations directly caused by Iraq's unlawful invasion and occupation of Kuwait in 1990–91.

[21]   Sam F Halabi and Saad B Omer, 'A Global Vaccine Injury Compensation System' (2017) 317 *JAMA: The Journal of the American Medical Association* 471 <http://dx.doi.org/10.1001/jama.2016.19492>; Katie Attwell and Mark C Navin, 'Childhood Vaccination Mandates: Scope, Sanctions, Severity, Selectivity, and Salience' (2019) 97 *The Milbank Quarterly*; Sam Halabi and others, 'No-Fault Compensation for Vaccine Injury – The Other Side of Equitable Access to Covid-19 Vaccines' (2020) 383(23) *New England Journal of Medicine* e125.

[22]   Melissa Farris, 'Compensating Climate Change Victims: The Climate Compensation Fund as an Alternative to Tort Litigation' (2009) 2 *Sea Grant Law and Policy Journal* 49; Julie-Anne Richards and Liane Schalatek, 'Not a Silver Bullet: Why the Focus on Insurance to Address Loss and Damage Is a Distraction from Real Solutions' (Heinrich Böll Stiftung North America 2018).

[23]   'No-Fault Compensation Programme for COVID-19 Vaccines Is a World First' <https://www.who.int/news/item/22-02-2021-no-fault-compensation-programme-for-covid-19-vaccines-is-a-world-first>.

[24]   Helmut Koziol, *Basic Questions of Tort Law from a Germanic Perspective* (1st edn, Jan Sramek Verlag 2012) 1, 262; Bjarte Askeland and others in Helmut Koziol (ed), *Basic Questions of Tort Law from a Comparative Perspective* (1st edn, Jan Sramek Verlag 2015) 698, 710, 713.

[25]   For example the starting principle in France is *neminem laedere* – see Olivier Moréteau, 'Basic Questions of Tort Law from a French Perspective' in Helmut Koziol (ed), *Basic Questions of Tort Law from a Comparative Perspective* (1st edn, Jan Sramek Verlag 2015) 3. See also Corjo Jansen, 'Accidental Harm Under (Roman) Civil Law' in Klaas Landsman and Ellen van Wolde (eds), *The Challenge of Change – A Multidisciplinary Approach from Science and the Humanities* (Springer Open 2016).

[26]   Ken Oliphant, 'Liability for Road Accidents Caused by Driverless Cars' [2019] *Singapore Comparative Law Review* 190, 192.

loss-allocation tool of 'fault' resulting in damages, by replacing it with a no-fault structure.[27] Unlike strict liability-based frameworks, no-fault compensation funds generally do not require a legal standard of causation to be met, preferring a simple statutory test based on factual causative links. Compensation funds aim to enable swift calculation and payment of compensation to real person victims by way of a public or quasi-public administrative scheme.

A central dynamic in the field of compensation funds is the dissolution of the bond between liability and compensation, and the factual and legal consequences of that dissolution. A jurisdiction's social security and insurance frameworks underpin that dynamic. At one end of the spectrum, some jurisdictions have a generous complementary financial support framework for their citizens and residents in the form of sophisticated social insurance.[28] At the other end of the spectrum, victims of misfortune who are ineligible for court awarded damages, insurance or compensation fund support may have to make do with more austere flat-rate social security support.[29] Similarly, some jurisdictions have advanced mandatory and optional insurance markets that are heavily regulated and that force and/or enable citizens to protect themselves against most kinds of loss via insurance.[30] This includes the social insurance systems already mentioned, which reveal the significant overlap that naturally exists in many jurisdictions between social security and insurance legal systems. In other jurisdictions, the use of insurance to cover most risks for the individual citizen is more limited and focused on life cover and major assets. Compensation funds therefore exist at the intersection between different fields of law and functions of loss allocation. They raise important questions and contrasting philosophies about how legal systems and societies believe loss should be allocated.

There is currently insufficient coherence between and within different countries' compensation fund systems and other private (tort) and public (social security and public law damages) compensation mechanisms.[31] The causes of these differences are political, factual and legal.[32]

---

[27]   Cane and Goudkamp (n 3) 442. As will be discussed later, schemes in the Nordic countries use an 'avoidability standard', which is slightly different to strict liability.

[28]   This includes European systems which have a 'Bismarck-ian' contributions-based social insurance structure such as Belgium, the Netherlands and France. It also includes Scandinavian countries, which generally follow a 'demogrant' system which guarantees universal entitlement to social security benefits if citizenship or residency requirements are met.

[29]   This can include 'Beveridge-style' systems, such as those in the United Kingdom and New Zealand which incorporate a 'needs-based' approach to some or all social security payments, with means-tested support.

[30]   For example, Western European nations and the United States. See OECD, 'Global Insurance Market Trends' (2019) <www.oecd.org/daf/fin/insurance/oecdinsurancestatistics.htm>.

[31]   For a specific analysis of the Irish jurisdiction's incoherence on the topic of compensation funds, see Kim Watts, 'Managing Mass Damages Liability via Tort Law and Tort Alternatives, with Ireland as a Case Study' (2020) 11 *Journal of European Tort Law* 57 <https://www.degruyter.com/view/journals/jetl/11/1/article-p57.xml>.

[32]   van Boom and Faure (n 7) 13–15.

Given compensation funds' proximity to other loss allocation systems, they often merit a brief mention in a wide range of legal literature that is relevant to tort, social security and insurance law. There are also a number of individual legal articles and studies that consider certain functions of compensation funds, or undertake a broad comparison with non-fund compensation structures in other jurisdictions. There have been some useful recent in-depth studies of the nature and legality of individual compensation funds within one jurisdiction (with relevant comparisons with other systems where necessary).[33] However there are some key twenty-first-century landmarks in the comparative law literature on compensation funds that are the theoretical departure points for this book:

a. *Shifts in Compensation Between Private and Public Systems* (2007), edited by Willem H. Van Boom and Michael Faure,[34] was the first major study in this century of why tort has been abandoned in favour of other (often public) systems. It covers both no-fault and strict liability as the 'tort alternative' systems, but was nevertheless instrumental in defining a scope for a modern reassessment of no-fault compensation.

b. Jonas Knetsch's doctoral thesis *Le droit de la responsabilité et les fonds d'indemnisation: analyse en droits français et allemande*[35] (2011, published 2013) undertook a thorough comparative law analysis of the French and German approaches to compensation funds. This study gave more definition to no-fault compensation as being a distinct field of its own, and identified the key legal difficulties with its current formulation.

c. Sonia Macleod and Christopher Hodges' *Redress Schemes for Personal Injuries* (2017) attempted the first systematic comparative study of non-litigious personal injury redress schemes in multiple jurisdictions.[36] Ambitious in scope, it consolidates for the first time a wealth of descriptive data on very different themes of compensation funds (or 'redress schemes'). There are general conclusions on and analyses of the ideal compensation fund structure that advance the law further from the conclusions found in Van Boom and Faure and Knetsch. However the enormous scope of the volume means the conclusions are ultimately quite general in nature, revealing the need for more targeted research.

---

[33] Such as the focus on the Belgian no-fault medical injury fund in the recent study by Wannes Buelens, *Het Medisch Ongeval Zonder Aansprakelijkheid* (Intersentia 2019). A recent proposal for a criminal injuries compensation fund in South Africa was set out in Albertus Bernardus Wessels, 'Developing the South African Law of Delict: The Creation of a Statutory Compensation Fund for Crime Victims' (Stellenbosch University 2018).

[34] Willem H van Boom and Michael Faure (eds), *Shifts in Compensation between Private and Public Systems (Tort and Insurance Law Vol. 22)* (Springer 2007).

[35] Knetsch (n 2).

[36] Macleod and Hodges (n 2).

d. Matti Urho's 2015 doctoral thesis on drug compensation funds in Nordic countries is summarised in a 2018 English language article appearing in the *European Review of Private Law*. Matti Urho is a Finnish researcher who contributed to the Macleod and Hodges book. In the article 'Compensation for Drug-Related Injuries',[37] he sketches out the optimal functions of a drug compensation fund that could be applied across the European Union member states.

e. *Atiyah's Accidents, Compensation and the Law* is a seminal tort law text, now in its ninth edition (2018) and currently edited by Peter Cane and James Goudkamp.[38] The final chapter dealing with the role of accident compensation in the twenty-first century deals most specifically with the justifications for choosing a no-fault system and the desperate need for further study in this area.

The following recent literature of which I am an author or contributing author also forms relevant reference points, and expands of some of the key themes of this book:

a. *Compensation Funds in Comparative Perspective*, edited by Thierry Vansweevelt and Britt Weyts, contrasts and analyses both well-known and lesser known compensation funds in Belgium, France, Germany, the Netherlands, New Zealand (including the ACC Scheme), Spain, and the United Kingdom. It deals with some important jurisdictions that were not or were only partially considered in Macleod and Hodges' work. Some of the key outstanding questions for further research are identified in this text, including questions that are addressed in this book.

b. My article 'Potential of No-fault Comprehensive Compensation Funds to Deal with Automation and other 21st Century Transport Developments'[39] gives a broad overview of the four large no-fault compensation funds analysed in depth in this book. The article sketches out some broad arguments about why this kind of legal framework is suitable for addressing the liability and insurance challenges posed by new transport developments such as e-scooters and automated vehicles.

c. My article 'Managing Mass Damages Liability via Tort Law and Tort Alternatives, with Ireland as a Case Study'[40] analyses how the Irish government has, over decades, used compensation funds, whether *ex gratia*

---

[37] Urho (n 2).

[38] Cane and Goudkamp (n 3).

[39] Kim Watts, 'Potential of No-Fault Comprehensive Compensation Funds to Deal with Automation and Other 21st Century Transport Developments' (2020) 12 *European Journal of Commercial Contract Law* 1–21.

[40] Watts (n 31).

Chapter 1. Introduction

or statutory in nature, to manage and avert its liability for a number of different mass harm events.

d. My article co-authored with Tina Popa, 'Injecting Fairness Into COVID-19 Vaccine Injury Compensation: No-Fault Solutions',[41] critically analyses why a liability exemption approach to COVID-19 vaccine injury compensation (that has been favoured by the European Commission and Australian federal government) is inferior to a no-fault compensation framework of some kind.

3.2. FOCUS: NO-FAULT COMPREHENSIVE COMPENSATION FUNDS

There are four key examples of a thoroughly comprehensive no-fault compensation fund in modern jurisprudence. These funds meet my specific definition of a no-fault comprehensive compensation fund, which is a subset of a general legal definition of a compensation fund. The four compensation funds are:

a. In New Zealand, the accidental personal injury scheme, administered by the Accident Compensation Corporation.
b. In Australia, the Victorian traffic injury scheme, administered by the Transport Accident Commission.
c. In Canada, the Québécois traffic injury scheme, administered by the Société de l'assurance automobile du Québec.
d. Also in Canada, the virtually identical Manitoba traffic injury scheme, administered by Manitoba Public Insurance.

New Zealand operates a universal and comprehensive no-fault compensation fund for injury. It provides coverage for every person in New Zealand (including tourists) if they are injured in an accident, no matter their age, social security status or occupation.[42] Individuals forego the right to sue for compensatory damages for injury under the common law, in exchange for this comprehensive cover and compensation. Personal injury victims eligible for New Zealand's relatively generous and expansive no-fault compensation system, ACC,[43] will be much better off than non-eligible disabled people, sick people and other victims

---

[41] Kim Watts and Tina Popa, 'Injecting Fairness into COVID-19 Vaccine Injury Compensation: No-Fault Solutions' (2021) 12 *Journal of European Tort Law* 1–39.

[42] Accident Compensation Corporation, 'What We Do' <https://www.acc.co.nz/about-us/who-we-are/what-we-do/>.

[43] The scheme is managed by the Accident Compensation Corporation and established by the Accident Compensation Act 2001.

of misfortune.[44] The New Zealand system has provided cover for all types of injury from 1974 onwards, including medical treatment injury and criminally-caused injuries. The New Zealand approach – which covers all injuries – has not been wholly replicated in another major common law jurisdiction, but it does share some similarities with Nordic compensation fund systems.

Victoria has a well-established statutory no-fault compensation fund for transport accident injuries,[45] managed by the Transport Accident Commission (TAC). This system compensates 'anyone injured in a transport accident'[46] in the state of Victoria (or interstate if a Victorian-registered vehicle is involved).[47] The system offers loss of earnings compensation,[48] compensation for medical and rehabilitation costs and funeral lump sum payments.[49] The system is funded by annual motor vehicle registration fees, not by an insurance levy.[50] With its coverage of all types of transport accident injuries, the support offered by the TAC is probably the closest equivalent system in Australia to the New Zealand ACC system. In contrast to the New Zealand system, however, 'common law' damages claims are still possible for transport accident victims who have a serious injury[51] and can show that their injury occurred through no fault of their own.[52] Because of the comprehensive indemnity offered to all Victorian drivers, these common law damages are almost always paid by the TAC itself.

Québec has a public automobile no-fault compensation fund that covers all Québec road users involved in traffic accidents in the province and anywhere

---

[44] Macleod and Hodges (n 2) 46. See also Māmari Stephens, 'The Right to Social security' in Margaret Bedggood and Kris Gledhill (eds), *Law into Action Economic, Social and Cultural Rights in Aotearoa New Zealand* (Thomson Reuters 2011) 150.

[45] Transport Accident Act 1986 (Victoria).

[46] A transport accident is defined as 'an incident directly caused by the driving of a motor car or motor vehicle, a railway train or a tram' – ibid s 3(1). Since 2013 this definition has been given a more expansive interpretation that includes out-of-control motor vehicles, trains and trams, and certain types of cyclist accidents (involving stationary vehicles, vehicles opening doors or cyclists on their way to or from work) – ibid s 3(1A).

[47] Transport Accident Commission, '2017/18 Annual Report' p 8 <http://www.tac.vic.gov.au/__data/assets/pdf_file/0009/298629/2017-18-TAC-Annual-Report.pdf>.

[48] 'Work and income' <http://www.tac.vic.gov.au/clients/work-and-income>. TAC will pay for loss of earnings for the first 18 months after an accident, if the victim is unable to return to work. After the first 18 months, benefits may be paid for another 18 months or (in the case of very serious injuries) for the rest of the victim's life until retirement age (when the victim becomes eligible for the old age pension). For such long-term cases, the TAC compensation fund system operates in a way similar to that of the general social security system.

[49] 'What we can pay for' <http://www.tac.vic.gov.au/clients/what-we-can-pay-for>.

[50] Transport Accident Commission (n 47) 54.

[51] A 'serious injury' is defined as '(a) a serious long-term impairment or loss of a body function; (b) a permanent serious disfigurement; (c) a severe long-term mental or severe long-term behavioural disturbance or disorder; or (d) loss of a foetus' – Transport Accident Act 1986 (Victoria) s 93(17).

[52] ibid ss 93, 93A, 93D.

else in the world.[53] This is called the Société de l'assurance automobile du Québec (SAAQ). This means that the government pays compensation for personal injury resulting from automobile accidents, and it will not be possible to file court proceedings in relation to such an injury. Tourists and newcomers (other than drivers or passengers in a Québec-registered vehicle) may also be eligible for compensation, based (curiously for a no-fault scheme) on a calculation of the degree to which they were not responsible for the accident. There are exclusions for some kinds of accidents, including accidents that occur during a race or which are affected by an external machinery part or animal. The courts have given a liberal interpretation towards the definition of a qualifying motor accident.[54] Manitoba operates a virtually identical scheme to the SAAQ, which is administered by Manitoba Public Insurance.

In terms of the choice between a no-fault and some-fault or strict liability approach, it has been argued by Helmut Koziol that (in the European medical law field at least) debate has largely subsided about introducing no-fault compensation funds.[55] Gerhard Wagner continues to dismiss the relevance and sustainability of no-fault funds generally.[56] However, these assertions do not match the evidence presented recently by Macleod and Hodges that there are a wide range of established and emerging no-fault schemes in multiple jurisdictions, both common and civil law.[57] Further, Finnish drug injury compensation scholar Matti Urho has also concluded that no-fault funds are likely to develop further in Europe where jurisdictionally and culturally possible.[58] As noted already, the world's largest no-fault framework has recently been established for COVID-19 vaccine injuries in low- and middle-income countries. As a counterbalance to their ongoing legal complexity, there is also clear empirical evidence that pure no-fault funds (which completely separate compensation from fault)

---

[53]   Société de l'assurance automobile Québec, 'If You Have an Accident in Québec' <https://saaq. gouv.qc.ca/en/tourists-and-newcomers/accident/>.

[54]   Jean-Louis Baudouin and Allen M Linden, 'Canada' in Britt Weyts (ed), *The International Encyclopaedia for Tort Law* (Wolters Kluwer 2015) 74. Three types of accidents are excluded from the system's coverage: accidents caused while the car is not moving and caused by an independently operated device (e.g. a crane), accidents caused by certain types of work vehicles and accidents that take place during a show or event.

[55]   Helmut Koziol, 'Compensation for Personal Injury: Comparative Incentives for the Interplay of Tort Law and Insurance Law' (2017) 8 *Journal of European Tort Law* 41, 43. See also James Goudkamp, 'Reforming English Tort Law: Lessons from Australia' in Eoin Quill and Raymond Friel (eds), *Damages and Compensation Culture: Comparative Perspectives* (Bloomsbury Publishing 2016) 76.

[56]   Gerhard Wagner, 'Comparative Tort Law' in Mathias Reimann and Reinhard Zimmermann (eds), *The Oxford Handbook of Comparative Law* (2nd edn, Oxford University Press 2019) 1027.

[57]   Macleod and Hodges (n 2) 628.

[58]   Urho (n 2) 513.

have a positive financial impact on public healthcare spending,[59] and that a mixed system that retains victims' access to tort litigation is the most expensive option of all.[60, 61] No-fault compensation alternatives to tort damages are still being advocated in relation to Canadian and Australian medical treatment incidents,[62] medical research injuries,[63] self-driving vehicles[64] and artificial intelligence applications in healthcare.[65] The Canadian provinces of British Columbia and Alberta have, respectively, recently passed and show intention

---

[59] Tom Vandersteegen and others, 'The Impact of No-Fault Compensation on Health Care Expenditures: An Empirical Study of OECD Countries' (2015) 119 *Health Policy* 367 <https://www.healthpolicyjrnl.com/article/S0168-8510(14)00240-1/pdf>.

[60] Royal Commission into Institutional Responses to Child Sexual Abuse, 'Redress and Civil Litigation' (2015) 384 <http://www.childabuseroyalcommission.gov.au/policy-and-research/redress>; PriceWaterhouseCoopers, 'Accident Compensation Corporation New Zealand Scheme Review' (2008) 74–76.

[61] Kirsten Armstrong and Daniel Tess, 'Fault versus No Fault – Reviewing the International Evidence', *Institute of Actuaries of Australia 16th General Insurance Seminar* (November 2008) 34 <https://actuaries.asn.au/Library/Events/GIS/2008/GIS08_3d_Paper_Tess,Armstrong_Fault versus No Fault – reviewing the international evidence.pdf>. This actuarial review of international systems found that there was 'no clear evidence that fault, no fault or blended schemes are, overall, more expensive than the other scheme types in aggregate, but we note that more people are compensated under no fault schemes, hence the per claimant cost is overall cheaper under no fault schemes ... No fault schemes come out ahead on this evaluation, with a higher portion of claimants covered, a higher portion of scheme cost going to claimants, better claimant outcomes, a more equitable distribution of claimant outcomes and a similar level of scheme costs, average benefits and prevention effects. This needs to be weighed up against potentially less equitable allocation of scheme costs and the freedom of people to pursue tort law remedies in response to their injuries and grievances.'

[62] Elaine Gibson, 'Is It Time to Adopt a No-Fault Scheme to Compensate Injured Patients?' (2016) 47 *Ottawa Law Review* <https://commonlaw.uottawa.ca/ottawa-law-review/sites/commonlaw.uottawa.ca.ottawa-law-review/files/olr_47-2_02_gibson_final.pdf>; Tina Popa, 'Practitioner Perspectives on Continuing Legal Challenges in Mental Harm and Medical Negligence: Time for a No-Fault Approach?' (2017) 25 *Tort Law Review* 19.

[63] Joanna M Manning, 'Does the Law on Compensation for Research-Related Injury in the UK, Australia, and New Zealand Meet Ethical Requirements?' (2017) 25 *Medical Law Review* 397 <https://academic.oup.com/medlaw/article-abstract/25/3/397/3769302>. In the case of medical incident compensation funds, the historical and social context of their development is affected by the dynamic between different stakeholders and ideas about how to improve care – see Janine Barbot, Isabelle Parizot and Myriam Winance, '"No-Fault" Compensation for Victims of Medical Injuries. Ten Years of Implementing the French Model' (2014) 114 *Health Policy* 236.

[64] Maurice Schellekens, 'No-Fault Compensation Schemes for Self-Driving Vehicles' (2018) 10 *Law, Innovation and Technology* <https://www.narcis.nl/publication/RecordID/oai:tilburguniversity.edu:publications%2F5dc6cc56-ce7a-46ff-986b-0b2f8a28010a>. See also Georg Borges, 'New Liability Concepts: The Potential of Insurance and Compensation Funds' in Sebastian Lohsse, Reiner Schulze and Dirk Staudenmayer (eds), *Liability for Artificial Intelligence and the Internet of Things* (Hart Publishing 2019).

[65] Søren Holm, Catherine Stanton and Benjamin Bartlett, 'A New Argument for No-Fault Compensation in Health Care: The Introduction of Artificial Intelligence Systems' (2021) 29 *Health Care Analysis* 171 <https://doi.org/10.1007/s10728-021-00430-4>.

of passing legislative frameworks to create their own no-fault comprehensive compensation funds for automobile injury.[66] As noted already, the Canadian federal government has recently chosen to launch a national no-fault vaccine injury compensation fund.

4. GENERAL LEGAL DEFINITION OF COMPENSATION FUNDS

A fund can be defined as 'a sum of money saved or made available for a purpose'.[67] The term 'compensation' can be defined as 'rendering of an equivalent, requital, recompense'.[68] Based on the overlapping and reflexive nature of compensation structures, it seems logical to include in this definition of compensation fund any type of centralised system that distributes funds with the purpose of compensation, or a system that purchases compensatory services for victims. A specific purpose of compensation funds has been defined as the financial compensation of victims of a certain accident or disaster described and limited by law.[69] We can also see in the no-fault comprehensive compensation funds (all operating in predominantly common law jurisdictions) that there is a greater overlap of compensation funds in areas that civil European jurisdictions would classify as the realm of compulsory social insurance.

A common distinction in the classification of compensation funds in civil European jurisdictions is between 'guarantee' and 'damage' funds.[70] This classification is related to tort and liability law concepts of compensation. Guarantee compensation funds are used when a tortfeasor is unavailable, untraceable or insolvent (or has inadequate insurance). Damage compensation funds, conversely, are funds that completely replace liability in particular circumstances (tortfeasor can't be found, specific events, damage caused without liability). No-fault compensation funds in the common law tradition are probably most similar to the 'damage' classification. No-fault *comprehensive*

---

[66] Attorney General Statutes (Vehicle Insurance) Amendment Act 2020; Province of British Columbia, 'Better Benefits, Lower Rates: Moving to a Care-Based Insurance Model' (2020); Automobile Insurance Advisory Committee, 'Report on Fundamental Reform of the Alberta Automobile Insurance Compensation System' (2020).

[67] 'fund, n.' OED Online, Oxford University Press, March 2018, www.oed.com/view/Entry/75490.

[68] 'compensation, n.' *OED Online*, Oxford University Press, March 2018, www.oed.com/view/Entry/37549.

[69] Larissa Vanhooff, Thierry Vansweevelt and Britt Weyts, 'So Many Funds, so Many Alternatives: Compensation Funds as a Solution for Liability Issues in Belgium, the Netherlands and the United Kingdom' (2016) 8 *European Journal of Commercial Contract Law* 42, citing Knetsch (n 2).

[70] Vanhooff, Vansweevelt and Weyts (n 7); Vansweevelt and others (n 4).

compensation funds are also most similar to 'damage' funds. However they can also operate as 'guarantee' funds in the sense that they provide compensation to a victim *and* the fund can impose some kind of legal or financial consequences on the other party. To give a simple example, under the New Zealand Accident Compensation Corporation scheme, an employer may face higher levies if his or her employees have many accidents at work.[71] A further example can be found in Manitoba's MPI scheme, where the MPI can recoup compensation costs via subrogation from unlicensed drivers or drivers of unregistered cars who cause accidents.[72]

In relation to terminology, there is some interchangeability between the terms 'scheme' and 'fund' in academic literature on compensation.[73] What matters for the purposes of this book is that the compensation payment is administered centrally by a public or quasi-public structure, even if the monies it distributes may have different primary sources. As noted previously, a 'compensation fund' is generally understood by scholars to mean a simple 'pot of money' structure that has been made available by legislation for a specific purpose. This could include a situation where all the compensation funding comes from central government for all or certain classes of victim. The term 'compensation scheme' suggests a slightly more complex structure, where the monies for the compensation payments are drawn from different sources. Where these two different structures ('fund' versus 'scheme') have the same purpose and practical operation, their compensatory effect is identical – therefore they can be properly analysed together.

5. SPECIFIC DEFINITION OF A NO-FAULT COMPREHENSIVE COMPENSATION FUND

Recent literature in the compensation funds field, such as Macleod and Hodges' text, has grouped together similar compensation funds that are intended to have a similar effect: redress for personal injury by way of a (usually no-fault) administrative scheme. This is of a very broad scope, and the sheer volume of material addressed in Macleod and Hodges' work has led to criticisms that it has

---

[71] s 178 Accident Compensation Act 2001.
[72] s 26(2) The Manitoba Public Insurance Corporation Act.
[73] For example, Macleod and Hodges' recent comparative law text which refers to no-fault compensation 'schemes' – Macleod and Hodges (n 2). Meanwhile the term 'system' is preferred in Cane's analysis of the intersection between tort law compensation, compensation systems and social security systems in common law jurisdictions – Cane and Goudkamp (n 3) ch 18. This can be contrasted with the continental civil and international law approaches that classify such compensation systems as 'funds' – Knetsch (n 2).

failed to be a truly comparative study.[74] A choice has been made to focus in this book on no-fault comprehensive compensation funds because:

a. They are the kind of compensation fund that is the most revolutionary departure from traditional compensation options like tort law, insurance and social security.

b. There has not previously been a comparative law study of no-fault comprehensive compensation funds in isolation from the general compensation funds field. Such 'big' funds are generally compared only with less comprehensive schemes in the same functional category or with traditional compensation structures operating in the same function. Comparison with less extreme schemes and with traditional compensation structures is of course important (especially when focused on a specific function), but so is comparison between the most revolutionary compensation funds themselves. This enables us to determine whether all no-fault comprehensive compensation funds have the same structure and effect in law and practice. It also enables us to see what conclusions are relevant (and not relevant) to less comprehensive funds.

c. There has not been any extensive scholarly comparative law analysis of no-fault comprehensive compensation funds in the Australian state of Victoria and the Canadian territories of Québec and Manitoba, despite those funds sharing remarkable similarities with New Zealand's ACC Scheme.[75]

d. A set of criteria based on the features 'no-fault' and 'comprehensive' enables a precise comparison of funds. It also allows for some limited comparison on a functional basis between other jurisdictions which use no-fault compensation in a different purposive way.

In contrast, a 'sliding scale' comparative law analysis that includes both no-fault comprehensive and smaller compensation funds from more than two jurisdictions quickly runs the risk of becoming very expansive and/or possibly unmanageable. This is a valid methodological critique that can be levied against Macleod and Hodges' work. This approach can also reinforce perceptions that compensation funds in general are incomparable, or that no-fault *comprehensive*

---

[74] Per Laleng, 'Redress Schemes for Personal Injuries – Book Review' (2018) 25 *European Journal of Health Law* 469; Sebastian Peyer, 'Sonia Macleod and Christopher Hodges, *Redress Schemes for Personal Injuries* (Book Review)' (2019) 27(3) *Medical Law Review* 534 <https://academic.oup.com/medlaw/advance-article-abstract/doi/10.1093/medlaw/fwy037/5146517>.

[75] Professor Daniel Gardner of the Université Laval in Québec did some useful comparative law work in this area in the early 2000s that is worth revisiting and updating. See Daniel Gardner, 'Quelques Points de Comparaison Entre Les Deux plus Anciens Régimes Intégrés d'indeminisation Des Victimes d'accidents d'automobile: Québec et Nouvelle-Zélande' (2004) 71 *Assurances et Gestion des Risques* 591; Daniel Gardner, 'Automobile No-Fault in Québec as Compared to Victoria' (2000) 8 *Torts Law Journal* 89.

funds are so extreme that they are legal 'orphans', and it is unrealistic to compare them with other structures at all.

For similar reasons, the specific definition of very large no-fault compensation fund used in this book relates only to *publicly* administered and underwritten no-fault compensation funds, rather than some larger no-fault models that are administered by one or more private insurers. This is a specific choice that has been made for accuracy and manageability reasons. If this book were to include privately underwritten and managed large no-fault schemes, it would be necessary, for accuracy, to include (at the very least) the Nordic no-fault motor transport schemes,[76] the Ontario no-fault automobile framework in Canada, the Israeli no-fault transport injury scheme,[77] and the Northern Territory's no-fault transport framework in Australia (and the structural complexities of how it moved from public to private management). Thus, even a small extension of scope automatically draws in a number of extra funds – which in turn have also close functional and structural similarities to a number of other smaller no-fault compensation schemes. Where should one then draw the methodological line with other structural and functional relatives? This very quickly leads to the 'expansive and unmanageable' criticism of analyses of these kinds of alternative liability schemes. By maintaining a very strict definition that is limited to the pure public no-fault type of large scheme, it is possible to complete a detailed and novel analysis of this particular subset of scheme. This is vitally important for issues like financial sustainability (including taxpayer funding and underwriting) and the contextual impact of a single large public scheme on the wider legal system, for which there is presently a large research gap. These conclusions are in turn relevant to separate comparisons that can be made with private schemes. It is therefore justified to focus the definition in this book on the publicly administered type of scheme – however, there are of course further research gaps relating to the choice between a public and privately administered no-fault scheme.

The precise definition of a no-fault comprehensive compensation fund for the purposes of this book is therefore:

a. A fund-based system that provides compensation to real (human) persons. This can include financial compensation, income replacement and provision of equivalent compensatory services.

---

[76] Sonia Macleod and Christopher Hodges, 'An Introduction to the Schemes' in Sonia Macleod and Christopher Hodges (eds), *Redress Schemes for Personal Injuries* (1st edn, Hart Publishing 2017) 6.

[77] That scheme is of a similar age to the four funds studied in this project, and is governed by the Israel Road Accident Victims Compensation Law 1975. For an overview, see Ilan Kaner, 'The Israeli System of Road Accidents Victim Compensation', *HILA-AIDA Summit* (Athens May 2014) <http://ilankaner.co.il/assets/files/Articles/Israeli-System-of-Road-Accidents-Victims-Compensation---Ilan-Kaner-May-2014 (1).pdf>.

Chapter 1. Introduction

b. The question of fault will *never* be relevant to whether the person will be eligible to receive the core benefits of the compensation fund – the scheme is no-fault. However, beyond core benefits, the *factual behaviour* of an individual or their *breaches of law* may have some impact on whether extra or non-core compensation is available.

c. The fund is comprehensive, which means that a broad scope of functionally or thematically-linked events or losses will be eligible for compensation under the fund.[78] By contrast, a non-comprehensive compensation fund only compensates for injuries that occurred in a very specific way.

d. The compensation is paid or administered by a single public or quasi-public centralised body. Compensation is paid and benefits are provided to an individual (real) person (rather than a corporate entity or other kind of legal person). A specific single, publicly administered 'pot' is used to fund the entitlements under the compensation fund, but the funding of that pot may come from different sources.

e. The framework for the compensation fund system must be established by statute. This therefore excludes niche compensation funds set up solely by political or executive direction (with no legislation) and privately established and managed compensation structures for mass harm, such as class action settlement funds.

f. The compensation is intended to compensate the person in relation to an adverse event or circumstance[79] that caused the person damage, hardship or suffering (this includes physical or emotional suffering). Mixed purposes are permissible, but compensation must be one of the purposes of the benefits available.

g. The compensation provided is a compulsory alternative in (nearly) *all* circumstances to a tort law compensatory damages action or a public law damages action before the courts. Where there is access to fault-based benefits within the relevant legislation, this will only be in very limited circumstances. In effect, there is no ability under a no-fault comprehensive compensation fund for a victim to choose between systems.

---

[78] Simon Connell has defined 'comprehensive' in relation to New Zealand's ACC Scheme as meaning coverage of a particular type of harm (accidental personal injury) regardless of cause. He contrasts this with compensation schemes which are focused on worker injury or motor vehicle injury. I believe this is too narrow a definition of 'comprehensive' for comparative law purposes, because it effectively orphans the New Zealand system from all other compensation funds. No-fault comprehensive compensation funds focused on all types of traffic accidents or worker injury may appear to be non-comprehensive from a New Zealand perspective, but are in fact relatively comprehensive. Simon Connell, 'Community Insurance versus Compulsory Insurance: Competing Paradigms of No-Fault Accident Compensation in New Zealand' (2019) 39(3) *Legal Studies* 1 <https://www.cambridge.org/core/product/identifier/S0261387518000508/type/journal_article>.

[79] Circumstances can include disability and long-term illness, for the purposes of my definition.

Intersentia

h. The compensation provided can be a specific substitute for what would otherwise be available (theoretically or in reality) under that jurisdiction's social security structures. The system may be the primary means of compensation for that kind of loss, or subsidiary in nature. However, the definition of a compensation fund in this research does not include schemes that entirely fall within the social security system. Systems that provide compensation for ongoing need that may not be linked to an individual event of misfortune are therefore not included.

i. To be clear, the definition does not include compensation funds or schemes created to cover bad conduct or unexpected financial problems by actors in regulated industries such as bankers, lawyers and travel agents. These are compensation funds and schemes that relate to professional conduct issues, contractual obligations, fiduciary duties and financial solvency. Such structures could be understood as more likely to fall within the sphere of equity law or the fulfilment of contractual relations, rather than tort law or social security law.

j. Additionally, the definition of a 'no-fault comprehensive compensation fund' does not include government-backed or government-underwritten insurance schemes, where the benefits are only available following the payment of a premium or levy. In other words, the victim himself or herself does not need to have personally paid any premium in order to be eligible for the compensation fund. Although a no-fault comprehensive compensation fund may use levies or insurance structures as a fund-generating device, a victim's eligibility for some degree of compensation should not depend on the payment of any levy.

6. FURTHER COMMENTS ON COMPENSATION THEORY

Broadly speaking, when considering the relevance or need for a no-fault compensation fund, there is a need to consider what choices and changes are to be made to existing structures and the way that an individual society or group of societies want to think about loss allocation. If an individual suffers physical, emotional and financial loss due to misfortune (of any kind), is he expected to carry the burden of this loss himself unless he can show another's fault (as per the classic principles of law), or should society carry some or all of that burden by compensating him (as per more modern concepts of social security and social solidarity)?

The choice of a no-fault (comprehensive) compensation fund is not just a selection between private and public law options, or a decision to use a 'social' approach instead of classic tort principles of loss allocation. The use of compensation funds reveals what human societies think contemporaneously about how we manage the most difficult parts of human life *today* – loss, and specifically how loss should be shared between the individual and wider society.

Chapter 1. Introduction

This is relevant to every kind of loss – accidental injury, loss suffered by crime victims, congenital and degenerative conditions, disability, loss caused by mental illness, loss caused by natural or environmental disaster or climate change, loss suffered by victims of abuse, loss suffered by individuals in the course of their employment, loss caused by war, pandemics, and many more.

If a compensation fund has been selected as a legal tool by a jurisdiction, generally that is because the existing legal structures and philosophical decisions made by that society in the past for the allocation of loss have been found unsatisfactory. The philosophical choices about how non-contractual loss is allocated in a society are manifested in the form of tort law, insurance law, social security law, other public law mechanisms, political choices and public displays of charity and compassion.[80] In the mid-twentieth century, arguments favouring the elimination of tort law for injury and misfortune and the expansion of social security were popular and novel. Later, Patrick Atiyah made the argument that tort damages for injury should be abolished in favour of first-party insurance (and no-fault compensation for motor accidents).[81] In the late twentieth-century and beyond, tort law and law and economics scholars rigorously critiqued the merits and failings of no-fault compensation schemes.[82] Despite those critiques, compensation funds of various shapes still exist, are still being established, and require updated analysis in light of their continuing and evolving existence. There is also a particular gap in the research about whether no-fault compensation facilitates or hinders access to justice and is compatible with human rights law.

As noted by Peter Cane, it is necessary to accept that the further wholesale abolition of tort law is probably unrealistic, because such an endeavour faces fundamental changes to the way loss is allocated.[83] Aside from the sheer logistics and cost, this would face massive opposition from interest groups (like lawyers

---

[80] This book uses the term non-contractual loss, because in a situation of two or more contracting parties, the individual parties have chosen between themselves how loss is allocated in the event of contract breach. In different jurisdictions there is often a statutory gloss on top of contract law that specifies, in accordance with society's and lawmakers' philosophical and policy choices, restrictions on how loss is allowed to be allocated if the parties have not expressly dealt with the topic. Because compensation systems for contractual loss do not form part of the definition of a compensation fund system in this book, they are not being considered here.

[81] Atiyah (n 1). Peter Cane and James Goudkamp have criticised the concept of the freedom to choose a private first-party insurance policy to compensate for injury as being inadequate for 'the poor, the ill-educated and the vulnerable … The freedom to be inadequately insured against personal injury and disability is no freedom at all.' – Cane and Goudkamp (n 3) 466.

[82] From a common law perspective in particular, the articles found in volume 73 of the *California Law Review* from 1985 (based on a symposium about compensation and tort law) provide a valuable overview of the landscape of tort law's engagement with no-fault compensation funds in the late twentieth century.

[83] For a useful discussion of 'abolitionist' versus 'incrementalist' approaches to the reform of tort law from a political economy perspective, see Peter Cane, *The Political Economy of Personal Injury Law* (University of Queensland Press 2007).

Intersentia

21

and insurers) whose livelihoods and philosophical beliefs are invested in the maintenance or incremental development of the status quo. Further, for many types of harm, tort is an effective tool to pursue those who have caused it and to allow an evolving definition of justiciable societal obligations.[84] However, dissatisfaction remains with the practical effects of both tort law (large costs to all parties, inconsistency of compensation outcomes, complexity and inefficiency) and social security law (inadequate compensation, inefficiency, discrimination between classes of loss) as manifestations of philosophical choices about loss allocation. This is demonstrated by the fact that no-fault compensation funds (as a general category) have been chosen, and are continuing to be chosen, as an answer to that dissatisfaction. A comparative law study of now-mature comprehensive and publicly managed no-fault funds surely provides necessary guidance on co-ordination efforts and legal system design.

This book's specific contribution is a specific comparative law understanding of how comprehensive no-fault compensation funds work, how they could work better as legal tools of loss allocation, in accordance with human rights law, and what they reveal about the development of hybrid public and private law compensation solutions. Understanding philosophical choices about loss allocation – and challenging their orthodoxy – enables proposed new solutions for compensation funds generally that are achievable, consistent and ideally reflective of best international practice. In plain language – if we take a fresh look at revolutions in compensation, we can understand how and when it is possible and appropriate to replicate them in other contexts. We can also understand the limits of their usefulness. This study thus evolves the understanding of the law a step further from Peter Cane's bipolar abolitionist and incrementalist camps.

The future of how jurisdictions use compensation fund systems and other kinds of loss allocation legal tools is not set in stone. Research that seeks to understand jurisdictions' philosophical perceptions, their practical choices and the effect of those perceptions and choices in action provides results that can inform the best development of compensation fund system theory and practice.

7. A NOTE ON METHODOLOGY

In terms of methodology, a 'pluralist's toolbox' of functional, analytical, structural, historical and in-context sub-methodologies has been used.[85] This is

---

[84] For example, in May 2021 a Dutch court allowed the general tort obligation in that country's civil code to be used as successful grounds for a ruling that the oil giant Royal Dutch Shell must comply with the Paris Climate Agreement obligations – see *Vereniging Milieudefensie et al v Royal Dutch Shell plc* C/09/571932, ECLI:NL:RBDHA:2021:5337.

[85] Mark Van Hoecke, 'Law and Method Methodology of Comparative Legal Research' [2015] *Law and Method* 1, 28–29 <https://www.bjutijdschriften.nl/tijdschrift/lawandmethod/2015/12/RENM-D-14-00001.pdf>.

in line with recognised trends in comparative law.[86] Limited qualitative surveys of the relevant compensation funds were undertaken on specific points to enhance the comparative law conclusions. Regrettably, more extensive surveys and information gathering were rendered impossible because of the COVID-19 pandemic.

There is an ever-present (but rarely directly addressed) question in this field of what is the right (or best) methodology to use to analyse no-fault compensation funds. This reflects compensation funds' multi-faceted nature as simultaneously a tort law damages alternative, a social security structure, an alternative to private first-party insurance and a public insurance structure. This book uses a comparative law methodology. Other methodologies that can be used to analyse compensation funds include law and economics, socio-legal methodology, and critical legal studies. From a comparative law standpoint, law and economics can perhaps be used directly in partnership with comparative methods.[87]

It is worthwhile making a critical comment here on the use of a law and economics approach to analyse no-fault comprehensive compensation funds. The overlap of compensation funds with insurance law and tort philosophy has led to a law and economics approach being favoured by many academics. This is particularly the case for scholars in the Dutch tradition, who often consider the intersection between compensation funds and other forms of first-party and third-party insurance for different types of harm.[88] Michael Faure and associated scholars have championed a law and economics approach that sets strict limits on the use of compensation funds, arguing that it is better from a fairness and efficiency perspective to make different types of harm more insurable *ex ante* than to use a publicly administered no-fault compensation fund.[89] This may certainly be appropriate when considering, for example, the specific proximity of no-fault systems to other structures of insurance and liability law (when using a law and economics analysis to evaluate insurance systems in particular). And generally speaking, welfare economics – being concerned with the impact of economic policies on community and individual well-being – will of course provide useful economic tools for assessing the impact of legal systems (like no-fault compensation funds) on community and individual welfare.

---

[86] Mathias Siems, 'New Directions in Comparative Law' in Mathias Reimann and Reinhard Zimmermann (eds), *The Oxford Handbook of Comparative Law* (2nd edn, Oxford University Press 2019).

[87] Florian Faust, 'Comparative Law and Economic Analysis of Law' in Mathias Reimann and Reinhard Zimmermann (eds), *The Oxford Handbook of Comparative Law* (2nd edn, Oxford University Press 2019) 848–850.

[88] See also Ronen Avraham, 'The Law and Economics of Insurance Law – A Primer' (2012), University of Texas Law, Law & Economics Research Paper No 224 <http://ssrn.com/abstract=1822330>.

[89] Michael Faure, Ton Hartlief and Gerrit van Maanen, 'Compensation Funds in the Netherlands' in Thierry Vansweevelt and Britt Weyts (eds), *Compensation Funds in Comparative Perspective* (Intersentia 2020).

However, a law and economics approach is not the best default tool for analysing no-fault comprehensive compensation funds as a category or the shape of their relationship with tort law and the wider legal landscape. The purpose and scope of no-fault comprehensive funds is to provide redress (both monetary and non-monetary) for a wide variety of harms. There is not an individualised calculation of loss, but an individualised calculation of *need* based on income replacement, medical need and severity of harm. The impossibility or undesirability of existing legal, contractual and social welfare mechanisms to compensate for a group of losses is the motivation for the creation of these wide-ranging compensation funds. The no-fault comprehensive compensation funds analysed in this book were all designed – and continue to exist – without reference to law and economics principles.[90]

Importantly, recent actuarial and econometric analyses of no-fault and no-fault comprehensive compensation funds reveal that they are the cheapest and most effective method of compensating for loss on multiple measures. Increased risk of injury or harm in no-fault systems in fact appears to result from ancillary functions, such as whether experience rating is used in the calculation of premiums and the effect of safety campaigns.[91] In other words, classic hypotheses (from a law and economics perspective) about the downsides of no-fault comprehensive compensation funds[92] have not been proven in recent statistical and scientific evidence of compensation funds' operations across and within multiple functions.[93] This is an issue that would be best addressed by further empirical study in multiple disciplines in collaboration with legal researchers.[94] The relevance of law and economics to the future study of no-fault

---

[90] Although law and economics principles were a catalyst for a number of the confusing – and ultimately repealed – convulsions of the New Zealand ACC Scheme in the 1990s and early 2000s. See Richard Gaskins, 'Accounting for Accidents: Social Costs of Personal Injuries' (2010) 41 *Victoria University of Wellington Law Review* 37, 46–48; Richard Gaskins, 'Reading Woodhouse for the Twenty-First Century' [2008] *New Zealand Law Review* 11.

[91] Kay Winkler, 'Effects of No-Fault Auto Insurance on Safety Incentives' (2016) <https://ssrn.com/abstract=2747006>.

[92] Michael J Trebilcock, 'Incentive Issues in the Design of No-Fault Compensation Systems' (1989) 39 *University of Toronto Law Journal* 19; Gerhard Wagner, 'Tort, Social security, and No-Fault Schemes: Lessons from Real-World Experiments' (2012) 23 *Duke Journal of Comparative & International Law* <https://pdfs.semanticscholar.org/0849/1023d1456ce49ab 02483101a6b5ddcfa988d.pdf>; Gerhard Wagner, '(Un)Insurability and the Choice between Market Insurance and Public Compensation Systems', *Shifts in Compensation between Private and Public Systems (Tort and Insurance Law Vol. 22)* (Springer 2007).

[93] PriceWaterhouseCoopers (n 60) 74–76; Armstrong and Tess (n 61) 34; Kelly Dickson and others, 'No-Fault Compensation Schemes: A Rapid Realist Review to Develop a Context, Mechanism, Outcomes Framework' (2016) <https://eppi.ioe.ac.uk/CMS/Portals/0/PDF reviews and summaries/No Fault Comp Schemes 2016 Dickson.pdf>; Vandersteegen and others (n 59) 36; Gibson (n 62).

[94] As advocated in Genevieve Grant and David M Studdert, 'Poisoned Chalice? A Critical Analysis of the Evidence Linking Personal Injury Compensation Processes with Adverse Health Outcomes' (2009) <http://papers.ssrn.com/sol3/papers.cfm?abstract_id=1484340>.

Chapter 1. Introduction

compensation funds should, in the future, be assessed with reference to whether its hypothesises are proven or disproven by multidisciplinary data resulting from the operation of different functions of compensation funds.[95] This is of course also true of any other methodological prism through which law is observed, such as socio-legal studies and critical legal studies.

No comments are made here about the merits of law and economics as a philosophy and discipline generally. It is a perspective which has had a powerful influence on legal systems and legislative choices since the 1960s.[96] However, it is not an appropriate primary methodology or perspective to use when considering no-fault comprehensive compensation funds. This kind of fund is ultimately a legal system of rules to govern and support the behaviour and needs of human beings – it is *not* primarily an economic system. Recent works on legal theory have also made a renewed challenge to the notion that people, communities and individuals are merely human resources in a world of competitive encounters.[97]

Specifically, normative economic analyses of law are not suited to no-fault (comprehensive) compensation funds. For example, use of the Kaldor-Hicks test[98] to determine the efficiency of legal compensation (e.g. damages, or no-fault compensation paid by a fund) is most useful when one is considering financial gains and losses. However as Florian Faust has noted, this kind of test is very difficult to apply in relation to other losses, because the size of an individual's emotional or other non-financial losses is neither observable nor reliably measurable.[99] No-fault compensation funds – comprehensive ones in particular – tend to take a rehabilitative approach to compensation that aims to address the economic, social *and* personal costs of injury.[100] An economic analysis of the

---

[95] The need for a data-focused approach also been supported by Faure and van Boom: 'We would therefore hope that in the future policymakers think more seriously about data collection rather than continuing to engage in various shifts without a clear idea of the effects (*ex ante* or *ex post*) of these shifts.' – Michael Faure and Willem H van Boom, 'Concluding Remarks' in *Shifts in Compensation between Private and Public Systems (Tort and Insurance Law Vol. 22)* (Springer 2007) 236.

[96] Due in at least part to the vast quantity of private sector funding that the field of law and economics received from politically conservative right-wing sources. See Radhika Balakrishnan and Joshua Curtis, 'Advancing Human Rights through Economics', *Series on Economics and Law in Conversation* (Laboratory for Advanced Research on the Global Economy, Centre for the Study of Human Rights, London School of Economics 2016) <http://www.lse.ac.uk/sociology/assets/documents/human-rights/HR-SO-5.pdf>; Robert Van Horn, 'Corporations and the Rise of Chicago Law and Economics' (2018) 47 *Economy and Society* 477.

[97] Scott Veitch, 'The Sense of Obligation' (2017) 8 *Jurisprudence* 415, 433–434 <https://www.tandfonline.com/action/journalInformation?journalCode=rjpn20>.

[98] Kaldor-Hicks efficiency is said to occur when an alteration in the allocation of resources produces more benefits than costs overall. See 'Kaldor-Hicks efficiency' in Jonathan Law (ed), *A Dictionary of Law* (9th edn, Oxford University Press 2018).

[99] Faust (n 87) 831–832.

[100] s 3 Accident Compensation Act 2001. The Victorian Transport Accident Commission scheme legislation has the object of providing, *inter alia*, 'in the most socially and economically

effectiveness of a compensation fund is therefore limited to an analysis of the *economic* consequences flowing from injury, which are impossible to precisely divorce from non-economic consequences.[101] This also therefore makes it difficult, for example, to apply a law and economics perspective in isolation from the calculation of levies under a no-fault comprehensive compensation fund.

No-fault compensation funds do not sit wholly within private law. And the terms 'justice' and 'fairness' do not mean the same thing in law as they do in economics. An attempt to force such legal terms to have equivalence *in all circumstances of compensation* with economic interpretations of 'fairness' and other terms like 'efficiency' is inappropriate and has no methodological basis or conclusive legislative or judicial support. Richard Posner's speculation that an economic analysis would eventually assimilate itself fully with law[102] is not a *fait accompli*.[103] This is especially the case when issues like access to justice and the compatibility of compensation funds with human rights law must be considered – a important gap in the law surrounding compensation funds that this book aims to (at least partially) address. An economic perspective is not primarily relevant to whether a compensation fund facilitates or hinders access to justice as a question of fact and law. A law and economics perspective will at times be relevant to an analysis of no-fault comprehensive compensation funds.[104] However, there should be strong resistance to any proclaimed inevitability or undisclosed presumption of the application of a law and economics prism to no-fault (comprehensive) compensation funds as a default or best approach.

---

appropriate manner, suitable and just compensation in respect of persons injured or who die as a result of transport accidents ... [and] to provide suitable systems for the effective rehabilitation of [injured] persons'. s 8 Transport Accident Act 1986 (Victoria). The Québec's SAAQ and Manitoba's MPI 'may take any necessary measures to contribute to the rehabilitation of a victim, to lessen or cure any disability resulting from bodily injury and to facilitate his return to a normal life or his reintegration into society or the labour market.' See – s 83.7 Automobile Insurance Act (Québec); s 138 The Manitoba Public Insurance Corporation Act.

[101] Particularly in a tort law action – see Stanley Ingber, 'Rethinking Intangible Injuries: A Focus on Remedy' (1985) 73 *California Law Review* 772.

[102] Richard A Posner, *Economic Analysis of Law* (9th edn, Wolters Kluwer Law & Business 2014) 28.

[103] A useful recent literature review that summarises critiques of law and economics is David M Driesen and Robin Paul Malloy, 'Critiques of Law and Economics' (2015) <http://ssrn.com/abstract=2572574>.

[104] For example, one interesting topic that could be studied from a law and economics perspective is the effect of a no-fault comprehensive compensation fund on the efficient operation of the private insurance market for add-on or extra insurances. An ancillary discovery of this study was that the operation of insurance markets in Québec, Manitoba and New Zealand for add-on insurances have been radically affected in their size and scope by the existence of no-fault comprehensive compensation funds in the automobile injury function.

CHAPTER 2

ANALYSIS OF CORE PROBLEMS IN THE CLASSIFICATION OF COMPENSATION FUNDS

1. INTRODUCTION

This chapter analyses some of the core problems afflicting the classification and analysis of compensation funds generally, and no-fault comprehensive compensation funds specifically. The inconsistent legal philosophical and technical definitions and usage of compensation funds across different jurisdictions illustrate a number of key problems that require proper framing and analysis.

2. THE DISTINCTION BETWEEN SOCIAL SECURITY SCHEMES AND NO-FAULT COMPREHENSIVE COMPENSATION FUNDS

The design of social security systems globally varies widely depending upon legal tradition and other political and economic influences. European systems in states like Belgium, the Netherlands and France generally have a 'Bismarck-ian' contributions-based social insurance structure.[1] The United Kingdom, New Zealand and Scandinavian countries generally follow a 'demogrant' system, which guarantees universal entitlement to social security benefits if citizenship or residency requirements are met.[2] Other countries, including Canada, Australia and the United States take a blended approach involving social insurance,

---

[1] John M Kleeberg, 'From Strict Liability to Workers' Compensation: The Prussian Railroad Law, the German Liability Act, and the Introduction of Bismarck's Accident Insurance in Germany, 1838–1884' (2003) 36 *NYU Journal of International Law and Politics* 53.

[2] See William Beveridge, 'Beveridge Report' Social Insurance and Alllied Services (1942) HMSO Cmd 6404 <https://www.sochealth.co.uk/national-health-service/public-health-and-wellbeing/beveridge-report/>.

universal social security and private insurance/out-of-pocket principles depending on the particular social security purpose.[3]

There are differing theories from legal scholars about the social security overlap with compensation funds generally and no-fault comprehensive compensation funds in particular. A no-fault comprehensive compensation fund has been described by Cane and Goudkamp as a 'social welfare solution' to the problem of compensation.[4] Some tort law scholars have classified no-fault comprehensive compensation funds as a complete social insurance system that follows from the logical extension of loss distribution to all accidental losses.[5]

Knetsch classified compensation funds generally as being distinct from social security because they provide compensation without means-testing, evidence of prior contributions or affiliation and operate in a narrow field related to the circumstances of damage.[6] Macleod and Hodges have most recently described an international trend towards compensating personal injury on a no-fault basis as a shift to compensating on a 'wider social basis' that may also (depending on the jurisdiction) be infused with concepts of social solidarity.[7] Wagner has pointed to the failure in the UK and the Netherlands of general social security schemes with substantial benefits for disability, and distinguished them from 'focused, no-fault schemes like workers' compensation', which in his view sit apart from social security.[8]

There is clearly therefore a close and sometimes overlapping relationship between social security and compensation funds. The wide coverage of the New Zealand ACC scheme and the expansive goals of the twin Australian National Disability Insurance Scheme and National Injury Insurance Scheme (described in Chapter 3) are an example of the common border between social security (Beveridge-style), social insurance (Bismarckian-style) and compensation funds. From the perspective of civil European jurisdictions, which have complex social insurance infrastructures, it is *prima facie* easier to simply place such schemes and compensation funds squarely into the box of 'social insurance' or 'social security'. However, to do so fails to realise that the kinds of losses covered

---

[3]   TR Reid, *The Healing of America : A Global Quest for Better, Cheaper, and Fairer Health Care* (Penguin 2010).

[4]   Peter Cane and James Goudkamp, *Atiyah's Accidents, Compensation and the Law* (9th edn, Cambridge University Press 2018) 461.

[5]   'Introduction: The Functions of Tort Law' in Allen M Linden and others, *Canadian Tort Law* (11th edn, LexisNexis Canada) 5.

[6]   Jonas Knetsch, *Le Droit de La Responsabilité et Les Fonds d'indemnisation : Analyse En Droits Français et Allemand* (LGDJ 2013) 506 <https://docassas.u-paris2.fr/nuxeo/site/esupversions/f60b2840-bda3-453e-8626-788d7c4de001>.

[7]   Sonia Macleod and Christopher Hodges, *Redress Schemes for Personal Injuries* (Hart Publishing 2017) 618–621.

[8]   Gerhard Wagner, 'Tort, Social Security, and No-Fault Schemes: Lessons from Real-World Experiments' (2012) 23 *Duke Journal of Comparative & International Law* 1 <https://pdfs.semanticscholar.org/0849/1023d1456ce49ab02483101a6b5ddcfa988d.pdf>.

by expansive compensation funds might simultaneously be of a social security nature *and* of a tort *and* an insurance nature – for example, long-term injury following a catastrophic vehicle or workplace accident. This indicates that no-fault comprehensive compensation funds sit in a category of their own.

How can we therefore properly demarcate the boundary between social security schemes and compensation funds, for the purposes of analysis? This book has defined a compensation fund as including a system that compensates for a type of loss that *may* (but for the compensation fund) be covered by social security, but is not completely different from the kinds of losses that (but for the compensation fund) would be covered by tort or insurance. For example, conclusions that can be made about the New Zealand ACC scheme (which covers many types of loss) could theoretically be compared and applied to the Belgian Fund for Medical Accidents (which has proximity to the possibility of compensation through insurance and tort), but not to the Belgian occupational injury body *Fedris* (which sits wholly within the social security system, for the purposes of claimants). This gives clarity to a way of defining the compensation fund, and enables us to then separately make a conclusion about whether the further expansion of comprehensive compensation funds to fully mesh with social security infrastructure (as is currently being advocated by New Zealand disability and law reform advocates)[9] is a desirable next step.

There are three key differences between social security and a no-fault comprehensive compensation fund:

a.　Firstly, a social security or social insurance scheme requires a claimant to at least be legally domiciled in the jurisdiction in some way to benefit from the scheme. This is not a requirement of any no-fault comprehensive compensation fund – all provide quite significant coverage to eligible non-residents.

b.　Secondly, a no-fault comprehensive compensation fund has separate funding arrangements from the rest of the state's social security structures. Although there may be aspects of the scheme's funding that come from the central taxation revenue pool, the day-to-day management and distribution of funding is done by the fund itself and is separate from the public social security system.

c.　Thirdly, a no-fault comprehensive compensation fund always compensates for loss based on *both* a defined causation harm event and the victim's evidence-based ongoing need for assistance. The low threshold for entry and wide causation criteria for a no-fault comprehensive fund do not mean that there are no causation eligibility criteria whatsoever. Funding sustainability

---

[9]　Forster & Associates, 'Expansion of ACC' <https://www.forster.co.nz/beyond-injury/expansion>.

Intersentia

requirements of the funds mean that the claimant must meet an ongoing evidentiary threshold to keep receiving compensation and other assistance. This distinguishes no-fault comprehensive compensation funds from, for example, the failed former universal disability social security system in the Netherlands.[10]

These three differences show that even this most extreme of compensation funds, the no-fault comprehensive type, stands apart functionally and structurally from the wider social security system.

3. THE DISTINCTION BETWEEN INSURANCE AND COMPENSATION FUNDS AS A REDRESS SOLUTION

Different jurisdictions have different systems of mandatory or optional insurance available to cover possible instances of loss. The importance of different types of insurance as a societal loss allocation structure is greater in continental European civil jurisdictions, for example, than in common law jurisdictions like New Zealand and Australia.[11] There are therefore varying levels of tension in different jurisdictions about when and how it is appropriate to choose a compensation fund as a redress option instead of more insurance solutions. Leading European scholars such as Michael Faure, for example, continue to argue in favour of increasing the insurability against and *ex ante* preparation for misfortune, instead of expanding the use of compensation funds (whether niche or comprehensive).[12] However *ex ante* preparation seems to be most suitable for primarily economic or pecuniary losses associated with harm, and not specifically injury losses which tend to have a very personal and continually evolving recovery dimension.[13]

---

[10] Sandra Resodihardjo and others, 'The Reform of Dutch Disability Insurance: A Crisis-Induced Shift of Preferences and Possibilities' in *Reform in Europe* (1st edn, Routledge 2018) 107.

[11] To compare the situation with New Zealand, see PriceWaterhouseCoopers, 'Accident Compensation Corporation New Zealand Scheme Review' (2008) 108. For a recent discussion, see Helmut Koziol, 'Compensation for Personal Injury : Comparative Incentives for the Interplay of Tort Law and Insurance Law' (2017) 8 *Journal of European Tort Law* 41.

[12] Veronique Bruggeman and Michael Faure, 'Compensation for Victims of Disasters in Belgium, France, Germany and the Netherlands' (2018) 90 <https://www.wrr.nl/binaries/wrr/documenten/working-papers/2018/10/10/wp30-compensation-for-victims-of-disasters-in-belgium-france-germany-and-the-netherlands/WRR+WP+30+Compensation+for+victims+of+disasters.pdf>; Koziol (n 11). This working paper is targeted to the development of better disaster risk management solutions for the Netherlands, but Michael Faure's work has influence throughout the Netherlands, France, Belgium and Germany, given the broad similarities of insurance structures in those jurisdictions.

[13] For example, although New Zealand has a comprehensive no-fault compensation fund for personal injury, it successfully uses *ex ante* compulsory flat-rate insurance to cover earthquake

Chapter 2. Analysis of Core Problems in the Classification of Compensation Funds

The legal tradition of a scholar likely influences their perception of whether compensation funds are either an appropriate replacement for insurance or an illustration of inadequate insurance possibilities. For example, in contrast to Faure, leading common law accident compensation scholars Peter Cane and James Goudkamp have rejected simply turning to non-mandatory insurance coverage as a panacea for tricky types of loss, noting that the freedom to be inadequately insured is no freedom at all.[14] Specifically, academics from a law and economics tradition tend to favour an economic efficiency-based approach to compensation.[15]

A study of no-fault comprehensive compensation funds reveals a unique dimension to this generalised tension with general insurance principles. Is a no-fault comprehensive compensation fund simply a mandatory public insurer? What if, as in the New Zealand ACC Scheme, the fund is (rather surreally) not providing insurance, but may provide 'insurance-related' services,[16] whilst simultaneously calling itself a social insurer?[17] What about where the fund itself is categorised and described as a type of public insurance? For example, the comprehensive no-fault traffic accident compensation fund in the Canadian province of Québec (and Manitoba) considers itself to be a type of public insurer,[18] but its standardised no-fault benefits are actually immediately available to all injured Québec residents (such as passengers, cyclists and pedestrians), even though they may not have paid any premium or levy to the scheme.[19] There is acknowledgement within the Canadian schemes themselves that the funds

---

and other natural disaster-related property damage. This is in contrast to the compensation fund approach that seems to be favoured in Japan, another country on the Pacific Rim with a risk of natural disaster damage. See Kim Watts, 'New Zealand' in Thierry Vansweevelt and Britt Weyts (eds), *Compensation Funds in Comparative Perspective* (Intersentia 2020) 108; Cuong Nguyen and Ilan Noy, 'Insuring Earthquakes: How Would the Californian and Japanese Insurance Programs Have Fared after the 2011 New Zealand Earthquake?' (2020) 44(2) *Disasters* 367.

14   Cane and Goudkamp (n 4).
15   See Alexia Herwig and Marta Simoncini, *Law and the Management of Disasters: The Challenge of Resilience* (Routledge 2016); Tom Baker and Peter Siegelman, 'The Law and Economics of Liability Insurance: A Theoretical and Empirical Review' (2011) <http://scholarship.law. upenn.edu/faculty_scholarshiphttp://scholarship.law.upenn.edu/faculty_scholarship/350>; Ronen Avraham, 'The Law and Economics of Insurance Law – A Primer' (2012) 224 <http:// ssrn.com/abstract=1822330>; Mark Harrison, 'Evidence-Free Policy: The Case of the National Injury Insurance Scheme' (2013) 20 Agenda <http://ro.uow.edu.au/cgi/viewcontent. cgi?article=2384&context=eispapers>.
16   Accident Compensation Act 2001 s 262(2).
17   Accident Compensation Corporation, 'Annual Report 2020' 31.
18   Comments made by Nancy LaRue, Expert Advisor on Insurance Coverage at the Société de l'assurance automobile du Québec, in interview on 6/5/2019. The legislation governing the scheme is called the 'Automobile Insurance Act', yet judicial descriptions of the scheme characterise it as a 'societal choice reflected in a social compromise' – see *Godbout v Pagé et al* [2017] SCC 18.
19   The Société de l'assurance automobile du Québec is funded by driver licensing fees and annual vehicle registration costs.

go beyond insurance and have a social or public character.[20] Further, benefits (on a fault basis) will be available even to non-residents. This is one example of the problem of a lack of clear legal definition of compensation funds generally merging with different semantic uses of terms like 'insurance'.

There are three key differences between a no-fault comprehensive compensation fund and (mandatory public) insurance, as it is generally understood:

a. There is a fundamental social benefit dimension and a social contract aspect to no-fault comprehensive compensation funds, which differentiate it from (non-mandatory) insurance. This goes beyond socialising common risks – it is to do with the intrinsic well-being of society and individuals. This does not mean that ordinary insurance frameworks cannot have such a social benefit as an objective, and it is therefore necessary to make some clarifications in relation to this point. For example, in many European jurisdictions where there are dynamic and well-populated insurance markets, there are a galaxy of mandatory and voluntary insurance products offered by insurers to protect individuals from a variety of life's ills and misfortunes. The social necessity of these insurances (for participation in everyday life) is reflected in the regulatory design of these insurance products and the rules governing how private insurers operating in the relevant market may approve or deny cover. There is a clear parallel here with the social benefit and public interest aura that surrounds no-fault comprehensive compensation funds. However there is a key difference: who has the public interest objective? In the case of regulations relating to 'socially important' insurance or setting rules for how private insurers may conduct their business or treat consumers, the regulator and/or legislature are the bodies who are required to act in the public interest and may impose this obligation on private insurers operating in the market (who comply with these socially beneficial requirements in order to participate in the market – and leaving the market perhaps, if those requirements become too onerous). In contrast, in the case of the no-fault comprehensive compensation fund, it is the public authority administering the fund itself which has a socially beneficial nature at the heart of its design. As will be observed by the analyses in this book, this can influence the fund's behaviour in relation to matters such as rehabilitation, its treatment of claimants and the way it gathers monies. Therefore, the no-fault comprehensive compensation fund is a wholly socially beneficial compensation framework, whereas the socially beneficial regulatory insurance framework is something that applies to other parties and in relation to specific types of insurance.

---

[20] Comments made by Glenn Andersen, Director of Injury Claims Management at Manitoba Public Insurance in call on 21 October 2019.

b.   A levy or fee is not required to be paid under a no-fault comprehensive compensation fund in order for a claimant to be eligible for compensation. Nor does a written contract of insurance need to be concluded in order for a claimant to be eligible for coverage.

c.   In no-fault comprehensive compensation funds that have been studied in this volume, there is no possibility for large institutions or state bodies to completely contract out statutory obligations, self-insure, or access equivalent insurance using a private provider.[21]

These three differences show that no-fault comprehensive compensation funds stand apart from other kinds of 'insurance' as they are understood in law. However, it is important to recognise that the funds still use functional tools of insurance to administratively manage their liabilities. This point is explored in further detail in Chapter 4.

4.   THE RELATIONSHIP AND DISTINCTION BETWEEN THE CONCEPTS OF 'NO-FAULT' AND '*EX GRATIA*'

Two (non-)liability concepts that are frequently found in compensation funds of all shapes and sizes in different jurisdiction are 'no-fault' and '*ex gratia*'. What is the difference between the concepts of no-fault and *ex gratia*? What is the true relationship between these concepts? Is the presence of one of these characteristics in a compensation fund determinative of whether the other will also occur? A specific analysis of this point is helpful, because it does not appear to have been addressed by other scholars. Properly understanding and analysing the differences and relationship between no-fault and *ex gratia*, as they relate to a compensation fund, are important to developing a proper analytical approach.

Firstly, the concept of 'no-fault' appears to have as many different shades of definition as there are compensation funds. Ken Oliphant describes it as 'a term applied to a variety of alternatives of compensation by way of traditional, private law processes, not a unitary phenomenon.'[22] Macleod and Hodges ultimately rejected the term 'no-fault' in favour of 'no-blame.'[23] More recently, Macleod

---

[21]   Under the ACC Accredited Employers' Programme, certain New Zealand employers may take on more of the compensation requirements of injured workers themselves, in exchanged for a reduced premium. However this is far short of a total 'self-insurance' option or private choice that is available for worker compensation programmes that are administered by private insurers.

[22]   Ken Oliphant, 'Landmarks of No-Fault in the Common Law', *Shifts in Compensation between Private and Public Systems (Tort and Insurance Law Vol. 22)* (Springer 2007) 43 <http://link.springer.com/10.1007/978-3-211-71554-3_3>.

[23]   Macleod and Hodges (n 7) 615.

and Chakraborty have noted that the term 'no-fault' is problematic in itself, as it describes a feature of a scheme that is absent rather than present.[24] The issue of fault is a matter that is determined at the loss allocation stage of the compensation problem. Allan Hutchinson claimed that both no-fault and fault depend on 'rarely articulated foundational assumptions about the nature of human personality and social organization'.[25]

In contrast to no-fault, the concept of an *ex gratia payment* can be defined as a payment that is made on a voluntary basis, without any legal obligation or duty.[26] Where a compensation payment is *ex gratia* or in accordance with a schedule, this indicates that the financial compensation provided under the scheme is (1) not intended to be fully compensatory in nature, or (2) wholly symbolic in nature. The issue of liability does not need to be considered at all, because of the voluntary, almost gift-like nature of an *ex gratia* payment. There appears to be no comprehensive scholarly analysis of *ex gratia* and *ex gratia compensation* in contrast with no-fault.

If a compensation fund is no-fault, and the determination of liability is not relevant, does this mean that the payments made under that fund are therefore also *ex gratia* (because of the absence of any determination of fault or liability)? There are three key reasons why *ex gratia* is different to no-fault, whilst the two concepts are nevertheless still very closely aligned. These may appear to be rather obvious, but in the absence of any precise authoritative scholarly literature on this point, these reasons are worth formally articulating:

a. The absence of liability with an *ex gratia payment* is primarily relevant to the payer – the compensation payment is made without any establishment of obligation on the authority administering the fund. In contrast, a well-designed no-fault compensation fund – such as a no-fault comprehensive fund – will make payments on the basis of obligations set out in statute and regulatory guidelines. The legislation will also set out whether other types of compensation (e.g. damages) may be sought from another source. In a no-fault (comprehensive) compensation fund, the absence of liability therefore relates to the irrelevance of fault and liability concepts at the points of (1) determining eligibility for compensation and (2) a claimant attempting to seek further compensation by way of e.g. court damages.

---

[24]   Sonia Macleod and Sweta Chakraborty, *Pharmaceutical and Medical Device Safety* (Hart Publishing 2019) 11.

[25]   Allan C Hutchinson, 'Beyond No-Fault' (1985) 73 *California Law Review* 756.

[26]   Definitions of *ex gratia* and *ex gratia payment* in *Black's Law Dictionary* (11th edn, Thomson Reuters 2019), and *ex gratia* in the Oxford English Dictionary (2019).

b. The behaviour of the compensation recipient is often highly relevant under an *ex gratia* fund. For example, in the field of crime victim compensation funds, which are often classified as *ex gratia*, the behaviour and actions of the applicant victim can still be relevant to the success of a claim for compensation. This is slightly different to standard concepts of fault that are relevant to a claim of negligence. A payment trigger under an *ex gratia* compensation fund may therefore include some sociological consideration of 'fault' or 'worthiness',[27] rather than a legal standard. In contrast, no-fault comprehensive compensation funds still allow access to at least basic compensatory benefits in virtually all cases, even for victims who are criminally liable for the events that lead to their injury (or perhaps redirect it to dependant family members, as occurs in Québec and Manitoba).

c. With *ex gratia* compensation, the claimant usually has no ability to challenge the amount of compensation or their eligibility to receive it. This is in contrast with a no-fault comprehensive compensation fund, which typically allows for a range of internal and external dispute resolution possibilities. This means that less legal scrutiny of *ex gratia* compensation is possible. In my view, an *ex gratia* scheme is a preferred choice for public authorities and governments that wish to avoid legal scrutiny and institutional reform – it is a gap-stopping solution that does not call into question the rest of the legal compensation landscape.[28]

What we can conclude about the intersection between these two ideas is that they are relevant at different stages of the compensation process, but there is a link between them. The link between them is concerned with the divorce of the issue of liability from the issue of compensation. The difference between them is that no-fault schemes suspend or erase the liability of the actors who factually caused the loss or harm, whereas *ex gratia* schemes suspend or erase the liability of the public authority that pays the compensation. Therefore, under a no-fault comprehensive compensation fund it is still possible to assign some kind of legal responsibility to the 'responsible party' in a different field of law – for example workplace safety law, or motor vehicle licensing law. Under an *ex gratia* scheme, there is no possibility of this, and the legal effects of the events that lead to the loss are rendered null and void.

---

[27] David Miers, 'Victims, Criminal Justice and State Compensation' (2019) 9 *Societies* 29 <https://www.mdpi.com/2075-4698/9/2/29>.

[28] This is especially the case where multiple *ex gratia* schemes are implemented for mass liability incidents, such as in Ireland. See Kim Watts, 'Managing Mass Damages Liability via Tort Law and Tort Alternatives, with Ireland as a Case Study' (2020) 11 *Journal of European Tort Law* 57 <https://www.degruyter.com/view/journals/jetl/11/1/article-p57.xml>.

5. SHOULD HISTORICAL ABUSE COMPENSATION SCHEMES BE INCLUDED WITHIN THE DEFINITION OF A COMPENSATION FUND?

In a number of countries, evidence has emerged publicly since the late twentieth century about large numbers of vulnerable children and adults being abused in different ways by institutions and individuals that held a position of responsibility, were responsible for pastoral care, or wielded other types of power. The individuals affected and wider society have demanded justice and redress for this abuse. In light of the recent #MeToo movement, many more victims are becoming empowered to reveal instances of abuse and seek redress and recognition.

Civil damages claims, including multi-party actions, have been one avenue used by victims and their advocates to seek redress and accountability from alleged abusers and the institutions protecting them. However, tort law can only be a remedy for historical injustice under specific circumstances.[29] Compensation funds, or redress schemes as they are also called, have been another legal tool used to channel and manage claims and compensation.

Historical abuse compensation funds can be broadly defined as funds that provide financial redress to individuals who have suffered sexual, physical and/or emotional abuse, usually while they were children in the care of large (often religious) institutions or state-associated institutions. They are an alternative to court damages claims – which may or may not be practically feasible due to a lack of evidence, the death of perpetrators, or statutory time bars on bringing proceedings. The amount of compensation paid is usually dependent upon what compensation is available to a victim from other sources, and is usually seen as a fund of last resort.[30] This kind of fund could be seen as a second generation of historical abuse funds, with the first generation being those established to compensate victims of Nazi war crimes and genocide in World War II.[31]

---

[29] This is because of issues such as the difference in strength (in terms of moral force in tort law theory) between the principles of restitution and compensation. See Marc Loth, 'How Does Tort Law Deal with Historical Injustice?' (2020) 11 *Journal of European Tort Law* 181.

[30] When comparing the UK, Belgian and Dutch crime victim compensation funds, Vanhooff notes that there are minor differences in how strict different victim compensation funds are in regard to compensation that may be available from other sources. Larissa Vanhooff, Thierry Vansweevelt and Britt Weyts, 'So Many Funds, so Many Alternatives: Compensation Funds as a Solution for Liability Issues in Belgium, the Netherlands and the United Kingdom' (2016) 8 *European Journal of Commercial Contract Law* 41.

[31] Such as the schemes administered by the Conference on Jewish Material Claims Against Germany (Claims Conference). The Claims Conference is a compensation advocacy group for Jewish Holocaust survivors and their heirs. Some of the schemes managed or linked to the Claims Conference are privately administered, and others are at least partially publicly administered. See Claims Conference, 'Learn More About Compensation Programs' <http://www.claimscon.org/what-we-do/compensation/background/>.

Chapter 2. Analysis of Core Problems in the Classification of Compensation Funds

There is some uncertainty in academic writing and legal doctrine about whether historical abuse compensation funds (or redress schemes, as they are often called) of any kind should be included in the wider pool of compensation funds, and compared with funds that compensate for other (and usually contemporaneous) types of misfortune like injury, natural disaster and uninsurable and unrecoverable loss. I believe that there is a certain symmetry in their application and use, not least because crime victim compensation funds are commonly included in general and comparative law analyses of compensation funds. Both crime victim compensation funds and historical abuse compensation funds aim to provide compensation to individuals who have been harmed in a criminal way, and are often structured with reference to principles of restorative justice.

This book is a study of what can be learned from a specific incarnation of compensation fund – the *no-fault comprehensive* type that is administered by a public authority. There are also conclusions about what can be learned from this specific type of very broad public fund that is more widely relevant to the field of compensation funds generally. It is not possible to answer generally the question of whether historical abuse compensation funds can *always* be grouped together and analysed with other compensation funds. That is a separate issue that is worthy of further analysis. However, the issue of overlap between historical abuse compensation funds and other/general non-abuse funds must be at least partially addressed, primarily because there may be coverage for historical abuse injury under a *no-fault comprehensive* compensation fund. This chapter will address the following questions that relate to historical abuse compensation funds, in order to better define and analyse the relationship between different kinds of funds:

a.   How have historical abuse schemes been addressed by other legal scholars in the field of compensation funds?
b.   What is the purpose of payments within a historical abuse scheme – compensatory or symbolic?
c.   Do any historical abuse compensation funds fit within the definition of a no-fault comprehensive compensation fund?
d.   What further information is needed to better study this field and the overlap between general compensation funds and historical abuse compensation funds?
e.   Can general research findings about *no-fault comprehensive* compensation funds also be applied to existing historical abuse compensation funds?

5.1.   HOW HAVE HISTORICAL ABUSE SCHEMES BEEN ADDRESSED BY OTHER LEGAL SCHOLARS?

Compensation fund legal scholars have taken different approaches to whether historical abuse compensation funds should be analysed alongside more typical categories of compensation funds (like medical or vaccine injury, disaster or uninsurable motor vehicle injury funds).

Jonas Knetsch excluded historical abuse funds from the scope of his research because of the generally symbolic value of compensation payments under those schemes, but has left the door open to the possibility of including historical abuse schemes in the general definition of a compensation fund.[32] In contrast, Sonia Macleod and Christopher Hodges' comprehensive recent comparative law analysis of redress schemes for personal injury included Irish redress schemes for historical abuse[33] within its comparison of compensation funds for patient injuries,[34] as well as classifying them as 'social' schemes.[35] Other legal and social science scholars have analysed historical abuse funds in relation to concepts of restorative justice and their effectiveness compared to a tort law damages claim. Stephen Winter argues that in implementing a public redress scheme for historic abuse and injury, a state is attempting to engage with claimants on a moral basis, providing restorative justice through redress to repair the damage caused by injury.[36] In the context of an analysis of New Zealand's comprehensive personal injury compensation fund, Mijatov, Barraclough and Forster interpret restorative justice in the same vein as access to justice reforms that reject legalism and advocate direct dispute resolution between parties[37]

This difference in approach between scholars does not directly resolve whether historical abuse compensation funds should be compared and analysed with other functional types of compensation funds. This is a question made more difficult to answer because of the already imprecise framing in legal literature and doctrine of what constitutes a compensation fund generally.

As a category, publicly administered historical abuse redress schemes have been established in common law jurisdictions (alongside or instead of civil law damages claims).[38] In the civil law world, notable (partially) publicly administered

---

[32] Knetsch (n 6) 114–115; Jonas Knetsch, 'Compensation Funds in France and Germany' in Thierry Vansweevelt and Britt Weyts (eds), *Compensation Funds in Comparative Perspective* (Intersentia 2020) 65.

[33] In state-linked residential institutions and religious order-administered Magdalene Laundries.

[34] Macleod and Hodges (n 7).

[35] ibid 28.

[36] Stephen Winter, 'Australia's Ex Gratia Redress' (2009) 13 *Australian Industrial Law Review* 49 <http://www.austlii.edu.au/au/journals/AUIndigLawRw/2009/3.pdf>.

[37] Tiho Mijatov, Tom Barraclough and Warren Forster, 'The Idea of Access to Justice: Reflections on New Zealand's Accident Compensation (or Personal Injury) System' (2016) 33 *Windsor Yearbook of Access to Justice* 197, 28.

[38] Examples would include Ireland's Residential Institutions Redress Board and Magdalene Laundries Scheme, and Australia's National Redress Scheme for Victims of Sexual Abuse. By contrast in Canada, a settlements approach was favoured – the largest example of this is the Indian Residential Schools Settlement Agreement. In New Zealand, there is a Historic Claims Unit within the Ministry of Social Development that pays monetary redress to certain categories of individuals who were abused in state care. However the New Zealand scheme

equivalents include a Dutch hybrid tort-compensation fund scheme for Catholic Church sexual abuse that enabled the payment of monetary and non-monetary compensation,[39] German funds for Nazi-era forced labourers[40] and children abused in post-War foster homes.[41]

It should be noted that many legal analyses of compensation funds across multiple jurisdictions generally include crime victims' compensation funds.[42] Thematically there is a close parallel in purpose between crime victim compensation funds and historic abuse compensation funds. The victims of a criminally convicted perpetrator of historical child abuse (or indeed any historical crime) may be eligible for compensation under such a fund – this strengthens the thematic and direct factual overlap between these two different categories of compensation fund.[43] In the European Union, all Member States are required to establish a redress scheme of some kind for crime victims, however the shape of these schemes varies widely by jurisdiction.[44] The traditional purpose of crime victims' compensation funds is to provide an avenue for

---

     is not widely advertised and is likely to be affected by the recommendations of the ongoing Royal Commission of Inquiry into Historical Abuse in State Care and in the Care of Faith-based Institutions. In the United Kingdom, locally targeted schemes exist, as well as a scheme for child migrants who were sent away from the UK. Wider schemes covering Northern Ireland and Scotland have been proposed, but the landscape remains complicated. See Winter, 'Australia's Ex Gratia Redress' (n 36); Stephen Winter, 'Two Models of Monetary Redress: A Structural Analysis' (2018) 13 *Victims & Offenders* 293; Stephen Winter, 'Redressing Historic Abuse in New Zealand: A Comparative Critique' (2018) 70 *Political Science* 1 <https://www.tandfonline.com/action/journalInformation?journalCode=rpnz20>; Alison Millar, 'Redress for Survivors of Abuse – Could It Be a Reality across the UK?' (*Leigh Day Blog*, 2018) <https://www.leighday.co.uk/Blog/September-2018/Redress-for-survivors-of-abuse---could-it-be-a-rea>; Department of Health and Social Care, 'Payment Scheme for Former British Child Migrants' (*Gov.UK* 2019) <https://www.gov.uk/government/news/payment-scheme-for-former-british-child-migrants>.

39   Gijs van Dijck, 'Victim Oriented Tort Law In Action: An Empirical Examination of Catholic Church Sexual Abuse Cases', *Conference on Empirical Legal Studies* (2018) <https://www.law.ox.ac.uk/sites/files/oxlaw/ssrn-id2738633_3.pdf>.

40   'German Fund Ends Payments to Nazi-Era Forced Laborers', *DW.com* (11 June 2011) <https://www.dw.com/en/german-fund-ends-payments-to-nazi-era-forced-laborers/a-2584879>.

41   Tony Paterson, 'Germany Admits Enslaving and Abusing a Generation of Children' *Independent.co.uk* (14 December 2010) <https://www.independent.co.uk/news/world/europe/germany-admits-enslaving-and-abusing-a-generation-of-children-2159589.html>.

42   Macleod and Hodges (n 7) 501–508; Stephen D Sugarman, 'Quebec's Comprehensive Auto No-Fault Scheme and the Failure of Any of the United States to Follow' (1998) 39 *Les Cahiers de droit* 303, 624; Simon Connell, 'Justice for Victims of Injury: The Influence of New Zealand's Accident Compensation Scheme on the Civil and Criminal Law' (2012) 25 *New Zealand Universities Law Review* 181; Vanhooff, Vansweevelt and Weyts (n 30); Bruggeman and Faure (n 12).

43   However some crime victim compensation funds limit or preclude access to compensation where the applicant has criminal convictions of their own.

44   Council Directive 2004/80/EC of 29 April 2004 relating to compensation to crime victims. See also European Convention on the Compensation of Victims of Violent Crimes 1983.

financial redress for crime victims who may be unable to bring a successful tort-based claim against the relevant defendant, or because there may be no other source of compensation.[45]

This acceptance for including crime victims' compensation funds within the general 'family' of compensation fund categories, yet excluding historical abuse funds, is not justifiable when crime victim funds have such a similar structure and purpose to historical abuse funds. Current legislative and policy developments seem likely to make crime victim compensation funds operate even more like historic abuse funds, which also supports the argument that they should be classified together. A 2019 report by a Special Adviser to the European Commission President has recommended that there should be a paradigm shift on a European level for crime victim compensation funds from mere financial compensation to 'reparation', which includes non-financial support and rehabilitation.[46, 47]

Newer, 'second generation' historic abuse funds (for general mistreatment suffered by a range of individuals) also have more in common with other types of compensation funds than earlier, 'first generation' compensation funds (for specific targeted harm). Knetsch distinguished historic abuse funds that were established to compensate for or provide redress for the systemic or intentional attack on the fundamental rights of certain people, from funds established for the compensation for victims of a negligent act.[48] He argued that historical abuse redress schemes for groups such as Holocaust survivors, with their heavy political dimension, were more likely to fall into the former category. However, historical abuse of children in institutional settings is not an example of a concerted systemic attack on a group. This kind of abuse is an example of systemic negligence by individuals and institutions, harm inflicted by powerful individuals on vulnerable individuals, a failure to adequately address the abuse at the time, and a failure to create or enact safeguarding procedures to prevent future abuse. This kind of harm has much more in common with other kinds of (often otherwise tortious) harm that no-fault compensation funds typically seek to address.

---

[45]   Macleod and Hodges (n 7) 502; Vanhooff, Vansweevelt and Weyts (n 30).

[46]   Joëlle Milquet, 'Strengthening Victims' Rights: From Compensation to Reparation' (2019) <https://ec.europa.eu/info/sites/info/files/strengthening_victims_rights_-_from_compensation_to_reparation_rev.pdf>.

[47]   Recent revisions to other crime victim compensation funds have recommended a more victim-centred approach, which has direct parallels with the stated objective of most historical abuse compensation funds. See, for example, the proposed reforms set out in Victorian Law Reform Commission, 'Review of the Victims of Crime Assistance Act 1996' (July 2018) <www.lawreform.vic.gov.au/wp-content/uploads/2021/07/VLRC_Victims-of-Crime-Assistance-Act-Report_Web.pdf>.

[48]   Knetsch (n 6) 115.

5.2. THE PURPOSE OF PAYMENTS IN A HISTORIC ABUSE SCHEME: SYMBOLIC OR COMPENSATORY?

The symbolic purpose of the financial payments made by a historical abuse fund was another criterion that Jonas Knetsch used to differentiate historical abuse compensation funds from compensation funds with other functions.[49] However, compensation payments under current and emerging historic abuse schemes in multiple jurisdictions typically display a mixed compensatory and symbolic nature. This is in a wider context of mixed purposes to compensation and redress under no-fault comprehensive compensation funds generally.

The previous section considered the relationship and distinction between the concepts of no-fault (in terms of removing the requirement of proving liability as a requirement to access compensation) and *ex gratia* (in terms of the classification of the payment as not demonstrating the existence of liability in the payer).

Looking at some important publicly administered historical abuse compensation funds[50] in different jurisdictions, the aim of the payments tends to be categorised in a way that mixes compensatory and symbolic purposes. In light of the empirical evidence about the complex long-term consequences of child abuse injury,[51] it may not be useful for traditional definitions of 'full' or 'complete' financial compensation to be strictly followed anyway for this field of harm.[52] The consequences and effect of child abuse vary depending on the individual (as well as the nature of the abuse),[53] and financial compensation is likely to be insufficient on its own to 'repair the harm done'.[54]

---

[49] ibid 114–115.

[50] By the term 'compensation funds' I mean here a publicly administered fund that is established on a no-fault basis. It can include funds that are '*ex gratia*' in nature.

[51] The consequences of child abuse and maltreatment can disrupt children's brain development, and impair the development of the nervous and immune systems. A range of physical and psychological problems can follow in adolescence and adulthood, as well as substance abuse. See World Health Organization, 'Child Maltreatment' (2016) <https://www.who.int/news-room/fact-sheets/detail/child-maltreatment>.

[52] In any event, the Olivier Moréteau and other scholars (and French judges) have suggested that the concept of 'full' compensation is a fallacy. See Olivier Moréteau, 'Basic Questions of Tort Law from a French Perspective' in Helmut Koziol (ed), *Basic Questions of Tort Law from a Comparative Perspective* (1st edn, Jan Sramek Verlag 2015) 87–88.

[53] Royal Commission into Institutional Responses to Child Sexual Abuse, 'Final Report – Preface and Executive Summary' (2017) 15–17.

[54] Patricia Lundy, 'What Survivors Want From Redress Introduction: The Project and Panel of Experts on Redress' (March 2016) 16 <https://www.amnesty.org.uk/files/what_survivors_want_from_redress.pdf>. For a deeper discussion of why money is inadequate to redress historical abuse, see Ingunn Studsrød and Elisabeth Enoksen, 'Money as Compensation for Historical Abuse: Redress Programs and Social Exchange Theory' (2020) 13 *The Journal of the History of Childhood and Youth* 288 <https://doi.org/10.1353/hcy.2020.0039https://muse.jhu.edu/article/754490>.

Firstly, in Ireland the now-closed Residential Institution Redress Board (a statutory redress scheme for historic residential school abuse) classified the payments made under the scheme as being 'financial awards to assist in the recovery' of former child residents.[55] Meanwhile, the ongoing Magdalen Restorative Justice Ex Gratia Scheme offers *ex gratia* payments that do not purport to offer full and complete compensation to Magdalen women. The report that set out the framework for the Magdalen scheme said full compensation payments could 'only be calculated and awarded after a detailed [and usually lengthy] adversarial process'.[56] However, in at least one case a woman who was initially denied compensation under this fund has since been awarded a five-figure settlement for her years of 'unpaid work' within the laundry by the Irish Ombudsman.[57] Evidence of loss or at least the fact of making a complaint was an eligibility factor in another Irish school abuse *ex gratia* compensation fund for claimants who were restricted from accessing the court for a remedy.[58] The compensation offered under these schemes cannot be categorised as only symbolic.

Secondly, in Australia the 'redress payment' available to successful claimants under the National Redress Scheme for Institutional Child Sexual Abuse is simply described in the relevant statute as being 'for the sexual abuse, and related non-sexual abuse, of the person that is within the scope of the scheme'.[59] The amount of compensation paid is decided according to a matrix that is based on severity of abuse and physical contact (e.g. penetration), to a maximum of A$150,000. For the purposes of relevant social security entitlements, veteran entitlement and other legislation, the redress payment is *not* treated as a payment of compensation or damages.[60] A legislative explanatory memorandum shows a symbolic element to the financial payment – it aims to 'recognise the wrong the person has suffered.'[61] The straightforward Australian wording of the

---

[55] Residential Institutions Redress Act 2002. Further, s 22 of the Act noted that financial awards made were equivalent (for tax purposes at least) to an award of damages following a civil action.

[56] John Quirke, 'The Magdalen Commission Report' (May 2013) 36 <https://www.justice.ie/en/JELR/THE%20Quirke%20report.pdf/Files/THE%20Quirke%20report.pdf>.

[57] 'Magdalene Laundry Survivor Awarded Compensation for Unpaid Work', *The Irish Times* (21 August 2019) <https://www.irishtimes.com/news/social-affairs/magdalene-laundry-survivor-awarded-compensation-for-unpaid-work-1.3992743>.

[58] Iarfhlaith O Neill, 'Independent Assessment of Claims for Ex Gratia Payment Arising from the Judgment of the ECtHR in the Louise O'Keeffe v Ireland Case' (2019) <https://www.education.ie/en/Learners/Information/Former-Residents-of-Industrial-Schools/ECHR-OKeeffe-v-Ireland/independent-assessment-process/okeeffe-v-ireland-decision-of-the-independent-assessor.pdf>.

[59] National Redress Scheme for Institutional Child Sexual Abuse Act 2018 s 17.

[60] ibid s 49(1).

[61] Explanatory Memorandum: National Redress Scheme for Institutional Child Sexual Abuse (2018) 8.

National Redress Scheme statute reveals a hybrid symbolic and compensatory purpose. It is not full compensation, but nor is it a mere symbol. It is not inferior to compensatory damages, but simply different. This is supported by the conclusions of the Royal Commission into Institutional Responses to Child Sexual Abuse (the body that recommended the establishment of the Redress Scheme). The Royal Commission noted the distinction in purpose between compensatory damages obtained via civil litigation and monetary payments made under redress schemes, but based on the findings of its investigations and public inquiry, concluded that 'civil litigation is not an effective way for all survivors to obtain redress that is adequate to address or alleviate the impact on them of institutional child sexual abuse.'[62] The Commission's finding that 'justice is an inherently individual and subjective experience' indicates that both financial and non-financial compensation measures may need to be used in order for a victim to consider they have received adequate, full or sufficient redress.[63]

Also relevant is the fact that non-compensatory elements have always been a part of the package of redress available under no-fault comprehensive compensation funds.[64] Critics of no-fault compensation funds have historically always focused on comparisons between pure financial compensation elements under no-fault comprehensive schemes and what could be available in a civil damages claim.[65] However, it is inappropriate and artificial to separate out financial payments (for example a lump sum, or an income-linked payment) from the wider package of rehabilitation and support benefits under a no-fault comprehensive scheme, because they form part of the same overall holistic redress package to the individual. No-fault comprehensive compensation funds all have rehabilitation as one of their legislative objectives.

The partial or wholly symbolic nature of the payments made under historic abuse compensation funds should therefore not be a barrier to their inclusion

---

[62]   Royal Commission into Institutional Responses to Child Sexual Abuse, 'Redress and Civil Litigation' 92–93 <https://www.childabuseroyalcommission.gov.au/redress-and-civil-litigation>. That report also made recommendations for the reform of civil litigation to better facilitate compensatory damages claims by abuse victims.

[63]   Royal Commission into Institutional Responses to Child Sexual Abuse, 'Redress and Civil Litigation' (2015) 93 <http://www.childabuseroyalcommission.gov.au/policy-and-research/redress>. The need for non-financial compensation has also been recognised and facilitated in schemes that are not publicly administered, such as the Dutch (hybrid tort and compensation fund) child sexual abuse redress scheme that was administered by the Catholic Church. See van Dijck (n 39).

[64]   For example, fixed payments for funeral expenses and one-off payments that do not specifically compensate for any particular loss are available under the New Zealand ACC Scheme.

[65]   Daniel Gardner, 'Quelques Points de Comparaison Entre Les Deux plus Anciens Régimes Intégrés d'indeminisation Des Victimes d'accidents d'automobile: Québec et Nouvelle-Zélande' (2004) 71 *Assurances et Gestion des Risques* 591.

A Comparative Law Analysis of No-Fault Comprehensive Compensation Funds

for comparison with other schemes. The logical conclusion of this and the previous subsection is that historical abuse redress schemes are a type of general compensation fund.

5.3. DO ANY EXISTING HISTORICAL ABUSE COMPENSATION FUNDS FIT WITHIN THIS DEFINITION?

Given the argument in the previous subsection that historical abuse compensation funds can and should be included in the wider compensation funds group, we should now consider whether any historical abuse funds fit within this book's definition of a no-fault comprehensive compensation fund, and could be included in a comparative law analysis.

Comprehensive no-fault compensation funds represent and encapsulate the extreme dimensions of arguments about compensation funds generally: a utopian compensation and redress dream versus an unrealistic and expensive bureaucratic nightmare; a trend towards more socialised compensation for loss versus an ill-thought out curiosity that leads to discrimination against those who do not qualify for compensation; and finally an escape from the expensive and slow litigation process versus a barrier to exercising one's fundamental right to justice before a court. The argument about whether historical abuse compensation funds are functionally and purposively comparable to general (non-comprehensive) compensation funds is an important related argument, but not one that is at the centre of existential questions about no-fault comprehensive compensation funds overall.

Until recently, publicly administered historical abuse compensation funds have generally not been comprehensive. Ireland has been a front-runner in creatively using compensation funds in the context of the Irish government's engagement in processes of acknowledgment, restitution and compensation for large-scale historical abuse, injury and trauma inflicted on vulnerable Irish citizens. However, these compensation funds have been limited causally to individuals who were abused within specific, named state residential institutions[66] or Magdalen laundries.[67] In that jurisdiction there has been no

---

[66] Residential Institutions Redress Act 2002 s 7. An individual was only eligible for compensation if he or she could establish that he was resident in a listed institution during his or her childhood, that he or she was injured while resident, and that the injury was consistent with abuse that was alleged to have occurred while resident.

[67] Around 10,000 Irish women and girls spent time in Catholic Church-operated Magdalen laundries, where many endured forced labour and physical, sexual and emotional abuse. However there was a critique by the Irish Ombudsman of, among other issues, the limited definition of the eligible category of claimants. The scheme was recently extended to include women and girls who were living in similar or annexed institutions. See Office of the Ombudsman, 'Opportunity Lost: An Investigation by the Ombudsman into the

44   Intersentia

Chapter 2. Analysis of Core Problems in the Classification of Compensation Funds

comprehensive compensation fund for historical abuse applicable to multiple settings on a statutory basis.

The Netherlands[68] and Germany[69] have established compensation funds for some specific (non-comprehensive) categories of historical child abuse. Scotland launched an advanced payment compensation scheme for childhood abuse victims, in advance of the establishment of a more comprehensive statutory scheme.[70]

In New Zealand, the ACC Scheme will provide coverage for some types of historical abuse. There are often evidentiary challenges for the ACC Scheme in processing these kinds of claims, but there will be cover where a qualifying injury can be shown to have been caused by the historical abuse on the balance of probabilities.[71] In that jurisdiction, there is currently an ongoing Royal Commission of Inquiry investigating the nature, extent and impact of institutional child abuse linked to state care in New Zealand, and what kind of monetary and non-monetary redress is appropriate.[72]

In 2018, Australia established the National Redress Scheme for Victims of Sexual Abuse (National Redress Scheme). This compensation fund was a recommendation of the Royal Commission into Institutional Responses to Child Sexual Abuse.[73] It will operate for 10 years.[74] This scheme is an alternative to tort liability damages claims. The scheme is made up of individual state and territorial-level institutions and many non-governmental institutions (including the Catholic Church, the Anglican Church, Salvation Army, Scouts Australia, YMCA and the Uniting Church).[75] The National Redress Scheme has a wide

---

Administration of the Magdalen Restorative Justice Scheme' (November 2017) <https://www.ombudsman.ie/publications/reports/opportunity-lost/>; Patsy McGarry, 'Government Plans to Broaden Magdalene Redress Scheme Welcomed', *The Irish Times* (18 April 2018) <https://www.irishtimes.com/news/social-affairs/government-plans-to-broaden-magdalene-redress-scheme-welcomed-1.3465533>.

[68] van Dijck (n 39).

[69] 'Stiftung Anerkennung Und Hilfe – Wer Kann Sich Anmelden?' <http://www.stiftung-anerkennung-und-hilfe.de/DE/Infos-fuer-Betroffene/Wer-kann-sich-anmelden/wer-kann-sich-anmelden.html>.

[70] The Scottish Government, 'Child Protection: Justice and Support for Child Abuse Survivors' <https://www.gov.scot/policies/child-protection/supporting-child-abuse-survivors/>.

[71] Comments of ACC Principal Solicitor Michael Mercier in email correspondence dated 28/5/2019. See also *Accident Compensation Corporation v Ambros* [2007] NZCA 304.

[72] Royal Commission of Inquiry into Historical Abuse in State Care, 'Terms of Reference' (2018) <https://www.dia.govt.nz/diawebsite.nsf/Files/Royal-Commission-of-Inquiry-into-Historical-Abuse-in-State-Care/$file/Royal-Commission-Terms-of-Reference-for-consultation.pdf>. Amendments 2021: https://www.abuseincare.org.nz/our-progress/library/v/3/terms-of-reference.

[73] Royal Commission into Institutional Responses to Child Sexual Abuse, 'Final Report Recommendations'.

[74] National Redress Scheme for Institutional Child Sexual Abuse Act 2018 (n 59) s 193(1).

[75] 'Institutions That Have Joined the Scheme' <https://www.nationalredress.gov.au/institutions/joined-scheme>.

Intersentia

scope and no-fault principles,[76] but its non-compulsory nature means it does not fall within the definition of a no-fault comprehensive compensation fund. Recent parallel changes to civil procedure rules (that were recommended by the Royal Commission into Institutional Responses to Child Sexual Abuse) mean that it is now more feasible in some Australian states for abuse survivors to seek civil damages based on negligence and even overturn previously negotiated compensation settlements.[77] Further, the existence of the National Redress Scheme does not appear in practice to have had a dampening effect on the number of civil claims presently being lodged in relation to historical abuse.[78] Courts have also thus far shown a reluctance to overturn previously negotiated settlements between victims and institutions.[79]

There are currently therefore no existing historical abuse compensation funds that precisely meet the definition of a no-fault comprehensive compensation fund.

5.4. WHAT FURTHER INFORMATION IS NEEDED TO BETTER STUDY THIS FIELD?

The key barrier currently to analysing the overlap between general compensation funds and the historical abuse compensation funds category is the fast-changing

---

[76] For all claims, the Scheme assesses whether one or more participating institutions are *responsible* for the claimed abuse for the purposes of the Scheme. This is different to a finding of civil liability, and no finding of fault is required – the simpler causal 'reasonable likelihood' is the required standard (s 12(2)(b) National Redress Scheme for Institutional Child Sexual Abuse Act 2018 (n 59)). A finding of partial or whole 'liability' for abuse has the effect of requiring the relevant institution(s) to fund the compensation payment to the applicant. By accepting an offer of compensation via the Scheme, the applicant releases the relevant institution and its associates and officials from any liability for sexual abuse and related non-sexual abuse that is within the scope of the Scheme. An institution is automatically deemed to be responsible for the abuse where the Government had parental responsibility of a child (e.g. ward of the state), the person was a defence force cadet or was a child migrant to Australia. Equally, an institution will automatically not be responsible if it has already paid court damages for the abuse, and there were minor links between the government and the abuse. See '2.2.1 What does "reasonable likelihood" mean?', '6.4 Effect of accepting an offer of redress', '7.7 Determining institution is responsible', '7.7.1 Automatic deeming an institution responsible', '7.7.2 Automatic deeming an institution not responsible' in Australian Government, 'The National Redress Guide (v1.02)' (2019) <http://guides.dss.gov.au/national-redress-guide>.

[77] The Limitation of Actions Amendment (Child Abuse) Act 2015 removed civil claim time limits in Victoria for survivors of child abuse. Mirror legislation was introduced in 2016 in New South Wales and Queensland.

[78] Comments made in a telephone interview with Victorian institutional abuse lawyer Judy Courtin on 27 June 2019. In 2019 the Victoria Supreme Court established a special list for handling historical abuse cases. At the time of the interview, around 100 cases were in progress under that list.

[79] *TRG v The Board of Trustees of the Brisbane Grammar School* [2019] QSC 157.

nature of legal developments in the field of abuse compensation and redress. Legal and policy developments that are changing the redress landscape are still in play at the time of writing, which means that there cannot be a definitive analysis of the intersection between general and historic no-fault comprehensive compensation fund structures.

New Zealand's Royal Commission of Inquiry into Historical Abuse in State Care and in the Care of Faith-based Institutions was established in 2018. The findings of this Royal Commission will affect how victims of historical child abuse are compensated in New Zealand, and this will have a legislative interaction with ACC where there is an overlap of eligibility.[80] The Royal Commission is scheduled to issue its final report in January 2023.[81] If a redress scheme is proposed, it is not guaranteed to mirror the Royal Commission's recommendations and it may take some time before it is implemented. Because of thematic overlap, there will almost certainly be modifications to the entitlements available to relevant potential claimants under the ACC Scheme.

There is therefore inadequate information available at this time to undertake a proper comparative law analysis of no-fault comprehensive compensation funds that includes both general and historical abuse compensation funds, and considers the interaction and relationship between them. However, there is a very strong case for including historical abuse compensation funds in future comparative law analyses. The overlap between the purpose and function of existing niche crime victim compensation funds and wider historical abuse funds is a suitable departure point for a comparative law analysis.[82]

5.5. ARE RESEARCH FINDINGS ABOUT NO-FAULT COMPREHENSIVE FUNDS APPLICABLE TO HISTORICAL ABUSE FUNDS?

Despite the exclusion of historical abuse funds from analysis, conclusions on the interaction between no-fault comprehensive compensation funds and human rights will still be relevant to historical abuse compensation funds. Firstly, child abuse of any kind can be considered a breach of fundamental personal integrity

---

[80]   Royal Commission of Inquiry into Historical Abuse in State Care and in the Care of Faith-based Institutions Order 2018 s 32(b).

[81]   ibid, ss 34 and 39.

[82]   For example, the recent conviction and dismissed appeal of Cardinal George Pell in Australia has focused popular thought on what compensation options are available to victims. In the Australian state of Victoria, Catholic Church abuse victims can launch a civil claim, or make an application to a compensation scheme created by the Church itself (The Melbourne Response), the Victorian Victims of Crime compensation fund, or the National Redress Scheme. Accumulation rules apply to applications seeking compensation from multiple sources, but there is no clear guidance for victims or single application window.

rights. Secondly, the tendency for historical abuse funds to restrict a claimant's access to court as a pre-condition for accepting a redress award is relevant to whether compensation funds generally breach human rights or access to justice principles. Conclusions about the interaction between human rights and no-fault comprehensive compensation funds could be applied in future analyses of historical abuse compensation funds.

6. CAN SUCH VARIED COMPENSATION FUNDS AND LEGAL TRADITIONS BE EFFECTIVELY COMPARED?

There are certainly legal doctrinal, contextual and societal differences between the no-fault comprehensive compensation funds analysed in depth in this book, and the other compensation funds to which the resulting research conclusions can be applied. This leads naturally to the question of whether it is appropriate to undertake a comparative law analysis of such different compensation funds – of either comprehensive no-fault funds themselves as a specific category, or of no-fault compensation funds in general. It must be acknowledged that this is a common issue in the field of comparative law, and a (justified) critique that has been applied to Macleod and Hodges' ambitious and widespread review of personal injury redress schemes.[83] The answer to that question must surely be yes, for the following reasons:

a. There has been inadequate legal comparison in scholarly literature of the differences between the use of compensation funds in non-UK/non-US major common law jurisdictions and major European civil jurisdictions. In particular, the decades of New Zealand, Victorian, Québécois and Manitoban experiences are particularly instructive for whether a no-fault comprehensive fund is viable for other jurisdictions, yet they have been inadequately considered together within recent tort and other legal scholarly literature.

b. Non-legal academic disciplines have recently compared and analysed the outcomes of similar functional categories of compensation funds in different jurisdictions, using statistical and econometric data.[84] It is surely desirable

---

[83] Per Laleng, 'Redress Schemes for Personal Injuries – Book Review' (2018) 25 *European Journal of Health Law* 469.

[84] Kirsten Armstrong and Daniel Tess, 'Fault versus No Fault – Reviewing the International Evidence', *Institute of Actuaries of Australia 16th General Insurance Seminar* (2008) <https://actuaries.asn.au/Library/Events/GIS/2008/GIS08_3d_Paper_Tess,Armstrong_Fault versus No Fault – reviewing the international evidence.pdf>; Tom Vandersteegen and others, 'The Impact of No-Fault Compensation on Health Care Expenditures: An Empirical Study of OECD Countries' (2015) 119 *Health Policy* 367 <https://www.healthpolicyjrnl.com/article/S0168-8510(14)00240-1/pdf>.

for the development of legal compensation structures to be founded on a good scientific, analytical and evidential basis, rather than simply on legal theory. Therefore, at the very least a functional comparison of equivalent compensation fund structures used in different jurisdictions to deal with similar loss incidents (that applies empirical data) will always be a valuable comparative law research exercise. Helmut Koziol has drawn attention to the (often overlooked) point that the common law understanding of torts (a loose group of around 70 individualised torts) is very different to the civil European conception of tortious damages (and the differences within civil law jurisdictions[85]), thus limiting the usefulness of comparative exercises. But he points to compensatory damages alone as being the only 'tort' concept that can be effectively compared across different world views of tort.[86] It is not an overreach to say that equally, no-fault compensation funds can therefore also be compared together across different legal traditions.

c.   In the future, compensation funds may be used to address new loss incidents that involve citizens, state actors, and multi-national organisations. These loss incidents may result from such topical issues as climate change and artificial intelligence applications.[87] During the writing of this book, a global COVID-19 vaccine no-fault compensation fund was created.[88] This means it will be vitally necessary in the future to understand how compensation funds could be harmonised or be made reasonably procedurally consistent across very different jurisdictions in order to obtain equitable, efficient and equivalent compensation results – regardless of differences in legal traditions.

---

[85]   For example, the difference between the rule of *casum sentit dominus* that is derived from Roman law, and French jurisprudence's preference for the perspective of *neminem laedere*.

[86]   Helmut Koziol, 'Comparative Conclusions' in Helmut Koziol (ed), *Basic Questions of Tort Law from a Comparative Perspective* (1st edn, Jan Sramek Verlag 2015) 697.

[87]   There has already been some useful academic scholarship on this, including arguments for further research to be done. See Georg Borges, 'New Liability Concepts: The Potential of Insurance and Compensation Funds' in Sebastian Lohsse, Reiner Schulze and Dirk Staudenmayer (eds), *Liability for Artificial Intelligence and the Internet of Things* (Hart Publishing 2019); Maurice Schellekens, 'No-Fault Compensation Schemes for Self-Driving Vehicles' (2018) 10(2) *Law, Innovation and Technology* 314 <https://www.narcis.nl/publication/RecordID/oai:tilburguniversity.edu:publications%2F5dc6cc56-ce7a-46ff-986b-0b2f8a28010a>; Julie-Anne Richards, Liane Schalatek and Heinrich Böll Stiftung North America, 'Not a Silver Bullet: Why the Focus on Insurance to Address Loss and Damage Is a Distraction from Real Solutions' (2018) <https://us.boell.org/sites/default/files/not_a_silver_bullet_1.pdf>.

[88]   Sam Halabi and others, 'No-Fault Compensation for Vaccine Injury – The Other Side of Equitable Access to Covid-19 Vaccines' (2020) 383(23) *New England Journal of Medicine* e125; 'No-Fault Compensation Programme for COVID-19 Vaccines Is a World First' <https://www.who.int/news/item/22-02-2021-no-fault-compensation-programme-for-covid-19-vaccines-is-a-world-first>.

As a general statement, the 'unicorn' status of New Zealand's ACC Scheme does of course present some framing and analytical challenges from a comparative law perspective. Its gargantuan size and function, compared to most other compensation funds, makes it more challenging to find even one immediately logical equivalent comparator. The comprehensive nature of the scheme (covering many different injury classes, and funding a variety of types of rehabilitative compensation) and its successful implementation beg the question of what are the intrinsic successful features that could be replicated elsewhere. By limiting deep analysis to no-fault comprehensive compensation funds, this practically limits the comparative law analysis to the most logical comparators of the very broad New Zealand ACC Scheme.

Setting precise criteria for the comparative law analysis hopefully avoids the pitfalls of an analysis that ends up including far too many funds, because of a (completely understandable) desire to compare relatively similar 'compensation fund' or 'redress scheme' structures that are being used for different functions and purposes in multiple jurisdictions. Ultimately, the reason why a comparative law analysis of no-fault comprehensive compensation funds will advance the law and should be pursued is because these funds all face the same kind of problems – such as the issues of whether they breach human rights or restrict access to justice, give inadequate redress for harm, or are unsustainable to replicate in other jurisdictions.

7. CONCLUSIONS

The conclusions from this chapter are set out below. They partially answer the first and second key questions.

a. No-fault comprehensive compensation funds *stand apart functionally and structurally from social security.*
b. No-fault comprehensive compensation funds have a *wider social purpose and cover than most insurance systems* (even if they are described as insurance). This is because unlike a private insurer, a no-fault compensation fund has an intrinsic social nature at its heart.
c. The differences between *ex gratia* and no-fault for the purposes of compensation are considered. *The key difference between* ex gratia *compensation and no-fault compensation is that the former erases the liability of the compensation payer, whereas the latter erases the relevance of the conduct of the claimant.* Therefore it is still possible to assign legal or factual responsibility to another party under a no-fault compensation fund.

d. *Historical abuse funds can be validly compared* with other functions of compensation funds. However, this is a field that is rapidly evolving. There are inadequate data and finalised legislative developments to enable such funds to be included in this book.

e. There is *enough commonality between different no-fault comprehensive compensation funds* to enable them to be compared, especially when a precise definition is used.

CHAPTER 3

REVIEW OF EXISTING NO-FAULT COMPREHENSIVE COMPENSATION FUNDS

1. INTRODUCTION

This chapter considers the four existing no-fault comprehensive compensation funds, and analyses their purpose, scope and effect. Firstly, each jurisdiction is described and analysed using a pluralist comparative law approach (considering functional, structural, and in-context elements). After this, the selected funds are compared and analysed by their function – how they deal with the same kinds of loss incidents (traffic injury, medical/pharmaceutical, employment injury and everyday risks of life). Next, the learnings from the no-fault comprehensive approach are compared to functionally relevant French, Belgian and Nordic[1] no-fault compensation funds. The European funds have functional and purposive relevance to our four no-fault comprehensive compensation funds. They are not as comprehensive as the key New Zealand, Australian and Canadian funds, but they represent a significant departure from standard compensation and liability law approaches in those jurisdictions. The European funds have also been compared in the past with one another. Finally, conclusions are drawn about this comparative law analysis of existing systems. This partially answers the first and third key questions, and forms the departure point for further comparative law analyses in the subsequent chapters on issues of administration, human rights, access to justice and possible future applications.

2. NEW ZEALAND'S ACCIDENT COMPENSATION CORPORATION (ACC)

When jurists consider the issue of tort law losses, social insurance protections and insurance coverage in the New Zealand jurisdiction, the impact of one compensation fund is always addressed before any other consideration. That fund is the universal single-window statutory scheme for personal injury

---

[1]   Denmark, Finland, Norway and Sweden.

Intersentia

compensation, administered by the Accident Compensation Corporation (hereafter 'the ACC Scheme').[2] Under this scheme, individuals forego the right to sue for compensatory damages for injury under the common law, in exchange for this comprehensive cover and compensation. The fund also has a mirror injury prevention and rehabilitation focus, which makes the purpose and scope of the scheme wider than financial compensation.

The ACC Scheme is something of a legal 'unicorn' because, despite being in effect for the best part of 50 years, it has not been wholly replicated (i.e. its multi-function coverage) in any other major common law or civil law jurisdiction.[3] The New Zealand approach to its major compensation fund can be broadly characterised as a successful twentieth-century private law revolution. But it now needs further evolution with a broad community consensus[4] in this century to meet the original New Zealand vision and address existing and future compensation problems.[5]

The following subsections analyse the legislative structures and relevant doctrines of the ACC Scheme from a comparative law perspective, and the fund's scope and effect. There is also a comparison with other New Zealand compensation structures.

2.1. THE BACKGROUND TO THE ACC SCHEME

The ACC Scheme's beginnings were a Royal Commission established in 1966; it was charged with surveying and reporting on the existing law relating to compensation and claims for damages for incapacity or death arising out of workplace accidents (including industrial diseases).[6] Prior to this, New Zealand had a patchwork of compensation possibilities for injury and loss that was broadly similar to the United Kingdom. In 1900, New Zealand became one of the first countries in the world to create a (limited) worker injury compensation scheme.[7] The New Zealand legislation was modelled on United Kingdom legislation passed three years earlier, and the roots of the UK scheme could be

---

2   The system is governed by the Accident Compensation Act 2001.
3   However it has been replicated recently by one of New Zealand's smaller South Pacific neighbours. In 2018 a comprehensive no-fault compensation fund system for all kinds of personal injury came into force in Fiji, following a need to replace outdated injury insurance legislation. The system is administered by the Accident Compensation Commission Fiji. This can be seen as a logical choice for a small jurisdiction that is heavily influenced by New Zealand (Fiji's nearest wealthy neighbour).
4   Geoffrey Palmer, *Reform: A Memoir* (Victoria University Press 2013) 216.
5   Geoffrey Palmer, 'Sir Owen Woodhouse Memorial Lecture 2018' (Wellington September 2018).
6   Royal Commission to Inquire into and Report upon Workers' Compensation, *Compensation for Personal Injury in New Zealand* (Government Printing Office 1967) 30.
7   Workers' Compensation for Accidents Act 1900.

Chapter 3. Review of Existing No-Fault Comprehensive Compensation Funds

found in 1884 German legislation.[8] By the late 1960s personal injury litigation dominated New Zealand's law of negligence, and was a significant area of activity for lawyers, the Courts and the trade unions.[9]

After a comprehensive national and international fact-finding mission,[10] in 1967 the Royal Commission published its findings. These are commonly known as the Woodhouse Report (named after its author and Commission chairman, Sir Owen Woodhouse, at that time a judge). The Woodhouse Report considered that personal injury, as a consequence of social progress, required that victims of all kinds 'receive a co-ordinated response from the nation as a whole'.[11] The existing negligence action under the common law was considered unjust because it is a form of lottery, and the report said that it was time for a new universal scheme to replace the status quo.[12]

The proposal of a comprehensive no-fault compensation fund was an unexpected result for a Royal Commission that was established only for the purpose of investigating compensation and law reform issues relevant to workplace injury.[13] There was no major crisis of insurance, injury or calamity that spurred the establishment of the Royal Commission or the implementation of a no-fault comprehensive compensation fund. A White Paper and a Select Committee report immediately followed the Woodhouse Report;[14] legislation

---

[8]   Royal Commission to Inquire into and Report upon Workers' Compensation, *Compensation for Personal Injury in New Zealand* (n 6) 33.

[9]   Peter McKenzie, 'The Compensation Scheme No One Asked For: The Origins of ACC in New Zealand' (2003) 34 *Victoria University of Wellington Law Review* 193, 206 <https://www.victoria.ac.nz/law/research/publications/vuwlr/prev-issues/vol-34-2/mckenzie.pdf> 195.

[10]   Royal Commission to Inquire into and Report upon Workers' Compensation, *Compensation for Personal Injury in New Zealand* (n 6) 27–28.

[11]   Royal Commission to Inquire into and Report upon Workers Compensation, *Compensation for Personal Injury in New Zealand* (Government Printing Office 1967) ibid 19. There is mention in particular of the 'grave risks of the road' – the technological advances which lead to greater number of motor vehicles on the road in the mid-20th century had opened up new and much greater dimensions of personal injury risk for the community.

[12]   ibid 41.

[13]   ibid 11–12. Although the focus of the Royal Commission was intended to be law reform proposals relating to workplace injury, the Commission's scope did also hint at an interest in learning more widely about alternative compensation systems. The Commission was tasked with investigating and reporting on 'The desirability of adopting, in whole or in part or with suitable modifications, any scheme or system of compensation, medical care, retraining, and rehabilitation in operation in any other country which the Commission feels justified in investigating.' There was also interest in the 'relationship between money payable by way of compensation or allowances or damages in respect of persons incapacitated or killed in employment and money payable pursuant to legislation concerned with social security or welfare or pensions.'

[14]   New Zealand Parliament, *Personal Injury: A Commentary on the Report of the Royal Commission of Inquiry into Compensation for Personal Injury in New Zealand* (Government Printer 1969); Select Committee on Compensation for Personal Injury in New Zealand and George F Gair, *Report of Select Committee on Compensation for Personal Injury in New Zealand.* (Government Printer 1970).

was passed without controversy in 1972[15] and the scheme came into effect in 1974 (without any major changes from what was proposed in the Woodhouse Report).

Compared to the normally incremental pace of law reform in most jurisdictions, the proposal and implementation of the ACC Scheme was an astounding divergence from established norms. Such a significant departure from the status quo requires consideration of the legal and political context to law reform. Firstly, it should be noted that New Zealand is a small and highly stable common law jurisdiction, with a British Westminster system of government and an uncodified constitution.[16] The development of legislation and case law in the jurisdiction has always been broadly in line with that of other common law Westminster and Commonwealth systems, and relevant case law from those jurisdictions will often be persuasive in New Zealand judicial precedent.[17] It is also worth noting that New Zealand has had a unicameral legislature since 1951 and has a strong history of centralised government.[18] The New Zealand legal system at the time of the Woodhouse Report's publication can therefore be characterised as having few constitutional and legislative barriers to major law reform.

But whatever the constitutional and legislative simplicities, one might have expected political forces and vested interests (such as the personal injury legal bar or insurance businesses) to have affected the ACC Scheme's implementation or secured key modifications to its operation. This was not the case. In terms of politics, the farming sector was New Zealand's dominant political lobby in the early and mid-twentieth century. Other lobby groups and interest groups existed but did not hold the same degree of influence and political leverage as the farming sector.[19] The Woodhouse Report affected the insurance industry, the legal profession and the trade union movement. None of the groups opposed the scheme to an extent that progress could not be made.[20] Geoffrey Palmer gives

---

[15] Accident Compensation Act 1972.

[16] Like the United Kingdom, New Zealand has no written constitution. Key differences from the UK are New Zealand's mixed member proportional voting system (introduced in 1996), and the fact that New Zealand has only one legislative house (Parliament). New Zealand is ranked internationally as having strong legal rights across public and private indicators – World Bank, 'Strength of Legal Rights Index' <https://data.worldbank.org/indicator/IC.LGL.CRED. XQ?locations=NZ>; Kim Watts, 'New Zealand' in Thierry Vansweevelt and Britt Weyts (eds), *Compensation Funds in Comparative Perspective* (Intersentia 2020) 93.

[17] Diarmuid F O'Scannlain, 'What Role Should Foreign Practice and Precedent Play in the Interpretation of Domestic Law' (2005) 80 *Notre Dame Law Review* 893.

[18] Geoffrey Palmer, *Compensation for Incapacity: A Study of Law and Social Change in New Zealand and Australia* (Oxford University Press 1979) 63.

[19] BH Easton, *In Stormy Seas: The Post-War New Zealand Economy* (1st edn, University of Otago Press 1997) 213.

[20] Palmer, *Compensation for Incapacity: A Study of Law and Social Change in New Zealand and Australia* (n 18) 115.

one possible explanation for the lack of insurance industry clout at the time of the Woodhouse Report's implementation: the industry's low political profile and lack of donations to the private-enterprise focused centre-right National Party which was in government at the time.[21]

The legal profession was divided on the Woodhouse Report's proposals but ultimately the New Zealand Law Society took a balanced view. New Zealand has a fused legal profession, where the majority of lawyers hold practising certificates as both barristers and solicitors. In 1971, fewer than 20 per cent of lawyers handled personal injury work (but those who did undertook a significant amount).[22] Lawyers had a few years' advance warning of the ACC scheme's implementation, and thus had time to adapt their practices.[23] Trials relating to accidental injury before 1974 continued to appear before courts until 1978. Additionally, in 1969 a comprehensive civil legal aid scheme came into effect, and there was a simultaneous increase in town planning-related tribunal work. A prosperous legal environment and adequate adjustment time for this small jurisdiction's legal profession seems likely to have smothered any significant legal profession opposition to the ACC Scheme. The political and business interests at the time of the ACC Scheme's implementation can therefore be characterised as being not in direct conflict with a major change to tort law or the introduction of a novel no-fault comprehensive compensation fund structure.

2.2. LEGISLATIVE STRUCTURES AND RELEVANT DOCTRINES

This subsection sets out the legislative structure of the ACC Scheme, and discusses relevant doctrinal issues. Subsequent chapters analyse specific operational issues in more detail from a comparative law perspective, so the focus here is on the key legislative points that are relevant for comparison.

The purpose of the ACC Scheme, as set out in the current legislation, is to 'enhance the public good and reinforce [a] social contract' by providing for a fair and sustainable scheme for managing personal injury, with the twin goals of minimising the incidence of injury and the impact (economic, social and personal) of injury in the community.[24] The stated intention of the Royal Commission in the Woodhouse Report was to completely revolutionise the existing system. To illustrate this, it is useful to directly

---

[21]   ibid 122–123.
[22]   ibid 123.
[23]   ibid 128.
[24]   Accident Compensation Act 2001 s 3; Accident Compensation Corporation, 'Briefing to the Incoming Minister' (2017) 6 <https://www.acc.co.nz/assets/corporate-documents/minister-briefing-2017.pdf>.

A Comparative Law Analysis of No-Fault Comprehensive Compensation Funds

quote the Commission's summarised explanation of its guiding principles for a proposed new scheme:[25]

> 'First, in the national interest, and as a matter of national obligation, the community must protect all citizens (including the self-employed) and the housewives who sustain them from the burden of sudden individual losses when their ability to contribute to the general welfare by their work has been interrupted by physical incapacity;
>
> Second, all injured persons should receive compensation from any community financed scheme on the same uniform method of assessment, regardless of the causes which gave rise to their injuries;
>
> Third, the scheme must be deliberately organised to urge forward the physical and vocational recovery of these citizens while at the same time providing a real measure of money compensation for their losses;
>
> Fourth, real compensation demands for the whole period of incapacity the provision of income-related benefits for lost income and recognition of the plain fact that any permanent bodily impairment is a loss in itself regardless of its effect on earning capacity;
>
> Fifth, the achievement of the system will be eroded to the extent that its benefits are delayed, or are inconsistently assessed, or the system itself is administered by methods that are economically wasteful'.

These five pillars still inform the operation of the ACC Scheme today.[26]

The original 1972 legislation[27] created comprehensive, compulsory coverage for all victims of accidental personal injury in New Zealand, in exchange for a bar on the right to sue or claim workers' compensation. The new ACC Scheme took effect in April 1974. 'Personal injury by accident' was not fully defined in the statute, allowing the concept to be defined further by decision-making bodies and processes created by the legislation. A statutory body, called the Accident Compensation Commission, was created to administer the regime. Compensation generally took the form of medical expenses and associated costs and weekly earnings-related payments, with lump sums available in limited circumstances. Funding came from employers and the self-employed, motor vehicle owners and general taxation. The model created by the 1972

---

[25]   Royal Commission to Inquire into and Report upon Workers Compensation, *Compensation for Personal Injury in New Zealand* (n 6) 39.

[26]   Accident Compensation Corporation, 'What We Do' <https://www.acc.co.nz/about-us/who-we-are/what-we-do/>.

[27]   Accident Compensation Act 1972. Following a change in government after its enactment, the ACC Scheme's coverage was extended by legislative amendments before it came into force to cover all types of personal injury victims, including the unemployed and tourists. A Committee established in 1975 to investigate extending the scheme to sickness was curtailed by another change in government.

58

Intersentia

legislation was neither social insurance (as understood in the New Zealand sense, i.e. funded by general taxation with means-tested flat-rate payments) nor commercial insurance, but rather a unique type of social insurance (funded by compulsory levies with earnings-related compensation and universal entitlement).[28] The 1972 legislation can be seen as largely fulfilling the original spirit of the Woodhouse Report.

The 1982 legislation[29] made some significant administrative and funding changes. The Accident Compensation Corporation company entity replaced the Accident Compensation Commission. Funding was changed to a pay-as-you-go model, meaning that levies for the year paid all costs (old and new claims), but did not cover continuing costs of claims in future years. The government then faced (successful) political pressure from employers to reduce levies.[30] This led to funding reserves being depleted during the 1980s (reserves which had been accumulated since 1974 under the prior quasi-full funding model).

The 1992 legislation[31] introduced stricter definitions about what constituted accidental personal injury (for the purposes of cover under the legislation) and removed judicial discretion to define the limits of statutory definitions. This has to be understood in the context of a seismic political shift in the jurisdiction from a social democratic worldview to a centre-right free market perspective.[32] The 'medical misadventure' definition introduced in the 1992 legislation required consideration of fault-based elements, which a 2003 ACC and Department of Labour review found to be problematic given the no-fault nature of the

---

[28] Stephen Todd and others, *The Law of Torts in New Zealand*, Stephen Todd (ed) (8th edn, Thomson Reuters 2019) 26.

[29] Accident Compensation Act 1982.

[30] Todd and others (n 28) 27.

[31] Accident Rehabilitation and Compensation Insurance Act 1992.

[32] A 1988 government-commissioned Law Commission review of the scheme firmly recommended that the ACC Scheme be extended to include sickness and non-accidental incapacity (in line with the original Woodhouse Report vision) – see New Zealand Law Commission, 'Personal Injury: Prevention and Recovery – Report on the Accident Compensation Scheme' (1988) paras 83–102 <http://www.lawcom.govt.nz/sites/default/files/projectAvailableFormats/NZLC R4 part 1.pdf>. Meanwhile, international economic pressures (diversification, technology and consumer choice) and the favouring of market-focused economic theories led to the New Zealand economy's major market liberalisation in the second half of the twentieth century. For the ACC Scheme, this led to political and ideological clashes in the 1980s and early 1990s about the ambit and funding of the ACC Scheme. The Law Commission disagreed with the dominant public and political perception of the time that the ACC Scheme was facing a financial crisis, and concluded that an extension of the scheme would not lead to a cost blow-out. However legislative attempts to bring the 1988 Law Commission review's recommendations into legislative reality were curtailed by a change of government. The new centre-right conservative government concluded (following its own policy review) that the scheme was too expensive and took a different policy approach. See Bill Birch, *Accident Compensation: A Fairer Scheme* (Office of the Minister of Labour 1991). See also Easton (n 19); BH Easton, 'The Historical Context of the Woodhouse Commission' (2003) 34 *Victoria University of Wellington Law Review* 207.

ACC Scheme. In a cost-cutting move, the 1992 legislation abolished lump sum payments and allowed for some unemployed claimants to be moved off the ACC Scheme's books and onto social welfare. Pay-as-you-go funding was retained, but the funding pool was extended to all earners, including employees.[33]

The 1998 legislation[34] introduced some privatisation elements and reversed the 1982 legislation funding changes. The new legislation required employers to provide statutory benefits for workplace injury via private insurance companies or a new state-owned insurer (set up to compete with the private insurers). ACC administered the rest of the scheme (i.e. for non-workplace injuries). There was a switch from pay-as-you-go to full funding. The government's justification for both of these changes was the need for an increased focus on safety and rehabilitation, which it believed could be delivered through competition and a funding scheme that rewarded injury prevention innovation.[35] The privatisation elements of the 1998 legislation were quickly reversed in 2000 following a change in government.[36]

The 2001 Act retained the full funding model. It also re-introduced lump sum compensation for some situations. A 2003 amendment changed the medical error and mishap definitions (called 'medical misadventure', introduced by the 1992 legislation) to a broader 'treatment injury' definition. Cover for some types of work-related mental injury was introduced in 2008. A 2008 government proposal to reintroduce privatisation never came to fruition.[37]

Today, the ACC organisation itself is a type of Crown Entity,[38] a government-controlled entity that includes corporations created by statute. This means that ACC is a Crown agent which must give effect to government policy when directed by the government's minister for ACC.[39] ACC's board is appointed by the relevant minister,[40] and the corporation's board, in consultation with the minister, selects ACC's chief executive.[41] ACC must adhere to a Code of ACC Claimants' Rights, which confers rights on claimants and obligations on the ACC.[42]

---

[33] Todd and others (n 28) 29.
[34] Accident Insurance Act 1998.
[35] Accident Insurance Bill (203-1) 1999.
[36] Todd and others (n 28) 30.
[37] ibid 31–32. In my view this could be because the results of a PriceWaterhouseCoopers Australia review commissioned by the government showed that the existing ACC structure was preferable to any international comparators involving privatisation. See the Executive Summary in PriceWaterhouseCoopers, 'Accident Compensation Corporation New Zealand Scheme Review' (2008).
[38] Accident Compensation Act 2001 s 259(2).
[39] Crown Entities Act 2004 s 7.
[40] Accident Compensation Act 2001 s 267.
[41] ibid sch 5, cl 17.
[42] ibid ss 39–47; Code of ACC Claimants' Rights 2002. This code was provided for under the 2001 Act following criticism that ACC behaved in in an unduly adversarial and harsh way towards claimants. See Todd and others (n 28) 92–93.

The legislative evolution of the ACC Scheme reveals a scheme that began with bold objectives, which had to make adjustments over time in light of internal funding challenges and external macroeconomic and political factors. The developments from the late 1990s also show a push-pull tension between whether the ACC Scheme should mimic a private insurer or act as a social scheme. The creep of the concept of 'fault' into the fund in 1992, its total obliteration in 2003 – and no further developments – reveals satisfaction up until now with the broadly no-fault status of the ACC Scheme.

From a structural perspective that is relevant to a comparative law analysis, the ACC Scheme has therefore created a codified framework of statutory entitlements to compensation in the case of personal injury[43] – in effect a 'right' to compensation. This contrasts to New Zealand's needs-based social welfare system, under which there is no standing entitlement to social security, and financial support is only available as a last resort.[44] Under the ACC Scheme, prevention, rehabilitation and injury-related data collection have equal importance to compensation for loss.[45] From the outset, the fund was characterised as a hybrid replacement for equivalent injury compensation options under tort, social insurance and insurance that sought to avoid their various pitfalls.[46] More recently, Simon Connell has argued that the ACC Scheme can be characterised as having either a community insurance scheme *or* a compulsory insurance scheme.[47] This dual categorisation argument seems accurate, because the ACC Scheme has continued to exist (nearly 20 years after the last major legislative review) in broad harmony with whichever flavour of political and

---

[43]   Accident Compensation Act 2001 ss 67, 69.

[44]   Social Security Act 2018 s 3. There has not been any significant policy change in purpose from the previous version of the legislation (s 1A Social Security Act 1964). Mamari Stephens, a social welfare law scholar, argues that there is an implicit and explicit right to social security in New Zealand, but this entitlement is not codified in legislation or enshrined in case law precedent. See Māmari Stephens, 'The Right to Social Security' in Margaret Bedggood and Kris Gledhill (eds), *Law into Action Economic, Social and Cultural Rights in Aotearoa New Zealand* (Thomson Reuters 2011).

[45]   Accident Compensation Act 2001 s 3.

[46]   Royal Commission to Inquire into and Report upon Workers Compensation, 'Part 9 – Conclusions and Recommendations' (Government Printing Office 1967). In the case of tort, these pitfalls included the inability to prevent injuries from happening or to aid in their rehabilitation, the 'erratic and capricious' operation of the fault principle, its inefficiency and the fact that complete indemnity is only available to a small group of people. In the case of social security, this included the potential of claimants to receive double compensation for the same injury, the unsuitability of flat-rate benefits for 'varied income losses or permanent physical impairment' after injury and the disincentive effect of a means-test on rehabilitation. In the case of an insurance system, the pitfalls were its inability to offer 'central impetus in the important areas of accident prevention and rehabilitation', its costliness and its inability to avoid adversarial problems.

[47]   Simon Connell, 'Community Insurance versus Compulsory Insurance: Competing Paradigms of No-Fault Accident Compensation in New Zealand' (2019) 39(3) *Legal Studies* 499 <https://www.cambridge.org/core/product/identifier/S0261387518000508/type/journal_article>.

economic theory holds power in government. However, it means that there is no *precise* existing definition of its legislative structure and philosophical basis that allows for the proper principled extension or modification of the fund's statutory entitlements as required.

Most recently this has been exemplified by government attempts to manage compensation and loss flowing from the 2019 Christchurch mosque terrorist attack. After a public and political outcry about the lack of mental trauma cover for some victims of the terrorist attack, the government minister responsible for ACC sought Cabinet approval to extend the fund's coverage to relevant mental trauma victims. A key argument behind this proposal was that ACC had the necessary claims management infrastructure in place to contact the relevant victims (because it was already handling claims from eligible physical personal injury victims of the terrorist attack). However the proposal was not implemented, in part it seems because Treasury identified (accurately) that it would lead to unequal treatment of different victims. Treasury noted that it would be better to review the purpose of ACC generally in tandem with other healthcare, disability and social welfare legislative reforms.[48] Although the proposal by ACC itself to extend coverage to unfairly excluded categories of victims is morally laudable and was well-reasoned, Treasury's caution was right to be heeded to ensure the proper development of the scheme and protect it from inconsistency. Proposing to extend the ACC Scheme to include mental trauma victims from this one particular terrorist attack (rather than terrorism generally[49]), would have been effectively creating a new *ex gratia* compensation fund under ACC's auspices.[50] It would not have bound the government to compensate equivalent future victims in the same way, and would have been funded solely out of general taxpayer revenues allocated to ACC.[51]

The incongruities of combining (or erasing) tort, social insurance and (public) insurance principles under a single statutory scheme of compensation entitlements have mostly been handled by New Zealand courts with a view to maintaining scheme integrity. Judges have been quick to recommend that most

---

[48] Ministry of Business Innovation and Employment, 'Extended Mental Health Support for Those Affected by the 15 March 2019 Terrorist Attack'; Cabinet Business Committee, 'Minute of Decision CBC-19-MIN-0014'.

[49] The Cabinet paper identified that extending ACC Scheme compensation to terrorism victims generally had a high risk of unintentional scheme expansion. See Ministry of Business Innovation and Employment (n 48) 23.

[50] It would not have been directly funded out of existing ACC Scheme funds, due to legislative controls. 'This will require ACC to be provided with new funding for these services. New funding cannot be sourced from ACC's levied accounts, as the use of those funds is tightly specified in legislation. Estimated costs would be up to approximately $35 million lifetime costs, including $1.4 million for 2018/19. This is based on current information available that an estimated potential population of 200 people directly witnessed the event, and potentially an additional 480 people are family members of those injured or killed in the attack.' – ibid 8.

[51] The proposal was to be funded out of new funding sourced via the non-levied parts of the ACC Scheme funds, the 'Non-Earners' Account' – in shorthand, central taxpayer funds.

Chapter 3. Review of Existing No-Fault Comprehensive Compensation Funds

potentially problematic inconsistencies either be directed back to the legislature for correction, or be accepted as a fact of the broad social purpose of the scheme. Expansions of statutory entitlement to accidental personal injury compensation may, however, be possible if medical evidence about the impairment allows a particular case to fall within the natural wording of the legislation. The three cases set out below are key illustrations of the attempt by judges to both maintain the coherence of the regime and allow for specific, fact-based expansion.

2.2.1. Davies v New Zealand Police

In *Davies v New Zealand Police*[52] the Supreme Court overturned a (criminal) sentence of reparation imposed on the appellant, that made up the shortfall between his victim's lost earnings and the weekly compensation received under the ACC scheme. The majority judgment of the Supreme Court noted that if reparation could be ordered under criminal sentencing legislation to make up for perceived inadequacies in the ACC scheme, then crime victims would stand outside the ACC statutory bar on civil wrong victims seeking compensation through the courts. The court viewed such a result as incompatible with the social contract created by the ACC scheme. In response, Parliament amended the Sentencing Act 2002 to allow for such 'top-up' reparation payments.[53] Connell has suggested that inconsistent outcomes between victims of injury may be acceptable as long as all receive adequate compensation.[54] However it is unsatisfactory because Parliament is sanctioning different levels of compensation for different categories of victims – in effect violating its own principle of fairly compensating different victims of unexpected misfortune.[55]

2.2.2. McGougan v DePuy International Limited

In *McGougan v DePuy International Limited*,[56] the New Zealand High Court and Court of Appeal both rejected an attempt to circumvent the statutory bar against a compensatory damages claim, on the ground that the overseas 'tortfeasor' was escaping financial consequences of its negligent conduct. This case related to hip implants manufactured by DePuy that were later

---

[52]   *Davies v New Zealand Police* [2009] NZSC 47.

[53]   Victims of Crime Reform Bill 2011.

[54]   Simon Connell, 'Justice for Victims of Injury: The Influence of New Zealand's Accident Compensation Scheme on the Civil and Criminal Law' (2012) 25 *New Zealand Universities Law Review* 181, 320.

[55]   For a similar argument in the context of an earlier critique of the ACC Scheme, see James A Henderson, 'New Zealand Accident Compensation Reform' (1981) 48 *University of Chicago Law Review* 781, 794.

[56]   *McGougan v DePuy International Limited* [2016] NZHC 2511; *McGougan v DePuy International Limited* [2018] NZCA 91.

discovered to have safety and operational problems. The plaintiffs in this case represented a larger group of 38 New Zealanders who received DePuy hip implants in New Zealand, between 2006 and 2009. DePuy is a company registered in England and does not carry out business in New Zealand. The hip implants in question were designed and manufactured in England and distributed in New Zealand by related companies. The problems suffered by the plaintiffs due to the hip implants were covered by the ACC Scheme as treatment injuries, and the plaintiffs had therefore received various entitlements and benefits from ACC. However the plaintiffs had sought further compensatory damages from DePuy via personal injury proceedings in England.[57] The English judge determined that New Zealand law applied to the claims, and that the ACC Scheme statutory bar prevented the plaintiffs from seeking common law compensatory damages.[58] The question to be decided by the New Zealand courts was whether a common law claim for compensatory damages could be brought in New Zealand relating to ACC Scheme-covered injuries, where the conduct that resulted in the claims (the manufacturing of faulty hip implants) occurred overseas. The New Zealand High Court and Court of Appeal both agreed with the English court and found that the plaintiffs' claims were barred by the 2001 Act. The courts said that the plaintiffs' injuries occurred in New Zealand (an interpretation consistent with private international law principles) and focusing on the place of the defendant's conduct would lead to ambiguity and unacceptable uncertainly. The plaintiffs also argued that the ACC Scheme's 'integrity and economic viability' would be compromised if DePuy could escape liability, because DePuy had contributed nothing to the scheme by way of levies (because they did not carry out business in New Zealand), giving DePuy an 'unexpected windfall'. Collins J disagreed and said linking levies to tortious liability was at odds with the no-fault comprehensive nature of the ACC Scheme. The judge also pointed to the scheme's rehabilitative goals and the scheme's funding model (which is linked to the type of injured victim rather than the type of putative defendant).[59] Justice Asher in the Court of Appeal affirmed this, and pointed out the continued availability of exemplary damages, despite the tort bar.[60] The 'windfall' argument was rejected on the ground that the ACC Scheme's focus is on the victim's rehabilitation. The judicial conclusions in *DePuy* are surely a sound statutory interpretation of the current

---

[57] In jurisdictions such as the United States and Ireland, courts have awarded very large amounts of compensatory damages to plaintiffs injured with the faulty DePuy hip implants.

[58] *Allen and others v DePuy International Ltd* [2015] EWHC 926 [87].

[59] Collins J in *McGougan v DePuy International Limited* [2016] NZHC 2511 also quoted (at paragraph [54]) a 1974 Torts and General Law Reform Committee report on which noted that 'Dangerous and defective products produce a number of injuries, yet once the accident compensation scheme is in force, those enterprises whose products cause injuries will not be directly liable to finance the risk in the same manner as the industry operator is called upon to finance the risk of injuries to earners.'

[60] *McGougan v DePuy International Limited* (n 56) para 29.

Chapter 3. Review of Existing No-Fault Comprehensive Compensation Funds

bar against common law action. The New Zealand plaintiffs' position may seem inequitable compared to similar classes of victims internationally who could participate in class actions, but the answer to this is surely that the plaintiffs have benefited from efficient compensation (that they were statutorily entitled to) and access to rehabilitation via the ACC Scheme. A further point to note here is that the reasoning in the *DePuy* judgments would not be inconsistent with a future legislative choice to tweak the tort bar and give ACC subrogation powers to pursue the likes of DePuy – but this is an issue that will be considered in subsequent chapters.

2.2.3. Accident Compensation Corporation v Calver (Estate of Trevarthen)

Accident Compensation Corporation v Calver (Estate of Trevarthen)[61] is a recent and ground-breaking NZ Court of Appeal decision, approving a 2019 High Court decision, which has used medical evidence to allow the ACC Scheme's scope to be expanded to include non-workplace asbestos-related mesothelioma. The High Court judge's reasoning in this 'Hug of Death' case[62] was made on the basis of known medical science about the development of the mesothelioma disease, rather than skewing the statutory interpretation of eligibility under ACC Scheme. The appellant, Deanna Trevarthen, had died from mesothelioma following childhood exposure to asbestos via her father, an electrician. ACC had declined cover on the basis (of its view) that mesothelioma was an ineligible non-workplace gradual process condition.[63] Justice Mallon relied on known medical evidence and international mesothelioma-related case law, which showed that mesothelioma could, theoretically, be caused by a single exposure to asbestos. She held that the development of mesothelioma was indeed an accidental personal injury resulting from that exposure (and thus qualified for ACC Scheme cover). Expert medical evidence showed there was no current scientific knowledge about what exact dosage level or accumulation would lead to the development of mesothelioma – one exposure could quite possibly be sufficient to lead to a latent diagnosis of mesothelioma cancer.[64] Existing ACC precedent on the definition of personal injury requires consideration of the claimant's whole condition and says that personal injury will exist so long as there are physical impacts (even progressive ones).[65] The sub-definition of an accident in the legislation (that was

---

[61]   *Accident Compensation Corporation v Calver (Estate of Trevarthen)* [2021] NZCA 211.
[62]   *Calver v Accident Compensation Corporation (Estate of Trevarthen)* [2019] NZHC 1581.
[63]   Accident Compensation Act 2001 s 26(2). There is no cover under the ACC Scheme for injuries resulting from non-workplace gradual processes or disease.
[64]   *Calver v Accident Compensation Corporation (Estate of Trevarthen)* (n 62) para 98.
[65]   *Allenby v H* [2012] NZSC 33. In *Allenby v H*, pregnancy was found to be a ACC-covered personal injury for a mentally ill patient who became pregnant following sterilisation. However, there was only cover in relation to the pregnancy itself and its associated physical impacts, not for the costs to the mother of raising the child.

Intersentia

applicable in this case) says that an injury meets the 'accident' requirement where there is 'the inhalation of any solid, liquid, gas, or foreign object on a specific occasion'.[66] Justice Mallon took an appropriately generous approach to the plain meaning of this sub-definition,[67] and concluded that 'a specific occasion' could include multiple single exposures to asbestos fibres.[68] Therefore Ms Trevarthon's mesothelioma could be properly regarded as qualifying for ACC Scheme cover – it flowed from an accident (asbestos fibre inhalation) that lead to personal injury (her eventual mesothelioma), and was *not* a gradual process. A comparison was made with tetanus – although it is a disease, nobody would contest factually the fact of an accident causing the damage (that leads to the tetanus infection).[69]

The Court of Appeal agreed with this reasoning and said that

> 'it is artificial to draw a distinction between being inflicted with a disease and experiencing the physical manifestations of the disease and then, by reference to such a distinction, to nominate the disease (as distinct from its external cause) as the cause of the personal injury. We cannot discern the intentional drawing of a such a distinction in the legislation. Certainly it could not be said to derive from the confusing structure of s 26(2) which deploys the phrase "personal injury" three times'.[70]

This judgment does not distort the existing legislative framework – it was medical evidence about mesothelioma's pathology that meant the appellant's case was able to meet the threshold of eligible accidental personal injury. The case shows that judges are willing to take a facts-based approach to scheme coherency. The judgment does, of course, have significant practical expansion consequences that must be managed – but there is no misapplication of the law. The best conclusion here might be that *assumptions* (by the government, legislature and the fund itself) about the breadth of scheme cover no longer match the results of an actual application of the law to scientific knowledge. Further, general remarks about the confusing drafting of the relevant definition of personal injury indicate that significant scheme revision (particularly in terms of eligibility and fairness issues) is overdue.

2.2.4. *The Status Quo: Consistent Inconsistency*

Where does this leave us, for the purpose of understanding the ACC Scheme's legislative structure and how it fits into a comparative law context? Firstly, there is a hybrid purpose enshrined in the ACC Scheme legislation that shows it

---

[66]   Accident Compensation Act 2001 s 25(1)(b).

[67]   *Harrild v Director of Proceedings* [2003] 3 NZLR 289 (CA) at [19], [37] and [130] requires judges to look for a generous, un-niggardly interpretation of legislation.

[68]   *Calver v Accident Compensation Corporation (Estate of Trevarthen)* (n 62) para 106.

[69]   ibid 75.

[70]   *Accident Compensation Corporation v Calver (Estate of Trevarthen)* (n 61) para 74.

Chapter 3. Review of Existing No-Fault Comprehensive Compensation Funds

can be classified expansively as a tort replacement structure, a type of social insurance support, and mandatory insurance structure. It therefore stands apart on its own, as a special hybrid fund. The courts have attempted to maintain the coherence of the ACC Scheme as it is presently described in legislation, but will allow for limited expansion where this matches the factual evidence about injury and disease. But as Connell notes, it appears there is no longer clear political, public or institutional consensus about the true purpose of the ACC Scheme.[71] There is ongoing lobbying by claimant advocates and legal scholars to extend the scheme to include sickness and disability, and re-imagine the ACC Scheme for the twenty first century.[72] But the normative foundations of the ACC Scheme need to be clarified – with comparative reference to other no-fault compensation fund developments – before any extension of cover is possible.

In 2011, the architect of the ACC Scheme Sir Owen Woodhouse said that his 1967 Report

'spoke of [the fund's] purpose as the delivery of a system of social insurance to provide for injured persons. But the 'social' and the hyphen have been ignored by those who imagine the ACC is merely commercial insurance under another name.'[73]

This encapsulates the problem: the legislative scheme in practice is a hybrid system of no-fault comprehensive compensation, rehabilitation and prevention. This hybrid approach does not need to be abandoned, but it must be recognised as the *current* departure point for the future development of the ACC Scheme. From a comparative law perspective, any future re-interpretation of how the ACC Scheme is defined or operates will impact on how it should be compared with compensation funds in other jurisdictions. A tilt towards social insurance will place it more closely to social insurance and security systems of European jurisdictions, whilst a tilt towards private insurance concepts and privatisation will require the ACC Scheme to be analysed through an insurance law prism. The government appears to have some awareness of a need to reconcile the ACC Scheme's legislative and purposive relationship with other legal structures because it delayed a major overhaul of the ACC Scheme legislation until after it has received advice from various expert groups.[74]

---

[71] Connell (n 47).

[72] Forster & Associates, 'Expansion of ACC' <https://www.forster.co.nz/beyond-injury/expansion>; Palmer, 'Sir Owen Woodhouse Memorial Lecture 2018' (n 5); Warren Forster, Tom Barraclough and Tiho Mijatov, 'Solving the Problem: Causation, Transparency and Access to Justice in New Zealand's Personal Injury System' (New Zealand Law Foundation Research Reports 2017) <http://www.nzlii.org/nz/journals/NZLFRRp/2017/10.html>.

[73] Owen Woodhouse, 'The ACC Concept' <http://docs.business.auckland.ac.nz/Doc/ACC-Forum-2011-17-Woodhouse-ACC-Concept-Paper-revised.pdf>.

[74] Michael Fletcher, 'Towards Wellbeing? Developments in Social Legislation and Policy in New Zealand' (Max Planck Institute for Social Law and Social Policy 2018) 19 <http://www.mpisoc.mpg.de>. One of these working groups, the Welfare Expert Advisory Group, has recommended that the relationship between the ACC Scheme, social welfare, and the health

2.3. THE SCOPE OF THE ACC SCHEME

This subsection considers the scope and the effect of the ACC Scheme. 'Scope' means the space in law and practice in which the compensation fund operates, what it provides (in terms of compensation) and what it takes away (in terms of entitlement to access other remedies). Closely related, the 'effect' of the ACC Scheme is its effect on both related legislation and its effect on tort law.

The scope of the ACC Scheme is coverage for a wide range of statutorily defined qualifying personal injuries. A qualifying personal injury is defined as including death, physical injuries (for example, a strain or a sprain), mental injury caused by physical injury, mental injury caused by some types of sexual crimes, some kinds of work-related injury and out of the ordinary damage to prostheses.[75] There is also cover for some types of injury as a result of medical treatment (called 'treatment injury'); those injuries are not considered to be 'an accident' but they still have cover under the legislation.[76] As a broadly no-fault scheme, fault or contributory liability for the relevant injury is almost always irrelevant to the payment of compensation or provision of treatment and rehabilitation services.[77] Although the system is stated to be no-fault, in the 1990s elements of fault were introduced to the scheme for 'medical error' and 'medical mishap'. Upon review a decade later, the medical mishap criteria were found to be confusing and arbitrary; meanwhile the medical error category required considerations of fault (in contrast to the no-fault ethos of the rest of the ACC scheme) and was found to have resulted in a 'blaming culture'.[78]

Set out in the table below is an overview of the broad types of harm ('functions') that ACC covers, what these functions include, and any specific limitations to cover.[79]

---

and disability system be reviewed by New Zealand Health and Disability System Review. See Welfare Expert Advisory Group, 'Whakamana Tāngata – Restoring Dignity to Social Security in New Zealand' (2019) <www.weag.govt.nz>. However that Review put much of the ACC Scheme outside of its scope of review, and solely focused on the long-term planning and case management approaches of ACC being a useful reference point. See *Health and Disability System Review: Final Report / Pūrongo Whakamutunga* (2020) 138 <www. systemreview.health.govt.nz/final-report>. The most recent relevant announcement is a plan to introduce an unemployment social insurance scheme, but that is still at a conceptual stage – see 'Building Stronger Support for Workers Post COVID' (*Beehive.govt.nz*) <https://www. beehive.govt.nz/release/building-stronger-support-workers-post-covid>.

[75] Accident Compensation Act 2001 s 26.

[76] ibid s 25(2).

[77] There are some narrow exceptions to this for certain categories of claimants. Section 119 of the Accident Compensation Act 2001 says there can be some limitation of entitlements in cases of suicide and self-harm. Section 120 restricts the availability of fatal injury entitlements to claimants convicted of murdering the dead person. Sections 121 and 122 limit the availability of ACC Scheme entitlements for prisoners.

[78] Ken Oliphant, 'Beyond Misadventure: Compensation for Medical Injuries in New Zealand' (2007) 15 *Medical Law Review* 357, 370.

[79] The functional divisions in this table are those that are used in the Accident Compensation Act 2001 and Chapter 2 of Todd and others, *The Law of Torts in New Zealand* (n 28).

Table 1. Overview of the ACC Scheme

Function of cover	What this includes	Limitations/Noteworthy points
Personal injury (s 20; definition of personal injury in s 26)	In any circumstances: death, physical injuries (eg strain or sprain); mental injuries caused by physical injuries; damage to dentures or prostheses.	No cover for a gradual process, disease or infection unless it is work-related, caused by treatment injury or another covered injury.
	The cover is universal and extends to all situations, anywhere in New Zealand – it includes workplace injuries (s 28(1)), transport-related injuries and all everyday circumstances. No distinction is made between the venue of the injury; there are only distinctions between the types of harm (as described in this table).	No cover for injuries caused substantially by the ageing process. No cover for suicide or injuries flowing from self-harm. Limitations on fatal injury entitlements if the claimant is convicted of murdering the relevant deceased person.
Personal injury by an accident (accident defined in s 25)	Generally a specific event(s) that is not a gradual process and involves an external force being applied to the body, or the body reacting to such a force. This includes inhalation of a foreign substance (but not a virus or bacteria, unless criminally inflicted), a burn or exposure to the elements.	This strict statutory description was introduced in the 1992 statutory reforms, to wind back the expansive approach to 'accident' that courts had taken.[80] Does not include personal injuries by accident that fall within the 'treatment injury' definition. Does not include ecto-parasitic infestations or diseases carried by an arthropod unless they are work-related.
Mental injury (s 26(1)(c), (d) and (da); s 27)	Mental injury that is caused by physical injury, certain criminal acts (ss 21 and 21A), work-related mental injury (s 21B).	All other kinds of mental injuries.

(continued)

---

[80]   ibid 43–44.

Table 1 *continued*

Function of cover	What this includes	Limitations/Noteworthy points
Treatment injury (ss 32, 33)	Personal injury that was caused by a treatment that was delivered by or at the direction of a registered healthcare professional. If the injury is an infection (caused by the treatment), cover extends to other specific persons that get infected by the primary victim. Includes injuries suffered in certain types of clinical trials.	No cover if the injury was a necessary part or ordinary consequence of the treatment, taking into account all the circumstances of the case (the victim's health condition and clinical knowledge). No cover simply because the treatment did not achieve the desired result. No cover where the injury is wholly or substantially caused by victim's underlying condition, by a resource allocation decision, or by the victim unreasonably withholding or delaying consent to treatment.
Work-related diseases and other non-accident work ailments (s 30)	There is cover for work-related gradual processes, diseases and infection where those occurred in a work setting, and that work setting had a 'particular property or characteristic' that has some extra degree of risk (that does not exist for other types of employees who do not perform that task). There is cover for specific diseases flowing from work-related exposure to agents, dusts, compounds, radiation and other things (s 30(3) and Schedule 2).	There is no cover for work-related exposures to gradual processes, diseases or infections *unless* the person was ordinarily resident in New Zealand at the time of the exposure (s 30(4A)). No cover for non-physical stress (for example, a heart attack brought on by general employment-related stress).
Visitors to NZ and NZers overseas (ss 22 and 23)	All visitors to New Zealand are covered for their personal injuries suffered while in the country. Persons ordinarily resident in New Zealand have cover for injuries that occur overseas, if they are of a kind that would be covered if they were in New Zealand.	No cover if injury occurred on a ship or aircraft travelling to, from or around New Zealand.

Source: Compiled by the author.

Chapter 3. Review of Existing No-Fault Comprehensive Compensation Funds

The healthcare provider (e.g., doctor, or hospital emergency room) makes the initial causal assessment of whether an individual's injury falls within the scope of the ACC Scheme and submits the necessary documentation to ACC.[81] This streamlined non-legal determination of eligibility widens further the potential scope of the scheme. There is some discretion available to ACC Scheme staff in the determination of whether a claim is eligible for cover. For a covered accidental injury, ACC will pay most or all of the treatment costs directly to the healthcare provider. Confirmation of coverage is by letter to the injured person. Applications should normally be made within 12 months of the qualifying injury or treatment,[82] but ACC will still accept claims after this time unless the lateness affects their ability to make a decision.[83] Claimants of all kinds can manage an increasing number of their claims via an agile online platform.[84]

Other than treatment costs, the main scope of compensation paid is weekly compensation of the injured person's lost earnings (at an 80 per cent rate) from one week after the injury date until there has been adequate recovery. In the case of a work-related personal injury sustained as an employee, the employer must pay the injured person's earnings for the first week (at an 80 per cent rate).[85] This is to incentivise good health and safety practices in the workplace.[86] This means that people injured in non-workplace accidents must bear the first week's loss of earnings themselves.[87] There are various formulae in the statute for calculating the weekly earnings of self-employed people and those with irregular or multiple sources of income.[88] The current legislation also allows weekly compensation payments to be stopped after a period of time if a claimant is fit to return to work.[89] Weekly compensation is payable to a surviving spouse/partner and child

---

[81]   Accident Compensation Corporation, 'What to Do If You're Injured' (2017) <https://www.acc.co.nz/im-injured/what-to-do/>; Accident Compensation Act 2001 s 49.

[82]   Accident Compensation Act 2001 s 53.

[83]   'Making a Claim and Dealing with ACC' (*Communtity Law Manual: Accident Compensation*) <https://communitylaw.org.nz/community-law-manual/chapter-18-accident-compensation-acc/making-a-claim-and-dealing-with-acc/>.

[84]   For a recent overview of the ACC Scheme's recent improvements to case management, see Controller and Auditor-General, 'Accident Compensation Corporation Case Management: Progress on Recommendations Made in 2014' (2020).

[85]   Accident Compensation Act 2001 s 98.

[86]   Todd and others (n 28) 79–80.

[87]   However, the employee may be entitled to sick leave during this first week under the Holidays Act 2003 and the terms of their employment contract.

[88]   Accident Compensation Act 2001 ss 9, 14, 15, 100 and Holidays Act 2003 s 49.

[89]   Accident Compensation Act 2001 ss 6, 107, 112. Fitness to return to work is called 'vocational independence' under the legislation. This is defined under s 6 as meaning the claimant's capacity to engage in work (that he/she is suited to by experience, education and/or training) for 30 hours or more a week. A strict work capacity test had been introduced by the 1992 legislation, but it was found to be unworkable in practice – see Todd and others (n 28) 81–82. The 1991 government report that preceded the 1992 legislative changes noted that rehabilitation 'cannot be forced on an individual, but an insurer must have the right to terminate income maintenance if the injured person refuses to cooperate in rehabilitation.' – see Birch (n 32) 57.

in the event of a fatal accident.[90] More rarely, lump sum compensation will be paid for permanent impairment.[91] A feature of the original 1972 legislation, lump sum payments were abolished under the 1992 legislation. This was controversial and viewed by some as a breach of the social contract underlying the ACC Scheme.[92] Lump sums are still available for permanent impairment, and this amount is indexed in line with inflation.[93] ACC also makes one-off payments to the dependants and survivors of a fatal accident victim.[94]

From a structural perspective, the compensation offered under the ACC Scheme is distributed via a social insurance model. There is a focus on the speedy and streamlined payment of the costs of treatment and income replacement as the main form of compensation. Rehabilitation is also relevant to the financial compensation payable to claimants, and is one of the key goals of the ACC Scheme.[95] ACC's key obligation is the identification of a suitable rehabilitation plan to meet this goal,[96] and claimants have a responsibility to co-operate with the rehabilitation plan.[97] The claimant's compensation and redress process is therefore effectively administered by ACC itself. There is a presumption of entitlement when the initial statutory conditions are met. In contrast, a more active demonstration of entitlement will be needed to show an ongoing entitlement to compensation on a longer term basis.[98] The fund's wide scope means that the ACC Scheme handles a very large number of claims – ACC

---

[90]   Accident Compensation Act 2001 sch 1, cll 66, 70, 76.

[91]   ibid sch 1, cl 54. Permanent impairment is defined by cl 54(1)(c) as a personal injury resulting in 'a degree of whole-person impairment of 10% of more'. Assessment of permanent impairment is based on ACC guidelines and American Medical Association guidelines – see Accident Compensation Corporation, 'Impairment Assessment Lump Sum/Independence Allowance Operational Guidelines' (2014) <https://www.acc.co.nz/assets/contracts/imp-og. pdf>.

[92]   Todd and others (n 28) 84. Lump sum payments for loss of faculty were replaced in 1992 with a graduated 'independence allowance'. Lump sum payments for emotional loss and pain and suffering were abolished on the grounds that they were 'very difficult to administer in a fair and consistent manner, reflecting the essential problem of assessing monetary compensation for a non-economic loss' – see Birch (n 32) 52. These kinds of lump sum payments have not been reintroduced.

[93]   Accident Compensation Act 2001 sch 1, cl 56.

[94]   ibid sch 1, cll 64–65.

[95]   ibid s 3(c).

[96]   ibid s 70; Todd and others (n 28) 76.

[97]   Accident Compensation Act 2001 s 72.

[98]   Sections 103–112, ibid. The need to show ongoing entitlement can be stressful and difficult for the applicant – see Anne-Maree Farrell, Sarah Devaney and Amber Dar, 'No-Fault Compensation Schemes for Medical Injury: A Review' (2010) <http://www.ssrn.com/ abstract=2221836>; Miriam Dean, 'Independent Review of the Acclaim Otago (Inc) July 2015 Report Into Accident Compensation Dispute Resolution Processes' (2016) <http://www. mbie.govt.nz/info-services/employment-skills/legislation-reviews/accident-compensation-dispute-resolution/document-and-images-library/independent-review.pdf>.

receives around 2 million claims each year, out of a total country population of around 5 million.[99]

2.4. THE EFFECT OF THE ACC SCHEME

The wide scope of this no-fault comprehensive compensation has associated effects for the legal framework that would (in other jurisdictions) deal with personal injury, as well as related bodies of legislation. This subsection discusses the effect of the ACC on tort law, health and safety legislation and product liability and consumer legislation.

The most important effect is that the right to sue for tort law compensatory damages is removed in exchange for the comprehensive cover afforded to every person in New Zealand (including tourists) if they are injured in an accident, no matter their age, social insurance status or occupation.[100] Because of its obliterating effect on tort law, the ACC Scheme is most commonly conceptualised by lawyers from the perspective of tort law (i.e. as a replacement).[101] Focus on the tort law perspective alone, however, inhibits a structural analysis. At the most basic structural level, the ACC Scheme prevents the burden of losses being left to an individual who has suffered a personal injury that meets the criteria set out in the relevant legislation. It covers losses that *could*, under a different legal framework, be sorted under the headings of tort, social insurance and private insurance. From a functional comparative law perspective, this means that the compensation fund scheme is therefore a complete substitute – in multiple functions – for tort law compensatory damages for personal injury,[102] private personal injury liability insurance cover and some types of social insurance benefits.[103]

---

[99] Accident Compensation Corporation, 'Annual Report 2017' (2017) 8 <https://www.parliament.nz/resource/en-NZ/PAP_75085/cd5473578a0a648b7c15d0d819d2f36d8ba477c2>. In 2020, the ACC Scheme experienced an 8% reduction in claims (1.86 million claims) due to COVID-19 restrictions – see Accident Compensation Corporation, 'Annual Report 2020' 55.

[100] Accident Compensation Act 2001 ss 317 and 318. These are core provisions in the legislation that create the statutory bar against common law proceedings for personal injury.

[101] This is evidenced by the fact that New Zealand law students primarily study the ACC Scheme in tort law courses, and the most comprehensive domestic textbook analysis of the ACC Scheme can be found in the dominant tort law tome. See Todd and others (n 28).

[102] The ACC Scheme provides personal injury victims with a replacement for common law compensatory damages, but the legislation expressly leaves open the possibility of exemplary damages for ACC-covered personal injury, and commentary and case law say that vindicatory damages might also be possible. See Accident Compensation Act 2001 s 319; Todd and others (n 28) 67–69.

[103] The Woodhouse Report itself saw merit in the idea of modifying or supplementing New Zealand's social security system with a form of income-related benefits (with a view to merging the ACC Scheme with the social security system) but could not anticipate whether this was likely to happen. See Royal Commission to Inquire into and Report upon Workers' Compensation, *Compensation for Personal Injury in New Zealand* (n 6) 106.

As the ACC Scheme is only a complete replacement for tort law *compensatory* damages, in theory common law damages will still be available where the personal injury is not covered by ACC, or alternatively (and more rarely) where non-compensatory damages are sought.[104] Exemplary damages are expressly retained within the legislation.[105] However, it can be difficult factually for a court to determine which of the victim's injuries are ACC-covered and which are not. Where it is difficult to divide them up, the statutory bar will generally apply.[106] If the injury is ACC-covered, but there is no compensation under the statute, then the statutory bar still applies and a common law claim will be barred.[107] Concerns about the fact that an identified party responsible for injury might escape without any cost or censure, due to the strong no-fault ethos of the ACC system, were dismissed in the *DePuy* litigation as irrelevant to the purpose of the system.[108] The legislature has, in contrast, allowed criminal injury victims to 'top-up' their accident compensation entitlements with reparations paid by the perpetrator under criminal sentencing law.

In Davies v New Zealand Police,[109] the Supreme Court overturned a sentence of reparation on the appellant that would make up the shortfall between the victim's lost earnings and the weekly compensation received under the ACC scheme. The majority judgment of the Supreme Court noted that if reparation could be ordered under sentencing legislation to make up for perceived inadequacies in the ACC scheme, then crime victims would stand outside the ACC statutory bar on civil wrong victims seeking compensation through the courts. The court viewed such a result as incompatible with the social contract created by the ACC scheme. Section 35(2) of the Sentencing Act 2002 was an explicit intervention by Parliament to amend the Davies judgment. This action of the legislature can be seen as inconsistent and incoherent with the rest of the ACC Scheme, and as a decision by the legislature to prioritise criminal sentencing legislative choices.

---

[104] Some examples of where common law claims may be possible in special cases outside the ACC Scheme definition of personal injury include: mental injury for secondary victims (*Queenstown Lakes District Council v Palmer* [1998] NZCA 190), non-accidental injury such as the inhalation of gases (*L v Robinson* [2000] 3 NZLR 499), and disease that does not fit within one of the approved categories of injury (such as cancer caused by smoking – *Pou v British American Tobacco (New Zealand) Limited* [2006] 1 NZLR 661). In the medical context, it remains unclear whether an unwanted pregnancy and the costs of raising the resulting child can be classified as an ACC-covered personal injury – see Todd and others (n 28) 57; *Allenby v H* [2012] NZSC 33. Another example of the very narrow category of injuries not covered by ACC is injuries caused during pharmaceutical industry clinical trials – the exclusion of which has been regarded as a policy misstep – see Joanna M Manning, 'Does the Law on Compensation for Research-Related Injury in the UK, Australia, and New Zealand Meet Ethical Requirements?' (2017) 25 *Medical Law Review* 397 <https://academic.oup.com/medlaw/article-abstract/25/3/397/3769302>.

[105] Accident Compensation Act 2001 s 319.

[106] *P v Attorney-General* [2010] NZHC 959.

[107] *van Soest v Residual Health Management Unit and Ramstead* [1999] NZCA 206.

[108] *McGougan v DePuy International Limited* (NZHC and NZCA) (n 56).

[109] *Davies v New Zealand Police* [2009] NZSC 47.

Another lesser known effect of the ACC Scheme's wide scope and suppressive effect on tort law is the fact that very few New Zealand lawyers (less than one per cent) now practise law relating to personal injury tort and ACC generally.[110] The consequences of this for access to justice issues will be discussed further in subsequent chapters, because it relates to some major critiques of no-fault comprehensive compensation funds. However in short, concerns about the way ACC handled disputes over coverage and entitlements led to a critical independent review in 2016 conducted by a senior lawyer. The government concurred with all the recommendations.[111] ACC claims it has implemented all of the recommendations, but lawyers and claimant advocate groups still say that the complaints procedure is unfair and unbalanced.[112]

There are also a number of effects that the ACC Scheme has on other legislation. The scheme has a co-operative relationship with health and safety legislation. Injury prevention is a key focus of the 2001 legislation and ACC's activities. Minimising the incidence and impact of injury on the community is one of the express purposes of the 2001 Act.[113] There has been an increasing focus on safety and injury prevention over the ACC Scheme's legislative history, for both social good reasons and in order to minimise claim costs to the ACC. The general unavailability of tort damages and other remedies for personal injury means that there is no common law hypothetical incentive for a defendant to avoid wrongful conduct.

A primary function of ACC is to promote injury prevention measures that reduce the incidence and severity of personal injury.[114] However, ACC itself is not legally responsible for ensuring compliance with health and safety measures. In practical terms this means that ACC's focus is targeted financial investment in injury prevention. This means investment in community programmes that seek to reduce the incidence and mitigate the effect of every kind of injury, including motorcycle and driver safety education, first aid training, sports injury prevention and programmes that aim to prevent sexual violence. ACC is also considering financial incentives (probably levy reductions) to encourage improved health and safety performance.[115]

Detailed workplace health and safety law is enshrined in legislation separate to the ACC Scheme, and its enforcement is the responsibility of a separate agency (that reports to the same government minister responsible for the ACC Scheme). In 2015 Parliament passed the Health and Safety at Work Act (HSWA),

---

[110] Dean (n 98) 53.

[111] New Zealand Government, 'Further Work to Improve ACC Dispute Resolution' (2016) <https://www.beehive.govt.nz/release/further-work-improve-acc-dispute-resolution>.

[112] Fletcher (n 74) 18–19.

[113] Accident Compensation Act 2001 s 3.

[114] ibid s 263.

[115] Accident Compensation Corporation, 'Annual Report 2017' (2017) <https://www.parliament.nz/resource/en-NZ/PAP_75085/cd5473578a0a648b7c15d0d819d2f36d8ba477c2> 21.

one of the most significant reforms to workplace health and safety in decades. The incentive for this legislative reform was to improve New Zealand's poor health and safety performance compared to similar jurisdictions (such as the UK and Australia).[116] The HSWA introduced amendments to the Accident Compensation Act 2001 to enable the ACC to work collaboratively with WorkSafe, New Zealand's new workplace safety regulatory agency.[117] Earlier health and safety legislation also aimed to complement the ACC Scheme.[118] An example of practical collaborative injury prevention activities by ACC and WorkSafe are online toolkits for businesses to manage health and safety risks.[119] WorkSafe is the agency responsible for bringing prosecutions for breaches of the HSWA. WorkSafe is also responsible for administering and enforcing legislation relating to mines rescue, hazardous substances, electricity and gas. ACC's role in health and safety law is therefore one of collaboration and financial investment, rather than enforcement.

New Zealand's comparatively poor workplace health and safety outcomes naturally beg the question of whether the no-fault ACC Scheme results in worse preventative safety outcomes, compared to a liability-based system. A 2008 independent review of the ACC Scheme noted that there is no consistent systematic evidence of a liability-driven deterrence effect on injury.[120] That review noted that ACC had a relatively small role in the area of prevention compared with other accident compensation schemes internationally.[121] The 2015 health and safety legislative reforms and the creation of a new regulatory agency can be seen as fulfilling many of the 2008 ACC Scheme review's recommended structural changes to New Zealand's approach to health and safety. ACC's injury prevention activities should be viewed as (potential) victim-centred and directly connected to reducing the incidence of claims and thus improving the fund's

---

[116] New Zealand Government, 'A Blueprint for Health & Safety at Work' (2013) 5 <http://www.mbie.govt.nz/info-services/employment-skills/workplace-health-and-safety-reform/document-and-image-library/working-safer-key-documents/safety-first-blueprint.pdf>. The New Zealand government has set a target of a 25% reduction in workplace injuries and fatalities by 2020.

[117] Accident Compensation Act 2001 s 264A; Health and Safety at Work Act 2015 s 196.

[118] Doug Tennent, *Accident Compensation Law* (LexisNexis New Zealand 2013) 348.

[119] WorkSafe, 'Role and Responsibilities' <https://worksafe.govt.nz/about-us/who-we-are/role-and-responsibilities/>.

[120] PriceWaterhouseCoopers (n 37) vi. Interestingly, on the issue of system costs, the PWC review noted that evidence indicated 'that access to common law benefits, even where significantly limited in nature, has been one of the primary drivers of cost blow-outs in workers compensation schemes in Australia.' In relation to treatment injury, that review noted that there is evidence that no-fault schemes have a positive patient safety impact in the long run.

[121] PriceWaterhouseCoopers, 'Accident Compensation Corporation New Zealand Scheme Review' vi <https://accfutures.org.nz/uploads/sites/accfutures/files/images/pricewaterhousecoopersaccreport.pdf> xi.

financial position. Actions to punish or sanction the person or company who caused the injury are outside ACC's ambit.

The ACC Scheme has deeply affected the shape of safety and liability legislation in New Zealand. Product liability, an expansive field of jurisprudence in the European Union and its member states, for example, is effectively non-existent in New Zealand. This is because personal injuries caused by a defective product are not treated differently to another type of personal injury for the purposes of the victim's compensation. A person injured by a defective product will likely be eligible for coverage under the ACC Scheme, but due to the statutory bar the injured person will not be able to sue the defective product manufacturer or distributor for compensatory damages in relation to their injury.

Product safety is regulated by the Fair Trading Act 1986, and the Consumer Guarantees Act 1993 provides a general consumer rights framework. There are civil and criminal penalties for breaches of the Fair Trading Act,[122] whereas the Consumer Guarantees Act mandates simpler practical remedies for consumers.[123] The Commerce Commission is the relevant regulator for product safety, and sets mandatory safety standards (via the Fair Trading Act) for a very small number of products. The Commerce Commission is the most frequent plaintiff (and prosecutor) in proceedings involving an alleged breach of the Fair Trading Act. Because the issue of compensation for injury is disconnected from liability in New Zealand, consumer protection and product safety legislation is also philosophically disconnected from the ACC Scheme. Tort liability under negligence may sometimes be relevant in this area, remembering of course that the ACC Scheme litigation bar will block any cases involving compensatory damages claims for personal injury.

This effect of the ACC Scheme leaves New Zealand curiously out of kilter with other jurisdictions, especially when it comes to multi-jurisdictional product liability cases. The *DePuy* hip replacement case mentioned already is a perfect example.[124] In that case the plaintiffs argued that the defendant company was receiving a financial windfall because it was escaping any financial liability for its defective product (because of the statutory bar), yet it had made no contribution as a taxpayer or levy-payer to the ACC Scheme. Justice Collins in the High Court accepted this outcome as a natural consequence of a no-fault comprehensive compensation fund. At paragraph [54] of the judgment he quoted a 1974 Torts and General Law Reform Committee report which noted that

> 'Dangerous and defective products produce a number of injuries, yet once the accident compensation scheme is in force, those enterprises whose products cause injuries will

---

[122] Fair Trading Act 1986 s 40.
[123] Additionally, the Sale of Goods Act 1908 provides various implied warranties and conditions in contracts for the sale of goods. However, the parties can contract out of the statute's provisions either expressly or by their conduct or trade usage.
[124] *McGougan v DePuy International Limited* (n 56).

not be directly liable to finance the risk in the same manner as the industry operator is called upon to finance the risk of injuries to earners'.

O'Sullivan and Tokeley have argued recently argued that the ACC Scheme should be adapted to include a subrogation or 'public tort liability' option in cases of product failure, allowing ACC itself to pursue manufacturers of faulty products in tort.[125] They also propose extra ACC levies and increased HSWA legislative oversight for manufacturers. The authors argue that these changes should be made on the grounds of distributive fairness (to the ACC Scheme as whole), because there is no evidence to suggest that a liability to compensate leads to a deterrent effect. This is a compelling proposal for reform, because it does not undermine the victim-focused nature of the scheme's purpose, weaken the scheme's integrity or remove statutory entitlements to compensation. Product liability is a matter that needs to be addressed in any substantive review of ACC Scheme entitlements – specifically the questions of who, in a globalised world, the legislature intends should be covered by the scope of no-fault and also what extra financial burden for product liability/mass harm it is fair to place on taxpayers and levy-payers.

2.5. COMPARISON WITH OTHER COMPENSATION FUND STRUCTURES

The ACC Scheme is the only current New Zealand compensation fund structure that meets our definition of a no-fault comprehensive compensation fund. However there are some other New Zealand compensation fund structures that can be contrasted with the ACC Scheme.

In other jurisdictions, natural disasters (or more specifically, the uninsurable consequences of natural disaster) are a common function of niche compensation funds.[126] In terms of a disaster compensation fund, New Zealand has a Natural Disaster Fund that is managed by a state body called the Earthquake Commission (EQC).[127] It is made up of contributions from compulsory

---

[125] Trish O'Sullivan and Kate Tokeley, 'Consumer Product Failure Causing Personal Injury Under the No-Fault Accident Compensation Scheme in New Zealand – a Let-off for Manufacturers?', *Product Safety, Consumers' Health and Liability Law Conference* (Springer 2017) <https://doi.org/10.1007/s10603-018-9383-2>.

[126] Larissa Vanhooff, Thierry Vansweevelt and Britt Weyts, 'So Many Funds, so Many Alternatives: Compensation Funds as a Solution for Liability Issues in Belgium, the Netherlands and the United Kingdom' (2016) 8 *European Journal of Commercial Contract Law* 41.

[127] Earthquake Commission, 'The Natural Disaster Fund' <https://www.eqc.govt.nz/about-eqc/our-role/ndf>.

flat-rate levies on individual home insurers and reinsurance purchased by the Earthquake Commission. It is backed by a government guarantee. In the event of a natural disaster,[128] EQC pays out compensation for loss or damage. However, compensation is only paid out of the National Disaster Fund in relation to *insured* residential buildings and land. Home insurance is not compulsory in New Zealand (although mortgage providers will normally require borrowers to take out a policy). Because eligibility for compensation depends upon the payment of a levy, this means that the Natural Disaster Fund is a type of government-guaranteed insurance and is not a no-fault comprehensive compensation fund like ACC.

The consequences of this contribution requirement for EQC coverage are also a point of contrast with the ACC Scheme. Unlike personal injury, the New Zealand government has *not* viewed natural disaster compensation through the lens of solidarity and community responsibility – and legislated accordingly. Uninsured homeowners will in principle receive no compensation out of the Natural Disaster Fund,[129] although the government has in some cases elected to provide *ex gratia* compensation for the uninsured.[130] On its face this difference seems surprising, given the geologically active nature of New Zealand and its propensity to natural disaster – there is a very real risk of all New Zealand residents being affected by a natural disaster at some point in their lives. Yet when one takes the fiscal consequences of the recent natural disasters into account, a wider solidarity approach seems unlikely. The 2010 natural disasters completely exhausted the Natural Disaster Fund and its reinsurance policies on international markets, necessitating a top-up from central taxpayer funds.[131] Since 2017, EQC has increased levies to hopefully rebuild the National Disaster Fund within 10 years – barring any further disaster events.[132] The sobering consequences of recent severe natural disasters on New Zealand's existing risk

---

[128] A natural disaster is defined as an earthquake, a natural landslip, a volcanic eruption, hydrothermal activity or a tsunami. There is some coverage for storm and flood damage, fire resulting from a natural disaster, and imminent damage following a natural disaster. See EQC Earthquake Commission, 'EQC Insurance' <https://www.eqc.govt.nz/what-we-do/eqc-insurance>.

[129] Additionally, uninsured owners of uninhabitable Christchurch homes affected by the 2010 and 2011 earthquakes were only compensated for land value in a government property buy-back. See *Quake Outcasts v Minister of Canterbury Earthquake Recovery* [2017] NZCA 332.

[130] Thomas Mead, 'Government to Pay $12m to Uninsured Christchurch Red Zone Homeowners', *Newshub* (21 August 2018) <https://www.newshub.co.nz/home/new-zealand/2018/08/government-to-pay-12m-to-uninsured-christchurch-red-zone-homeowners.html>.

[131] Michael Hayward, 'EQC Gets Another $45m Top up from the Public Purse', *Stuff.co.nz* (11 June 2019) <https://www.stuff.co.nz/national/politics/113373906/eqc-gets-another-45m-top-up-from-the-public-purse#comments>.

[132] Earthquake Commission (n 127).

management laws and financial provision have led to calls for law and economic reform.[133] Natural disaster compensation in New Zealand lacks the social contract and solidarity dimension (summarised in the ACC Scheme catchphrase 'community responsibility') that is present in personal injury compensation, and is better characterised as a matter involving tensions between private and mandatory public insurance coverage for natural disaster.[134]

Nevertheless, the success of the ACC Scheme and the entrenchment of other insurance-based fund solutions into the fabric of New Zealand law and society mean that it is conceivable that other compensation funds will appear in the future. A compensation fund system or compensation mechanism to compensate for bio-security related damage has been mooted.[135] As noted in the previous chapter, New Zealand's ongoing Royal Commission of Inquiry into Historical Abuse in State Care may suggest a compensation fund scheme in its redress process recommendations.[136] Both the ACC Scheme and the EQC/ Natural Disaster Fund have made New Zealanders familiar with the concept of broad state-administered compensation for injury and natural disaster loss – so there is a ready acceptance for government to lead the design of compensation

---

[133] Stephen Kós, 'Disaster & Resilience – The Canterbury Earthquakes and Their Legal Aftermath', *Supreme and Federal Courts Judges' Conference* (Brisbane 2016); Sally Owen, 'Regressivity in Public Natural Hazard Insurance: A Quantitative Analysis of the New Zealand Case' <https:// wzukusers.storage.googleapis.com/user-30969499/documents/5b44142c06e87eKoIwKZ/ Owen_Sally.pdf>; New Zealand Treasury, 'New Zealand's Future Natural Disaster Insurance Scheme: Proposed Changes to the EQC Act 1993' (2015) <http://www.treasury.govt.nz/ publications/reviews-consultation/eqc/pdfs/eqc-rev-discussion-doc.pdf>.

[134] In fact, the predecessor to the EQC, the Earthquake and War Damage Commission, was established in response to slow rates of repairs in the 1930s and '40s after two major earthquakes. A guaranteed right to affordable disaster insurance with flat-rate pricing, backed by a Crown funding guarantee, was seen in New Zealand as a fairer approach than the *ad hoc* support after natural disasters that was observed in other jurisdictions. In Belgium, France and the Netherlands, those kind of *ad hoc* schemes have eventually morphed into today's no-fault disaster guarantee funds that supplement uninsurable losses. See New Zealand Treasury (n 133) 15–16.

[135] Isaac Davison, 'Farmers Could Be Asked to Contribute to New EQC-like Fund for Biosecurity Threats' *New Zealand Herald* (20 May 2018) <https://www.nzherald.co.nz/nz/news/article. cfm?c_id=1&objectid=12055129>; Alexandra Moore, 'ACC for the Cows? Analysing How Best to Deal with the Losses Caused by Biosecurity Breaches' (2019) 26/2019 <https://ssrn. com/abstract=3477020>.

[136] Royal Commission of Inquiry into Historical Abuse in State Care, 'Terms of Reference' (2018) <https://www.dia.govt.nz/diawebsite.nsf/Files/Royal-Commission-of-Inquiry-into-Historical-Abuse-in-State-Care/$file/Royal-Commission-Terms-of-Reference-for-consultation.pdf>, para 5.6. It is likely that New Zealand will closely observe the operation of the Australian National Redress Scheme for Victims of Sexual Abuse. A little-known financial settlement scheme for historical abuse in state care is available through the Confidential Listening and Assistance Service and the Crown litigation service. This is not a no-fault scheme; it requires demonstration by the applicant of some degree of state liability. See Stephen Winter, 'Redressing Historic Abuse in New Zealand: A Comparative Critique' (2018) 70 *Political Science* 1 <https://www.tandfonline.com/action/journalInformation? journalCode=rpnz20>.

options. However there is not a clear modern restatement by government, Parliament or other actors about *which* kind of losses should be compensated for on a social, community or solidarity basis and which should be compensated for on insurance-based principles.[137] As it currently stands, the existence of the ACC Scheme has not encouraged the New Zealand government to experiment with wider, social-based compensation for other kinds of losses.[138]

3. AUSTRALIA: VICTORIA'S TRANSPORT ACCIDENT COMMISSION (TAC)

There is a much different compensation fund ecosystem in New Zealand's largest neighbour, the federal Commonwealth of Australia. Compensation funds and other redress systems in Australia exist amidst a patchwork of individual state and territory choices between fault and no-fault, traditional tort litigation and alternative compensation mechanisms. The federal government is attempting to effect change in this landscape to deliver more consistent compensation fund systems in individual states and territories, but this is a work in progress and faces many legal, political and practical challenges.

Despite the physical distance between the two countries, Australia has a close cultural and legal proximity to its neighbour New Zealand. The histories of compensation fund system development in the two jurisdictions are intertwined, and they are the most natural comparators for each other. Two new Australian schemes, the National Disability Insurance Scheme (NDIS) and the National Injury Insurance Scheme (NIIS), aim to bridge the gap between existing social insurance concepts in different states and provide compensation based on need and a no-fault basis. They embody the ongoing duality and tension between social insurance schemes and compensation funds. In the field of historical child abuse, the National Redress Scheme provides an alternative to tort or public law compensatory damages. Existing compensation fund systems for workplace and

---

[137] For a recent statement about themes for a potential future (re)vision of ACC that would bring superannuation and social welfare issues under the same lens, see Susan St John, 'Reflections on the Woodhouse Legacy for the 21st Century' (2020) 51 *Victoria University of Wellington Law Review* 295 <https://ojs.victoria.ac.nz/vuwlr/article/view/6572/5734>.

[138] A recent New Zealand Productivity Commission report recommended that the ACC weekly compensation model, levying and experience-rating procedures could be applied to a hypothetical unemployment insurance scheme. If such a scheme were successful, then it could be expanded to include sickness and disability, as is common in European jurisdictions. See Kathy Spencer, 'Unemployment Insurance: What Can It Offer NZ?' Report for the Technology and the Future of Work Inquiry (Productivity Commission July 2019) 27. As noted earlier, the New Zealand government has recently announced its intention to establish such a scheme – see 'Building Stronger Support for Workers Post COVID' (n 74).

accident injury sit on the border between tort alternatives and social insurance systems.

Since 1987 Victoria has operated a no-fault comprehensive compensation fund for transport accident injuries that limits access to court damages.[139] The scheme is managed by the Transport Accident Commission (hereafter 'TAC'). The TAC scheme compensates 'anyone injured in a transport accident'[140] in the state of Victoria (or interstate if a Victorian-registered vehicle is involved).[141] The system offers loss of earnings compensation,[142] compensation for medical and rehabilitation costs and funeral lump sum payments.[143] The system is funded by annual motor vehicle registration fees, not by an insurance levy.[144]

With its coverage of all types of transport accident injuries, the support offered by the TAC is probably the closest equivalent system in Australia to the New Zealand ACC system. In contrast to the New Zealand system, however, tort law damages claims may still (rarely) be possible for transport accident victims who have a serious injury[145] and can show that their injury occurred through no fault of their own.[146] However, because most traffic accidents will, logically, involve Victorian-registered vehicles that have TAC scheme no-fault coverage, it will almost be always be the TAC itself who will pay common law damages (often by agreed settlement) to a seriously injured person.

3.1. THE BACKGROUND TO THE TAC

Australia in the 1970s dabbled at the federal level with the potential for an ACC-style no-fault compensation fund system. In 1973 the newly elected

---

[139] Transport Accident Act 1986 (Victoria).

[140] A transport accident is defined as 'an incident directly caused by the driving of a motor car or motor vehicle, a railway train or a tram' – ibid s 3(1). Since 2013 this definition has been given a more expansive interpretation that includes out-of-control motor vehicles, trains and trams, and certain types of cyclist accidents (involving stationary vehicles, vehicles opening doors or cyclists on their way to or from work) – ibid s 3(1A).

[141] Transport Accident Commission, '2017/18 Annual Report' 8 <http://www.tac.vic.gov.au/__ data/assets/pdf_file/0009/298629/2017-18-TAC-Annual-Report.pdf>.

[142] 'Work and income' <http://www.tac.vic.gov.au/clients/work-and-income>. TAC will pay for loss of earnings for the first 18 months after an accident, if the victim is unable to return to work. After the first 18 months, benefits may be paid for another 18 months or (in the case of very serious injuries) for the rest of the victim's life until retirement age (when the victim becomes eligible for the Age Pension). For such long-term cases, the TAC compensation fund system operates in a way similar to that of the general social security system.

[143] 'What we can pay for' <http://www.tac.vic.gov.au/clients/what-we-can-pay-for>.

[144] Transport Accident Commission, '2017/18 Annual Report' (n 141) 54.

[145] 'A serious injury' is defined as '(a) a serious long-term impairment or loss of a body function; (b) a permanent serious disfigurement; (c) a severe long-term mental or severe long-term behavioural disturbance or disorder; or (d) loss of a foetus' – Transport Accident Act 1986 (Victoria) s 93(17).

[146] ibid ss 93, 93A, 93D.

82   Intersentia

Chapter 3. Review of Existing No-Fault Comprehensive Compensation Funds

(and eager to reform) Australian Labor Government invited Owen Woodhouse, the architect of the New Zealand scheme, to chair an inquiry on national rehabilitation and compensation for personal injury in Australia. The scope of the inquiry became wider than was undertaken in New Zealand prior to the establishment of the ACC Scheme, because it was extended in 1974 to include sickness and disability. The Australian inquiry had greater complexities to consider, given Australia's federal structure, bicameral federal legislature, individual state legislatures and written constitution. Powerful lobby interests ultimately blocked the enactment of such a scheme,[147] in addition to cost concerns and doubts about whether the federal Commonwealth government had the power to abolish individual states' tort rights.[148]

Meanwhile, in the state of Victoria the country's first purportedly 'no-fault' scheme for motor vehicle accident injuries was established via the Motor Accidents Act 1973, and administered by a body called the Motor Accidents Board.[149] However, the fund was not comprehensively no-fault, and the right to sue at common law was retained. No-fault compensatory benefits were available in most, but not all cases – disqualifying circumstances included drink driving, being an unlicensed driver, or the car being used to help commit a crime at the time of the accident.[150] For accidents after September 1980, no-fault benefits continued for life if no common law claim was possible.[151] This double system was alleged by one contemporaneous commentator to be deficient because there was 'no justification … for perpetuating a system which discriminates between two classes of accident victims – those who can prove fault, and those who cannot.'[152] There was also evidence that around a third of claimants receiving no-fault benefits were using that money to finance common law actions. The funding structure of the 1973 scheme and Board was also generally inadequate – by 1986, the Motor Accidents Board had A$1.6 billion of estimated unfunded liability and an anticipated cash-flow shortage of A$91 million.[153]

The Victorian state government was eager to reform the compensation fund in a way that would completely remove the right to sue at common law, and bring

---

[147] Palmer, *Compensation for Incapacity: A Study of Law and Social Change in New Zealand and Australia* (n 18) 174–196.

[148] Mark Harrison, 'Evidence-Free Policy: The Case of the National Injury Insurance Scheme' (2013) 20, Agenda <http://ro.uow.edu.au/cgi/viewcontent.cgi?article=2384&context=eispapers> p 57.

[149] A detailed history of the immediate legislative background to the Transport Accident Commission scheme establishment can be found in Ian Malkin, 'Victoria's Transport Accident Reforms – In Perspective' (1987) 16 *Melbourne University Law Review* 254.

[150] Motor Accidents Act 1973 s 16.

[151] 'History of the TAC – Accident Compensation in Victoria' <https://www.tac.vic.gov.au/about-the-tac/our-organisation/what-we-do/history-of-the-tac>.

[152] Mark A Robinson, 'Accident Compensation in Australia – No-Fault Schemes' 25 <http://www.robinson.com.au/Accident Compensation in Australia-No-Fault Schemes-book.pdf>.

[153] Malkin (n 149) 260.

Intersentia

the scheme more in line with the comprehensive no-fault nature of the New Zealand ACC Scheme.[154] However the prospect of a complete elimination of court damages was swiftly and strenuously opposed by a slick private and public lobby campaign by the legal profession. The resulting political impasse led to the 1980s traffic accident compensation reforms being ultimately largely in line with what the legal profession proposed – the right to sue would be retained for seriously injured individuals.

3.2. LEGISLATIVE STRUCTURES AND RELEVANT LEGAL DOCTRINES

This subsection sets out the legislative structure of the TAC scheme, in a similar way to how the ACC Scheme was detailed in the previous section.

The purpose of the TAC scheme is simply stated as 'to establish a scheme of compensation in respect of persons who are injured or die as a result of transport accidents.'[155] Unlike the New Zealand scheme, there is therefore no infusion within the legislation itself of ideas like 'social insurance' or a social contract, or any other infusion of policy or philosophy.[156] Nor is there any expression of insurance-type principles, or a purposive description of the balance between the provision of a statutory scheme with the restriction of the right to sue in court. References to 'social insurance' can be found on the TAC's website and other materials.[157]

The 1986 legislation established a statutory scheme of entitlements to compensation from 1 January 1987 that was to be administered by a new body, the Transport Accident Commission (TAC). The eligibility criteria for the scheme were very wide from the launch of the scheme – an individual would be eligible for compensation for an injury resulting from a transport accident (defined as 'an incident arising from the use of a car, train or tram') that occurred in Victoria.[158] Extra-territorial coverage has also always been available for Victorian residents in Victorian-registered cars. The most significant major extension of scheme eligibility occurred in 2018, when future and retrospective

---

[154] See Government Statement, 'Victoria: Transport Accident Compensation Reform' (May 1986) which built on ideas in New South Wales Law Reform Commission, 'Accident Compensation: A Transport Accidents Scheme for New South Wales', LRC series vol 43 (1984).

[155] Transport Accident Act 1986 (Victoria) s 1.

[156] The explanatory memoranda to the original legislation are both surprisingly devoid of policy or legal philosophy discussion – see 'Transport Accident Bill 1986 – Explanatory Memorandum'; 'Transport Accident Bill 1986 (No. 2) – Explanatory Memorandum'.

[157] Transport Accident Commission, 'What We Do' <https://www.tac.vic.gov.au/about-the-tac/our-organisation/what-we-do>.

[158] Transport Accident Act 1986 (Victoria) s 35.

coverage was introduced for cyclists injured following a collision with a stationary motor vehicle.[159]

Access to the scheme is by way of a victim's application to the TAC within 12 months of the accident (or within 12 months of the accident injury becoming evident). This is the shortest claims window of all the no-fault comprehensive compensation funds studied. There is a procedural similarity with the New Zealand ACC scheme, because the initial application step may be completed by the hospital or attending healthcare provider.[160]

In terms of compensation, there is a focus (much like the New Zealand ACC Scheme) on supporting an individual during recovery (and paying for medical treatment and capped income-replacement benefits), with a view to enabling an individual to return to work (with corresponding time-based cut-off points for compensation eligibility). Until recently, an important key difference from the New Zealand ACC was the existence of an insurance excess on all medical treatment claims.[161] Separately, further financial compensation will be available in two situations – firstly, where a transport accident victim has a serious injury, and secondly where a transport accident victim has a permanent psychological or physical impairment. The former category is the most significant example of incoherence within the scheme.

The TAC is a public statutory corporation whose existence is wholly governed by the Transport Accident Act itself, rather than other general legislation relating to state corporations.[162] Unlike New Zealand's ACC, the TAC has subrogation powers under the legislation to 'claw back' compensation costs from an identifiable party (or their insurer) who is not entitled to enjoy the coverage of the TAC Scheme.[163] In practice, these powers are limited in their practical application (because most traffic accidents in the state of Victoria will involve persons who are entitled to TAC Scheme coverage), but this is an important difference from New Zealand's ACC Scheme, which does not confer such powers on the ACC.

The legislative evolution of the TAC Scheme can be characterised as surprisingly unremarkable, especially when compared to the wild political evolutions in the New Zealand ACC Scheme or even when compared to the

---

[159] Treasury and Finance Legislation Amendment Act 2018; Transport Accident Commission, 'TAC Legislation Changes' <http://www.tac.vic.gov.au/providers/for-service-providers/for-legal-professionals/tac-legislation-changes>.

[160] Transport Accident Commission, 'Making a Claim for Compensation' <https://www.tac.vic.gov.au/clients/what-we-can-pay-for/policies/other/making-a-claim-for-compensation>.

[161] Until February 2018, the first A$651 of medical treatment expenses had to be covered by the claimant themselves, thus removing the most minor of injuries from the scope of the scheme. This was repealed by the Compensation Legislation Amendment Act 2018 (Victoria).

[162] Part 2 Transport Accident Act 1986 (Victoria).

[163] ibid s 107.

Intersentia

evolutions that have occurred in Victorian worker no-fault compensation legislation.[164]

From a structural perspective that is relevant to a comparative law analysis, the TAC Scheme has therefore created a codified framework of statutory entitlements to compensation in the case of personal injury, which is broadly comparable to the New Zealand ACC Scheme. However, as will be discussed in the next subsections, there are tensions created by the scheme that have been managed in two very different ways. The scope of eligibility for the scheme (i.e., what is a qualifying transport accident injury?) is a question that has been adjusted in a principled way to ensure the coherent development of the scheme. In contrast, the continued availability of common law damages for serious injury is a glaring, expensive and arbitrary anomaly for a no-fault comprehensive compensation fund that is unlikely to be adequately addressed by the introduction of a national serious injury compensation scheme (in the form of the NIIS).

3.3. THE SCOPE OF THE TAC SCHEME

This subsection discusses the scope and the effect of the TAC Scheme. As with the review of the ACC Scheme, 'scope' means the space in law in which the compensation fund occupies, what it provides (in terms of compensation) and what it takes away (in terms of entitlement to access other remedies). Closely related, the 'effect' of the TAC is dealt with in this subsection and concerns the fund's effect on both related legislation and tort law. First, there is a review of the 'serious injury' carve-out within the no-fault comprehensive compensation structure that still allows for a form of common law damages to be claimed. Next, there is consideration of the statutory benefits that are available for permanent impairments. Finally, there is discussion of how the TAC manages the overlap between its scheme and compensation entitlements available under other statutes.

Transport accident victims with a serious injury (legally defined as 30 per cent or more impairment, *or* if determined by the TAC itself to be a 'serious injury' within the definition of the legislation) who can show that someone else was at least partly at fault for the accident may be eligible for common law compensation that recognises the long-term impact the accident has had on the victim's life. This is the sole area where the TAC Scheme retains some overlap with tort law, but it is financially very significant. The legal definition of 'serious injury' is complex. The legislation itself defines a 'serious injury' as a serious long-term impairment or loss of a body function, a permanent serious disfigurement,

---

[164] Judicial College of Victoria, *Serious Injury Manual* (2019) section 1.3 <http://www.judicialcollege.vic.edu.au/eManuals/SIM/index.htm#53962.htm>.

Chapter 3. Review of Existing No-Fault Comprehensive Compensation Funds

a severe long-term mental or behavioural disturbance or disorder, or the loss of a foetus.[165] It can be especially challenging to determine what qualifies legally as a 'serious injury', especially in cases of mental injury flowing from a transport accident. The Transport Accident Amendment Act 2013 limited the availability of common law damages for psychiatric injury,[166] but these restrictions were rolled back in 2016.[167]

> *Case study – Transport Accident Commission v Katanas* – A recent important decision from Australia's highest court concerns mental injury flowing from a covered traffic accident, and whether or not it is 'serious'. In *TAC v Katanas*, the High Court of Australia found that there is no particular scale that needs to be used in calculating seriousness.[168] The key test is whether the injury is serious for the particular applicant, and also serious when compared to a range of similar cases. The court recognised that unlike a physical injury, mental injury is particularly difficult to clinically diagnose and legally establish.[169] The *Katanas* case provides clarity on the correct test to be used by a court in the determination of a serious injury. However it highlights the stark contrast between the (relative) clinical certainty of a serious injury assessment when undertaken by the TAC itself (which is made with reference to American Medical Association clinical guidelines[170]), and the much more fluid contextual legal test afforded by court precedent. This model might be advocated by lawyers as the best of both worlds, in that it allows for a statutory calculation with the backup of a highly personalised judicial assessment if the claimant is unsatisfied with the TAC view. However, such an imprecise and highly personalised test is also an invitation for a claimant and their lawyer to chance the 'damages lottery' – which (due to the indemnity offered to all Victorian-registered drivers by the statute) is ultimately paid for by the taxpayer/motorists who fund the TAC no-fault comprehensive scheme.

The financial implications for the TAC fund of the carve-out for serious injury are significant. In the 2017/18 financial year, for example, there were over 10 times as many no-fault claims as common law damages claims under the TAC Scheme. However, the total cost to TAC of common law payments in that year was A$535 million, compared with a total of A$1.14 billion for no-fault treatment, income replacement and lump sum payments.[171]

---

[165] Transport Accident Act 1986 (Victoria) s 93(17).

[166] Section 93(17A) restricted the meaning of psychiatric injury for the purpose of obtaining leave to bring common law proceedings. Section 93(2A) abolished rights to common law damages for some kinds of indirect psychiatric injuries, e.g. those of third parties not directly involved in the accident.

[167] The Transport Accident Amendment Act 2016.

[168] *Transport Accident Commission v Katanas* [2017] HCA 32 [25].

[169] ibid 29.

[170] Transport Accident Act 1986 (Victoria) s 46A.

[171] Transport Accident Commission, 'Claims Statistics' <https://www.tac.vic.gov.au/about-the-tac/our-organisation/what-we-do/claims-statistics>.

Intersentia

In contrast, transport accident victims who are assessed by TAC as having a permanent psychological or physical impairment of more than 10 per cent may be eligible for a category of statutory 'impairment' benefits. This range of statutory benefits is not truly no-fault, because they are not available to drivers who are convicted of a driving-related offence or were under the influence of alcohol or drugs.[172] Unlike the legal 'serious injury' test, the calculation of a psychological or physical permanent impairment is made with reference to clinical criteria, and the personalised, subjective 'disabling' effects of the impairment are not given any weight. This is a point of contrast to calculation of 'serious injury' common law damages under the TAC and the calculation of non-traffic accident personal injury damages. The impairment benefit can be seen as logically and procedurally consistent with the rest of the benefits of TAC, but inconsistent (especially from a tort lawyer's perspective) with the principles of damages calculation generally and serious injury common law damages in particular.

Despite the existence of a dual system of compensation recovery for serious injury, there are protections within legislation and case law against double recovery. The legislation says that damages may be reduced if the claimant has already received a statutory payment.[173] The highest Victorian court, the Supreme Court, has interpreted that this probably applies to both court damages and a common law damages settlement with the TAC itself.[174] Given the large proportion of common law claims that are resolved by settlement, it seems to be an appropriately logical interpretation (that, regardless, would probably benefit from a clearer restatement in the legislation).

Another limitation on the scope of no-fault benefits is the limitation on recovery for anything other than medical treatment benefits for people who are convicted of driving-related criminal offences, or are found to be unlicensed at the time of the accident.[175] This can be characterised as a normative view of what kinds of entitlements are the purest form of no-fault that are available to everyone (medical treatment for injury and basic rehabilitation), and which kind of no-fault benefits can be affected by the behaviour and characteristics of the applicant (regardless of whether those factors had a causative relationship to the accident that occurred).

Because the Victorian scheme carves out a space for compensation only in relation to eligible road traffic accidents, and not *all* personal injuries in Victoria,

---

[172]   Transport Accident Commission, 'Impairment Benefits – Policy' <http://www.tac.vic.gov.au/clients/compensation/impairment-benefits#tabs-3>.

[173]   Transport Accident Act 1986 (Victoria) ss 93(11) and 93(11A).

[174]   *Tanska v Transport Accident Commission* [2000] VSC 56.

[175]   Transport Accident Act 1986 (Victoria) ss 35, 39, 40, 40(A).

the legislation sets out how there can be exclusion or interaction with other types of statutory compensation arrangements.[176] This also aids in the prevention of double recovery by claimants. The most important of these interactions is with the Victorian no-fault compensation system for workplace injuries. Compensation under the TAC scheme is generally not payable for transport accidents that result 'arising in the course of employment', and this includes journeys to and from work.[177] The Victorian WorkCover scheme does not count as a no-fault comprehensive compensation fund under my definition, because it is not entirely managed by a single public authority (in short: because private insurers can act as 'agents' and there is also the possibility of self-insurance for some very large employers). The TAC legislation manages interaction and reimbursement between the two schemes,[178] and these provisions are mirrored in the equivalent workplace compensation legislation.[179] Ultimately, it means that the compensation 'safety net' can be managed in a contractual way between the two systems in a comprehensive way (beyond the boundaries of the TAC) that minimises any potential compensation gaps for injury victims.

3.4. THE EFFECT OF THE TAC SCHEME

Although the TAC scheme is quite comprehensive in terms of the cover it provides for traffic accident injury, it is not as universal in effect as the New Zealand ACC Scheme. In terms of the TAC's effect on other statutory compensation structures, there is a strong level of coherence with other Victorian statutory schemes. As noted above, the problem of transport accidents that occur in the course of employment is deftly managed by clear statutory provisions in both regimes that allow for the two relevant authorities to work together co-operatively. This subsection summarises the general effects of the scheme, the consequential inconsistent legal effects, and the effect of the TAC scheme on those who are outside its scope of cover (in particular, non-residents).

Generally, the scheme, by virtue of its continued and mostly unchanged existence, has created a comprehensive set of (mostly) no-fault statutory entitlements to compensation and recovery assistance following a transport accident. This has been connected closely, as in New Zealand, with extensive

---

[176] Section 37 ibid. These were all mostly older statutory compensation structures that were already in existence at the time of the TAC's creation: the Country Fire Authority Act 1958, the Police Assistance Compensation Act 1968. Some newer statutory compensation schemes that exclude the coverage of the TAC relate to state emergencies and juries.

[177] ibid ss 38, 38A, 38AA.

[178] Sections 38, 38A, 38AA ibid.

[179] Accident Compensation Act 1985 (Victoria) ss 137, 137A.

public engagement on the themes of rehabilitation and road safety (which aims to reduce the cost to the TAC of liabilities to victims, as well as improving public health outcomes). The TAC has an ambitious strategy to end road deaths and serious injuries, and be a 'world leader in social insurance'.[180] The mixed no-fault and common law damages elements of the TAC – with correspondingly higher levels of compensation available to severely injured claimants, and world-class catastrophic care – have been described as 'a functional approach to meeting the compensation needs of people injured in transport accidents … Very stable with a strong financial position'.[181] However this functional success must be contrasted with the legal incoherency of a no-fault comprehensive compensation fund offering fault-based common law damages (with limited possibilities of reimbursement) for some claimants.

Because the scheme is limited to traffic accident injuries and allows some interaction with the common law system, this means that the TAC has not had the same (obliterating) effect on the tort law system as the New Zealand ACC Scheme. However, the maintenance of a dual system, even though it is only limited to serious injuries, is a troubling inconsistency of the TAC scheme. From a financial perspective, it certainly appears as though Victorian motorists (who are the sole funders of the TAC scheme) are financially subsidising the maintenance of a quasi-tort system (and all of its associated costs) for a very small category of claimants. This is because in virtually all cases the relevant defendant will be the TAC itself (because the TAC will be the effective 'insurer' of the relevant 'tortfeasor' if s/he was the driver of a vehicle covered by the scheme). This is a practical manifestation of Patrick Atiyah's critique that the guilty party does not pay in a damages claim.[182] If there were greater (and more generous) entitlement to long-term statutory benefits for serious injuries, then conceivably it would be possible to eliminate the common law damages category and move towards pure no-fault. However, given the significant number of lawyers that practise in the field of transport accident injury in Victoria,[183] it is likely there would be strenuous legal lobbying efforts to oppose such a change.

---

[180] Transport Accident Commission, 'What We Do' (n 157); Transport Accident Commission, 'TAC 2020 Strategy' <https://www.tac.vic.gov.au/__data/assets/pdf_file/0009/192753/TAC_Strategy2020_UPDATE_WEB.pdf>; Samantha Cockfield, 'Road Safety – the Experience of the Transport Accident Commission in Victoria, Australia' (2011) 2011–24.

[181] PriceWaterhouseCoopers (n 37) 153.

[182] PS Atiyah, *The Damages Lottery* (Hart Publishing 1997) ch 5.

[183] A search of the Law Institute of Victoria's and the Victorian Bar's public registers of lawyers in September 2019 showed that there were 779 solicitors and 41 barristers (out of a total of 20,588 solicitors and 2,102 barristers) who practised in the field of transport accident compensation.

Chapter 3. Review of Existing No-Fault Comprehensive Compensation Funds

The traffic accident compensation systems in other Australian states and territories are not as consolidated or comprehensive in scope as the TAC.[184] This means that there is potential for TAC entitlements to conflict with other Australian motor insurance and compensation systems, and have an extraterritorial effect upon individuals in other states and territories within the Australian Commonwealth. The courts have not commented on the merits or difficulties of having inconsistent schemes available across different jurisdictions, but have simply said it is a permissible level of difference and discrimination.

Case study – Sweedman v Transport Accident Commission[185] is a key case that tested the conflict between the very different transport accident compensation systems across Australian states and territories. Mrs Sweedman, a resident of neighbouring New South Wales (NSW) had a car accident in NSW with the Suttons, who were Victoria residents. The parties' respective vehicles were registered in their own jurisdictions. The Suttons claimed TAC benefits in the aftermath of the accident, as they were entitled to do. As Mrs Sweedman was not covered by the scope of the TAC, the TAC brought an indemnity action against Mrs Sweedman.[186] Mrs Sweedman argued (unsuccessfully) that she should not be subject to the scope of the Victorian scheme, and she was been unfairly discriminated against (because, unlike the Suttons, she could not benefit from the scheme as the owner of a NSW-registered car). The High Court of Australia dismissed her appeal but chose not to venture into the substantive choice of law and fairness consequences of one state (Victoria) operating a vast no-fault comprehensive compensation fund, quite different to other Australian jurisdictions.[187] The key point that is relevant to a comparative law analysis is that Victoria's TAC has been allowed to have the effect of applying extraterritorially to individuals (and their insurers) in the case of transport injuries involving out-of-state drivers or occurring out of state. The fact that the no-fault comprehensive nature of the TAC is much more extensive than compensation structures in other states has not been addressed as a substantive problem, but merely found not *inconsistent* with the choice of law and constitutional rules.

---

[184] The Northern Territory has a no-fault comprehensive compensation system for motor accidents that is very similar in scope to the TAC. However, because the administration of the scheme is outsourced to a private insurance company, this means that it is excluded from my definition of a no-fault comprehensive compensation fund. A comparison between the TAC and other Australian transport accident compensation schemes is made in the next subsection.

[185] *Sweedman v Transport Accident Commission* [2006] HCA 8.

[186] Transport Accident Act 1986 (Victoria) s 104(1).

[187] See also Amelia Simpson, '*Sweedman v Transport Accident Commission*: State Residence Discrimination and the High Court's Retreat into Characterisation' (2006) 34 *Federal Law Review* 363.

This kind of reasoning may well be relevant to how no-fault comprehensive injury compensation could operate (or simply co-exist with neighbouring jurisdictions) within other federalised nations or collective bodies such as the EU.

3.5. COMPARISON WITH OTHER AUSTRALIAN COMPENSATION FUNDS AND SCHEMES

3.5.1. Summary

The scheme managed by the Transport Accident Commission is the only Australian system that meets the definition of being a no-fault comprehensive compensation fund.

3.5.2. Traffic Accident Compensation

A degree of national consistency is emerging in Australia in relation to no-fault cover for catastrophic injuries from traffic accidents, thanks to the NDIS and the NIIS. Regarding the scope of compensation for those kind of extreme losses, it seems, at least, that there will be functional similarity between schemes. However, overall, the wider traffic accident compensation landscape is still very varied.

Set out below is a table of the different traffic accident compensation systems that are available in other Australian states and territories, and the key aspects that contrast them from Victoria's TAC. The Australian Capital Territory and Northern Territory systems are now probably the closest in scope and effect to Victoria's TAC, but their private insurer involvement takes them outside this research project's definition of a no-fault comprehensive compensation fund. In both Western Australia and the ACT, public consultation during recent legislative reforms showed a significant public appetite for no-fault compensation in at least some circumstances.[188] The ACT's decision to restrict access to common law claims in most cases is the most significant revolutionary development – it remains to be seen whether other states and territories will be similarly influenced.

---

[188] Insurance Commission of Western Australia, 'Proposal to Add No-Fault Catastrophic Injury Cover to Western Australia's Compulsory Third Party Insurance Scheme' (2015) <https://www.icwa.wa.gov.au/__data/assets/pdf_file/0014/1274/ctp_consultation_report.pdf>; Motor Accident Injuries Bill 2019 (ACT) – Explanatory Statement.

Table 2. Comparison of the TAC with traffic accident compensation schemes in other Australian states and territories

State/Territory	Nature of traffic accident compensation	Key points of difference with TAC
Australian Capital Territory	Private insurance cover with access to the tort system is the main system of cover, but third-party cover for personal injury liability (offered by a choice of private providers) is compulsory. The NDIS has had effect in the Territory since 2014 – via the ACT Lifetime Care and Support Scheme there is no-fault compensation available for most types of catastrophic motor vehicle or workplace accidents.[189] No-fault compensation has recently been extended to include defined benefits regardless of fault for all motor vehicle injuries. Access to common law damages will be restricted to cases of serious injury (more than 10 per cent whole person impairment).[190]	Until recently, in ACT there was only no-fault defined compensation for catastrophic injury. Since 2020, the ACT system has offered no-fault compensation for all traffic accidents with a common law damages option only for serious injury. This brings the scheme, from the ordinary person's perspective, *purposively* in line with what is offered in TAC. However there are key *functional* differences from the TAC. The claims management and underwriting of the scheme is effectively handled by the four private insurers licensed to operate under the new ACT system (but some reimbursements from the public fund will be available to insurers). The limitation on common law damages was strenuously opposed by the ACT Law Society.[191] *Key difference:* *Comprehensive no-fault cover similar to TAC, but costs of statutory benefits in ACT will be privately administered and underwritten by the licensed private insurer[192] except where the driver was at fault/broke relevant driver laws. Then the insurer (or the nominal insurer, in the case of an uninsured or unknown driver) can claim a reimbursement from the Motor Accident Injuries Commission for the statutory no-fault benefits that were paid out.[193]*

(continued)

---

[189] 'Lifetime Care and Support Scheme' <https://apps.treasury.act.gov.au/ltcss>.

[190] By Sally Whyte, 'Jury's in: More People Covered, Lower Premiums in New CTP Scheme', *The Canberra Times* (24 April 2018) <https://www.canberratimes.com.au/story/6021573/jurys-in-more-people-covered-lower-premiums-in-new-ctp-scheme/>; Katie Burgess, 'Workers Injured on Roads Will Have to Choose between Insurance Schemes', *The Canberra Times* (12 November 2018) <https://www.canberratimes.com.au/story/6000552/workers-injured-on-roads-will-have-to-choose-between-insurance-schemes/>.

[191] The Law Society of the ACT, 'ACT CTP – Don't Trade Away a Fair and Stable Scheme for Illusory Savings' <https://www.actlawsociety.asn.au/news-media/media-releases-2018/act-ctp-dont-trade-away-a-fair-and-stable-scheme-for-illusory-savings>; The Law Society of the ACT, 'ACT CTP – Cheaper Premiums Come at a Cost' <https://www.actlawsociety.asn.au/news-media/media-releases-2018/act-ctp-cheaper-premiums-come-at-a-cost>.

[192] Motor Accident Injuries Act 2019 (ACT) s 295(2). 'The MAI insurer for an MAI policy is, despite any other law, liable to indemnify each MAI insured person for the MAI policy for the liability that the policy purports to insure against.'

[193] ibid Part 6.10; Motor Accident Injuries Bill 2019 (ACT) – Explanatory Statement 75.

Table 2 *continued*

State/Territory	Nature of traffic accident compensation	Key points of difference with TAC
New South Wales	Private insurance cover with access to the tort system is the main system of cover, but third-party cover for personal injury liability (offered by a choice of private insurers) is compulsory. Insurance and Care NSW (icare) has an expanding role as a state[194] and nominal insurer managing a patchwork of specific no-fault schemes. In the field of traffic injury compensation, it manages and distributes no-fault catastrophic motor vehicle injury compensation (which, on a legislative basis, is now an off-shoot of the NIIS).[195]	No-fault defined benefits for catastrophic injury, compared to common law benefits for serious injury. The closest similarity between TAC and the NSW system is for catastrophic injury. *Key difference:* *Lifetime no-fault compensation will only be available for catastrophic motor vehicle injury victims.*
Northern Territory	The NT Motor Accidents Compensation Commission provides statutory no-fault compensation for all injuries following any motor vehicle accident in the Northern Territory,[196] and interstate accidents involving Northern Territory-registered vehicles. The system bars all tort damages claims for motor vehicle injury,[197] and the Commission indemnifies owners of Northern Territory-registered vehicles for accidents in other Australian states and territories.[198] The system is funded by annual motor vehicle registration fees, not by an insurance levy.[199] Disputes about claims are determined by the Motor Accidents (Compensation) Appeal Tribunal. The system also handles claims that qualify for support under the NIIS.[200]	Functionally, this scheme is virtually identical to the TAC. The key difference between the NTMACC and the TAC is *structural* – TIO manages all aspects of the MACC scheme, including the administration of the fund that underpins the scheme. TIO was formerly a state insurance body called the Territory Insurance Office, but it was sold to Allianz in 2014.[201] Because the MACC is effectively administered by a private insurer, this means that the MACC does not fit within my definition of a publicly administered no-fault comprehensive compensation fund. The public dimension of this kind of extensive fund is a key point of difference from other compensation funds and systems; hence its exclusion. *Key difference:* *The administration and operation of the MACC scheme has been outsourced to a private insurer.*

---

194 But it also competes with private insurers.

195 'Caring for people severely injured on the road' < https://www.icare.nsw.gov.au/injured-or-ill-people/motor-accident-injuries/who-we-care-for/>. The compensation participants receive under this scheme is the cost of 'reasonable and necessary' treatment, rehabilitation and care.

196 Motor Accidents (Compensation) Act (Northern Territory) s 7. There are exclusions for situations involving unregistered vehicles – see 'Exclusions and Benefit Reductions' <https://www.ntmacc.com.au/exclusions>.

197 ibid s 5.

198 ibid s 6.

199 Northern Territory Motor Accidents (Compensation) Commission, 'Annual Report 2016–17' 2 <https://www.ntmacc.com.au/MACC_Annual_Report_2017.pdf>.

200 ibid 5.

201 Territory Insurance Office (Sale) Act (Northern Territory) 2014; 'NT Government Confirms $424m TIO Sale after Months of Speculation' ABC News (2014) <https://www.abc.net.au/news/2014-11-24/nt-government-confirms-$424m-tio-sale/5912838>.

Queensland	Private insurance cover with access to the tort system is the main system of cover, but third-party cover for personal injury liability (offered by a choice of providers) is compulsory. Since July 2016 the National Injury Insurance Scheme Queensland (NIIS Queensland) has provided no-fault compensation for serious motor vehicle (and workplace) injuries.[202] The motor vehicle injuries aspect of the system is funded by Queensland motor vehicle registration fees, not by an insurance levy.[203] Common law rights to bring a tort claim for damages have not been excluded by the legislation.[204]	No-fault defined benefits for catastrophic injury, compared to common law benefits for serious injury. The closest similarity between TAC and the Queensland system is for catastrophic injury. *Key difference:* *Lifetime no-fault compensation will only be available for catastrophic motor vehicle injury victims.*
South Australia	Private insurance cover with access to the tort system is the main system of cover, but third-party cover for personal injury liability (since 2019, offered by a choice of providers) is compulsory. The Lifetime Support Authority manages a statutory no-fault compensation fund system for serious motor vehicle accident injuries.[205] This was a pre-existing system that is now being adapted to incorporate the requirements of the NIIS.[206] Common law damages claims will still be possible for economic loss in serious injury cases.[207]	No-fault defined benefits for catastrophic injury, compared to common law benefits for serious injury. The closest similarity between TAC and the South Australian system is for catastrophic injury. *Key difference:* *Lifetime no-fault compensation will only be available for serious motor vehicle injury victims.*

(continued)

---

[202] National Injury Insurance Scheme (Queensland) Act 2016. The compensation payable under the system will be for necessary and reasonable treatment, care and support services.

[203] National Injury Insurance Agency Queensland, 'Annual Report 2017–18' 23 <www.niis.qld.gov.au>.

[204] See 'Workers' Compensation and Rehabilitation (National Injury Insurance Scheme) Amendment Act 2016' at <https://www.worksafe.qld.gov.au/laws-and-compliance/workers-compensation-laws/laws-and-legislation/workers-compensation-and-rehabilitation-national-injury-insurance-scheme-amendment-act-2016>.

[205] 'Motor Vehicle Accidents (Lifetime Support Scheme) Act 2013 (South Australia)' <https://www.legislation.sa.gov.au/lz?path=%2FC%2FA%2FMOTOR%20VEHICLE%20ACCIDENTS%20(LIFETIME%20SUPPORT%20SCHEME)%20ACT%202013>. The compensation provided under the system is for necessary and reasonable treatment, care and support – see Lifetime Support Authority, 'Lifetime Support Scheme Rules' (2017) <http://lifetimesupport.sa.gov.au/wp-content/uploads/Final-LSS-Rules.pdf> rule 2.1.2.

[206] Government of South Australia, 'Lifetime Support Authority of South Australia's 2020 Strategy' 3 <http://lifetimesupport.sa.gov.au/wp-content/uploads/2020-Strategy.pdf>.

[207] 'Motor Vehicle Accidents (Lifetime Support Scheme) Act 2013 (South Australia)' s 56A.

Table 2 *continued*

State/Territory	Nature of traffic accident compensation	Key points of difference with TAC
Tasmania	Statutory no-fault compensation is available for *all* motor accident injuries via the Motor Accidents Insurance Board (MAIB).[208] There is coverage for all kinds of injuries caused by motor accidents, with some exclusions for situations including criminal conduct, uninsured vehicles and non-Tasmanian vehicles.[209] There is lifetime cover for catastrophic injuries. The scheme is fully funded by motor vehicle insurance premiums.[210] There is no restriction on the tort system – common law claims are still possible where negligence can be proven.[211]	The MAIB system *appears* to be functionally identical to the TAC – but a key difference is the continued unlimited access in the Tasmanian system to common law damages. This means that Tasmania is operating a dual system, so the functional effects of tort law bar are not present in this jurisdiction. *Key difference:* *There is no limitation on access to court damages.*
Western Australia	Statutory fault-based compensation for motor vehicle injuries is administered by a single public authority, the Insurance Commission of Western Australia (ICWA).[212] Amid overwhelming community consensus,[213] no-fault life-time compensation has been available for serious motor vehicle injury victims via the Catastrophic Injuries Support system since July 2016.[214] A catastrophic injury is specifically defined as a spinal cord injury, a traumatic brain injury, certain amputations, certain serious burns and permanent blindness.[215] The option of tort law damages has been retained for seriously injured claimants who can establish fault.[216]	Although publicly administered, the ICWA is a fault-based system for all but catastrophic motor vehicle injury. In those serious cases, a dual system is still retained because there is no restriction on the ability to claim tort damages if fault can be established. *Key difference:* *System is almost entirely fault-based. Even in the no-fault portion of the system, it is still possible to bring a tort damages claim.*

Source: Compiled by the author.

---

[208] Motor Accidents (Liabilities and Compensation) Act 1973 (Tasmania). Compensation payable under this system is temporary income support, reasonable medical and rehabilitation costs (including daily care costs for catastrophic injuries) and death benefits. See 'What MAIB covers' <http://www.maib.tas.gov.au/already-have-a-claim/>.

[209] 'Claim exclusions' <http://www.maib.tas.gov.au/been-in-an-accident/claim-exclusions/>.

[210] Motor Accidents Insurance Board, 'Annual Report 2017–2018' 2 <http://www.maib.tas.gov.au/wp-content/uploads/2018/10/AnnualReport2018.pdf>.

[211] Motor Accidents (Liabilities and Compensation) Act 1973 (Tasmania) s 22.

[212] Compensation will only be paid to injured persons who were not at fault or only partially at fault. Compensation payable under this system is for the necessary and reasonable costs of medical treatment, rehabilitation, temporary income loss, and pain and suffering – see 'What Can You Claim?' <https://www.icwa.wa.gov.au/motor-injury-insurance/claims/what-can-you-claim>.

[213] 'Catastrophic Injuries Support Scheme' <https://www.icwa.wa.gov.au/motor-injury-insurance/product-information/catastrophic-injuries-support>.

[214] Motor Vehicle (Catastrophic Injuries) Act 2016.

[215] Motor Vehicle (Catastrophic Injuries) Regulations 2016 (Western Australia) regs 6–11.

[216] No-fault compensation was theorised as a complementary choice for claimants, and retaining the possibility of tort law damages was seen to give flexibility and independence. See Insurance Commission of Western Australia (n 188) 4.

Chapter 3. Review of Existing No-Fault Comprehensive Compensation Funds

3.5.3. *Worker Injury and Work-Related Disease Compensation*

In the field of worker injury and disease, compensation arrangements in Australia are managed at the level of individual states and territories (except for federal and defence force employees). Mary Walker's contribution to Macleod and Hodges' *Redress Schemes for Personal Injury* included most of the Australian worker compensation landscape. It is a very descriptive chapter but its broad functional scope means that very differing systems are lumped together because they ostensibly have the same task – compensating for injuries and diseases incurred in the workplace. Her analysis also does not consider the state of Victoria (and the close structural interplay between the TAC and WorkSafe Victoria), the impact of the NDIS and NIIS at the state/territory or federal level, or (separately) the impact of the National Redress Scheme for Victims of Sexual Abuse.[217]

It is true that all Australian states' and territories' worker compensation schemes have no-fault elements to them that divert away from the tort system and classic private insurance principles in some way. However, all of them have features that mean they fail the test of being a no-fault comprehensive compensation fund, so they cannot be compared with Victoria's TAC or other no-fault comprehensive compensation funds internationally. They are best compared between themselves or with other funds with the worker compensation function, perhaps contrasting the varying levels of access to the courts and outsourcing to private insurers. Set out in the table below are the reasons why all Australian worker injury compensation funds have been excluded from the scope of this research project:

Table 3. Worker injury compensation funds by state/territory, their differences from a no-fault comprehensive compensation fund and why not included in this research

Difference and why fund is not included	State or Territory
Incomplete tort law/court-based damages bar for participants – i.e., dual system access is possible	Western Australia;[218] Victoria;[219] Northern Territory;[220] Queensland.[221]

(continued)

---

[217] Part 2 Chapter 3 'Australia' in Sonia Macleod and Christopher Hodges, *Redress Schemes for Personal Injuries* (Hart Publishing 2017).

[218] In Western Australia, common law tort claims will still be possible in all cases where it can be determined that a third party or the employer was negligent. However, it is worth noting that the scheme is very comprehensive. WorkCover WA has a generous definition of a worker, that truly stretch the bounds of eligibility for a worker compensation scheme. Also interesting is the presumed inclusion of dust diseases (which makes sense given the strong presence of the mining industry in that state, and the corresponding high level of dust-disease claims).

[219] In Victoria, a tort law damages claim is possible in cases of serious injury.

[220] Northern Territory allows a common law claim if a third party was negligent. However, a common law claim cannot be brought against an employer alone – it is only by way of a claim against a third party that an employer could be included in such an action.

[221] In Queensland, workers can sue their employers for negligence for common law compensatory damages.

Intersentia

97

Table 3 *continued*

Difference and why fund is not included	State or Territory
Not comprehensive	New South Wales (many niche schemes under one umbrella);[222] the Commonwealth (only applies to Commonwealth/federal employees).[223]
	The default or nominal insurer funds which exist in each state and territory are only applicable where no other worker benefits are available (because e.g. the employer did not take out insurance or the insurer has collapsed).[224] This means that they will only be utilised in rare cases and therefore cannot be considered to be 'comprehensive' funds on their own.
	In all Australian states and territories there is the possibility of large employers self-insuring for workplace injury compensation (with the approval of the relevant regulator). However, they are required to comply with statutory compensation entitlements and are subject to strict supervision. New Zealand's ACC Scheme operates a similar, but highly restricted, self-insurance option for large employers, called the Accredited Employers' Programme. Self-insurance is therefore not always incompatible with the 'comprehensive' criteria.
Not publicly administered (the handling of claims is outsourced to one or more private insurer or claims agent)	Australian Capital Territory, South Australia;[225] Tasmania;[226] Northern Territory;[227] Victoria.

Source: Compiled by the author.

---

[222] In New South Wales, many different redress schemes, including worker compensation, have been folded under the management of a body called icare. However, icare is excluded from analysis. In the future, the borders between the individual schemes may be blurred so that icare is closer to a comprehensive no-fault compensation fund, but currently it is best regarded as an umbrella organisation managing a number of niche schemes that still have a significant private insurance dimension.

[223] The Commonwealth (federal employee) worker compensation scheme is no fault and generous in nature, but as it only applies to a very small subset of workers for a particular employer (the federal government), it cannot properly be considered comprehensive.

[224] S 166 of the Workers Compensation Act 1951 (Default Insurance Fund, Australian Capital Territory).

[225] South Australia's ReturntoWorkSA is broadly no-fault, but it is excluded from this research project because the claims management process is outsourced to private bodies.

[226] WorkerCover Tasmania is excluded because the scheme is underwritten by private insurers, who manage individual policies.

[227] In the Northern Territory, the Return to Work Act 1986 allows four specified insurance companies to handle policies and claims.

3.5.4. Medical Injury

In 2017 the Australian federal government's Treasury officials published a discussion paper with possible minimum benchmarks for a medical treatment injury no-fault compensation fund, within the context of the National Injury Insurance Scheme (NIIS).[228] Coverage was proposed in this paper for specific catastrophic traumatic injuries from medical treatment by a registered medical provider: spinal cord injuries, brain injuries, multiple amputations, burns, and permanent blindness. These were directly comparable to already agreed NIIS benchmarks for catastrophic motor vehicle injury. Birth defects, injuries resulting from unreasonable withholding or delay of consent by a patient, and injuries to patients over 65 years of age would be specifically excluded. Primary funding would be an insurance premium charged on health professionals. A complete abolition of common law tort rights would be left to individual states and territories. The New Zealand ACC model and definitions of medical treatment injury were specifically favoured in this report – meaning that negligence concepts like medical misadventure should not be included. However this legislative policy development work appears to be dead in the water, with no further developments at the time of writing.[229] There is, however, widespread support in Australian medico-legal literature for the implementation of a no-fault compensation fund for medical injury[230] and vaccine injury.[231] The Australian federal government had specifically ruled out setting up a no-fault compensation fund for COVID-19 vaccine injuries,[232] but has since changed its position.

---

[228] Australian Government, 'Medical Treatment Injury Discussion Paper' (2017) <https://static. treasury.gov.au/uploads/sites/1/2017/06/Medical_treatment_injury_discussion_paper-1. pdf>.

[229] Council of Australian Governments, 'COAG Meeting Communiqué, 9 June 2017' (2017) <https://www.coag.gov.au/meeting-outcomes/coag-meeting-communique-9-june-2017>.

[230] Tina Popa, 'Practitioner Perspectives on Continuing Legal Challenges in Mental Harm and Medical Negligence: Time for a No-Fault Approach?' (2017) 25 *Tort Law Review* 19; Deborah Marshall, 'No-Fault Compensation for Medically Caused Injury: A Comment on the Current Proposal' (1991) 21 *Western Australia Law Review* 336 <http://www.austlii.edu. au/au/journals/UWALawRw/1991/14.pdf>; David Wiesbrot and Kerry J Breen, 'A No-Fault Compensation System for Medical Injury Is Long Overdue' (2012) 197 *Medical Journal of Australia* 296 <www.mja.com.au>.

[231] Nicholas Wood and others, 'Australia Needs a Vaccine Injury Compensation Scheme – Upcoming COVID-19 Vaccines Make Its Introduction Urgent' (2020) 49 *Australian Journal of General Practice*. doi 10.31128/AJGP-COVID-36.

[232] Rachel Clun, 'Coronavirus Australia: Johnson & Johnson Vaccine Not Purchased as Sector Calls for Compensation Scheme' *Sydney Morning Herald* (12 April 2021) <https://www. smh.com.au/politics/federal/no-johnson-and-johnson-covid-19-vaccine-for-australia-as-sector-calls-for-compensation-scheme-20210412-p57ih9.html>; Kim Watts and Tina Popa, 'Injecting Fairness into COVID-19 Vaccine Injury Compensation: No-Fault Solutions' (2021) 12 *Journal of European Tort Law* 1.

3.6. THE TAC IN THE CONTEXT OF THE NATIONAL INJURY INSURANCE SCHEME ROLL-OUT

Two recently implemented twin schemes, the National Disability Insurance Scheme (NDIS) and the National Injury Insurance Scheme (NIIS), aim to bridge the gap with existing social insurance frameworks in different Australian states and provide compensation based on need and a no-fault basis. From a compensation fund perspective, the NIIS is more relevant to analyse in terms of whether it leans further towards the social insurance end of the spectrum (like the NDIS) or whether it operates on the tort replacement end of the spectrum in a similar fashion to New Zealand's Accident Compensation Commission. Neither scheme has been analysed in existing comparative law literature in context with other no-fault comprehensive compensation funds.

The two schemes were proposed in 2011 by the Australian Productivity Commission.[233] These new systems are an embodiment of tensions between public and private systems of compensation, and the question of whether compensation fund systems are a type of social insurance or a tort law alternative. Despite the new national framework, inconsistencies in compensation and support mechanisms available between different Australian states and territories are still likely to occur because of the way legislative power is divided between the Australian Commonwealth, and individual states and territories.

The National Disability Insurance Scheme (NDIS) is a social insurance system.[234] It aims to provide consistent levels of compensation and support to all persons who are affected by disability. It is centrally funded by State and Commonwealth governments, by way of tax increases and other indirect levies, rather than by individual contributions.[235]

The National Injury Insurance Scheme (NIIS) is the proposed sister scheme to the National Disability Insurance Scheme. The Productivity Commission

---

[233] The Productivity Commission is the Australian government's independent research and advisory body, which considers a range of economic, social and environmental issues affecting the welfare of Australians.

[234] The term 'social insurance' is not used within the legislation, but the legislative objects and principles described in Part 2 of the Act are focused on facilitating the social and economic participation of all Australian residents who are affected by disability. This kind of broad social purpose and the fact that it is described as an 'insurance' scheme mean that the NDIS can be properly categorised as a social insurance scheme. See National Disability Insurance Scheme Act 2013.

[235] There is a statutory agency responsible for the scheme: the National Disability Insurance Agency (NDIA). Certainty and sustainability are key principles underpinning compensation under the NDIS. To prevent double recovery, the NDIA has claw-back powers against claimants in relation to personal injury compensation payments the latter receive from outside judgments and settlements. See Luke Buckmaster, 'The National Disability Insurance Scheme: A Quick Guide' (2017) <http://parlinfo.aph.gov.au/parlInfo/download/library/prspub/4790922/upload_binary/4790922.pdf>.

Chapter 3. Review of Existing No-Fault Comprehensive Compensation Funds

recommended the establishment of separate, fully-funded schemes to provide lifetime care, support and compensation, on a no-fault basis, for all people suffering from catastrophic injury, whatever the cause.[236] The Productivity Commission identified huge inconsistencies in compensation and support for individuals across Australia affected by disability and injury.[237] Echoing the conclusions of the Woodhouse Report in New Zealand, the Commission said there was little rationale for the differences between the existing compensation mechanisms for catastrophic injury forming a patchwork of provision (workers' compensation, no-fault third-party motor vehicle insurance, fault-based compensation for motor accidents, crime victim compensation funds and fault-based medical indemnity and public liability insurance).[238] The Productivity Commission did question whether the administrative 'neatness' of rolling existing, well-functioning injury compensation schemes into a larger no-fault disability compensation system would result in any worthwhile gains.[239] However the efficient contractual model of interaction between the TAC and the Victorian workplace compensation system was recommended by the Productivity Commission as a way to manage the transfer of catastrophic injury from individual worker compensation systems to the NIIS.[240]

Each state or territory is supposed to implement its own version of the NIIS scheme, to cover catastrophic injuries caused by motor vehicle accidents, workplace accidents, medical accidents and general accidents. As noted later in this chapter, there have been significant developments in relation to no-fault NIIS compensation for catastrophic motor vehicle injuries. Negotiations between the Australian Commonwealth and individual States are ongoing in relation to the roll-out of the NIIS to other categories of injury.[241]

---

[236]   Productivity Commission, 'Productivity Commission Inquiry Report – Disability Care and Support, Volume 2' (2011) 789 <http://www.pc.gov.au/inquiries/completed/disability-support/report/disability-support-volume2.pdf>.

[237]   The Productivity Commission undertook a fact-finding mission, and actively sought submissions from the public and interested stakeholders. It also consulted relevant Australian and international organisations and held public hearings. For further details about the inquiry processes used by the Productivity Commission, see Productivity Commission, 'Productivity Commission Inquiry Report – Disability Care and Support, Volume 1' (2011) 107–108 <http://www.pc.gov.au/inquiries/completed/disability-support/report/disability-support-volume1.pdf>.

[238]   Productivity Commission, 'Productivity Commission Inquiry Report – Disability Care and Support, Volume 2' (n 236) 790.

[239]   Productivity Commission, 'Productivity Commission Inquiry Report – Overview and Recommendations' (2011) 48 <http://www.pc.gov.au/inquiries/completed/disability-support/report/disability-support-overview-booklet.pdf>.

[240]   Recommendation 18.4 Productivity Commission, 'Productivity Commission Inquiry Report – Overview and Recommendations' (n 239).

[241]   Australian Treasury, 'National Injury Insurance Scheme' <https://treasury.gov.au/programs-initiatives-consumers-community/niis/>. As of early 2020, the governments of New South Wales, Queensland and Victoria are apparently working together to discuss the feasibility of a general accident stream of the NIIS – see Lucy Kent and Norman Hermant,

Intersentia

101

But the original vision of the NIIS scheme has stalled politically, particularly in relation to medical accidents. In 2017 the Council of Australian Governments agreed not to proceed with the medical accident stream of the NIIS.[242] However the Australian (federal) Treasury remains interested in a medical accidents approach for NIIS, modelled closely on the New Zealand system, that would eliminate fault and concepts of negligence as much as possible.[243] As foreshadowed by public officials,[244] there is a risk, with time, of an ever-decreasing incentive for the establishment of NIIS systems as the NDIS is fully implemented. This is because the costs of any significant and permanent disabilities (caused by injuries) would be captured by the publicly funded NDIS, in the absence of an applicable existing NIIS no-fault scheme (which would be user funded or would create major changes to existing liability and insurance structures).

The political stall on the NIIS roll-out does not reflect an ambivalence or disinterest towards no-fault comprehensive compensation generally. As noted above, in Western Australia and the ACT, there was overwhelming public support for reforms that would increase the availability of no-fault compensation for catastrophic transport injuries. Australian medico-legal scholars have also advocated a no-fault system for medical injuries, arguing that an Australian shift in this direction is long-overdue and should be based on detailed medical evidence and modelling.[245] One legal commentary on the NIIS scheme claims that the accident rate will be increased by the introduction of a no-fault scheme.[246] However this kind of view appears to prioritise law and economics theories and ignores both the lack of actual data about whether no-fault actually leads to an increase in accidents and multiple actuarial and econometric findings that no-fault compensation funds are the cheapest and most effective system of compensation for injury.[247]

'Catastrophically Injured Australians Still Waiting for National Insurance Scheme Meant to Roll out with NDIS' *Australian Broadcasting Corporation News* (19 February 2020) <https://www.abc.net.au/news/2020-02-20/national-injury-insurance-scheme-injured-australians-waiting/11796928>.

[242] Productivity Commission, 'Study Report – National Disability Insurance Scheme (NDIS) Costs' (2017) <http://www.pc.gov.au/inquiries/completed/ndis-costs/report/ndis-costs.pdf>; Council of Australian Governments (n 229). There has been no update since then to the COAG's position.

[243] Australian Government (n 228).

[244] Council of Australian Governments Senior Officials' Working Group, 'ATTACHMENT A – Interactions between the National Injury Insurance Scheme (NIIS) and the National Disability Insurance Scheme (NDIS)' <https://treasury.gov.au/sites/default/files/2019-03/Document-7-7.pdf>.

[245] Wiesbrot and Breen (n 230). In relation to the state of Victoria, see Popa (n 230).

[246] Harrison (n 148).

[247] PriceWaterhouseCoopers (n 37) 74–76; Kirsten Armstrong and Daniel Tess, 'Fault versus No Fault – Reviewing the International Evidence', *Institute of Actuaries of Australia 16th General Insurance Seminar* (2008) 34 <https://actuaries.asn.au/Library/Events/GIS/2008/GIS08_3d_Paper_Tess,Armstrong_Fault versus No Fault – reviewing the international evidence.pdf>;

Chapter 3. Review of Existing No-Fault Comprehensive Compensation Funds

The NIIS's current roll-out only relates to providing lifetime no-fault compensation and support for victims of catastrophic injuries sustained in motor vehicle accidents. The NIIS could (if fully implemented), as a set of individual schemes with some degree of federal co-ordination, be compared in future legal analyses with other no-fault comprehensive compensation funds. If more states and territories begin to roll-out the scheme to other functional streams (such as medical injury and general accident cover), then this will be a truly comprehensive no-fault system for catastrophic injury. It could lead in turn to questions about whether such a no-fault comprehensive approach is also suitable for some types of non-catastrophic injury.[248] However, because there is no certainty (and something of a legislative and policy information void) over whether the NIIS will roll-out further as originally envisaged, analysis of it must be limited in this book to a contextual description and comparison with Victoria's TAC.

4. CANADA: NO-FAULT COMPREHENSIVE COMPENSATION FUNDS FOR TRANSPORT INJURY IN QUÉBEC AND MANITOBA

No-fault compensation in Canada can be characterised as being either very entrenched or barely present, depending on the province and the causal category of misfortune. The concept of no-fault is dominant in the areas of worker compensation (in all provinces) and automobile injury in the Québec and Manitoba provinces (and also vaccine injury in Québec). The concept is *partially* present in some provinces for motor vehicle injury, and then much less developed for medical incidents and other types of misfortune. This patchwork of differences between provincial systems is similar to Australia. Québec and Manitoba[249] are the provinces that have used compensation funds most expansively on a no-fault basis to compensate all residents (and some non-residents) for automobile injury.

Tom Vandersteegen and others, 'The Impact of No-Fault Compensation on Health Care Expenditures: An Empirical Study of OECD Countries' (2015) 119 *Health Policy* 367 <https://www.healthpolicyjrnl.com/article/S0168-8510(14)00240-1/pdf>.

[248] Other types of compensation fund structures have also been proposed, for example, a disaster fund to benefit individuals and communities affected by heatwaves, bushfires and other effects of climate change in Australia – see The Australia Institute, 'The National Climate Disaster Fund' (2019) <https://www.tai.org.au>.

[249] As well as Saskatchewan, but as will be seen, it lacks the compulsory requirement to be considered in this study.

Intersentia

103

An added dimension of interest is the fact of Canada's mixed common law and civil law heritage.[250] The Québec legal system has a unique shape and is a uniquely bi-juralist or mixed jurisdiction, where the private law is codified in line broadly with the French Napoleonic tradition. Québec public law, in contrast, follows the English common law tradition.

The Québec public automobile statutory no-fault compensation fund that is administered by the Société de l'assurance du Québec (hereafter 'SAAQ') covers all Québec residents involved in traffic accidents in the province and anywhere else in the world.[251] This means that the public authority pays compensation for personal injury in automobile accidents, and it will not be possible to file court proceedings in relation to an injury. There is also some coverage for property damage, but in a different part of the legislation. Tourists and newcomers may also be eligible for compensation, based (curiously for a no-fault scheme) on a calculation of the degree to which they were not responsible for the accident. There are exclusions for some kinds of accidents, including accidents that occur during a race or are affected by an external machinery part or animal. The courts have given a liberal interpretation to the definition of a qualifying motor accident.[252]

The province of Manitoba operates a very similar scheme to Québec, which provides basic compulsory automobile insurance for all Manitoba residents, with an entitlement to compensation for injury that occurs in a qualifying automobile accident anywhere in Canada or the United States. There is no-fault coverage for all bodily injury[253] and a bar against tort actions relating to bodily injury[254] – this is described as the Personal Injury Protection Plan.[255] As in Québec, non-residents may be eligible for some compensation (depending on their degree of responsibility),[256] and there are similar exclusions relating to animals.[257]

---

[250] French-style civil law applies in Québec, whilst the other provinces are common law jurisdictions and the federal law that applies to all jurisdictions is based on common law. A general point of interest in the Canadian common law is a general shift away from fault and closer to strict liability – see Jean-Louis Baudouin and Allen M Linden, 'Canada' in Britt Weyts (ed), *The International Encyclopaedia for Tort Law* (Wolters Kluwer 2015) 155.

[251] Société de l'assurance automobile Québec, 'If You Have an Accident in Québec' <https://saaq.gouv.qc.ca/en/tourists-and-newcomers/accident/>.

[252] Baudouin and Linden (n 250) 74. Three types of accidents are excluded from the system's coverage: accidents caused while the car is not moving and caused by an independently operate device (e.g. a crane), accidents caused by certain types of work vehicles and accidents that take place during a show or event.

[253] The Manitoba Public Insurance Corporation Act s 73.

[254] ibid s 72.

[255] Manitoba Public Insurance Corporation, 'Personal Injury Protection Plan' <https://www.mpi.mb.ca/Pages/personal-injury-protection-plan.aspx>.

[256] The Manitoba Public Insurance Corporation Act s 75(1).

[257] ibid s 70(1).

Chapter 3. Review of Existing No-Fault Comprehensive Compensation Funds

Québec's SAAQ and the Manitoba Public Insurance (hereafter 'MPI'), with their comprehensive cover for virtually all transport accident injuries (and some economic losses) on a no-fault basis, therefore fit this project's definition of a no-fault comprehensive compensation fund. Both can be functionally and structurally compared with New Zealand's ACC Scheme and Victoria's TAC. SAAQ and MPI are specifically described as 'public insurance' in their legislation, but they have been also described as a type of social welfare or a 'social good' measure.[258] By contrast, the no-fault worker compensation funds in each Canadian province do not fit within this comparative framework, because they are not truly comprehensive in coverage for that type of injury: in each province, a significant minority of workers (like contractors, or particular industries) are or may be excluded. This puts those funds at odds with the comprehensive coverage available for workplace injury under New Zealand's ACC. The very small scale of the no-fault Québec Vaccine Injury Scheme means that it must also be excluded from the comparative framework. There is some small comparative treatment in this section of the Canadian worker compensation schemes, the Québécois Vaccine Injury Scheme and blood products injury scheme[259] with the no-fault comprehensive transport injury compensation funds in Québec and Manitoba, for the purpose of a contextual analysis.

4.1. THE BACKGROUND TO THE SOCIÉTÉ DE L'ASSURANCE AUTOMOBILE DU QUÉBEC (SAAQ) AND MANITOBA PUBLIC INSURANCE (MPI)

The concept of no-fault as applied to automobile accidents was a popular feature of 1970s Canadian legal developments, but mostly as a way to supplement recovery through a tort claim.[260] The introduction of no-fault was not seen as necessitating a major alternation to the tort landscape or significantly changing how the compensation system for automobile accidents was managed. In Québec and later Manitoba, however, a more significant change did take place – no-fault comprehensive compensation funds were established to provide a statutory scheme of benefits for all province residents (and some non-residents) for bodily injury flowing from automobile accidents.

---

[258] Jeffrey Schnoor, 'No-Fault Automobile Insurance in Manitoba: An Overview. Les Cahiers de Droit' (1998) 39 *Les Cahiers de droit* 335, 339; Jean-Louis Baudouin, 'La Nouvelle Législation Québécoise Sur Les Accidents de La Circulation' (1979) 31 *Revue internationale de droit comparé* 381, 393.

[259] Act respecting Héma-Québec and the biovigilance committee.

[260] Craig Brown, *No Fault Automobile Insurance In Canada* (Carswell 1988).

Intersentia

105

The motivation for the development of these schemes was political, rather than because of a specific legal inadequacy of the existing system or a liability crisis. In Québec, these changes occurred in the context of a political desire to reduce road accidents and provide equitable and fair compensation to victims.[261] In Manitoba, these changes occurred in the context of a public outcry over car insurance costs.[262]

From the start of the twentieth century, the Québec legislature took an active approach towards the design of liability rules in a way that would solve the legal and social problems resulting from traffic accidents.[263] In 1971, the Québec government nominated an actuary, Jean-Louis Gauvin, to survey the causes of accidents and consider how to best compensate the relevant victims. The critique that followed in his 1974 report shares many similarities with the criticisms found in New Zealand's Woodhouse Report – the arbitrariness of a fault-based system, inadequate compensation, slow resolution of claims, and complex insurance pricing were all noted as problems with the status quo.[264] The Gauvin Report concluded that the abolition of the fault principle was necessary, and a universal compulsory[265] no-fault insurance covering bodily injury and property damage was needed. The status of automobiles as a 'social risk' to be managed was identified by Gauvin. As in the Australian state of Victoria, the response of the legal profession and the insurance industry to the report and the proposed introduction of a pure no-fault system was immediate and fierce.[266] Tensions were high and the debate about the introduction of the scheme dominated the political sphere and played out extensively in the media. Against all (political) odds, the *Loi sur l'assurance automobile* passed into law in March 1978, establishing the body that would eventually be come to known as the Société de l'assurance automobile du Québec (the SAAQ).[267] The core provisions concern the coverage provided for automobile-related personal injury under 'Title II – Compensation for Bodily Injury'.

---

[261] Québec Government, 'Rapport Du Comité d'étude Sur l'assurance-Automobile' (1974) 7–8.

[262] Schnoor (n 258) 338.

[263] Baudouin and Linden (n 250) 73. From 1912, a presumption of fault against both the owner and driver of a motor vehicle was introduced. The legislature later attempted to impose mandatory liability insurance.

[264] Québec Government (n 261) 9–11.

[265] Gauvin proposed that the scheme initially be managed by private insurance for five years, but if the results were unsatisfactory then a single public insurer should manage the scheme.

[266] Baudouin (n 258) 384.

[267] 'Il y a 40 Ans, Lise Payette Créait l'assurance Automobile Au Québec' *Radio Canada* (2018) <https://ici.radio-canada.ca/nouvelle/1086058/lise-payette-assurance-automobile-quebec-archives>.

Manitoba's pure no-fault comprehensive compensation fund for the compensation of personal injuries (called the Personal Injury Protection Plan) was established in 1993. This was an expansion of a more limited existing statutory cluster of no-fault benefits for personal injury that 'topped up' what could be available under a damages claim in negligence. Echoing the Woodhouse Report process in New Zealand, a judge (Provincial Court Judge Robert Kopstein) had been appointed by the Manitoba government to carry out a public consultation and review of motor insurance and the operations of the (previously established) Manitoba Public Insurance Corporation.[268] The review of traffic injury compensation that led to the Kopstein Report was largely a consequence of a public backlash against significant automobile insurance rates increases in 1987.[269] The stability of motor vehicle insurance rates under a new no-fault scheme was a clearly stated purpose of the Manitoba legislature when the relevant legislation was passed, and remains a key focus of the scheme today.[270]

In both provinces, the new schemes were a significant departure from the status quo. At the time, there was significant insurance industry and legal profession opposition to the changes in both jurisdictions.[271] The final legislation introducing both schemes was passed following elections where the issues of motor injury compensation (and automobile insurance costs) were key issues, so it is logical to deduce that there was an electoral mandate from at least a majority of the public for such changes. The Canadian Supreme Court has recently recognised that the creation of the SAAQ was a marked 'societal choice that reflected a social compromise by which all drivers were to collectively assume the financial consequences of bodily injuries caused by automobile accidents.'[272] Because of the legislative similarity of the Manitoba MPI to the SAAQ, it seems logical to apply this description to both schemes. Since their establishment, there have been high levels of both public and insurance industry satisfaction

---

[268]   Robert L Kopstein, 'The Report of the Autopac Review Commission – Volume 1' (Government of Manitoba 1988).

[269]   Schnoor (n 258) 338.

[270]   ibid; Manitoba Public Insurance Corporation, 'Our History' <https://www.mpi.mb.ca/pages/our-history.aspx>.

[271]   'Il y a 40 Ans, Lise Payette Créait l'assurance Automobile Au Québec' (n 267); Daniel Blaikie, 'Manitoba History: The Origins of Autopac: An Essay on the Possibility of Social Democratic Government in Manitoba' (2008) <http://www.mhs.mb.ca/docs/mb_history/59/autopac.shtml>.

[272]   *Godbout v Pagé et al* 2017 SCC 18; [2017] 1 SCR 283 [29].

with both funds, and no serious efforts to move back to a tort-based system or a hybrid system in either province.[273]

4.2. LEGISLATIVE STRUCTURES AND RELEVANT LEGAL DOCTRINES

This subsection sets out the legislative structure of the SAAQ and MPI schemes, in a similar way to how the ACC and TAC schemes were detailed in previous subsections. The Manitoba legislation was closely modelled on that of Québec, although they are not completely identical.[274] However, in terms of the universal coverage that they provide to all province residents and effective elimination of access to the courts, they are identical.

Unlike the New Zealand and Victorian schemes, there is no 'purpose' section of the SAAQ and MPI statutes. However a study of historical documents, parliamentary debates and case law reveals that the legislators had different goals in mind when establishing these virtually identical no-fault comprehensive compensation funds. Comprehensive no-fault insurance and the abolition of tort remedies were the same means to two different ends. For the SAAQ, the relevant Québec National Assembly debates from the establishment of the no-fault compensation scheme reveal a social justice purpose that, like the New Zealand ACC Scheme, aimed to create a community responsibility for the sharing of road risks.[275] In contrast, the Manitoba scheme was established with the objectives of

---

[273] David Gambrill, 'David Marshall on Why Quebec's Auto Insurance System Works – and Ontario's Doesn't Canadian Underwriter', *Canadian Underwriter* (25 September 2019) <https://www.canadianunderwriter.ca/insurance/david-marshall-on-why-quebecs-auto-insurance-system-works-and-ontarios-doesnt-1004168833/>; Paul Waldie and Peter Cheney, 'Quebec, Manitoba Systems Called the Best', *The Globe and Mail* (14 June 2003) <https://www.theglobeandmail.com/news/national/quebec-manitoba-systems-called-the-best/article1017430/>. In their most recent annual reports, the SAAQ had an overall rate of 80% user satisfaction and the MPI an overall rate of 90% user satisfaction. See Manitoba Public Insurance Corporation, 'Annual Report' (2017); Société de l'assurance automobile du Québec, 'Rapport Annuel de Gestion 2018' (2018) <https://saaq.gouv.qc.ca/fileadmin/documents/publications/rapport-annuel-gestion-2018.pdf>.

[274] 'There can be little doubt that the Manitoba legislation was modelled on the Québec plan. It is worded similarly, but is not identical to that plan', according to the Manitoba Court of Appeal in *McMillan v Thompson (Rural Municipality)* (1997) 144 DLR (4th) 53, [64]. The legislative scope and design of the MPI scheme was 'essentially lifted and shifted' from the SAAQ, according to the MPI's Director of Injury Claims Management, Glenn Andersen (Email correspondence dated 16 October 2019).

[275] 'Puisque nous savons tous que ce n'est pas à l'assurance de pénaliser les coupables, puisque nous savons tous que mes collègues de la Justice et des Transports verront à écarter de la

Chapter 3. Review of Existing No-Fault Comprehensive Compensation Funds

reducing the cost and volume of litigation,[276] and to maintain premium stability for motorists.[277]

The initial application process for the SAAQ and MPI is generally by way of a telephone application, followed by an official form. Because of the nature of the Canadian public health system, the SAAQ and MPI do not need to cover the costs of, for example, immediate primary care and hospital treatment following an accident.[278] However both the SAAQ and MPI make monthly rebate payments to their provincial public health services.[279] Claims must be made within three years of the date of the accident or onset of injury to SAAQ,[280] and within two years for MPI.[281]

Like New Zealand's ACC Scheme and Victoria's TAC, the SAAQ and MPI's 'Personal Injury Insurance Plan' both provide most of their compensation benefits in the form of treatment costs and lost income replacement costs. Under both SAAQ and MPI there is a statutory entitlement to:

a. Direct time-limited financial compensation for loss of income (for both earners and non-earners),[282] as well as (in the case of SAAQ) compensation for small-value personal property (like clothing) that was damaged during the traffic accident.[283] There are indemnities for students of all ages and minors for the loss of a school year or semester[284] (and further compensation if the injury affects his or her employment prospects[285]).[286]

---

route les conducteurs imprudents ou dangereux, nous avons essayé de trouver une meilleure expression qui colle davantage au concept de la mise en commun des risques routiers, car c'est cela que nous voulons instaurer, c'est cela, notre "no fault", c'est cela que nous appelons une plus grande justice sociale, la mise en commun des risques routiers' – quoted in *Godbout v Pagé et al* (n 272) 345–346.

[276] *McMillan v Thompson (Rural Municipality)* (n 274) para [54].

[277] Schnoor (n 258) 338–339.

[278] However, in the case of the SAAQ at least, an annual reimbursement payment is made to the government that specifically relates to healthcare costs.

[279] Comments made in interviews with SAAQ and MPI staff in May and October 2019.

[280] Automobile Insurance Act (Québec) s 11. This provision gives some discretion to the SAAQ to allow an out-of-time application in the case of 'serious and valid reasons'.

[281] The Manitoba Public Insurance Corporation Act s 141(1).

[282] Title II, Chapter II Automobile Insurance Act (Québec); The Manitoba Public Insurance Corporation Act ss 81–86.

[283] Automobile Insurance Act (Québec) s 2.

[284] ibid ss 27–33; The Manitoba Public Insurance Corporation Act ss 87–98.

[285] Automobile Insurance Act (Québec) ss 34–39; The Manitoba Public Insurance Corporation Act ss 90(1), 90(3), 96(1), 97(3).

[286] Société de l'assurance automobile du Québec, 'Indemnity for Students' <https://saaq.gouv.qc.ca/en/traffic-accident/public-automobile-insurance-plan/covered-how/financial-compensation/students/>.

Intersentia

Lump sum death benefits (the quantum of which is linked to the victim's age and income) and funeral expenses are available to the family members of fatal traffic accident victims.[287]

b. Compensation by way of direct and indirect payment for medical costs (that are not already covered by Canadian public healthcare services). Non-public healthcare services that relate to traffic accident victims may be covered – such as chiropractic care, physiotherapy, occupational therapy, psychotherapy, dental therapy and acupuncture.[288]

c. Compensation by way of rehabilitation services – this can include home adaptation, and other rehabilitation to help the victim return to full function in society or manage a long-term catastrophic injury.[289]

In terms of non-residents, both schemes offer complete no-fault coverage if the victim was driving or a passenger in a locally registered automobile at the time of the accident. In the case of a non-resident in a non-resident vehicle, the default position is that both schemes offer compensation to victims in inverse proportion to their responsibility for the accident (for example, a non-resident who was 20 per cent responsible for the accident will receive only 80 per cent of the no-fault benefits).[290] Where the home jurisdiction (normally another

---

[287] 'In the Event of a Death in a Traffic Accident' <https://saaq.gouv.qc.ca/en/traffic-accident/death/?ADMCMD_prev=IGNORE>; The Manitoba Public Insurance Corporation Act ss 119–125.

[288] 'Private Health Care Covered by the Public Automobile Insurance Plan' <https://saaq.gouv.qc.ca/en/traffic-accident/public-automobile-insurance-plan/covered-how/health-care/?ADMCMD_prev=IGNORE&cHash=433a574c7ff36b131fcd8f373a95e879>; Manitoba Public Insurance Corporation, 'Personal Injury Protection Plan' (n 255).

[289] Société de l'assurance automobile du Québec, 'Automobile and Home Adaptation' <https://saaq.gouv.qc.ca/en/traffic-accident/public-automobile-insurance-plan/covered-how/automobile-home-adaptation/>; Société de l'assurance automobile du Québec, 'Personal Home Assistance' <https://saaq.gouv.qc.ca/en/traffic-accident/public-automobile-insurance-plan/covered-how/personal-home-assistance/>; Société de l'assurance automobile du Québec, 'Occupational, Educational or Social Reintegration' <https://saaq.gouv.qc.ca/en/traffic-accident/public-automobile-insurance-plan/covered-how/occupational-reintegration/>; Manitoba Public Insurance Corporation, 'Injury Rehabilitation' <https://www.mpi.mb.ca/Pages/injury-rehabilitation.aspx>.

[290] Société de l'assurance automobile du Québec, The Insurance Policy for All Quebecers (2019) <https://saaq.gouv.qc.ca/fileadmin/documents/publications/automobile-insurance-policy-quebec.pdf>; Manitoba Public Insurance Corporation, 'Personal Injury Protection Plan – Your Guide' <https://www.mpi.mb.ca/Documents/PIPPGuide.pdf>; Manitoba Public Insurance Corporation, 'Personal Injury Protection Plan' (n 255); Automobile Insurance Act (Québec) s 83.61; The Manitoba Public Insurance Corporation Act s 75(1).

Chapter 3. Review of Existing No-Fault Comprehensive Compensation Funds

Canadian province or a US state) has a reciprocal agreement with the SAAQ and MPI, then the terms of that agreement will be applied.

From a functional perspective, the no-fault comprehensive funds managed by the SAAQ and MPI are therefore virtually indistinguishable.[291] There are, however, two minor differences between the schemes that are worth noting in a comparative analysis. Firstly, the worldwide entitlement to protection for traffic accidents afforded to all Québec residents and their dependents[292] indicates that a wider degree of social protection is intended to be offered. The second key difference between the SAAQ and the MPI is that there are specific measures in place prohibiting the Manitoba government from privatising of the scheme without a public referendum.[293] This indicates that although the Manitoba scheme does not have the same kind of 'social good' inspiration as the SAAQ, the fund has been deemed by the Manitoba legislature to be an important enough piece of 'legal infrastructure' to warrant protection from political interference unless absolutely justified and in accordance with the public's wishes.

In terms of the evolution of the legislative structures during their history, both the Québec and Manitoba schemes have been relatively stable with no significant legislative changes to the scope of their application (especially when compared to the tumultuous politically-influenced revolutions of the New Zealand ACC Scheme).

Both the SAAQ and the MPI can be categorised in the Canadian insurance law context as monopolistic public insurers.[294] Like New Zealand and Victoria, the MPI administrative body is created and governed by the same primary legislation that creates the no-fault comprehensive compensation fund. The SAAQ is created and governed under separate legislation that also details the SAAQ's trustee relationship with the financial fund underpinning the scheme.[295] The SAAQ took its current Crown corporation form in 1990 after different motoring regulatory functions were folded under one umbrella corporation.[296] The organisations

---

[291]   Further effective differences between the schemes are very difficult to quantify. MPI undertook a jurisdictional scan in 2017, and determined that the average cost per injury claim between 2012 and 2016 was nearly identical under MPI and SAAQ.

[292]   Chapter I, Division II, Automobile Insurance Act (Québec) s 7.

[293]   The Manitoba Public Insurance Corporation Act s 14.1.

[294]   Chapter 17, 'Different Classes of Insurance' in Craig Brown and Andrew Mercer, *Introduction to Canadian Insurance Law* (4th edn, LexisNexis Canada 2018).

[295]   Act respecting the Société de l'assurance automobile du Québec.

[296]   Société de l'assurance automobile du Québec, 'A Brief History of the SAAQ' <https://saaq.gouv.qc.ca/en/saaq/a-brief-history-of-the-saaq/accessible-version/>.

Intersentia

111

themselves consider their purpose and existence to be those of a public insurer, rather than a branch of social insurance or an unconventional compensation structure,[297] but there is recognition of their special social status.[298]

Both the SAAQ and MPI have the statutory subrogated right to pursue other parties who are not entitled to scheme cover for a recoupment of compensation costs.[299] These powers primarily relate to the ability of the corporations to recover costs from at-fault out-of-province drivers, and in practice usually result in a negotiated settlement with the relevant third party's insurer. The SAAQ and MPI have both put bilateral procedures in place with a limited number of neighbouring Canadian provinces.

From a structural perspective that is relevant to a comparative law analysis, the Québec and Manitoba schemes have created a codified framework of statutory entitlements to compensation in the case of automobile personal injury – in effect a 'right' to compensation for injury. This is primarily because the entitlement to compensation extends beyond motorists with registered SAAQ or MPI policies. All residents and non-residents (with limits) are entitled to compensation. The effect of the tort bar and of creating an entitlement to no-fault benefits amounts to the establishment of an entitlement to socialised compensation in what would otherwise be a private law sphere. From this departure point we can go on to discuss and analyse the scope and effect of the SAAQ and MPI.

4.3. THE SCOPE OF THE SAAQ AND MPI

As with New Zealand and Victoria, in terms of scope we can refer to the space in law in which the Québec and Manitoba schemes occupy, what they provide (in terms of compensation) and what they take away (in terms of entitlement to access other remedies). Both schemes provide no-fault compensation for injuries flowing from an automobile accident as specifically (yet generously) defined in the legislation.

Set out below is a table describing the key legislative scope of both the SAAQ and the MPI, and where some minor differences exist between them. In terms of their most restrictive provision – the statutory bar against tort proceedings – they are identical.

---

[297] Comments made in interview with Nancy LaRue, Expert Advisor on Insurance Coverage at the Société de l'assurance automobile du Québec, 6/5/2019.

[298] Comments made in interview on 21/10/2019 with Glenn Andersen, Director of Injury Claims Management at Manitoba Public Insurance.

[299] The Manitoba Public Insurance Corporation Act s 26; Automobile Insurance Act (Québec) ss 83.60–83.62.

Table 4. Scope of the SAAQ and MPI schemes

Concept	SAAQ	MPI
General scope of cover for injury	Every person who suffers a bodily injury in an accident is a qualifying victim (s 6).	Same as SAAQ (s 71(1)).
What is a bodily injury?	A bodily injury is any physical or mental injury, including death, suffered by a victim in an accident. It also includes damage to the clothes that the victim was wearing at the time of the accident (s 2).	Similar to SAAQ, but includes clarification that permanent physical or mental impairment is definitely included (s 70(1)). Clothes not included.
What is an accident?	Any event in which damage is caused by an automobile (s 1).	Slightly narrower than SAAQ – any event in which 'bodily injury' is caused by an automobile (s 70(1)).
What is an automobile?	Any vehicle propelled by power (other than muscular force) and adapted for transportation on public highways (s 1). 'Public highways' specifically excludes land that is mainly accessed by farm vehicles, snow mobiles and off-road vehicles. 'Damage caused by an automobile' is defined as excluding the act of an animal that is part of the automobile's load or the ordinary maintenance of a vehicle (s 1).	Mostly identical to SAAQ (s 70(1)). Same exclusions for animals and ordinary vehicle maintenance.
Specific exclusions?	As well as the general exclusion under s 1, s 10 specifically says there will be no entitlement to compensation where the injury happened when vehicle is not in motion, is caused by a farm vehicle off a public highway, or caused by a snowmobile anywhere,[300] or if the injury occurred during a special event. There is also an exclusion under s 10 for mobility aids and personal mobility devices. In the case of farm vehicles and snow mobiles, if another normal qualifying automobile is involved, that will reactivate entitlement.	Similar to SAAQ. Exclusions exist within the statute for farm equipment, mobility scooters, electric bicycles, golf carts and other 'prescribed personal transport device[s]'. (s 71(2)). The SAAQ legislation leaves it to the SAAQ itself to make relevant regulations about these kinds of non-typical vehicles (s 195 SAAQ).
Statutory bar against tort actions	'Notwithstanding the provisions of any other Act, compensation under this Part stands in lieu of all rights and remedies arising out of bodily injuries to which this Part applies and no action in that respect may be admitted before any court.' (s 72).	Identical to SAAQ (s 72).
Coverage for non-residents	Complete coverage exists if driving a locally registered vehicle. Otherwise, coverage is in inverse proportion to responsibility for the accident (unless there is an agreement in place with the non-resident's home jurisdiction on this point) (s 83.61).[301]	Identical to SAAQ (s 75(1)).

Source: Compiled by the author.

---

[300] Prior to 1990, snowmobiles on public roads did enjoy SAAQ scheme coverage, but this was abolished because it was too difficult to determine practically what did or did not occur on a public road.

[301] Société de l'assurance automobile du Québec, *The Insurance Policy for All Quebecers* (n 290) 6.

As in both New Zealand and Victoria, there can be a limitation on the scope of no-fault compensatory benefits for individuals who are convicted of a driving-related or other relevant criminal offence. However, in Québec this restriction is not as severe, because any reductions in benefit are offset by the number of dependants that person has, and the benefits in question are paid directly to the dependants.[302] This shows a clear social fairness intent – access to compensation is reduced for someone whose behaviour contributed to the accident, but there is an attempt to mitigate the effect of that restriction on the 'guilty' person's innocent family members. Manitoba also uses this 'dependant'-focused approach but in the case of some criminal offences (such as motor vehicle theft), the MPI can seek an order for reimbursement of compensation from the victim.[303]

In terms of their scope, the Québec and Manitoba schemes remain different from the insurance and tort schemes that are available in other provinces. Although both the MPI and the SAAQ are specifically described as 'insurance' (of a public nature), this does not mean that from a structural perspective the statutory no-fault benefits they provide are the same as what is available under a contract of insurance with a private insurer. The Canadian Supreme Court has allowed a peaceful inconsistency to prevail on this issue – it remains unclear whether statutory benefits are the same as a contract of indemnity, but for practical purposes this might not matter so long as undesirable outcomes such as double recovery are avoided. This mirrors the approach taken by the High Court of Australia in *Sweedman v Transport Accident Commission*. The scope of the Québec and Manitoba schemes can therefore be categorised (in terms of the space they occupy in law relating *specifically to automobile-related personal injury*) as being structurally apart from insurance, but not inconsistent with it.[304]

The treatment of this issue by Canadian courts supports the view that as a structure, these two no-fault comprehensive compensation funds stand apart from other structures in law.

Nordquist v Gurniak[305] concerned the automobile death of a Québec resident in British Columbia. The Supreme Court of Canada had to determine whether SAAQ

---

[302] Automobile Insurance Act (Québec) s 83.30. This exception is only applicable during the period where the victim is imprisoned, and is not imposed automatically.

[303] The Manitoba Public Insurance Corporation Act s 161.1. MPI staff commented that this legislative amendment was a specific adjustment following a perceived car theft problem in the province.

[304] The MPI also offers a variety of extension insurance products for automobiles and other special vehicles (including off-road vehicles that are not covered within the no-fault scheme). It competes in theory with private insurance companies, but according to MPI itself, it holds a more than 97% market share in the extension insurance market. The relevance of this is to show that outside of the no-fault personal injury statutory benefits, the MPI *does*, as a near monopolistic public insurer, operate within the sphere of insurance. In contrast, Québec's Automobile Insurance Act requires all vehicle owners to hold at least C$50,000 of civil liability coverage (i.e. for non-personal injury cover) under a prescribed regulated and standardised contract of insurance, but this is provided by a choice of private providers.

[305] *Nordquist v Gurniak* 2003 SCC 59.

Chapter 3. Review of Existing No-Fault Comprehensive Compensation Funds

no-fault benefits received in relation to the deceased should be deducted from damages that were awarded in a British Columbian tort action (and would therefore be deductible under the double recovery provisions of the relevant British Columbia insurance legislation). The majority judgment found that there was broad equivalence between the 'general nature and character' of the benefits themselves, and it was not necessary to consider the fundamental differences between the British Columbia and Québec insurance regimes (even though it had been a major point of contention between the parties).[306] The BC Court of Appeal had categorised the SAAQ death benefit payments as being the same as insurance indemnity benefits, but the majority judgment of the Supreme Court refused to make a specific ruling on this point (on the ground that it was not necessary for the particular facts of the case, and in order to prevent double recovery). A simple functional conclusion that statutory no-fault benefits could serve the same purpose as a compensatory tort award was as far as the Supreme Court was willing to take this line of reasoning.[307] This approach is reflective of the theme of flexible interpretative consistency towards automobile insurance, which has also been favoured by at least one Canadian insurance scholar.[308]

There is a generous scope of what is a qualifying automobile accident under these two schemes, but there remain limitations on what kind of vehicles are covered. Both the SAAQ and the MPI specifically exclude snowmobiles and off-road vehicles from cover. As already discussed in relation to the New Zealand jurisdiction, anywhere there is a threshold of eligibility for compensation under a no-fault comprehensive compensation fund, there is the risk of unequal treatment of similar victims.

J.A. v SAAQ[309] concerned a child, X, who had suffered a catastrophic injury after being struck by an uninsured snowmobile on a public road. The city where X lived was in Nunavik, the far northern portion of the Québec province. In Nunavik, the Arctic climate conditions mean that the snowmobile is the main form of transportation (rather than an automobile). The appellant (who sought SAAQ scheme coverage for X), argued that the SAAQ legislative definition of automobile should be interpreted to include snowmobiles, because north of the 49th parallel snowmobiles were the dominant road vehicle. The Court of Appeal rejected these arguments, denying coverage for X, whilst acknowledging the factual reality of snowmobile use in Nunavik. The purpose of the legislative scope of the SAAQ scheme legislation was found to be clear and justified within its framework. The appellant's arguments, if successful, would have the effect of greatly expanding the legislative scope of the scheme. Clearly, the inconsistency of treatment in this case had very serious and painfully unfair consequences for now-paraplegic X (who only had recourse to the normal civil liability regime, against an uninsured defendant).

---

[306] ibid 653–654.

[307] ibid 674.

[308] Erik S Knutsen, 'Auto Insurance as Social Contract: Solving Automobile Insurance Coverage Disputes Through a Public Regulatory Framework' (2011) 48 *Alberta Law Review* 715.

[309] *J.A. v Société de l'assurance automobile du Québec* 2010 QCCA 1328.

Intersentia

115

The only justification for this judgment is the maintenance of a clearly defined compensation fund scope, because an inclusion of *all vehicles* on both public and private roads would be a step towards a wholly universal 'everyday risks' compensation fund, more akin to the New Zealand scheme. That kind of adjustment would fundamentally change the nature of the SAAQ scheme and should only be effected by way of an express legislative choice.

4.4. THE EFFECT OF THE SAAQ AND MPI AND THEIR ROLES IN CONTEXT

The principal effect in law of both the SAAQ and the MPI is to completely eliminate the possibility of tort damages for traffic accident bodily injury, and to establish a new, divergent scheme of comprehensive statutory no-fault benefits for automobile injury in its place. The lack of a special carve-out for serious injuries, as in Victoria's TAC, gives the Canadian schemes an obliterating effect that is more akin to the New Zealand ACC Scheme. The scope of a qualifying automobile accident and the breadth of the statutory bar against tort actions have been upheld by the Canadian Supreme Court in an absolute way (at least in relation to the SAAQ) that is very similar to how New Zealand judges have approached these issues.

Godbout v Pagé[310] concerned two linked cases about the right to sue third parties for injuries that had some factual (but not causative, in the tortious sense) connection to a qualifying SAAQ automobile injury. The first appellants, Ms Godbout and her family members, suffered various subsequent additional injuries because of alleged failures by the medical staff that treated them after their car accident. The second linked appellant, Mr Gargantiel, said that the failure of police to find his crashed vehicle (where he lay injured and unconscious in freezing conditions for nearly three days, despite the fact that his car's on-board computer had sent multiple alerts via satellite to the police) caused his severe injuries. Both Godbout and Gargantiel received SAAQ compensation and assistance for their injuries, but they wanted to get around the tort bar so that they could also sue the allegedly negligent third parties for further damages. The majority judgment of the Supreme Court dismissed both appeals. Firstly, it said it was inappropriate to use civil liability concepts of causality, because the SAAQ legislation only required a sufficiently close factual link between the accident and the injury. Secondly, the judgment spoke specifically about the social purpose of the scheme and the intention to take the problem of automobile injury wholly out of the reach of civil liability. This was done to 'ensure that the victim need not engage in costly and uncertain court proceedings in order to obtain compensation

---

[310]   *Godbout v Pagé et al* (n 272).

116   Intersentia

Chapter 3. Review of Existing No-Fault Comprehensive Compensation Funds

for the whole of his or her injury.[311] The decision to create a comprehensive tort bar was a 'societal choice that reflected a societal compromise'.[312] In other words, the purpose of the scheme would be undermined if accident victims were forced to start splitting up causally the sources of their injuries that, on a simple factual basis, had occurred because of the fact of an accident – even though the normal civil liability rules would require such a forensic division of the injuries.

Downer v Attorney General of Québec[313] is a Québec Superior Court decision, confirmed by the Québec Court of Appeal,[314] that confirms the strength and breadth of the bar against court-based damages within the SAAQ legislative framework – even in relation to a punitive damages claim on a human rights basis. It concerned the late Mrs Downer, who was killed in a 2017 car accident, and her related co-plaintiffs who were seriously injured in the same accident. The death and personal injuries associated with the accident were of course automatically covered by the SAAQ scheme. The plaintiffs, however, alleged that the accident was caused by various Québec provincial agencies' negligent installation and maintenance of signs, and therefore sought punitive damages for the infringement of their right to life and security, guaranteed and enabled by sections 7 and 24 of the Canadian Charter of Rights and Freedoms. The Superior Court applied *Godbout* and confirmed that compensation paid under the no-fault scheme for bodily injury suffered in an automobile accident takes the place of *all* rights and remedies arising from such injury. The Court said that the 'watertight'[315] or comprehensive nature of the no-fault compensation scheme excluded any possibility of punitive or exemplary damages.

Westmount (City) v Rossy[316] is an earlier Supreme Court decision that was applied in *Godbout*. It concerned the deceased, R, who was killed when a tree fell on his car in the Québec city of Westmount. R's family members wanted to bring a claim for civil damages against the City of Westmount on the grounds that, as owner of the tree, it had failed to properly maintain it. Like in *Godbout*, the Supreme Court relied on a simple causal connection between the automobile and the injury – the accident occurred while he was using the car as a form of transportation, and this was sufficient to trigger SAAQ no-fault cover and the statutory bar. The court cautioned that taking a more restrictive interpretation of

---

[311] ibid para 30.

[312] ibid para 29.

[313] *Downer v Procureure générale du Québec et Société de l'assurance automobile du Québec* 2019 QCCS 1280.

[314] *Downer v Procureure générale du Québec et Société de l'assurance automobile du Québec* (CA) 2019 QCCA 1893. The Supreme Court of Canada subsequently denied the appellants leave to further appeal.

[315] '… qu'en raison du régime étanche d'indemnisation sans égard à la faute stipulé à l'art. 83.57 LAA, une victime d'un accident d'automobile ne peut intenter un recours en vertu du par. 24(1) de la Charte canadienne pour obtenir des dommages exemplaires.'

[316] *City of Westmount v Rossy* 2012 SCC 136.

Intersentia

117

the legislation, and importing civil liability principles of causation, 'risks unduly restricting the intended application of the Québec's no-fault scheme and must therefore be rejected.'[317]

The Supreme Court has indeed taken a 'large and liberal' interpretation of SAAQ's social purpose.[318] But does this large and liberal interpretation also apply to the Manitoba MPI scheme? The majority judgment in *Godbout* noted that that although the schemes were very similar in structure, on the scope of 'no-fault' the Québec scheme had a wider scope than Manitoba. This was because although both schemes say that compensation is payable 'regardless of who is at fault',[319] the Manitoba scheme adds the words 'for the accident' at the end of that sentence. The dissenting judgment, however, noted that overall the intention and meaning of the relevant statutory provisions were identical in the two schemes. It appears as though the Supreme Court majority in *Godbout* were seeking to clearly distinguish a much older Manitoba case, *Mitchell v Raman*, which allowed a subsequent injury to break the factual nexus with the automobile accident.[320] However *Mitchell* was decided long before *Rossy*. Now, there is certainly a wider 'social purpose' envisaged by the Québec scheme – simply because there are more words to that effect in the legislative documents surrounding the SAAQ's establishment. It is arguable that there are simply not enough clearly stated differing points of purpose in the legislative provisions of the Québec and Manitoba schemes to indicate that future cases relating to third parties and subsequent events would be treated much differently in the two provinces. This is especially the case given two clear Supreme Court statements favouring an expansive approach to the tort bar (which, incidentally, in both the Manitoba and Québec schemes is worded identically) and the scheme coverage of a no-fault comprehensive compensation fund. If the Manitoba legislature were to introduce clarification on this point within the legislative provisions, that could change things – but the attempt to introduce a 'nexus' point between an accident and subsequent events would introduce a mass of (unwelcome and unwieldy) uncertainty to the Manitoba scheme.

Ultimately, *Godbout*, *Downer* and *Rossy* show that the creation of no-fault comprehensive compensation funds leads to a new hybrid field of compensation law on a rough 'social good' basis that is not bound by traditional principles of loss allocation, and would be artificially complicated by an attempt to fuse ordinary tort principles with a no-fault basis for compensation.

---

[317] *City of Westmount v Rossy* 2012 SCC 136 [54].
[318] *Godbout v Pagé et al* (n 272) para 38; Thérèse Rousseau-Houle, 'Le Régime Québécois d'assurance Automobile, Vingt Ans Après' (1998) 39 *Les Cahiers de droit* <https://doi.org/10.7202/043491ar>; Baudouin and Linden (n 250) para 191.
[319] Automobile Insurance Act (Québec) s 5; The Manitoba Public Insurance Corporation Act s 75.
[320] *Mitchell v Rahman* 2002 MBCA 19.

Does this expansive effect have a negative impact on SAAQ and MPI compensation recipients, compared to what they would receive under a civil liability claim? This may be easier to estimate in Canada than in New Zealand, for example, because there will be some kinds of road-related injuries that are not covered by the schemes. From a comparative perspective, another catastrophic snowmobile accident (and thus ineligible for SAAQ cover) involving a child is interesting to consider.

The plaintiff in *Bouliane v Commission scolaire de Charlesbourg* was awarded C$3 million, the largest ever civil damages award in Québec at the time.[321] Daniel Gardner, a prominent Québécois liability law professor, analysed this case and demonstrated that hypothetical SAAQ benefits available to a victim like Bouliane over her lifetime (roughly C$20 million) would be larger and more adaptive to addressing her changing needs than would be possible under a structured settlement – not least because she would not have had to pay 25–30 per cent of her damages in legal fees.[322] In this case, the plaintiff would, under SAAQ, have benefited from particularly generous provisions within that scheme that allow the scheme to estimate the claimant's hypothetical future income (had the injury not occurred) and pay it out to her. This is far more generous than what would be available to such a victim under the New Zealand ACC Scheme. Under Victoria's TAC the basis of calculation would be 'common law' damages, so it is conceptually slightly different. The best comparative conclusion we can probably make on this point is that the *possible* lifetime financial benefits, as well as the value of recognised social benefits[323] of a no-fault comprehensive compensation fund, combine to balance out any negative effect of a lack of access to a 'full' calculation of compensatory damages in tort law.

4.5. COMPARISON OF THE SAAQ AND MPI WITH TRAFFIC INJURY SCHEMES IN SASKATCHEWAN AND ONTARIO

From a functional perspective, there is a basic degree of philosophical agreement between all Canadian provinces – the concept of no-fault is useful and logical to the management within the legal system of the consequences of injury and loss flowing from an automobile accident of some kind. However beyond that, from a structural perspective, the Québec and Manitoba schemes stand far apart from other provinces because no-fault insurance is not just compulsory – it

---

[321] *Bouliane v Commission scolaire de Charlesbourg* [1984] CS 323.

[322] Daniel Gardner, 'Automobile No-Fault in Québec as Compared to Victoria' (2000) 8 *Torts Law Journal* 89.

[323] The social benefit is the greatly improved equity in the distribution of resources, as identified by PriceWaterhouseCoopers in their review of the ACC Scheme. See PriceWaterhouseCoopers (n 37) 85.

is used *comprehensively* and there is *no choice* to use the tort system instead. The provinces of Saskatchewan and Ontario bear the closest similarity with Manitoba and Québec, but their reluctance to take the step of completely barring tort claims is a key difference and shows less clarity in the use of the concept of no-fault.

In the province of Saskatchewan we find the current closest other Canadian example of the Québec and Manitoba schemes. The Saskatchewan Auto Fund is managed by Saskatchewan Government Insurance (a Crown corporation) under the framework set out in the Automobile Insurance Act. Under this scheme, the default is no-fault statutory compensation coverage, but individuals retain the choice to select the tort system (at the time of purchasing their car insurance cover). The reality is that the vast majority of individuals choose the no-fault scheme, but the fact of the availability of choice makes this scheme legislatively different from the no-fault comprehensive schemes enjoyed in Manitoba and Québec.[324] The Saskatchewan scheme also allows the victim of motor vehicle accident injuries (or his or her surviving spouse or dependant) to sue for both economic and non-economic loss in excess of the statutory no-fault coverage.[325]

There is thus a wider scope of access to tort remedies for multiple classes of victims in Saskatchewan than is possible in Québec and Manitoba (and, if comparing internationally, wider access than the limited tort law carve-out for catastrophic injury damages under Victoria's Transport Accident Commission in Australia). The Saskatchewan scheme can therefore not be described as sufficiently 'comprehensive'. The Canadian Supreme Court in *Rossy* also concluded that the Saskatchewan system had a 'different legislative intent' from that of the Manitoba and Québec schemes.[326]

Ontario operates a no-fault automobile compensation system which requires private insurers to pay out benefits regardless of fault. It is also possible to make a tort law claim under this system. Where a motor vehicle accident occurs and none of the parties involved have insurance, the Motor Vehicle Accident Claims Fund will provide some last-resort statutory accident benefits, as well as compensation for personal injury and property damage.[327] In this scheme we

---

[324]   See also Saskatchewan Government Insurance, 'The Ability to Sue'.

[325]   The Automobile Accident Insurance Act (Saskatchewan) ss 41.15 and 41.16. Accidents for bereavements are also possible for immediate family members of a fatal motor vehicle accident victim under section 4.1 of The Fatal Accidents Act (Saskatchewan). In the case of non-economic loss and bereavement actions, the responsible driver must have been convicted of a criminal offence that is specified in the Automobile Accident Insurance Act. See also 'Injury Manual – Tort Actions Available to Part VIII Beneficiary: The Ability to Sue' 1 <https://www.sgi.sk.ca/documents/625510/627089/1_Ability_to_Sue.pdf/7557ceba-0271-4283-b100-11a113370358>.

[326]   *City of Westmount v Rossy* (n 317) para 31.

[327]   Financial Services Commission of Ontario, 'Motor Vehicle Accident Claims Fund' <https://www.fsco.gov.on.ca/en/auto/mvacf/pages/default.aspx>.

see a statutory entitlement to no-fault benefits as in Manitoba and Québec, but not the key step of eliminating access to damages in tort entirely. Also, private insurance companies (rather than one public insurer) offer the statutory no-fault benefits, a factor which probably increases overall costs.[328]

From an empirical perspective, it is worth noting that Canadian insurance research has found that government-run, pure no-fault automobile injury and property damage compensation probably results in lower average costs overall than private tort actions and modified no-fault coverage (such as in Saskatchewan and Ontario).[329] However Rose Anne Develin has recently found that in order to truly compare no-fault comprehensive public and other compensation systems in a meaningful way, it would be necessary for data to be gathered and analysed with a more consistent method.[330]

4.6. REFORM EFFORTS TOWARD COMPREHENSIVE NO-FAULT IN BRITISH COLUMBIA AND ALBERTA

It seems very likely that more Canadian comprehensive no-fault compensation funds will be established in the function of automobile transport injury. The provinces of British Columbia and Alberta have both made significant recent reform efforts towards comprehensive no-fault compensation for automobile injury.

In February 2020 the government of British Columbia introduced legislation to completely transform its fault-based automobile insurance framework (currently run by a single mandatory public insurer) into a no-fault model that would be broadly in line with the schemes in Québec and Manitoba.[331] This legislation was passed in August 2020 and came into effect in May 2021.[332] The legislation bars all civil actions or proceedings for bodily injury arising out of an accident (meaning bodily injury caused by a vehicle).[333] The only narrow exception to this is where a victim is injured in a crash and the at-fault driver

---

[328] Rose Anne Devlin, 'A Comparison of Automobile Insurance Regimes in Canada' (2019) 86 *Assurances et gestion des risques* 55, 57.

[329] Mary Kelly, Anne Kleffner and Maureen Tomlinson, 'First-Party versus Third-Party Compensation for Automobile Accidents: Evidence from Canada' (2010) 13 *Risk Management and Insurance Review* 21.

[330] Devlin (n 328) 77.

[331] Province of British Columbia, 'Better Benefits, Lower Rates: Moving to a Care-Based Insurance Model' (February 2020); Jason Contant, 'The Story behind ICBC's Bold Change to Auto Insurance', *Canadian Underwriter* (12 February 2020) <https://www.canadianunderwriter.ca/insurance/the-story-behind-icbcs-drastic-change-to-auto-insurance-1004173792/>.

[332] Attorney General Statutes (Vehicle Insurance) Amendment Act 2020.

[333] ibid ss 113, 115.

is convicted of certain criminal driving-related offences (such as impaired driving). In that case, the victim can still sue the other party in a civil claim for certain damages.[334]

In September 2020 the government of Alberta released the detailed findings of an expert advisory committee tasked with exploring options to reform Alberta's automobile insurance system.[335] The report conclusively recommended a no-fault comprehensive compensation fund model, with an associated statutory bar on tort compensation claims. This report was based on a detailed analysis of the existing Alberta framework, the Ontario framework, pure no-fault systems including the Québec and Manitoba schemes, and the New South Wales experience in Australia of trying to combine a no-fault system with retained access to tort. The Alberta report concluded that 'emerging scientific data has produced equally compelling evidence that tort models impede health outcomes and recovery of traffic injured.' Actuarial analysis undertaken for the report revealed that price control of insurance premiums would be best achieved with a pure no-fault system, because the

> 'primary cause of high and continuing increases in auto insurance premiums in Alberta and in other tort jurisdictions is that uncapped bodily injury loss costs continually increase and at a rate well in excess of Consumer Price Index increases for other market commodities'.[336]

Based on the observations of attempts at incremental or partial no-fault measures in Alberta and other jurisdictions, a half-hearted approach was likely to lead to failure. In terms of administrative structure, the committee recommended establishing a public authority with regulatory powers and different arms responsible for compensation, claims administration and the independent medical assessment of injury.[337] However, underwriting, the issuing of policies and other insurance activities would still be undertaken by the private insurance industry. The public body responsibility for injury compensation would be funded by insurers with a small amount of additional funding from the provincial government. The Albertan legal profession, which was not consulted upon or involved in the report, voiced its strong objection to the proposals on the basis that they would negatively affect civil rights and the rights of injured victims to

---

[334] 'Less Legal Costs' (ICBC 2021) <https://2021.icbc.com/less-legal-costs>.
[335] Automobile Insurance Advisory Committee, 'Report on Fundamental Reform of the Alberta Automobile Insurance Compensation System' (2020).
[336] ibid 29.
[337] ibid 20.

Chapter 3. Review of Existing No-Fault Comprehensive Compensation Funds

receive pain and suffering-related non-pecuniary damages.[338] A no-fault scheme managed by private insurers, similar to the Ontario model, ultimately came into force.

The British Columbia scheme changes will bring that framework within this project's definition of a no-fault comprehensive compensation fund, but it came into effect after much of the research in this project was finalised and therefore there are inadequate results and impacts currently available for it to be analysed in detail.

4.7. COMPARISON WITH THE CANADIAN NO-FAULT COMPREHENSIVE WORKER COMPENSATION LANDSCAPE

Some of the most progressive thinking of the twentieth century on no-fault comprehensive compensation emerged from Canada, and this was influential on developments in other jurisdictions. In 1913 the Ontario lawyer, politician and judge Sir William Meredith published a Royal Commission report on worker injury compensation. It outlined the basic principles of no-fault compensation benefits received by the worker in exchange for relinquishing the right to sue his or her employer.[339] Canadian lawyer and academic Terence Ison did much to develop legal understanding in the area of compensation system design, and his work was very influential on the Royal Commission that designed New Zealand's universal no-fault compensation fund system.[340]

Each individual province has its own no-fault worker injury compensation system, and most types of employees are covered by their state-run fault-based compensation fund systems[341] (like Australia, federal employees are covered by

---

[338] Michelle Bellefontaine, 'No-Fault Auto Insurance Should Be No-Go in Alberta, Lawyers Say' *CBC News* (30 October 2020) <https://www.cbc.ca/news/canada/edmonton/no-fault-auto-insurance-should-be-no-go-in-alberta-lawyers-say-1.5784807>.

[339] William Ralph Meredith, 'The Meredith Report' (1913) <http://awcbc.org/wp-content/uploads/2013/12/meredith_report.pdf>.

[340] Palmer, *Compensation for Incapacity: A Study of Law and Social Change in New Zealand and Australia* (n 18) 73; Terence Ison, *The Forensic Lottery: A Critique on Tort Liability as a System of Personal Injury Compensation* (Staples Press 1968).

[341] WorkplaceNL (Newfoundland and Labrador); Workers' Compensation Board of Prince Edward Island; Workers' Compensation Board of Nova Scotia; WorkSafeNB (New Brunswick); Commission des normes, de l'équité, de la santé et de la sécurité du travail (Québec); Workplace Safety and Insurance Board (Ontario); Workers Compensation Board of Manitoba; Saskatchewan Workers' Compensation Board; Workers Compensation Board of Alberta; WorkSafeBC (British Columbia); Workers' Safety and Compensation Board (Yukon); Workers' Safety and Compensation Commission (Northwest Territories/Nunavut); there is also an agreement in place to co-ordinate worker compensation for employers and employees who work in more than one Canadian jurisdiction.

an equivalent federal workers compensation scheme[342]). There are high levels of participation in these compensation systems, with an average of 86.03 per cent of the workforce across all Canadian provinces covered in 2016.[343] This high level of entrenchment and acceptance of no-fault worker compensation systems is to be expected given the history of extensive theoretical development of this area in the twentieth century.

The Canadian worker compensation system is, in one way, a perfect example of a highly successful nationally aligned and publicly administered no-fault approach to injury compensation. However, the permissible exclusions within each scheme means that they cannot meet my definition of a *comprehensive* fund (within their function) and they must be excluded from in-depth analysis in this book. This is because each provincial worker compensation scheme allows for certain categories of workers to be excluded or have cover on an optional basis, as set out in the table below.[344] This is different to the transport accident coverage under the SAAQ and MPI (and Victoria's TAC and New Zealand's ACC), which by default cover *all* motorists on public roads (unless they are covered by another specified no-fault scheme – usually worker injury compensation for work-related motor accidents). Where some classes of victims are allowed or required to be excluded from the scope of no-fault compensation, that fund or system can never truly stand apart from the ordinary landscape of civil liability.

It is important to note here that Québec's occupational accident and industrial disease scheme is perceived *functionally* and *structurally* by lawyers and scholars within that province as being the 'sibling' of the SAAQ. There are many structural and contextual similarities between the SAAQ and the legislative framework[345] administered by CNESST.[346] However, due to the need to maintain strict definitional boundaries, only the SAAQ has been selected for analysis.

---

[342] Government Employees Compensation Act 1985.

[343] Association of Workers' Compensation Boards of Canada, 'Canadian Workers' Compensation System – Year at a Glance' <http://awcbc.org/?page_id=11803>.

[344] This data is taken from a summary of benefits and exclusions prepared by the Association of Workers' Compensation Boards of Canada – see Association of Workers' Compensation Boards of Canada, 'Scope of Coverage – Industries/Occupations' (2016) <http://www.statcan.gc.ca/tables-tableaux/sum-som/l01/cst01/demo31a-eng.htm>.

[345] Act respecting industrial accidents and occupational diseases.

[346] Commission des normes de l'équité de la santé et de la sécurité du travail (CNESST) – for an overview of compensation entitlements under this framework, see 'Compensation' <https://www.cnesst.gouv.qc.ca/en/procedures-and-forms/workers/compensation-and-reimbursements/compensation>.

Chapter 3. Review of Existing No-Fault Comprehensive Compensation Funds

Table 5. Canadian provincial worker compensation schemes

Province	% of working population covered	Carve-outs allowed
Alberta	92.63	There are a number of exempted industries, for example service industries and professional sport. There is optional coverage for the self-employed/owner-operators.
British Columbia	97.34	Contractors, owner-operators and some specific industries are excluded.
Manitoba	76.28	A variety of industries – such as banking and finance, computer services, domestic employment, family farms, healthcare services and universities – are excluded.
New Brunswick	91.40	Businesses with fewer than three workers and fishing businesses with fewer than 25 workers are excluded.
New Territories/Nunavut	100	Although there are no excluded industries, the self-employed and workers under 'temporary employers' are excluded from the scheme.
Newfoundland & Labrador	97.63	The scheme does not include employees of non-incorporated entities (e.g. owner-operators), but they can choose optional coverage. Also excluded are professional athletes, domestic workers and commercial fishers (in some circumstances).
Nova Scotia	74.12	A range of specific industries, classes of workers and employers are excluded by regulation.
Ontario	74.48	Individual owner-operator businesses can get optional coverage. Large service industries such as banking and finance and daycare are not required to registered for coverage. Sportspeople, stuntpeople and circuses are excluded.
Prince Edward Island	97.06	Owner-operators, CEOs and directors can choose optional coverage. A range of industries – including farming, fishing, taxi drivers, salespeople and performers – are excluded.
Québec	93.17	Generally quite generous, but contractors, domestic workers, care workers, sportspeople and executive officers are excluded. Contractors can choose to pay the relevant premium and be included in the scheme.
Saskatchewan	73.33	Individual owner-operators can get optional coverage, and some industries are excluded.
Yukon	99.76	The self-employed and casual employees can get optional coverage, but no industries are specifically excluded.

Source: Compiled by the author.

4.8. COMPARISON WITH THE WIDER CANADIAN COMPENSATION LANDSCAPE

4.8.1. Québec Vaccine Injury Compensation Program and the Impending Federal Vaccine Injury Support Program

In the 1980s Québec established a Vaccine Injury Compensation Program.[347] This compensation fund system was a direct result of a damages claim brought against the Government of Québec by the family of a young girl who had a severe adverse reaction to the measles vaccine.[348] Since 1988, 271 claims have been submitted, with only 43 being accepted (and a handful of others accepted following disputes about causality and compensation amounts).[349] The level of compensation is identical to the levels of compensation awarded in an automobile accident. Although indeed no-fault, comprehensive and compulsory, the tiny number of claimants under this scheme means that it is most of relevance or interest to a comparison with other vaccine or pharmaceutical injury schemes. No other Canadian province has such a scheme in place, but very few vaccine injury compensatory damages claims reach the courts anyway.[350] This suggests that vaccine injury claimants in other Canadian provinces face more intrinsic barriers to seeking compensation than Québecois victims.

Québec also operates a blood products injury compensation programme, which pays compensation to individuals injured by blood products distributed to public health institutions in the province via the Héma-Québec body.[351] Compensation is paid on the same basis as the SAAQ scheme,[352] showing a legislative desire for coherency and harmonisation across compensation frameworks.

In December 2020, the Canadian federal government announced that it would implement a nationwide no-fault vaccine injury support programme for all approved vaccines, including COVID-19 vaccines.[353] However, unlike the Québec scheme, the new federal no-fault compensation fund will be privately administered (with public health authority oversight).[354]

---

[347] 'Vaccine Injury Compensation Program' <http://sante.gouv.qc.ca/en/programmes-et-mesures-daide/programme-d-indemnisation-des-victimes-d-une-vaccination/>.

[348] *Lapierre v Attorney General (Quebec)* [1985] 1 SCR 241.

[349] In 2017 and 2018, no awards of compensation were made. 'Vaccine Injury Compensation Program' (n 347).

[350] Eve Dubé and others, 'Vaccine Injury Compensation Programs: Rationale and an Overview of the Québec Program' (2020) 46 *Canada Communicable Disease Report* 305.

[351] Chapter II.1 Act respecting Héma-Québec and the biovigilance committee.

[352] ibid s 54.3.

[353] 'Government of Canada Announces Pan-Canadian Vaccine Injury Support Program' <https://www.canada.ca/en/public-health/news/2020/12/government-of-canada-announces-pan-canadian-vaccine-injury-support-program.html>.

[354] 'A third-party administrator will be selected to administer the VISP via an open solicitation process. Canadian not-for-profit and for-profit organizations and corporations can apply.

Chapter 3. Review of Existing No-Fault Comprehensive Compensation Funds

4.8.2. Wider Canadian Compensation Landscape

Throughout the rest of Canada, the field of medical injury is dominated by tort law. There is, however, a framework of ongoing and now-closed compensation fund systems for compensating individuals who have contracted HIV and Hepatitis C via blood products. The Extraordinary Assistance Plan is the primary federal government scheme, that provides a lump sum tax-free payment of C$120,000.[355] Further periodic payments are available to HIV blood product infection victims via the Multi Provincial/Territorial Assistance Plan for HIV infection; to Nova Scotian HIV blood product infection victims via the Nova Scotia Compensation Plan; and to Manitoba Hepatitis C blood product infection victims via the Manitoba Hepatitis C Compassionate Assistance Program.[356] There have also been class action settlement agreements for victims of tainted blood products.

All other medical injuries and treatment injuries in Canada are resolved via the common law tort system (or the civil law tort/delict system in Québec). A move to a no-fault system has been advocated by some in response to ever-increasing medical practitioner liability insurance premiums, the government's role in subsidising these fees at the expense of taxpayers, and the growth of a stronger public safety agenda.[357] It is yet to be seen whether there will be any development of a compensation fund system for medical incidents in Canada at a provincial or Commonwealth level.[358] In 1998 the Québec Medical Council

---

The successful applicant will work independently to achieve the program's objectives, based on criteria outlined by the Public Health Agency of Canada. The Public Health Agency of Canada requires that the third-party administrator have experience and expertise in administering similar support programs.' – 'Call for Applications: Vaccine Injury Support Program – Canada.Ca' <https://www.canada.ca/en/public-health/services/funding-opportunities/grant-contribution-funding-opportunities/call-applications-vaccine-injury-support-program.html>.

[355] Government of Canada, 'Extraordinary Assistance Plan – Financial Assistance to Individuals Infected with HIV Through the Canadian Blood System' <https://www.canada.ca/en/public-health/services/infectious-diseases/extraordinary-assistance-plan-financial-assistance-individuals-infected-hiv-through-canadian-blood-system.html>.

[356] Canadian Hemophilia Society, 'Compensation Programs for Individuals with HIV or Hepatitis C' (2014) <https://www.hemophilia.ca/files/EN Compensation Programs-HIV, HepC-English – final14-11-2014.pdf>; Province of Manitoba, 'Manitoba Hepatitis C Compassionate Assistance Program (MHCAP)' <http://www.gov.mb.ca/health/hcv/index.html>.

[357] Elaine Gibson, 'Is It Time to Adopt a No-Fault Scheme to Compensate Injured Patients?' (2016) 47 *Ottawa Law Review* 303 <https://commonlaw.uottawa.ca/ottawa-law-review/sites/commonlaw.uottawa.ca.ottawa-law-review/files/olr_47-2_02_gibson_final.pdf>.

[358] Unlike in the French and Belgian systems, the existing Canadian medical liability insurance and tort damages frameworks protect medical practitioners and pose a barrier to all but the strongest claims. Thus there is no obvious motivation from the insurer or practitioner side to reform the law. See Colleen M Flood and Bryan Thomas, 'Canadian Medical Malpractice Law in 2011: Missing the Mark on Patient Safety' (2011) 86 *Chicago-Kent Law Review* 1053.

unanimously recommended the implementation of a no-fault compensation fund for medical accident victims.[359] Outside of the medical sphere and vaccine injury, it remains to be seen whether broad harmonisation of motor vehicle compensation systems will take place or if further compensation fund systems will be developed.[360]

5. COMPARISON AND ANALYSIS OF SELECTED COMPENSATION FUNDS BY PURPOSE

The four no-fault comprehensive compensation funds analysed in this chapter (ACC, TAC, SAAQ and MPI) all display some core common structural features that can be easily identified: a comprehensive tort claims bar; a single public authority administering all claims; broad no-fault benefits enshrined in statute; and income replacement and rehabilitation services forming the core of compensation payments.

The no-fault comprehensive compensation funds also share a common proactive purpose to compensate future, yet-to-be-identified victims of a certain broad category of loss.[361] This kind of proactive purpose can also be found in other less comprehensive compensation funds (such as compensation funds in France, for example, that compensate certain victims of medical injuries and terrorism victims), but it is always a feature of a no-fault comprehensive compensation fund.

What can also be identified about comprehensive funds is that they represent either a complete or a partial departure from compensation norms. The difference between a complete and partial revolution of purpose is specifically related to whether any access to principles of tort is retained. The reader might logically ask at this point – firstly, what is the importance of this distinction, and secondly, what is novel about such an argument?

---

[359] Gardner (n 322) 106.

[360] This may also be influenced by the stated policy goal of the Canadian government to harmonise regulations in a range of areas with its southern neighbour, the United States. This is relevant to compensation fund systems because the United States is not a jurisdiction that favours systemic use of publicly administered compensation fund systems for resolving liability and compensation issues. See Government of Canada, 'Canada-United States Regulatory Cooperation Council (RCC)' <https://www.canada.ca/en/health-canada/corporate/about-health-canada/legislation-guidelines/acts-regulations/canada-united-states-regulatory-cooperation-council.html>. Nevertheless, recent comments in the media suggest that the Québec medical regulator has no objection to a no-fault compensation fund for medical injury – Yves Boisvert, 'Un Système Injuste, à Jeter', *La Presse* (13 September 2019) <https://www.lapresse.ca/actualites/201909/12/01-5241027-un-systeme-injuste-a-jeter.php>.

[361] Thierry Vansweevelt and others, 'Comparative Analysis of Compensation Funds' in Thierry Vansweevelt and Britt Weyts (eds), *Compensation Funds in Comparative Perspective* (Intersentia 2020) 197.

Chapter 3. Review of Existing No-Fault Comprehensive Compensation Funds

On the first point, the idea of a complete or partial departure from tort law is certainly an important distinction to be made in law. This is because the degree of revolution determines whether we can describe the comprehensive fund as a wholly separate field of compensation jurisprudence. In other words, the *comprehensive* no-fault fund does not just 'abolish' tort law to some degree, it creates a new, quite separate field of law. The evidence of a new field of law is found in the successful ongoing existence, as described in this chapter already, of such funds for many decades now in New Zealand, Australia and Canada. The evidence is also found in the affirmation by courts of these funds' broad purpose (*Calver v ACC* in New Zealand, *Godbout v Pagé* in Canada), the effect of the tort bar (*DePuy* in New Zealand), and their wholly different nature to more traditional tort-based systems (*Sweedman v TAC* in Australia).

A fund which constitutes a complete revolution stands apart from tort and does not always have to be immediately compared with tort principles of compensation as a first point of reference or comparison. A fund which constitutes a *partial* revolution still retains a close link with its tort law ancestor, although this leads to less desirable (or simply more inconsistent) outcomes. This is not to say that tort is completely irrelevant after a complete revolution. The possibility of subrogation powers for the fund has already been mentioned. It will also be useful for some comparison to be made, for example, with civil litigation damages tables when calculating lump sum payments that might be available under a fund. But a no-fault comprehensive fund is not a vacuum created by an absence of tort, in the way that atheism is the absence of belief. It is argued here that a no-fault comprehensive compensation fund is its own standalone system, that has more in common with its equally mature cousins in other jurisdictions, than it does with the remaining domestic tort landscape.

Second, the novelty of this argument is the fact that it goes a step further from typical 'abolitionist' and 'incrementalist' views of tort law development. Peter Cane has described the abolitionist view as one that sees the inefficiencies and expenses in a tort law system (as famously stated by the likes of Woodhouse, Meredith, Atiyah, Kopstein and others), and ends logically in a conclusion that tort should be abolished.[362] However, Cane says this is a utopian vision that may be difficult to realise in modern times due to the political difficulty of realising such a scheme. Cane contrasts abolitionism with the more practical incrementalist view, which accepts tort law as a fixed feature of the legal universe.[363] Incrementalism busies itself with developments such as caps on tort damages and adjustments to the tort landscape in the case of unexpected problems such as insurance crises.

---

[362]   Peter Cane, *The Political Economy of Personal Injury Law* (University of Queensland Press 2007) 3–4, 98.

[363]   ibid 5–7.

Intersentia

129

No argument is made in this book about whether tort compensation (for personal injury damages) *should* be abolished in other systems, in the way already done fully or partially New Zealand, Victoria, Québec and Manitoba. Rather, it is simply possible to point to what has actually emerged, over decades, from the act of abolition: a standalone system of law that is no longer immediately relevant to tort for the purposes of compensation (especially where a complete revolution has occurred). There are learnings to be found in this for other compensation funds (of all kinds).

The heart of this argument is that no-fault comprehensive principles of compensation *for victims* are, fundamentally, incompatible with tort principles of liability leading to compensation and the two sets of principles cannot co-exist with one another without resulting in inconsistency or injustice. Better results flow from a complete revolution, and a partial revolution (Cane's incrementalism) is not an ideal compromise (from a theoretical perspective). However, if for normative reasons a partial revolution is preferred, there should be adequate justification for this choice. Reference is made here to tort law principles that apply to *the compensation of victims*, because this is different to tort law principles (or indeed, some kind of specific injury regulation laws) being used by the compensation fund itself in an action to pursue one or more third parties for a recoupment of the compensation that was paid (or perhaps a fine, if that were provided for in the relevant laws). The concepts of subrogation and 'public tort liability' will be analysed further in subsequent chapters. Cane said that a risk of the abolitionist view was that it stifled the possibility of creative thinking about compensation.[364] This view underestimates the potential of no-fault comprehensive funds – however the existing four funds have not been as creative as they could about creating equitable and novel compensation.

5.1. COMPLETE DEPARTURE IN PURPOSE

No-fault comprehensive compensation funds can amount to a complete revolution in purpose because they disconnect from a tort world-view on compensation. This is in addition to their proactive purpose as a structure that is designed to deal with future, yet-to-be-identified losses. The New Zealand ACC, Québec SAAQ and Manitoba MPI can all be classified as having this complete revolution in purpose. Set out below is the evidence for such a 'complete' revolution.

First and foremost, the act of complete revolution was undertaken when the legislatures undertook the major reformatory step of establishing a no-fault comprehensive compensation fund and introducing a statutory bar against

---

[364] ibid 5.

Chapter 3. Review of Existing No-Fault Comprehensive Compensation Funds

common law damages claims for covered victims. As noted above already in the 'Background' subsections in relation to each jurisdiction, this legislative step faced differing levels of political challenge because of anti-reform lobbying from the legal and insurance professions.

More importantly is the second point – over the three-to-four decades of their existence, there has not been a permanent retreat from the complete step of revolution. Legislative attempts at retreat have been reversed, and judicial decisions have mostly embraced an expansive scope to the funds.

In New Zealand, had the 'fault creep' of medical misadventure (introduced in 1992) or even the privatisation of work injury compensation (introduced in 1998) remained in place, then this would certainly have made a 'complete revolution' description inapplicable.

Most recently and controversially in New Zealand, it has been shown that developments in scientific knowledge about injury can affect the legal definition of covered and not covered injuries. In *Accident Compensation Corporation v Calver (Estate of Trevarthen)*, scientific evidence about what kind of asbestos exposure could lead to mesothelioma meant that the court could allow the facts to 'fit' what was legislatively possible and grant ACC coverage.

In Canada, the Supreme Court has not imposed limits on the scope and effect of the statutory bar so long as there is a basic factual connection (rather than a legally defined causative link) between the injury and the statutory scope of cover. We see this reflected in case law – it is the key difference between, on one hand, the *J.A. v SAAQ* judgment (where snowmobiles expressly did not fit the legislative eligibility), and on the other hand *Godbout v Pagé*. In *Godbout*, there was a factual connection between the qualifying accident and all the events (medical error) that flowed from the accident.

This complete revolution, however, has led to inequalities and inconsistencies between those who are eligible for coverage and those who are not. In terms of the border between qualifying personal injury and other kinds of illness and misfortune, a recent Organisation for Economic Co-operation and Development (OECD) report noted that New Zealand has effectively created a two-tier healthcare system which disadvantages people with mental health conditions. The OECD recommended that the ACC system be expanded to include illness, as was originally envisaged by the Woodhouse Report.[365] In Canada, the unavailability of compensation for the appellant in *J.A. v SAAQ* was because of the complete specific exclusion of her class of injury from scheme coverage.

What is necessary at this point, to confirm the fact of this revolution and to define the scope of future no-fault compensation fund development, is a restatement from legislatures about the intended future scope of each of these

---

[365] *Mental Health and Work: New Zealand* (OECD 2018) 19 <https://www.oecd-ilibrary.org/social-issues-migration-health/mental-health-and-work-new-zealand_9789264307315-en>.

Intersentia

131

no-fault comprehensive schemes. This is certainly necessary in New Zealand (as identified most recently by that country's Treasury in relation to mental health cover for terrorism victims). It would also be helpful in Manitoba and Québec to iron out the differences between the funds and confirm (or refute) the position taken by the Supreme Court of Canada in *Godbout*.

5.2. PARTIAL REVOLUTION IN PURPOSE

Victoria's TAC is a complete revolution in most parts for transport injuries in that particular jurisdiction. But the retention of the potential for common law damages for very serious injuries within Victoria's TAC means that no-fault comprehensive compensation fund has ultimately effected only a partial revolution when compared to the funds in New Zealand, Québec and Manitoba.

The primary evidence of this is the fact that a study of the background of the TAC shows that the decision to retain common law damages for very serious injuries was never because of a clearly elucidated fundamental philosophical choice by the legislature that no-fault was an inappropriate choice for serious injuries. The restriction was because of a political compromise on the back of lawyers' lobbying efforts.[366] The effect has been to maintain a two-tier system that does, on a positive note, give the possibility of more generous damages to 'top-up' no-fault damages in the most serious cases. However, there is no principled legal basis for the maintenance of this duality, especially given the fact that in most cases the TAC is the 'defendant' who will be settling or paying the common law damages. On a negative note, the maintenance of common law damages has resulted in highly complex and unclear legal tests needing to be applied (in a system that is supposed to be less complex than the tort system). There has also been a marked blow-out in costs compared to other no-fault comprehensive compensation funds and even an ordinary fault-based system.[367] There is no evidence to suggest that a more generous scheme of no-fault benefits (compensatory and symbolic) for seriously injured victims would fail to achieve equally good compensatory and rehabilitative results (from the perspective of the victim) with fewer administrative costs and less complexity.

As it stands, there appear to be no moves to undertake further reform of the TAC model to progress towards a complete revolution. The reversal of legislation to restrict access to common law damages for some types of psychiatric injury shows a system-wide commitment to a two-system model. In 2013, the Transport Accident Act was amended to remove access to common law damages for indirect psychological injuries to third persons, where the relevant accident

---

[366] Malkin (n 149) 260–262.
[367] However, as will be discussed in Chapter 5, the TAC still maintains a sustainable financial position despite these cost blow-outs.

Chapter 3. Review of Existing No-Fault Comprehensive Compensation Funds

was predominantly caused by a driver's negligence or intention to commit suicide. An example of the relevant third persons would be emergency services staff or the family members of the accident victims.[368] This was repealed in 2016 (with retrospective application) in light of criticisms about the unfairness of the restrictions regarding third persons.[369] Any restriction on access to common law benefits would undoubtedly be viewed as unfair by the affected group. However where there is an attempt to maintain a dual system of no-fault benefits and tort access there will always be a heightened degree of tension and potential perception of unfairness where some victims are excluded from the option of accessing more generous compensation.

The wider context of the 2013 legislative amendment was primarily to introduce a clinical definition of the concept of mental injury for the purposes of serious injury (with more consistency with physical injury), and more overall coherency.[370] The 2016 repeal shows that scheme coherency (with reference to clinical standards) was ultimately seen as less important than *perceived* distinctions of fairness between classes of victims. Where there are two purposively different systems maintained within a single compensation fund structure, it is very challenging to objectively assess which system is more 'fair' and whether relevant limitations are proportional and justified.

6. COMPARISON AND ANALYSIS OF SELECTED COMPENSATION FUNDS BY FUNCTION

No-fault comprehensive compensation funds can also be analysed by function, as well as purpose. The classification of compensation funds for comparative law and other types of scientific analysis purposes does generally tend to occur according to function. This is logical because it is most obvious to compare different legal frameworks that have the same function or goal that they seek to address.[371] In terms of methodology, a functional analysis is one of the most common approaches in comparative law. It allows us to consider the way practical problems are dealt with in different jurisdictions, enabling us to step outside the doctrinal limitations and caveats of that jurisdiction.[372]

---

[368] Transport Accident Amendment Act 2016 s 93(2A).

[369] Glenys Wilkinson, 'Letter to Hon Gordon Rich-Phillips MLC (28/10/2013)'.

[370] Section 4.3 – 'Is the injury a serious injury?' in Judicial College of Victoria, *Serious Injury Manual* (n 164).

[371] Macleod and Hodges' *Redress Schemes for Personal Injury*, for example, proceeds with a descriptive horizontal jurisdictional comparison as well as analysis by function.

[372] Mark Van Hoecke, 'Law and Method Methodology of Comparative Legal Research' [2015] *Law and Method* 1, 9 <https://www.bjutijdschriften.nl/tijdschrift/lawandmethod/2015/12/RENM-D-14-00001.pdf>.

Intersentia

This section considers some functional issues that can be identified in relation to the four selected compensation funds (ACC, TAC, SAAQ and MPI). Obviously compensation funds can exist in relation to many more functions (for example natural disaster damage, consumer or medical product failure, historical abuse, and consumer financial protection to name just a few), but considered here are only the ones that are applicable to the selected no-fault comprehensive compensation funds. The New Zealand ACC Scheme is the only compensation fund that has application across all four functions, but the comprehensive scope of the other funds means that there is some tendency for them to overlap into the 'everyday risks of life' function.

6.1. TRAFFIC-RELATED INJURY

Traffic-related injury is the one function where all four no-fault comprehensive compensation funds have common ground.

The first functional point that can be made is that various traffic injury-related regulatory issues will intersect with compensation concepts in this type of fund. In Québec, Manitoba and Victoria, the compensation fund aspect of the statutory schemes forms just one (albeit very important) part of the relevant organisations' operation. This is because in those jurisdictions, the SAAQ, MPI and TAC have all taken over the entire motor vehicle regulatory framework and are responsible for driver testing and licensing. In the case of the SAAQ and MPI, they even have regulatory oversight for vehicle roadworthiness. The consequence of this standalone 'motor vehicle ecosystem' in the three jurisdictions is that functionally, all three are set apart from the rest of the loss and compensation landscape in their jurisdictions. The sole exception is to the extent that all three interact with relevant worker injury compensation (for example, when there is a car accident involving an employee who is driving their employer's vehicle).

In contrast, the New Zealand ACC Scheme is not responsible for driver licensing and registration. Because it covers more functional types of injury, it would not be sensible for it to also take on other motor vehicle or transport regulatory functions. This difference between New Zealand and the other jurisdictions shows that where comprehensive compensation is limited to one function, it will be logical for compensation issues to have an overlap with other regulatory issues relevant to that function. For example:

a. The payment of motor vehicle registration and other licensing fees can be used as the most basic eligibility criteria for immunity from a tort damages claim if simple residency or demogrant criteria are not used. For example, in the TAC, immunity from a damages claim (a common law damages claim in particular) results from the payment of the Transport Accident Charge, which is incorporated within the motor vehicle registration renewal fee

Chapter 3. Review of Existing No-Fault Comprehensive Compensation Funds

(there is a short grace period if an unpaid charge is paid within 28 days of an accident).[373] This does also mean that immunity from a tort damages claim is not available to vehicles and people who do not have to pay that charge (such as cyclists and e-scooter users), resulting in different treatment for different modes of transport.

b. Issues of deterrence can be handled internally within the same body of legislation and administered by the same organisation. This means that deterrence no longer needs to affect access to compensation or the use of no-fault. For example, the MPI has the power to seek reimbursement of costs from uninsured drivers (and can cancel their driver licences and motor vehicle registrations if they don't comply), even though those uninsured drivers still enjoy *prima facie* access to no-fault compensatory benefits flowing from the accident.[374] In Québec, a driver can have his or her driver's licence suspended for not registering for cover with SAAQ or letting another (unregistered) person use his or her vehicle (even though no-fault compensation is always available for Québec residents and their dependants).[375] Any potential increased moral hazard relating to motor accidents that might be associated with no-fault benefits can therefore be managed by way of other regulatory powers relevant to transport law as a function, rather than tort.

In the past few years there have been significant developments in the field of personal transport, with more changes underway. For example, rapid advancements are being made to automobile driver-assistance technology, with the ultimate goal of rolling out self-driving personal vehicles on public roads. E-scooter share schemes and other types of micro-mobility services are now found in many cities around the world. In a no-fault comprehensive compensation fund, the risks of new transport technologies and services can be more easily accommodated and managed, compared with a fault-based system. This is obviously dependent upon the exact wording of the legislation and the surrounding transport regulatory landscape – there is broader coverage for transport accidents of all kinds in New Zealand and most kinds in Québec and Manitoba (because all residents are automatically covered and the relevant definitions of a qualifying accident are wide) than in Victoria. There are also data-gathering benefits to this sub-function, that allow for the evidence-based development of any extra legislation that may be required. Ultimately, a study of the selected jurisdictions reveals that a no-fault comprehensive compensation fund for transport accidents enables a jurisdiction to respond more rapidly and

---

[373] Transport Accident Act 1986 (Victoria) ss 3, s 94(1) and s 109(4).
[374] The Manitoba Public Insurance Corporation Act ss 39(8), 39(a), 71(1).
[375] Accident Insurance Act 1998 ss 7, 186, 187, 188.

Intersentia

accurately to new liability and harm challenges.[376] The potential for no-fault comprehensive compensation funds to be a model solution for the challenges associated with new transport technologies is considered in more detail in Chapter 6. However a comparative analysis of our four big funds and their usefulness in relation to harms associated with e-scooters and automated vehicles is considered in the subsections below, as well as harms associated with out-of-jurisdiction drivers.

6.1.1. E-Scooters

Low-speed electric scooters[377] (whether personally owned or accessible via a short-term hire/mobility service) have rapidly appeared in different cities around the world. They have recently become rapidly popular as both a personally owned transport device and as a publicly accessible private hire transport device through ride-share.[378] They are no passing fad either: a study of the impact of e-scooters across 10 major global cities has concluded that they could be a micro-mobility catalyst (particularly in historic high-density city centres, such as those in Europe), but further study is still required about how e-scooters are replacing traditional transport modes or meeting transport gaps.[379] The rise of e-scooter share schemes is socially and legally significant because it can be linked to an increase in minor and major injuries associated with their use.[380] E-scooters fit within a wider trend in transport called micro-mobility.[381] There has been little

---

[376] Kim Watts, 'Potential of No-Fault Comprehensive Compensation Funds to Deal with Automation and Other 21st Century Transport Developments' (2020) 12 *European Journal of Commercial Contract Law* 1.

[377] An e-scooter can be broadly defined as a device with a footboard, two or three wheels, and a long steering handle. An e-scooter is powered by one or more electric motors, with a wattage of around 300 to 500 watts. It should have a braking system but not a seat. See Reg 244A, Road Safety Rules 2017 (Victoria), 'E–Scooters (Declaration Not to Be Motor Vehicles) Notice 2018', *New Zealand Gazette* <https://gazette.govt.nz/notice/id/2018-au4674>; SAAQ, 'Low-Speed Electric Scooters' <https://saaq.gouv.qc.ca/en/saaq/documents/pilot-projects/low-speed-electric-scooters/>.

[378] 'Lime Electric Scooter Rentals' <https://www.li.me/electric-scooter>; 'How to Bird' <https://www.bird.co/how/>.

[379] Stefan Gössling, 'Integrating E-Scooters in Urban Transportation: Problems, Policies, and the Prospect of System Change' (2020) 79 *Transportation Research Part D: Transport and Environment* 9 <https://doi.org/10.1016/j.trd.2020.102230>.

[380] Austin Badeau and others, 'Emergency Department Visits for Electric Scooter-Related Injuries after Introduction of an Urban Rental Program' (2019) 37 *American Journal of Emergency Medicine* 1531; Mark Nagy Zaky Bekhit, James Le Fevre and Colleen J Bergin, 'Regional Healthcare Costs and Burden of Injury Associated with Electric Scooters' (2020) 51 *Injury* 271 <https://linkinghub.elsevier.com/retrieve/pii/S0020138319306084>; Yee Kent Liew, Choon Peng Jeremy Wee and Jen Heng Pek, 'New Peril on Our Roads: A Retrospective Study of Electric Scooter-Related Injuries' (2020) 61 *Singapore Medical Journal* 92 <https://doi.org/10.11622/smedj.2019083>.

[381] This trend includes devices and vehicles weighing up to 350 kg and whose power supply, if any, is gradually reduced and cut off at a given speed limit (at most 45 km per hour).

Chapter 3. Review of Existing No-Fault Comprehensive Compensation Funds

comparative law study of the impact of micro-mobility devices like e-scooters on the legal liability landscape. New electric-supported micro-mobility devices let users travel quickly in a busy urban setting with little physical effort, and this has resulted in an increase in certain types of (sometimes severe) injury.[382] In terms of e-scooters – both individually owned and those available via share schemes – there is clearly a liability challenge posed by the current liability incoherence and insurance coverage gaps in this area.[383] E-scooters, as a risk-generating phenomenon, have been dealt with by the four big funds considered here to greater and lesser degrees.

The universal nature of the ACC Scheme and the broad definition of personal injury[384] mean that all transport-related personal injuries, including those caused by new transport technologies, will be automatically covered for no-fault compensation (regardless of their legal status). E-scooters have been declared, under the relevant New Zealand transport regulations, to not be a motor vehicle.[385] All injuries resulting from the use (or misuse) of these devices on public roads and elsewhere are automatically covered by the scope of the ACC Scheme. This will be true whether an e-scooter is privately owned or accessed through a share scheme. This has obviously facilitated a rapid public uptake of this new technology.[386] Consequently ACC, in a short space of time, has been enabled to gather precise statistical information about the injuries and costs of compensation flowing from this mode of transport.[387] ACC has reported that the number and cost of e-scooter injuries is low in that jurisdiction compared to other forms of micro-mobility transport.[388]

In Québec the highway code ordinarily prohibits their use on public roads, but there were recently two pilot projects in place to assess their use by

---

This can include traditional individual transport devices like bicycles. See International Transport Forum, 'Safe Micromobility' (2020) <https://www.itf-oecd.org/sites/default/files/docs/safe-micromobility_1.pdf>.

[382] Nikan K Namiri and others, 'Electric Scooter Injuries and Hospital Admissions in the United States, 2014–2018' (2020) 155 *JAMA Surgery* 357; Badeau and others (n 380); Bhavin Trivedi and others, 'Craniofacial Injuries Seen With the Introduction of Bicycle-Share Electric Scooters in an Urban Setting' (2019) 77 *Journal of Oral and Maxillofacial Surgery* 2292.

[383] For example, due to gaps in empirical data it is still unclear whether these devices should always be considered equivalent to traditional personal transport devices like bicycles. This is for injury-related reasons. For example, some studies have shown higher rates of head injuries from e-scooter users than cyclists. It appears that there has not yet been enough data gathered about e-scooters to make sound conclusions on this point. See Namiri and others (n 382); International Transport Forum (n 381) 20–33.

[384] Accident Compensation Act 2001 s 26.

[385] 'E–Scooters (Declaration Not to Be Motor Vehicles) Notice 2018' (n 377).

[386] Helen Fitt and Angela Curl, 'E-Scooter Use in New Zealand: Insights around Some Frequently Asked Questions' (2019) <https://ir.canterbury.ac.nz/handle/10092/16336>.

[387] Accident Compensation Corporation, 'E-Scooters: Wellington City, It's Your Turn' <https://www.acc.co.nz/newsroom/stories/e-scooters-wellington-city-its-your-turn/>.

[388] ibid.

Intersentia

private users[389] and through ride-share schemes.[390]Any injuries occurring during this pilot project were specifically not covered by the SAAQ scheme unless the accident involved a qualifying motor vehicle.[391] Specific exclusions were included relating to compensation for bodily injury caused by 'motorized personal mobility device[s]'.[392] Distributors and manufacturers of share scheme e-scooters are required to hold a liability policy (with minimum coverage of C$5 million per event) for the duration of the pilot scheme.[393] The SAAQ is acting in an information-gathering and evaluation role at this point in time, together with the provincial government – both the manufacturers and distributors of private e-scooters and share scheme e-scooters are required to submit regular reports on e-scooter sales and accidents.[394] In significantly less populous Manitoba, these devices are neither insurable nor registrable, and are effectively treated like ordinary bicycles because of their low speed.[395] This means that there will only be MPI coverage if they have an accident with an automobile, but there will be no coverage for other kinds of accidents. The Québec and Manitoba legislatures have thus not yet made the active social and legal choice to include micromobility devices within their schemes' scope (unless, of course, an accident also involves an automobile in motion).

In terms of e-scooters, Victoria has (like Québec) taken a restrictive approach to their introduction. The kind of e-scooters commonly seen elsewhere are prohibited from public roads and footpaths as they can travel faster than

---

[389] 'Arrêté Numéro 2018-18 Du Ministre Des Transports, de La Mobilité Durable et de l'Électrification Des Transports', *Gazette officielle du Québec* (29 August 2018); SAAQ (n 377). In Montreal, the rental of e-scooters has now been banned but there is some allowance for privately owned e-scooters – 'Montreal Pulls the Plug on E-Scooters on Its Territory', *Montreal Gazette* (19 February 2020) <https://montrealgazette.com/news/local-news/montreal-pulls-the-plug-on-e-scooters-on-its-territory>.

[390] Transports Québec, 'Trottinettes Motorisées' <https://www.transports.gouv.qc.ca/fr/modes-transport-utilises/trotinettes-motorisees/Pages/trotinettes-motorisees.aspx>. In February 2020, the city of Montreal announced that it would end the trial and not renew the licences of the participating e-scooter share scheme providers, because of non-compliance with traffic rules. See 'Montreal Pulls the Plug on E-Scooters on Its Territory' (n 389).

[391] SAAQ (n 377).

[392] Automobile Insurance Act (Québec) s 10(5). For the definition of a motorized personal mobility device see clause 9.1 of Regulation respecting the application of the Automobile Insurance Act.

[393] Art 13 Projet pilote relatif aux trottinettes électriques en location libre-service (C–24.2, r. 39.1.3) 2019.

[394] Chp V 'Arrêté Numéro 2018-18 Du Ministre Des Transports, de La Mobilité Durable et de l'Électrification Des Transports' (n 389); Art 20 & Chp VI Projet pilote relatif aux trottinettes électriques en location libre-service (C–24.2, r. 39.1.3).

[395] Section 71(2) of the Manitoba Public Insurance Corporation Act excludes bodily injury cover for a motorized mobility aid or a prescribed personal transportation device – unless an automobile in motion is involved in the accident.

10 km/h (and have a power output over 200 watts).[396] Under existing road rules they would effectively be required to register as motorcycles and thus require a licence (and pay a TAC contribution), which has severely limited their (legal) use.[397] There is therefore currently no TAC coverage for e-scooter injuries, unless they involved a collision with a motor vehicle. A federal-level investigation of the regulatory challenges associated with e-scooters and other micro-mobility devices, and the increased likelihood of their conflict with other road users, produced a set of regulatory recommendations in 2020.[398] There remains scope for the existing TAC legislative framework to be adapted to include e-scooters, along the lines of how future and retrospective coverage was introduced for cyclists injured following a collision with a stationary motor vehicle (e.g. a car door opening out onto a passing cyclist).[399]

From a functional perspective, a no-fault comprehensive compensation fund therefore allows (in conjunction with the operation of public highways regulations) an automatic safety net of no-fault compensation to be immediately available (without significant further legislative action), while the risks and viability of new technology and services are assessed. Data gathered by the funds about injuries can be used to accurately calculate the right level of levies that might be applied to the sale or hire of these devices (or the licensing of services) and the scope of any new laws in the transport law field that might need to be designed. A recent study from New Zealand, for example, shows that there is a disproportionate burden being placed on primary care and hospital facilities in Auckland from e-scooters.[400] The precise cost calculations provided in this study, which was facilitated by ACC data (in combination with public health service data), are a valuable and accurate evidential basis for the calculation of levies and the design of suitable laws to regulate the use of e-scooters. This kind of thorough data from both primary and tertiary care settings could only realistically be captured by a no-fault comprehensive compensation fund that

---

[396] VicRoads, 'Scooters & Wheeled Recreational Devices' <https://www.vicroads.vic.gov.au/safety-and-road-rules/road-rules/a-to-z-of-road-rules/scooters-and-wheeled-recreational-devices>; Aubrey Perry, 'Electric Scooters Work Brilliantly in Europe – so Why Not Here?', *The Age* (14 September 2019) <https://www.theage.com.au/national/victoria/electric-scooters-work-brilliantly-in-europe-so-why-not-here-20190913-p52r1e.html>.

[397] Rachel Clayton, 'Calls for E-Scooter Laws to Change as People Flout the Rules and Police Turn a Blind Eye', *ABC News* (14 December 2019) <https://www.abc.net.au/news/2019-12-14/calls-for-escooter-laws-to-be-relaxed-across-australia/11800280>.

[398] National Transport Commission, 'Barriers to the Safe Use of Personal Mobility Devices' (2019) <www.ntc.gov.au>; National Transport Commission, 'Barriers to the Safe Use of Innovative Vehicles and Motorised Mobility Devices' (2019) <www.ntc.gov.au>.

[399] Treasury and Finance Legislation Amendment Act; Transport Accident Commission, 'TAC Legislation Changes' (n 159).

[400] Bekhit, Le Fevre and Bergin (n 380).

A Comparative Law Analysis of No-Fault Comprehensive Compensation Funds

compensates for *all* injuries, including those of tourists.[401] There is no need for lawmakers to resort to unproven theories from tort about deterrence or from law and economics about the costs of accidents, when one has access to a complete statistical data set.[402]

6.1.2. *Automated Vehicles*

Automated vehicles are presently a 'hot topic' in motor liability law (despite the fact that this mode of transport is not currently available for sale commercially in any jurisdiction), and there currently is much scholarly debate about what form of liability and/or insurance coverage is appropriate for this kind of technology.[403] There also remains a degree of inconsistency and incoherency about the term 'automated vehicle' or 'self-driving car'. One broad definition of an automated vehicle system is 'a combination of hardware and software (both remote and on-board) that performs a driving function, with or without a human actively monitoring the driving environment'.[404] In other words, and

---

[401] ibid 2. 'Because [the ACC Scheme] provides financial compensation and support to citizens, residents, and temporary visitors who have suffered personal injuries, ACC provides a data set that contains virtually all electric scooter injuries that have presented both to primary and tertiary care settings.' In contrast, studies about e-scooter injuries from other jurisdictions have only been able to capture emergency care visits and not outpatient or primary care clinic visits. See Tarak K Trivedi and others, 'Injuries Associated With Standing Electric Scooter Use' (2019) 2 *JAMA network open* e187381.

[402] ACC has made its datasets on e-scooter injuries publicly available. As of June 2020, ACC had 426 active claims in this category with NZ$593,221 of active costs. The most common kind of injuries associated with this harm is soft tissue injuries, lacerations/punctures/stings and fractures/dislocations. Less common injuries include dental injuries and concussions/ brain injuries. See 'E-Scooter Injuries – Datasets' (*data.govt.nz*, 2020) <https://catalogue. data.govt.nz/dataset/e-scooter-injuries#dataset-resources>.

[403] Kenneth S Abraham and Robert L Rabin, 'The Future Is Almost Here: Inaction Is Actually Mistaken Action' (2019) 105 *Virginia Law Review Online* 91 <http://www.virginialawreview. org/sites/virginialawreview.org/files/Abraham%26Rabin_Book.pdf>; Ryan Calo, 'Commuting to Mars: A Response to Professors Abraham and Rabin' (2019) 105 *Virginia Law Review Online* 84 <http://www.virginialawreview.org/sites/virginialawreview.org/files/Calo_Book.pdf>; 'Motor Accident Injury Insurance and Automated Vehicles: Discussion Paper' (2018) <www. ntc.gov.au>; Mark Brady and others, 'Automated Vehicles and Australian Personal Injury Compensation Schemes' (2017) 24 *Torts Law Journal* 32; Matthew Blunt, 'Highway to a Headache: Is Tort-Based Automotive Insurance on a Collision Course with Autonomous Vehicles' (2017) 53 *Williamette Law Revew* 107; Tracy Pearl, 'Compensation at the Crossroads: Autonomous Vehicles and Alternative Victim Compensation Schemes' (2018) 60 *William & Mary Law Review* 1827; Ken Oliphant, 'Liability for Road Accidents Caused by Driverless Cars' [2019] *Singapore Comparative Law Review* 190. Separately, for a recognition of the suitability of the New Zealand no-fault approach to managing the risks and social benefits of artificial intelligence, see Jin Yoshikawa, 'Sharing the Costs of Artificial Intelligence: Universal No-Fault Social Insurance for Personal Injuries' (2019) 21 *Vanderbilt Journal of Entertainment Technology Law* 1155.

[404] US Department of Transportation and National Highway Traffic Safety Administration, 'Federal Automated Vehicles Policy: Accelerating the Next Revolution In Roadway Safety' (2016) 10.

Chapter 3. Review of Existing No-Fault Comprehensive Compensation Funds

most relevant for liability purposes, this is technology that allows the transfer of driving control functions from a human driver to a computer.[405] One of the main advantages of automated vehicles is the potential for increased safety: it is estimated that around 90 per cent of road accidents involve human error of some kind.[406] The most widely agreed and precise definition of vehicle automation is encapsulated in six levels by the international engineering standards agency SAE International.[407] This range comprises a conventional vehicle (Level 0), a basic level of assistance (Levels 1 and 2 being the kind of driver supports that are already widely commercially available), a bridging level of AI assistance where the human must only be available to supervise (Level 3, such as a traffic jam chauffeur feature) and finally full degrees of AI control of the vehicle (in specific situations under Level 4, or in all situations under Level 5). The first commercially available Level 3 automation system, Audi's Traffic Jam Pilot system, was recently withdrawn worldwide.[408] This was reportedly due to regulatory approval issues, and concerns about legal liability in the event of a crash. Other manufacturers are still testing vehicles targeted to consumers and commercial enterprises,[409] possibly with a focus on Level 4's strictly con-fined/area limited level of automation.[410]

Existing fault-based liability or strict liability frameworks may produce inconsistent or undesirable results when applied to automated vehicles because the 'driver' of a vehicle with a very high level of automation may have little more control over the vehicle's behaviour than an ordinary passenger would. It is *prima facie*

---

[405] Susanne Pillath and European Parliamentary Research Service, 'Briefing: Automated Vehicles in the EU' (2016) <https://www.europarl.europa.eu/RegData/etudes/BRIE/2016/573902/EPRS_BRI(2016)573902_EN.pdf>.

[406] European Commission, 'Report on the Safety and Liability Implications of Artificial Intelligence, the Internet of Things and Robotics' (2020) 2 <https://ec.europa.eu/info/sites/info/files/report-safety-liability-artificial-intelligence-feb2020_en_1.pdf>; European Commission, 'Saving Lives: Boosting Car Safety in the EU (COM(2016) 787 Final)' (2016) 4.

[407] SAE International, 'Taxonomy and Definitions for Terms Related to Driving Automation Systems for On-Road Motor Vehicles'; 'SAE International Releases Updated Visual Chart for Its "Levels of Driving Automation" Standard for Self-Driving Vehicles' (December 2018) 1 <https://www.sae.org/news/press-room/2018/12/sae-international-releases-updated-visual-chart-for-its-"levels-of-driving-automation"-standard-for-self-driving-vehicles>. For a more detailed analysis of the liability intersections of the different SAE levels, see Watts (n 376) 5; Pearl (n 403).

[408] 'Audi Quits Bid to Give A8 Level 3 Autonomy' <https://europe.autonews.com/automakers/audi-quits-bid-give-a8-level-3-autonomy>.

[409] An AI vehicle project associated with Ford may target goods delivery rather than passenger transport/ride sharing for its automated vehicles. This is partially due to the impact of the Covid-19 pandemic. See 'Ford Delays Commercial Automated Vehicle Launch To 2022' <https://www.forbes.com/sites/samabuelsamid/2020/04/28/ford-delays-commercial-automated-vehicle-launch-to-2022/#74c49447083c>.

[410] Mark Anderson, 'Surprise! 2020 Is Not the Year for Self-Driving Cars', *IEEE Spectrum* (22 April 2020) <https://spectrum.ieee.org/transportation/self-driving/surprise-2020-is-not-the-year-for-selfdriving-cars>.

Intersentia

A Comparative Law Analysis of No-Fault Comprehensive Compensation Funds

unjust and inconsistent for a driver/vehicle owner in such circumstances to have no coverage for his or her own 'first-party' injuries under, for example, a strict liability or fault-based system.[411] Further, insurance companies rely on clear liability rules in order to calculate risk and claim reimbursement from liable parties.[412] When individual claimants must prove liability to access compensation, opaqueness about the allocation of liability for artificial intelligence-related harm adds a complexity hurdle and a risk of unexpected coverage gaps. 'No-fault insurance' and artificial intelligence guarantee funds have had some brief treatment in legal research from various jurisdictions.[413] However what has not been extensively recognised in most of the recent scholarly literature[414] is that the selected no-fault comprehensive compensation funds would already automatically cover injuries flowing from such novel vehicles.[415]

In Québec the SAAQ has worked with the provincial government to anticipate the arrival of automated vehicles and their testing via pilot projects, with regulatory controls for liability and compensation issues.[416] In 2018, Québec's highway legislation was amended to specifically define an autonomous vehicle (with direct reference to SAE Levels 3, 4 and 5),[417] and prohibit their operation on public roads[418] other than as part of an authorised pilot project.[419] Autonomous vehicle manufacturers and distributors can be required to reimburse SAAQ for all bodily injury compensation costs, as well as taking out adequate liability insurance for property damage costs. However, in a current

---

[411] 'SAE International Releases Updated Visual Chart for Its "Levels of Driving Automation" Standard for Self-Driving Vehicles' (n 407); EFD Engelhard and RW de Bruin, 'EU Common Approach on the Liability Rules and Insurance Related to Connected and Autonomous Vehicles.' (2017) 42–43.

[412] European Commission, 'Report on the Safety and Liability Implications of Artificial Intelligence, the Internet of Things and Robotics' (n 406).

[413] Florin Costinel Dima, 'Fully Autonomous Vehicles in the EU: Opportunity or Threat?' (University of Twente 2019) 44–45 <https://essay.utwente.nl/72945/2/DIMA_MA_PA.pdf>; Olivia J Erdélyi and Gábor Erdélyi, 'The AI Liability Puzzle and A Fund-Based Work-Around' (2019).

[414] Maurice Schellekens, 'No-Fault Compensation Schemes for Self-Driving Vehicles' (2018) 10 *Law, Innovation and Technology* 314 <https://www.narcis.nl/publication/RecordID/ oai:tilburguniversity.edu:publications%2F5dc6cc56-ce7a-46ff-986b-0b2f8a28010a>. However, Brady and others do briefly recognise that the complex liability issues posed by automated vehicles to fault-based and hybrid third-party liability schemes will simply not arise for no-fault schemes. See Brady and others (n 403) para 51. There is near silence on the topic of no-fault coverage in Mark Chinen, *Law and Autonomous Machines: The Co-Evolution of Legal Responsibility and Technology* (Edward Elgar Publishing 2019).

[415] Watts (n 376).

[416] Société de l'assurance automobile du Québec, 'Autonomous Vehicles' <https://saaq.gouv. qc.ca/en/road-safety/modes-transportation/autonomous-vehicles/>.

[417] Highway Safety Code s 4.

[418] ibid s 492.8. There is an exception for Level 3 vehicles that are permitted for sale in Canada.

[419] ibid s 633.1.

Chapter 3. Review of Existing No-Fault Comprehensive Compensation Funds

automated minibus project that is operational in Montreal, the requirement for participating distributors to reimburse the SAAQ has been dropped (although the property damage insurance requirements remain).[420] This is possibly because the minibuses may only operate in designated lanes in a small number of specifically named streets, and all other road users are prohibited from accessing those lanes.

Victoria's TAC is also active (in a co-ordination and funding capacity) in a number of projects to test and manage the implementation of autonomous vehicle technology.[421] This activity is due to the overarching accident prevention and injury reduction objectives of the TAC, as applied to new technologies.[422] The TAC-involved projects are therefore among the most advanced in Australia (i.e. targeted applications, rather than general or awareness-raising activities as seen in other states and territories).[423] A study at the Australian federal level concluded that a no-fault universal access compensation approach would the simplest and best solution to insurability issues associated with automated vehicles.[424] There are attempts underway to try and reconcile the varying interstate no-fault and fault-based approaches to motor vehicle injury in a way that produces nationally consistent results,[425] although it seems unclear how this can be achieved, given the liability challenges of using a fault-based model in artificial intelligence applications.

As with the e-scooter technology, the threshold for compensation cover can generally be managed (in Victoria, Québec and Manitoba) by way of whether the automated vehicle is required to be registered and licensed to operate on a public road. This can be complemented with lateral regulatory controls and direct involvement by the fund in the testing and authorisation of automated vehicles on local roads.

The New Zealand ACC scheme will clearly offer blanket compensation coverage without the need for any law changes, regardless of where the use

---

[420] Autonomous Bus and Minibus Pilot Project, CQLR c. C-24.2, r. 37.01.

[421] Transport Accident Commission, 'Victoria Leads The Way With Self Driving Vehicles' <http://www.tac.vic.gov.au/about-the-tac/media-room/news-and-events/2016/victoria-leads-the-way-with-self-driving-vehicles>.

[422] Transport Accident Commission, 'Towards Zero 2016–2020' (2016) 24–28.

[423] Austroads, 'Trials' <https://austroads.com.au/drivers-and-vehicles/future-vehicles-and-technology/trials>.

[424] 'Motor Accident Injury Insurance and Automated Vehicles: Discussion Paper' (n 403). See also the discussion under the heading 'Legal responsibility and insurance' in House of Representatives Standing Committee on Industry Innovation Science and Resources, 'Social Issues Relating to Land-Based Automated Vehicles in Australia' (2017) 39–46.

[425] National Transport Commission, 'Motor Accident Injury Insurance and Automated Vehicles' (2019) 46 <www.ntc.gov.au>.

Intersentia

of the automated car occurs and whether or not licensing approval has been granted.[426] This is because of the broad definition of both a personal injury and a motor vehicle injury.[427] Further, there is no immediate regulatory impediment to their introduction on public roads, because New Zealand's existing vehicle regulations do not preclude the use of a vehicle on a public road without a driver.[428] It is currently possible to apply for a permit to test an automated vehicle under a straightforward procedure, with no specific insurance requirements.[429] The identified liability challenges[430] of automated vehicles for the New Zealand jurisdiction are therefore likely to be centred on property damage liability and apportionment of criminal responsibility for road safety law offences. Any bodily injuries (whether to driver/operators, passengers, other road users, pedestrians or other by-standers) are automatically covered by the existing ACC Scheme. One point worth noting here is that New Zealand is a small automobile market that does not manufacture its own vehicles, and is generally a 'taker' of technology.[431] This leads to a policy and fairness difficulty caused by the existing ACC framework and its broad statutory bar against tort law actions for personal injury. As we know from the *DePuy* litigation, it would currently not be possible for the New Zealand government (or any injured individual) to bring a tort or product liability claim for compensatory damages against an overseas-owned distributor of automated vehicles for personal injury damage flowing from such a vehicle's use, even if that took the form of participation in class action proceedings filed in another jurisdiction.

Under either the transport function or total personal injury function model, an immediate safety net of no-fault compensation is therefore available while accurate data about the actual risks of harm is gathered. This allows for the formulation of new targeted legislation (where necessary), and appropriate levies

---

[426] Michael Cameron, *Realising the Potential of Driverless Vehicles: Recommendations for Law Reform* (The Law Foundation New Zealand 2018) ch 7 <https://www.lawfoundation.org.nz/wp-content/uploads/2018/04/Cameron_DriverlessVehicles_complete-publication.pdf>.

[427] Accident Compensation Act 2001 ss 26, 35.

[428] Land Transport Act 1998 s 7. This key section of legislation prohibiting reckless driving refers to driving a vehicle or causing a vehicle to be driven. A generous interpretation would easily include use of an autonomous vehicle within the scope of being 'caused' to be driven. The definition under s 2 of 'operate' in relation to a vehicle clearly states that the relevant person does not have to be 'present with the vehicle'. For further analysis of these regulatory issues in a New Zealand context, see Zane Fookes, 'Navigating the Law Reform Route for Driverless Cars in New Zealand' (2016).

[429] New Zealand Transport Agency, 'Testing Autonomous Vehicles in New Zealand' <https://www.nzta.govt.nz/vehicles/vehicle-types/automated-and-autonomous-vehicles/testing-autonomous-vehicles-in-new-zealand/>.

[430] Ministry of Transport, 'Overview of Ministry's Autonomous Vehicles Work Programme' (2019).

[431] Ministry of Transport, 'Ministry of Transport AV Work Programme' <https://www.transport.govt.nz/multi-modal/technology/specific-transport-technologies/road-vehicle/autonomous-vehicles/ministry-of-transport-av-work-programme/>.

Chapter 3. Review of Existing No-Fault Comprehensive Compensation Funds

or experience-rating costs that could be applied to the registration or sale costs of such vehicles. No-fault comprehensive compensation funds therefore appear to be a satisfactory and efficient way to manage the risk of this new technology, without any significant scheme adjustment.

6.1.3. Out-of-Jurisdiction Drivers

Accidents involving out-of-jurisdiction drivers pose a particular challenge for the coherency of the funds and the compensation that is available in the case of accidents. They lead primarily to risks of the tort action bar being undermined (or a non-resident having no entitlement to no-fault benefits and also being blocked from accessing civil remedies). In Victoria, Manitoba and Québec, this problem has been managed by providing coverage for all locally registered vehicles, followed by subrogation where necessary. The provision of coverage for all locally registered vehicles is a practical way that the Victorian and Canadian funds use their involvement in the wider regulation of transport to primarily minimise the number of in-state accidents that do not qualify for complete no-fault coverage.[432] It also means that the non-resident driver has contributed either directly (as the vehicle owner) or indirectly (as the renter of a local car, for example) towards the levies that maintain the funds.

In Victoria, there is blanket no-fault coverage for all transport accidents that occur in the state,[433] with the possibility of common law damages where the 'serious injury' threshold is met. Subrogation powers found in the statute[434] are then used after the fact to recoup compensation costs paid by non-Victorian drivers in non-Victorian registered vehicles.[435] This is the same power that the TAC uses to recoup costs from other third parties, such as the manufacturer of a defective motor vehicle part or doctors whose negligence leads to worsened injuries for transport injury victims (the latter point is detailed in the next section).[436]

In Manitoba and Québec, non-resident rules will only apply to non-resident vehicles being driven by non-residents. The default position (access to no-fault

---

[432] However this only relates to in-state accidents. There is a key difference between Victoria, Québec and Manitoba in the case of out of state accidents. No TAC benefits are available to a Victorian resident who is injured or dies in an interstate accident if no Victorian registered vehicle is involved. Conversely, Québec and Manitoba provide some demogrant benefits here – Québec residents have worldwide coverage for automobile injury, and Manitoba residents have North American coverage.

[433] Transport Accident Act 1986 (Victoria) s 35.

[434] ibid s 104(1).

[435] Because the owners/drivers of these out-of-state vehicles won't have the immunity from costs recoupment that is granted from the payment of the Transport Accident Charge – see s 94 Transport Accident Act 1986.

[436] Transport Accident Commission, 'Overpayments and Recoveries' <https://www.tac.vic.gov.au/clients/what-we-can-pay-for/policies/other/recoveries#nontacindem>.

Intersentia

145

benefits in inverse relation to the degree of non-resident responsibility for the accident) is supplanted where the MPI or SAAQ has an agreement in place with another jurisdiction.

By contrast in New Zealand, blanket coverage for everyone (including tourists) is the most logical approach. This is because, as a geographically isolated island nation, it will simply not be possible for a foreign-registered vehicle to drive on New Zealand public roads.[437] Out-of-jurisdiction drivers will always be driving New Zealand licensed vehicles (for example rental vehicles), and will contribute in a small way to the fund in the form of ACC levies that are charged on the sale of petrol and diesel.[438] The introduction of subrogation arrangements against potentially negligent or criminally convicted individual foreign drivers would certainly introduce unacceptable incoherency to the pure no-fault nature of the ACC Scheme and increase administrative costs.[439]

6.2. MEDICAL AND PHARMACEUTICAL

Only New Zealand's ACC scheme offers no-fault compensation for the function of medical and pharmaceutical injury, i.e. treatment injury.[440] As mentioned earlier in this chapter, there is specific cover under the legislation for personal injury that was caused by a treatment that was delivered by or at the direction of a registered healthcare professional. However there are some wide exclusions – primarily, there will be no cover if the injury was a necessary part or ordinary consequence of the treatment, taking into account all the circumstances of the case (including the victim's health condition and clinical knowledge). Similarly, there will be no cover simply because the treatment didn't achieve the desired result, nor where the injury was wholly or substantially caused by the victim's underlying condition, a resource allocation decision, or the victim unreasonably withholding or delaying consent to treatment.

---

[437]   In any event, s 242 of the Land Transport Act 1998 says that a motor vehicle cannot be operated on a New Zealand road unless it is registered and licensed in accordance with that statute.

[438]   This is at a rate of 6c per litre – see cl 5 Accident Compensation (Motor Vehicle Account Levies) Regulations 2019.

[439]   For example, an attempt by a tourist (who was convicted of careless driving resulting in two deaths) to voluntarily repay his medical bill was rejected by ACC on the grounds that it would signal a move towards a system where tourists no longer enjoyed no-fault benefits. Overseas travel insurance providers might then seek to recoup their losses and want to identify an at-fault party to sue or seek reimbursement from ACC itself, a consequence that the relevant government minister said was not 'where we want to go'. See Zac Fleming, 'Tourist's ACC Refund Offer Rejected', *Radio New Zealand News* (8 June 2017) <https://www.rnz.co.nz/national/programmes/checkpoint/audio/201846823/tourist-s-acc-refund-offer-rejected>.

[440]   Accident Compensation Act 2001 ss 32, 33.

Chapter 3. Review of Existing No-Fault Comprehensive Compensation Funds

The Canadian Supreme Court's very broad interpretation in *Godbout v Pagé* of the SAAQ's reach, however, means that there will be application of the scheme to *all* the actions and conduct of medical practitioners who treat automobile injury victims. So there is a small subset of coverage for medical injury under the SAAQ scheme (and probably the MPI too, if we assume that these kinds of cases will be interpreted in the same vein). However, this is only really relevant to the victim and their entitlement to no-fault benefits (whether they want it or not). Subrogation could be used to recover SAAQ's costs, especially in relation to a private provider.

There is an interesting point of correlation here with the situation in Victoria. The TAC's subrogation powers to pursue non-covered persons for a recoupment of costs are also used in practice to pursue doctors whose negligent treatment leads to worse recovery outcomes for the transport accident victims.[441] However, the individual victim's new (worsened) condition will be accepted for the purposes of no-fault benefits, even if it is significantly different from the original transport injury and/or is serious or life-altering.[442] This means that in Victoria, the functional reach of the no-fault compensation fund is linked factually to injuries directly flowing from the accident, as well as those exacerbated by third parties such as doctors and other healthcare providers.

Aside from this narrow point, there is no obvious direct functional comparator for ACC in the no-fault comprehensive compensation fund field for medical and pharmaceutical injuries. Therefore the best way to proceed on this function, within this project, is to make a more limited comparison with no-fault compensation possibilities available for medical injuries in the Nordic countries, France and Belgium.[443] A simple functional and purposive comparison is made in the next two subsections relating to Franco-Belgian and Nordic no-fault funds.

---

[441] Comment made by Transport Accident Commission legal and policy staff in email correspondence dated 11 July 2019. This relates to the practical use and application of s 104(1) of the Transport Accident Act 1986, which states: 'If an injury or death arising out of a transport accident in respect of which the Commission has made payments under this Act arose under circumstances which, regardless of section 93, would have created a legal liability in Victoria or elsewhere in a person (other than a person who is entitled to be indemnified under section 94) to pay damages in respect of any loss suffered by reason of the injury or death, the Commission is entitled to be indemnified by the first-mentioned person for such proportion of the amount of the liability of the Commission to make payments under this Act in respect of the injury or death as is appropriate to the degree to which the injury or death was attributable to the act, default or negligence of the first-mentioned person.'

[442] Comment made by Transport Accident Commission legal and policy staff in email correspondence dated 30 October 2019. In one given example, a TAC client was administered an incorrect blood type (in the course of their treatment for a transport injury) and this resulted in blindness. The client was eligible for no-fault benefits (presumably incapacity benefits as well as common law damages due to the seriousness of the injury). The TAC turned to the relevant third party's insurer under s 104(1) for a recoupment of costs.

[443] This is the approach that has been taken by other scholars. See Joanna M Manning, 'Plus ça change, plus c'est la même chose: Negligence and treatment injury in New Zealand's accident compensation scheme' (2014) 14 *Medical Law International* 22.

Intersentia

147

What can be said generally is that the stalling in Australia of the NIIS stream for medical injuries, despite strong arguments in favour of its benefits,[444] shows that it will be especially difficult for contextual reasons to establish a no-fault *comprehensive* compensation fund for the function of medical and pharmaceutical injury.

6.3. EMPLOYMENT INJURY

As noted earlier in this chapter, the employment injury compensation landscapes of Australia and Canada do not meet the definition of being a no-fault comprehensive publicly administered compensation fund. This means that New Zealand's ACC stands alone functionally within this category. A glance internationally confirms that there are no other obvious comparators with New Zealand.[445] A comparative law analysis for the function of no-fault *employment* injury and loss compensation is therefore best done separately. It is not within the scope of this project, which focuses on no-fault comprehensive compensation funds more generally, that tend to cover transport injury (TAC, SAAQ and MPI) or all accidental personal injury risks (ACC).[446]

In terms of the intersection between transport injury and workplace injury in the context of a no-fault comprehensive compensation fund, the best functional conclusion that can be observed from the legislative structure of the four schemes is that if there is not blanket coverage (as in New Zealand) there should be a direct and overlapping legislative relationship between the two fields that defines precisely when the claimant will fall under worker compensation legislation, and when he or she will fall under the transport accident compensation legislation.

This is has been handled well in Québec, with a clear legislative framework to manage the boundaries between the two systems.[447] New Zealand has recently implemented a similar model of strengthened collaborative ties as part

---

[444] Tina Popa, 'Don't Look for Fault, Find a Remedy! Exploring Alternative Forms of Compensating Medical Injuries in Australia, New Zealand and Belgium' (2019) 27 *Tort Law Review* 1.

[445] For example, France, Belgium and Norway's workplace injury schemes fall wholly within the realm of social security. There are carve-outs for the self-employed in Germany. Denmark's system uses private insurers. In Finland there are different rules in place for small employers, the state, and all other employers.

[446] A recent doctoral study which proposed a reform of ACC through a labour law approach with health and safety prevention functions is Dawn Duncan, 'Beyond Accident: A Model for the Compensation of Work-Related Harm in New Zealand' (Victoria University of Wellington 2019).

[447] Automobile Insurance Act (Québec) ss 83.66 and 83.67. In Victoria, the key point of overlap is where TAC common law damages will be available for a workplace vehicle accident and where they will not be.

Chapter 3. Review of Existing No-Fault Comprehensive Compensation Funds

of an attempt to improve its workplace safety performance.[448] The relationship structure is more fluid in Manitoba, where the worker can elect to choose between MPI benefits and workers' compensation.[449] What must be recognised here that it is not fundamentally challenging from a functional or structural perspective for a *no-fault* workplace injury scheme to have overlap with a *no-fault* transport injury scheme. If a *no-fault* transport injury compensation fund has to intersect with a *strict-liability* or *fault-based* worker injury scheme, it is difficult to see how this could be managed in a coherent way. The high degree of complexity that is involved in the determination of the small common law damages carve-outs for worker and transport accidents in Victoria is evidence of this.[450]

6.4. GENERAL INJURY RISKS

The New Zealand ACC scheme is the only no-fault comprehensive fund that completely covers the everyday risks of life. Arguably, widespread personal vehicle ownership in most developed countries means that traffic-related injury compensation funds address a sort of 'everyday' general injury risk, but this is nowhere near on the same scale as the New Zealand coverage of all accidental personal injury and treatment injuries. However, the widening of the SAAQ's scope by the Canadian Supreme Court in *Godbout v Pagé* shows that that scheme (and Manitoba's) will now cover all risks, both expected and unexpected, that have a basic causal connection with a single automobile accident event.

It may be possible to make a limited functional comparison here between the New Zealand ACC Scheme and the various 'guarantee' funds that are found in Belgium and France. Some of these guarantee funds cover 'everyday' (or rather practically uninsurable) risks like injury from terrorism and non-automobile traffic accidents such as e-scooter accidents. These are funds that compensate on the basis of the specific concept of *solidarity* which, as will be discussed later in this chapter, can be broadly translated as equivalent to the New Zealand concept of 'community responsibility'.

Thinking specifically about the 'everyday risks of life' concept, this is the precise aspect that puts no-fault comprehensive compensation funds in a

---

[448]   New Zealand Government (n 116); s 246A Accident Compensation Act 2001 s 246A; Health and Safety at Work Act 2015 s 196.

[449]   The Manitoba Public Insurance Corporation Act s 195.

[450]   Transport Accident Commission, 'WorkCover – Transport Accidents and Accidents Arising out of the Use of Vehicle Claims' <http://www.tac.vic.gov.au/clients/what-we-can-pay-for/policies/other/workcover-transport-accidents-and-accidents-arising-out-of-the-use-of-vehicle-claims>. Confusingly, there are also different legal standards applied in case law to the definitions of serious injury, depending on whether it is a transport or workplace accident – analysis of this distinction can be found in Section 4.3 'Is the injury a serious injury?' in Judicial College of Victoria, *Serious Injury Manual* (n 164).

Intersentia

149

sphere most functionally similar to a universal social welfare benefit, where compensation is also paid on the basis of a set of conditions caused by a specific circumstance (on a demogrant basis). This leads to challenges in the definition of what amounts to an eligible 'everyday risk of life' and how (and whether) the compensation fund should be further expanded. Now, case law is generally where we see the limits of eligibility being tested – but these reflect only the most extreme issues of eligibility. Decisions about eligibility or ineligibility for scheme coverage are being made by no-fault comprehensive compensation funds every day, possibly with inadequate guidance for the claimant about how the compensation fund navigates equivalent cases of eligibility.[451] Looking across all four funds, the following points emerge as common issues in the 'everyday risks of life' function.

6.4.1. What is an Eligible Form of Harm?

The precise statutory definition of harm is the primary departure point, with reference to the purpose of the scheme as the secondary consideration. The policy results flowing for claimants about whether or not there is coverage, and the treatment of the claimant under a tort (or other field of law) if there is no coverage are both irrelevant in individual cases, according to judicial interpretation in Canada and New Zealand.[452] It is also not necessary for the (in)consistency of the no-fault comprehensive compensation fund with other legal structures to be resolved when determining eligibility – a broad compatibility is sufficient.[453]

For individual cases this is mostly a satisfactory answer and does not need to be resolved, but in the long term the inconsistency with other legal structures needs to be addressed by the legislature. The inconsistency with social insurance system supports in New Zealand, for example, has been well-documented.[454]

Turning to historic abuse, a regrettably common risk of life for many children, there is already ACC Scheme coverage of some categories of claimants where they can show evidence of a covered harm (e.g. mental injury resulting from a personal injury) on the balance of probabilities.[455] But some claimants

---

[451] In New Zealand, a review of ACC dispute resolution procedures recommended public distribution of case notes and guidance about how it makes decisions, in accessible language. Dean (n 98) 39–40.

[452] *Queenstown Lakes District Council v Palmer* (n 104); *Godbout v Pagé et al* (n 272); *J.A. v Société de l'assurance automobile du Québec* (n 309); *McGougan v DePuy International Limited* (n 56).

[453] *Sweedman v Transport Accident Commission* (n 185); *Nordquist v Gurniak* (n 305).

[454] And recognised by recent official studies – Welfare Expert Advisory Group (n 74) 147.

[455] As per the test in *Accident Compensation Corporation v Ambros* [2007] NZCA 304. An example of this might be the conclusions of a ACC-approved clinical psychologist that the

Chapter 3. Review of Existing No-Fault Comprehensive Compensation Funds

will be unable to show this basic causal connection.[456] If, as expected, a compensation fund is recommended by New Zealand's Royal Commission of Inquiry into Historical Abuse in State Care, then the overlap between three possible sources of compensation (ACC Scheme, social welfare and a proposed historic abuse scheme) will need to be very actively and closely managed to avoid both double recovery by some applicants and total exclusion for others. This may be less of an issue in a function that is well-supplemented by insurance for non-covered losses, for example in the way that snowmobiles and off-road vehicles are excluded from the Manitoba and Québec traffic injury funds. Although catastrophic exclusions can result in non-covered cases (such as in *J.A. v SAAQ*),[457] the healthy functioning of a well-regulated insurance market for snowmobiles and off-road vehicles (that is cross-supported by the stability offered by the no-fault comprehensive funds) has (according to SAAQ and MPI staff) neutralised arguments for an extension or revision of eligibility under the no-fault fund.[458]

Eligibility criteria for everyday risks of life thus need to be more actively managed in a no-fault comprehensive fund than for other functions that are easily insurable. This can include express exclusion for a particular category of individuals, but, as Goudkamp and Cane note, there must be adequate explanation of exclusion from a no-fault fund.[459]

6.4.2. What is the Right Way to Extend or Limit the Scope of Eligibility?

Extension of eligibility is possible where facts and new scientific evidence show that a previously ineligible harm *does* factually fit within the statutory definition. This is exemplified by the approach taken by the New Zealand High Court and Court of Appeal in *Calver* to non-workplace mesothelioma caused by asbestos.

The approach taken in *Calver* is logical, as the alternative is that the application of statute would be made without regard to developments in accepted medical knowledge. However in most cases it is surely better for a restatement of scope to come from the legislature itself after consideration of the impact of scheme expansion on funding or its relevance to other compensation sources. This does mean that the fund or judiciary may not be able act 'nimbly' to resolve

---

mental harm was caused by historical physical or sexual injury. The establishment of cover might also be assisted by evidence of a criminal conviction or other investigatory findings about the historical abuse for a certain class of victims.

[456] And could only have recourse to the little-known *ex gratia* Confidential Listening and Assistance Service operated by the Ministry of Social Development. This is critiqued in Winter (n 136).

[457] Discussed in section 4.3, text to n 309 above.

[458] Comments made in interviews with MPI and SAAQ staff in May and October 2019.

[459] Peter Cane and James Goudkamp, *Atiyah's Accidents, Compensation and the Law* (9th edn, Cambridge University Press 2018).

Intersentia

eligibility issues[460] – but this is probably a good thing to avoid the creation of inconsistencies.[461]

6.4.3. Why are Economic Losses not Included, as these are also a General Injury Risk?

Coverage of economic loss is best limited (for cost reasons) to the income replacement aspects of the schemes (and small amounts of economic loss, like the coverage under the SAAQ for clothing worn at the time of accident). The Canadian funds do show that it is possible to incorporate a limited degree of economic loss under separate headings of the same legislation. However that is only possible because the scheme is limited to automobile injury (albeit with expansive reach) and is also responsible for other regulatory issues in relation to automobile transport. It would not be feasible for more general economic losses to be included solely within the New Zealand ACC scheme, for example, which does not have responsibility for other regulatory issues.

In all four jurisdictions, coverage for non-injury economic losses flowing from car accidents (to continue the example) is offered via the ordinary insurance market. In Manitoba, the MPI itself holds a near-monopolistic position in this market (even though competition is possible in theory). MPI's extension insurance revenues are required to be held strictly separate from its compulsory (personal injury and economic) coverage revenues and no cross-subsidisation is allowed.[462] Automobile insurance for non-injury economic losses is not mandatory in New Zealand or Victoria, but is widely purchased. In Québec, drivers are required to take out a minimum of C$50,000 of cover.[463] In Manitoba the minimum requirement is C$200,000.[464] There are higher coverage requirements for commercial drivers.

We see, therefore, that there is a principled difference applied to everyday risk of life *economic* losses in no-fault comprehensive compensation funds. There has been no attempt in any of the four funds to extend coverage widely

---

[460] Such as the decision to not allow an extension of the New Zealand scheme to cover terrorism 'mental injury' victims (because, as the New Zealand Treasury hinted, it could inadvertently lead to cost blow-outs, and all scheme expansions should be considered on a proactive basis). See Ministry of Business Innovation and Employment (n 48) 10. See also the sympathetic comments of the Québec Court of Appeal towards to the (ultimately unsuccessful) appellant in *J.A. v SAAQ* 2010 QCCA 1328 at paragraph [40] – 'The debate brought before us by the appellant is basically political. She is arguing in favour widening [sic] the *AIA*'s scope. This objective is not merely defensible but certainly praiseworthy … [but] we cannot grant the application.'

[461] Like the 'top-up' of ACC payments that is now possible for crime victims by way of a criminal reparation order against the perpetrator.

[462] The Manitoba Public Insurance Corporation Act s 6.3.

[463] Automobile Insurance Act (Québec) s 87.

[464] Highway Traffic Act (Manitoba) s 160(4).

Chapter 3. Review of Existing No-Fault Comprehensive Compensation Funds

to general economic losses, revealing the fallacy of a 'slippery slope' argument about no-fault comprehensive funds. The holistic cost of human injury and harm to the individual and to society is therefore prioritised over economic consequences (beyond immediate income replacement).

What is clearly not included in the scope of this study is compensation fund management of economic losses flowing from a different type of everyday risk of life – natural disasters. This is because no natural disaster funds fit my definition of a no-fault comprehensive compensation fund. Natural disasters will obviously have major economic losses (e.g. property loss) as a consequence of the harm event. Therefore a distinction may need to be made between the principles that underpin general economic loss compensation for *injury* no-fault compensation funds and those governing *natural disaster* no-fault compensation funds.

6.4.4. Should Anybody have Limits Placed on their Ability to Recover Compensation?

All four schemes *do* place limits on income-related and special compensation for injuries that flow from certain criminal conduct and self-harm. This reflects a series of political and ideological choices about corrective, retributive and distributive justice, which should be seen as specific to each jurisdiction and not based on a logical 'meta-principle'.[465] The Canadian schemes, with their redirection of compensation to the family of victims of criminally convicted drivers, probably do the best job of attempting to impose justified limits on compensation in the case of criminal behaviour, but mitigating any negative impacts by redirecting that compensation to any innocent dependent family members.

Ultimately this is a question of policy for the legislature (and the wider public), but it should be handled with extreme caution by the legislature – and never in policy or legislative isolation – because of the significant risks of inconsistent treatment emerging that will undermine the comprehensive nature of the scheme.

7. PRINCIPLED COMPARISON WITH THE FRENCH AND BELGIAN APPROACH

Before we contrast our four examples of no-fault comprehensive compensation with the functional and purposive approach in France and Belgium, there are some basic issues of legal systems and doctrinal compatibility to be addressed.

---

[465]   Connell (n 54) 18.

Intersentia

The four no-fault comprehensive compensation funds studied in this book all exist within major common law jurisdictions. This begs the fundamental comparative law methodology question: if all the funds identified come from common law jurisdictions, is it possible or relevant to make comparisons with the (less comprehensive) compensation funds in other jurisdictions, particularly those from a civil law tradition?[466] The answer must certainly be yes. As noted already, there are relevant functional dimensions of no-fault comprehensive compensation funds that can be identified for comparison with their more limited civil jurisdiction cousins.

But there is also a fundamental legal systems point to be addressed here. No-fault comprehensive compensation funds should never be thought of as 'incompatible' with civil law jurisdictions. This is because one of the most expansive and socially-purposed examples is found in Québec, a hybrid common law and civil law jurisdiction. Although much of Québec civil law does not have a high profile within Canada or internationally, the operation of the SAAQ within this hybrid civil jurisdiction is particularly instructive in any comparative law analysis of compensation funds across common and civil law traditions.[467]

Secondly, why should the French and Belgian approaches to compensation funds be considered together? The French and Belgian legal systems have many similarities in terms of the influence and relevance of the Napoleonic code to legislative structures. The development of Belgian law has also organically evolved in its own pragmatic way to reflect the societal and legal differences between Flanders and Wallonia.[468] In terms of the development of compensation funds, developments in Belgium have links to systems in both France and the Netherlands.[469] The close functional and structural similarity of the medical incident compensation funds in France and Belgium is most relevant to compare together with the no-fault comprehensive model on the function of medical injury.[470] Separately, the French single-window guarantee funds model can also

---

[466] Especially given the sense of a very 'common law evolution' that no-fault is given in Ken Oliphant, 'Landmarks of No-Fault in the Common Law', *Shifts in Compensation between Private and Public Systems (Tort and Insurance Law Vol. 22)* (Springer 2007) <http://link.springer.com/10.1007/978-3-211-71554-3_3>.

[467] Although Québec's civil law system – as a Napoleonic system – shares a common legal historical bond with France and Belgium, some important doctrinal differences have developed. These differences are directly related to issues of compensation. The late-nineteenth-century French movement to replace 'fault' in civil liability with the concept of general risk (that eventually evolved into the concept of strict liability) was not fully replicated in Québec. However the notion of 'risk' did filter through into the development of the province's worker compensation schemes. See Baudouin and Linden (n 250) paras 33–35.

[468] Dirk Heirbaut, 'The Belgian Legal Tradition: Does It Exist?' in Marc Kruithof and Walter De Bondt (eds), *Introduction to Belgian Law* (Wolters Kluwer 2017).

[469] Vanhoof, Vansweevelt and Weyts (n 126).

[470] In France it is Office National d'Indemnisation des Accidents Medicaux (ONIAM) and in Belgium it is the Fonds voor de medische ongevallen or Fonds des accidents médicaux (FMO/FAM).

Chapter 3. Review of Existing No-Fault Comprehensive Compensation Funds

be compared on a limited basis with the 'everyday risk of life' and automobile injury functions of no-fault comprehensive compensation funds.

7.1. THE FRENCH AND BELGIAN COMPENSATION FUND LANDSCAPE

From a comparative law perspective, French and Belgian compensation funds can be characterised as flexible mechanisms to 'fill the gap', when needed, between tort remedies, insured benefits and social insurance support. They are not intended as a comprehensive alternative to insurance or a private law damages claim. This could be thought of as a reactive approach that addresses gaps in the system where they are needed, but remaining subordinate to private law solutions, where available. They demonstrate 'social solidarity' in terms of accessing compensation, but this does not mean the same thing as access to justice.[471] Nor does it enshrine a firm right to compensation in law.

The French medical incident compensation fund (ONIAM) was established in 2002,[472] and the very similar Belgian system (FMO/FAM) was established in 2010.[473] Both countries have also established specific compensation funds for motor accidents (where no responsible insured party can be found), terrorism victims[474, 475] and asbestos victims.[476] France has consolidated a number of its 'guarantee funds' for different types of misfortune into a single administrative structure. Belgium has a separate statutory compensation fund for technological accidents,[477] and a general disaster fund that provides compensation for

---

[471] Macleod and Hodges (n 217) 625.

[472] Loi n° 2002-303 du 4 mars 2002 relative aux droits des malades et à la qualité du système de santé [Act nr 2002-203 of 4 March 2002 on the Rights of Patients and on the Quality of the Health System].

[473] Wet van 31 maart 2010 betreffende de vergoeding van schade als gevolg van gezondheidszorg [Act of 31 March 2010 on the Compensation of Damage as a Consequence of Health Care].

[474] In France, it is Fonds de garantie des victimes d'actes de terrorisme et d'autres infraction. In Belgium, it is the Fund for Redress to Victims of Intentional Offences and to the Occasional Rescuers.

[475] An overview of Belgian compensation fund systems (as well as Dutch and UK compensation fund systems) can be found in Vanhooff, Vansweevelt and Weyts (n 126). French compensation funds (in comparison to German funds) were analysed in depth in the doctoral thesis of Jonas Knetsch, *Le droit de la responsabilité et les fonds d'indemnisation: Analyse en droits français et allemand* (LGDJ 2013) <https://docassas.u-paris2.fr/nuxeo/site/esupversions/ f60b2840-bda3-453e-8626-788d7c4de001>.

[476] In France, it is Fonds d'indemnisation des victimes de l'amiante (FIVA). In Belgium, it is the Asbestfonds or Fonds Amiante.

[477] This fund was established on a special statutory basis following a gas explosion. See Wetsvoorstel betreffende de schadeloosstelling van lichamelijke en geestelijke letsels ingevolge een technologisch ongeval [Private Members' Bill on the Compensation of Physical and Non-Physical Damage from a Technological Accident], Parl. St. Kamer 2010–2011, nr 1286/011, 5, cited in Vanhooff, Vansweevelt and Weyts (n 126) 43.

Intersentia

155

uninsurable loss following an officially recognised disaster.[478] France has general natural disaster and agricultural disaster compensation funds that are available to top-up compensation for insured property owners.[479] The occupational injury and disease compensation systems in both countries can be considered fully a part of their social insurance frameworks (rather than a replacement or alternative for them).[480]

7.2. OVERVIEW OF THE BELGIAN AND FRENCH MEDICAL INJURY FUNDS

The motivation for the establishment of the ONIAM in France was a regulatory crisis where the insurers of medical practitioners threatened to leave the market, claiming that courts were diluting the strictness of the fault standard and compensation costs were rising unsustainably.[481] The French legislature re-asserted the importance of fault for compensation for treatment injury and missed diagnosis, but also created a no-fault compensation option for serious[482] and unpredictable injuries that are unrelated to patients' pre-existing conditions.[483] An out-of-court settlement system aimed to provide claimants with a faster and cheaper option than the court system, with stakeholder involvement in decision-making in individual cases.[484] Compensation for contaminated blood and other specific types of medical harm is also managed by the ONIAM on a direct and non-subsidiary basis; in 2004 an existing compensation system

---

[478] The administration of the Disaster Fund has been devolved to the individual Belgian regions. See 'Rampenfonds' <https://overheid.vlaanderen.be/organisatie/rampenfonds> in relation to Flanders and 'Calamités naturelles – Fonds Régional des Calamités: Actualités' in relation to Wallonia <http://pouvoirslocaux.wallonie.be/jahia/Jahia/site/dgpl/accueil/calamites>. At the time of writing, the website for the Brussels region Disaster Fund was not working.

[479] Eligibility for these schemes appears to be dependent upon having purchased fire insurance for the affected farm or property. In other words, they require a premium to have been paid by the victim in order to access the system. See 'Natural disasters compensation scheme' <https://www.ccr.fr/en/-/plaquette-indemnisation-des-catastrophes-naturelles-en-france> and 'Loi n°64-706 du 10 juillet 1964 organisant un regime de garantie contre les calamites agricoles' <https://www.legifrance.gouv.fr/jorf/id/JORFTEXT000000691714>.

[480] See The French Social Security System: II – Accidents at work and occupational diseases <https://www.cleiss.fr/docs/regimes/regime_france/an_2.html> and 'Wie zijn we?' <https://www.fedris.be/nl/over-het-fonds/wie-zijn-we>.

[481] Janine Barbot, Isabelle Parizot and Myriam Winance, '"No-Fault" Compensation for Victims of Medical Injuries. Ten Years of Implementing the French Model' (2014) 114 *Health Policy* 236, 237.

[482] 25% or more bodily impairment.

[483] Genevieve Helleringer, 'Medical Malpractice and Compensation in France: Part II: Compensation Based on National Solidarity' (2011) 86 *Chicago-Kent Law Review* 1125.

[484] But the system always retains the option for claimants to bring court proceedings. However, once there has been compensation determined under the ONIAM mechanisms, there may be no cause of action available to bring a court proceeding.

for HIV contamination was folded into the scheme, and new types of blood contamination, vaccine-related infection, growth hormone damage, and harm caused by a medical practitioner acting outside their normal field of specialisation were added as compensation categories. The ONIAM system has been successful in enabling many claims to be resolved more quickly;[485] however, there have been challenges in ensuring that as many claimants as possible access compensation and a tension about whether the threshold for accessing the no-fault compensation element should be adjusted.[486]

The Belgian FMO/FAM operates on a similar basis to the ONIAM and is both a guarantee and damage fund.[487] As well as the fast-track alternative dispute resolution procedures for medical incidents, the system offers compensation (as a guarantee fund) when the liable doctor or hospital is uninsured, the insurer refuses to pay, or there is a dispute about the liability quantum. Claimants always retain the right to bring court proceedings and fault remains the default principle for determining compensation. Access to the no-fault compensation element (the damage fund) requires demonstration of severe disability, as in France. Compensation for blood contamination victims is also included. In contrast to the French model, there is not the same stakeholder participation in decision-making.[488]

7.3. FUNCTIONAL AND PURPOSIVE COMPARISON OF MEDICAL INJURY COMPENSATION

In terms of the purposive classifications we have already identified for no-fault comprehensive compensation funds, the French and Belgian medical injury no-fault funds show a partial, rather than a complete revolution in purpose. This is primarily because of the full retention of access to the tort system. But there remain hints at the possibility of a more complete revolution – although this would probably be fraught with philosophical and practical difficulty.

The New Zealand ACC Scheme currently offers no-fault comprehensive compensation for the function of treatment injury.[489] This is defined in

---

[485] This is evidenced by the steady increase in the number of claims the scheme has received during its existence, of which a third have been accepted. It takes on average eight months for a claim to be decided by the Conciliation and Compensation Commissions that process claims at regional levels. For an English-language summary of the ONIAM's operational statistics between 2003 and 2015, see chapter 18 of Macleod and Hodges (n 217).

[486] Barbot, Parizot and Winance (n 481) 244–245.

[487] Vanhooff, Vansweevelt and Weyts (n 126) 48–49.

[488] 'Onze hulp bij een medisch ongeval' <https://www.riziv.be/nl/themas/medische-ongevallen/Paginas/default.aspx#.W9eTjXpKgzV>.

[489] The costs of which are spread through risk pooling, but most treatment injury compensation is funded specifically by scheme levies paid by registered health professionals or organisations – s 228 Accident Compensation Act 2001.

legislation[490] as being a personal injury, suffered by someone receiving treatment from a registered health professional, that is caused by treatment and isn't a necessary or ordinary consequence of the treatment. The patient's whole health condition, whether or not they unreasonably withheld consent to treatment, and other clinical considerations, are all relevant to a determination of whether there has been a treatment injury.

Between 1992 and 2005 it was necessary for claimants to the New Zealand scheme to show either a medical error or a medical mishap that resulted in a 'medical misadventure' personal injury. The medical error concept was a translation into legislation of an objective concept of 'fault' from the law of negligence.[491] The concept of medical mishap related to non-negligent errors, but there was only cover for restrictively defined cases of 'rarity' and 'severity'.[492] However, a number of legal and practical problems resulted from this approach. Firstly, the requirement of claimants to show an individual healthcare provider's fault (for the purposes of medical error), combined with ACC's legal requirement to report all cases of medical error to the medical regulatory authorities, resulted in an 'overly blaming' culture.[493] Secondly, the 'rarity' and 'severity' criteria were found to be too restrictive and arbitrary, leading to unfair results. Overall, the move to a 'treatment injury approach' aimed to reduce delays and complexity, encourage a co-operative approach with healthcare providers and improve patient safety.[494] However, as Joanna Manning has observed (and Ken Oliphant and Stephen Todd predicted[495]), the tortious concept of fault is still creeping informally into internal ACC decisions on cover and in challenges to cover that appear before the courts.[496] This problematic inability to 'stamp out' fault has been directly acknowledged in recent NZ District and High Court decisions, particularly in relation to the failure to treat (or to provide treatment in a timely manner), and therefore still requires further legislative or senior court clarification.[497]

---

[490]   ibid ss 32 and 33.

[491]   Manning, 'Plus ça change, plus c'est la même chose: Negligence and treatment injury in New Zealand's accident compensation scheme' (n 443) 27; Accident Rehabilitation and Compensation Insurance Act 1992 s 5(1); Accident Insurance Act 1998 s 36(1); Injury Prevention, Rehabilitation and Compensation Act 2001 s 33(1).

[492]   Accident Rehabilitation and Compensation Insurance Act 1992 ss 5(3) and (4).

[493]   Accident Compensation Corporation and Department of Labour, 'Review of Medical Misadventure' (2003).

[494]   Explanatory Note Injury Prevention, Rehabilitation, and Compensation Bill 90-3 2001.

[495]   Oliphant, 'Beyond Misadventure: Compensation for Medical Injuries in New Zealand' (n 78); Stephen Todd, 'Treatment Injury in New Zealand' (2011) 86 *Chicago-Kent Law Review* 1169.

[496]   Manning, 'Plus ça change, plus c'est la même chose: Negligence and treatment injury in New Zealand's accident compensation scheme' (n 443) 50.

[497]   *Accident Compensation Corporation v Ng* [2018] NZHC 2848; *Crawford v Accident Compensation Corporation* [2019] NZACC 77.

The now-repealed 'medical mishap' criterion has the most obvious specific functional equivalent in the French and Belgian medical injury schemes' requirement of 'severity' for eligibility for the no-fault medical injury schemes. The key difference of course, is that the no-fault offerings in French and Belgian schemes are purposively different to the rest of the fault-based liability landscape. The inclusion of a severity criterion in the New Zealand scheme (along with the infusion of fault-based principles, which have been surprisingly difficult to stamp out) was what was out of step with the rest of the comprehensive (non) liability landscape in that jurisdiction. It is on the point of 'severity' – and the inability to define this accurately, even with reference to expert evidence – that we can see a common difficulty between the old New Zealand approach and the current French and Belgian schemes.[498] The problems in defining severity accurately, and the number of patients that it excludes (although Vandersteegen points out that the data on claims to the fund shows that a significant number of applicants *do* meet this criterion) appear to be completely at odds with the object of establishing a streamlined, user-friendly no-fault scheme.

Placing a requirement for a technical calculation of severity before eligibility for no-fault compensation is considered is a significant practical barrier for claimants. It only appears to make sense when one considers whether an inclusive or restrictive approach to no-fault appears to be intended by the legislature. In a liability system that is predominantly designed to funnel most injuries through a lens of fault, it is logical to place a high threshold of initial eligibility and insist that no-fault compensation exist only for subsidiary ('last-resort') purposes. However, in my view, it is illogical to take this approach in a system which *predominantly* has wider purposive intensions to compensate most injuries and facilitate patient learning outcomes – like the New Zealand scheme and, as will be noted in the next section, the Nordic countries' patient injury schemes.

Wannes Buelens' recent ground-breaking comprehensive study of the FMO/FAM put some of scheme's difficulties (the problem of delays) down to its newness and 'teething issues', but also noted that the fund should perhaps be allowed to intervene regardless of the injury severity (even where the caregiver's insurer disputes liability), if only to determine what compensation should be received.[499] Buelens' study concluded that the Belgian FMO/FAM is a truly evolutionary step in that jurisdiction's legal system, because it allows previously un-reimbursable

---

[498] Tom Vandersteegen, Wim Marneffe and Dominique Vandijck, 'Advantages and Disadvantages of the Belgian Not-Only-Fault System for Medical Incidents' (2017) 72 *Acta Clinica Belgica* 36 <https://www.tandfonline.com/doi/full/10.1080/17843286.2016.1202371>; Macleod and Hodges (n 217) ch 18.

[499] Wannes Buelens, *Het Medisch Ongeval Zonder Aansprakelijkheid* (Intersentia 2019). See also Wannes Beulens, 'Fonds Medische Ongevallen – Quo Vadis?' *De Specialist* (2019) <https://www.despecialist.eu/nl/nieuws/beroepsnieuws/fonds-medische-ongevallen-ndash-quo-vadis-nbsp-wannes-buelens.html>.

losses to be compensated. An extension of the scheme to include injuries of all degrees of severity would certainly put the FMO/FAM functionally and purposively on a closer footing to the New Zealand ACC Scheme and the Nordic country model. But it is hard to see how an extension or further evolution of no-fault compensation could actually be achieved without a purposive wholesale re-imagining of liability law for the function of medical injury. For example, if all levels of medical injury severity (without responsibility) were compensated by the French and Belgian funds, this would probably lead to financial problems under the existing legal system designs and in comparison to wider liability jurisprudence. This is because, coming from a French and Belgian view on compensation, victims would end up (unacceptably) having to accept less than 'full' compensation. The fact that empirical evidence demonstrates that no-fault rehabilitative-focused compensation for medical injury is cheaper and more effective overall (for victims and society) than fault-based medical malpractice approaches is not going to solve the legal puzzle of creating coherency with the rest of liability law.[500] If, as Buelens points out, what would ordinarily fall to the victim's own pocket is now being compensated by a fund, then the question of extension is not going to be solved by a slow march of careful incrementalism in liability law reform.

Belgium and France also need only to look at Australia and the stalling of the NIIS medical injury stream to see the challenges a jurisdiction will face to when it tries to reimagine liability concepts (in a fault-based system) for a single broad function. As we have seen already, no-fault is purposively always going to be fundamentally at philosophical odds with an ordinary fault-based liability system. Vigorous management of reform and the fundamental incoherency of fault with no-fault would seem to be the only path forward for the coherent continued development of both the fault and no-fault dimensions of compensation.

Meanwhile, Knetsch's research on compensation funds has shown that it is unlikely that the concept of 'national solidarity' (which is a foundational concept underpinning both French and Belgian medical injury schemes) has strong enough normative foundations to properly direct the establishment and development of no-fault compensation funds.[501] The impact of the COVID-19 pandemic has disrupted and refreshed the concept of public solidarity, but there is no clear picture yet whether a defined new perspective and agreed definition of solidarity will emerge in European jurisdictions. Buelens has rightly concluded that it will be necessary to specifically have regard to developments in the Nordic countries and New Zealand to inform any further law reform.[502] But again, it is

---

[500] Vandersteegen and others (n 247).
[501] Knetsch (n 475) 506. See also Helleringer (n 483).
[502] Buelens (n 499) 506.

160

Intersentia

far from clear whether there is an appetite among French and Belgian jurists to take no-fault compensation out of its tightly drawn subsidiary box, to challenge private law liability rules – no matter what the scientific and econometric evidence is in favour of a no-fault approach in these jurisdictions.[503]

The key learning to be found here from a functional comparison is that there are significant theoretical pitfalls to an 'incrementalist' approach to the development of no-fault compensation (either edging forwards towards comprehensiveness, or edging backwards towards the inclusion of fault-based principles). This is because distortions will emerge when policy choices informed by scientific evidence (about patient safety and patients' rights, for example) are forced to co-exist in the same system with inconsistent (or at least not precisely aligned) legal principles like fault, no-fault, solidarity and community responsibility. This finding is relevant to both the medical injury function and other functions of no-fault (comprehensive) compensation. More active management of the effect of policy choices on legal principles, and *vice versa*, is a possible way to mitigate this problem.

7.4. OVERVIEW OF FRENCH AND BELGIAN GUARANTEE FUNDS FOR AUTOMOBILE AND TERRORISM VICTIMS

In France the motor accident and terrorism victim schemes are presently handled together by one single *administrative* and public relations structure (governing two guarantee funds which remain nevertheless legally separate) that emphasises the concept of solidarity towards victims in its organisational structure.[504] What was originally the motor accidents fund has grown from its original mandate and now (as the *Fonds de garantie des assurances obligatoires de dommages* (FGAO)[505]) also covers accidents involving animals, uninsured cyclists and pedestrians, and some kinds of economic loss related to property damage caused by mining and technological accidents.[506] The system is not simply a passive organ that dispenses compensation: it is empowered to seek damages from responsible parties via the tool of subrogation (if those parties

---

[503] Vandersteegen and others (n 247); Barbot, Parizot and Winance (n 481); Kenneth Watson and Rob Kottenhagen, 'Patients' Rights, Medical Error and Harmonisation of Compensation Mechanisms in Europe' (2018) 25 *European Journal of Health Law* 1. But if the body of empirical evidence about the benefits of no-fault compensation for injury eventually grows to be overwhelming, then the morality (from a public interest perspective) of lawyers and legal scholars opposing wider no-fault law reform may need to be debated.

[504] See 'Mettre en œuvre la solidarité nationale envers les victimes' <https://www.fondsdegarantie.fr/en/guarantee-fund/the-missions-of-compensation/>.

[505] Article 15 Loi n° 51-1508 of 31 December 1951. The guarantee fund was most recently extended and modified by the Loi n° 2003-706 of 1 August 2003.

[506] See 'Les missions d'indemnisation' <https://www.fondsdegarantie.fr/fgao/missions/>.

can be identified).[507] The French terrorism victim compensation fund, *Fonds de garantie des victimes des actes de terrorisme et d'autres infraction* (FGTI),[508] covers both compensation for criminal offences and terrorism attack victims. Reminiscent of Québec's SAAQ coverage, the FGTI compensates French citizens and their dependants *worldwide* for loss flowing from terrorism attacks.

Meanwhile in Belgium, the motor guarantee fund (established in 1956,[509] and broadly equivalent to the French fund set up in the same era), has eventually morphed into a 'Common Guarantee Fund'. This general fund also has partial responsibility for the compensation of victims of technological accidents, which is a recent addition to its scope of responsibility.[510] Terrorism victims can be compensated via a recent legislative expansion[511] to the general Victim Compensation Fund, which was established in 1985.[512] There have been attempts to make accessing compensation administratively easier for terrorism victims,[513] but overall the fund has, according to some critics, proven to be rather awkward, complex and ultimately unjust for victims.[514] This is especially due to differing levels of compensation depending on social and immigration status, an approach that is not taken by the French FGTI. However, this fund has provided access to compensation for victims who previously would have had no recourse, and so the general impact of that innovation and extension of access to compensation should not be overlooked or underrated.

---

[507] 'Le recours contre les auteurs' <https://www.fondsdegarantie.fr/le-fonds-de-garantie/le-recours/>.

[508] The fund has its legislative underpinnings in Loi n° 77-5 of 3 January 1977. It was expanded to its current scope of covering terrorism victims and other crime victims by Loi n° 85-1407 of 30 December 1985; Loi n° 90-589 of 6 July 1990.

[509] Article 16 wet van 1 juli 1956 betreffende de verplichte aansprakelijkheidsverzekering inzake motorrijtuigen.

[510] Article 18 Wet van 13 november 2011 betreffende de vergoeding van de lichamelijke en morele schade ingevolge een technologisch ongeval. See also Larissa Vanhooff, 'Compensation Funds in Belgium' in Thierry Vansweevelt and Britt Weyts (eds), *Compensation Funds in Comparative Perspective* (Intersentia 2020); Jonas Knetsch, 'Compensation Funds in France and Germany' in Thierry Vansweevelt and Britt Weyts (eds), *Compensation Funds in Comparative Perspective* (Intersentia 2020).

[511] Wet van 18 juli 2017 betreffende de oprichting van het statuut van nationale solidariteit, de toekenning van een herstelpensioen en de terugbetaling van medische zorg ingevolge daden van terrorisme.

[512] Wet van 1 augustus 1985 houdende fiscale en andere bepalingen.

[513] Such as a single point of contact email address and phone number.

[514] Ryan Heath, '"Treat Every Victim the Same" Urges Brussels Terrorist Attacks Widow' *Politico Europe* (21 March 2017) <https://www.politico.eu/blogs/playbook-plus/2017/03/treat-every-victim-the-same-urges-brussels-terrorist-attacks-widow-charles-michel-jim-cain-cameron-cain-karen-northshield/>. More recently, United Nations Special Rapporteur Fionnuala Ní Aoláin has criticised the exclusion and discrimination in terms of compensation and other support available to victims of Belgian terrorist attacks – see 'Preliminary Findings of the Visit to Belgium' (United Nations Office of the High Commissioner for Human Rights 2018) <https://www.ohchr.org/EN/NewsEvents/Pages/DisplayNews.aspx?NewsID=23164&LangID=E>.

Terrorism victim compensation is an area where the French compensation funds seem likely to make some innovative developments (such as how to efficiently compensate both international and domestic victims) that would extend the application of no-fault to a broader category of claimants.[515]

7.5. FUNCTIONAL AND PURPOSIVE COMPARISON OF GENERAL RISKS COMPENSATION

As noted above, the FGAO and the FGTI in France have been directed since September 2017 to take a 'single shop' administrative and public-facing approach to their operations.[516] This undoubtedly comes across, on its face, as a sensible consolidation from a public administration and user-friendliness perspective. However, from a legal coherency perspective, the lack of a legal framework to regulate the overlap (or purposive consolidation) of the two guarantee funds is deeply concerning.

From a (non-legal) functional perspective, the creation of a simplified website with clear, plain-language information about possible entitlements to benefits closely mirrors the public facing portals of the four no-fault comprehensive compensation funds. This is the kind of 'single window' approach mooted by Knetsch (that the French legislature undertook in relation to medical and blood injuries compensation when it created the ONIAM),[517] but without the necessary legal underpinnings. It is not immediately clear why there have not been necessary legislative steps taken to formalise this administrative consolidation. Other than a shared national solidarity motivation,[518] it is not immediately obvious whether the FGAO and FGTI should continue functionally to 'live' together. Therefore, although there is some (legal) functional equivalence here between New Zealand and France in the 'everyday risks of life' category, it is impossible to draw further comparative conclusions at this point in time without legislative clarification about the FGAO/FGTI's joint operation and the precise definition of 'solidarity'.

---

[515] See 'France organizes international conference at UNESCO for aid to victims' (9 January 2017) <https://en.unesco.org/news/france-organizes-international-conference-unesco-aid-victims/> and 'Cap 2020: l'excellence au service des victimes' <https://www.fondsdegarantie.fr/en/guarantee-fund/the-guarantee-fund-corporate-project/>.

[516] Fonds de Garantie, 'The Guarantee Fund Corporate Project – Cap 2020: L'excellence Au Service Des Victimes' <https://www.fondsdegarantie.fr/en/guarantee-fund/the-guarantee-fund-corporate-project/>.

[517] Knetsch (n 510); Knetsch (n 475) para 639.

[518] The administratively combined funds have a slogan of *'Agir pour les victims au nom de la solidarité nationale'* or 'Act for the victims in the name of national solidarity' [sic].

7.6. PROBLEM: DOES 'SOLIDARITY' MEAN THE SAME THING AS 'COMMUNITY RESPONSIBILITY'?

The current legislative murkiness surrounding the FGAO and FGTI, glossed over by the concept of 'national solidarity', begs a further question from a comparative law perspective. Does 'national solidarity' (especially as it is conceived from the French perspective) mean the same thing as 'community responsibility' (which underpins the New Zealand ACC Scheme) for the purposes of compensation? And what conclusions can be drawn that are relevant to the principled development of no-fault (comprehensive) compensation funds?

From a comparative law perspective, the French concept of solidarity is challenging to pierce and to translate into equivalence with similar principles in other jurisdictions. It has not been extensively analysed in English-language academic liability law literature.[519] Solidarity has a specific political root, most specifically nineteenth-century French ideals about an idealistic fraternal society based on republican ethics.[520] The state, as a structure that is fully representative of all its citizens, guarantees support to its citizens – this is at the heart of solidarity. The financial cost of that guarantee is carried by contributions made by all individuals to the state. The principle of solidarity therefore also underpins the French social insurance system, which according to Dominique Thouvenin, is the antithesis of private insurance principles (which levies premiums based on individualised risk factors).[521] It also means that public (i.e. taxpayer) funding will generally be the source of any structure that has the 'solidarity' classification. But as Knetsch identified, there is significant vagueness in the precise boundaries of solidarity and particularly in terms of how it should apply to alternative redress systems.[522]

As mentioned above,[523] Knetsch's research on French and German compensation funds ultimately concluded that a compensation fund as a structure stands apart from the social welfare system. So, what does that then mean for the principle of solidarity, as it relates to a comparative analysis of no-fault comprehensive compensation funds? Because there is already functional equivalence between some of the French (and Belgian) compensation funds and

---

[519] But a useful overview of the concept for English-language legal scholars can be found in an appendix to a 2011 paper by Dominique Thouvenin on the ONIAM system. Dominique Thouvenin, 'French Medical Malpractice Compensation since the Act of March 4, 2002: Liability Rules Combined with Indemnification Rules and Correlated with Several Kinds of Proceedings' (2011) 4 *Drexel Law Review* 165.

[520] Gerard Soulier, 'Verbo Solidariti' [Solidarity], in Alain Rey (ed), *Le Dictionnaire Culturel en Langue Française* (2005) 864 cited in Thouvenin (n 519) 192.

[521] Thouvenin (n 519) 193.

[522] Knetsch (n 475) paras 89–91.

[523] Chapter 3, section 2.

Chapter 3. Review of Existing No-Fault Comprehensive Compensation Funds

the New Zealand ACC Scheme, the right approach here is to determine whether there is conceptual equivalence between solidarity and the New Zealand notion of 'community responsibility'.

The original Woodhouse Report defined 'community responsibility' as follows:[524]

> 'First, in the national interest, and as a matter of national obligation, the community must protect all citizens (including the self-employed) and the housewives who sustain them from the burden of sudden individual losses when their ability to contribute to the general welfare by their work has been interrupted by physical incapacity'.

The notions of national obligation and the protection of all citizens from unexpected loss burdens in this classic founding definition of community responsibility, has clear equivalence with core French solidarity ideals. The guarantee of support from the state to individual citizens is identical, when one undertakes a straightforward interpretative reading of both concepts. How that has been realised legislatively in the context of compensation funds – structures with general functional equivalence to one another and coverage for *all* individuals (not just those who have paid a contribution or levy) – also has equivalence.

There is also little difference between French-style solidarity and New Zealand-style community responsibility in terms of the actions of the hypothetical citizen within this bargain. The French solidarity concept recognises every citizen's contribution to social development,[525] and the New Zealand community responsibility concept recognises how modern society benefits from citizens' productive work.[526] In relation to compensation funds, what both concepts are theoretically silent on is why non-citizens should also be able to access entitlements. This can probably simply be best placed under an umbrella of fairness and non-discrimination and minimising the risk of incoherency within the schemes for identical victims. The consequences of discriminating between citizens and non-citizens in the everyday risks of life function are exemplified by the complications encountered by the Belgian (solidarity-based) terrorism compensation fund.[527]

One key point of difference that one might point to is that solidarity in the French sense is a guaranteed entitlement in exchange for a contribution towards the state coffers that funds that entitlement. But that argument only really

---

[524] Royal Commission to Inquire into and Report upon Workers Compensation, 'Part 2 – Introductory Survey' (Government Printing Office 1967) para 55.

[525] Thouvenin (n 519) 192.

[526] Royal Commission to Inquire into and Report upon Workers Compensation, 'Part 2 – Introductory Survey' (n 524) para 56.

[527] See n 514.

Intersentia

165

applies to social insurance systems where entitlement is limited to residents and taxpayers. A no-fault compensation fund – even French ones, such as the FGTI – can be available to someone who has paid no contribution. And the FGTI and FGAO are both completely funded by levies, returns on investments and the proceeds of subrogation actions, with no recourse to public funds.[528]

There has not been a clear restatement of the definition of New Zealand-style community responsibility in the legislation (which is unsurprising given the political convulsions in the ACC Scheme's scope), but the purpose of the 2001 Act is to 'enhance the public good and reinforce the social contract represented by the first accident compensation scheme'.[529] There is recent legislative affirmation of the goal that the ACC Scheme 'continues to meet society's expectations'.[530] Ken Oliphant has characterised modifications to the New Zealand ACC Scheme in the 2000s as demonstrating a shift towards 'personal injury viewed as a shared responsibility of the community and the individual'.[531] Richard Gaskins has argued that ACC's evolution has reflected a social contract based on individual will (and giving up the right to sue) rather than a concept of social solidarity.[532] However, Gaskins' comments were premised on the theories about decay of 'a shared sense of solidarity' and social cohesion in English-speaking countries and the import of law and economics analyses to the conceptualisation of compensation entitlements. Gaskins' comments are certainly in line with the purpose of the ACC Scheme as regards the application to the bar against civil proceedings,[533] but he did not consider the relevance or equivalence of French solidarity principles to the scheme generally.

From a public policy perspective, 'community responsibility' can be distilled as allowing a guaranteed automatic entitlement to reasonable compensation in exchange for the relinquishment of rights.[534] Most recently Simon Connell has said that the notion of community responsibility underpinning the ACC Scheme is predominantly embraced by those of a left-leaning political persuasion

---

[528] Fonds de Garantie, 'Chiffres Financiers – Rapport Annuel' (2017) <https://rapportdactivite. fondsdegarantie.fr/chiffres-financiers>; Fonds de Garantie, 'The History of FGAO' <https:// www.fondsdegarantie.fr/en/fgao-2/the-history-of-fgao/>; Fonds de Garantie, 'The History of FGTI' <https://www.fondsdegarantie.fr/en/fgti-2/the-history/>.

[529] Accident Compensation Act 2001 s 3.

[530] Explanatory Note Accident Compensation Amendment Bill 49-1 2018.

[531] Oliphant, 'Beyond Misadventure: Compensation for Medical Injuries in New Zealand' (n 78) 388.

[532] Richard Gaskins, 'The Enigma of Community Responsibility: Ethical Reflections on Accident Compensation' (2015) 46 *Victoria University of Wellington Law Review* 789.

[533] As was the issue at hand in *McGougan v DePuy International Limited* (n 56).

[534] Grant Duncan, 'New Zealand's Universal No-Fault Accident Compensation Scheme: Embedding Community Responsibility' in Joannah Luetjens, Michael Mintrom and Paul 't Hart (eds), *Successful Public Policy Lessons from Australia and New Zealand* (ANU Press 2019) 352 <http://press-files.anu.edu.au/downloads/press/n5314/pdf/ch14.pdf>.

Chapter 3. Review of Existing No-Fault Comprehensive Compensation Funds

(in contrast to a 'compulsory insurance' perspective preferred by those with a right-leaning political persuasion).[535] Simon Connell did not consider whether the French solidarity principle could be cross-referenced with community responsibility.

An extra point to be considered here is whether solidarity is relevant to the conceptual underpinnings of Québec's SAAQ. Solidarity is a philosophical concept is well-known within the Québec legal system (and Canadian society more widely since World War II), especially in relation to social insurance and taxation redistribution programmes.[536] But the SAAQ takes on functions wider than compensation – it is active in the regulatory management and administration of virtually all aspects of automobile transportation in the province. Accordingly, the Québec Ministers of Transport and Finance are responsible for the administration of the SAAQ legislative scheme (and the administration of the financial fund that underpins it), and *not* the Minister of Employment and Social Solidarity and the Minister of Health and Social Services.[537] The Canadian Supreme Court in *Godbout v Pagé* expanded the effective scope of the SAAQ scheme and affirmed the scheme's status as a 'social choice that reflected a social compromise'.[538] But there was no reference in this judgment to the concept of solidarity. The SAAQ is an example of a decision to actively manage the risk landscape with the creation of a complete legal system to both regulate behaviour and provide compensation. Functionally, it is obviously on the same footing as the New Zealand ACC Scheme for the purposes of compensating for transport injury, but this absence of solidarity principles is noteworthy. The SAAQ certainly matches Gaskins' formulation of a social contract based on individual will and the relinquishment of the right to sue.

What conclusions can therefore be drawn on this point? Firstly, there is sufficient evidence that, for comparative law purposes, the French concept of solidarity has equivalence with the New Zealand concept of community responsibility. Secondly, there also evidence that the classic formulations of both concepts do not completely explain and justify *all* the compensation entitlements available under French and New Zealand no-fault compensation funds (for example, the entitlements of non-citizens or non-residents). This leads to a third conclusion that both solidarity and community responsibility

---

[535] Connell (n 47) 17.

[536] Janine Brodie, 'Citizenship and Solidarity: Reflections on the Canadian Way' (2002) 6 *Citizenship Studies* 377 <https://www.tandfonline.com/action/journalInformation?journal Code=ccst20>.

[537] Automobile Insurance Act (Québec) s 204; Act respecting the Société de l'assurance automobile du Québec s 25.

[538] *Godbout v Pagé et al* (n 272) para 29.

Intersentia

167

need a political and legal clarification or re-statement *specifically* for the purpose of no-fault compensation funds. The structural proximity of compensation funds to insurance – which, as a concept, is fundamentally antithetical in nature to solidarity – reinforces the necessity of this restatement. As a subcategory, the difference between (or proximity of) solidarity and community responsibility for the purposes of social welfare schemes (which are separate to compensation funds) must also be addressed. As Knetsch concluded, solidarity/community responsibility does not have adequate normative underpinnings to carry the principled development of no-fault (comprehensive) compensation funds in the twenty-first century, nor can it address current problems within such funds. If it is too difficult to accurately define solidarity/community responsibility in a twenty-first-century compensation fund context, then the 'social compromise' approach of the SAAQ can give useful guidance (especially if regulatory prevention and deterrence/subrogation functions are given to a compensation fund for a specific function). Finally, it remains to be seen what long-term impacts the COVID-19 pandemic will have on the definition of solidarity and the expectations of citizens towards the state. The term 'solidarity' has certainly had renewed use and application during the pandemic, but it is not clear whether there has also been renewed exploration of its definition and purpose in the context of compensatory or extra-legal support structures.

8. PRINCIPLED COMPARISON WITH THE NORDIC APPROACH

Denmark, Finland, Norway and Sweden are civil jurisdictions that have enacted advanced medical incident and pharmaceutical schemes for different kinds of injuries in similar ways, featuring some parallels with the New Zealand approach in their effective elimination of tort litigation for injury. Their schemes illustrate a particularly Nordic approach to dispute resolution, social insurance and risk protection that favours mutual support, multiple insurance pools and avoiding adversarial dispute management.[539] From a comparative law perspective, it is therefore essential to understand that the costs of most losses flowing from tortious behaviour are socially distributed to taxpayers.[540] This has impacts on the comparative law conclusions we can draw.

---

[539] Macleod, Urho and Hodges (n 217) 163.
[540] Bjarte Askeland, 'Basic Questions of Tort Law from a Norweigan Perspective' in Helmut Koziol (ed), *Basic Questions of Tort Law from a Comparative Perspective* (1st edn, Jan Sramek Verlag 2015) 103.

Chapter 3. Review of Existing No-Fault Comprehensive Compensation Funds

8.1. OVERVIEW OF THE NORDIC COMPENSATION FUNDS FOR MEDICAL AND PHARMACEUTICAL INJURY

The most important thing to know about the Nordic compensation fund systems from a comparative law perspective is that they are part of a holistic dispute resolution culture that aims to make private law solutions like litigation the rare exception rather than the default redress solution.[541] In contrast to the reactive approach detailed above in relation to the French and Belgian compensation fund systems, this could be thought of as a proactive approach to managing redress, that rounds out the edges of other compensation and support structures. Tort law does of course exist in Nordic jurisdictions, but tort liability is viewed in those jurisdictions as unsatisfactory as a default solution in the context of traditional litigation or compensation fund systems. This is particularly relevant to the design of compensation funds for medical incidents, because tort liability is viewed in Nordic states as downright dangerous and not conducive to information sharing and learning in a medical context.[542] However, tort principles of damages calculation are relevant to all the Scandinavian compensation funds.[543]

Macleod and Hodges' text on redress schemes includes a useful and thorough chapter co-authored by Matti Urho, a Finnish no-fault compensation funds researcher.[544] This gives a consolidated overview of the compensation landscape across multiple functions in Sweden, Denmark, Finland and Norway, and where no-fault (or rather 'no-blame') fits within it. Medical injury and pharmaceutical injury are the functions that are most relevant to compare with New Zealand, and also my findings about France and Belgium. It is also possible to make a limited comparative analysis on the general risks function.

---

[541] In the mid-twentieth century there was a significant reshaping of basic legal principles (including tort) in Scandinavian countries that coincided with rapid development of expansive social security frameworks. 'It was emphasised, in particular with regard to personal injury, that the goal must be to secure the needs of everyone. The vision was to replace tort law – at least in the area of personal injuries – with a collective insurance system.' Within legal thinking there is also a deep scepticism of notions of 'traditions' (like tort liability) which are thought by Scandinavian jurists to disguise value judgements rather than being based on evidence or critical reasoning. For a general overview of the development of Scandinavian tort law theory, see Håkan Andersson, 'The Tort Law Culture(s) of Scandinavia' (2012) 3 *Journal of European Tort Law* 210. The quote cited here can be found at page 217 of that article. For an overview of the similar Norwegian tort landscape, see Trine-lise Wilhelmsen and Birgitte Hagland, 'Norway' in Britt Weyts (ed), *International Encyclopaedia for Tort Law* (Wolters Kluwer 2017).

[542] Macleod and Hodges (n 217) 164.

[543] ibid 165.

[544] Sonia Macleod, Matti Urho and Christopher Hodges, 'Part III: Nordic States' in Macleod and Hodges (n 217).

Intersentia

8.2. FUNCTIONAL AND PURPOSIVE COMPARISON OF GENERAL RISKS COMPENSATION IN THE NORDIC COUNTRIES

There are obvious purposive similarities between the Nordic and New Zealand approaches – they both widely exclude or minimise the relevance of tort liability and private law compensation for most types of injury. But in Nordic countries, this is done by 'sending the loss elsewhere', rather than eliminating liability through a universal no-fault scheme. This is because the Nordic funds typically do not aim to be the primary source of compensation. Insurance companies, social insurance, and local and central government can be seen to work co-operatively in Nordic jurisdictions to manage the allocation of a victim's loss. Separately, it is only the Danish medical injury and drug injury compensation fund system that takes a roughly similar publicly-funded single entity approach, like New Zealand, with a government minister having ultimate responsibility for the scheme.

This matches a structured approach generally to general risks in the Nordic states – there are multiple tiers that compensate need of all kinds – national social insurance, compulsory employer insurance for workplace injury, social insurance and compensation fund systems.[545] This has the effect of reducing the functional burden of the no-fault compensation funds and effectively eliminating most of any unallocated loss. In contrast, the New Zealand ACC Scheme is limited in its statutory purpose to the creation of a 'fair and sustainable scheme for managing personal injury'[546] in order to minimise the occurrence and impact of injury. Comparing the models functionally and structurally, the Nordic approach can be classified as a completely socialised and holistic perspective on the management of losses flowing from the general risks that present themselves in daily life. Specific functions of compensation fund exist to 'catch' losses that are not captured elsewhere in the system, using an active management approach to replace ordinary civil liability concepts. In contrast, New Zealand has tried to simply 'catch' as many losses as possible in one large structural net that replaces civil liability for most functions but does not *manage* the landscape further.

In one sense, there is actually closer legal and purposive proximity between the Nordic and the current French and Belgian approaches (than to New Zealand) – the Nordic, French and Belgian compensation funds do not bear as heavy a burden because they are not responsible for so much loss. But in contrast to the Franco-Belgian 'add-on' characterisation of a no-fault compensation fund, the Nordic approach is a complete evolutionary change to the framing of liability. The Nordic systems round off a multi-layered state and private insurance

---

[545] Andersson (n 541).
[546] Accident Compensation Act 2001 s 3.

Chapter 3. Review of Existing No-Fault Comprehensive Compensation Funds

structure in a way that is theoretically consistent with those jurisdictions' general approach to liability and theory. The French and Belgian medical injury compensation funds do not appear to be theoretically consistent with the rest of their (sometimes differing) liability law landscape, except perhaps where the nebulous concept of 'solidarity' comes into play.[547] The New Zealand legal landscape, meanwhile, does not have the theoretical consistency of the Nordic states – the purposive basis of access to support under the ACC Scheme and the social welfare system (and the disqualifications for them) are currently vastly different.[548] New Zealand, like the Nordic countries, has actively carved away the relevance of the principle of *casum sentit dominus* by using a compensation fund – but (unlike the Nordic states) New Zealand has not continued to actively manage what that then means for non-accidental or non-covered loss and civil liability generally.

8.3. FUNCTIONAL AND PURPOSIVE COMPARISON OF MEDICAL INJURY COMPENSATION IN THE NORDIC COUNTRIES

Turning to the specific function of medical injury, the key point to analyse from a comparative law perspective is the nature of the triggers for compensation under the Nordic and New Zealand funds. This means the policy choice (and its corresponding translation into law) about the actions of the health professional that will lead to the claimant being allowed to claim compensation (because the negative results that flowed from the treatment were not simply an ordinary or expected consequence of treatment).

---

[547] Although French society has accepted a more socialised distributive approach to losses, that includes subsidisation of compensation funds – fundamentally the French legal system still requires victims to bear their own losses, and those who have can show they have suffered a loss through the fault of another are entitled to full compensation (even if the idea of 'full compensation' is in reality, somewhat of a fallacy). See Olivier Moréteau, 'Basic Questions of Tort Law from a French Perspective' in Helmut Koziol (ed), *Basic Questions of Tort Law from a Comparative Perspective* (1st edn, Jan Sramek Verlag 2015). Belgian courts in the past century have not adhered to the same interpretation of civil liability principles as their French neighbours. But fundamentally the function of Belgian liability law is also to force losses to fall where they lie, and compensation is only available when a victim can show responsibility against a liable party. As in France, an injured party is entitled to reparation/full compensation once he or she can show causation and liability. See Marc Kruithof, 'Tort Law' in Marc Kruithof and Walter De Bondt (eds), *Introduction to Belgian Law* (2nd edn, Wolters Kluwer 2017); Marc Kruithof, 'Belgium' in Britt Weyts (ed), *International Encyclopaedia for Tort Law* (Wolters Kluwer 2017) 33–37, 133.

[548] There is no clearly stated entitlement to social welfare benefits under the Social Security Act 2018, and this is significantly different to the clearly stated entitlements within the Accident Compensation Act 2001. The courts have recognised and allowed this inconsistency within the broader social security system. See Stephens (n 44); *Trevethick v Ministry of Health* [2008] NZCA 397.

Intersentia

171

'Avoidable' patient injuries are compensated for by compulsory statutory compensation fund systems in all four Nordic jurisdictions, that are funded by a mix of healthcare providers' insurance premiums and state monies (depending on the jurisdiction). Sweden historically had voluntary insurance arrangements for compensating patient injuries, but these were replaced in 1997 by a mandatory statutory scheme that requires compensation to be paid in the case of avoidable patient injury[549] in a public or private setting (with no reference to the opinion or behaviour of the caregiver).[550] The other jurisdictions follow a similar route. In Denmark, all patient injury compensation claims (as well as vaccine and medicine injury compensation) are managed by the statutory Patient Compensation Association system.[551] In Finland patient claims are processed by the Patient Insurance Centre, and compensation is a top-up to social insurance benefits.[552] In Norway the Patient Compensation System processes patient claims, and compensation will generally only be paid if there was a treatment failing that caused more than NOK10,000 (approximately €1,000) of defined financial loss.[553]

The first drug injury compensation funds system was established in Sweden in 1978, and this scheme operates on a voluntary basis, using insurance principles.[554] Finland's voluntary drug injury system was established as an insurance pool and horizontal insurance-based network.[555] Norway established a mandatory scheme under product liability legislation in Norway, and it has close

---

[549] The six categories of compensable injury under the legislation are avoidable treatment injury, material-related injury, diagnostic injury, infection injury, accident-related injury (in a medical setting) and medication injury. See Macleod and Hodges (n 217) 177–178.

[550] Most patient injury compensation is processed and paid by a mutual insurer (used by most public health service providers) called Löf (Landstingens Ömsesidiga Försäkringsbolag) – see 'If you are injured in healthcare' <https://lof.se/other-languages/>. Any claims not covered by Löf are handled by the Patient Insurance Association – see 'Patient Insurance Association' <https://www.pff.se/extra/information-in-english/>.

[551] See 'FAQ for patients' <https://pebl.dk/en/faq-for-patients>.

[552] See 'Types of injury' <http://www.pvk.fi/en/For-those-suspecting-an-injury/types-of-injury/>.

[553] See 'Hva skal til for å få erstatning for en pasientskade?' ['What is required to receive compensation for patient injury?'] <https://www.npe.no/no/Erstatningssoker/Soke-erstatning/Hva-skal-til-for-erstatning-pasientskade/>.

[554] Läkemedelsförsäkrings (insurance for injuries caused by pharmaceuticals). This was an entity established by pharmaceutical companies, following political pressure from the Swedish government, for the purpose of purchasing insurance to pay pharmaceutical injury claims. There have been some recent modifications to the governance and insurance management structure of the compensation fund system. There is close practical and structural involvement of all relevant stakeholders – the pharmaceutical companies, patients, hospitals and doctors. See Urho (n 2) 471–473 and 'A unique type of insurance' <https://lff.se/a-unique-type-of-insurance/for-patients/>.

[555] Urho states that the Thalidomide disaster was the key motivation for the establishment of the Finnish system. A network or 'co-operative' insurance approach was preferred, with the active involvement of industry. As of 2012 the relevant insurance coverage is provided

Chapter 3. Review of Existing No-Fault Comprehensive Compensation Funds

operational links with the medical incident compensation fund.[556] Denmark's mandatory system has close links to the public health system introduced as a supplement to the medical incident compensation fund system.[557] The publicly funded single entity approach of the Danish medical injury and drug injury scheme also has similarities to the Québec vaccine injury scheme.

As discussed in the section on France and Belgium (section 7.2), the New Zealand legislature attempted in 2005 to eliminate fault-based concepts for medical injury that were introduced in 1992 (medical error leading to leading to misadventure).[558] The trigger now is that the injury must be caused by treatment (by a registered healthcare provider), and was not a necessary part or ordinary consequence of treatment (taking all the circumstances of clinical knowledge and the patient's underlying health condition).[559] In contrast, the Nordic countries' 'no-blame' approach (to specifically exclude fault) is used when reviewing an *irregularity* in treatment that triggers an entitlement to compensation. The standard of the trigger is an 'avoidable treatment injury' from the perspective of an experienced specialist (Sweden and Denmark)[560] or experienced medical professional (Finland).[561] Norway allows for distinctions to be made between different kinds of practitioners (e.g. specialists and general practitioners) and different clinical settings (e.g. small local hospitals vs large tertiary care hospitals).[562]

On the face of it, it therefore looks like different tests are being used in the Nordic countries and New Zealand. The New Zealand ACC scheme does

---

by Suomen Keskinäinen Lääkevahinkovakuutusyhtiö (LVY) (the Pharmaceutical Injuries Insurance), which was established by the pharmaceutical company network (called the Finnish Co-operative for Pharmaceutical Injury Indemnities). See 'Insurance pays' <https://www.laakevahinko.fi/in-english/insurance-pays/> and ibid 477–479.

[556] The system was established by the Product Liability Act of 1988. All pharmaceutical manufacturers must be members of the Legemiddelansvarsforeningen (LAF) association, which gathers contributions to purchase the necessary insurance to fund compensation (that insurance is now provided by a captive state insurance entity). Claims under the pharmaceutical compensation fund system are processed by Norsk pasientskadeerstatning, the Norwegian medical incident compensation fund system. Urho's research revealed that the scheme has been particularly successful because it is folded under product liability legislation, thus avoiding the boundary issues present in the Swedish and Finnish schemes. For an overview see 'Norsk pasientskadeerstatning gjennom 30 år' <https://www.npe.no/en/About-NPE/Organisation/historien-til-norsk-pasientskadeordning/> and ibid 473–475.

[557] As in Norway, Danish drug injury compensation is thought of in the product liability legislative context. A key contrast with the other Scandinavian systems is that the Danish system is publicly funded. This, as well as the management of all claims by a single entity, makes the system the closest European comparator to the New Zealand compensation fund system. See 'History' <https://pebl.dk/en/about-the-danish-patient-compensation-association/history>, 'FAQ' <https://pebl.dk/en/faq-for-patients> and ibid 475–476.

[558] Accident Rehabilitation and Compensation Insurance Act 1992.

[559] Accident Compensation Act 2001 s 32.

[560] Macleod and Hodges (n 217) 177, 198.

[561] ibid 241.

[562] ibid 270.

Intersentia

173

not immediately *appear* to require a reference to a standard of treatment, but as noted above this is a reference point (to varying degrees) in the different Nordic states. Joanna Manning in 2014 pointed specifically to medical injury cases involving a failure to treat (or to give timely treatment) as the location of the continued festering of fault within New Zealand no-fault treatment injury compensation.[563] That trend she identified in 'failure to treat' cases has been continued in recent judicial decisions, and thus the relevance of a fault-based standard of conduct by practitioner continues to (paradoxically) exist in a comprehensive no-fault fund.[564] Manning argued that the Swedish and Danish retrospective 'avoidability' standard of a specialist would have been preferable and would have eliminated the need to reference to negligence concepts.[565] Although the New Zealand Court of Appeal in *Adlam v ACC* allowed a type of Danish and Swedish 'experienced specialist' standard to be used,[566] that standard has not since been applied consistently.[567]

Now, what is the relevance of this specific medical injury point to no-fault comprehensive compensation funds generally? If there are slightly different tests being used, what is the point of these different jurisdictions' funds being compared in this function? I believe that the usefulness of a comparison is the revelation of an important contextual issue about the impact of the legal landscape on a no-fault compensation fund's operations and legal effects. Based on what has been observed about the existence and operation no-fault comprehensive compensation funds generally, compared in a limited functional way with the Nordic states, I submit that no different results would flow from an official 'avoidability'-based standard in New Zealand. Avoidability is likely to end up being interpreted (even where the legislation pointed expressly to the Swedish and Danish schemes) with an infusion of negligence based principles.[568]

---

[563] Manning, 'Plus ça change, plus c'est la même chose: Negligence and treatment Injury in New Zealand's accident compensation scheme' (n 443) 33–37.

[564] Most notably Joanna M Manning, '"Fair, Simple, Speedy and Efficient"? Barriers to Access to Justice in the Health and Disability Commissioner's Complaints Process in New Zealand' (2018) 4 New Zealand Law Review 611 <http://www.legislation.govt.nz/act/public/1994/0088/latest/viewpdf.aspx>; *Crawford v Accident Compensation Corporation* (n 497); *Adlam v Accident Compensation Corporation* [2017] NZCA 457.

[565] Manning, 'Plus Ça Change, plus c'est La Même Chose: Negligence and Treatment Injury in New Zealand's Accident Compensation Scheme' (n 443) 51.

[566] *Adlam v Accident Compensation Corporation* (n 564) para 72.

[567] The High Court in *ACC v Ng* refers to a standard of a 'reasonably competent health professional' and the District Court in *Crawford v ACC* mention simply 'a departure from a professional standard'. Thus both cases cite *Adlam v ACC*, but they do not actually apply the specific Swedish-Danish specialist 'avoidability' standard set by the Court of Appeal. See *Accident Compensation Corporation v Ng* (n 497) para 93; *Crawford v Accident Compensation Corporation* (n 497) para 38.

[568] In my view, this confusing situation is not helped by recent tort law commentary which approves of a Swedish-Danish avoidability standard, but then couches it in negligence terms. 'The approach taken in *Adlam*, with the focus simply on what an experienced specialist in

Chapter 3. Review of Existing No-Fault Comprehensive Compensation Funds

In my view, this is for contextual reasons that can be observed from a comparative law analysis. The tort and social compensation landscape is more actively managed and strictly controlled in the Nordic states. The compensation fund is not the primary and most essential source of compensation for the claimant. The consequences of a decision about compensation fund coverage are not as loaded and devastating as they are in New Zealand, where a claimant can only look at meagre social insurance offerings for help if there is no ACC 'treatment injury' cover. The impact of the concepts 'avoidability' and 'no-blame' are therefore not as loaded with consequences in Nordic countries, and it is easier overall for the system to utilise a simple factual retrospective test. It has already been recognised that an 'avoidability' test with reference to a specialist standard could result in all undiagnosed or incorrectly treated illnesses falling within the scope of the ACC Scheme. Judges are likely to be extremely reluctant to issue judgments which significantly expand the scope of the ACC Scheme on the basis of a legal standard that is not expressly set out in the legislation.[569] A reversion to a standard that is closer to the ordinary common law negligence-based standard (that of an ordinary skilled doctor, which is much harder for the applicant to meet) has already been observed in both *ACC v Ng*[570] and *Crawford v ACC*.[571]

What is therefore actually causing the difference in effect between the Nordic and New Zealand landscape is both the formulation of the relevant test *and* the surrounding functional and structural compensation landscape. For a no-fault comprehensive compensation fund to function as intended it is therefore clear that you have to solve both issues to have logical and coherent legal results. Using contextual comparative law considerations here, we can solve the problem of why a similarly structured no-fault tool to solve the same functional problem in one jurisdiction is leading to different results in another jurisdiction.

9. CONCLUSIONS

There are number of key learnings that can be concluded from the descriptions and analysis in this chapter. These conclusions partially answer my first and third

---

the field would have done or decided, may help in achieving such a result [avoiding a blame culture and fostering co-operation]. Nothing done or not done by the doctor concerned needs to be characterised as negligent, even if negligence would in fact be established in a common law action.' – Todd and others (n 28) 57.

[569] In contrast to using advancements in known medical knowledge to allow for more cases to fall within the existing legal framework, as with non-work related asbestos cover in *Calver (Estate of Trevarthen) v Accident Compensation Corporation* (n 62). See section 2.2 above.

[570] *Accident Compensation Corporation v Ng* (n 497) para 93.

[571] *Crawford v Accident Compensation Corporation* (n 497) para 38.

Intersentia

175

research questions, and reveal issues that need to be addressed more deeply in subsequent chapters.

a. A no-fault comprehensive compensation fund is *harder to establish* than a more limited scheme, for political and legal incompatibility reasons. The Victorian, wider Australian, French and Belgian experiences show that a step-by-step transition from a limited to a more comprehensive model is also unlikely to be successful. This is because of the irreconcilable incompatibility between a no-fault and a fault-based system. *This partially answers the first research question.*

b. Once established, a no-fault comprehensive compensation fund is in the long run *easier to maintain* than its more limited cousins, especially if the courts have some freedom to modestly refine and confirm the limits of a wide scope of cover. This is displayed by the Canadian and New Zealand funds. *This partially answers the first research question.*

c. Significant changes to the fund's legal scope are best handled by the legislature. However a no-fault comprehensive fund will be difficult to modify incrementally without creating significant inconsistencies. The wider the functional scope of the fund, the more magnified the effects of even slight changes will be, even where there are attempts to limit the changes functionally. This has been experienced by the New Zealand ACC Scheme recently in relation to an attempted extension for mental health cover for specific terrorist attack victims. Periodic scheme review might be the only way to manage this, and would both allow inconsistencies that have emerged in individual cases and new scientific knowledge about injury to be accommodated. *This partially answers the first and third research questions, and will be explored more deeply in later chapters.*

d. A *clear definition* of how the fund interacts with other fields of compensation and liability and compensation structures will prevent legal inconsistencies and mitigate unexpected consequences. An incrementalist approach limited to specific functions is unlikely to be sufficient. We see that this has been done well by the Canadian and Victorian funds in relation to the intersection with work-related injury, but less well by the New Zealand scheme across a number of functions (including crime victim reparation top-up payments). This might be affected by the universal nature of the New Zealand ACC Scheme, which can never achieve legal and regulatory 'dominance' over one field, as the Victorian and Canadian transport funds can. However it could be managed by periodic scheme review, as noted at the previous point. This kind of periodic scheme review would also avoid administrative consolidations that have no legislative underpinnings, which has been observed in France. *This partially answers the first research question.*

Chapter 3. Review of Existing No-Fault Comprehensive Compensation Funds

e. Once a total bar against tort proceedings has been established, it puts the no-fault comprehensive compensation fund structure into *a separate hybrid legal structure*. This point of divergence is now well-established, because of the longevity and stability of all four comprehensive funds. It has been affirmed by judicial statements in New Zealand, Australia and Canada. Comparison with tort and social insurance compensation functions *for the purposes of delivering no-fault compensation to the victim* should be limited to where there is specific reference within legislation and regulation to those form of entitlements. *This is a general conclusion that partially answers the first research question, but raises points to be considered in subsequent chapters to answer the second research question.*

f. *Any maintenance of access to tort actions by claimants* for compensation, even in very limited cases as in Victoria, *leads to significantly increased cost and complexity*. Where there is a universal indemnity offered in statute by the fund to most 'defendants', the public end up shouldering the financial burden of the carve-out. Given the fact that the defendant usually does not 'pay', there is no apparent legal or philosophical justification for this choice within a no-fault comprehensive compensation fund. This is a reflection of the fundamental incompatibility of a no-fault system with a fault-based system for the purposes of compensating the victim. *This partially answers the first research question. This conclusion also raises further questions in relation to the use of subrogation and public tort liability that will be more deeply explored in subsequent chapters.*

g. The fusion of the concepts of rehabilitation and prevention with the concept of compensation in no-fault comprehensive funds represents *a marriage of a legal structure with scientific knowledge*. Instead of a tort *theory* of deterrence linked to the payment of compensation, strategies and programmes for the reduction of future harm risk are based on scientific knowledge of actual harm that has occurred (and been compensated). No-fault comprehensive compensation funds have therefore proven themselves to be well suited to deftly handling the *liability and compensation risks of new technologies such as e-scooters and automated cars. This partially answers the first and third research questions, and will be explored more deeply in subsequent chapters to fully answer the third research question.*

h. Based on a limited functional comparison, the *French concept of 'solidarity'* is *broadly equivalent to the concept of 'community responsibility'* that underpins the New Zealand ACC Scheme. However this is not the same as the 'social choice' that has underpinned the Québec SAAQ. Both solidarity and the community responsibility principle have also shown themselves to be inadequate to alone underpin the further development of no-fault comprehensive compensation funds (or indeed any compensation funds). A legislative restatement of the meaning of these principles is required.

For the purposes of compensation funds design and development, this restatement should have reference to both French and New Zealand funds, because of this philosophical equivalence. *This partially answers the first research question.*

i. The *no-blame/avoidability tests for medical treatment injury in Nordic countries will be difficult to replicate in a no-fault comprehensive fund,* because they will lead to significant increases in the number of claims. In the absence of a legislative confirmation that this increase is permissible, the attempted use of Nordic-style avoidability tests in New Zealand have resulted in the continued creep of negligence-based legal standards into determinations of entitlement. This has produced uneven results that are not consistent with the current purpose of the ACC Scheme provisions on treatment injury. A contextual comparison reveals that Nordic country standards are actually successful because most losses are already managed by other efficient statutory compensation structures before they reach the compensation fund. *This partially answers the first research question.*

CHAPTER 4

KEY PILLARS

1. INTRODUCTION

Much of the existing research about no-fault compensation funds in general has been focused on the legal benefits and drawbacks compared to a fault-based system. However these studies have been often approached from a sceptical viewpoint – are these funds ever a realistic alternative, in limited cases, to traditional liability (including strict liability) or insurance frameworks? Only recently have there been attempts to undertake comparative law analysis of how successful these schemes are in fact, and what are the core elements of their success – and what are their key problems.[1] An identification of the key pillars of no-fault comprehensive compensation funds allows for the next step of analysis to be undertaken on a more thorough and informed basis – specifically the more precise identification of these schemes' benefits, their fundamental drawbacks and areas for improvement, and the circumstances to which they are suited (or not).

The comparative law analysis of four large mature systems in the previous chapter enabled an identification of the key characteristics of these big funds, and a limited functional comparison with some relevant European non-comprehensive funds. In this chapter, there is an analysis of some the key pillars common to multiple jurisdictions, for the successful establishment, administration, and operation of no-fault comprehensive compensation funds. There is also an assessment of some of the common difficulties and problematic elements of these schemes.

There are many possible key pillars that could be identified, but those most relevant to a comparative legal analysis have been selected. It is interesting to identify and analyse these key pillars because the ACC, the TAC, the SAAQ and the MPI are all mature compensation and liability exclusion ecosystems. There has not been a comparative law study of these four compensation funds as

---

[1] Sonia Macleod and Christopher Hodges, 'Part IX: Conclusions' in Sonia Macleod and Christopher Hodges (eds), *Redress Schemes for Personal Injuries* (1st edn, Hart Publishing 2017); Thierry Vansweevelt and others, 'Comparative Analysis of Compensation Funds' in Thierry Vansweevelt and Britt Weyts (eds), *Compensation Funds in Comparative Perspective* (Intersentia 2020).

mature, standalone systems that identifies the common key positive and negative elements of their structures. In order to gather further useful information, the funds themselves were surveyed on various aspects of these key pillars. This facilitates an analysis that goes beyond the issues already discussed and also considers the payment of compensation, disputes and funding.

The key learnings in this chapter relate to:

a. The balancing of legal philosophy in the establishment of a compensation fund.
b. The speed of processing claims and paying compensation, contrasted with the legal and operational challenges this poses for the fund itself.
c. The calculation of quantum in a no-fault comprehensive compensation fund and the purpose of compensation and its calculation.
d. The core elements of dispute resolution that are common to all comprehensive no-fault compensation funds, including their advantages and disadvantages.
e. The methods of funding no-fault comprehensive compensation funds. This includes an assessment of their suitability to underpin this kind of legal structure as well as their sustainability.
f. The possibilities for subrogation within no-fault comprehensive compensation funds, and the results that flow from the selected approach to subrogation.

2. ESTABLISHMENT: KEY PHILOSOPHICAL STEPS AND CHALLENGES

It is a significant undertaking for a jurisdiction to create a no-fault comprehensive compensation fund. Unlike an add-on compensation fund that covers merely limited losses where the tortfeasor is unavailable or absent,[2] we have seen that a comprehensive fund that is publicly administered (almost) completely supplants the tort system in the relevant functions and replaces a private insurance market for a particular broad category of loss in most circumstances. As discussed in Chapter 3, there were also varying degrees of resistance from interested stakeholders (such as lawyers' associations, insurers, workers' unions) in each of the selected jurisdictions to the proposed shift from a fault-based system to a comprehensive no-fault environment. A comparative law analysis of these establishment challenges is therefore relevant and useful to the development or expansion of compensation funds, both large and small.

---

[2] The 'impossibility' justification is a feature of the classic guarantee fund that exists in European jurisdictions for, for example, hit-and-run motor vehicle accidents – see Vansweevelt and others (n 1) 193–195.

In this section, the big four funds are used as examples to analyse how it is possible to define and choose no-fault as a liability choice for the compensation of a very broad category of victims. This analysis reveals the key theoretical pillars of establishing a comprehensive no-fault compensation fund.

When a jurisdiction decides to implement a no-fault compensation fund it amounts to either a complete or partial departure from tort law. We have seen in the four funds that their framework results in a broad, but statutorily specified, category of injury victims being compensated for their losses on a no-fault basis. This compensation source is made the compulsory and default source of redress; access to other sources of compensation is severely limited.

What is the purpose of (non-contractual) liability, as a concept? The classic principle underpinning tort law in most jurisdictions is *casum sentit dominus* 'the owner bears the loss' (modified in the form of *neminem laedere* 'general duty of care/duty not to harm anyone' in French tort law), which creates a default position of the victim carrying the loss unless he or she can show that someone else is responsible for it. This section discusses the challenges of defining and choosing no-fault, and the divorcing of liability from the calculation of compensation.

In the establishment of all four big funds that are analysed in this project, the choice of no-fault was not made purely because of legal theoretical choices and a desire to conduct an experiment in liability. The problems with an existing fault-based model were identified at the time of these systems' establishment, but the use of no-fault was mostly a means to an end. For example:

a. The current purpose of the New Zealand legislative scheme is to 'enhance the public good and reinforce the social contract represented by the first accident compensation scheme' by providing for a fair and sustainable scheme for managing personal injury, with the twin goals of minimising the incidence of injury and the impact (economic, social and personal) of injury in the community.[3] The purpose of the original establishing legislation of the ACC Scheme was to

> 'promote general safety with a view to preventing accidents and minimising injury … to promote … rehabilitation … so as to seek to restore all such earners and persons to the fullest physical, mental, social, vocational, and economic usefulness of which they are capable … [and] to make provision for [their] compensation.'[4]

Therefore, the use of no-fault and the alteration of liability structures have always been the means of facilitating this social contract that establishes

---

[3] Accident Compensation Act 2001 s 3; Accident Compensation Corporation, 'Briefing to the Incoming Minister' (2017) 6 <https://www.acc.co.nz/assets/corporate-documents/minister-briefing-2017.pdf>.

[4] Accident Compensation Act 1972 s 4.

a statutory right to personal injury compensation, rather than being an end in itself. There has never been a suggestion that no-fault should be expanded to non-injury liability, such as economic or property loss caused by natural disaster.

b.   The TAC scheme did not have the same social purpose set in its legislation as the New Zealand scheme. There was a significant degree of philosophic grappling with the effect of no-fault and its impact on individuals' civil justice rights, i.e. the elimination of the right to sue – a matter that was brought into the public sphere by the relevant legal practitioner bodies.[5] However the specific practical motivation was the financial unsustainability of the add-on no-fault scheme that existed at that time.[6] The way that no-fault was ultimately chosen and selected in Victoria was due to political compromise. In recent times, the TAC itself has taken on the mantle of defining its own purpose, specifically that it aims to be the 'the world's best social insurer. Social insurers are responsible for prevention, compensation and rehabilitation, and we are striving to be the best in the world. We identify as a social insurer because our outcomes are about people'.[7] Therefore, at the time of establishment, no-fault was used as a means to address existing problems within the previous motor vehicle injury compensation framework – but there was no consensus on the philosophical merits of no-fault for all injury as an end in itself. More recently, no-fault is the means by which the TAC aims to achieve its self-described goals.

c.   In the development of the SAAQ scheme the arbitrariness of a fault-based system, inadequate compensation, slow resolution of claims, and complex insurance pricing were all noted as problems with the status quo.[8] The Gauvin Report concluded that the abolition of the fault principle was necessary and that a universal compulsory[9] no-fault insurance covering bodily injury and property damage was also necessary. Therefore, no-fault was a means by which the aim of better management of the financial and negative societal costs of a social risk could be achieved. There was no consensus on no-fault as a legal philosophical choice, because there was significant resistance to the removal of access to court-based remedies.

d.   The review of traffic injury compensation that led to the report that established the MPI was largely a consequence of a public backlash against

---

5   Ian Malkin, 'Victoria's Transport Accident Reforms – In Perspective' (1987) 16 *Melbourne University Law Review* 254.

6   ibid 260.

7   Transport Accident Commission, 'TAC 2020 Strategy' 7 <https://www.tac.vic.gov.au/__data/assets/pdf_file/0009/192753/TAC_Strategy2020_UPDATE_WEB.pdf>.

8   Québec Government, 'Rapport Du Comité d'étude Sur l'assurance-Automobile' (1974) 9–11.

9   Gauvin proposed that the scheme initially be managed by private insurance for five years, but if the results were unsatisfactory then a single public insurer should manage the scheme.

significant automobile insurance premium increases in 1987.[10] The stability of motor vehicle insurance rates under a new no-fault scheme was a clearly stated purpose of the Manitoba legislature when the relevant legislation was passed, and remains a key focus of the scheme today.[11] No-fault was and remains a means to an end of financial stability in insurance costs for road users. Therefore, we cannot point to any strong theoretical underpinnings for this legislative choice. It is worthwhile therefore, to sketch out a definition of no-fault and its relationship to liability in the context of a comprehensive no-fault compensation fund.

Based on the observation of the establishment of these four funds, we do not have a clear theoretical definition of no-fault for the purpose of establishing such funds. Technically, for the benefit of legal theory purists, it is arguable that the creation of a no-fault comprehensive compensation fund is not necessarily an erasure of the *casum sentit dominus* principle, as it is simply creating an avenue for the loss to automatically fall under a statutory scheme in a given set of circumstances. In some ways this is no different to strict liability. However in practice the creation of a no-fault scheme, whether large or small, is certainly a displacement of the default position that exists in both common and civil law jurisdictions (often enshrined by civil law codes in the latter). Both strict liability and no-fault schemes, as alternatives to ordinary tort liability, remove the need for the claimant to show the liability of another party in order to claim compensation. The key difference between them is that a strict liability scheme *automatically assigns* liability to a particular party, whereas a no-fault scheme completely *eliminates the relevance of liability* to the calculation of compensation for the victim.[12] Ultimately, it appears that no-fault was used as a means to achieve sweeping social and financial goals for a certain category of physical losses, with significant legal consequences. The use of no-fault in a very broad way is therefore a non-legal and social choice that supplants traditional legal frameworks.

However, given the haphazard diversity of no-fault compensation funds in different jurisdictions, a more forensic approach needs to be taken to determine where *exactly* a statutory no-fault scheme sheers away from the classic tort law position. This pinpointing exercise is clearly overdue and is not present in existing literature, which leads to a lack of adequate understanding of the legal

---

[10] Jeffrey Schnoor, 'No-Fault Automobile Insurance in Manitoba : An Overview' (1998) 39 *Les Cahiers de droit* 335, 338.

[11] ibid; see also Manitoba Public Insurance Corporation, 'Our History' <https://www.mpi.mb.ca/pages/our-history.aspx>.

[12] Kim Watts, 'Potential of No-Fault Comprehensive Compensation Funds to Deal with Automation and Other 21st Century Transport Developments' (2020) 12 *European Journal of Commercial Contract Law* 17.

A Comparative Law Analysis of No-Fault Comprehensive Compensation Funds

consequences of a no-fault choice. This pinpointing is particularly important for the large funds studied in this book, which all exert a significant impact on the daily lives of individuals living in the jurisdictions to which they apply – yet lack a clear definition of no-fault that is independent of the ends sought to be achieved. In Chapter 2 a modern and clear definition of the distinction between no-fault and *ex gratia* was proposed (the distinction between these two concepts being a fundamental problem in the proper comparative law study and analysis of no-fault compensation funds generally). But the 'rarely articulated'[13] nature of no-fault is no longer acceptable, particularly in light of how widely it is used across the world in different incarnations. If no-fault results in different legal consequences for the individual and the system as a whole, then this choice should be properly justified or explained on a legal basis. An attempt is made in the following paragraphs to set out a clear definition of the *precise co-ordinates of no-fault's shearing away from tort*, based on what has been observed in the establishment and operation of the four big funds. This will hopefully allow for a more principled approach to be taken to the justification of the creation of a very large no-fault compensation fund. Similarly, such a definition hopefully also provides tools for a proper and principled justification for why no-fault might *not* be appropriate for particular circumstances or in a particular jurisdiction.

As discussed in Chapter 2, no-fault does not actually have a precise legal definition. Being somewhat atheistic in nature, no-fault is at first glance akin to the creation of a vacuum. If fault is the default position in tort law for the determination of eligibility for compensation, then no-fault is, logically, defined primarily by its absence or the non-presence of the default criteria of liability. It does not describe what system or legal framework should replace the default liability structures. A void in nature likes to be filled, and thus a rush of different views on the exact definition of no-fault has attempted to fill this gap. These were set out in Chapter 2, but in summary: no-fault is not a unitary phenomenon;[14] it could perhaps better be rephrased as 'no-blame'[15] but the concept is ultimately problematic in nature.[16]

A clearer defining statement can be made in relation to no-fault, which is supported by the observational analysis of the initial choice in favour of no-fault that was made in relation to each of the four analysed funds, and the shape of 'no-fault in practice' that has emerged from these mature compensation schemes.

---

[13] Allan C Hutchinson, 'Beyond No-Fault' (1985) 73 *California Law Review* 756.

[14] Ken Oliphant, 'Landmarks of No-Fault in the Common Law', *Shifts in Compensation between Private and Public Systems (Tort and Insurance Law Vol. 22)* (Springer 2007) <http://link.springer.com/10.1007/978-3-211-71554-3_3>.

[15] Macleod and Hodges (n 1) 615.

[16] Sonia Macleod and Sweta Chakraborty, *Pharmaceutical and Medical Device Safety* (Hart Publishing 2019).

Much like the definition of atheism,[17] no-fault should be defined on the basis of it being a *negation*, rather than *absence*. What this means is that no-fault means the rejection of the relevance or necessity of fault and/or the determination of liability, rather than its dissolution from existence entirely. This matches the earlier definition of no-fault in relation to *ex gratia*, where it is only the latter concept that erases the existence of liability – no-fault simply suspends liability or makes it irrelevant for the purposes of the victim claiming and receiving compensation.

But with regard to what, specifically, is the relevance or necessity of liability being suspended by a no-fault compensation fund? Liability in law can be generally defined as 'responsibility that someone has for their actions, for example the responsibility to pay another person for harm or damage that is a result of these actions'.[18] This definition implies that there can be multiple dimensions to legal liability, depending upon the circumstances. Jurists know this to be objectively true from the various ways that statutes or civil codes and case law shape how liability operates in particular factual scenarios. In relation to a no-fault compensation fund, the most relevant dimension of liability is the responsibility to pay another person for harm or damage, to compensate the victim for that loss. A no-fault compensation fund therefore extinguishes the link in law between the requirement to pay compensation and the legal and factual existence of liability generally. However, it does not extinguish legal liability for all purposes – an assertion which is supported by the legislative design of the four big funds studied in this project. Specifically:

a. The bar against tort proceedings in the New Zealand ACC scheme legislation nevertheless specifically allows space for property and contractual damages claims, employment law claims, some human rights infringement claims in relation to healthcare practitioners, and damages claims relating to the carriage of passengers that are subject to relevant international conventions.[19] The New Zealand ACC scheme also specifically enshrines the right of victims to seek *exemplary damages*,[20] even if in practice this might be factually challenging to separate from ACC-covered compensation.[21]

---

[17] Paul Draper, 'Atheism and Agnosticism' in Edward N Zalta (ed), *The Stanford Encyclopedia of Philosophy* (August 2017) <https://plato.stanford.edu/archives/fall2017/entries/atheism-agnosticism/>.

[18] 'Definition of Legal Liability' (*Cambridge English Dictionary*, 2020) <https://dictionary.cambridge.org/dictionary/english/legal-liability>.

[19] Accident Compensation Act 2001 s 317(2), (4), (5).

[20] ibid s 319.

[21] New Zealand courts have said that when determining which of the victim's injuries are covered and which are not, the statutory bar will generally apply where it is difficult to divide them up. See *P v Attorney-General* [2010] NZHC 959.

A Comparative Law Analysis of No-Fault Comprehensive Compensation Funds

b.   The TAC scheme in Victoria carves out a space for serious injury claims to be eligible for common law damages.[22] As already discussed, this 'partial revolution' approach is fraught with practical difficulty – but it is evidence that 'no-fault' does not mean a total dissolution of liability for all purposes.

c.   Both the Québec and Manitoba schemes bar proceedings arising out of bodily injury (which means that other liability issues related to the context might still be actionable), unless other statutes say otherwise.[23] This shows that liability is only suspended in relation to compensation for bodily injury as expressly provided for under the governing Act, and *not* in all circumstances.[24] The legislature retains the freedom to change or create different scopes to liability.

Additionally, the factual causes of a loss incident are still relevant to the determination of eligibility for compensation under the four studied schemes. A no-fault comprehensive compensation fund requires *both* a defined causal harm event and the victim's evidence-based ongoing need for assistance (in order to access compensation). The low threshold for entry and wide causation criteria for a no-fault comprehensive fund do not mean that there are no causation eligibility criteria whatsoever. What this means, for the purposes of defining no-fault, is that there is a factual causative identification which can be relevant to other legal, preventative and rehabilitative actions.

Therefore, a revised legal definition of no-fault could be:

'the rejection of a legal definition of fault or liability as being relevant to the determination of legal or factual compensation responsibility for an adverse event. In a no-fault compensation fund this means the rejection of fault or liability as being relevant to the victim's eligibility for and/or entitlement to categories of financial compensation for pecuniary and non-pecuniary losses. The rejection of the utility or relevance of a legal definition of fault or liability does not, however, mean that liability or responsibility is extinguished in all senses. However, in the case of a very broad no-fault compensation fund, there may be very few practically remaining avenues for alternative liability possibilities'.

---

[22]   Transport Accident Act 1986 (Victoria) s 93.

[23]   Automobile Insurance Act (Québec) s 83.57; The Manitoba Public Insurance Corporation Act s 72.

[24]   Elsewhere in Canada, we see examples of liability being suspended for the purposes of compensation, but re-activated for the purposes of insurance premium adjustment. Under the Ontario province's statutory no-fault compensation system for automobile accidents (which is administered on a day-to-day basis by private insurers and therefore not extensively studied here), fault is not relevant to eligibility for compensation for bodily injury. However under the Fault Determination Rules (regulations issued under the main insurance legislation), fault will be relevant to an individual's future car insurance premiums and whether a person must pay a collision-related deductible/excess for their vehicle damage. See R.R.O. 1990, Reg. 668: Fault Determination Rules.

186   Intersentia

What is the benefit of such a revised definition? Primarily, it helps to put to rest the 'moral hazard' argument that is often associated with critiques of no-fault schemes. This argument postulates that without the threat of a potential liability claim, there is no incentive for individuals to take appropriate care to reduce harm. Non-legal scholars have recently disproven any inextricable or unavoidable link between no-fault and moral hazard (at least in relation to automobile accidents),[25] yet the tort law scholars' consensus has not moved on.[26] A no-fault compensation fund system, in suspending liability for compensation, raises the possibility of identifying another party who should be responsible for deterrence – for example, the fund itself (if it is tasked with injury prevention), other bodies (such as health and safety regulators, or road transport regulators) or the legislature (which should, in an ideal world, create holistic liability and deterrence frameworks). Combined with the lack of any evidence for the proposition that tort has deterrent or safety incentive effects,[27] this shows that the real hazard comes from legislatures failing to consider how to deal with responsibility for harm in a broad factual or legal sense.

This new definition thus reinforces the importance of legislatures appropriately directing remaining legal liability and factual responsibility questions (including issues of deterrence) to other fields of law that may be better suited to their management – for example, workplace safety law, professional regulation, criminal law, road safety law and product liability. This includes giving a certain limited scope for victims to bring a liability claim directly against defendants in certain circumstances – the TAC serious injury carve-out is an example of this; however it lacks adequate legal justifications for the inconsistency it represents. Other, non-legal, activities can also be undertaken to deal with prevention of the type of harm that is covered by the no-fault compensation fund. For example, extensive activities and investment in public safety initiatives have been commonplace features of all four of the studied funds. This is not to say that the relevant legislatures here have always legislated appropriately or adequately in practice – see, for example, the failings of the New Zealand Health and Disability Commissioner to provide acceptable and effective legal

---

[25] Kay Winkler, 'Effects of No-Fault Auto Insurance on Safety Incentives' (February 2015) <https://ssrn.com/abstract=2747006>.

[26] For example, the arguments made by Michael J Trebilcock, 'Incentive Issues in the Design of No-Fault Compensation Systems' (1989) 39 *University of Toronto Law Journal* 19, that remain mirrored in the arguments of the likes of Gerhard Wagner, 'Tort, Social Security, and No-Fault Schemes: Lessons from Real-World Experiments' (2012) 23 *Duke Journal of Comparative & International Law* 1 <https://pdfs.semanticscholar.org/0849/1023d1456ce49ab02483101a6b5ddcfa988d.pdf>.

[27] Kirsten Armstrong and Daniel Tess, 'Fault versus No Fault – Reviewing the International Evidence', *Institute of Actuaries of Australia 16th General Insurance Seminar* (Coolum Qld, November 2008) 27 <https://actuaries.asn.au/Library/Events/GIS/2008/GIS08_3d_Paper_Tess,Armstrong_Fault versus No Fault – reviewing the international evidence.pdf>.

mechanisms for medically injured individuals to assert their legal rights and secure just outcomes.[28]

In summary then, this section has explained why the philosophical motivation for the creation of (comprehensive) no-fault schemes has generally been non-legal in nature. A properly legally justified and coherent definition of the principle of no-fault has also been proposed, based on an observational analysis of the manifestations and consequences of no-fault that are common to all four studied funds.

3. OPERATIONS: PAYING COMPENSATION TO CLAIMANTS

We can turn now to an analysis of one of the key operative elements of no-fault comprehensive compensation funds, specifically that related to the payment of compensation to claimants. The descriptive study of the four funds made in Chapter 3 shows that they all share these same core characteristics in terms of paying compensation to claimants:

a. The primary form of compensation received 'cash in hand' by the claimant is regular income replacement.
b. Medical costs are compensated for mostly by way of direct payments to the public or private healthcare providers, with some direct reimbursements to the individual victim. There may be a co-payment contributed by the claimant.
c. Lump sum compensation is available in limited cases, including death and severe injury. In the case of fatal accidents this is paid to the survivors and/or dependants.
d. The compensation is framed as a statutory entitlement when certain causative qualifications are present. This enables a fast processing of compensation and minimal consideration of legal issues in most claims.
e. The application for compensation has an informal or non-legalistic nature, with no legal assistance required for most initial applications. Healthcare providers are often responsible for, or can assist with, the completion and submission of relevant paperwork. Compensation fund staff are available by telephone or via online contact to assist with applications.

---

[28] Joanna M Manning, '"Fair, Simple, Speedy and Efficient"? Barriers to Access to Justice in the Health and Disability Commissioner's Complaints Process in New Zealand' (2018) 4 *New Zealand Law Review* 611 <http://www.legislation.govt.nz/act/public/1994/0088/latest/viewpdf.aspx>.

f. The ongoing payment of compensation is linked to the rehabilitation of the claimant. Rehabilitation can variously mean medical recovery or fitness to return to an equivalent category of work, or some general category of work.

g. The payment of compensation in the future may be linked to the original event, leading to a reactivation of the claimant's file rather than a fresh application.

To add to these observations, the four funds were all surveyed for this research project on elements of their claims handling processes. The goal of these surveys was to discover up-to-date information on the speed of processing claims, how causation challenges were triaged, and the legal training of staff handling causation issues. These topics were chosen for the following reasons:

a. The speed of processing claims was selected because this is one of the most significant perceived advantages of a no-fault comprehensive compensation fund over other kinds of legal frameworks for delivering compensation for harm. A comparative analysis of the speed of processing claims in these very large funds reveals legal issues that may arise or were previously unknown. There is also a need to consider the legal impact of new claims processing technologies – this is something that has not been identified in existing literature.

b. The triaging of causation issues was selected because this is where distinctions could be made between how decisions are being made in practice within big no-fault compensation funds about the eligibility of borderline cases. This triaging is useful to compare in practice the speed of processing claims, to reveal the effects of the 'law in action'.

c. The legal training of staff handling causation issues was chosen as a survey question because it is relevant to analysing how difficult cases are handled in practice. It is unclear whether problematic issues from a legal perspective are being directly grappled with or simply glossed over in the name of the speed and efficiency of the administration procedure. In other words, are potential legal issues being actively dealt with, or simply ignored given the generally non-legalistic nature of these schemes? What are the relevant legal conclusions that can be made from these observations?

The empirical information gathered from these surveys and from other conversations and correspondence with fund staff enables a comparative law analysis that more precisely identifies the common key operational pillars of the four no-fault comprehensive compensation funds. The speed of processing claims is one of the key perceived advantages of a no-fault comprehensive compensation fund compared to other legal frameworks. However there has been little recent analysis of the veracity of this claim, particularly in a comparative legal context. Renewed analysis based on new information is particularly urgent, given rapidly

A Comparative Law Analysis of No-Fault Comprehensive Compensation Funds

evolving technological advances that lead to the possibility of increased claims processing speeds and higher customer/claimant expectations in the (parallel) private insurance sector.[29] The answers of the four funds to this question are set out in the table below.

Table 1. Survey responses on claims processing time

Question: What is the average claims processing time?			
ACC	TAC	SAAQ	MPI
'In the 2019/20 reporting year (1 July 2019–30 June 2020) there were 1.9 million decisions made in total with an average decision time of 2.07 days from receipt of the claim to the first decision of accept or decline. Of those 1.9 million decisions, 1.6 million were auto-accepted with an average timeliness of 0.29 days (6.85 hours). Of those 1.6 million, 1 million were made within 60 seconds of receipt.'	'From lodgement to acceptance: 90% in 5 days and close to 100% within 28 days. If the question relates to [the time from] claim lodgement to claim closure there are no statistics, as technically TAC [claims] are never closed.'	[translated] 'The corporation does not generate this data. However, there is another indicator that may be of interest, namely the percentage of clients with disabilities who have returned to their initial activities (employment or studies): • Before one year: 73.4% (2019) • Before two years: 84.2% (2019)'	'Though claims processing time has a direct correlation to claims costs, we have found that this metric does very little to help us understand risk or exposure due to the vast variability in the claims profiles; therefore, we do not track this specifically.'

Source: Compiled by the author.

The answers to this question reveal on the one hand, an almost instant approval timeframe for the ACC and TAC schemes. The ACC scheme in particular has approvals executed at such a high speed that determination of causative eligibility in the majority of cases can clearly be nothing more than a mere box-checking exercise. The answers of the Canadian schemes, however, are more curious. The discovery that both funds do not track claims processing time at all was an unexpected response. It means, firstly, that it is not possible to make a complete and accurate comparison of the speed of accessing compensation, other than making an assumption that (based on the broad popularity of all the schemes[30])

---

[29]   Ramnath Balasubramanian, Ari Libarikian and Doug McElhaney, 'Insurance 2030: The Impact of AI on the Future of Insurance' (2018, updated March 2021) <https://www.mckinsey.com/industries/financial-services/our-insights/insurance-2030-the-impact-of-ai-on-the-future-of-insurance>.

[30]   The SAAQ is very popular with residents, with 80% of the population expressing confidence in the scheme. The MPI enjoys very high satisfaction ratings with Manitoba residents. Like its Canadian cousins, the TAC is extremely popular with Victorian residents. Meanwhile, the ACC scheme is generally popular, and there are significant efforts underway to improve customer experience. See 'Les Faits Saillants' in Société de l'assurance automobile du Québec, 'Rapport Annuel de Gestion' (2019); Manitoba Public Insurance Corporation, 'Annual Report 2018' (2019) 15 <https://www.mpi.mb.ca/Documents/2018-Annual-Report.pdf>;

Chapter 4. Key Pillars

simple claims are probably not unduly delayed. It also reveals a difference between the Canadian and the Antipodean schemes: processing claims at high speed has obvious key priority in both ACC and TAC, even though this goal is not expressly stated within the legislation. This may mean that a focus on speed in those funds ends up driving the way that the stated legislative goals of the funds are actually executed. In relation to the Canadian schemes, there is clearly a preference for focusing on wider rehabilitation and acknowledging the huge variety of claims, but there is no way of assessing the efficiency or speed of claims handling. The Australian and New Zealand approach makes it impossible to objectively determine frequently occurring problems with causation and areas for improvement – or whether those funds facilitate access to justice through increased speed.

The Canadian approach makes it difficult to assess the efficiency of claims processing there in comparison with their Antipodean cousins. However, one key operative conclusion can be made here. Where there is an active interest in claims processing speed in a big no-fault fund (as in ACC and TAC), this correlates with a lower focus on causative issues or the long-term impact of claims (in contrast with MPI and SAAQ) at the time of claim triaging.

On a related note, the funds were also asked about whether they used automated claims processing algorithms or were considering including any kind of automation in their claims processing procedures. This question was primarily motivated by the fact that New Zealand's ACC recently launched an automated claims processing tool, to replace manual claims processing by ACC staff. This 'Cover Decision Service' tool was designed to

> 'identify characteristics of a claim that are relevant to whether a claim will be accepted. Straightforward claims – where the information provided shows that an injury was caused by an accident – will be fast-tracked and immediately accepted. Complex or sensitive claims will be referred for review by an ACC staff member, as all claims are now'.[31]

Therefore, the automated claims processing tool does not have the ability to decline claims. Those claims that cannot be auto-approved will be directed to a human claims processing staff member for closer review. The complementary 'Accident Description Service' tool identifies free text in the claim form, 'looking for key words that could help categorise the type of accident being claimed for, e.g. "rugby accident", or "fall". The data generated from this second tool is used

---

Transport Accident Commission, 'Annual Report 2018/19' (2019) 22; Accident Compensation Corporation, 'Annual Report 2019' (2019) 38.

[31] Accident Compensation Corporation, 'Statistical Models to Improve ACC Claims Approval and Registration Process Statistical Modelling to Support the ACC Automation Cover Decisions and Accident Description' (2018) 4.

Intersentia

'for injury prevention, monitoring and reporting purposes as well as by the Actuarial team.'[32] Combined, the new system 'can complete several tasks that are currently done manually, using a combination of business rules and predictive modelling.'[33]

Importantly, the use and impact of these kinds of new technologies was not foreseen by the original legislative design of each of these schemes, nor has it been considered within legal analysis of any of these funds (or in wider no-fault compensation fund or alternative liability scheme literature, anywhere in the world). The comprehensive and compulsory nature of these compensation funds means that the known and unknown legal impact of these technology developments will affect large numbers of claimants in relation to the main (and often, only) source of compensation for their harms.

ACC was questioned specifically on issues to do with the operation of its Cover Decision Tool. The other funds were informed about the ACC tool and questioned on whether they had considered or planned to use any kind of automation tool for claims processing.

Table 2a. Survey responses on automated claims processing (ACC)

Question 1: Can you provide any updated data on the effectiveness/efficiency gains of your automated claims processing algorithm?
'We don't have any stats on the effectiveness/efficiency, but the automated system did allow us to lower the thresholds (let more claims through) at the beginning of [the Covid-19] lockdown when there were concerns about [staffing] capacity for cover assessment. The thresholds have since been raised.'
Question 2: Have any claims eligibility problems (or other problems) resulted from the introduction of your automated claim processing system?
'No problems with cover/eligibility as far as we know. We did make some changes to the Accident Description Service (ADS) since go-live, but this was intended to improve our own data and did not impact any cover decisions.'
Question 3: Do you have any way of estimating how many 'false positives' might be resulting from the process? For example, simple claims that would probably be declined for ineligibility if they were manually processed?
'The registration team completes a random audit of 400–600 claims each week. If they identify one that needs investigation it will be sent to the cover assessment team. These claims are tracked to measure how many end up being declined for cover (i.e. false positives). It was recommended that we run the models when we have more than 30 false positives per 20,000 audits. We are currently running at 3/20,000.'

Source: Compiled by the author.

---

[32]   ibid 6.
[33]   ibid 5.

Chapter 4. Key Pillars

Table 2b. Survey responses on automated claims processing (TAC, SAAQ and MPI)

Question (for the other funds): Are you considering introducing any automation of your claims processing procedure? If yes, for what kinds of claims?		
TAC	**SAAQ**	**MPI**
'The TAC continues to employ human resources to review claims and make claims decisions as opposed to using data analytics and algorithms to automate decisions. The TAC's payment system does automatically process payments for claims-related services provided these have been approved by a claims manager. The TAC has developed several different analytical models to support our claims decision making. The TAC is also in the process of improving our data environment to be able to better use our data to further support claims decision making.'	[translated] 'In the short term, the Company does not envision automation. However, some activities in the compensation process are already automated, including the automatic payment for drugs at pharmacies.'	'Back in September of 2010, we implemented a "no touch" or "low touch" claims process for medical expense only claims. Once a claimant registered their claim, we allowed the system to manage the claim within set parameters. If those parameters were approached or exceeded, then it would be reviewed. However, though we continue to allow claims to essentially run within a low touch work process, we have significantly narrowed the criteria, and now ensure the details of a claim are understood to prevent claims that are not actual compensable losses. This increased our staff numbers slightly, but the cost benefit remained favourable and helped protect the integrity of the plan.'

Source: Compiled by the author.

The design of automated claims processing tools, or tools that may use artificial intelligence or machine learning in the future and that are focused on processing claims at high speed may not be compliant with the original legislative intent in relation to causative assessment of whether claims are valid. Indeed, questions were raised in relation to the ACC model before its implementation about the lack of privacy or independent oversight in relation to the design of this tool.[34]

The operation of the ACC Scheme's automated claims processing tool seems nevertheless to have been successful so far. It was recognised that faster claims processing enabled injured individuals to begin their rehabilitation process more quickly.[35] However, ACC claims were already processed manually at such a high speed (around 30 seconds for a non-work injury and two minutes 30 seconds for a work-related injury) that cost saving, stability and consistency were stronger motivations for the creation of the automation tool.[36] The ACC developments indicate a preference to give claimants the benefit of the doubt and approve injuries claims, so long as there is no more than a statistically insignificant number of false positives. There is no wording in the legislation that specifically requires ACC to

---

[34]   Kirsty Johnston, 'Privacy and Profiling Fears over Secret ACC Software', *New Zealand Herald* (14 September 2017).

[35]   Accident Compensation Corporation, 'Privacy Impact Assessment: Statistical Models Used to Improve the Claim Registration and Approval Process' (2018) 2.

[36]   ibid 3–4.

Intersentia

193

take this approach, so this can be best described as an operational manifestation of the statutorily described social contract. Meanwhile, the MPI's revisions of its 'no touch' or 'low touch' approach to claims processing shows a preference to maintain strict control of eligibility and maintain legal integrity of the scheme, even where this may result in additional administrative costs. The TAC and SAAQ do not show any significant use of automated claims processing at this time.

The difference in approach reveals that the larger a no-fault comprehensive compensation scheme is in (functional) scope, the easier it is to take a less strict approach to causation and eligibility in simple cases. In other words, it appears that it is easier and less time consuming (in economic terms, more efficient) from an operational perspective to allow a minimal number of false positives to pass through a big system than to engage personnel resources to police the borders of eligibility in simple cases. The operation of the ACC automation tool does not appear so far to have led to a significant number of false positives, so perhaps this approach is justifiable. And certainly, from a justice and fairness perspective, it is appropriate that the automated claims tool does not have authority to decline claims and directs 'tricky' cases to human input. However, from a purely legal perspective, the MPI approach is preferable. This is because there is greater control of scheme integrity and easier identification of causative difficulties that may arise, as well as other legal complexities. The MPI approach is also probably more suitable for environments where there may be other possible sources of compensation for a claimant, depending on what the factual and legal cause of an injury may be. The complete digitisation of claims processing in insurance and the quasi-insurance sector[37] means that it is unlikely that big compensation funds can resist the encroachment of automation long-term. The TAC appears to have recognised this, with its comment that it is working on improving its data environment to be able to more effectively use technology in claims management. The use of automated processing is generally logical, given the large number of claims that these big funds deal with – and is likely to be a significant point of difference with smaller non-comprehensive funds that deal with a smaller number of claimants.

All four funds were questioned on what kind of legal training their staff had, how 'tricky' cases (from a causative perspective) were initially triaged, and whether they were always sent for an initial legal review. The answers of the four funds on these initial eligibility questions are set out in the tables below. This was to determine to what degree there is a consideration of legal issues in the causative doorway to cover, and whether there were any broad similarities in how causative issues were managed.

---

[37] 'The insurance industry is in the midst of a radical, digitally infused shake-up ... [insurers] must move quickly to integrate digital technologies into their operations.' – Pia Brüggemann and others, 'Claims in the Digital Age: How Insurers Can Get Started' (2018) <https://www.mckinsey.com/industries/financial-services/our-insights/claims-in-the-digital-age>.

Chapter 4. Key Pillars

Table 3. Survey responses on legal training of fund staff

Question: What kind of legal training (if any) do your claims processing staff have?			
ACC	TAC	SAAQ	MPI
'The assessors do not have any legal training per se. They are provided with training as part of their role on how to assess a claim within ACC's legislative frameworks. They also have the ability to access technical services support and if necessary refer the query to Legal Services if there is a technical query.'	'Mainly on the job training in issues of negligence, liability and negotiation. Encouraged to keep abreast of case law and precedent decisions. As what we do is half art and half science we utilise mentors and case forums for consistency and ongoing development.'	[translated] 'No legal training.'	'We do not provide our Benefit Administrators or Case Manager's [sic] with any formal legal training. We do train our staff on the Act and Regulations that govern the Personal Injury Protection Plan, as well as the correlating policies and procedures. Most legal training would be considered as "on the job" and through experience in managing claims. If there are any disputes that cannot be resolved through the case owner or their direct leadership, our claimants can then file for a Review and Appeal. Our Internal Review Office staff are not lawyers, but do receive specific training, and any claim that advanced to the external appeal process are defended by an internal lawyer from the Legal Department.'

Question: How are 'tricky' cases (from a causation perspective) triaged? Are they always sent for legal review?			
ACC	TAC	SAAQ	MPI
'As above – whether a claim requires legal rather than technical support (or both) depends on how "tricky" the issue is. It's the exception rather than the rule for a cover issue to be "tricky" enough to require legal referral though.'	'We treat these claims with a higher level of scrutiny.'	[translated] 'No, they are not sent for legal review. However, the Company has a dedicated team for handling claims admissibility. Also, eligibility deemed complex is discussed in a working committee, which includes legal resourcing.'	'Causation reviews are not determined by a legal review; rather by a medical review that is based on "a balance of medical probabilities" or more simply stated, more likely to be true than not. We need to be satisfied on a medical balance of probabilities that the medial evidence supports a cause and effect relationship between the accident and the injuries. These reviews are first completed by the benefit administrator / case manager, and may advance to an in-house medical consultant for their professional medical opinion as the complexity increases. Legal reviews only take place at the time of review and appeal, or if we have questions about the interpretation of the Act and Regulations. Tricky cases will be reviewed by an established Claims Coverage Committee, which is comprised of senior leaders who review the specifics of a claim to determine if coverage applies. Examples would be unidentified hit and run vehicles, intentional acts, residency reviews, vehicles not in motion, and the like. Cause and effect of accident to injury, however, is a medical review.'

Source: Compiled by the author.

Intersentia

195

The responses from the funds on these two questions reveal that legal perspectives do not form a central part of the payment of compensation, except when the claim is complex enough to warrant closer review (or indeed if a dispute is raised about legislative entitlements). Legal concepts of causality are not relevant to the vast majority of cases and will not be applied in practice, as claims management staff in general do not have any specific legal training. In contrast, it is far more likely that medical or empirical issues will be relevant. This indicates that significant importance is given (or should be given) to proper legislative design and definitions within the statute itself. This is to ensure that there is clarity about the legal scope intended for cover that can be interpreted and applied, in most cases, by non-legal staff. The responses also reveal that a no-fault comprehensive compensation fund cannot be accurately described as a wholly legal framework – it is a socio-legal and medical framework for compensation that operates, for most simple cases, outside of the legal sphere. The longevity and stability of these four funds indicate that it is not inherently problematic overall to make the compensation of personal injury for a certain wide category a matter for non-legal determination. However, from a strictly legal perspective, one could certainly voice concern over the lack of legal attention given to claims. There appears to be little opportunity in all four schemes – but especially in ACC, SAAQ and the TAC – to identify causative trends and ensure firm compliance with the legislative scope of the scheme. This is not to suggest that compliance and trends identification can only be undertaken by legally-trained staff and only at the time of initial claim. However, it is appropriate to caution that it may be more difficult to pinpoint problematic elements with the overall *legal* system design if there is no regular legal quality assurance process in place for initial claims.

What is the relevance of the findings made above on paying compensation to claimants? Clearly, most claimants will experience an effectively seamless or procedurally simple process to access compensation for personal injury. This streamlined effect would appear to be reflected by the schemes' popularity. The SAAQ is very popular with residents, with 80 per cent of the population expressing confidence in the scheme. The MPI enjoys very high satisfaction ratings with Manitoba residents. Like its Canadian cousins, the TAC is extremely popular with Victorian residents. Meanwhile, the ACC scheme is generally popular, and there are significant efforts underway to improve the customer experience.[38] For claimants with non-complex injuries that fall squarely within the obvious statutory definitions of eligibility, there is an obvious focus on speed. The balance with analysis becomes more relevant when a claimant's injury is more complex – the most obvious example here is the medical treatment

---

[38] See 'Les Faits Saillants' in Société de l'assurance automobile du Québec, 'Rapport Annuel de Gestion' (n 30); Manitoba Public Insurance Corporation, 'Annual Report 2018' (n 30) 15; Transport Accident Commission, 'Annual Report 2018/19' (n 30) 22; Accident Compensation Corporation, 'Annual Report 2019' (n 30) 38.

Chapter 4. Key Pillars

injury category.[39] Medical and any relevant legal opinions and analysis on eligibility and the scope of cover take more time to access, and the claimant's engagement with this process is heavily affected by the legislative framework.

Non-legal empirical research reveals that there are significant perceived advantages for victims from a comprehensive no-fault compensation fund. Empirical research on traffic accident victims within a no-fault comprehensive compensation system has revealed that claimant satisfaction with the compensation system is proportional to claimants' own subjective apportionment of responsibility for the relevant accident.[40] Other empirical research has demonstrated significantly worse fairness perception outcomes for injury victims in a fault-based compensation system compared to a no-fault comprehensive compensation fund.[41] There is also evidence of improved socio-economic outcomes for individuals able to benefit from a no-fault comprehensive compensation fund.[42]

What is the relevance to the fund itself and the legislature of the findings on processing claims and paying compensation? From an operational perspective, all four funds have had to strike a balance between the statutory direction given to them by the legislature and operational necessity. All four funds have shown a broad trend to make legal definitions of causality and definition not relevant to the vast majority of claimants, in order to facilitate strong operational efficiency. This is understandable given the wide scope and coverage of the schemes. A focus on speed is particularly noticeable in the ACC and TAC schemes, and this has heavily influenced the former's use of new data technology tools. Different choices about oversight of the legal integrity of the scheme are showcased by the four different funds, which illustrate different options for big no fault funds to balance the requirements of speed and analysis.

However, on a negative point, the results of the survey undertaken for this project also indicate the lack of any regular legal oversight or quality control processes at the time of initial claims assessment. This may impact on the ability of the funds to have enough legally-framed information to accurately communicate legal and causative issues to the legislature. Although these

---

[39] For example, treatment injury claims will typically require submission of case notes, a Clinical Incident Review form, laboratory reports, a referral letter, x-ray reports, MRI reports, operative notes, consent forms, and discharge summaries. See Accident Compensation Corporation, 'Treatment Injury Claim Lodgement Guide' 8 <https://www.acc.co.nz/assets/provider/405074f420/treatment-injury-claim-lodgement-guide.pdf>.

[40] Jason Thompson and others, 'The Association between Attributions of Responsibility for Motor Vehicle Accidents and Patient Satisfaction: A Study within a No-Fault Injury Compensation System' (2015) 29 *Clinical Rehabilitation* 500.

[41] Nieke A Elbers and others, 'Differences in Perceived Fairness and Health Outcomes in Two Injury Compensation Systems: A Comparative Study' (2016) 16 *BMC Public Health* 1 <http://dx.doi.org/10.1186/s12889-016-3331-3>.

[42] Susan McAllister and others, 'Do Different Types of Financial Support after Illness or Injury Affect Socio-Economic Outcomes? A Natural Experiment in New Zealand' (2013) 85 *Social Science and Medicine* 93.

Intersentia

four big funds are a clear manifestation of a policy choice to take a non-legal approach to a broad category of personal injury, the funds are ultimately a legal design structure and replace legal remedies for victims. Better regular assessment and evaluation of legally relevant data could help to inform the coherent maintenance and development of the funds.

4. ESTABLISHMENT AND ADMINISTRATION: QUANTUM AND PURPOSE OF COMPENSATION

4.1. THEORETICAL UNDERPINNINGS

We turn now to the analysis of the key elements of the calculation of compensation quantum under no-fault comprehensive compensation funds. The Oxford English Dictionary defines compensation as 'something, typically money, awarded to someone in recognition of loss, suffering, or injury'.[43] Compensation (financial or otherwise) is very important: behavioural economics theory suggests that compensation of the victim to restore equity is more important than punishment.[44]

The compensation quantum issue is the real practical trade-off that a claimant under our four funds experiences compared with a system of compensation that is based on ordinary liability law. The claimant has a statutory entitlement to compensation (which is processed very quickly) if s/he is eligible, but it is within set statutory rates and is associated with his or her income and immediate medical need, rather than a full imagining of the loss that s/he has suffered. In contrast, the entitlement to full or individualised (perhaps subject to caps) compensation of an injured party who can prove another person's fault is a core principle of liability law and tort generally in most jurisdictions. Under the law of obligations frameworks that exist in both civil and common law jurisdictions, those who can show that they have suffered a loss through the fault of another are generally entitled to full compensation of their loss. This remains true even in jurisdictions which might take a socially distributive approach to loss – and even if the idea of 'full compensation' may in reality be somewhat of a theoretical fallacy.[45] No-fault compensation funds of all sizes generally do not provide full compensation (although there are some exceptions),[46] and this is a point upon

---

[43] 'Compensation' (*Oxford Dictionary*) <https://www.lexico.com/definition/compensation>.

[44] Janne van Doorn and others, 'An Exploration of Third Parties' Preference for Compensation over Punishment: Six Experimental Demonstrations' (2018) 85 *Theory and Decision* 333 <https://doi.org/10.1007/s11238-018-9665-9>.

[45] Olivier Moréteau, 'Basic Questions of Tort Law from a French Perspective' in Helmut Koziol (ed), *Basic Questions of Tort Law from a Comparative Perspective* (1st edn, Jan Sramek Verlag 2015) 86.

[46] Vansweevelt and others (n 1) 200–201. For example, 'in Belgium the fund for medical accidents can offer full compensation that is measured according to the standards of court damages'.

198   Intersentia

which they are often criticised by private law scholars and practitioners.[47] This core problem is even more significant for the very large no-fault comprehensive compensation funds studied in this text, because the main form of compensation paid by all four funds is income replacement and reimbursement or direct payment of medical and rehabilitation costs relevant to the injury – *not* a one-off calculation of all current and future pecuniary and non-pecuniary losses.

This issue is an area of much debate in the field of tort law alternatives. Cane and Goudkamp define the trade-off between tort compensation and alternative systems as being rooted in full and generous compensation under the former, and more entitlement for a wider range of people at a lower level under the latter.[48] They note that tort is in fact the outlier compared to most other compensation frameworks, because only tort seeks to compensate on a fully individualised basis. Cane and Goudkamp also argue that calculating future pecuniary loss is difficult, costly and speculative – but an earnings-linked compensation framework (as exemplified by our four big funds) tends to provide more compensation to higher earners than the poor.[49] Helmut Koziol insists, within a comparative European perspective, on the essential nature of full compensation.[50] However, legal analysis by Prue Vines and other Australian academics suggests that the notion of 'full' compensation is erroneous because recipients of lump sum awards may end up running out of money and having to 'double dip' into the social security system – leading to the conclusion that tort-based lump sum awards are in fact under-compensation and do not restore the victim to the position s/he was in before the loss occurred.[51] Daniel Gardner has argued that a comprehensive no-fault compensation fund with wide lifetime cover for catastrophic injury, such as SAAQ, may actually provide a higher total value of financial compensation over the victim's lifetime than under a classic lump sum damages model where 'full' damages are merely estimated.[52] This value can also be combined with the identified social benefits to victims of a fast compensation process, the significantly reduced legal costs and the low administration costs of a well-designed comprehensive no-fault compensation fund.[53] Further, a restriction of a large no-fault compensation fund to bodily injury means that classic full compensation for property damage

---

[47] Helmut Koziol, 'Comparative Conclusions' in Helmut Koziol (ed), *Basic Questions of Tort Law from a Comparative Perspective* (1st edn, Jan Sramek Verlag 2015) 719–720; Wagner (n 26).

[48] Peter Cane and James Goudkamp, *Atiyah's Accidents, Compensation and the Law* (9th edn, Cambridge University Press 2018) 447.

[49] ibid 448–449.

[50] Koziol (n 47) 825.

[51] Prue Vines, Matthew Butt and Genevieve Grant, 'When Lump Sum Compensation Runs Out : Personal Responsibility or Legal System Failure?' (2017) 39 *Sydney Law Review* 365.

[52] Daniel Gardner, 'Automobile No-Fault in Québec as Compared to Victoria' (2000) 8 *Torts Law Journal* 89, 101–105.

[53] PriceWaterhouseCoopers, 'Accident Compensation Corporation New Zealand Scheme Review' (2008) ix–x.

through insurance or a liability claim can be retained. However, scholars such as Gerard Wagner still insist that 'full' tort compensation is the best restorative compensation mechanism for the victim.[54] Clearly, there remains significant legal debate about the proper quantum of compensation for victims, and there remains inadequate empirical data[55] to inform the resolution of this theoretical problem.

Yet it should be remembered that the theoretical underpinnings of 'no-fault' or 'no-blame' compensation are actually silent about the level of compensation that should be available. Choices about the level of compensation available under a no-fault scheme are therefore entirely normative and a legal construct, unless they have been specifically informed by evidence-based policy. These are legislative policy choices related to the surrounding legal landscape of the fund, the appetite of the legislature, lobbying efforts by lawyers and other interested parties, and – most obviously – funding possibilities. As noted already, there is empirical data that shows that the absence of full compensation has no actual impact on a victim's perceptions of fairness.[56] This may to some readers be an obvious point, but it is an important one to state for comparative (tort) law purposes because there are fundamental differences between jurisdictions in the default standards for compensation in civil claims, that are often overlooked by readers not familiar with systems and legal families other than their own. This can then impact views about what is fundamentally acceptable or not acceptable (in terms of quantum of compensation) under a no-fault compensation fund. Anything less than full compensation in a tort claim is anathema in some systems,[57] but in other jurisdictions permissible compensation levels for even ordinary civil claims can be happily limited and regulated by civil procedure rules or case law. This means that the theory of 'no-fault' actually presents a blank canvas for each individual jurisdiction when it comes to the question of compensation quantum.

Therefore, a pre-conception that a no-fault system with limited compensation would offer a 'poor' level of compensation is just as erroneous as a pre-conception that it should offer equivalent 'full' compensation to an ordinary damages claim. These assumptions are imported (consciously or unconsciously) by individual legal thinkers and those designing the system. Further, there is an emerging theory in Europe of a victim's right to reparation[58] which begs the question: does an entitlement to limited compensation for a wide category of loss victims ensure

---

[54]   Wagner (n 26) 7.
[55]   For example, qualitative socio-legal research on the experiences and perceptions of different categories of victims who receive compensation via either a liability framework or an alternative compensation framework, including longitudinal studies.
[56]   Elbers and others (n 41).
[57]   Such as in France – see 'The myth of full compensation as a basic principle' in Moréteau (n 45).
[58]   Joëlle Milquet, 'Strengthening Victims' Rights: From Compensation to Reparation' (March 2019) 36–37 <https://ec.europa.eu/info/sites/info/files/strengthening_victims_rights_-_from_compensation_to_reparation_rev.pdf>.

better fairness and justice outcomes than a system that fully compensates only those who can show fault? Ultimately these are all normative choices that rest with legislatures, who must be mindful of the legal context in which they operate – but from a theoretical standpoint, the issue of quantum of compensation under a no-fault comprehensive compensation fund is something that is completely open to legislative choice, with reference to the wider legal context. However, it should be noted that the recognised cost blow-outs in the TAC scheme from even a modest allowance for common law claims (in the case of seriously injured victims where fault is shown) show that it will never be realistic for a *large* no-fault compensation fund (i.e. one that is open to lots of potential claimants) with a single public administrator to offer full compensation to most or all claimants.[59] Therefore, when designing a comprehensive no-fault compensation fund, a legislative and philosophical choice always has to be made about whether the income and medical need associated with 'real' compensation and the societal benefits offered by a no-fault comprehensive fund can be an acceptable alternative in most cases to the classic theory of 'full' or individualised compensation. This calculation might mean that it would be *legally* inappropriate and incoherent (given the wider legal context) for some jurisdictions to ever choose a large no-fault compensation scheme, unless this could be overridden by clear empirical evidence or other non-legal factors. Therefore, it is possible to conclude on a comparative legal basis that the issue of compensation quantum under a large no-fault compensation fund is dependent on both funding and existing normative perceptions about compensation quantum, that may or may not be informed by empirical data.

After distilling some of these theoretical key points, we can now turn to a practical exposition of how compensation is actually structured in our four large comprehensive compensation funds.

4.2. STRUCTURING OF COMPENSATION

What kind of compensation does each of our four large funds offer to eligible claimants? Set out below are three tables with summaries of the key kinds of compensation offered by each of the four funds. There is then identification of the key characteristics in common about compensation across all four funds, what we can identify as the objective purpose of the compensation, and how the continuing adequacy of compensation quantum can be ensured.

We turn first to the ACC Scheme, as it offers compensation for the widest range of injuries, being a universally comprehensive scheme. The comprehensive but functionally limited compensation under the other three schemes is then considered.

---

[59] For example, see the comments made in Chapter 3 in relation to the financial impossibility (for legal contextual reasons) of offering full compensation on a wider basis within the Belgian no-fault compensation fund for medical accidents. See also Wannes Buelens, *Het Medisch Ongeval Zonder Aansprakelijkheid* (Intersentia 2019).

A Comparative Law Analysis of No-Fault Comprehensive Compensation Funds

Table 4a. Analysis of compensation available under ACC (New Zealand)

ACC	Categorisation of loss
Treatment costs[60]	Predominantly pecuniary loss. There is mixed pecuniary and non-pecuniary loss in relation to cover for mental harm associated with a covered personal injury, and other kinds of specifically covered loss.[69]
Includes acute[61] and ongoing treatment.[62] ACC generally has to authorise compensation approval for ongoing treatment.[63] Treatment costs include contributions to or all the ancillary costs of treatment for a covered injury, such as pharmaceutical costs, transport and laboratory tests.[64]	
Includes social rehabilitation[65] and vocational rehabilitation,[66] the details of which are specified in a personalised rehabilitation plan developed by ACC in liaison with the claimant.[67]	
The treatment has to be necessary and appropriate and of the required quality. This must take into account the nature and severity of the injury, the generally accepted means of treatment for that injury and a cost–benefit analysis.[68]	
Weekly earnings compensation	Pecuniary loss
Is available only to a claimant who was an earner 'immediately before' the injury occurred.[70] There are different calculations specified in the legislation for the different possible types of employment, including permanent employment, casual employment and self-employed person.[71]	
The claimant has to bear the loss of the first week's earnings him or herself unless the injury was work-related.[72]	
The rate of payment is 80 per cent of the claimant's weekly pre-injury earnings.[73]	
Lump sum compensation for permanent impairment	Mixed pecuniary and non-pecuniary loss, because this compensation category is linked to physical and mental impairment rather than financial loss.
Is available to claimants who have suffered a degree of permanent whole-body impairment of 10 per cent or more.[74]	
The assessment of permanent impairment is made when the injury has been medically assessed as stable.[75]	

(continued)

---

60   Accident Compensation Act 2001 s 69(1)(a) and Sch 1 Part 1.

61   Meaning the cost of the first visit and subsequent urgent visits associated with that first visit – see s 7 ibid.

62   ibid Sch 1 cll 1–6.

63   ibid Sch 1 cl 4.

64   ibid Part 1 cl 3.

65   Social rehabilitation means any of the following supports that are specified in the legislation: aids and appliances; attendant care; child care; education support; home help; modifications to the home; training for independence and transport for independence. ACC also has some discretion to provide some other kinds of rehabilitations that may be necessary. See ibid s 81; ibid Sch 1 cll 12–23.

66   Vocational rehabilitation is aimed at achieving vocational independence, which means the claimant's capacity to return to work 'for which he or she is suited by reason of experience, education, or training, or any combination of those things ... for 30 hours or more a week' – see s 6 ibid. Services such as medical assessments, special equipment or adjustments or training programmes might be included in the vocational rehabilitation.

67   ibid ss 75–80 and Sch 1 cll 7–10.

68   ibid Sch 1 cl 2.

69   ibid ss 26(c), (d), (da) and 27.

70   ibid Sch 1 cl 32.

71   ibid ss 97–106, 112, 113 and Sch 1 cll 32–53.

72   ibid s 98.

73   ibid Sch 1 cl 32(3).

74   ibid Sch 1 cl 54.

75   ibid Sch 1 cl 57.

Chapter 4. Key Pillars

Table 4a *continued*

ACC	Categorisation of loss
The maximum amount of possible lump sum compensation is not currently published by ACC, but is at least NZ$133,000 in line with annual indexing (the statutory base amount is NZ$100,000).[76] This amount is only available to a claimant with a whole body impairment of 80 per cent or more.[77]	
Support for dependants of a fatal injury victim Survivor's grant – a one-off payment of NZ$7,043.38 to the deceased's spouse or partner, and NZ$3,521.71 to each child younger than 18.[78] ACC will also pay a funeral grant of NZ$6,569.53.[79] This amount is indexed annually in line with inflation.[80] Weekly compensation for deceased's spouse – if the deceased was an earner, 60 per cent of the deceased's weekly earnings will be paid to the surviving spouse for five years or until the youngest child turns 18.[81] Weekly compensation for deceased's child – if the deceased was an earner, 20 per cent of the deceased's weekly earnings will be paid to the child until s/he is 18 (or 21 if in full-time study).[82] Childcare costs of the deceased's child(ren) for five years or until the age of 14.[83] If the child is disabled, ACC has the discretion to extend this cover for longer.	Mixed pecuniary and non-pecuniary loss. The survivors' grant is the compensation that falls most squarely within the non-pecuniary category.

Source: Compiled by the author.

Table 4b. Analysis of compensation available under TAC (Victoria)

TAC	Categorisation of loss
Treatment and rehabilitation costs All medical and like[84] rehabilitation costs causatively linked with the accident for the first 90 days are paid by the TAC, with no prior approval required. This includes acute care (such as ambulance and hospital care) and associated immediately necessary therapies and home adaptations.[85] The costs of treatment that occurs 90 or more days after the accident require TAC approval.	Predominantly pecuniary, non-pecuniary in relation to cover for mental health injury. Pecuniary costs of certain third parties are also foreseen.

(continued)

---

[76] Don Rennie, 'ACC and the Woodhouse Principles: Real Compensation' (*New Zealand Law Society* 2019) <https://www.lawsociety.org.nz/news/lawtalk/issue-926/acc-and-the-woodhouse-principles-real-compensation/>.

[77] Accident Compensation Act 2001 Sch 1 cl 56(4).

[78] ibid Sch 1 cl 65.

[79] 'Financial Support If Someone Has Died from an Injury' <https://www.acc.co.nz/im-injured/financial-support/financial-support-after-death/>.

[80] Accident Compensation Act 2001 s 116.

[81] ibid Sch 1 cl 66.

[82] ibid Sch 1 cl 70.

[83] ibid Sch 1 cl 77.

[84] Transport Accident Act 1986 (Victoria) s 60.

[85] Transport Accident Commission, 'Treatments and Services' <https://www.tac.vic.gov.au/clients/how-we-can-help/treatments-and-services>.

Intersentia

A Comparative Law Analysis of No-Fault Comprehensive Compensation Funds

Table 4b *continued*

TAC	Categorisation of loss
Childcare costs and income replacement costs for parents of injured children are also available.[86] Transport costs for family members are also available. Rehabilitation costs associated with helping the claimant to return to work.[87] The claimant's employer may also receive financial assistance with the costs of helping the claimant return to work or adapting the workplace.	
Income replacement For an employee claimant who has had a total loss of earnings due to an injury, compensation of up to 80 per cent of gross weekly earnings is available, up to a maximum of A$1,490 per week. However, low earners (earning less A$740 gross per week) will receive a proportionally higher amount – there is a compensation floor of A$740 per week. Within the legislation a distinction is made between partial and whole loss of earnings.[88] For a self-employed claimant, equivalent levels of compensation are available. Reference will be made to the self-employed person's earnings in recent financial years.[89] Income replacement in both cases is only payable if the claimant required more than five days off work because of the injury. Severely injured claimants (defined as 50 per cent or more bodily impairment) can access a special earnings replacement compensation if, after being injured, they are terminated from employment or no longer able to sustain their self-employment.[90] The compensation rates under this special 'Safety Net Income Benefit' are the same as under the other earnings compensation categories. Claimants who are still unable to work 18 months after their injury can be assessed on their entitlement to receive Loss of Earning Capacity benefits.[91] Earnings information, medical information and other sources of compensation or financial assets are taken into account in this calculation. After a period of three years, only those claimants who have a bodily impairment of 50 per cent or more can continue to access earnings compensation.	Pecuniary

(continued)

---

[86] Transport Accident Act 1986 (Victoria) s 60(2C)–60(2CE); Transport Accident Commission, 'Support for Family Members' <https://www.tac.vic.gov.au/clients/how-we-can-help/support-for-family-members?tab=2>.

[87] Transport Accident Commission, 'Return to Work Support' <https://www.tac.vic.gov.au/clients/how-we-can-help/return-to-work-support>.

[88] Transport Accident Act 1986 (Victoria) ss 44–45; Transport Accident Commission, 'Income Support for Employees' <https://www.tac.vic.gov.au/clients/how-we-can-help/income-support/income-support#howmuch>.

[89] Transport Accident Commission, 'Income Support for Self-Employed People' <https://www.tac.vic.gov.au/clients/how-we-can-help/income-support/income-support-for-self-employed-people>.

[90] Transport Accident Act 1986 (Victoria) s 54A(1).

[91] Transport Accident Commission, 'Loss of Earnings Capacity (LOEC) Benefits' <https://www.tac.vic.gov.au/clients/how-we-can-help/treatments-and-services/policies/other/loss-of-earnings-capacity-loec-benefits>.

Table 4b *continued*

TAC	Categorisation of loss
Death benefits A lump sum payment of up to A$195,190 to a dependent partner or child(ren), depending on the deceased's age, circumstances and any previously received TAC compensation payments.[92] Income replacement payments if the deceased was an earner, at the same 80 per cent rate as other income replacement costs.[93] Counselling costs of up to A$17,410 per family, including transport costs.[94] Childcare costs, fortnightly dependent child payments and an annual education allowance for each child up to the age of 18 years.[95]	Mixed pecuniary and non-pecuniary
Impairment benefits for claimants with more than 10 per cent impairment A one-off lump sum payment is available to claimants who have suffered a permanent impairment of 11 per cent or more due to their transport accident. This is to compensate for the permanent loss of function and movement. The level of impairment is medically assessed by specialist doctors once the injury has stabilised, to determine the impairment rating.[96] The maximum possible impairment benefit is A$371,610.[97] Claimants who are convicted of a driving-related offence (related to the accident in question), such as drink driving, are not entitled to impairment benefits.	Mixed pecuniary and non-pecuniary, as some dimensions (such as psychological impairment and the holistic impact of permanent impairment) are difficult to precisely quantify
Common law compensation for seriously injured claimants Claimants who have suffered a 'serious injury', defined in the legislation as a serious long-term impairment or loss of a body function,[98] may be entitled to common law compensation if they can show the fault of another party (even if that person cannot be identified). The scope of this carve-out from the no-fault scheme is described in more detail at Chapter 3 section 3.3. The nature of the TAC liability indemnity means that, in the vast majority of cases, it is the TAC itself who is paying this compensation.	Pecuniary and non-pecuniary, determined separately

(continued)

---

[92] Transport Accident Act 1986 (Victoria) ss 57–59; Transport Accident Commission, 'When a Family Member Dies' <https://www.tac.vic.gov.au/what-to-do-after-an-accident/how-to-claim/when-someone-dies>.

[93] Transport Accident Act 1986 (Victoria) ss 58–59.

[94] 'Mental Health and Wellbeing Services' (*Transport Accident Commission*) <https://www.tac.vic.gov.au/clients/how-we-can-help/treatments-and-services/services/mental-health-and-wellbeing-services>.

[95] Transport Accident Commission, 'When a Family Member Dies' <https://www.tac.vic.gov.au/what-to-do-after-an-accident/how-to-claim/when-someone-dies>.

[96] Transport Accident Act 1986 (Victoria) ss 46A, 47 and 48.

[97] Transport Accident Commission, 'Impairment Benefits – Policy' <http://www.tac.vic.gov.au/clients/compensation/impairment-benefits#tabs-3>.

[98] Transport Accident Act 1986 (Victoria) s 93.

Table 4b *continued*

TAC	Categorisation of loss
The minimum amount of common law compensation is currently A$57,690. The maximum amount of pecuniary compensation (for loss of current or future earnings) is A$1,298,980. The maximum amount of non-pecuniary compensation (for pain and suffering) is A$577,280.[99]	
The receipt of common law benefits may affect the claimant's entitlement to no-fault benefits and benefits under other compensation sources.	

Source: Compiled by the author.

Table 4c. **Analysis of compensation available under SAAQ (Quebec) and MPI (Manitoba)**

SAAQ	MPI	Categorisation of loss
Treatment and rehabilitation costs	**Treatment and rehabilitation costs**	Pecuniary
Personal assistance and care expenses. This includes childcare expenses and the cost of replacement labour if the claimant worked in a family business.[100]	Personal assistance and care expenses.[102] This includes childcare expenses and the cost of replacement labour if the claimant worked in a family business.[103]	
Essential acute treatment costs are not part of the main compensation scheme, as this is covered by the provincial public health service (but as noted later in this chapter, a monthly contribution is paid by SAAQ to the public health service.) The scheme specifically covers medical and paramedical care not otherwise covered by a social security scheme, and associated miscellaneous costs like transport, prostheses and orthopaedic devices.[101] The SAAQ has some discretion determining compensation under this head.	Essential acute treatment costs are not part of the main compensation scheme, as this is covered by the provincial public health service (but as noted later in this chapter, a monthly contribution is paid by MPI to the public health service). The scheme specifically covers medical and paramedical care not otherwise covered by the public health system or other compensation framework.[104]	

(continued)

---

[99]   Transport Accident Commission, 'Common Law Compensation' <https://www.tac.vic.gov.au/clients/how-we-can-help/compensation/common-law-compensation>.

[100]   Automobile Insurance Act (Québec) ss 79–83.1.

[101]   ibid s 83.2.

[102]   The Manitoba Public Insurance Corporation Act ss 131–134.

[103]   ibid s 135.

[104]   ibid s 138; Manitoba Public Insurance Corporation, 'Personal Injury Protection Plan – Your Guide' 2 <https://www.mpi.mb.ca/Documents/PIPPGuide.pdf>.

Chapter 4. Key Pillars

Table 4c *continued*

SAAQ	MPI	Categorisation of loss
Earnings compensation	**Earnings compensation**	Pecuniary
If the claimant was in full-time employment at the time of the accident, 90 per cent of income up to a gross annual salary cap of C$83,000.[105]	If the claimant was in full-time employment at the time of the accident, 90 per cent of income up to a gross annual salary cap of C$101,000.[109] It is possible for individuals who earn higher amounts than this to buy extension coverage from MPI.[110]	
If the claimant was in part-time employment, 90 per cent of income for six months.[106] If the claimant is still unable to work at that point, this will be reassessed by SAAQ and possibly paid at the full-time employed rate.[107]	If the claimant was in part-time employment, 90 per cent of income for six months.[111] If the claimant is still unable to work at that point, this will be reassessed by MPI (but will not be paid at a rate less than was paid in the first six months).[112]	
Earnings compensation is gradually reduced and then stopped for claimants of pensionable age (and not available at all for those aged over 65).[108]	Earnings compensation is gradually reduced for claimants of pensionable age and then transitions to a 'retirement income' payment.[113] No income replacement or retirement income payment is available to unemployed accident victims aged 65 or over at the time of the accident.[114]	
Earnings compensation is not available for the first seven days after the accident.	Earnings compensation is not available for the first seven days after the accident.	

(continued)

---

[105] Automobile Insurance Act (Québec) ss 14–15; Société de l'assurance automobile du Québec, 'Compensation Table for 2021' (2021).

[106] Automobile Insurance Act (Québec) s 19.

[107] ibid s 21.

[108] ibid s 41.

[109] The Manitoba Public Insurance Corporation Act ss 81–82; Manitoba Public Insurance Corporation, 'Personal Injury Protection Plan' <https://www.mpi.mb.ca/Pages/personal-injury-protection-plan.aspx>.

[110] 'Additional Extension Products' <https://www.mpi.mb.ca/Pages/other-extensions.aspx>. Policyholders can buy up to $200,000 over the compulsory no-fault limit. This also provides extra coverage for fatality payments to survivors and dependants, and extra retirement income replacement benefits.

[111] The Manitoba Public Insurance Corporation Act ss 83(1)–83(3).

[112] ibid s 84(4).

[113] ibid ss 102–103(3).

[114] ibid s 101.

Intersentia

207

A Comparative Law Analysis of No-Fault Comprehensive Compensation Funds

Table 4c *continued*

SAAQ	MPI	Categorisation of loss
Quasi-earnings compensation for students and the unemployed	**Quasi-earnings compensation for students and the unemployed**	Non-pecuniary, because the precise impact of this kind of loss is not otherwise easily calculable
Students at all levels of education are entitled to an indemnity for every missed year of education.[115]	Students at all levels of education are entitled to an indemnity for every missed year of education.[118]	
Students over 16 who are unable to complete their studies due to an injury or are unable to work may be able to receive an income replacement indemnity based on the average Québec industrial wage (currently set at C$50,429).[116]	Students who are unable to complete their studies due to an injury or are unable to work may be able to receive an income replacement indemnity based on the average Manitoban industrial wage (currently set at C$49,540.22).[119]	
Claimants who were unemployed but able to work at the time of the accident will receive income replacement compensation for six months, calculated at the gross hypothetical wage s/he would have received, had s/he been employed.[117] This income replacement benefit can be extended if necessary.	Claimants who were unemployed but able to work at the time of the accident will receive income replacement compensation for six months, calculated at the gross hypothetical wage s/he would have received, had s/he been employed and their earnings history over five years.[120] This income replacement benefit can be extended if necessary.	
Death-related benefits	**Death-related benefits**	Mixed pecuniary and non-pecuniary
Surviving family members are entitled to receive a lump sum death benefit payment that is calculated with reference to the deceased victim's income at the time of the accident and how many dependants s/he had. There is the option to convert this to periodic instalments.[121]	Surviving family members are entitled to receive a lump sum death benefit that is calculated with reference to the deceased victim's income at the time of the accident and how many dependants s/he had.[122] The current maximum survivor	

(continued)

---

115 Automobile Insurance Act (Québec) ss 34–36.
116 ibid ss 36.1-39; Société de l'assurance automobile du Québec, 'Compensation Table for 2021' (n 105).
117 Automobile Insurance Act (Québec) ss 24–26.
118 The Manitoba Public Insurance Corporation Act ss 87(1)–88(3). The current maximum lump sum rates are C$5,581 for a primary school aged child, C$10,343 for a secondary school age child and C$20,690 for a higher education student. See Manitoba Public Insurance Corporation, 'Personal Injury Protection Plan' (n 109).
119 The Manitoba Public Insurance Corporation Act ss 89(1)–(3); Manitoba Public Insurance Corporation, 'Personal Injury Protection Plan' (n 109).
120 The Manitoba Public Insurance Corporation Act ss 85(1)–86(2).
121 Automobile Insurance Act (Québec) s 71.
122 The Manitoba Public Insurance Corporation Act s 120.

Table 4c *continued*

SAAQ	MPI	Categorisation of loss
The current maximum spouse payment, not including extra lump sums that may be available for relatives including dependent children is C$415,000. Annual tables published by the SAAQ explain how death benefits are to be calculated, and current rates. A funeral expenses payment of C$5,534.[123] Psychological treatment costs for surviving family members.[124]	payment, not including extra lump sums that may be available for relatives including disabled dependent children, is C$505,000.[125] A funeral expenses payment of up to C$8,951.[126] Grief counselling costs for surviving family members, including transport and accommodation costs to access counselling.[127]	
Permanent and temporary impairment 'For loss of enjoyment of life, pain, mental suffering and other consequences of the temporary or permanent injuries or functional or cosmetic sequelae that a victim may suffer following an accident, a victim is entitled, to the extent determined by regulation, to a lump sum indemnity'.[128] The maximum amount of this indemnity is currently set at C$258,947.[129] The coverage of temporary impairment is a unique feature of the SAAQ compared to the other four schemes.	**Permanent impairment** Lump sum impairment compensation is available for permanent impairments.[130] This is currently set at a maximum of C$164,181.[131] Further lump sum compensation is available for catastrophic injury victims. This is currently set at a maximum of C$259,245.[132] Catastrophic injury victims may also be paid extra discretionary amounts by MPI, up to a lifetime maximum total of C$1,205,794, to top up compensation that the claimant expects to receive from other compensation sources or government programmes.[133]	Non-pecuniary

Source: Compiled by the author.

---

[123] ibid s 70; Société de l'assurance automobile du Québec, 'Compensation Table for 2021' (n 105).

[124] Automobile Insurance Act (Québec) s 62.

[125] Manitoba Public Insurance Corporation, 'Personal Injury Protection Plan' (n 109).

[126] ibid; The Manitoba Public Insurance Corporation Act s 124(1).

[127] Manitoba Public Insurance Corporation, 'Personal Injury Protection Plan' (n 109).

[128] Automobile Insurance Act (Québec) s 73.

[129] Société de l'assurance automobile du Québec, 'Compensation Table for 2021' (n 105).

[130] The Manitoba Public Insurance Corporation Act s 127(1).

[131] Manitoba Public Insurance Corporation, 'Personal Injury Protection Plan' (n 109).

[132] The Manitoba Public Insurance Corporation Act s 127(2); Manitoba Public Insurance Corporation, 'Personal Injury Protection Plan' (n 109).

[133] Manitoba Public Insurance Corporation, 'Personal Injury Protection Plan' (n 109); Manitoba Public Insurance Corporation, 'Personal Injury Protection Plan – Your Guide' (n 104) 37.

Looking at the range of compensation available under the TAC Scheme, the most notable difference is, as signposted earlier, the availability of common law damages based on an individualised calculation of loss for seriously injured claimants.

Meanwhile, as noted in the table above, the SAAQ and MPI have broad equivalence in their legislative compensation structures. As done elsewhere in this book it is logical to describe and compare them at the same time. The compensation available under both schemes is broadly equivalent, although there are some key differences worth noting. For example, the SAAQ offers compensation for loss of enjoyment of life, pain and mental suffering for both permanent *and* temporary injuries.

What common conclusions can we draw about how compensation is structured and calculated across all four funds? There are four obvious broad elements in common.

The first core compensation pillar of all four schemes is the earnings-related compensation, which is set at a minimum of 80 per cent for earners. All employed and self-employed persons are entitled to some kind of earnings compensation across all four schemes, with the Canadian schemes extending this to include unemployed (but employable) persons and higher education students. The requirement in all four schemes for claimants to bear their own loss of wages for the first week means that, for claimants with minor eligible injuries, there may be no engagement at all with this primary pillar of compensation. Additionally, the cap on lost earnings compensation means that high earners may have significantly less of their income compensated than middle or low income earners – however the MPI scheme allows for the purchase of extension cover from its wider insurance business. Earnings-based compensation is therefore clearly the most dominant type of compensation paid under all four schemes.

Medical and rehabilitation benefits are the second core compensation pillar. The New Zealand and Victoria schemes have direct control over the payment and invoicing of all elements of this compensation, whereas the Canadian schemes do not include acute public hospital care directly (although they do make separate contributions to the public health budget).

Fatality and permanent impairment harms are the third core compensation pillar. The severity of the injury and the impact of the injury and/or death on dependants is a central consideration in calculations of this third pillar, but the quantum varies widely across different schemes. The Manitoba and TAC schemes' specific attention to catastrophic injury allows for some more generosity to severely injured claimants – not including the TAC's carve-out from the no-fault scheme for serious injuries.

Another noticeable pattern across all four funds is the strict control of compensation payments beyond an initial recovery period, and the very active role taken by the funds in the claimant's rehabilitation and recovery.

Specific approval is required for treatments beyond the initial acute injury period. This may limit the claimant's freedom to choose treatments if those treatments are unconventional or if they do not directly further the goal of rehabilitating the claimant's injuries.

Some kind of compensation of third parties affected by the injury is also foreseen in each scheme, beyond the obvious category of spouses and dependants of a seriously injured or deceased victim. However there is no fixed pattern to this compensation across all four schemes. Depending on the scheme, there is the possibility of such varied heads of compensation as counselling costs, childcare costs, income replacement for parents of injured children, and reimbursement for the value of lost labour within family businesses.

All four funds use indexing extensively to ensure that the value of various statutory entitlements to compensation (with statutorily specified minimum values) keeps pace with increased costs of living.

There is never any possibility of 'unlimited' or 'full' compensation. The continued availability of earnings-related compensation and medical and rehabilitation costs means that, theoretically, there is no fixed limit to the quantum of what could be compensated for under these two categories. However, ongoing access to this compensation is entirely dependent on the fund's determination about ongoing need, and subject to limitations on what kind of claimants can access long-term earnings compensation (for example, seriously injured claimants only). For other categories of compensation, particularly lump sum benefits, there are maximum caps on compensation available. Therefore, this means that for the predominantly pecuniary categories of loss there is a theoretically uncapped level of compensation available (for medical costs compensation at least) dependent on the fund's subjective assessment of the claimant's need for that compensation. However, there is never any possibility of unlimited compensation for non-pecuniary losses, which are often compensated by way of permanent impairment or death-related compensation. The exception to this, of course, is the TAC's carve-out for common law damages for serious injury – but even that category of compensation is subject to caps.

The Canadian schemes show that it is possible for a category of specific non-pecuniary compensation to be available within a comprehensive no-fault compensation fund, if only to a limited category of catastrophically injured claimants. This is an alternative approach to the common law carve-out for serious injury that is allowed by the TAC scheme.

Beyond these practical elements that all four funds share, what is the common legal purpose to compensation that can be identified across all four funds? A key issue here is understanding what is the underlying purpose of the financial compensation or payment being offered under these schemes. We can consider the issue of the 'purpose' of compensation in two dimensions. The first is the legal distinction between and combination of pecuniary and non-pecuniary compensation. The second is the broader question of whether the compensation is intended to be fully compensatory, partially compensatory, or merely symbolic.[134]

In relation to the classification of pecuniary versus non-pecuniary compensation, we can see that all four schemes have pecuniary compensation for personal injury as their core compensation: income replacement and medical and rehabilitation losses. Pecuniary compensation for other associated losses, such as property damage, is left to the ordinary rules of liability and/or the claimant's private insurance policy. A mixed pecuniary and non-pecuniary dimension exists for those losses that are more difficult to quantify: for example, mental injury losses as a part of rehabilitation, and the lump sum payments for the spouse and dependants of a fatal injury victim. The nature of the compensation that will be available depends on the severity of the injury and its ongoing impact. Severe injuries that require ongoing rehabilitation are likely to result in longer entitlements to and greater amounts of compensation, compared to injuries that crystallise quickly. Aside from the limited circumstances in which lump sum payments will be available, the claimant's whole loss is not crystallised at any one point in time. The entitlement to access compensation remains open (even where it is limited to ongoing rehabilitative costs, and no further income replacement). The compensation received may be divided between pecuniary and non-pecuniary compensation at different times. Therefore, we can conclude that although pecuniary compensation – linked to *current* income loss and *current* healthcare needs – is the primary form of compensation, there is the potential for a mixed pecuniary and non-pecuniary approach to be taken, and no fixed total cap on the amount of compensation that might be received under those heads.

We turn next to the broader question of whether the compensation is intended to be compensatory, non-compensatory or merely symbolic.

In *current* legislative and external communications statements on their strategy and purpose, all four schemes do not explicitly state that 'compensation' (or equivalent words like 'redress' or 'damages') is their core purpose. Instead, we see these kinds of statements:

a.   ACC says its role is

> 'improving [New Zealanders'] quality of life by minimising the incidence and impact of injury ... cover we provide helps pay for the costs of your recovery. This includes payment towards treatment, help at home and work, and help with your income';[135]

b.   The TAC says its 'role is to promote road safety, support those who have been injured on our roads and help them get their lives back on track';[136]

---

[134]   This was also a key issue relevant to earlier discussions about whether historical abuse funds that offer symbolic/non-compensatory/*ex gratia* payments are in the same category of compensation funds as those that deal with other types of injuries.

[135]   Transport Accident Commission, 'What We Do' <https://www.tac.vic.gov.au/about-the-tac/our-organisation/what-we-do>.

[136]   ibid.

Chapter 4. Key Pillars

c. The SAAQ speaks of 'two key concerns that define the purpose of the SAAQ's existence ... improvement of the road safety record [and] client satisfaction';[137] and

d. The MPI states that its mission is 'Exceptional coverage and service, affordable rates and safer roads through public auto insurance.'[138]

The four funds all have a broad dual purpose to prevent accidents and to restore claimants back to health and societal function. To the extent that this involves compensation for injury, this mixes compensatory, non-compensatory and symbolic elements of compensation. Compensation forms part of the restorative function of the funds, but it is *not* the defining element. The financial support provided is compensatory to the extent that it replaces income during the time of recovery and the costs of other injury losses. However it is non-compensatory in the sense that the restorative effect of the support is to return the claimant back to a good degree of social function. It is critical to understand that this may not be at the same level of social or vocational function that s/he had before the accident. The simple focus on a return to vocational independence in all four schemes underlines this. The symbolic element is the infusing of the compensation elements of all four schemes with social purpose – the fund does not simply make a financial calculation of pecuniary and non-pecuniary losses, but rather takes a holistic restorative approach that is focused on the claimant's rehabilitation and a community responsibility approach to a broad category of injury compensation. The symbolic element is infused with a limited degree of moral hazard and a large dose of normative policy choices. In the ACC Scheme there are exclusions to entitlements for wilfully self-caused injuries and suicide, and a ban on survivor benefits for persons convicted of the victim's murder.[139] The other three schemes all restrict access to income replacement and non-core benefits where the claimant is convicted of a driving-related offence.

The objective purpose of compensation under all four schemes can therefore be identified as restorative and all are underpinned with a social contract. The divisions between pecuniary, non-pecuniary, compensatory, non-compensatory and symbolic compensation are blurred. This blurred approach in turn influences quantum because the amount of compensation provided is designed to restore the claimant to the best achievable level of rehabilitation *given the current reality of the claimant's injuries*. This is different to a classic tort calculation of compensation, which tries to conceptualise what the claimant's life would have been like had the injury not occurred, with a specific division of losses under different heads of damages. Examples of different kinds of injured claimants illustrate this point. A catastrophically injured claimant who needs ongoing care, and whose aspects of injury and need may change, will be able to access theoretically unlimited

---

137 SAAQ, 'Strategic Plan' <https://saaq.gouv.qc.ca/en/saaq/performance/strategic-plan/>.
138 Manitoba Public Insurance Corporation, 'Who We Are' <https://www.mpi.mb.ca/pages/who-we-are.aspx>.
139 Accident Compensation Act 2001 ss 119–120.

Intersentia

levels of compensation and rehabilitative support – more than could be accessible under a tort calculation.[140] There is no attempt to finalise the whole scope of the loss, compared to the claimant's pre-injury life – the income replacement costs such a claimant would receive are the best approximation of this. However, a claimant who has a crystallised and stable permanent impairment that can be quantified will received a capped level of lump sum compensation. An injured claimant who must retrain and take a different job (potentially at a lower salary) because of their injury, will be considered equally compensated and rehabilitated as a person whose injury means they did not need to change their job or retrain. A claimant who has a simple whiplash injury but is approved to return to work after a few days will only receive compensation in the form of medical treatment – and no income replacement or pain and suffering compensation. Therefore, quantum of compensation will always be subject to these big funds' mixed restorative purpose, with individualised unlimited compensation only available where that is necessary to fulfil this purpose for a particular class of severely injured victims. This broad-brush restorative approach may certainly lead to unfair results in certain cases.

In terms of ensuring the ongoing adequacy of compensation, all four schemes use annual indexing to adjust the levels of compensation in line with inflation. This is sensible, but it does not address underlying inadequacies that may exist in relation to lump sum payments and compensation more generally. For example, the New Zealand ACC Scheme has significantly lower minimum and maximum levels of lump sum payments for fatalities and permanent impairments than the other three schemes. The Canadian schemes in particular have much more generous compensation possibilities that include non-pecuniary compensation for catastrophically injured claimants. And as discussed earlier, public and legislative discontent led to the incoherent statutory enshrinement of the availability of 'top-up' compensation for sexual crime victims.[141] Periodic statutory reassessment of the purpose of specific heads of compensation under the schemes, and therefore also a potential revision of quantum, seem necessary to ensure both continued appropriateness of the compensatory elements of the scheme and legislative coherency.

4.3. CONCLUSIONS ON QUANTUM AND PURPOSE

The review and analysis of the quantum and purpose of compensation allows some conclusions to be drawn that are applicable to all four schemes.

---

[140] Gardner (n 52).

[141] See the discussion in relation to the case *Davies v New Zealand Police* [2009] NZSC 47 in Chapter 3 and Simon Connell, 'Justice for Victims of Injury: The Influence of New Zealand's Accident Compensation Scheme on the Civil and Criminal Law' (2012) 25 *New Zealand Universities Law Review* 181.

Firstly, there is no requirement within the theory of no-fault that a compensation fund established on a no-fault basis should offer a particular level of compensation. There is also no clear empirical evidence that the best outcomes are achieved by the payment of hypothetical 'full' compensation. Choices about quantum are therefore a normative legal choice made by the legislature and influenced by the wider context of a jurisdiction's legal landscape.

The formulation of compensation reveals that all four funds provide a mixed purpose compensation payment or support. This combines what would ordinarily be described in law as pecuniary and non-pecuniary losses. Compensation under these schemes is not intended to be full compensation in the tort sense but it is available to all eligible claimants, a much broader group than would otherwise be eligible. There is also a symbolic element to the compensation that is associated with a fund's restorative social purpose. This may come at the price of not having specifically compensatory pecuniary and non-pecuniary damages available.

The dual preventative and restorative social purposes have a direct impact upon the quantum of compensation in all four schemes. Compensation is calculated with reference to what is necessary to restore the claimant to his or her best achievable social and vocational participation in a post-accident reality. The financial and social potential of the accident victim in their pre-injury world is not regarded as relevant, except with regard to calculation of income replacement compensation. This is certainly a practical approach to take, but it may lead to unfair and uneven results – for example, when a victim post-rehabilitation can only access lower paying work compared with their pre-accident state.

The annual indexing of compensation benefits ensures that existing benefits keep in line with inflation. However this does not address basic inadequacies that may exist in the levels of compensation. Those inadequacies would be best addressed by scheme review, with a consideration of the purpose and policy behind each head or category of compensation available.

5. OPERATIONS: RESOLVING DISPUTES ABOUT CLAIMS EFFECTIVELY

No-fault comprehensive compensation funds have as their legislative objective the payment of compensation for harm on the basis of statutory eligibility rather than a calculation of legal liability. This means that liability allocation systems using insurance or litigation structures, as are common in other countries, are not used. However not all claimants will be satisfied with the decision that the fund makes about their claim, or their claim might have been wholly rejected by the fund. These claimants may seek to challenge the decision of the fund.

The simplest solution, in terms of legislative design, would be to allow claimants to appeal all decisions made by the fund via the court or relevant administrative tribunal that might apply in that jurisdiction. However none of the four large funds studied and surveyed in this project take this approach. All four funds have some kind of structured review and appeal processes designed by legislation, regulation and sometimes by agreement with legal professional bodies. This can be perceived as part of the legislative choice to move the covered harms one step away from the liability or court-based arena for ordinary dispute resolution. This means that despite philosophically eschewing disputes for as many harm victims as possible, some kind of legislatively specified and operationally refined dispute resolution structure is a key pillar of the no-fault comprehensive fund operational structure. A comparison of these structures and processes allows conclusions to be drawn about how this works most effectively, and what kinds of processes lead to difficulty.

This section sets out the dispute resolution procedure in place for each of the four studied compensation funds. These procedures are then analysed with reference to the funds' empirical responses to survey questions. Conclusions are then drawn about what are the key pillars of dispute resolution common to all no-fault comprehensive compensation funds.

5.1. OVERVIEW OF DISPUTE RESOLUTION PROCESS FOR EACH FUND

The four funds all share in common a dispute resolution procedure that is, at a basic level, sketched out in the main legislative framework of the fund. Other elements of dispute resolution procedure are specified variously in regulations, internal policy documents and agreements with other relevant bodies (such as mediation agencies and legal practitioner bodies). A broad overview is given in the following paragraphs of the dispute resolution processes in each fund, starting with ACC and then turning to TAC, SAAQ and MPI. Most attention is given to the New Zealand ACC Scheme, because that fund has recently undertaken a significant review and adjustment of its initial dispute resolution processes, in response to claimant and advocacy group complaints.

5.1.1. ACC Dispute Resolution

The ACC Scheme's current dispute resolution process can be characterised as offering multiple administrative and mediation-based choices, with a very limited avenue of appeal to the ordinary courts, rather than a specialist tribunal. This is in a marked contrast to how the scheme was originally designed, with an inquisitorial style dispute resolution procedure followed by a full right of appeal to a specialist tribunal and then the ordinary law courts.[142] The significant changes introduced to the scheme's legislative framework in 1992 also led to the introduction of a more adversarial approach to dispute resolution. This was partly due to a political perception that common law courts would adopt a more restrictive interpretation of disputes, thereby limiting costs and potential scheme expansion.[143] Three categories of person can lodge a dispute in relation to an ACC decision: a claimant, a levy-payer (on very limited grounds[144]) and an employer (in relation to whether a personal injury was employment-related).[145] At the first stage, there are four possible options for dispute resolution, depending on the subject of the dispute and the preference of the parties: an internal administrative review, a formal independent review, an agreed mediation, or a complaint to the Ombudsman. The first two review processes are governed by the same basic legislation, but they operate practically in quite different ways. Mediation is obviously best suited to situations where ACC has some degree of discretion in relation to a claim, rather than a strict determination of eligibility under the statute or a causative determination on medical grounds.[146]

a. An internal administrative review is the simplest form of review, where ACC reconsiders its decision. This takes place entirely on the papers, but does consider further written submissions from the claimant and any new information that the claimant might provide. The application for review must be made within three months of ACC's decision.[147] The staff member undertaking the review must act independently, comply with principles of natural justice and undertake the review in a timely manner.[148] The review procedure is more than a formality: there is a requirement that ACC consider the whole application 'afresh', particularly in light of any new information available.[149]

---

[142] Review officers appointed under the 1982 legislation had the powers of a Commission of Inquiry and there were no statutory time limits on disputes. The ACC corporation also had no right of legal representation at review hearings. See Stephen Todd and others, *The Law of Torts in New Zealand*, Stephen Todd ed (8th edn, Thomson Reuters 2019) 94.

[143] Accident Rehabilitation and Compensation Insurance Corporation, *ACC Regulations and Legislation: Suggestions for Integrated Change* (December 1993), cited in Todd, ibid.

[144] In relation to the level of compensation available to self-employed persons, as a payer of levies (s 209(1) Accident Compensation Act 2001) or general dissatisfaction about a levy paid (s 236(1)).

[145] Accident Compensation Act 2001 s 134.

[146] 'Challenging an ACC Decision' (*Community Law Manual: Accident Compensation*) <https://communitylaw.org.nz/community-law-manual/chapter-19-accident-compensation-acc/challenging-an-acc-decision/mediation-and-other-alternative-ways-of-resolving-disputes/>.

[147] Accident Compensation Act 2001 s 135.

[148] ibid s 140.

[149] *Wikeepa v Accident Rehabilitation and Compensation Insurance Corporation* [1998] NZAR 402, 9.

Intersentia

217

b. An independent review occurs where the applicant formally applies for a review of ACC's decision on specified grounds. These grounds might relate to a claim, delays caused by ACC in deciding a claim, or ACC's response to a complaint under the Code of ACC Claimants' Rights. An oral hearing will be held (as well as a pre-hearing case conference), before one of the two independent dispute resolution agencies that are funded by ACC (but operate independently from it) – FairWay Resolution or the Independent Complaint and Review Authority (ICRA). This process also involves an internal ACC review, because ACC will undertake its own internal review before the independent external review hearing occurs. As with the internal administrative review, the complainant must submit the claim within three months of the original ACC decision, but accommodation can be made for challenging circumstances.[150] As with internal reviews, the assessment is a fresh look at the decision and there must be compliance with principles of natural justice. There are strict time demands placed on the independent reviewer within the statute: a decision and reasons must be communicated to the complainant within 28 days.[151] A failure to hold a hearing within three months, where no delay was caused by the complainant, will result in the dispute concluding by default in the complainant's favour.[152] The claimant does not have to be represented by a lawyer, but may engage a lawyer or non-legal advocate if desired. In terms of costs, the statute specifies that the complainant will be awarded costs where he or she is successful, or if the complainant was not successful but the reviewer thinks it was reasonable to make the application.[153] Costs may also be awarded against any relevant third party.

c. A mediation process via the newly established Talk Meet Resolve service. This is an independent body, funded by ACC, which independently mediates ACC disputes where both or all parties agree to the process. The key parties that attend a mediation session are the complainant and the relevant ACC case manager. There may be (legal) representation if the claimant and/or ACC feel it is necessary, but it is intended to be a non-legal dispute resolution process. The conciliator is a person who has prior expertise in ACC law or experience of adjudicating ACC disputes.[154]

d. A complaint to the Ombudsman. This is only possible if the complaint relates to procedural issues,[155] such as ACC taking too long to reply to claimant letters.

---

[150] Accident Compensation Act 2001 s 135.
[151] ibid s 144.
[152] ibid s 146.
[153] ibid s 148.
[154] Talk – Meet – Resolve, 'Why Use TMR?' <https://www.talkmeetresolve.co.nz/using-our-process/Why-try-TMR>.
[155] Ombudsmen Act 1975 s 13.

After an independent review, it is possible for a claimant to appeal directly to the District Court.[156] In practice ACC cases are heard by a select number of judges who have expertise in the area, and they can be assisted by expert assessors on technical matters. From the District Court it is possible to appeal (with leave) to the High Court on points of law,[157] and from there to the Court of Appeal (also only on points of law).[158] There is no possibility for ACC-related cases to be brought before the Supreme Court.[159] There is also a prohibition on accessing other tribunals during the review processes in relation to the dispute, such as the relevant employment tribunal or small claims court.[160]

The current overall dispute resolution legislative framework has remained largely the same for a number of years, but significant changes were implemented following the 2016 Miriam Dean QC review. This review was a consequence of the identification of dispute resolution process problems by a claimant advocate organisation.[161] The review's recommendations, which were wholly adopted by the government,[162] included the following steps to ensure that non-court dispute resolution in the ACC sphere met the same high standards as traditional avenues of justice:[163]

a. *Data and evidence*[164] – The review recommended that ACC explore better ways to analyse data about its claims and disputes.

b. *Access to law*[165] – The review recommended funding a third-party voluntary legal information website to provide access to all relevant case law, and a practical primer for (self-represented) claimants. The review also recommended that independent reviewers, ACC, the judiciary and the government use legal communication tools better to educate claimants about the dispute resolution process and understand better how claims and appeals are decided.

---

[156] Accident Compensation Act 2001 s 149.

[157] ibid s 162.

[158] ibid s 163.

[159] ibid s 163(4).

[160] ibid s 133(5).

[161] Acclaim Otago, 'Understanding the Problem: An Analysis of ACC Appeals Processes to Identify Barriers to Access to Justice for Injured New Zealanders' (2015) <http://www.acclaimotago.org>.

[162] New Zealand Government, 'Further Work to Improve ACC Dispute Resolution' (2016) <https://www.beehive.govt.nz/release/further-work-improve-acc-dispute-resolution>.

[163] Kim Watts, 'New Zealand' in Thierry Vansweevelt and Britt Weyts (eds), *Compensation Funds in Comparative Perspective* (Intersentia 2020) 123–130.

[164] Miriam Dean, 'Independent Review of the Acclaim Otago (Inc) July 2015 Report Into Accident Compensation Dispute Resolution Processes' (May 2016) 13–14 <http://www.mbie.govt.nz/info-services/employment-skills/legislation-reviews/accident-compensation-dispute-resolution/document-and-images-library/independent-review.pdf>.

[165] ibid 36–39.

c. *Access to medical evidence*[166] – The review recommended establishing better procedures (including dialogue between experts), easier access to costs and making the independence of medical experts known.

d. *The sense of being heard*[167] – This was an area that revealed the importance of good procedure and the optics of independence and impartiality. The review recommended structural changes relating to the independence of FairWay, which at that time was the only independent review provider. FairWay has since been transferred from Crown ownership to employee ownership.[168]

e. *Access to representation*[169] – ACC Scheme legislation and case law are complex, but only a small number of New Zealand lawyers have expertise in this area. The best and most experienced lawyers are usually retained by ACC. However, around 60 per cent of claimants represented themselves. The lack of legal expertise in this area is an unintended consequence of removing the legal profession from the sphere of personal injury law generally. The review recommended more ACC-funded quality independent advocacy services and giving the District Court power to appoint counsel to represent claimants in exceptional cases.

In my view, the modifications to ACC dispute resolution were clearly overdue. At the time of writing there are now far more options for complainants to choose from when faced with a dispute with ACC, all of which are focused on ideally securing a mediated, non-adversarial solution. However a stubborn problem that remains (and which ACC and its supervising ministry have themselves recently indicated they are unlikely to be able to resolve themselves)[170] is the lack of funded access to at least basic legal guidance on ACC disputes for all claimants, or any substantial increase in the number of advocacy or legal representatives operating in this field. Given the smothering effect of ACC on personal injury law practice generally – because virtually all claims will be resolved without the need for a lawyer – it is not clear how this problem can be

---

[166] ibid 42–50.

[167] ibid 20–33.

[168] New Zealand Government, 'FairWay Change Positive for Staff and Customers' (2017) <https://www.beehive.govt.nz/release/fairway-change-positive-staff-and-customers>.

[169] Dean (n 164) 52–58.

[170] 'MBIE [the Ministry of Business, Innovation and Employment] agrees that there is limited supply of ACC specialists on the legal market. However, MBIE does not consider that encouraging lawyers into the area will address distortions, if any, of the current market. MBIE also lacks the levers or expertise to influence individual decisions in terms of specialisation, including non-monetary considerations. This is more appropriately entrusted to professional organisations and education/training institutions.' – Ministry of Business Innovation and Employment and Accident Compensation Corporation, 'ACC and MBIE Briefing Paper: Update on the Response to the Miriam Dean Review and next Phase of Work to Improve Disputes Performance' (2018) 9.

solved without a dedicated funded legal service that is independent and free or heavily subsidised for users. Although the widely accepted purpose of the ACC Scheme is to remove personal injury disputes from the field of legal adversarial process, that does not mean that the public should not be entitled to access legal guidance about their entitlements and the potential to dispute ACC's findings. This problem sits within a wider context of poor access to legal aid services within New Zealand, and high legal fees in comparison with average wages.[171]

Ultimately, the ACC dispute resolution framework appears to be dogged by legal incoherency (in terms of legislative design) and a wealth of choice. However, in my view, there is a poverty of substantive and meaningful legal guidance for disgruntled claimants who need specialist advice – let alone basic guidance for ordinary claimants without any significant dispute with ACC. The ACC Scheme's success in moving compensation for personal injury away from the injustices of the 'damages lottery' has had the unintended consequence of depriving injury victims of basic access to legal information and guidance, as well as pitting them against a single highly-resourced organisation with expert knowledge of accident compensation law. This is a manifestation of acute unfairness within this large no-fault compensation fund framework.

5.1.2. TAC Dispute Resolution

We can turn next to Victoria's TAC. The dispute resolution procedure under this statutory framework can be characterised as offering a clearly defined choice between three different streams of dispute resolution, with a generous timeframe for making applications. Because of the carve-out from the tort bar for serious injury claims, these dispute resolution options apply to compensation decisions by TAC under the no-fault framework. These three options are:

a. An application for an informal internal review of the decision by TAC. This is carried by a specific independent Review Team, who has the power to 'maintain, overturn or compromise the original decision, depending on each individual situation'.[172] The TAC aims to complete all reviews within 60 days, but the median time of resolution is only 26 days.[173] In 2018/19, just over half (57 per cent) of the TAC's original decisions were upheld.[174] This dispute resolution option is free and is available to all TAC claimants.

---

[171]   Kayla Stewart and Bridgette Toy-Cronin, 'The New Zealand Legal Services Mapping Project: Finding Free and Low-Cost Legal Services' (2020).

[172]   Transport Accident Commission, 'Having a TAC Decision Reviewed' <https://www.tac.vic. gov.au/content/content/how-we-manage-your-claim/having-a-tac-decision-reviewed>.

[173]   Transport Accident Commission, 'Annual Report 2018/19' (n 30) 26.

[174]   ibid.

Intersentia

A Comparative Law Analysis of No-Fault Comprehensive Compensation Funds

b. An application for a review of the decision by the Victorian Civil and Administrative Tribunal (VCAT).[175] This is sometimes called a 'merits' review[176] and is governed by provisions under the main TAC legislation. This triggers an internal review of the decision (regardless of whether an informal internal review already occurred). Upon receiving the application, the TAC must review and respond to the complainant within 28 days or request more information from the claimant within that timeframe. The complainant has 90 days to respond to this request for further information. Upon receipt of further information, the TAC must conclude the review within 28 days. The matter then proceeds to a pre-hearing conference, where mediation is attempted. If this does not lead to resolution, there will be a hearing and the VCAT will issue a decision. It is not compulsory for the complainant to have legal representation, but claimants may choose to do so (at their own cost). This dispute option is also available to all TAC claimants, but there are fixed fees involved with the process (which may be reduced or waived for low income claimants).[177] VCAT decisions can be appealed on points of law to either the trial division or the Court of Appeal division of the Supreme Court of Victoria.

c. A special route for dispute resolution via TAC's Dispute Resolution Protocols.[178] These protocols were designed in consultation with two of the most significant legal practitioner representative organisations, and exist alongside protocols that were negotiated with those bodies in relation to common law TAC claims (i.e. serious injury claims that are within the scope of the carve-out from the no-fault scheme).[179] The claimant contacts a participating legal practitioner, who explains the process and begins the application. There is a dispute conference, which generally occurs within 90 days of the claim application.[180] The key advantage for the claimant under this framework is that the TAC pays the cost of the relevant mediator and joint experts. It will also pay the legal costs of the complainant if the TAC's decision is revoked or varied, 'or where the [dispute] is resolved by way of agreement'. The level of reimbursable costs is set out in the protocol.[181] This process is also not limited to certain types of disgruntled TAC claimants – it is available to all claimants who choose to engage legal representation. It is

---

[175] Transport Accident Act 1986 (Victoria) s 77.

[176] Transport Accident Commission, 'Annual Report 2018/19' (n 30) 26.

[177] Transport Accident Commission, 'Having a TAC Decision Reviewed' (n 172).

[178] Australian Lawyers Alliance, Transport Accident Commission and Law Institute Victoria, 'No Fault Dispute Resolution Protocols' (2016).

[179] 'Common Law Protocols' (2016); 'Supplementary Common Law Protocols' (2020).

[180] Transport Accident Commission, 'Dispute Resolution' <https://www.tac.vic.gov.au/clients/working-together/resolving-your-issues/dispute-resolution>.

[181] Section 16 'Legal Costs' Australian Lawyers Alliance, Transport Accident Commission and Law Institute Victoria (n 178).

important to note that if the claimant has retained a lawyer[182] at any time since the accident, it will be compulsory for disputes to go through this protocol mechanism before making a VCAT application.[183]

One immediately noteworthy difference in the TAC compared to New Zealand's ACC is that it is possible for complaints be directed to a specific administrative law tribunal. The timeframes are also more generous: in all cases, the complainant has 12 months from the date of the decision to begin the dispute resolution process. There is also an immediately obvious avenue to legal advice and guidance for claimants via the protocol route, the cost of which in many cases has a chance of being reimbursed by the TAC. It is noteworthy – and not surprising – that the protocol route is by far the most popular avenue for dispute resolution – in the year 2018/19, 565 disputes were lodged via the protocol route in comparison with 263 informal reviews and 179 (self-represented) VCAT reviews.[184] Interestingly, the number of protocol-based disputes is also reducing year-on-year, something that TAC attributes to 'effectiveness of The Protocols in promoting improved understanding and dialogue with stakeholders.' Further, TAC's recently revised strategy to be the 'world's leading social insurer'[185] also 'has allowed us to shift to more outcome focused decisions. This has contributed to an ongoing reduction in disputes.'[186] This seems logical, as lawyers who are participants in the protocol programme can advise claimants at the outset of their likely chances of success – and claimants are never denied some form of review, because they can always at least request an internal review, followed by a VCAT application if they choose not to take on legal representation. The three-pronged approach therefore appears to be a very effective way to manage all types of disputes and minimise the number of such disputes arising. It compares very favourably with the New Zealand ACC Scheme, because of the greater ease of access for all claimants to legal guidance and a greater chance of having the cost of that advice reimbursed. Therefore, although the partial revolution aspect of the TAC scheme – the retention of common law damages – has legal coherence problems, it does allow fairness and access to justice for a large number of claimants.

5.1.3. SAAQ and MPI Dispute Resolution

Moving to Canada, the SAAQ and MPI have similar two-step dispute resolution procedures, with an appeal to the court only possible on points of law. These are

---

[182]   This is defined as someone who is a member of the Law Institute of Victoria or the Australian Lawyers Alliance.

[183]   Transport Accident Act 1986 (Victoria) s 77(1A).

[184]   Transport Accident Commission, 'Annual Report 2018/19' (n 30) 26.

[185]   Transport Accident Commission, 'TAC 2020 Strategy' (n 7) 7.

[186]   Transport Accident Commission, 'Annual Report 2018/19' (n 30) 26.

very similar to the default options available under the TAC, but without the popular dispute resolution protocols that have been negotiated with Victoria's lawyer practitioner bodies. A key point of difference is that the MPI has introduced a formal mediation option, but this is only available at the point of appeal.

a. An internal review process is the first step for challenging a decision issued by either fund. This must be done within 60 days of the claimant receiving the claim manager's decision.[187] The SAAQ must respond to this application within 90 days,[188] whereas the MPI is prescribed just 30 days to respond.[189] Internal review processes in both funds are carried out by staff members independent from the original claims process. At the time of application, MPI complainants can request a hearing with the internal reviewer.[190]

b. If a complainant is unhappy with the outcome of the internal review, it is possible to lodge an appeal to an administrative tribunal. In Québec, this body is the general administrative tribunal that also handles disputes about decisions made by various government departments, commissions or municipalities. In Manitoba, appeal is to a dedicated Automobile Injury Compensation Appeal Commission (AICAC).[191] Complainants have either 60 days (Québec)[192] or 90 days (Manitoba)[193] from the date of the internal review decision to lodge a tribunal appeal. If the SAAQ had failed to respond to the internal review application, Québec complainants may be able to appeal directly to the Tribunal. In Manitoba, the AICAC is specifically excluded from making determinations about the MPI's discretionary compensation decisions in relation to catastrophically injured victims.[194] All appellants to the AICAC are entitled to free advice and support from the Claimant Advisor Office, an advocacy service that is funded by MPI but statutorily independent.[195] In Québec, claimants who need financial assistance to access legal advice need to apply for civil legal aid in the ordinary way. Further appeals from both tribunals to the ordinary courts are only possible on points of law. Concerns have been raised about delays in resolving transport injury cases before the Québec administrative

---

[187] Automobile Insurance Act (Québec) s 83.45; The Manitoba Public Insurance Corporation Act s 172(1).
[188] 'Contesting a Decision by the SAAQ' <https://saaq.gouv.qc.ca/en/traffic-accident/contesting-decision/>.
[189] The Manitoba Public Insurance Corporation Act s 172(3).
[190] 'Appealing an Injury Claim' <https://www.mpi.mb.ca/Pages/injury-claim-appeals.aspx>.
[191] The Manitoba Public Insurance Corporation Act s 175.
[192] Automobile Insurance Act (Québec) s 83.49.
[193] The Manitoba Public Insurance Corporation Act s 174(1).
[194] ibid ss 137.1, 175.1.
[195] ibid s 174.

tribunal, and the fact that most decisions are decided in favour of the SAAQ.[196]

c. A notable feature of the MPI dispute resolution process is that a formal mediation process has been introduced at the appeal stage. The mediation process was introduced partly because of a backlog of cases waiting for appeal. A quantitative and qualitative analysis of the mediation process during its trial phase found that the mediation process achieved its goal of reducing the appeal case backlog, and was significantly faster (around 5 months, compared to around 2.5 years for an appeal) than the ordinary appeal process (so long as a mediated solution was achieved).[197] Surveyed claimants were also significantly more satisfied with the mediation process than with the ordinary appeal process, and mediation was significantly cheaper.[198] In terms of qualitative matters, the personal interaction and claimant's sense of being heard in the mediation process was identified as a core element of satisfaction with the process. One notable critique of the mediation process came from the Claimant Advisor Office, whose representatives helped to prepare and support claimants during the mediation process. This critique was that a thorough investigation of the dispute should occur before mediation occurs, and that claimant advisors should know the difference between mediation-style advising and adversarial-style advocacy (the latter being necessary at tribunal hearings, but not in mediation).[199]

The two Canadian systems both take a two-step internal review and tribunal approach, but the Manitoba system appears to have been more effectively developed and adjusted to respond to case backlogs. The Claimant Advisor Office in Manitoba is also a particularly helpful development and ensures that claimants bringing an appeal can have certainty of accessing specialised legal guidance at no cost. This is superior to the TAC's protocol approach, because the Manitoban complainant does not have to risk being out of pocket to gain legal advice (if his or her claim is unsuccessful). The addition of an optional mediation stream before an appeal is also a logical choice, and is equivalent to the pre-hearing conferences that exist under the ACC Scheme and TAC dispute resolution processes.

---

[196] 'Going up against the SAAQ? You'll Probably Lose', *CBC News* (28 March 2019) <https://www. cbc.ca/news/canada/montreal/going-up-against-the-saaq-you-ll-probably-lose-1.5074039>.

[197] Jennifer L Schulz, 'Evaluating Manitoba's Automobile Injury Mediation Pilot Project' (2018) 41 *Manitoba Law Journal* 21 <https://movisa.org.mx/images/NoBS_Report.pdf>.

[198] 'The cost per concluded mediation was $3,776.66 while the cost per concluded appeal was $9,102.36.19. On this method of comparison, mediation is $5,325.70 cheaper per case than an appeal.' – see ibid 33.

[199] ibid 42–44.

Intersentia

5.2. SURVEY OF FUNDS AND ANALYSIS

Obviously, the legislative framework does not give a complete picture of the dispute resolution process in action. Therefore, the funds were all specifically surveyed on certain elements of their dispute resolution operations, in order to facilitate a comparative law analysis. The specific topics were chosen because they related to some simple factual gaps in the existing comparative law literature on no-fault compensation funds. As noted already, there was not scope to undertake a full socio-legal study with qualitative data-gathering within this project. However, it was worthwhile and possible to gather simple qualitative information from the funds in relation to the following issues:

a.   What kind of subsidised *legal* support is available to individuals who seek to challenge or review their compensation eligibility or entitlements? This was motivated by the findings in relation to the ACC Scheme that inadequate legal support or resources were available to individuals seeking to challenge an ACC decision,[200] as well as the apparent success of the Claimant Advisor Office under Manitoba's MPI framework.

b.   Questions were asked of each fund, specific to each fund's legislative framework, about how often it either settles disputes with dissatisfied claimants or how it can otherwise assess the perceptions or satisfaction of claimants who have engaged in a dispute resolution process. This was asked because the claimant who brings a dispute under these statutory compensation frameworks is a category of claimant who may have specific concerns about a no-fault system that effectively bars access to other remedies. These points relate to normative theories about the purpose of tort law and the elimination of any retributive justice possibilities[201] in a no-fault comprehensive compensation fund. The differences between the legislative frameworks and contexts of each fund meant that it was not appropriate or logical to ask exactly the same questions of each fund. However, all questions were linked to the same methodological objective of identifying comparative functional and structural issues present in a big no-fault compensation fund's dispute resolution framework.

c.   The funds were also questioned on the most common categories or themes of disputes that they encountered. This was to identify new information (that is not commonly reported in corporate documents) about what kinds of claims commonly lead to disputes. This reveals new information about which kinds of harms and losses may commonly cause problems

---

[200]   Acclaim Otago (n 161); Dean (n 164).
[201]   Allan Beever, 'Justice and Punishment in Tort: A Comparative Theoretical Analysis', *Obligations III* (2006).

226

Chapter 4. Key Pillars

(for causative and other reasons) across these kinds of funds, which enables functional and structural comparative law conclusions to be made.

In relation to the legal support that is available to individuals who seek to challenge a fund decision, the responses of the funds were as follows.

Table 5. Survey responses on legal support for claimants challenging a decision

Question: What free or subsidised legal support is available to claimants who seek to challenge a decision of your organisation?			
ACC	TAC	SAAQ	MPI
'ACC funds 3 providers as part of what it calls its "navigation" service. ACC's current total spend across these providers is [NZ]$117,000 per month regardless of the number of people the service supports.'	'None. Clients have the option of Informal Review. However we also make a contribution to a client's legal costs as part of our pre-litigation Protocol agreements.'	[translated] 'In administrative review and court recourse requests, clients may obtain legal aid when eligible, free of charge or for a fee. However, it is important to know that clients do not have to be represented in [their] appeals, both at review and in court. Also, legal aid is not administered by the Society, but rather by the Ministry of Justice. There are eligibility criteria to be met in order to be entitled to it, such as annual income, family situation, the value of certain assets, cash flow, etc.'	'At MPI we do not pay for legal representation of our claimants. However, the Manitoba Government did establish the Claimant Advisor Office, which is an independent office that our claimant[s] who advance their dispute to appeal may use to represent them at appeal at no cost to the customer. MPI funds this office, but they report to a different ministry within government.'

Source: Compiled by the author.

Three out of the four funds now offer some degree of direct and indirect financial support to at least some categories of claimants. It is only in Québec where claimants have to rely upon general legal aid entitlements to support a challenge to a SAAQ claim decision.[202] The location of the help and stage at which the advice is available varies, however, between each fund. At one end of the spectrum is the SAAQ, with no specific assistance available and a reliance on the ordinary legal aid system in the event of a dispute. Further along the spectrum are TAC and MPI, with their contribution to either private legal counsel or access to an independent legal service for certain categories

---

[202] It is also unclear whether reliance upon the legal aid system is appropriate or if its supports are widely available to transport injury claimants: after three years of dispute and negotiation, the Québec government and the provincial bar association only recently reached an agreement to raise legal fees and to establish an independent working group to conduct an exhaustive review of the tariff structure. See Luis Millán, 'Legal Aid Agreement Reached with Quebec Government', LexisNexis The Lawyer's Daily (16 October 2020) <https://www.thelawyersdaily.ca/articles/21654/legal-aid-agreement-reached-with-quebec-government>.

Intersentia

227

of claimants launching a challenge. In the case of TAC, this contribution is primarily for serious injury claimants,[203] meaning that the MPI-funded legal support is in practice available to a wider category of claimants. For non-serious injury TAC disputes, the claimant will only be able to receive a reimbursement of legal costs incurred during the internal review process if his/her challenge is at least partially successful.[204]

Meanwhile, recent changes to the ACC Scheme and the introduction of its 'Navigation Service'[205] now means that some degree of advice – *legally informed*, if not formal legal advice – is available to all claimants from the very start of their claim. This represents, on its face, a much wider availability of guidance than under the other funds, but some problems become more apparent on closer investigation. The establishment of this service was in direct response to the critiques about dispute resolution made by the Dean report. This report said that claimants had inadequate levels of access to legal advice and representation when they needed it, and recommended the establishment of ACC-funded advocacy services.[206] However the Navigation Service that was established cannot be properly described as a full legal advice service. Rather, it is a general guidance and advocacy service. Critics have argued that it would have been better to establish a Personal Injury Commissioner alongside a fully-funded advocacy service.[207] The suitability of a navigation service throws up two issues, from a legal perspective. The first issue relates to the necessity of an independent assistance and advocacy service for all claims – the streamlined and mostly automated nature of the claims application process means that most claims will be automatically approved and raise few problems. The second issue is that actual problematic cases that have been declined or involve a dispute between the claimant and ACC would appear to be the kind of situations where specialist legal and/or clinical advice would probably be immediately required, rather than a generic advice service. In this sense, the navigation service does not appear to be well-matched to the needs of individuals who are having problems with their claims. Further, the creation of this navigation service and the Talk Meet Resolve mediation service indicates a firm intention by the ACC Scheme to resolve disputes outside of the formal legal sphere. That seems logical from a structural perspective, because the whole ACC Scheme framework aims to make the compensation and resolution of personal injury issues a non-legal

---

[203] Legal Costs and Disbursements 'Supplementary Common Law Protocols' (n 179).

[204] In other words, only if the claim is varied, revoked or replaced. See Transport Accident Commission, 'Dispute Resolution' (n 180).

[205] 'Way Finders ACC Navigation Service' <https://www.wayfinders.org.nz/>.

[206] Dean (n 164) 3–4.

[207] Acclaim Otago, 'New Advocacy Service a Start, but Not the Solution' (2018) <https://www.scoop.co.nz/stories/PO1804/S00309/new-advocacy-service-a-start-but-not-the-solution.htm>; Warren Forster, Tom Barraclough and Tiho Mijatov, 'Solving the Problem: Causation, Transparency and Access to Justice in New Zealand's Personal Injury System' (2017).

matter. However, this does not mean that this is the best approach from a legal fairness and access to justice perspective.

Most of the funds do not appear to offer or fund an adequate level of basic free legal advice or assistance to claimants from the beginning of their claims challenge process. Although the intention of all four funds is to achieve personal injury compensation with minimal recourse to lawyers and legal advice, there is a specific point at which at least a basic degree of legal assistance will be necessary. This is because disputes that arise in the context of a no-fault comprehensive compensation fund are likely to be automatically complex for either causative or evidential reasons, because they have not been covered by the wide umbrella scope of the scheme. The Manitoba Claimant Advisor Office appears to do the best job of ensuring adequate access to basic legal advice for claimants. It should be noted that this is only open to claimants who intend to launch an appeal of an MPI internal review decision. However, given the paper-based and largely informal nature of internal reviews in the MPI, it seems logical that recourse to legal advice should be had after the fund itself has taken the prescribed statutory steps[208] to reassess the decision (but has once again made a conclusion denying or limiting the claimant's entitlements). In relation to New Zealand's ACC Scheme, the specialist training of Talk Meet Resolve mediation staff *may* mean that this becomes an avenue by which legal and clinical problems are flagged effectively, but the scheme is too new to thoroughly assess in comparison with the Manitoba approach.[209]

In relation to claimants who have raised disputes with the funds, the responses of the funds in relation the different questions asked of them are set out in the tables below.

Table 6. Survey responses on claimants' satisfaction with dispute resolution (ACC)

Question for ACC: In your annual report you mention client satisfaction ratings. Do you have a breakdown of these satisfaction ratings for clients who have engaged in a dispute of their claim? Do you take steps to assess the satisfaction with the disputes process of successful and/or unsuccessful claimants?
[This question was asked because of the legislative context in which internal reviews are the main form of dispute resolution set out in the act, with a limited scope for appeal to courts on points of law.[210] Further, in light of a 2016 review of dispute resolution procedures by Miriam Dean QC[211] and the wholesale adaptation of her recommendations,[212] it was appropriate to gather

(continued)

---

[208] The Manitoba Public Insurance Corporation Act ss 170(2), 170(3), 171.

[209] Talk – Meet – Resolve (n 154).

[210] Accident Compensation Act 2001 Part 5.

[211] Dean (n 164).

[212] 'Further Work to Improve ACC Dispute Resolution' <https://www.beehive.govt.nz/release/further-work-improve-acc-dispute-resolution>.

A Comparative Law Analysis of No-Fault Comprehensive Compensation Funds

Table 6 *continued*

some basic updated information about how this had translated into the experiences of claimants who brought a challenge of an ACC decision.]

A copy of a May 2020 internal report detailing survey responses of clients who had applied for reviews of ACC decisions within the past six months was supplied as the response to this question.[213] The survey specifically excluded sensitive claims or clients with a serious injury indicator.[214] At the time of taking the survey, 58 per cent of surveyed claimants had resolved their dispute, over half (52 per cent) by simply withdrawing their review claim. The
 	
    'main reasons clients give for why they applied for a review are their healthcare provider suggested they do (29%), not being able to afford treatment without ACC (24%) and their experience with ACC staff member/s handling their claim (22%).
 	
    …
 	
    Before lodging a review, clients indicated the most common ways they tried to resolve the issue was contacting the ACC staff member/s who handled their claim (67%), through contacting a healthcare provider (39%) or contacting ACC's call centre (26%).'
 	
The report indicated a stubbornly low satisfaction rate with the review process – 25 per cent. There were multiple apparent drivers of this poor outcome.
 	
    'When looking at drivers of dissatisfaction (by theming client comments), 38% relate to pre-review experience, 52% to the review process and 10% to the review specialist/team. Pre-review, the most common drivers of dissatisfaction relate to initial declines: not feeling that this decision considered all available information, being declined based on age, or not feeling their personal circumstances were considered/lacking personal contact. Top dissatisfaction drivers for the review process include the process being too slow/time consuming, a difficult/stressful process, not feeling all information was being considered and questioning the independence of the process. Top dissatisfaction drivers regarding the review specialist/team include communication (or lack of), not being helpful, and requests for more personal contact (face to face contact or joining online calls using video). Of the 25% of clients who were satisfied with the review process, satisfaction drivers relate to the review process (53%) or review specialist/team (33%) with top themes mentioned including good communication, fair process, satisfied with outcome, and helpful & professional individuals.'

ACC identified improved communication and explanation of the process to clients, including likely timelines, as being possible solutions to the identified problems.

Source: Compiled by the author.

The persistent dissatisfaction with the review of claims, for even the straightforward category of claims included in the survey, is noteworthy and concerning. The unaffordability of treatment without ACC cover as the motivating factor for a quarter of survey respondents is also very instructive from a contextual comparative law perspective. The problem in those cases could be argued as being not actually the scope of ACC cover or entitlements *per se*,

---

[213]   Accident Compensation Corporation, 'Client Reviews – Heartbeat Survey May 2020' (2020). 584 responses to the survey were recorded, which was a response rate of 22%.

[214]   ibid 5.

230   Intersentia

but rather the fact that the wider public health system or alternative insurance options are inadequate as another route of care for a significant proportion of these particular complainants. This is a reminder that attacks on the adequacy of ACC as a legislative framework[215] might be better framed as an argument in favour of wider social security and public health reforms (of which the ACC Scheme is one overlapping portion relating to personal injury compensation), or indeed in favour of effecting increased options for voluntary and mandatory insurance. The May 2020 report did not propose an increase in review processing or resolution speed as a possible goal resulting from this survey, suggesting that there is no institutional capacity to improve this factor. Better communication about timeframes does, however, seem to be a logical and achievable improvement to strive for.

The difficulty and stress faced by a significant proportion of claimants during the review process indicates a need for greater legal, advocacy and informational support for claimants. It is worth remembering that resolution of disputes via the Talk Meet Resolve service may occur before or after a review application has been launched, and resolution via this service must be agreed to by ACC. However, there is certainly potential for the Talk Meet Resolve service to help the significant proportion of claimants who ultimately withdraw their claim, by helping them come to a mediated solution. If future data, taken in context with published outcomes of the Talk Meet Resolve service, do not indicate some real improvements to perceptions of the review process, then this could indicate that there are persistent intrinsic problems with the legislative structure and the practical manifestation of dispute resolution processes.

From a comparative legal perspective, the most problematic aspect of the data provided by ACC is the fact that it does not include the most sensitive or complex types of disputes. Those are the kinds of 'high stakes' claims which test the fairness and appropriateness of a no-fault comprehensive compensation fund for the most vulnerable claimants. This kind of data is obviously difficult to gather and objectively analyse for privacy and sensitivity reasons, and ACC indicated its unwillingness to share this kind of information for this project due to privacy concerns. However the accurate assessment of the scheme and its review process as justice mechanisms requires more efforts to be made in the gathering and publication of this kind of data.

The other three funds have less expansive initial review processes than the ACC Scheme. In the three funds, initial reviews are all handled by a (sometimes independent) staff member, with the claimant retaining a right of appeal to a specific administrative tribunal. These three funds were therefore asked what percentage of cases were settled before heading to a tribunal or court.

---

[215] See for example, Forster & Associates, 'Expansion of ACC' <https://www.forster.co.nz/beyond-injury/expansion>; Forster, Barraclough and Mijatov (n 207).

Intersentia

A Comparative Law Analysis of No-Fault Comprehensive Compensation Funds

Table 7. Survey responses on dispute resolution outcomes (TAC, SAAQ and MPI)

Question for TAC, SAAQ and MPI: Can you estimate how often legal disputes between claimants and your organisation are settled rather than heading to court? (Average percentages are fine) Of cases that proceed to court, what percentage are successful?		
TAC	SAAQ	MPI
'The vast majority (over 95%) are resolved without Court.'	[translated] 'For the year 2019: – 30% of cases were settled through transactions, without going to tribunal. – For the remaining 70%, a conciliation session or a hearing (in roughly equal proportion) has been set; • 16% of them were finalized with a withdrawal • 54% of them resulted in a conciliation agreement or a tribunal decision These statistics are similar for the year 2018.'	'At MPI, we have a legislated Review and Appeal process. When there is a dispute, the first step is to file an Internal Review, which is managed by the Internal Review Office, which is "arm's length" from claims. The claimant's next step is to advance the matter to an external appeal board. Once the appeal is files [sic], they have the option of attempting to resolve the matter through mediation. If after the appeal, if they are still not satisfied, they have the option of filing at the Manitoba Court of Appeal – which is exceptionally rare, with only a handful of applicants since 1994. On average we get around 800 Applications for Review per year. I don't know what percentage this is of all decisions that are made; that would depend on the number of decisions Claims makes, keeping in mind Claimants generally only seek review of adverse decisions. Of those 800 reviews, this will generate around 600 decisions a year. About 20% will be overturned or varied on average. Of the 500 or decisions that confirm the Claims decision, about 100 will be appealed to AICAC. Many will settle out or be resolved in Mediation. External appeal then does 40–50 decisions each year, with less than 10% being varied or overturned; the rest are confirmed.'

Source: Compiled by the author.

The SAAQ and MPI responses indicate that a focus on one or more mediation opportunities to resolve disputes comes always after an initial internal review of the merits of a decision. This is also presumably the case for the TAC, although less information was offered by that fund on this point. This is different to the current approach of the ACC Scheme, which has begun to offer different dispute resolution pathways to claimants from the beginning of the dispute process. The ACC Scheme approach to dispute resolution is now a significant step away from traditional processes of dispute resolution or review of administrative claims. The other three funds take an approach towards disputed claims that is broadly in line with the way that other administrative decision challenges or judicial reviews might be handled. The data to date about ACC Scheme claimant perceptions do not indicate that this model is significantly preferable to a more traditional administrative claim review process. Data that become available in the future may enable clearer conclusions to be made on this point.

The funds were all questioned about what were the most common categories of claim disputes that it encountered. These responses are set out in the table below.

232

Intersentia

Table 8. Survey responses on most commonly disputed issues (ACC, TAC, SAAQ and MPI)

Question: Can you provide a list of the most common subject of disputes/broad claim types? Naturally, this can be as anonymised as possible to protect the privacy of your claimants.			
ACC	**TAC**	**SAAQ**	**MPI**
'The most commonly disputed issues are: – ACC's liability to pay for elective surgery – Subsequent cover (i.e. where cover is accepted for a simple strain originally and the client subsequently claims for a more serious condition from the original accident) – Treatment injury cover [i.e. medical injury cover] – Work-related gradual process, disease, or infection cover – Mental injury cover (consequential on physical injury) – Mental injury cover (caused by work related single event) – Suspension of weekly compensation. Most of these disputes will turn on causation, and clinical evidence is pivotal.'	'The following services account for over half of the dispute types with the first two accounting for 30% of all dispute types: Section 60 – Medical Service, Section 60 – Physiotherapy Treatment, Impairment Degree, Section 60 – Home Services and Section 60 – Surgery.' [Section 60 refers to the provision in the TAC legislation which describes the entitlements of claimants to 'Medical and like benefits'. There is a strong causative thread within section 60, with the phrase 'because of the transport accident' being the qualifying indication of whether a claimant is entitled to specified medical and like benefits.]	[translated] 'The most contested topics are: – Compensation for *sequelae* [a condition which is the consequence of a previously existing disease or injury] – The injury versus accident relationship – The medical non-necessity of treatment – The end of the income replacement indemnity – Personal help at home – Medication reimbursement.'	'The most common issues Claimants seek review of are treatment (physiotherapy, athletic therapy, and chiropractic care), permanent impairment payments, income replacement, and personal care assistance. There is a common thread through many of these categories related to "causation", which overlaps these headings because the Claimant may be seeking for example, treatment, but the real issue is whether there is causation for that treatment.'

Source: Compiled by the author.

There are some striking parallels between the most common categories of disputes across all four funds. The most obvious and predictable parallel, noted in relation to the ACC, SAAQ and MPI, is disputes relating to the cessation of weekly income compensation. A decision by the fund that the claimant is no longer entitled to the main form of compensation is of course likely to result in a dispute from the claimant, if he or she is not back in full employment or otherwise 'financially rehabilitated'. Far more noteworthy is the common causation thread that is a common factor in disputes across all four funds. This indicates that disputes are likely to arise at the border of causative eligibility for cover in cases which are less than clear-cut under the statutory framework. It appears that despite the broad statutory scope of eligibility that is common to all four funds, it will be necessary to turn to specialised medical evidence concerning whether the sought-after cover and compensation is causatively linked to the required threshold of eligibility, or whether a new claimed-for injury is not actually associated with the relevant personal injury. Despite legislative best efforts at clarity – apart from the difficulty of defining a serious injury in the case of the TAC – it is impossible to completely eschew medico-legal complexity in causative issues. In my view, this begs the question of whether the dispute resolution processes are designed appropriately given the likely highly technical nature of causation questions. For example, how can informal mediation – now a core theme of the ACC Scheme approach – possibly resolve technical questions of causative eligibility for cover, unless this simply results in case-by-case settlements or discretionary cover acquiescence on the part of the fund?[216]

Also instructive, from a comparative law perspective, is the fact that medical treatment injury as a whole category is one of the ACC Scheme's most common categories of dispute. This is despite reforms in the 2000s that removed the quasi-fault requirements to establish cover, which had the aim of removing complexity. Despite the scheme now having universal cover for most types of injury associated with medical treatment, the causative complexity of this field means that claims in this category will still generate a not insignificant number of disputes. This is instructive for non-comprehensive compensation funds in other jurisdictions that are targeted solely to medical injury claims, and arguments in favour of an expansive ACC-style no-fault scheme for medical injury in other countries.[217] It shows that it is not possible to wholly eliminate causative

---

[216] In this context, a recent public relations campaign launched by ACC to educate the public on what its role was, is telling – perhaps initial mediation is necessary because of a lack of understanding about ACC entitlements? See Accident Compensation Corporation, 'New Campaign to Tackle Low Awareness of ACC's Role' <https://www.scoop.co.nz/stories/PO2001/S00017/new-campaign-to-tackle-low-awareness-of-accs-role.htm>.

[217] Tina Popa, 'Don't Look for Fault, Find a Remedy! Exploring Alternative Forms of Compensating Medical Injuries in Australia, New Zealand and Belgium' (2019) 27 *Tort Law Review* 120; Elaine Gibson, 'Is It Time to Adopt a No-Fault Scheme to Compensate Injured

Chapter 4. Key Pillars

complexity in relation to compensation for this kind of harm, regardless of the broadness of cover. Dispute resolution procedures may need to be specifically designed to be cognisant of this kind of causative theme.

5.3. CONCLUSIONS ON DISPUTE RESOLUTION

Some kind of legislatively specified initial review and dispute resolution procedure is a key pillar of the dispute resolution framework of all very large no-fault compensation funds. A default recourse to a court or administrative tribunal as a first and only option is not a common feature. This is a logical structural feature, given the broad intention of these large schemes to eschew legal adversarial processes.

A common key pillar of dispute resolution of all no-fault comprehensive compensation funds is the extensive use of mediation and alternative dispute resolution to manage *all* claim reviews. This is logical, given the non-adversarial scheme design that is common to these big funds. When designed well, with a positive approach towards mediation on the part of the fund and appropriate and practical advice provided to the claimant, mediation can be a very effective and important pillar of dispute resolution. However, mediation is unlikely to be appropriate in technical eligibility or causative disputes, which appear to be the most common types of dispute arising in these big funds.

Even though big no-fault funds move personal injury compensation slightly outside the legal sphere, where there is a dispute about a claim it will be necessary for legal and evidential issues to be properly considered. Across all four funds there is currently uneven access for claimants to legal and other expert guidance when they have a dispute about their claim. The best practice is exemplified by Manitoba, where the government established a free legal advice service funded by the MPI for claimants from the internal review appeal stage onward. Some kind of funding of or contribution towards at least a basic level of legal advocacy and advice costs should therefore be regarded as a key pillar for the improved design of big no-fault compensation funds on the issue of dispute resolution. If that is not possible, then a negotiated protocol arrangement with legal practitioner bodies, as occurs in Victoria, is a good second choice. The popularity of the TAC protocol-based approach indicates that where claimants are given a choice about whether to resolve a dispute with or without the assistance of a lawyer, they will overwhelmingly choose legal assistance. Although there is no confirmed link between access to legal advice and claimant satisfaction, this evidence from

---

Patients?' (2016) 47 *Ottawa Law Review* 303 <https://commonlaw.uottawa.ca/ottawa-law-review/sites/commonlaw.uottawa.ca.ottawa-law-review/files/olr_47-2_02_gibson_final.pdf>.

Intersentia

235

the TAC suggests that existing big funds should aim to increase access to basic legal assistance for free or at little cost, in order to improve claimant perception and satisfaction about the dispute resolution process. It is logical – and highly appropriate, from a fairness perspective – that claimants who have a dispute will want some kind of guidance, given that they are in a vulnerable position and recovering from an injury. It is also likely that facilitating greater access to legal advice would reduce frivolous claims, as lawyers would be able to advise claimants on the likely success of their claim at the outset. The strict application and wide scope of the tort bar in these four large funds means that it is unlikely that an increase in vexatious or unsubstantiated claims would result from increased claimant access to legal guidance.

Causative issues have been clearly shown to be the strongest common denominator in disputes in all four funds. Causation should therefore be expected to be a common feature in most disputes emerging from such a big fund, regardless of its functional scope. However it is unclear whether existing dispute resolution procedures are designed appropriately and consciously to address the dominance of causative issues. Related to this, coverage for medical injury (as under the ACC Scheme) will automatically lead to a large number of disputes being generated due to causative and evidential complexity. A key pillar of a successful big compensation fund will be the design of dispute resolution procedures to respond effectively to the most common categories of disputes that arise. None of the four funds currently meet what might be a considered a 'best practice' standard on this issue. This means that funds need to be more cognisant of disputes when conducting scheme design and revision.

There is currently insufficient readily available data on whether the existing dispute resolution methods used by no-fault comprehensive compensation funds are working effectively in relation to seriously or complexly injured claimants who seek a review of their dispute. Better tracking of these kinds of claimants would be desirable to assess the funds' dispute resolution processes. Overall, a conclusion can be drawn here that regular assessment of the outcomes and effectiveness of dispute resolution processes will be a necessary key pillar of comprehensive no-fault compensation funds. This is to ensure that claimants, particularly those with serious or complex injuries and disputes, are being treated fairly and that the legislative design of dispute resolution processes and financial supports is fit for purpose. There may indeed be merit to an independent agency, such as a personal injury commissioner or no-fault ombudsman, having oversight of this process.

6. ADMINISTRATION: FUNDING AND SUSTAINABILITY

Funding, and its sustainability, is one of the most practically important parts of any compensation fund. This is particularly the case for a fund that is intended

Chapter 4. Key Pillars

to operate proactively in relation to future losses, and does not exist only in relation to a time- or event-limited group of victims. A pro-actively designed fund that includes future injuries has a potentially unknowable level of future cost liabilities – depending upon scheme scope and the relevant actuarial calculations that were made at the time of the fund's establishment. The vast majority of compensation funds around the world (both comprehensive and non-comprehensive) are publicly funded.[218] However a distinction can be made here between those compensation funds that are funded out of the general taxation public purse, and those that are funded out of a specially allocated budget or special taxes. Some compensation funds are privately funded: for example, many European non-comprehensive compensation funds in the field of uninsurable transport injury are funded by contributions from private insurance companies.[219]

The four large no-fault compensation funds studied in this project all have a very large scope, and have each been operating for at least three decades. This *prima facie* implies a degree of sustainability; however, the fact of sustainability should not be presumed. Are these big funds truly sustainable in their own right, or only because of the sustained injection of taxpayer funds? This is a question that has not been thoroughly or recently answered in the literature or practice. The longevity of these funds also means that it is important to analyse the funding mechanisms of these structures in order to identify what are the common key pillars of funding in big compensation funds. Are these large funds indeed sustainable and self-sufficient in their own right? Or do they require some degree of ongoing support from the public purse? What commonalities and core elements can be discerned from an analysis of the four large funds?

Typically, there has been a critical view taken by tort law heavyweights about the financial sustainability of such large no-fault compensation funds. Patrick Atiyah famously criticised schemes such as New Zealand's ACC as being an undue burden on state expenditure and the public at large,[220] a criticism more recently repeated by Helmut Koziol.[221] However, these critiques do not account for and combine the value and impact of social costs to a no-fault comprehensive scheme, something which is admittedly difficult to estimate.[222] Yet the open-ended nature of comprehensive funds' liabilities, combined with some link to public taxation revenue, makes it impossible to minimise or disregard the

---

[218]   Vansweevelt and others (n 1) 198.

[219]   Kim Watts, 'Managing Mass Damages Liability via Tort Law and Tort Alternatives, with Ireland as a Case Study' (2020) 11 *Journal of European Tort Law* 57, 199 <https://www.degruyter.com/view/journals/jetl/11/1/article-p57.xml>.

[220]   PS Atiyah, *The Damages Lottery* (Hart Publishing 1997) 183–184.

[221]   Helmut Koziol, 'Compensation for Personal Injury : Comparative Incentives for the Interplay of Tort Law and Insurance Law' (2017) 8 *Journal of European Tort Law* 41, 45–46.

[222]   Richard Gaskins, 'Accounting for Accidents: Social Costs of Personal Injuries' (2010) 41 *Victoria University of Wellington Law Review* 37.

Intersentia

substantial financial risks. These issues therefore demand a proper investigation into the funding structures of these large funds, with reference to their publicly reported financial data, to ascertain whether these criticisms have empirical foundation. It also begs an updated and objective assessment of the current financial position of these large funds, to determine whether there are core similarities in the way that they are funded – and whether these features point to sustainability and stability of the funds. An updated assessment of the funding structures can point to positive and negative features of financial elements that were not previously known, and that may be relevant to the financial design of other no-fault compensation funds and schemes.

Naturally, the issue of funding is the other side of the coin to the quantum of compensation offered by the fund. None of these large funds offer theoretically unlimited or 'full' compensation to all claimants, although they do pay compensation to victims for as long as they are statutorily eligible. As noted earlier, the TAC offers serious injury claimants the possibility of large tort-equivalent 'common law damages'. Therefore, an immediate distinction can be drawn with non-comprehensive funds that offer 'full' or tort-equivalent compensation to all victims.[223] The key pillars of funding that are identified for these big no-fault funds therefore may not be completely applicable or relevant to other funds, especially where the latter strive to offer 'full' compensation. However, lessons we can draw about the sustainability of these funds may be relevant to considerations of whether, on balance, it is legislatively desirable or fiscally viable to operate a large scheme that compensates more victims, albeit at a generally lower rate. There may also be relevance to choices about funding and investment for certain *functional* types of injury.

6.1. NEW ZEALAND'S ACC SCHEME

We turn first to New Zealand's funding model.[224] This fund has the most complex funding structure out of the four funds, incorporating different streams of revenue from risk-takers, employers and other businesses, and from the general public by way of levies on products. This complexity is logical, given that the scheme covers the widest range of harms. The ACC Scheme's funding models have changed significantly over its history. Issues of funding have been closely linked over time to public conceptions of the ACC Scheme,[225] and where the scheme fits within the (often jurisdictionally different) definitions of insurance, welfare and social insurance.

---

[223] For example, like Belgium's medical injuries compensation fund *Fonds voor Medische Ongevallen.*

[224] The paragraphs on New Zealand's funding model are an updated version of the relevant section in Watts, 'New Zealand' (n 163).

[225] Gaskins (n 222) 37.

The costing of the ACC Scheme was carefully calculated in the Woodhouse Report on the basis that existing compulsory worker injury compensation and motor insurance levies should be diverted to fund the new accident compensation scheme.[226] This, in combination with savings made by self-insurers (like the Government), and savings to social security and healthcare budgets, would come close to financing the new scheme. The remaining gap would be closed by contributions from newly covered groups – the self-employed and motor vehicle licence-holders. The Woodhouse Report had identified administrative cost concerns with allowing social insurance schemes to be administered by private insurance companies, who retained profits from contributions paid into a scheme.[227]

Funding for the ACC Scheme has always been based on a combination of levies on activities and the general taxation pool.[228] The scheme currently operates on a full funding model, with a pay-as-you-go model for the small number of outstanding pre-2001 non-earner injuries.[229] A pay-as-you-go model for funding the whole ACC Scheme was utilised in the 1980s and 1990s, but this was changed by the 1998 legislation due to significant costs blow-outs following political tweaks to levies.[230] Ken Oliphant has noted that ACC's historic funding problems are attributable not to any intrinsic lack of viability in the fundamental vision, but rather to specific failures in the implementation.[231] Over 20 years have elapsed since the most recent major changes to the ACC Scheme's financial framework, so it is therefore useful to re-evaluate the key financial pillars and compare them with the other three big funds.

---

[226] Royal Commission to Inquire into and Report upon Workers' Compensation, *Compensation for Personal Injury in New Zealand* (Government Printing Office 1967) 171.

[227] Royal Commission to Inquire into and Report upon Workers' Compensation, *Compensation for Personal Injury in New Zealand* (Government Printing Office 1967) 181.

[228] Stephen Todd and others, *The Law of Torts in New Zealand*, Stephen Todd (ed) (7th edn, Thomson Reuters 2016) 96–97.

[229] Accident Compensation Corporation, 'Annual Report 2017' (2017) <https://www.parliament. nz/resource/en-NZ/PAP_75085/cd5473578a0a648b7c15d0d819d2f36d8ba477c2>. 'Our broad financial sustainability objective is to ensure each levied account is in a fully funded solvency position. Full funding means that, at any point in time, the value of our investment portfolio is enough to pay for the future costs of every claim we have received to date. The exception to this full funding objective is the costs of Government-funded non-earners' injuries incurred prior to 1 July 2001. These are funded on a pay-as-you-go basis.'

[230] As noted already, the 1998 legislation introduced a degree of privatisation to the ACC Scheme by allowing private insurers to compete for the provision of work-related injury cover. It was necessary to introduce a full funding requirement to ensure private insurers had 'sufficient assets to meet their contractual obligations.' An Insolvent Insurers Fund was to be established to ensure that statutory entitlements continued to be paid if 'an insurer has insufficient assets to meet its obligations under accident insurance contacts.' See Accident Insurance Bill (203-1) 1999, iii.

[231] Ken Oliphant, 'Basic Questions of Tort Law from the Perspective of England and the Commonwealth', *Basic Questions of Tort Law from a Comparative Perspective* (Jan Sramek Verlag 2015) 367.

From the outset, it is worth noting that although the ACC Scheme is 'aligned with professional standards' on insurer solvency and financial stability, this is only to the extent that these standards 'make sense for ACC'.[232] Unlike other insurers, the ACC Scheme does not have to comply with the New Zealand central bank's minimum solvency requirements. This is because it operates on a non-profit basis and is a 'statutory monopoly with the right to raise levies'.[233] The Reserve Bank, for its part, classifies ACC as an 'unlicensed government-owned general insurer', in the same category as two state-controlled natural disaster insurers.[234] Therefore, annual independent actuarial assessments of the financial health of the ACC Scheme are made with reference to 'the funding position of each of the Accounts compared to funding targets set by Government'.[235] The funding targets are the amount of investment assets available to cover the liabilities of claims, with the target of keeping the scheme fully-funded to cover the lifetime costs of claims. This therefore reveals that ACC is subject to fewer financial regulatory controls than other insurers, owing to its Crown entity status. However it is also subject to government-set targets and requirements to operate fairly and sustainably, with an eye to 'intergenerational equity' and the current Labour government's 'wellbeing approach'.[236] These goals can be perceived as a contemporary funding policy reinterpretation of the existing statutory commitment to the scheme being fully-funded or 'save-as-you-go', which is linked to the additional objective of minimising large levy fluctuations.[237]

ACC's current full-funding model has in recent years generally proved to be a sustainable one: after conquering the financial solvency challenges of the 1980s and 1990s,[238] the ACC now broadly has adequate financial reserves in place and

---

[232] Accident Compensation Corporation, 'Financial Condition Report 2020' 2 <www.acc.co.nz/about-us/corporate>.

[233] ibid 19.

[234] These are the Earthquake Commission (which is a compulsory co-insurer of residential dwellings for certain natural disasters) and Southern Response Earthquake Services (a government-owned insurer resulting from the bailout of private insurer AMI following the Canterbury earthquakes of 2010-11, and AMI's inadequate re-insurance and capitalisation to cover earthquake-related losses). See Insurance (Prudential Supervision) Act 2010 s 8 and 'Insurance' (*Reserve Bank of New Zealand*) <https://www.rbnz.govt.nz/financial-stability/overview-of-the-new-zealand-financial-system/insurance>.

[235] Accident Compensation Corporation, 'Financial Condition Report 2020' (n 232) 19.

[236] Innovation and Employment Ministry of Business, 'Changes to ACC Funding Settings' (2020) <https://www.mbie.govt.nz/dmsdocument/11596-changes-to-acc-funding-settings-proactiverelease-pdf>.

[237] Accident Compensation Act 2001 s 166A.

[238] In short, this is because a social security-style 'pay-as-you-go' model was used in the 1980s and early 1990s, while employers successfully lobbied to reduce ACC levies. See Watts, 'New Zealand' (n 163) 94. However, since 1998 all but one of the scheme's liability accounts have been required to be funded on an insurance/fully-funded basis. Only non-motor vehicle injuries suffered by non-earners (e.g. children) are funded by Treasury. See Todd and others (n 142) 96.

a long-term investment strategy to cover its claims obligations.[239] Specifically, in the year 2017/18 the fund had a solvency ratio of 96.7 per cent. This dipped in 2019 to 81.2 per cent, but this was largely because of matters outside of ACC's control, such as falling interest rates globally.[240] However, the financial health of the scheme declined significantly in the most recent financial year of 2019/20. Overall solvency (renamed 'funding ratio') was on average 90 per cent, but significantly worse for the government-supported accounts.[241] Again, this was mostly due to falling interest rates globally (resulting in a lower return on investment income), which is something that affects the investment income of 'other long-tail insurance schemes around the world'.[242] However, worsening claims performance and reduced levies and appropriation have also had a negative impact on the ACC Scheme's financial position.[243] These issues will be explored at greater length later in this sub-section, as they are a first hint at financial challenges specific to no-fault comprehensive compensation funds, that may upset ACC's generally stable recent financial picture.

The scheme's long-term investments generate significant amounts of income and so this income is currently subsidising levies.[244] In 2019, investment income generated NZ$5.1 billion, before investment costs. In 2020, investment income dipped significantly to NZ$3.4 billion due to financial market instability, although this was a higher return than expected.[245] In the longer term, lower investment returns could well have an impact on the sustainability of the scheme – in terms of keeping levies low and avoiding the need for significant injections of taxpayer funding. However this is no different to challenges faced by other publicly managed investment bodies such as sovereign wealth and pension funds, as well as major international insurers and reinsurers. Indeed, sovereign wealth funds have reported significant investment losses due to the COVID-19 pandemic,[246] while the running total of COVID-19 associated losses for the global insurance industry was US$34.523 billion as of March 2021.[247] Nevertheless, it is clear that ACC's broad financial sustainability in the past two decades has been underpinned by investment income successes, which cannot be presumed to reliably continue and guarantee the financial sustainability of this kind of comprehensive no-fault scheme.

---

[239] Accident Compensation Corporation, 'Annual Report 2019' (n 30) 43–49.

[240] ibid 42–43.

[241] Accident Compensation Corporation, 'Annual Report 2020' 57.

[242] Accident Compensation Corporation, 'Financial Condition Report 2020' (n 232) 5.

[243] ibid 4.

[244] Accident Compensation Corporation, 'Annual Report 2019' (n 30) 45.

[245] Accident Compensation Corporation, 'Annual Report 2020' (n 241) 12.

[246] 'Covid-19 and Sovereign Wealth Funds: What Does the Future Hold?' (*Oxford Business Group*) <https://oxfordbusinessgroup.com/news/covid-19-and-sovereign-wealth-funds-what-does-future-hold>.

[247] 'COVID-19 Insurer & Reinsurer Loss Reports', *Reinsurance News* <https://www.reinsurancene.ws/covid-19-insurer-reinsurer-loss-reports/>.

The ACC itself has specifically defined relevant key terms in relation to its financial stability and sustainability. This is helpful to our assessment of the scheme overall from a legal perspective. These definitions may also be relevant to comparison with the other big funds, other smaller no-fault compensation funds, and alternative compensation structures.

ACC defines the term 'fair' as 'achieving outcomes, in accordance with the purpose of the Scheme, that are equitable for individuals and groups of people with an interest in the Scheme.'[248]

Sustainability is defined in this way by ACC: 'A sustainable Scheme is one that can fulfil its purpose, withstand shocks and endure into the future.'[249] This can be presumed to refer to the purpose clause within the legislation, which states that the purpose of the scheme is to 'enhance the public good and reinforce the social contract represented by the first accident compensation scheme by providing for a fair and sustainable scheme for managing personal injury.'[250] The goals of minimising the incidence and impact of injury to the community are also relevant here. The longevity of the scheme is also strongly implied, but there are no direct statements made in any corporate documents about whether the fund needs to be self-sufficient (in the sense that levies and investment income are enough to satisfy its current and long-term liabilities, except perhaps for specific injury classes that are taxpayer supported), or whether the fund (and the legislature's) conception of financial sustainability includes long-term reliance on taxpayer funding to an increasing degree.[251]

We turn now to the operational elements of the ACC Scheme's funding structure. ACC manages five different accounts that relate to specific types of injuries. These are:[252]

a.   the Work Account (for work-related injuries, including private domestic workers and the self-employed);[253]
b.   the Earners' Account (for injuries to earners that are not work-related, motor vehicle injuries or treatment injures);[254]
c.   the Motor Vehicle Account (for motor vehicle injuries);[255]

---

[248]   Accident Compensation Corporation, 'Financial Condition Report 2020' (n 232) 2.
[249]   Accident Compensation Corporation, 'Financial Condition Report 2020' (n 232).
[250]   Accident Compensation Act 2001 s 3.
[251]   For example, the most recent Annual Report simply states that a strategic objective is to 'ensure that New Zealand has an affordable and sustainable scheme by improving the financial sustainability of the ACC Scheme' – Accident Compensation Corporation, 'Annual Report 2020' (n 241) 28.
[252]   Accident Compensation Act 2001 s 166.
[253]   ibid ss 167–180.
[254]   ibid ss 218–222.
[255]   ibid ss 213, 214, 216 and 217.

Chapter 4. Key Pillars

d.   the Non-Earners' Account (for non-earning individuals such as children and retirees)[256] and

e.   the Treatment Injury Account.[257]

The first three accounts are funded by levies on personal income (earnings), business income, vehicle fuel and vehicle registration.[258] An overview of these levies is set out in the table below.

Table 9. Levies on income and vehicle usage (ACC Scheme)

Levy	What the levy funds and how it is calculated	Amount
Work levy	Funds the Work Account for workplace related injuries. A degree of risk rating is associated with the calculation of the work levy.	This is different for each individual business, and is calculated with reference to three criteria: – the risk of injury at work (depending on the business category that is used for general taxation purposes);[259] – the ACC claims history associated with that business and its employees; and – the liable income or payroll of the business. Selected large employers may apply to join the Accredited Employers Programme.[260] This allows the employer to significantly reduce its Work levy, but then takes all financial responsibility for personal injury compensation and rehabilitation of any injured employees. Participants are audited annually. There have been inconsistent employee outcomes under the AEP, and the scheme is currently being reformed.[261] A separate flat levy of NZ$0.08 per NZ$100 of payroll or income is levied by ACC on behalf of WorkSafe New Zealand, to support workplace safety and injury prevention activities.[262]

(continued)

---

[256]   ibid s 227.
[257]   Accident Compensation Corporation, 'What Your Levies Pay For' <https://www.acc.co.nz/about-us/how-levies-work/what-your-levies-pay/>.
[258]   Accident Compensation Act 2001 ss 167, 213 and 218.
[259]   'ACC Levy Guidebook 2020/21' <https://www.acc.co.nz/assets/business/acc7686-levy-guidebook-2020-2021.pdf>.
[260]   Accident Compensation Act 2001 ss 181–189; 'Joining the Accredited Employers Programme (AEP)' <https://www.acc.co.nz/for-business/understanding-your-cover-options/accredited-employers-programme/>.
[261]   'Improving the Accredited Employers Programme' <https://www.shapeyouracc.co.nz/enhancing-the-accredited-employer-programme/improving-the-accredited-employers-programme/>.
[262]   'Understanding Levies If You Work or Own a Business' <https://www.acc.co.nz/for-business/understanding-levies-if-you-work-or-own-a-business/>.

Intersentia

243

Table 9 *continued*

Levy	What the levy funds and how it is calculated	Amount
Earners' levy	Funds the Earners' Account and the Earners' portion of the Treatment Injury Account. This is a flat-rate levy.	NZ$1.21 per NZ$100 (excluding goods and services tax/VAT, NZ$1.39 after GST[263]) of an individual's liable income. This is levied at the same time as payroll taxes.[264] Levies are only paid on income up to a maximum of NZ$130,911. This means that individuals who earn more than this amount will not pay more than NZ$1,819.66 in Earners' levies per year. Self-employed people pay levies to the Earners' Account on the basis of the same maximum level, but must also pay minimum levies (based on an income of NZ$36,816), unless they are only part-time self-employed (less than 30 hours per week). Self-employed people can also pay extra levies to participate in the CoverPlus scheme, which guarantees a specified amount of income replacement compensation (something useful for those with fluctuating earnings or are newly self-employed with no income history).[265]
Vehicle fuel levy	The Motor Vehicle Account (for motor vehicle-related injuries). Factors relevant to the levy calculation include the historical level of fuel consumption.[266]	NZ$0.06 per litre of petrol, paid at the point of sale.[267] Diesel is not taxed at the fuel pump, because diesel powers vehicles other than road vehicles (such as boats). Diesel road vehicles pay more registration tax. Electric vehicles are obviously not subject to a fuel levy, but are classed as petrol vehicles for the purposes of the vehicle registration levy.
Vehicle registration levy	The Motor Vehicle Account (for motor vehicle related injuries). Factors relevant to the levy calculation include the number of vehicle registrations.[268]	These are the levies for 2021: – Petrol cars and light passenger vehicles – NZ$46.04. – Non-petrol cars and light passenger vehicles – NZ104.65. – Mopeds and scooters – petrol NZ$124.33, non-petrol NZ$138.98.

(continued)

---

[263] 'ACC Earners' Levy Rates' <https://www.ird.govt.nz/income-tax/income-tax-for-individuals/acc-clients-and-carers/acc-earners-levy-rates>.

[264] 'Understanding Levies If You Work or Own a Business' (n 262).

[265] 'Types of Cover for Self-Employed' <https://www.acc.co.nz/for-business/understanding-your-cover-options/types-of-cover-for-self-employed/>.

[266] Accident Compensation Corporation, 'Financial Condition Report 2020' (n 232) 83.

[267] 'Paying Levies If You Own or Drive a Vehicle' <https://www.acc.co.nz/about-us/how-levies-work/paying-levies-if-you-own-or-drive-a-vehicle/>.

[268] Accident Compensation Corporation, 'Financial Condition Report 2020' (n 232) 83.

Table 9 *continued*

Levy	What the levy funds and how it is calculated	Amount
	A general distinction is made between light passenger vehicles; mopeds, scooters and motorcycles; goods service vehicles and vintage vehicles.	
	Mopeds, scooters and motorcycles pay higher levies because of the greater accident risk associated with these vehicle types (based on government crash data).[269]	
	In 2019, ACC eliminated the relevance of vehicle safety ratings to levies on passenger vehicles. This was because of a lack of evidence that this 'vehicle risk rating' contributed to injury prevention, and because (according to a public consultation) it placed a burden on low-income people who were less able to afford vehicles with better safety ratings.[270]	
	Due to a lack of crash data for goods service vehicles, those vehicles' levies are based on weight.	

Source: Compiled by the author.

The Non-Earners' Account – covering children, social welfare recipients (including pensioners), students and visitors – is funded by the Government out of general taxation.[271] The Treatment Injury Account is funded by both the Earners' and Non-Earners' Account, depending on whether the injured person is employed.[272] Interestingly, the power that exists within the ACC legislation to impose levies on registered health professionals and associated organisations has never been exercised.[273] This means that treatment injury costs are not

---

[269] 'Paying Levies If You Own or Drive a Vehicle' (n 267); Ministry of Transport, 'Safety Annual Statistics – Motorcyclists' <https://www.transport.govt.nz/statistics-and-insights/safety-annual-statistics/sheet/motorcyclists>.

[270] 'Vehicle Risk Rating (VRR) Removed from ACC Motor Vehicle Levy' <https://www.acc.co.nz/newsroom/stories/vehicle-risk-rating-vrr-removed-from-acc-motor-vehicle-levy/>.

[271] Accident Compensation Act 2001 s 227(2).

[272] ibid s 228; Accident Compensation Corporation, 'What Your Levies Pay For' (n 257).

[273] Todd and others (n 142) 97. The wording of s 228(2) implies a degree of executive discretion as to whether such levies on healthcare professionals may ever be implemented. The wording of the relevant section is as follows: 'The funds for the Treatment Injury Account are to be derived from (a) any levies payable by registered health professionals or any organisation that

A Comparative Law Analysis of No-Fault Comprehensive Compensation Funds

funded in any way by healthcare professionals, except to the extent that these individuals pay earner or employer levies.

In the late 2000s and early 2010s, the government sought to introduce private insurer delivery of elements of the Work, Earners' and Motor Vehicle Accounts, with a view to introducing competitiveness and risk rating that would reduce cross-subsidisation between individuals.[274] However these proposals never went ahead. There is no clear empirical information available about whether the New Zealand private insurers were willing to undertake widespread rating (given the comprehensive 'everyday risks of life' coverage of the ACC Scheme), or whether there was even a suitable methodology for doing this.[275] From the limited data available, it seems that there was unwillingness to either increase levies on employers or reduce claims costs to offset the 20–26 per cent increase in operational expenses that would have been incurred by private insurers.[276] There was also inadequate empirical information available (due to the unique effects of the monopolistic ACC Scheme being in operation since the 1970s) about likely risk profiles, as well as inadequate actuarial expertise in New Zealand to provide the information needed to facilitate these changes.[277] Had these changes been implemented, then New Zealand would have experimented with the type of universal (but private insurer provided) personal injury insurance that Helmut Koziol has more recently advocated.[278] In relation to treatment injury, there was also a proposal that medical practitioners and healthcare organisations should purchase malpractice cover as part of their general professional indemnity insurance, in order to support the cost of treatment injury cover. However medical professionals pointed out that any insurance premiums would be passed on to patients through user charges, thus curtailing legislative appetite for any further development of this proposal.[279]

---

provides treatment under this Act, or a prescribed class of such persons or organisations; and (b) if there is no such levy or the levy relates only to funding part of the Account, from the Earners' Account (in the case of an earner) or the Non-Earners' Account (in the case of a non-earner); and (c) in the case of injuries suffered before the prescribed date from which levies become payable, from the Earners' Account (in the case of an earner) or the Non-Earners' Account (in the case of a non-earner).'

[274] Grant Duncan, 'New Zealand's Universal No-Fault Accident Compensation Scheme: Embedding Community Responsibility' in Joannah Luetjens, Michael Mintrom and Paul 't Hart (eds), *Successful Public Policy Lessons from Australia and New Zealand* (ANU Press 2019) 340 <http://press-files.anu.edu.au/downloads/press/n5314/pdf/ch14.pdf>.

[275] ibid 340–341.

[276] Department of Labour, 'Regulatory Impact Statement: Response to the Recommendations of the ACC Stocktake' (2010) 17.

[277] Jamie Reid and Andrew Mackessack, 'New Zealand Accident Compensation: What's Happening?', *Institute of Actuaries of Australia Accident Compensation Seminar* (Brisbane, November 2011) 15–19.

[278] Koziol (n 221).

[279] Duncan (n 274) 341.

246

Intersentia

In 2019, ACC reported that most of its funding came from levy sources (employer levies – NZ$861 million; employee levies – NZ$1,614 million; vehicle owners and drivers – NZ$425 million) and investment income (by far the largest source of funding at NZ$5,092 million). Central government funding was less significant, and related to non-earner injuries (NZ$1,274 million) and treatment injury (NZ$332 million – although as noted above, a portion of this latter category was funded by employee levies).[280] In 2020, ACC reported a significant dip in investment earnings (NZ$3,444 million) but reasonable stability across other funding sources (employer levies – NZ$815 million; employee levies – NZ$1,664 million; vehicle owners and drivers – NZ$444 million; non-earner taxpayer funding – NZ$1,278 million; treatment injury funding from government and employees – NZ$267 million).[281]

There is currently a 100 per cent target funding (or solvency) ratio for each of the ACC's five accounts. This is calculated 'by dividing total assets, less payables, accrued liabilities, provisions, unearned levy liability and unexpired risk liability by the outstanding claims liability (including additional liability for work-related gradual process claims not yet made but excluding any risk margin)'.[282] Any necessary adjustment to the average levy rate to meet this target must be done as smoothly as possible, over a 10-year horizon, and must not exceed 15 per cent (in addition to any necessary inflation adjustments for the Motor Vehicle Account).[283] Levy rates have fallen in the past 10 years to bring over-funded accounts back to targeted levels,[284] ensuring that current levy-payers are not over-funding future risks. However economic impacts on investment income now mean that funding ratios have fallen further than was expected. The partially or fully non-levied Treatment Injury and Non-earners' Accounts have suffered the greatest shortfall, as they are the most supported by investment revenue.[285]

In terms of how the ACC's investment portfolio is managed, ACC holds investment funds in trust for levy-payers. The funds associated with each account can only be used for meeting the claims associated with that account, and no cross-subsidisation of accounts is permitted.[286] The ACC Scheme is currently not underpinned by reinsurance, and a 2017 scenario analysis

---

[280] Accident Compensation Corporation, 'Annual Report 2019' (n 30) 4.
[281] Accident Compensation Corporation, 'Annual Report 2020' (n 241) 26.
[282] 'Funding Policy Statement in Relation to the Funding of ACC's Levied Accounts', *New Zealand Gazette* (8 July 2020).
[283] ibid.
[284] Accident Compensation Corporation, 'Annual Report 2020' (n 241) 24.
[285] In the year ending June 2020, the Treatment Injury account has suffered a shortfall of NZ$371m, while the Non-Earners' account has suffered a shortfall of NZ$2,016m. This puts the Treatment Injury account at a funding ratio of 81.2% and the Non-Earners' account at a funding ratio of 58.8%. By contrast, the position in the year 2017/18 was over 110% for the Treatment Injury account and just under 90% for the Non-Earners' account. See ibid 57.
[286] ibid 63; Accident Compensation Act 2001 s 166.

concluded that reinsurance was not necessary to reduce risk to ACC's funding position, even though there could be material impacts on solvency and funding requirements.[287] This is because

> 'very long-term individual claims aren't large enough to materially affect the Scheme's net assets [and] the most extreme catastrophes and resulting claims wouldn't threaten ACC's ability to pay claims in the short term. The Scheme can also post-fund claims for these events.'[288]

ACC is also responsible for managing the funding intersection with New Zealand's public health system (for example, in relation to acute injury cases that are treated in public hospitals). ACC makes an annual acute care contribution to the Ministry of Health/central Treasury. There are also agreements between ACC and regional public health boards for the funding of non-acute care. However there is not an exact alignment between all non-acute personal injury care costs provided by public health boards and what is reimbursed by ACC,[289] which indicates there is some degree of overlap between the ACC Scheme and the general taxpayer-funded public system.[290] In the year 2019/20, ACC paid NZ$555 million to public health acute services, which was NZ$10 million more than forecast.[291]

The overall broad financial sustainability of the ACC Scheme in recent times appears also to be enhanced by the value of its significant social benefits, such as the greatly improved equity in the distribution of resources, as identified by PriceWaterhouseCoopers in their review of the ACC Scheme.[292] However this is offset by the scheme's already detailed financial shortfalls in the past year due to investment fluctuations. The ACC identifies that the social benefits currently provided by the scheme include the provision of injury compensation in a way that improves social inclusion and cohesion, evidence-based accident reduction programmes, risk pricing to incentivise behaviour, effective injury management and rehabilitation, and the elimination of injury as a driver of poverty.[293] However the actual outlook of injury prevention programmes is mixed, with some core programmes delivering good results but others having yet to give a significant return on investment.[294] Compensation and rehabilitation

---

[287] Accident Compensation Corporation, 'Financial Condition Report' (2017) 5 <https://www.acc.co.nz/assets/corporate-documents/acc7847-financial-condition-report-2017.pdf>.

[288] Accident Compensation Corporation, 'Financial Condition Report 2020' (n 232) 22.

[289] Comments in interview with ACC's Principal Solicitor AC Law, December 2019.

[290] Accident Compensation Corporation, 'Paying for Patient Treatment' <https://www.acc.co.nz/for-providers/invoicing-us/paying-patient-treatment/>; 'Accident Services: A Guide for DHB and ACC Staff' (2018) <https://forms.acc.co.nz/ACC32>.

[291] Accident Compensation Corporation, 'Annual Report 2020' (n 241) 123.

[292] PriceWaterhouseCoopers (n 53) 85.

[293] Accident Compensation Corporation, 'Annual Report 2020' (n 241) 31.

[294] Accident Compensation Corporation, 'Financial Condition Report 2020' (n 232) 32–39.

Chapter 4. Key Pillars

performance are closely linked together, but both metrics have worsened in the past six years – claims volumes and costs have been higher than expected, to the tune of NZ$3 billion more outstanding claims liabilities between 2014/15 and 2019/20.[295] ACC itself expects that there will need to be an increase in levies and taxpayer funding to the five accounts.[296] The drivers of increased costs are currently:[297]

a. Increases in weekly income-linked compensation payments, particularly for claims more than one year old. This means that rehabilitation rates are worsening and claims are remaining within the ACC Scheme for longer. This is something that has previously been a driver in cost blow-outs of weekly compensation.

b. The costs of serious and non-serious social rehabilitation. These have been larger than expected since 2014. Social rehabilitation means programmes for and help with the restoration of an individual to cope with everyday life. It appears that rehabilitation goals for long-term claimants are not being adequately met, and ACC itself is monitoring this.

c. A growth in sensitive claims since a dedicated service was established to deal with these kinds of claims. Sensitive claims mean mental harm caused by sexual abuse (i.e. a mental harm caused by the personal injury that is sexual abuse).

The late Sir Owen Woodhouse in recent years suggested that funding should move back to a pay-as-you-go model, because this would enable the Woodhouse Report's requirement of administrative efficiency to be met.[298] He claimed that the original notion of social insurance had been ignored by those who viewed ACC as analogous to commercial insurance. ACC's current reporting data and statements certainly reflect the fact that the organisation takes a commercial insurance approach to its financial operations and management.[299] Sir Woodhouse said a return to pay-as-you-go funding and amalgamating the funding accounts would make it realistic to consider extending the system to sickness and incapacity, thus fulfilling the original vision of the Royal Commission. This point neatly encapsulates the conflicting views within New Zealand of whether

---

[295]   ibid 6.
[296]   ibid 7–8.
[297]   ibid 6.
[298]   Owen Woodhouse, 'The ACC Concept' <http://docs.business.auckland.ac.nz/Doc/ACC-Forum-2011-17-Woodhouse-ACC-Concept-Paper-revised.pdf>.
[299]   Accident Compensation Corporation, 'Annual Report 2017' (2017) <https://www.parliament.nz/resource/en-NZ/PAP_75085/cd5473578a0a648b7c15d0d819d2f36d8ba477c2>; Accident Compensation Corporation, 'Service Agreement 2017/18' (2017) <https://www.parliament.nz/resource/en-NZ/PAP_75186/92e34677ae6c78c38354d975e2ad5eb774ab2c66>; Accident Compensation Corporation, 'Statement of Intent 2015–2019' (2015) <https://www.acc.co.nz/assets/corporate-documents/ACC6969-Statement-of-intent-2015-2019.pdf>.

Intersentia   249

ACC should be thought of as a type of public insurance (similar to private insurance, but compulsory and with a single monopoly provider) or as a type of social insurance (like social security in continental European jurisdictions).[300] Another commentator has also suggested that a pay-as-you-go approach would be 'simpler, more transparent and less risky financially. It would also lower the investment risk for New Zealand.'[301]

However, with great respect to the architect of the ACC Scheme, these arguments are not entirely convincing when one considers the recent significant financial stability and success that has been achieved with the full funding model – and the current financial pressures that the scheme now faces. Despite the scheme's admittedly significant operating costs, comparative actuarial analysis reveals that that ACC has added enormous economic value (including vast legal cost savings) and social value to New Zealand society.[302] However ACC is a long-tail compensation scheme with large lifetime liabilities. 'Long tail' is an insurance term that means that the liability or claim is not fully settled for a long time, often a number of years. This means that ongoing universal injury compensation is costly to deliver, and rehabilitation efforts are proving difficult to reliably control. New Zealand's ageing population will continue to lead to greater incidences of injury with correspondingly poorer rehabilitation rates – and hence greater costs.[303] ACC has a stated desire to ensure that the funding of the scheme is fair from an intergenerational equity perspective. The intergenerational point is something that is an objectively very valid goal, given the wider context of the New Zealand social security system's extremely generous pay-as-you-go universal basic income for pensioners – that is not pre-funded to any degree.[304] Political consensus around the broad design of the scheme has settled since the introduction of full funding over 20 years ago[305] – a return to a situation where annual costs could wildly vary with little pre-funding is likely to reopen old political chasms. ACC has stated that

> 'Investigating the implications of moving away from the full funding model, addressing the impact of economic volatility, or significantly lowering funding

---

[300] Simon Connell, 'Community Insurance versus Compulsory Insurance: Competing Paradigms of No-Fault Accident Compensation in New Zealand' (2019) 39(3) *Legal Studies* 499 <https://www.cambridge.org/core/product/identifier/S0261387518000508/type/journal_article>.

[301] Michael Littlewood, 'Why Does the Accident Compensation Corporation Have a Fund?' (Retirement Policy and Research Centre, University of Auckland 2009) *Pension Commentary* 18.

[302] PriceWaterhouseCoopers (n 53) ix–x.

[303] Accident Compensation Corporation, 'Annual Report 2020' (n 241) 63; Accident Compensation Corporation, 'Annual Report 2017' (n 229) 36; Watts, 'New Zealand' (n 163) 131.

[304] For a broad recent overview, see Jenesa Jeram, 'Embracing a Super Model: The Superannuation Sky Is Not Falling' (4 December 2018) <https://www.nzinitiative.org.nz/reports-and-media/reports/embracing-a-super-model-the-superannuation-sky-is-not-falling/>.

[305] Connell (n 300).

targets would have significant implications. These include for levy and appropriation volatility, impact on business, financial markets, the Crown balance sheet, and intergenerational equity.'[306]

These are all factors that overall militate very strongly in favour of a legal design for this large no-fault compensation fund that includes full-funding. The ACC itself and current Cabinet have indicated that there is some potential to review funding settings and legislation, now that a comprehensive parallel review of the health and disability system has been completed.[307]

Advocates of a return to a pay-as-you-go model also do not give enough weight to the fact that the current ACC Scheme and its liabilities are being substantially supported by investment income to cover the cost of its long-term liabilities and its daily operating costs. The scheme itself has warned that

'a sustained or growing funding gap can lead to the need for greater levy and appropriation increases in the future than would otherwise be needed. This results in possible intergenerational inequities, intended to be minimised by the design of the funding policy.'[308]

There is currently limited legislative possibility for the government to substantially raise levies to smooth any shortfall – funding rates are smoothed over a 10-year horizon (three years when the taxpayer-funded Non-Earners' Account is in surplus) to avoid sharp levy rises.[309] In the financial year 2019/20, one quarter of the reported deficit was due to levies and appropriations being inadequate to cover the expected lifetime cost of new claims.[310]

What can we therefore conclude about the funding structure of ACC and its sustainability? What can these conclusions tell us about the funding of comprehensive no-fault compensation funds generally?

The current division of injuries across the five accounts works well as a functional division and allows clear distinctions to be made between the different categories of victims and/or injuries. To ensure scheme coherency it is logical that cross-subsidisation is not permitted between accounts. It could certainly

---

[306] 'Funding Policy Statement in Relation to the Funding of ACC's Levied Accounts' (n 282) para 19.

[307] The Health and Disability System Review's final report was published in mid-2020. Announcements are expected in mid-2021 of any legislative reform proposals, including those that might be relevant to ACC generally or ACC funding specifically. As noted already, the most significant recent announcement that is relevant to ACC is the proposed introduction of an unemployment social insurance framework – 'Building Stronger Support for Workers Post COVID' (*Beehive.govt.nz*) <https://www.beehive.govt.nz/release/building-stronger-support-workers-post-covid>.

[308] Accident Compensation Corporation, 'Annual Report 2020' (n 241) 58.

[309] ibid 24.

[310] Accident Compensation Corporation, 'Financial Condition Report 2020' (n 232) 4.

Intersentia

be possible to classify injuries and claimants in a different way. However it does not seem necessary to change the current classifications unless there were a systematic reassessment and legislative reform of the ACC Scheme in parallel with social security system reform.[311]

In terms of levies, it certainly appears likely that levies may need to be increased in the future to cover ongoing and long-term liabilities, and to offset recent instability in investment income returns. The fact that the Treatment Injury Account and the Non-Earners' Account are both mostly supported by investment income – and have accordingly suffered the greatest shortfalls in the last financial years – begs the question of whether they, too, should be levied. It is entirely possible – and desirable – to introduce new levies to better support these two accounts and reduce reliance on central government taxation revenue or investment income.

We can look first to the possibility of a levy to support the Treatment Injury Account, to supplement the levies that are already available in relation to Earners for treatment injuries. The enormous absolution from liability that New Zealand healthcare providers (compared to other jurisdictions) enjoy, yet with no specific levy on their activities, surely cannot be justified any longer in the context of funding shortfalls and potential financial instability. There is certainly no urgent crisis of affordability at this time. However an increased levy base would be fairer to the community and the taxpayer as a whole, and could enable a greater balance to be struck between reliance on investment income, levies, and central government funding. There are different ways that such a levy could be captured.

The first could be a levy on the provision of healthcare services at the point of payment – whether that is by an individual patient or by a public or institutional purchaser of healthcare services. This is immediately analogous to the model used for the fuel levy and vehicle registration levy in the Motor Vehicle Account. A flat-rate levy, payable at the time of practitioner certificate registration (and therefore collected by the relevant professional bodies and passed on to ACC), would also be possible under this heading.

The second way is via levies on the activities of healthcare practitioners and organisations, much in the same way as the Work Account is funded. There could be an assessment of the type of healthcare provision (to identify riskier types of activities) and risk rating associated with previous treatment injury claims against the healthcare provider or organisation. This kind of risk rating would be difficult for relevant professional bodies to undertake, and so it would be appropriate for ACC to implement a risk rating system that has equivalence with the model used for the Work Account.

---

[311] A parallel legislative reform process that was recommended in 2019 by New Zealand's Welfare Expert Advisory Group. See Welfare Expert Advisory Group, 'Whakamana Tāngata – Restoring Dignity to Social Security in New Zealand' (2019) 153 <www.weag.govt.nz>.

Chapter 4. Key Pillars

There is no doubt that this kind of proposal would provoke push-back from the healthcare practitioner field and public health bodies, but either proposal set out here would be coherent with levying methods already used in the wider scheme. It is not unreasonable, from a fairness or justice perspective, to expect participants in the healthcare sector to contribute even modest levies to a scheme that has effectively iron-clad protections against medical malpractice and medical liability costs. Earners already support the funding of the Treatment Injury Account, so an introduction of levies simply helps to capture costs associated with those who cannot or do not pay levies. Further, the fact that Treatment Injury claim frequencies are predicted to stabilise means that healthcare providers would not have to fear huge inflation in levy rates. This also answers concerns that very high level rates would be passed on to patients or healthcare provision customers. The same strict controls on levy increases – and the guaranteed nature of ACC cover and eligibility – would ensure that medical practitioners in 'riskier' fields are not unduly punished or priced out of the market. Those kinds of pressures have caused insurance crises in other jurisdictions around medical injuries, and have been a catalyst for the creation of smaller, injury-specific no-fault schemes. The first option of a flat-rate levy at the time of practitioner registration could be selected instead to reaffirm a legislative commitment to strictly control levy costs and ensure certain fields are not 'priced out' of practice. An increase in funding may also, for example, enable ACC to take a more generous approach to treatment injuries that are currently being handled very restrictively by the scheme to limit the acceptance of long-recovery claims.[312]

In terms of non-earners, it is more difficult to precisely pinpoint a potential levy source that most accurately and fairly captures this category of potential victims. The non-earner category would broadly capture children, pensioners, the unemployed (including those unable to work through sickness and/or disability) and tourists. It mostly consists of children and the elderly. New Zealand's ageing population means that the elderly non-earner 'represents a significant and

---

[312] For example, ACC recently changed its perineal tears qualification criteria to exclude all tears caused only by the birthing process – therefore approving only those claims that were caused by a direct and erroneous 'treatment' such as forceps. This has led to existing claimants with very serious injuries having their cover terminated after retrospective review. ACC states that birth-related injuries (to both mother and baby) are the category of treatment injuries that require support for the longest period. See Anusha Bradley, 'Lawyers Question ACC's New Policy on Perineal Tears' *Radio New Zealand News* (31 March 2021) <https://www.rnz.co.nz/news/national/439591/lawyers-question-acc-s-new-policy-on-perineal-tears>; Accident Compensation Corporation, 'Perineal Tear Treatment Injury' (2020) <www.acc.co.nz/lodgementguide>; Accident Compensation Corporation, 'Financial Condition Report 2020' (n 235) 117; 'Midwives Urge ACC to Rethink "inequities" around Perineal Tear Cover', *Radio New Zealand News* (1 April 2021) <https://www.rnz.co.nz/news/national/439631/midwives-urge-acc-to-rethink-inequities-around-perineal-tear-cover>.

Intersentia

growing cost to the ACC Scheme in the future'.[313] These are fluid categories of individuals who may have very different degrees of financial capability to pay any levy, or may be wholly dependent on another person who is already levied in a different way (for example, the child non-earner who is dependent upon two employed earner parents). However it is critically urgent to identify new funding sources for the Non-Earners' Account – the current funding (or solvency) ratio has fallen to 55 per cent compared to a target of 88 per cent.[314]

The current legislative prohibition on Accounts cross-subsidising each other means that it would not be possible for levies on other accounts to be raised slightly to support the Non-Earners' Account. This would also probably add undesirable complexity. A specific levy that is clearly earmarked to support the Non-Earners' Account would appear more desirable from a simplicity perspective. As the Non-Earners' Account and its recipients are the purest example of the 'community responsibility' and comprehensive nature of the ACC Scheme, it would seem logical to make the levy source as wide as possible. In the future (after the recent health and disability expert review projects) New Zealand may choose to reform its social security system to be funded by a dedicated social security charge (currently all social security is funded out of general taxation). If that were to happen, then it seems logical for a specific Non-Earners' Account levy to be created as part of a package of new social security charges. Otherwise, the most logical way to raise a levy specific to the Non-Earners' Account could be a specific small increase to goods and services tax that is earmarked for ACC. This levy would therefore be paid by the whole population whenever GST is paid – and therefore captures earners as well as non-earners who purchase goods and services (the elderly, children and tourists). The disadvantage of a GST-linked levy is that it is not specifically linked to risk. However a levy specifically targeted to the elderly – the group that ACC has identified will contribute to the largest cost blow-outs of the Non-Earners' Account in the future – is likely to be politically toxic given the pay-as-you-go nature of the current universal basic income pension. Conversely, a dedicated levy on overseas tourists coming to New Zealand (such as an arrival tax, from which citizens and permanent residents are exempt) could be more palatable. However current and recent figures do not indicate that tourists are causing undue strain on the ACC system. There is already in fact a degree of unofficial cross-subsidisation from the Work Account to the injuries of non-earners, as a number of adventure tourism industries (for which New Zealand is famous) fall within higher-risk industry business codes for the purposes of Work

---

[313]   'Funding Policy Statement in Relation to the Funding of ACC's Levied Accounts' (n 282) para 20.

[314]   The government has applied a generous risk margin of 12% to this account. See 'Funding Policy Statement in Relation to the Funding of ACC's Levied Accounts' (n 282).

Account levies.[315] However, the fact that the New Zealand tourism industry is effectively being subsidised by the effect of the ACC Scheme[316] – to the potential disadvantage of international consumers (tourists) who are probably not aware of the scheme and its consequences on their potential for recovery – suggests that a targeted levy on tourism activities may be worth considering in the medium term to support the Non-Earners' Account.

We can conclude therefore that the ACC Scheme needs to achieve a greater balance between the different sources of scheme income – if the scheme wishes to keep operating on its existing comprehensive basis, and on a sustainable financial path. ACC has, overall, performed well and has overcome the financial difficulties it faced in the 1980s and 1990s, largely due to a commitment to full-funding and prudent financial management. However the scheme faces long-term financial risks on its present path. The decade-long strong performance of investment returns (until the last financial year) made this matter of diversification of income less pressing to address in recent years. However the severe fluctuations in these investment returns, and increasing demands on the non-levied accounts, make it important to address the question of how risk-takers (the whole community and specific groups) are contributing to the scheme's upkeep. It goes without saying that any significant expansion or change to the benefits or entitlements associated with the ACC Scheme would require a careful assessment of whether a proposed change matches the existing scheme scope and available revenue. New Zealand's Treasury has been quick to warn the executive that there are severe cost and coherency risks to entitlement changes, and a comprehensive ACC legislation modernisation project would be the best avenue to address these issues.[317] The distilled lessons for the field of no-fault comprehensive compensation funds are therefore:

a.   Full-funding is key.
b.   An appropriate balance needs to be struck between levies, investment income, and taxpayer funding.
c.   It is ideal to have clearly demarcated different sub-funds that are associated with different groups of victims.

---

[315]   For further discussion, see Tourism Industry Aoetearoa, 'Submission to Accident Compensation Corporation' (2018) <www.tia.org.nz>. New Zealand tourism companies' specialty in the field of adventure tourism would likely be significantly hampered or rendered prohibitive if they had to insure against possible injury costs in the ordinary way – see Duncan (n 274) 330.

[316]   Marie Callander and Stephen J Page, 'Managing Risk in Adventure Tourism Operations in New Zealand: A Review of the Legal Case History and Potential for Litigation' (2003) 24 *Tourism Management* 13.

[317]   Ministry of Business Innovation and Employment, 'Extended Mental Health Support for Those Affected by the 15 March 2019 Terrorist Attack' 10 <https://www.mbie.govt.nz/dmsdocument/5890-extended-mental-health-support-for-those-affected-by-the-15-march-2019-terrorist-attack-proactiverelease-pdf>.

A Comparative Law Analysis of No-Fault Comprehensive Compensation Funds

d. Weekly compensation costs and rehabilitation problems are the greatest source of compensation-linked financial difficulties for the scheme. These costs may be difficult for the scheme to control, but investments in safety and close monitoring of rehabilitation will deliver broadly satisfactory results over the medium- and long-term. However the fund itself – if it is as broad as ACC – cannot significantly control for societal issues such as ageing, obesity, and poor socio-economic issues[318] which will impact financial liabilities.

The problem that ACC faces, if it wishes to seek new sources of income, is the political sensitivity around increased levies. The scheme is a monopoly provider of a kind of wide social insurance that reports to a government minister. This means that ACC does not have the same freedom to increase levies as a private insurance scheme might do. The fund's recommendations about levy and funding changes are always subject to the final approval of the government of the day, and will be considered alongside all of the latter's current political problems and concerns. For example, in 2020 the government announced that current ACC levies would be frozen until 2022 (instead of being reviewed in 2021 as planned) due to the impacts of the COVID-19 pandemic[319] – despite the fact that the country's effective elimination of the virus meant that the economic impacts of the pandemic had been effectively reversed within a few months.[320] The wide scope of the ACC Scheme also gives it a much wider potential to be attacked for levy rises that are perceived to be 'unfair' or punitive. As discussed already in this book, a future-focused legislative review of the ACC Scheme and what it can and should cover is long overdue – and should preferably be undertaken at the same time as an overhaul of the social welfare system. The ACC Scheme has proven its broad sustainability and popularity over 50 years, and it seems unlikely that it would be abandoned. This is especially true given that there is no certainty that New Zealand's private insurance industry has the interest or capability – in terms of underwriting and actuarial expertise – to replace the broad cover of ACC. ACC has not gathered the type and volume of data over its existence that private insurers could use to accurately price risks – leading to likely speculative pricing.[321] An appropriate further conclusion here in relation

---

[318] Such as New Zealand's very high rates of sexual and domestic violence – Ruth Gammon, 'Family Violence: New Zealand's Dirty Little Secret' (*Massey University*) <https://www.massey.ac.nz/massey/about-massey/news/article.cfm?mnarticle_uuid=C61AEFE4-B1D7-0794-48A1-CFA90FEDDEFF>.

[319] 'Keeping ACC Levies Steady until 2022', *New Zealand Government* (6 July 2020) <https://www.beehive.govt.nz/release/keeping-acc-levies-steady-until-2022>.

[320] Jamie Smyth, 'New Zealand's "Go Hard and Early" Covid Policy Reaps Economic Rewards', *Financial Times* (17 December 2020) <https://www.ft.com/content/b8c4ab58-99db-4af2-9449-5fd70a9235ce>.

[321] Reid and Mackessack (n 277) 18.

256   Intersentia

Chapter 4. Key Pillars

to ACC's funding model is that the fund should be given greater independence and control over the setting of levies in order to achieve stronger financial stability, with the aim of neutralising political influence on financial matters of the scheme. This could be balanced with greater regulatory supervision from the central bank (in line with private insurers) and a legislative requirement to meet solvency requirements (perhaps modified to reflect the unique social nature of the scheme). This kind of independence would also appear to be desirable for other comprehensive no-fault compensation schemes.

6.2. VICTORIA'S TAC

We can now turn to the funding models used by the other schemes. We will consider first the TAC, and then the SAAQ and the MPI. The funding models of these three schemes display more similarities with one another than with the ACC Scheme. This is because these three funds operate exclusively in the automobile/transport sector, and therefore have a smaller scope of claims and of risk-takers upon which levies can be applied. All three funds are currently funded in the same way – by fees associated with the use of motor vehicles. In other words, the schemes are directly supported by levies on the activity or product directly or factually causatively associated with most harms. It is useful to compare these three schemes with one another to identify the key elements of their funding mechanisms, and also to identify what similarities or differences they have with the funding model underpinning the ACC Scheme. These conclusions are all relevant to understandings about the funding best practices of very large no-fault compensation funds. Specifically, can we draw any conclusions about the long-term financial sustainability and stability of a fund that covers one functional field (albeit a very broad one – transport injury) compared to a fund that covers many functional fields (like the ACC's universality)? Are there any key financial differences between these kinds of funds?

As noted in Chapter 4, the two-tier non-compulsory no-fault scheme that preceded the TAC suffered serious financial difficulties. From the outset, the modern TA has been a publicly underwritten pure no-fault scheme with a limited carve-out for serious injury. The financial structures of the TAC are set out quite simply within the supporting legislation. It is an ordinary statutory corporation.[322] Financial sustainability objectives are clearly set out:[323] the scheme must be managed as effectively, efficiently and economically as possible; compensation must be 'delivered in the most socially and economically appropriate manner'; and internal management structures and procedures

---

[322] Transport Accident Act 1986 (Victoria) ss 10(2)(a), 10A.
[323] ibid s 11.

Intersentia

257

must enable the TAC to perform 'effectively, efficiently and economically'. Its primary income is the Transport Accident Charge, which forms part of the registration charge paid periodically by all registered vehicle owners in the state of Victoria.[324] TAC also receives revenue from premiums charged to train and tram operators. This income is directed towards a single pot called the Transport Accident Fund,[325] which the TAC is responsible for managing.[326] The Transport Accident Fund is also sustained by investment income, borrowing by the TAC[327] and penalties and other monies received by virtue of the operation of the legislative scheme. The TAC's annual budget must be approved by the relevant Victorian government minister a year in advance.[328] The TAC may be required to make repayments of its capital to the Victorian State Treasury,[329] and it must periodically pay a dividend to the Victorian state.[330] However, the Victorian Treasurer is required to consider TAC's solvency margin and the scheme's 'long term financial viability' when calculating the relevant dividend policy.

The investment elements of TAC's Transport Accident Fund are managed on a day-to-day basis by the Victorian state's financial management agency, the Victorian Funds Management Corporation.[331] Its investment objective horizon for the TAC is a rolling 10-year basis with a return of 7.25 per cent,[332] which is logical given the long-tail nature of TAC's ongoing claims. Unlike the ACC, the TAC has actively contemplated the need to purchase reinsurance, but this is linked to specific risk. Catastrophic accidents 'are modelled and the TAC's exposures are, if elected by the TAC's Board, protected by arranging reinsurance to limit the losses arising from an individual event. The retention and limits are approved by the TAC's Board'.[333] In the financial years 2018/19 and 2019/20, TAC has chosen to retain catastrophic risk in-house, and has not entered into any reinsurance contracts.[334] As with ACC, the TAC is not under the supervision of the relevant insurance regulator (the Australian Prudential Regulation Authority). However, it is subject to ordinary financial reporting and audit requirements, as a statutory corporation.

In 2018/19, the TAC recorded a current operating loss of A\$3.8 billion, and yet an economic funding/solvency ratio of 137.7 per cent.[335] Similarly to the

---

[324] ibid s 109.
[325] ibid s 27.
[326] ibid s 12(1)(a).
[327] ibid s 28.
[328] ibid s 29.
[329] ibid s 29A.
[330] ibid s 29B.
[331] Victorian Funds Management Corporation, 'Annual Report 2019–20' 73.
[332] Transport Accident Commission, 'Annual Report 2018/19' (n 30) 7.
[333] ibid 54.
[334] ibid.
[335] ibid 7. However this was a significant solvency drop from the previous financial year, which recorded an economic funding/solvency ratio of 164.8%.

ACC Scheme, operating losses in that year were caused by a 'difference between actual investment returns and long-term expected returns', specifically, record low Australian Commonwealth bond rates and record low interest rates.[336] An increase in paramedic/ambulance costs (after the TAC began to automatically cover these costs for all clients) also contributed to the immediate shortfall in that financial year. In the most recent financial year, the TAC focused on improving 'claims management and operational efficiencies'. An operating profit was therefore reported the following year. Yet despite an insurance operations result of A$744 million, the weak investment position reduced TAC's overall profit down to A$179 million in 2019/20. The TAC's ability to continually generate a positive cash flow means that, for financial auditing purposes, it is appropriate to treat the scheme as a viable going concern – even though it may have an overall negative net asset position.[337] In 2020, the TAC recorded a negative net asset position of A$4,056 million, compared to a negative position of A$4,236 million in 2019.[338] The most significant element contributing to the negative asset position is the TAC's estimation of outstanding claims liabilities (A$19.8 billion in 2019/20, an increase of around A$160 million from the previous financial year).[339] The calculation by the TAC of its outstanding claims liabilities is undertaken in a very similar way to the ACC.

Given its good capitalisation/solvency rate, the TAC system can therefore, overall, be said to be financially sustainable. This is despite the cost blow-outs associated with the availability of common law damages for serious injury. TAC's current capitalisation gives the scheme adequate reserves to cover the lifetime cost of all current and projected claim liabilities.[340] As with ACC, however, lower interest rates globally and lower returns on government bonds mean that the Scheme has suffered unexpected financial instability. The TAC is publicly underwritten: it is required to repay capital and pay dividends to the state of Victoria, as required and agreed in consultation with the state government.[341] To accommodate the recent investment income instability, the Victorian government has in the last few financial years elected not receive a capital repayment or dividend.[342]

The Transport Accident Charge is set by the TAC, and increases in line with the consumer price index (at a rate of 2.05 per cent in the year 2019/20[343]).

---

[336] ibid 6–7.

[337] Transport Accident Commission, 'Annual Report 2019–2020' 55 <https://www.tac.vic.gov.au/__data/assets/pdf_file/0011/470576/TAC-ANNUAL-REPORT-WEB.pdf>.

[338] ibid 71.

[339] ibid 68.

[340] Transport Accident Commission, '2017/18 Annual Report' 54 <http://www.tac.vic.gov.au/__data/assets/pdf_file/0009/298629/2017-18-TAC-Annual-Report.pdf>.

[341] Transport Accident Act 1986 (Victoria) ss 29A, 29B.

[342] Transport Accident Commission, 'Annual Report 2019–2020' (n 337) 95.

[343] ibid 55.

The charge is calculated with reference to type and use of the vehicle and the postcode where the registered vehicle is usually kept. Some examples of the differences in annual rates are set out below:[344]

Table 10. Transport Accident Charge rates by vehicle type and geographical zone

Type of vehicle	High Risk Zone (metropolitan Melbourne)	Medium Risk Zone (outer metropolitan Melbourne)	Low Risk Zone (rural)
Standard passenger vehicle (including a taxi)	A$532.40	A$477.70	A$413.60
Rental passenger vehicle or motorcycle	A$843.70	A$707.30	A$610.50
Goods vehicle (under two tonnes/ over two tonnes)	A$533.50/ A$776.60	A$403.70/ A$678.70	A$279.40/ A$583
Motorcycles (range depending on CC level)	A$89.10 for under 61cc to A$561 for over 500cc	A$89.10 for under 61cc to A$491.70 for over 500cc	A$89.10 for under 61cc to A$421.30 for over 500cc
Police passenger vehicle	A$1885.40	A$1885.40	A$1885.40

Source: Compiled by the author.

There are concessions to the standard rates for pensioners and other persons such as apprentice tradespeople. Meanwhile, the annual charge that rail and tram operators must pay is set following an actuarial review of claims.

Specifically designed funding structures and procedures also ensure that hospital and medical treatment costs are largely taken out of the hands of individual claimants. These would appear to facilitate the controlling stake that the TAC takes in terms of claimant rehabilitation and the requirement for non-acute treatments to be approved. In terms of intersections with the public health system, there are specific procedures in place for the billing and reimbursement of the TAC in relation to patients.[345] In the past, conflicts emerged over whether to shift the TAC's medical costs to the federal medical budget.[346] These disputes are likely to re-emerge if there is further development of the National Injury Insurance Scheme in Australia.

---

[344] Transport Accident Commission, 'Transport Accident Charge' <http://www.tac.vic.gov.au/about-the-tac/our-organisation/transport-accident-charge>; 'Transport Accident Charges Including GST and Duty' (2020).

[345] 'Medical Services Reimbursement Rates' (*Transport Accident Commission*) <https://www.tac.vic.gov.au/providers/invoicing-and-fees/fee-schedule/medical-practitioners>; Victoria State Government, 'Transport Accident Commission Patients' <https://www2.health.vic.gov.au/hospitals-and-health-services/patient-fees-charges/admitted-patients/compensable-patients/tac>.

[346] Gardner (n 52).

Looking at the TAC's current funding model, we see some similarities with the investment income return challenges faced by the ACC in New Zealand. Unexpected market fluctuations in the late 2010s created huge operating losses. These losses are now stabilising, as the TAC adapts to the revised investment horizon over 10 years. The TAC's outsourcing of day-to-day investment management to the state investment agency is a sensible approach, because it gives a degree of independence to this side of the TAC's finances, and ensures that an objective approach to investment income is more likely to be achieved. In terms of levies, the TAC takes a more coherent and strictly focused approach than ACC, with all levies being specifically calculated with reference to actual risk data. It is probably easier for the TAC to achieve this kind of strict control of levies, as it only has to focus on the one function of transport injury. The lack of any targeted levies on actual usage by way of fuel levies can be explained by the fact that Australian states and territories are prohibited from imposing excise taxes (a form of tax that only the federal Commonwealth can levy).[347]

Overall, the TAC has substantial outstanding long-tail risk, but a strong annual position. Unlike an ordinary private insurer, the scheme is fully publicly underwritten. Although the scheme (and the state Treasurer) have the option to purchase reinsurance, this option has not yet been exercised. This means that ultimately that the Victorian state bears all the risk of the outstanding liabilities of the scheme, including catastrophic injury costs. However the TAC has specifically defined that it aims to be the world's best social insurer, so its wholly publicly underwritten nature is logical. The scheme's risk is further balanced by its aggressive approach to safety investments, public education and research and which form a much larger portion of its annual costs than administration – in 2019/20, A\$333 million was spent on investments and other proactive measures, compared with A\$191 million in administration costs.[348] This is an explicit social and ethical focus of the whole scheme,[349] which leads itself to a goal of sustainability and ongoing adequate solvency. If the TAC can come reasonably close to achieving its goals of zero deaths and serious injuries on its roads[350] then this will immediately reduce its long-term outstanding liabilities (i.e. transport injuries that require a lot of time and resources to rehabilitate and manage) and the scheme's overall risk. The TAC's investments in understanding

---

[347] *Ha v New South Wales* [1997] HCA 34.
[348] Transport Accident Commission, 'Annual Report 2019–2020' (n 337) 57.
[349] 'We all make mistakes, but no one deserves to die or be seriously injured as a result' – Transport Accident Commission, 'Annual Report 2019–2020' (n 337).
[350] In 2018, Victoria achieved a record low death rate of 213 road fatalities (out of a population of nearly 6.6 million, of which the vast majority live in Melbourne). The TAC approach evolved from the Swedish Vision Zero philosophy and the Sustainable Safety model developed in the Netherlands. See Carlyn Muir, Ian R Johnston and Eric Howard, 'Evolution of a Holistic Systems Approach to Planning and Managing Road Safety: The Victorian Case Study, 1970–2015' (2018) 24 *Injury Prevention* i19 <https://injuryprevention.bmj.com/content/24/Suppl_1/i19>.

how to prevent road injuries and improve rehabilitation outcomes are very significant by international standards.[351]

What can we therefore conclude about the funding and sustainability of the TAC scheme? The TAC Scheme is well-managed, but it appears that more work needs to be done to manage the risk of investment income fluctuations to the scheme's financial stability. The management of investment income already has a degree of independence and is handled in line with the Victorian state's other sovereign wealth or investment funds, which is positive. It may be beneficial for the scheme to have clearer solvency targets that are broadly in-step with equivalent insurance best practice (with explanations, where necessary, for why a different approach is necessary given the social and publicly underwritten nature of the scheme). Better prudential clarity and some further independent oversight of the TAC's investment activities can be seen as a positive extra step that could be taken.

In terms of a reduction in costs, the serious injury carve-out is a logical potential target. This is a costly element of the scheme that adds legal incoherency and complexity, and is at odds with the rest of the pure no-fault scheme. However any change to the common law damages model would need to be counterbalanced with a significant increase to no-fault compensation. It is not clear that there is political will to change the status quo, and could in fact undermine public satisfaction with the scheme. Take, for example, the public uproar and quick reversal of the TAC's revised policy to exclude certain categories of third-party victims from accessing common law damages.[352] This shows that, much like the ACC, the possibility for the TAC to be modified to improve financial sustainability may be hampered by political sensitivities about the public perception of perceived entitlements. A more conservative approach to spending on safety investments and incentives seems unnecessary, as these are delivering real results, meet the scheme's social objectives and mitigate long-term future risks. The TAC could therefore be summarised as being broadly sustainable for a long-tail public insurance scheme, but subject to some specific investment and long-term liability risks that may be difficult to comprehensively address due to political sensitivities. However, the targeted focus of the scheme (which is sharper and more safety focused than

---

[351] As just one example, in 2020 the TAC launched its 'Road Injury Dashboard', which analyses injury, crash, road and road user types, and a breakdown of the costs of claims to the TAC and broader health sector. The objective of this investment is to demonstrate to other jurisdictions the benefits of investing in mitigating road safety infrastructure. See 'TAC IRAP Road Injury Dashboard' (*Transport Accident Commission*) <https://www.tac.vic.gov.au/road-safety/statistics/online-crash-database/irap-road-injury-dashboard>; 'Road Injury Dashboard Shines a Light on Real Cost of Road Trauma – IRAP', *iRAP* (29 March 2021) <https://www.irap.org/2021/03/ausrap-news-road-injury-dashboard-shines-a-light-on-real-cost-of-road-trauma/>.

[352] 'Transport Accident Amendment Bill 2015 – Explanatory Memorandum'.

New Zealand's ACC), by its very operation, aims to improve holistic financial sustainability. The sustainability of the scheme is directly connected to its social insurer objectives and its funding design, which ultimately presents a more coherent picture than New Zealand's ACC.

6.3. QUÉBEC'S SAAQ

We can turn now to our large Canadian no-fault comprehensive compensation funds. Are these two schemes broadly equivalent to Victoria's TAC, being limited to the transport injury category? What comparative conclusions can we draw that are relevant to big no-fault funds in the transport injury functional category, and relevant to big no-fault schemes more generally? Firstly, we consider the SAAQ.

Like the TAC, the SAAQ is similarly underpinned by an automobile insurance fund (Fonds d'assurance automobile du Québec), of which SAAQ is a trustee.[353] Because SAAQ also has general responsibility for automobile regulation in the province, the no-fault fund is mostly funded by driver licensing and car registration fees.[354] Yet, like the ACC and the TAC, investment income also forms an important secondary stream for the SAAQ.

The framework for gathering levies and the basis for the calculation of levies are set out clearly in the relevant legislation. Specifically, the legislation states that factors like vehicle size, vehicle technical specifications, class, driver licensing and demerit points and Highway Code infringements may all be taken into account when determining the amount of annual levy that must be paid by individual drivers and car owners.[355] The SAAQ pays an amount each year to the public health service that correlates to the health costs of automobile injuries. This amount is negotiated by agreement with the relevant provincial health minister, but it must be at least C\$88.6 million.[356] The SAAQ also has option of issuing debt in the forms of notes, bonds and securities, at rates determined by the Québec government. Any monies obtained from such debts can only be used for the operation of the Scheme.[357]

The SAAQ's specific fonds d'assurance was created in 2004 after increasing claims and chronic underfunding (down to a solvency ratio of just 64 per cent) led to a risk of the scheme becoming financially insolvent by 2018.[358] Specifically, the

---

[353]   Act respecting the Société de l'assurance automobile du Québec s 23.0.4.

[354]   SAAQ, 'Insurance Contributions' <https://saaq.gouv.qc.ca/en/traffic-accident/public-automobile-insurance-plan/insurance-contributions/>.

[355]   Automobile Insurance Act (Québec) ss 151, 151.1, 151.2, 151.3, 151.3.1, 151.4. Demerit points are otherwise known as penalty points in some jurisdictions.

[356]   ibid ss 155.1 and 155.2.

[357]   Act respecting the Société de l'assurance automobile du Québec ss 21, 22, 23.

[358]   PriceWaterhouseCoopers (n 53) 142, 155.

funding ratio at that time would have led to funding drying up by 2018, with the SAAQ still being on the hook for C$15 billion in claim costs.[359] The dedicated pot of money specifically for SAAQ that was independent from other government monies was devised as a funding sustainability solution, along with a requirement to eliminate under-funding by 2015. From 2004 any changes to insurance contributions have had to be submitted to an independent panel of experts,[360] which then holds public consultations about the proposed changes. The SAAQ's financial performance has improved significantly in recent years, and it cleared its cumulative deficit 10 years ahead of schedule.[361] The scheme's fonds d'assurance currently has a capitalisation or funding rate of 148 per cent (146 per cent after counting a remittance to contributors),[362] and a financing ratio of 96 per cent.[363] The financing ratio relates to the amount of revenue in a given year, and must be 100 per cent at the time insurance contributions are reviewed. Meanwhile, the funding ratio relates to the ratio of assets (i.e. invested assets) that must be available to be paid out in compensation. A target ratio or 'stabilisation corridor' of 100 to 120 per cent is sought.

The need for the SAAQ to be financially sustainable is expressed in the legislation. The twin purposes of the funding pot (to which all SAAQ revenues are directed) are the payment of compensation for automobile injury, and the promotion of accident prevention and highway safety. However, only the payment of compensation has primacy. Accident prevention and highway safety efforts 'must not compromise the financial stability of the Fonds d'assurance'.[364] The core legislation also requires that indemnities/compensation are financed by the contributions of that particular year, and that levies are adequate to be capitalised to pay all long-term liabilities.[365] In this way, there is a balancing of needs of current contributors and those of all victims over the whole lifetime of the scheme.

For the purposes of financial standards and accountability, the SAAQ is treated slightly differently in some ways to other government statutory bodies. For example, the SAAQ does not have to submit strategic plans to government.[366] The SAAQ also does not have to ensure that payments it makes are linked to available appropriations, unlike other government agencies.[367] However the

---

[359] Société de l'assurance automobile du Québec, 'Proposed Insurance Contributions for 2019–2021' (2017) 14.

[360] 'Conseil d'experts Sur Les Contributions d'assurance Automobile' <http://conseilexpert. aauto.ca/index_en.htm>.

[361] Société de l'assurance automobile du Québec, 'Proposed Insurance Contributions for 2019–2021' (n 359) 15.

[362] Société de l'assurance automobile du Québec, 'Rapport Annuel de Gestion' (n 30) 38.

[363] ibid 72.

[364] Act respecting the Société de l'assurance automobile du Québec s 23.0.3.

[365] Société de l'assurance automobile du Québec, 'Rapport Annuel de Gestion' (n 30) 36.

[366] Act respecting the Société de l'assurance automobile du Québec s 23.0.13.1.

[367] ibid s 23.0.13.

SAAQ's accounts must be independently audited, and the SAAQ's president and chief executive officer are directly accountable to the Québec National Assembly.[368] As a fully publicly underwritten state corporation, the SAAQ is not subject to the same regulatory supervision as private insurers. However, it is subject generally to the laws applying to government statutory corporations, other than the carve-outs described in this paragraph.

The SAAQ's investment income increased from C$27.8 million in 2018 to C$74 million in 2019.[369] Like the TAC, an official government investment agency is used to manage investment funds – the Caisse de dépôt et placement du Québec. The SAAQ is in fact required by statute to deposit funds not being used for everyday operations with the investment agency.[370] The overall growth of investment income for this fund stands in stark contrast to the poor investment performance suffered by the ACC and the TAC. A look at the most recent financial statements appears to point to a stronger and more procedural control of risk exposure than in the ACC and TAC.

The SAAQ scheme's drive since 2004 to achieve financial sustainability has been incorporated into and defined in specific policies. These have aimed to reduce accident numbers through safety initiatives (which ultimately brings down long-term costs), have insurance contributions reflect the road safety record and be indexed annually, and to ensure better and more efficient administration of the scheme.[371] In 2019 the independent actuarial body set the following principles for the SAAQ scheme's funding:[372]

a. Contributions have to be calculated to ensure full financing for each new accident year (i.e. the scheme is fully-funded, like the ACC and the TAC).
b. Contribution categories are determined on the basis of the accident risk (taking into account the data on the number of accidents involving contributors and the severity of injuries).
c. Individual driver prudence is to be encouraged by rewarding good behaviour.
d. The Scheme's 'financial solidity' must be balanced with the need for stable levels of insurance contributions.
e. There may be no discrimination on the basis of age, sex, or region.
f. The cost of an accident should be allocated equally among the categories of the vehicles involved.

---

[368] ibid ss 23.0.18. and 23.0.19.
[369] Société de l'assurance automobile du Québec, 'Rapport Annuel de Gestion' (n 30) 37.
[370] Act respecting the Société de l'assurance automobile du Québec s 17.3.
[371] Société de l'assurance automobile du Québec, 'Proposed Insurance Contributions for 2019–2021' (n 359) 14.
[372] ibid 18; Conseil d'experts sur les contributions d'assurance automobile, 'Avis Du Conseil d'experts' (2019).

Intersentia

A Comparative Law Analysis of No-Fault Comprehensive Compensation Funds

g.   There is an annual limit on levy increases of 15 per cent, to which additional increases may be added based on finance requirements.

Some examples of the SAAQ's current annual rates are set out below for driver/ motorcycle licences and vehicle registration costs.[373] Because the funding/ capitalisation ratio has been above target in recent years, the excess funds from the fonds d'assurance have been used to subsidise the scheme's daily financing.

Table 11a. SAAQ's annual contribution rates by licence type

Licence type	Contribution amount
Regular passenger vehicle driver licence – no demerit points[374]	C$56.87, of which C$15.16 was subsidised by funding.
Regular passenger vehicle driver licence – with demerit points	Ranging from C$96.96 for one to three demerit points up to C$359.40 for 15 or more demerit points.
	Regardless of the number of demerit points, no more than C$15.16 of the fee is subsidised by funding.
Restricted driver licence[375]	C$142.46, of which C$15.16 was subsidised by funding.
Motorcycle licence, no demerit points	C$63.33, of which C$2.22 was subsidised by funding.
Motorcycle licence, with demerit points.	If the licence holder also holds a driver licence, then a flat rate of C$103.34 (of which C$2.22 is subsidised).
	Otherwise, a range of fees from C$103.34 to up to C$448.80, all of which are only subsidised by C$2.22.

Source: Compiled by the author.

Table 11b. SAAQ annual contribution rates by vehicle type

Vehicle type	Contribution amount
Regular passenger vehicle	C$65.54, of which C$2.48 is a contribution to the funding account.
Motorcycle	Ranging from C$219.52 for 125cc or less to C$569.40 for over 400cc.
	Of this, C$10.46 is deducted from the funding account.
	The registration fee for high-risk motorcycles is C$1512.59 (including a C$10.46 deduction).
	In recent years, the motorcycle registration contributions have increased significantly because of worse accident outcomes and reduced numbers of motorcyclists (i.e. fewer motorcycle licence fees being paid).
Buses	Depending on the type of use and weight, ranging from C$163.94 for school buses to C$1939.52 for city buses, both including a C$12.68 deduction from the fonds d'assurance.

(continued)

---

[373]   Société de l'assurance automobile du Québec, 'Proposed Insurance Contributions for 2019–2021' (n 359) 19–22.

[374]   This is the largest category of licence holders, with around 4.3 million people.

[375]   A driver licence that only authorises driving a vehicle equipped with an alcohol ignition interlock device.

266

Intersentia

Table 11b *continued*

Vehicle type	Contribution amount
Trucks	Depending on number of axles, weight and whether they are owned by the government – from C$101.54 to C$366.58. These rates all include a C$12.68 deduction from the fonds d'assurance.
Mopeds or scooters	C$230.49, including a C$12.68 deduction.
Taxis	C$816.22, including a C$12.68 deduction.

Source: Compiled by the author.

Looking at the financial elements of SAAQ, we see a model that is even more precisely targeted than its Australian and New Zealand big no-fault cousins. There is specific targeting of risks associated with individual kinds of road users, and rates are set independently by an actuarial panel. This is a cautious and logical response to the severe funding sustainability difficulties that the scheme faced in the early 2000s. Most usefully, the independent nature of the actuarial supervision body means that the determination of contributions is made with less political interference than in the other schemes reviewed. A comparison can be made, for example, with a decision in New Zealand's ACC to reverse a vehicle risk rating based on socio-economic policy concerns.

The SAAQ funding model also directly addresses issues of deterrence and punishment for risky behaviour within the scheme itself, by specifically (and significantly) raising premiums for riskier road users. This is possible because the SAAQ has wide responsibility for the regulation and management of the whole automobile transport sector in Québec. However, it is a different approach to the TAC and the ACC, which take a broad 'general increased risk of accidents' approach by way of fuel levies and postcode-based scales of levies. The SAAQ approach directly punishes riskier behaviour, much like private insurance premiums would do, whereas the Antipodean model takes a generalist approach that is linked to how much an individual 'participates' in the transport arena (rather than their own particular behaviour). The SAAQ approach has the advantage of directly addressing moral hazard concerns that are commonly associated with no-fault compensation funds.

The separation of the annual financing and long-term funding accounts allows for a balance to be struck between the immediate operational stability of the scheme and the long-term compensation funding risks. The recognition of these twin elements of the budget for a large no-fault compensation scheme is different to the 'all-in' consolidated method used by the ACC and the TAC. Although there has been some cross-subsidisation between the two funding pillars, this has only been to a small degree in recent years. There is a high level of transparency and public engagement about the SAAQ's funding policy (the independent actuarial periodic reviews, followed by public consultations), which enables a strong element of civic stake-holding in the financial stability of the SAAQ.

As with the TAC, a core part of the financial stability strategy for the scheme is the reduction in transport accident injuries through safety improvements. However, unlike the TAC, this cannot be done at the expense of the everyday financial stability of the SAAQ. Returns on safety investments appear to be fruitful, albeit over a number of years and with sometimes patchy results.[376]

6.4. MANITOBA'S MPI

We turn now to the SAAQ's sibling, the MPI in Manitoba. The legislative framework of the MPI is broadly equivalent to that of SAAQ, and we see a very similar funding structure. Like the SAAQ, the MPI's no-fault benefits are also fully-funded by driver licensing costs and premiums charged to drivers under the compulsory no-fault personal injury coverage.[377]

Unlike the other big no-fault compensation funds, the MPI also operates as an insurer in the field of general property damage for automobile injuries. At first glance, it might appear that the financial structure of the scheme would be different or incomparable with the single-focused injury compensation schemes. However, the compulsory no-fault personal injury cover within MPI is a carefully carved-out sub-element of the wider insurance corporation. The shape of the general (non-personal injury) automobile insurance landscape in Manitoba means that MPI is the dominant provider in all transport injury functions. The legislation specifically foresees that the personal injury arm is kept separate and 'the revenue from its plans of universal compulsory automobile insurance and its other revenues are not used to subsidize the corporation's plans of extension insurance'.[378] However a Consolidated Fund of all revenues is also used to fund the costs of dispute resolution (including the independent Claimant Advisor body).[379] For the purposes of this funding and sustainability analysis we will only consider the financial elements of the scheme that are relevant to the no-fault comprehensive compensation fund for personal injury within MPI.

The MPI is a Crown corporation and a wholly public insurer. This means that, just like the other three schemes, supervision of the no-fault compensation fund is undertaken by the executive.[380] There is also direct accountability to

---

[376] Société de l'assurance automobile du Québec, 'Proposed Insurance Contributions for 2019–2021' (n 359) 16.

[377] Manitoba Public Insurance Corporation, 'Where Do Your Premium Dollars Go?' <https://www.mpi.mb.ca/Pages/where-do-your-premium-dollars-go.aspx>.

[378] The Manitoba Public Insurance Corporation Act s 6.3.

[379] ibid ss 174.3, 177.

[380] Via the Lieutenant Governor in Council.

the Manitoba legislature for the timely filing of annual reports and financial statements.[381] The MPI is not subject to the same regulatory oversight via the Insurance Council of Manitoba as are private insurance companies operating in the Manitoba province. However, the MPI is also subject to supervision by the Public Utilities Board (PUB), 'an independent, quasi-judicial administrative tribunal that has broad oversight and supervisory powers over public utilities and designated monopolies ... The PUB considers both the impact to customers and financial requirements of the utility in approving rates.'[382] The PUB has a supervisory role in the setting of MPI levies,[383] which is a similar degree of supervision to that of Québec's actuarial supervisory body for the SAAQ.

In terms of the MPI's current solvency, it is a little bit more challenging to pin down the solvency elements of the no-fault personal injury compensation. This is because the Personal Injury Protection Plan (PIPP) (the compulsory comprehensive no-fault framework) forms one (albeit very important) part of the compulsory Autopac Basic plan for all Manitoba drivers. Autopac Basic is the standard compulsory third-party liability coverage for economic damage associated with an automobile accident, which also includes personal injury cover through PIPP. However, like its no-fault comprehensive cousins, PIPP is available to all Manitoba residents regardless of whether they own a vehicle. The MPI's financial statements fold PIPP costs and capitalisation targets within its reporting for all 'Basic' cover.

The Basic cover stream has a capitalisation target of 100 per cent, which is specified in regulation.[384] This capitalisation target is approved by the PUB, and is 'based upon the capital management framework of the Office of the Superintendent of Financial Institutions Canada and the Minimum Capital Test (MCT).'[385] This rate of 100 per cent contrasts with capitalisation targets of 200 and 300 per cent for its extension and special risk (e.g. commercial trucking) categories, for which MPI is the dominant (but not only) insurer. The reason for these differences in capitalisation is that the Basic cover stream operates on a monopoly basis, whereas the capitalisation of the extension and special risk categories 'reflects the higher risks of operating in a competitive environment.'[386] The alignment with national insurance regulation is an attempt to ensure compliance with industry best practice. Before 2019, a total equity approach to capitalisation was used.

---

[381]   The Manitoba Public Insurance Corporation Act ss 43(2), 44(1) and (2).

[382]   The Public Utilities Board Act, 'About the PUB' <http://www.pubmanitoba.ca/v1/about-pub/index.html>.

[383]   The Manitoba Public Insurance Corporation Act ss 6.4(2) and (3), 33(1.1).

[384]   Reserves Regulation 76/2019.

[385]   Manitoba Public Insurance Corporation, 'Annual Report 2019' (2020) 23 <https://www.mpi.mb.ca/Documents/2019-Annual-Report.pdf>.

[386]   ibid.

The change to an industry-aligned approach was to ensure that the capitalisation target 'remains appropriate given changes to the Corporation's risk profile and balance sheet as compared to the static total equity target and will provide more comparability to industry peers.'[387] The capitalisation of the Basic cover account was 104 per cent in 2020, up from a significantly lower level in 2019 (54 per cent). This drop can be explained by significant changes behind the scenes to adjust actuarial claims forecasting for PIPP claims. Specifically,

> 'beginning in 2017 and continuing into 2018, a new centralized case reserving methodology was implemented for long-term Personal Injury Protection Plan (PIPP) claims files. A dedicated central team has been established to determine the necessary life-time reserves for PIPP claimants which has led to greater consistency and reliability of reserving adequacy ... increase in injury claims incurred compared to last year is mainly due to the significant unfavourable actuarial adjustment of $50.9 million made in 2018/19 and unfavourable interest rate impact on unpaid claims of $40.9 million'[388]

The MPI scheme operates on a fully-funded basis like the other three funds and can be broadly described as sustainable. Its 2018/19 financial statements showed that the scheme had adequate reserves and reinsurance in place to cover all existing liabilities, across all its cover businesses.[389] For the Basic cover category, in 2019 out of every dollar of premium revenue, 22 cents were spent on bodily injury claims (PIPP).[390] This was half of the cost of economic damage claims, at 44 cents per dollar (e.g. vehicle and property damage claims). Operating expenses made up an equivalent of 20 cents per revenue dollar.[391]

Investment income contributes an equivalent of 7 cents per dollar of revenue for the Basic cover category. A new asset-allocation strategy was launched in 2018, which aimed to better match the MPI's asset holdings to the different categories of liabilities. The goal of this asset allocation strategy realignment was to reduce risk 'which will support the Corporation's objective of managing volatility and delivering rate stability.'[392] This has led to some uneven results in investment income over the past two years – there was a large, one-time sale of equities in 2018, making investment income appear disproportionately lower in 2019.[393] The performance of the MPI's new investment strategy can therefore not be wholly assessed at this time. Responsibility for management of

---

[387] Manitoba Public Insurance Corporation, 'Annual Report 2018' (n 30) 24.
[388] ibid 16.
[389] Manitoba Public Insurance Corporation, 'Annual Financial Statements 2018/19' (2019).
[390] Robert L Kopstein, 'The Report of the Autopac Review Commission – Volume 1' (1988).
[391] Manitoba Public Insurance Corporation, 'Annual Report 2019' (n 385) 17.
[392] Manitoba Public Insurance Corporation, 'Annual Report 2018' (n 30) 24.
[393] C$242.6 million in 2018, compared with C$107.2 million in 2019. See Manitoba Public Insurance Corporation, Annual Report 2019 (n 385) 17.

the MPI's investments rests with the Manitoba Minister of Finance; however, the management of its equities portfolio (about 10 per cent of current investments) has been outsourced to three private investment managers.[394]

Financial sustainability has always been a core goal of the MPI scheme, via the emphasis on stable and affordable basic automobile insurance rates. Cost blow-outs would lead to the possibility of a spike in insurance levies, which would go against the founding principles and ongoing focus of the scheme. Indeed, in the 2019 annual report it is noted: 'Affordable rates and exceptional coverage are only sustainable if we continue to practise fiscal prudence. Cost containment and fiscal responsibility remain a primary focus for this Board'.[395] There is a statutory restriction on privatising the scheme without public approval via referendum, which means that any private sector possibilities to change funding frameworks or outsource liabilities are not immediately available to the MPI.[396] MPI acknowledges that one of the most significant challenges to the maintenance of this stability is the potentially volatile nature of long-term PIPP injury claims – which are far less predictable than short-term property damage claims. The MPI's actuaries' assessment of the reserves to be held to cover Basic liabilities is necessarily imprecise: it 'relies on analysis of historical claim trends, investment rates of return, expectation on the future development of claims and judgement'.[397] The total equity underpinning the Basic cover is what makes up that category's capitalisation, and this is referred to as the Rate Stabilization Reserve (RSR). The purpose of the RSR is 'to protect motorists from rate increases that would otherwise be necessary due to unexpected variances from forecasted results, and due to events, and losses arriving from non-recurring events or factors'.[398] Therefore, the definition of financial sustainability for the purposes of the MPI scheme is closely linked to rates stability whilst maintaining comprehensive Basic cover.

MPI's strong financial position, and a decrease in claims due to the COVID-19 pandemic, meant that it was able to provide a refund of C$110 million to policyholders (i.e. drivers) in 2020.[399] The MPI has also identified a reduction in injury claims due to the pandemic; however, it has also warned that the pandemic has had negative impacts on investment revenue.[400]

---

[394] ibid 18.

[395] ibid 4.

[396] Manitoba Public Insurance Corporation Act ss 14.1(1), (2), (3).

[397] Manitoba Public Insurance Corporation, 'Annual Report 2019' (n 385) 22.

[398] ibid.

[399] Kayla Rosen, 'MPI Returning $110M to Provide Financial Relief to Policy Holders', *CTV news* (23 April 2020) <https://winnipeg.ctvnews.ca/mpi-returning-110m-to-provide-financial-relief-to-policy-holders-1.4908417>.

[400] Manitoba Public Insurance Corporation, 'Annual Report 2019' (n 385) 16. The scheme also reports that it has adjusted its asset-liability matching strategy to better protect the scheme's investments and long-term liability cover against market fluctuations.

In terms of MPI's intersection with the public health system, like SAAQ it also makes a monthly payment to Manitoba's public health department.[401]

The calculation of MPI Autopac Basic (and other cover category) premiums is based on a number of different factors. There are many similarities to the other three schemes in terms of how the premium is calculated. However the MPI takes the most individualised approach of all our large no-fault funds. Remember, the Basic Autopac premium includes both the no-fault injury cover and basic third-party property damage cover. Therefore the calculation of the relevant levy or premium has to take into account a wider range of risks, including economic risks, than pure no-fault injury-related levies. These are the factors that influence the calculation of an individual's MPI premium:[402]

a. The type of vehicle – year, make, model and extra safety features.
b. The location of the vehicle registration – the Manitoba province is split into four geographic zones. The driver is required to disclose whether they live in one zone and commute into another.
c. Vehicle use – this includes frequency of use.
d. The individual driver's driving record – this includes at-fault (property damage) claims, traffic convictions or drug or alcohol-related administrative suspensions.

What can we therefore conclude about the financial stability and sustainability of the MPI scheme? Of all the four schemes the MPI shows the most focused financial target. The stability of automobile premiums – and the financial sustainability of the scheme to ensure that stability – has been a primary focus of the MPI since its establishment. Therefore, investment strategy design and actuarial monitoring are revised and adjusted as necessary to maintain financial stability. This has resulted in very low exposure to international equity fluctuations, compared with the ACC Scheme and the TAC. There is clear recognition of the potential volatility of long-term personal injury claims, and the adjustment of assets to better reflect outstanding liabilities shows prudence.

The direct targeting of premiums to the individual circumstances of the driver and his/her vehicle is also the most precise of any of the four funds, but shows broad equivalence with the TAC and SAAQ. It shows the most coherence in terms of capturing individual risk, but admittedly this is because the single monopoly scheme covers all the risks associated with automobile use – both basic all-perils economic risks and personal injury.

The independent supervision of rate-setting by the PUB is in line with the independent actuarial supervision found in Québec for the SAAQ. This adds a

---

[401] Comments made by Glenn Andersen, Director of Injury Claims Management at Manitoba Public Insurance in email correspondence dated 16 October 2019.
[402] 'Determining Your Rates' <https://www.mpi.mb.ca/Pages/your-rates.aspx>.

272

Intersentia

welcome level of independence and expertise to rate-setting, and ensures that the setting of levies is done with a clear eye on fiscal prudence.

There is a clear legislative commitment to public underwriting and monopoly provision of core automobile insurance (both economic loss and personal injury), because of the requirement to hold a public referendum before any privatisation steps. This gives the MPI and the legislature less flexibility to choose a different financial and underwriting model if required. However the extreme public backlash against insurance rates increases by private insurers in the 1980s shows that both successive Manitoban governments and the public give stability and universal coverage a higher normative value than individual choice in insurance coverage and fault-based compensation possibilities for personal injuries.

6.5. CONCLUSIONS ON FUNDING AND SUSTAINABILITY

In conclusion, there is a broad degree of similarity between the four funds in terms of their funding structure, but some important key differences in the details of how they administer these funding structures. These details have a significant influence on the flexibility and sustainability of the schemes in terms of the ability to adapt to changed financial circumstances. In this section, the key pillars of funding and sustainability are described.

6.5.1. Fully-Funded

Very large no-fault comprehensive compensation funds should, as a rule, be *fully-funded*. The four schemes studied in this book are all fully-funded, which means that they aim to have enough financial reserves on hand at any one time to cover the lifetime costs of existing injuries on their books. This reflects the quasi-insurance dimension of their administrative structure. There have been some academic calls for the New Zealand ACC Scheme to return to a pay-as-you-go social security-type model, partially in order to facilitate an expansion of the scheme to cover more types of misfortune (specifically: sickness and disability). This does not appear justified, given the success and stability of the fully-funded approach both within New Zealand and in comparison with its big no-fault cousins elsewhere. Those arguments should be contextually understood as being caused by the failure of the wider New Zealand social security system to support sick and disabled people to a standard that is equivalent to other highly developed countries. There have been no arguments made in relation to the other three schemes about a diversion away from a full-funding model. The fully-funded nature of large no-fault compensation schemes is a key point of difference between this category of fund and non-comprehensive no-fault compensation funds.

6.5.2. Publicly Underwritten and Operating at a Low Capitalisation Rate

As well as being fully-funded, large no-fault compensation funds are *publicly underwritten and are not subject to the same prudential and financial supervision as private insurers*. In recent years there have been efforts by all four funds to ensure voluntary compliance with private insurance prudential standards, where relevant to their structure and operational objectives. Large no-fault compensation funds also *have lower capitalisation rates than private insurers, but still aim to operate at minimum 100 per cent solvency/capitalisation, but not in great excess of that rate*. Although not expressly stated for all four funds, this relatively low capitalisation rate is because large no-fault compensation funds have the statutory power to raise levies and operate on a monopolistic compulsory basis. There is also a frequent legislative concern with the fairness on current levy-payers and intergenerational equality – this is because too high a capitalisation rate would mean that the risk-taking public was paying over the odds for future accidents. Where a fund also operates in the market of competitive insurance cover for other kinds of losses (such as MPI's extended cover products for economic losses), a higher capitalisation is required for those non-compulsory products. These two points – the identified key pillars of prudential/financial supervision and capitalisation – point towards further financial stability issues. Firstly, the public purse remains as the unacknowledged final backstop to all four schemes, in the case of major loss or revenue collapse. None of the four examined schemes have clear legislative rules in place for the circumstances and conditions under which there may need to be a Treasury injection (or sale of investment income) to address shortfalls. It is likely that arguments equivalent to 'solidarity' or 'community responsibility' would be used to justify that kind of support. Secondly, there is no direct supervision by a financial or prudential regulator of the financial position of big no-fault funds. This means that the financial position and sustainability of big no-fault funds is ultimately the responsibility of the legislative and executive branches at any one time, and there are limited independent financial oversight mechanisms available.

The reasons for a continued preference for public underwriting (and similarly, a public authority operational model) of the four big funds are not clear, if one excludes the point of a solidarity/social contract theme. Actuarial analysis indicates that this is because of a desire on the part of legislatures to maintain long-term scheme viability and to appropriately balance scheme objectives,[403] a possible lack of necessary data or actuarial expertise to facilitate a shift to private

---

[403] Andrew Fronsko and Alan Woodroffe, 'Public vs. Private Underwriting and Administration of Personal Injury Statutory Insurance Schemes', *Actuaries Institute Injury & Disability Schemes Seminar* (Brisbane, November 2017).

Chapter 4. Key Pillars

underwriting, and concerns about speculative pricing by private insurers.[404] In summary, one could conclude that the choice of public underwriting is normative and because of the lack of a sufficiently dynamic private insurance market in the relevant jurisdictions.

6.5.3. Reliance on Levies and Investment Income

The two main pillars of revenue for big no-fault compensation funds are *levies and investment income*. The New Zealand ACC Scheme was the only big fund that had any significant degree of taxpayer funding injection, due to the existence of two funding accounts that have no specific levy stream attached to them. A balance needs to be struck between the reliance on the two streams of income (levies and investment). *Unexpected local and international investment market and interest rate fluctuations have significantly affected the investment incomes* of some of the schemes in recent years. This is a financial risk because big no-fault funds also typically have *a statutory restriction on the level of possible levies increases*, in order to ensure levy stability for the public. This is different to a private insurance company, which would typically have more flexibility to increase premiums to accommodate for investment income shortfalls. The current legislative designs of all four schemes currently do not explicitly address how the balance between levies and investment revenue should be managed, although all four schemes have attempted to navigate this at a secondary level through careful institutional design.

The *design of levies typically has a broad link to the risk profile of the levy-payer.* This may include elements that try to take account of matters such as residence location, type of vehicle or activity, previous injuries, and frequency of engagement with risky activity. However, there are significant variations across all four schemes about how precisely that risk is being captured. A big no-fault compensation fund with wide responsibility for a whole functional field will be able to risk-target levies more accurately than a big fund with responsibility for multiple fields. The Canadian schemes, with a broad horizontal regulatory responsibility in the field of transport, appear to most accurately capture the risk profile of individuals when setting levies (for example, by strongly linking levy rates to driver demerit points). In contrast, the New Zealand ACC Scheme has wide horizontal responsibility for setting levies, paying compensation and actioning general injury-prevention but is *not* responsible for the parallel criminal or regulatory punishment of risky individuals. That scheme appears to face political and public backlash when it tries to more precisely price and levy for risk. Further, the risk profile of non-direct users or levy-payers has proven difficult to capture in that scheme for political reasons – although it has been shown in this analysis that it is not impossible.

---

[404] Reid and Mackessack (n 277).

Intersentia

275

6.5.4. Supervision of Levy-Setting and Independent Investment Management

Some kind of independent actuarial supervision and setting of levies and the purpose of levies is common to most of the schemes, but is most entrenched in the financial framework of the Canadian schemes. This is a helpful element that ensures that the setting of levies is as accurate as possible and – importantly – free from political influence. *Limits on levy increases* are also a common feature, to prevent sudden shocks to the levy-paying public.

Also common is *independent investment management of some or all of the investment assets of the fund.* This adds a layer of independence and professionalism in the management of this key pillar of investment income and reserves for long-term risks. This is an important financial stability feature, because big no-fault compensation funds' coverage of long-term and sometimes catastrophic injuries creates significant long-term solvency risks. Where a fund does not have an independent agency managing its investment income (such as the ACC), then the scheme is closer in nature to a sovereign wealth fund. This is a financial and stability risk, because the fund is then entirely responsible for having expertise in the payment of compensation *as well as* expertise in the investment of income for the coverage of liabilities. A delegation of expertise to a supervised agency that handles other government investments is a wise hedge against internal governance and financial management failures on the part of the fund.

6.5.5. Reinsurance

Reinsurance of long-tail risks is a possibility for the big four no-fault compensation funds, but it is rarely used in practice. We see that the four funds (and the government ministers ultimately directing them) prefer to publicly underwrite the potential for large scale catastrophic personal injury risks. This is a financial risk because a sudden mass injury event may create a shock of liabilities. The size and income of the schemes and the capped compensation available under them means that any single mass event is not likely to bankrupt any of the funds.[405] However a sudden severe mass injury event, such as personal injuries resulting from a natural disaster (whether a general injury that would be covered by ACC, or injuries to motorists in cars at the time of the disaster for the other

---

[405] Indeed, personal injury claims resulting from recent mass harm events in New Zealand, such as the Christchurch terrorist attack and the White Island/Whakaari volcanic eruption (both in 2019), have not posed any difficulties for the ACC Scheme. In the case of the latter, this is partly to do with the fact of long-term rehabilitation costs of repatriated overseas victims (mainly tourists) not being funded by ACC. See Accident Compensation Corporation, 'Annual Report 2020' (n 241) 56; Accident Compensation Corporation, 'Financial Condition Report 2020' (n 232) 22.

three schemes) could certainly cause the kind of harms that would benefit from reinsurance coverage. One might quite realistically foresee, for example, Victorian drivers being trapped by climate change-induced annual bushfires. There have also been recent scientific warnings that a severe earthquake is likely to occur within the next 50 years on New Zealand's Alpine Fault – in locations where significant numbers of local and international tourists (i.e. covered only by the non-levied Non-Earners' Account) could be present.[406] We can therefore conclude that reinsurance is something that is a key pillar of a big no-fault compensation fund framework, but is not being adequately utilised at this time to cover the potential for large scale catastrophic damage. This means that there is a tacit acceptance that the taxpayer (via the government) will cover such risks – a point that is not explicitly made clear in the existing legislative framework.

6.5.6. Injury Prevention and Rehabilitation

Injury prevention and rehabilitation is an important element of the financial sustainability equation for these kinds of large funds. Managing and guaranteeing the success of injury rehabilitation (and the long-term costs associated with a failure to rehabilitate victims out of the scheme) has not been easy or predictable for the funds. All four funds work actively to monitor this issue. Some funds, like the TAC, take a very aggressive approach towards injury prevention as a more reliable form of financial costs management. For that big fund, significant investment in empirical research into the causes of accidents and the costs of injuries has delivered concrete data that can inform levy-setting, road and infrastructure design (in conjunction with other agencies) and other transport policies. This has most likely been aided by the singular focus of that fund on one wide sector – transport injury. In contrast, we see that the New Zealand ACC Scheme (with a multi-sector remit) has struggled to aggressively target injury causes because, *inter alia*, targeted levies are perceived as unfair to certain socio-economic groups. More general injury prevention education and investment programmes are the strategy favoured by this fund, and returns on these investments are expected in the longer term. In the Canadian schemes, there is also a focus on safety investment, but only if it does not come at the expense of rate stability.

---

[406] Jamie Howarth and Rupert Sutherland, 'NZ's next Large Alpine Fault Quake Is Likely Coming Sooner than We Thought, Study Shows' (*The Conversation*, 19 April 2021) <https://theconversation.com/nzs-next-large-alpine-fault-quake-is-likely-coming-sooner-than-we-thought-study-shows-159223>; 'Alpine Fault: Probability of Damaging Quake Higher than Previously Thought', *Radio New Zealand News* (20 April 2021) <https://www.rnz.co.nz/news/national/440834/alpine-fault-probability-of-damaging-quake-higher-than-previously-thought>.

6.5.7. Limited Scope for Financial Reform

There is currently *limited scope for major financial reform of the schemes* – for both practical and legislative reasons. No conclusions are drawn here on whether such reforms would be desirable or necessary – overall, the four big schemes have achieved financial stability in the past two decades, although, as discussed, there is certainly room for improvements. The popularity and stability of the schemes also indicate that major reform away from a publicly administered and publicly underwritten model is unnecessary and undesirable. However, it is worth objectively pointing out which obstacles currently stand in the way of the possibility of major financial reform. These observations are useful indications of the kinds of challenges that a legislature may face if it installs a big no-fault compensation fund, and later wants to repeal or abandon it. Firstly, the comprehensive nature of our four no-fault schemes means that the private insurance market has pivoted away entirely from the coverage of long-term personal injury for transport and (in New Zealand's case) broad risks. This appears to be a causative result of such a comprehensive scheme. It means that there is little scope to identify whether the private insurance sector has the capacity, data availability and expertise (or indeed willingness) to take on some of the covered risks if required by legislative change.[407] This can be mitigated if there is comprehensive data available about the costs and causes of risks. Such data would also ensure that erratic and speculative pricing during scheme change is avoided.

Secondly on the reform point, there can be a legislative restriction in place against major changes to the fundamental financial principles of the scheme. Manitoba's MPI has a legislative restriction on privatising any parts of the no-fault scheme without the approval of a public referendum. This ensures that there is societal buy-in for any major changes, but it means that decisions about the future financial direction of the scheme (if that involves a deviation from the current public model) are automatically infused with political issues.

6.5.8. Full Compensation for Limited Categories

It is *financially possible and sustainable to have full compensation for limited categories of injuries* under a no-fault comprehensive compensation fund. This is an important conclusion to be made about whether full or tort-like compensation is possible or sustainable under a publicly administered scheme. The maintenance of 'common law damages' for serious injury (that are effectively paid in most cases by the TAC) is an area of theoretical incoherence

---

[407] The issue of a lack of available actuarial expertise and data – in the context of possible privatisation of some ACC business – is specifically discussed in Reid and Mackessack (n 277) 15–19.

within the TAC scheme and adds significant complexity. However the actual financial performance of the TAC scheme shows that although common law damages are the cause of cost blow-outs within the scheme, the fund overall is nevertheless sustainable. Therefore, despite the legal philosophical difficulties of including 'fuller' or tort-style compensation within comprehensive no-fault comprehensive compensation funds, a conclusion can be drawn that it is not financially impossible or unsustainable to do so in limited cases. This, however, does not address the legal incoherency of such a carve-out, but it proves that such a choice is possible if carefully budgeted for.

6.5.9.   Financial Interaction with Other Health and Support Structures

It is important to include *design for the financial interaction of the fund with other health and support structures*. On the topic of broader financial stewardship, another funding key pillar of big no-fault compensation funds is the specific design of how the fund interacts with other structures that involve public finances or have public responsibility. In particular, there must be specific regulatory direction given to the interaction with between the medical system and relevant social security. Direct reimbursement and billing of individual claims and bulk funding (on an annual or monthly basis) are two approaches used by the four big funds. This is important to ensure that a big no-fault fund does not free-ride on the public health system.

7.   SUBROGATION, PUBLIC TORT LIABILITY AND/OR REIMBURSEMENT

When may a comprehensive no-fault compensation fund seek subrogation or reimbursement of compensation it has paid to a victim from a causatively relevant party? And what are the impacts of this on access to justice issues?

Subrogation is a concept that is most at home within insurance law. It is a process by which the rights of an insured person against a third party can be assigned to an insurer, usually in order to prevent excess recovery or more than full indemnity.[408] Outside of insurance, subrogation can be defined in equitable or restitution dimensions: 'an equitable doctrine holding that when a third party pays a creditor or obligee the third party succeeds to the creditor's rights against the debtor or obligor.'[409] In other words, a third party is assigned – by statute or contractual agreement – any civil law rights to pursue relevant persons

---

[408]   John Lowry, Philip Rawlings and Robert Merkin, *Insurance Law: Doctrines and Principles* (3rd edn, Hart Publishing 2011) 350.

[409]   Merriam-Webster, 'Subrogation' <https://www.merriam-webster.com/dictionary/subrogation#legalDictionary>.

for the monies paid to the first party in relation to the loss. Insurance scholars have argued that, in reality, subrogation may be of little practical use to private insurance businesses, but may serve public policy goals of deterrence (especially in the case of uninsured wrongdoers).[410]

Subrogation is a tool that can sometimes be used within no-fault compensation funds. However some clarity is required at this point about when it might be employed in a no-fault compensation fund and what it is not. Subrogation is different to money that the compensation fund receives from individuals or businesses who have undertaken risk or caused harm indirectly in the field of the compensation fund's scope. For example, some European compensation funds are primarily funded by fines from criminal offences or other legal violations.[411] However, because many compensation funds (especially in Europe) are subsidiary in nature, this means that they can only be accessed or come into relevance where no tortfeasor can found or realistically be pursued.[412] Examples of this would include the guaranteed third-party liability motor vehicle injury funds that exist in European Union Member States, or compensation funds established in relation to disasters or terrorist attacks. Therefore, subrogation is often irrelevant in those contexts because there generally is nobody from whom to seek a reimbursement – if there were, the claimant would not be entitled to access the compensation fund (or the compensation fund might not have been established in the first place). A reserve subrogation power might be helpful if, at a later point in time, a relevant tortfeasor could be found and the compensation fund could use that tool to seek recovery of its costs.[413]

In a comprehensive no-fault compensation fund, however, there is a causative-linked entitlement to compensation on a no-fault basis *and* a statutory bar against pursuing a tortfeasor in (nearly) all cases. This means that there may certainly be someone who factually could be pursued for compensatory damages, *but for* the compensation fund's restrictions.

There is little literature on the relevance or definition of subrogation in relation to no-fault comprehensive compensation funds. This would be a recovery action taken by the fund for the reimbursement of costs from an identified, causatively responsible party. The most recent scholarly literature on the usefulness of subrogation in relation to no-fault compensation generally

---

[410] Lowry, Rawlings and Merkin (n 408) 370–371.
[411] Vansweevelt and others (n 1) 199.
[412] ibid 193–195.
[413] In that case, the right to recover monies might be vested in the government or state itself, rather than in the compensation fund. An example of this is in national vaccine injury compensation programmes, where the state itself is granted the right to recover monies that its compensation programme has paid out. See John D Winter, Cassye Cole and Jonah Wacholder, 'Toward a Global Solution on Vaccine Liability and Compensation' (2019) 74 *Food and Drug Law Journal* 1, 9 <http://www.who.int/csr/don/7-september-2018-ebola-drc/en/>.

Chapter 4. Key Pillars

(whether a comprehensive or non-comprehensive fund) has used different terminology to describe this activity. This term is 'public tort liability'. Public tort liability has been advocated as a possibility for all no-fault compensation funds.[414]

A 2002 paper by Hassan El Menyawi considers the advantages and disadvantages of no-fault compensation (compared to tort liability) from the perspectives of distributive and corrective legal philosophy.[415] He sought to identify a third way that reconciled these advantages and disadvantages, and moved away from the classic perspective that the battle between tort and no-fault was a choice between tort liability and social insurance. Certainly, that kind of classic characterisation still dominates scholarly literature on no-fault or no-blame compensation,[416] although there is finally some recognition in more recent comparative law literature that there are intrinsic social differences between compensation funds and social security.[417] Menyawi argued in favour of a comprehensive no-fault compensation fund for all personal injuries regardless of cause, like the New Zealand ACC Scheme. However he also suggested that the state be vested with a complementary comprehensive power of subrogation:[418]

'Of course, the above recommendation (if taken by itself) is not unique and does not reconcile the corrective justice justifications of tort liability with the distributive justice justifications of no-fault compensation. The unique feature about our overall recommendation is that, although the state compensates all victims who suffer personal injury, the state also pursues wrongdoers (or defendants) who committed the faults that resulted in the suffering of victims. We recommend that the state demand, after having assessed whether the wrongdoer did commit a fault and the extent of the damages, as well as financial ability of the defendant, to come up with a figure that the defendant ought to pay to the state. This is analogical to criminal law where the state (instead of the victim) pursues the criminal'.

---

[414] Mark R Forwood, 'Whither No-Fault Schemes in Australia: Have We Closed the Care and Compensation Gap?' (2018) 43 *Alternative Law Journal* 166; Trish O'Sullivan and Kate Tokeley, 'Consumer Product Failure Causing Personal Injury Under the No-Fault Accident Compensation Scheme in New Zealand-a Let-off for Manufacturers?', *Product Safety, Consumers' Health and Liability Law Conference* (Springer 2017) <https://doi.org/10.1007/s10603-018-9383-2>; Hassan El Menyawi, 'Public Tort Liability: An Alternative to Tort Liability and No-Fault Compensation' (2002) 9(4) *Murdoch University Electronic Journal of Law* <http://www.bepress.com/gj/advances/vol3/iss1/art1>; Jeffrey O Connell and Craig Brown, 'A Canadian Proposal for No-Fault Benefits Financed by Assignments of Tort Rights' (1983) 33 *University of Toronto Law Journal* 434.

[415] El Menyawi (n 414).

[416] For example, Macleod and Hodges argue that no-fault compensation fund structures are representative of a trend of providing compensation on a wider social basis, which is an argument that can lead somewhat inevitably to a conclusion that compensation funds are a type of social insurance. See Macleod and Hodges (n 1) 620.

[417] Vansweevelt and others (n 1) 206.

[418] El Menyawi (n 414) 74.

Intersentia

281

The Menyawi proposal therefore expands the concept of subrogation to have key importance within the context of a comprehensive no-fault compensation fund. More recently, public tort liability has been mentioned as potentially having a role within the (currently stalled) Australian National Injury Insurance Scheme.[419] Public tort liability can therefore be defined as the most expansive type of subrogation possible that is specifically suited to a very large compensation fund. An obvious difficulty that has been identified in literature is the fact that public tort liability, as the most expansive form of subrogation possible, requires significant legislative operational design and some kind of supervision of the compensation fund's subrogation/prosecutorial activities (although Menyawi argued that the latter could be efficiently managed by way of judicial review).[420]

Another specific difficulty of the Menyawi proposal for public tort liability for a big no-fault compensation fund is the question of *who* might be a potential tortfeasor/defendant. If every person may hypothetically be sued for their role in another's personal injury, but are also always entitled to compensation, then everyone has a right to compensation but nobody actually has immunity from liability. In my view, this seems rather similar to, for example, the strict liability (and privately underwritten and operated) Swedish motor vehicle injury insurance framework, which (unlike most strict liability schemes) *always* also covers first-party injuries.[421] It also begs the question of whether it might be easier for legislatures to simply follow Koziol's proposal for universal mandatory liability insurance for personal injury,[422] especially in jurisdictions where there is a sufficiently competitive and well-populated insurance market.[423]

New Zealand academics Trish O'Sullivan and Kate Tokeley did not refer to public tort liability when they discussed the possibility of introducing proper subrogation to the ACC Scheme in the context of consumer product failures causing personal injury.[424] They specifically argued for a limited power of

---

[419]   Forwood (n 414). See also the discussion in Andrew Field, 'There Must Be a Better Way: Personal Injuries Compensation Since the Crisis in Insurance' (2008) 13 *Deakin Law Review* 67.

[420]   Forwood (n 414) 5; El Menyawi (n 414) paras 87–88.

[421]   Watts, 'Potential of No-Fault Comprehensive Compensation Funds to Deal with Automation and Other 21st Century Transport Developments' (n 12) 16; Sonia Macleod, Matti Urho and Christopher Hodges, 'Part III: Nordic States' in Sonia Macleod and Christopher Hodges (eds), *Redress Schemes for Personal Injuries* (1st edn, Hart Publishing 2017) 168–174. The limited circumstances where personal injury compensation can be reduced – but never removed – in the Swedish motor injury framework include situations of intentional or gross negligence by the driver, or the use of drugs or excessive alcohol.

[422]   Koziol (n 221).

[423]   Although as noted elsewhere in this text, Cane and Goudkamp argue that the freedom to be inadequately insured – which would inevitably result for poorer and disadvantaged persons under a Koziol-type model – is no freedom at all. See Cane and Goudkamp (n 48) 466.

[424]   O'Sullivan and Tokeley (n 414).

subrogation to be granted to the ACC body, to allow it to pursue consumer product failure claims against local or overseas manufacturers. One of the (possibly unintended) consequences of the existing ACC Scheme is that there is very little in the way of powerful public liability law to protect consumers against faulty goods. This has led to few legal solutions being available to pursue, for example, an overseas manufacturer of a defective product who has contributed nothing to ACC levies (as evidenced by the *DePuy* hip-replacement litigation). To maintain the integrity of the statutory bar, O'Sullivan and Tokeley argued that subrogation

> 'could be limited to circumstances where the extent of the product failure reaches a certain trigger point which indicates far reaching consequences ... In order to determine the appropriate trigger point, work would need to be done in relation to assessing the costs of making such a claim and the benefits in terms of pursuing manufacturers'.

As an example of subrogation that the New Zealand legislature could copy, the authors reference the SAAQ scheme's subrogation powers.

One can therefore see here two theoretical possibilities that have been sketched out for subrogation or reimbursement for a no-fault comprehensive compensation fund – the expansive Menyawi public tort liability approach on one hand, and the more limited defective products approach espoused by O'Sullivan and Tokeley on the other hand. The former creates a right to compensation for personal injury but vests a wide quasi-criminal type power of prosecution in the public authority administering the compensation fund. This attempts to tackle distributive and retributive justice issues simultaneously. The latter takes an approach to subrogation that appears to be focused on better regulating 'big players' who might benefit from a no-fault approach/elimination of tort liability with too little deterrence for risky actions, thereby enhancing retributive justice.

To assess the usefulness and relevance of all these ideas within the specific context of a no-fault comprehensive compensation fund, it is therefore appropriate at this point to consider the current shape and practical application of subrogation powers within existing comprehensive no-fault comprehensive compensation funds. This is because the subrogation powers in existence in those funds are directly linked to a corresponding immunity from liability. As noted already, New Zealand's ACC Scheme has no substantive subrogation possibilities within its existing statutory framework. The subrogation powers within the TAC, MPI and SAAQ regimes are set out in the table below. For comparative comprehensiveness, the very limited possibility of subrogation within the ACC Scheme is nevertheless also detailed.

Table 12. Subrogation rights (TAC, SAAQ, MPI and ACC)

	TAC	SAAQ	MPI	ACC
Key subrogation statutory provision(s)	Section 104 – indemnity by a third party.[425] Section 107 – TAC may take proceedings.[426]	Section 83.60 – where SAAQ compensates a person for an accident outside Québec, it is subrogated to the person's rights to pursue the relevant non-resident – this is effected by the decision of SAAQ to compensate the victim.	Section 26(1) – where MPI compensates someone, it is subrogated to and shall be deemed to be an assignee of all rights of recovery against any other person liable.[427] Section 26(2) – when subrogation rights apply. This is, broadly speaking, when a person is driving	Section 321 – if a claimant has the right to bring proceedings in New Zealand or elsewhere in relation to the covered personal injury, ACC can force the claimant to take 'reasonable steps' to act on that right.[428] ACC can also deduct any

---

[425] Section 104(1) of the Transport Accident Act 1986 states: 'If an injury or death arising out of a transport accident in respect of which the Commission has made payments under this Act arose under circumstances which, regardless of section 93, would have created a legal liability in Victoria or elsewhere in a person (other than a person who is entitled to be indemnified under section 94) to pay damages in respect of any loss suffered by reason of the injury or death, the Commission is entitled to be indemnified by the first-mentioned person for such proportion of the amount of the liability of the Commission to make payments under this Act in respect of the injury or death as is appropriate to the degree to which the injury or death was attributable to the act, default or negligence of the first-mentioned person.'

[426] Section 107(1) states: '(1) If – (a) the Commission has paid an amount under this Act in respect of an injury or death; and (b) a person (other than the Commission) who appears to be liable or who it appears would have been liable, but for section 93, to pay damages or an amount by way of indemnity in respect of the injury or death is not entitled to be indemnified against that liability under an indemnity to which section 94 applies; and (c) proceedings against that person for the purpose of recovering such damages or amount have not been instituted or have been instituted but have been discontinued or have not been properly prosecuted – the Commission may take over the conduct of the proceedings.'

[427] Specifically: 'Upon making any payment of benefits or insurance money or upon assuming liability for such payment, the corporation is subrogated to and shall be deemed to be an assignee of all rights of recovery against any other person liable in respect of the loss, damage, injury, or death of every person to whom, or on whose behalf, or in respect of whom, the benefits or insurance money are to be paid; and the corporation may enforce those rights of recovery as provided in subsection (6) to the extent that the corporation has paid or has assumed liability to pay the benefits or insurance money.'

[428] In practice, this power has rarely been used. A footnote in the *DePuy* litigation referenced a 2006 affidavit from an ACC staff member which said that she was 'aware only of 21 cases in the last 14 years'. See *McGougan v DePuy International Limited* [2016] NZHC 2511 fn 82.

	Section 83.61 – extra terms of the SAAQ subrogation powers.[429]	without a licence or vehicle registration, or without the vehicle owner's consent.[430] However, generally omissions or errors in the ordinary use of a vehicle are excluded.	damages or settlement received by the victim from ACC compensatory benefits paid to him/her.

(continued)

---

[429] Specifically: 'Notwithstanding section 83.57, where the Société compensates a person by reason of an accident that occurred in Québec, it is subrogated to the person's rights and is entitled to recover the indemnities and the capital value of the pensions that the Société is required to pay from any person not resident in Québec who is responsible for the accident to the extent that he is responsible therefor and from any person liable for compensation for bodily injury caused in the accident by such non-resident. The subrogation is effected of right by the decision of the Société to compensate the victim.

The remedy of the Société as subrogee is subject to decision of the court and is prescribed by three years from the date of the decision. Responsibility is determined according to the ordinary rules of law to the extent that sections 108 to 114 do not derogate therefrom.'

[430] Specifically, section 26(2) states: 'The rights conferred upon the corporation under this section apply only where the loss, damage, injury, or death for which the corporation has paid or has assumed liability to pay benefits or insurance moneys is caused or contributed to by the fault of

(a) a person who, at the material time, was driving a motor vehicle

  (i)   while not qualified to drive a motor vehicle, or
  (ii) while not authorized by law to drive a motor vehicle, or
  (iii) that was not designated in an unexpired owner's certificate, or
  (iv) that was towing an unregistered trailer that was required to be registered under The Drivers and Vehicles Act, or
  (v)   while under the influence of intoxicating liquor or drugs to such an extent as to be for the time being incapable of the proper control of the motor vehicle; or

(b) a person who, at the material time, was driving or operating a motor vehicle or trailer without the consent, express or implied, of the owner thereof or who otherwise is not a person entitled to the benefit of subsection 38(4); or

(c) a person whose fault did not consist of acts or omissions in the ownership, use, or operation of a motor vehicle or trailer; or

(d) a person not the owner of a vehicle causing the loss, damage, injury or death or sustaining the loss or damage who at the material time is engaged in the business of selling, repairing, servicing, storing or parking motor vehicles or the servant or agent of any such person.'

Table 12 *continued*

	TAC	SAAQ	MPI	ACC
Associated statutory provisions	Section 105 – amounts to be repaid to Commission where damages recovered. Section 106 – contributory negligence, These are both provisions governing historic accidents.	Section 83.59 – a Québec resident who has an out-of-state accident may recover *extra* costs, subject to SAAQ's subrogee powers.[431] Section 83.62 – other Québec bodies who also have subrogation powers in relation to a relevant automobile accident.[432] Section 83.58 – there is no restriction on other indemnities via private insurance.[433]	Section 26(6) – when using its subrogated powers, MPI may bring actions separately or join with other parties. Section 26(7) – person may also bring action in own name separate to MPI's subrogated action, but *only* for the amount that damages exceed MPI benefits and insurance money. Further minor definitional scope issues of the subrogation power are set out in section 26(3),[434] 26(4),[435] 26(5),[436] 26(8),[437] 26(9).[438]	

---

[431] Specifically: 'A person entitled to compensation under this title by reason of an accident that occurred outside Québec may benefit by the compensation while retaining his remedy with regard to any compensation in excess thereof under the law of the place where the accident occurred.
No person who exercises such remedy may, unless authorized by the Société, prevent the Société from exercising its remedy as subrogee pursuant to section 83.60. The Société is released from its obligation toward a person who prevents it from exercising that remedy.'

[432] For example, the relevant public health department bodies and workplace injuries bodies. Reference is made specifically to other relevant legislation here.

[433] Specifically: 'Nothing in this division limits the right of a person to claim an indemnity under a private insurance scheme, regardless of who is at fault.'

[434] Subrogation powers not affected by reduction in liability provisions elsewhere in the legislation.

[435] A clarification that there is no limitation on the persons who might be liable under the subrogation provisions, subject to subsection (5).

[436] Clarifications in relation to persons who live with the owner of a vehicle but used the vehicle without the owner's consent.

[437] The subrogation rights of [MPI] corporation are not to be prejudiced.

[438] 'Upon being notified in writing that the corporation has made or is making a claim or bringing an action or other proceeding under this section, no person shall negotiate or effect a compromise, settlement, or satisfaction of any claim of that person to the prejudice of the claim of the corporation'.

Conclusions		
The subrogation power is part of a wider statutory right of the TAC seek reimbursement from individuals who are not entitled to the section 94 indemnity. The subrogation/indemnity amounts are linked to the quantum of compensation paid by TAC. The TAC may not recover more than the relevant defendant would have been liable to pay under the relevant civil liability legislation (section 104(2)).	The subrogation power is focused on the recovery of costs from individuals not entitled to SAAQ coverage, i.e. non-Québec residents. The lack of any restriction on cumulation or double recovery from any extra private insurance policies (section 83.58) is a curious distinction, but this small allowance of double recovery allows the no-fault scheme and any subrogation powers to stand independently of the SAAQ scheme. The subrogation power is much wider than that of SAAQ, to include recovery from persons who *should not have* been driving the vehicle or were not properly licensed. The allowance for an individual to bring his or her own claim can be seen as roughly analogous to the allowance within the ACC Scheme for a person to bring a claim for exemplary damages.	This is not a subrogation power for ACC per se, but effectively a tool for ACC to prevent double recovery by a claimant who has a non-statutory barred right of recovery in New Zealand or elsewhere. In practice, it is very rarely used.[439]

Source: Compiled by the author.

---

[439] Email correspondence with ACC dated 29 October 2020.

Where do these subrogation powers sit with reference to the Menyawi proposal for public tort liability, or O'Sullivan and Tokeley's vision of a structured subrogated power? In relation to the latter, the SAAQ is a logical equivalent, as those authors' vision was directly based on their understanding of SAAQ's subrogation powers. The MPI's powers of subrogation could be viewed as something approximating to public tort liability, as, in theory, anyone is potentially within the scope of the subrogated power, aside from individuals using their own or licensed vehicle in an ordinary way. The TAC subrogated power is a step back from this, as it is focused on subrogation actions against individuals who are not captured by the (relatively generous) section 94 liability immunity provisions. Meanwhile, the ACC Scheme provision is not really a substantive subrogation provision at all, but rather a (rarely used) mechanism by which ACC can prevent double recovery by plaintiffs who have a right of recovery elsewhere (that is not restricted by the general statutory bar).

The TAC, SAAQ and MPI were specifically surveyed on their subrogation activities for this research project. ACC was obviously not surveyed on this point because there is currently no noteworthy possibility of subrogation under the existing ACC Scheme legislation, and the fund's legal staff have commented that this power is rarely used in practice.[440] This survey was undertaken in order to gather novel information about subrogation in no-fault comprehensive compensation funds to facilitate a relevant and impactful comparative law analysis. The specific questions asked were in relation to the internal allocation of costs in relation to subrogation in comparison to the reimbursement received; the allocation of internal and external legal activities; and estimations on settlements. The answers to these questions allow a comparative law analysis (with socio-legal qualities) of the legal effectiveness and coherency of subrogation activities within no-fault comprehensive compensation funds.

The three funds were firstly asked to roughly estimate what percentage of their organisation's administrative costs and/or legal costs were spent on subrogation activities. Effectively, the question was asked where the financial return provided by subrogation efforts is more or less than the administrative and legal costs of subrogation. In the table below, the response of each of the three compensation funds is set out, along with my conclusion on the effectiveness of subrogation for each fund.

---

[440] Email correspondence with ACC dated 29 October 2020.

Table 13. Subrogation costs (TAC, SAAQ and MPI)

TAC	SAAQ	MPI
'The percentage of administrative/legal costs spent on subrogated recoveries is very small in terms of the overall TAC (less than 1%). In raw numbers, the TAC has 123 subrogated recoveries listed on the database from 2003 onwards (average of 7–8 per year). There are many more matters subject to subrogation under the WorkSafe legislation; however no recovery ensues if the worker/client is at fault or negligence sits wholly or mainly with a TAC-insured party. Across these matters, the TAC has recovered around $17.7m from a potential pool of $30.5m whilst our incurred costs were less than $1.3m (excludes in-house time and effort).' * * All sums in A$.	[translated] 'Through subrogation activities, the Company recovers between $1.5m and $3m annually. To do this, the Company has two full-time professionals, a part-time technician, coordination by an expert and a manager, as well as advice from a lawyer. The approximate associated costs are as follows: Professionals $150k Technician $25k Coordination $25k Attorney $50k Total $250k' * * All sums in C$	'While I don't have hard numbers, the financial return can be substantial and is well worth the effort. The return in Manitoba is much easier as we control the rules and insurers have larger minimums, as opposed to the United States where coverages can be very low or non-existent.'
Conclusion: The well-regulated intersection with the Worksafe/worker injury scheme shows that the effectiveness of subrogation is best assessed with reference to that parallel no-fault or limited fault liability framework in a different functional field. This, however, makes it difficult to accurately assess whether the subrogation power is effective (or financially sustainable), although it is certainly coherent with the legislative scheme.	**Conclusion:** The subrogation power is neatly defined given the blanket coverage for Québec residents. The limitation of the subrogation power in this way allows for specific staff to be retained in-house for the implementation of subrogation activities. This appears to be an effective subrogation tool that is coherent with the rest of the scheme.	**Conclusion:** The subrogation power operates in the wider context of MPI's control of the insurance market within Manitoba. Outside of that jurisdiction, it is unclear whether subrogation is financially or practically effective. Therefore, within Manitoba the subrogation power is effective and coherent, but possibly not outside Manitoba.

Source: Compiled by the author.

Table 14. Handling of subrogation legal work: In-house or external handling?

TAC	SAAQ	MPI
'No. Identification occurs in tandem with WorkSafe via reporting, after which an initial review and feasibility is considered in-house (this may involve requesting further information). Once the TAC officer is confident the matter warrants a request for reimbursement and/or legal advice, the matter is allocated to specialist legal agents who perform this type of work under the WorkSafe legislation (in high volumes for WorkSafe). The legislation also involves an intricate recovery formula and the TAC simply does not see enough subrogated recoveries to build in-house expertise.'	[translated] 'Yes. However, the Company may occasionally hire a lawyer at the scene of the accident to make representations on behalf of the Company.'	'Yes, we manage this entirely in-house, and it falls under the umbrella of our Finance Department. The department comprises of 25 staff, one of which is a lawyer (the manager). As stated earlier, due to the statutory nature of the plan in Manitoba, we do not subrogate within our province – we quite simply have the right of recovery. A majority of our subrogation efforts take place in other Canadian provinces where we do not have a reciprocal agreement, and throughout the United States.'
Conclusion:	**Conclusion:**	**Conclusion:**
The true total costs of subrogation are actually carried to a significant degree by WorkSafe. The total actual legal costs of subrogation are difficult to accurately quantify here and may be quite significant (in comparison to what is recovered).	The costs appear well-controlled, as most of the work associated with subrogation is handled in-house. To practically manage legal risks of a scheme that is operational and effective on the roads of a large province 24 hours a day, it is logical that SAAQ would need to have some small expenditure to hire lawyers on location.	The ratio between legal and accounting staff within MPI indicates that the subrogation efforts are handled administratively within Manitoba and in provinces where there is a reciprocal agreement. Outside of Manitoba, there is an unquantified possibility of legal costs from external counsel and no clarity on how much might be recovered.

Source: Compiled by the author.

Table 15. What subrogation strategy is utilised in practice?

TAC	SAAQ	MPI
'Virtually all subrogated claims are litigated to the extent of issuing proceedings (serves the purpose of exerting some pressure and a requirement to engage, but proceedings also provide an avenue for claiming costs and interest). Very few actually get to hearing and most resolve via pre-hearing conferences or written settlement offers. The TAC does not proceed with matters involving an insolvent defendant, as experience has shown these to be troublesome and provide underwhelming returns.'	[translated] 'There are between 50 and 100 settlements a year, often settling [after] over a year. The Company always tries to negotiate with the insurer or its lawyer. Cases very rarely go to court as this is not an avenue the Company wishes to use. Before making any subrogation efforts, the Company analyses the liability of the parties, assesses the solvency of those responsible and the countries where the accidents occurred. When the chances of recovery are low, such as, for example, if the person responsible for the accident has no insurance, the Company does not move forward.'	'Most recovery claims are settled where there is an insurer on the other side. A very small minority are completely written off. Though the averages do fluctuate, we estimate we write off or abandon less than 10%. Virtually no subrogation cases within our no-fault scheme go to court; we manage that entirely in-house.'
Conclusion: The adversarial tools of litigation are actively used to cajole the relevant defendant into action, even though ultimately most claims are settled. Claims against insolvent defendants are, however, generally written off as a rule for practical reasons.	**Conclusion:** A notable point of interest here is the stated preference of the SAAQ to *not* bring subrogated matters to court where possible. A preference for a mediated settlement indicates that the SAAQ is willing to sacrifice possible recovery in some cases in order to avoid an adversarial approach and to quickly resolve subrogated cases in a just and efficient way.	**Conclusion:** A slightly different perspective is taken to that of the SAAQ, but the effect is the same – the vast majority of subrogated cases are settled with a relevant insurer. A small minority are written off for practical reasons.

Source: Compiled by the author.

As indicated in the tables on the preceding pages, the three funds were asked whether all elements of subrogated claim activities are handled in-house by their own legal team. This question helps to gauge whether the estimations of cost in the previous answers were accurate, or if there is potentially a large amount of legal costs associated with subrogation that are incurred as external legal counsel costs (which would relate to both subrogation and other activities of the compensation fund requiring external legal advice).

Finally, the three funds were asked to make an approximate comparison of how often a subrogated claim resulted in an insurance settlement, and how often a claim resulted in litigation or another result (for example, a claims write-off against an insolvent defendant).

As a reminder, this research project did not proceed on a socio-legal or empirical legal methodology and there was not space or capacity to undertake full empirical data gathering. There was a need for some basic qualitative data to be gathered to facilitate this novel comparative law analysis of these big no-fault compensation funds. The results of this limited qualitative survey reveal the following conclusions about subrogation and some questions that require further research.

It is not possible to easily determine the true costs of subrogation to a no-fault comprehensive compensation fund. Further empirical and statistical research is required to discover the total *actual* legal costs of subrogation to these large funds. This should include external and extra-jurisdictional legal costs and the costs incurred by other agencies handling cases on behalf of the fund. An averaging of costs over a number of years would ensure balance. Further research on this point would enable a clearer assessment to be made of whether there are indeed proper financial motivations to seek a recoupment of costs. If there are not, then the issue of subrogation has to be decided by a legislature on a purely philosophical or 'social choice' basis – whether subrogation powers have a moral or deterrent purpose that justifies the lack of any significant financial purpose to those activities. As it stands, it is not possible to currently draw any evidence-based conclusions on that point due to a lack of easily-accessible information.

There remains definitional uncertainty about the actual meaning of the term 'subrogation' within the context of a no-fault comprehensive compensation fund. It is notable that the MPI legal counsel did not recognise the equivalence of the term 'subrogation' with the concept of MPI's statutory right of reimbursement. TAC staff also sought clarification of what specifically was meant by the term, when answering the questionnaire. These kinds of definitional matters – things being 'lost in translation', so to speak – are perhaps to be expected in all comparative law exercises. However this specific point illustrates that the idea of 'subrogation' – in its classic insurance framing – may not be recognised as relevant or completely equivalent within the context of a no-fault comprehensive compensation fund. On the one hand, this may be because the statutory entitlement of a fund to seek a recoupment of costs is simply perceived as being different to an insurance contract that includes a freely given agreement to subrogate rights to recovery. On the other hand, it may be because a big no-fault compensation fund's statutory concurrent extinguishment of liability and of any claimant rights to bring a compensatory damages claim are not the same theoretical concept as subrogation. This latter point appears to be the more logical conclusion.

That conclusion means there is an extinguishment of a claimant's rights to bring a compensatory damages claim at the same time that a statutory entitlement to reimbursement from a causatively liable party *might* be created and vested in the compensation fund. There is not an exchange of rights, entitlements or restrictions between the big fund and the claimant: the entitlements and restrictions may be shaped independently of one another. In other words, the shape of the fund's statutorily vested right of reimbursement or subrogation does not have to be identical to what has been denied to individual claimants. For practical purposes, of course, in order to prevent double recovery by the victim, there should be no (or only minimal) overlap between the fund's reimbursement rights and the claimant's extinguishment of rights. This problem would best be solved by clarity within legislative drafting about the meaning of the term subrogation. The Manitoba legislation achieves the best level of clarity on this point, making it logical and obvious for that fund to interpret its subrogation rights as an independent statutory entitlement of the fund to reimbursement that can be managed as the fund sees fit (within the scope of the legislation). There is the least amount of clarity in the TAC subrogation powers (when compared to the funds' responses about its actual practice) because the strategy of the TAC indicates that it vigorously activates the otherwise extinguished liability of the injury victim – but in reality it simply settles the very small number of subrogation cases that occur or outsources them to its sister workplace injury organisation.

The logical next benefit that flows from this point is that subrogation, as imagined within a no-fault comprehensive compensation fund, does not require consideration of whether the victim should be entitled to receive some of the monies recovered by the compensation fund. The amount of compensation available to claimants is set out in statute, whereas what might be recovered by subrogation is far from certain and subject to the ordinary uncertainties of any claim for damages. This is logical, because to do otherwise would result in different calculations of compensation for claimants depending on whether there is a causative defendant available for the compensation fund to pursue. In that circumstance, it would be hard to see what the point would be of operating a large no-fault compensation fund. Claimants might lobby the compensation fund to pursue subrogated actions, or object to the amount of reimbursement awarded or negotiated through settlement. That is a point of difference with a no-fault compensation fund which does not operate so broadly or does not bar claimants from accessing other remedies.

From an access to justice perspective, the main benefit of subrogation is that it is part of the whole streamlined package available to claimants to obtain compensation for their losses in a timely manner and more efficiently and equitably than via the tort system. The (no) liability issues associated with a potential defendant are rendered irrelevant, unless the fund itself is empowered and wishes to pursue that person for a contribution to costs. If the legislature perceives, from a deterrence or retributive justice perspective, that the individual(s) causatively responsible for the loss should pay some financial penalty or contribute to the costs of compensation, that can be managed and pursued by the fund itself rather than the individual claimant. The individual sacrifices the hypothetical chance of extra damages or the emotional satisfaction of a judgment against the defendant in return for guaranteed immediate compensation. In a European context, this has been identified as a useful aspect of subrogation in the context of crime victim compensation funds.[441] There needs to be more direct comparative research undertaken on the exact costs of subrogation (compared with, say, the costs of an individual pursuing a defendant) to determine whether the use of subrogation by no-fault comprehensive compensation funds is both financially and philosophically justifiable. Overall, subrogation when used in a clearly defined way that is directly linked to reimbursement of costs and deterrence, with a focus on efficient settlement and resolution of matters, appears to be an ideal model for subrogation in this kind of big fund, which also facilitates access to justice.

8. CONCLUSIONS

The following conclusions can be drawn from the descriptions and analyses in this chapter. These further answer the first and third research questions:

- What are the key characteristics of no-fault comprehensive compensation funds and the key pillars, common to multiple jurisdictions, for the successful establishment, administration, operation and further development of no-fault comprehensive compensation funds?
- How can no-fault comprehensive compensation funds be used to address contemporary legal problems common to multiple jurisdictions?

---

[441] Milquet (n 58) 15.

The conclusions on dispute resolution partially answer the second research question:

- What is the interaction between comprehensive no-fault compensation funds and human rights law, principles of access to justice and practical dispute resolution issues?
  a. The four comprehensive no-fault comprehensive compensation funds studied in this project were not underpinned by a watertight theoretical definition of no-fault at the time of their establishment. The legal theory was simply applied as a means to a policy end. However, the operation of no-fault in practice over many decades means that we can better define no-fault as a legal theory and framework, and determine what dimension of it is a key pillar for the establishment of these big funds. The definition distilled here is:

    > the rejection of a legal definition of fault or liability as being relevant to the determination of legal or factual compensation responsibility for an adverse event. The rejection of the utility or relevance of a legal definition of fault or liability does not, however, mean that liability or responsibility is extinguished in all senses.

  b. The processing of claims and payment of compensation is generally undertaken at a very fast pace in these large funds. This processing time is tracked closely in two of the four big funds. There is no detailed consideration of legal issues at the time of processing for most claims. This is regardless of whether claims processing is predominantly carried out by human staff or via automated algorithm. The use of new technologies in claims processing was not foreseen in the original legislative design of the four funds, but appears so far to work well. The wider a fund's scope of operation, the less legal analysis of incoming claims there can be, leading to a more generous approach to causation issues.
  c. The theory of no-fault does not specify any particular type of quantum calculation. However in big no-fault compensation funds, the vast majority of compensation is paid at a capped or limited level. The core compensation payments are broadly pecuniary in character. The formulation of the whole compensation package available overall reveals a mixed pecuniary and non-pecuniary purpose of compensation payments and supports. Just one scheme, the SAAQ, offers non-pecuniary compensation for both temporary and permanent impairment. This also combines symbolic elements that are linked to the scheme's social purpose. Compensation is calculated with reference to what is necessary for restoring the claimant to his or

her best social and vocational status in a post-accident reality – their pre-accident potential is of limited relevance.

d. In terms of dispute resolution about claims, immediate or default access to court is not a feature of no-fault comprehensive compensation funds. A basic dispute resolution procedure will always be set out in the legislation, usually with an alternative dispute resolution infusion. An internal review of the file carried out by fund staff members (often independent from the staff member who processed the claim) is the basic starting point. There is no immediate access for disgruntled claimants to free or subsidised formal legal guidance at the start of the dispute process, which is unfortunate and should be addressed. However, a funded advocacy service and a guidance/ navigation service for claimants are two examples of dispute resolution support that work well – the former leading to more legal coherency and better support of claimants. A lack of funded legal support from an early stage may correlate with negative perceptions of the dispute resolution process. Another alternative is the fund negotiating an agreement with legal professional bodies to manage certain types of claimants with disputes to ensure overall consistency and adherence to a common dispute resolution procedure. Most claim disputes are settled in one way or another. Most disputes relate to causation issues, which are likely to be legally or medically technical and complex.

e. Full-funding is the gold standard funding model for all comprehensive no-fault compensation funds. This allows the schemes to be sustainable, especially if levies are indexed with inflation. Full-funding means that all four funds receive a substantial financial return from their investment portfolio, which supports operation and claim costs. These investment portfolios can be managed in-house, or (preferably) by an independent professional investment agency. This reliance on investment funds also means that the funds' sustainability can be seriously affected by international financial market fluctuations. Only one of the four funds receives some degree of taxpayer funding, and this makes up a minor part of the fund's total revenue stream. However, there are fairness and long-term stability issues associated with any reliance on taxpayer funding – but changes to address this appear to be hindered by political issues. It may also be necessary for the fund to pay a regular financial contribution to the public health service to ensure that the fund and its claimants are not 'free riding' on the public health system. Independent actuarial setting of levies and design of financial objectives is another common feature, although not universal.

f. Big no-fault compensation funds are not subject to the same financial and prudential regulation as insurers, although all four funds voluntarily harmonise their capitalisation approaches with the prevailing private sector standards, where possible. This is clearly a financial stability risk, and there could be exploration of whether further independent financial supervision is required. All four funds are currently not clear enough about the final taxpayer backstop/public underwriting of their financial structure. Big no-fault compensation funds have the option of reinsurance for catastrophic risks, but have tended not to use this tool, preferring the government/taxpayer to carry this risk. There should be more legislative and policy clarity about the nature and extent of public underwriting and taxpayer backstops for these large schemes, if these big funds are not subject to the same financial and prudential rules as other insurers.

g. Although a carve-out for individualised tort-style compensation is legally incoherent within a no-fault scheme, it is not actually financially unsustainable to do so – so long as the category of eligible claimants is very limited.

h. Subrogation has a potential role within a big no-fault compensation fund, but this role has not yet been fully defined in practice. The use of subrogation in practice reveals the fund's role as a vehicle for non-legal resolution of disputes and as the 'owner' of the liability entitlements that were divested from the individual. The use of subrogation in three of the four funds has a coherent structure, but it is unclear if it is actually financially justified. In terms of the design of subrogation powers, a narrowly structured power is possible, or a broader philosophical scope that gives the fund a quasi-prosecutorial scope ('public tort liability'). If subrogation is used, it should be used in a clearly defined way that has a focus on efficient and fair settlement. The shape of the fund's subrogation power does not have to be the same size and design as the private law rights that were withdrawn from the claimant by statute.

CHAPTER 5

HUMAN RIGHTS, ACCESS TO JUSTICE AND DISPUTE RESOLUTION

1. INTRODUCTION

A no-fault comprehensive compensation fund is a significant part of a jurisdiction's legal framework. In the four jurisdictions that are studied here, the fund framework affects the way that individuals access justice for specific types of injury-related harms. Most specifically, it restricts access to the courts and an individual's choice about whether to pursue potential defendants.

However there has been little or no analysis of how no-fault comprehensive compensation funds intersect with human rights and access to justice issues. There is a current knowledge gap about the intersection between human rights and no-fault compensation funds generally.[1] This chapter, however, focuses on the impact of comprehensive no-fault funds on human rights and access to justice issues, as a discrete sub-field. Large funds pose slightly different issues in the realm of human rights, compared with their smaller cousins. This is because they create a near or total restriction on the ability of a comprehensive category of claimants to access court-based remedies or settlements. As a trade-off for this, they offer a statutory entitlement to compensation for certain classes of injury, and a fast and streamlined claims process. However, a question that has not fully been analysed by research or practice remains: is this balancing act ultimately a fundamental problem from a human rights perspective, or an acceptable alternative approach?

The four big funds studied in this book are located in jurisdictions that do not all have a fundamental human rights framework equivalent to the European Convention on Human Rights (ECHR) or the United States Constitution. Only Canada's human rights frameworks are connected to its written constitution

---

[1]   Thierry Vansweevelt and others, 'Comparative Analysis of Compensation Funds' in Thierry Vansweevelt and Britt Weyts (eds), *Compensation Funds in Comparative Perspective* (Intersentia 2020) 210–211.

Intersentia

and/or have a fundamental nature. This leads to a natural or default presumption that a fundamental human rights framework may be incompatible with such a fund, or that the fund hinders access to justice in an unacceptable way. However, there has been no scholarly legal analysis of whether these presumptions or suspicions would be correct. This chapter makes comparative law conclusions about these big no-fault compensation funds that are relevant to all jurisdictions (including European Union Member States) that have fundamental human rights frameworks, as well as those that do not. The study of this element also helps to further clarify the intersections between human rights law and compensation funds more generally.

The key questions to be answered in this chapter are therefore:

a. Whether the existence or absence of a fundamental human rights framework affects the ability to establish and operate a no-fault comprehensive compensation fund. In other words, is a fundamental human rights framework an intrinsic barrier to the creation and operation of such 'big' funds?
b. In the European context specifically, would the ECHR and other fundamental rights instruments be an insurmountable barrier to the creation of a no-fault comprehensive compensation fund similar to the four schemes studied in this research project?
c. What are the specific characteristics of a no-fault comprehensive compensation fund that facilitate access to justice? What are the specific characteristics that hinder access to justice?
d. There has been little legal or socio-legal research to date on the human rights impacts of comprehensive no-fault compensation funds. This is a significant knowledge gap in the field of compensation funds. The analysis in this chapter can therefore be seen as a first attempt to tackle this gap from a comparative law perspective, rather than a comprehensive or final one. This analysis will also aid in the refinement of further relevant research questions.

It is important to note that the conclusions here are directly relevant to no-fault *comprehensive* compensation funds. There is no specific analysis of the human rights law issues associated with the multiple smaller no-fault schemes that already exist in multiple other jurisdictions. That is a research gap to be addressed by other researchers. However, it is likely that there are different human rights and access to justice impacts for comprehensive no-fault compensation funds compared to smaller compensation funds, and so they need to be analysed separately from one another. A comparative law analysis of the different impacts of larger and smaller compensation funds is a valuable question for further research, but there is unfortunately not space within this text to explore that. The research and state of the art on this sub-topic is still at such an elementary

Chapter 5. Human Rights, Access to Justice and Dispute Resolution

stage in both civil and common law jurisdictions, that much further work needs to be undertaken. The analysis and conclusions in this chapter could therefore be a departure point for future analyses.

Given the potential for inconsistent definitions in comparative law analysis, and the potential for similar words to have the same meaning, it is therefore useful to set out the methodological basis for analysis in this chapter. From a methodological perspective, the comparisons undertaken in this chapter can be classified as both:[2]

a. the classic comparative domestic human rights law (the horizontal comparison of two or more domestic systems); and

b. the emerging method of comparative international-domestic human rights law (the horizontal comparison of the influence of international human rights law in domestic law).

Even though the comparison of human rights frameworks has the hopeful objective of identifying some kind of common ground, it is important to remember that human rights must be placed very specifically in each individual political and legal context.[3] In the context of no-fault comprehensive compensation funds, this could mean that the correct comparative interpretation of relevant human rights in Australia, Canada and New Zealand may actually be affected by the very existence of these big funds.

There is also a distinction that should be made between what is a fundamental legal right and what is an ordinary legal right.[4] The analyses in this chapter are focused predominantly on the human rights issues associated with the most central civil rights issue posed by no-fault comprehensive compensation funds – the bar on civil litigation proceedings. As we will see, individual plaintiff access to a civil law claim before the courts has not generally been framed as an inalienable fundamental legal right in common law jurisdictions. However, access to the courts is an important element of the rule of law in all jurisdictions, regardless of whether or not access to the courts in all circumstances is fundamental. That is why it is critically important, as a first analytical step, to focus on access to court rights and how they are affected by big no-fault compensation funds. There are considerations of other human rights intersections that have appeared in case law and other significant events.

---

2   Samantha Besson, 'Comparative Law and Human Rights' in Mathias Reimann and Reinhard Zimmermann (eds), *The Oxford Handbook of Comparative Law* (2nd edn, Oxford University Press 2019) 1228–1229.

3   ibid 1233.

4   James J Spigelman, 'The Common Law Bill of Rights', *Statutory Interpretation and Human Rights: McPherson Lecture Series* (University of Queensland Press 2008) 39 <http://ssrn.com/abstract=1806775>.

Intersentia

It is also very likely that there are intersections between no-fault comprehensive compensation funds and socio-economic rights. However, that is a question for subsequent analysis, as there is not space to explore that issue in this project. Further, it is not yet clear whether socio-economic rights are fully justiciable,[5] even in jurisdictions where they are specifically protected (such as in Europe via the European Social Charter). This chapter first sets out the relationship of our four big no-fault compensation funds with the fundamental and non-fundamental human rights legislation and case law precedent in their jurisdiction. As Canada is the only one of our three jurisdictions that has a fundamental human rights framework, there is then a simple structural and analytical comparison of the identified issues with the European position. Next, there is consideration of the wider issue of the no-fault comprehensive compensation fund as either a facilitator or a barrier to access to justice. This balancing exercise and analysis puts the conclusions about the legislative and case law positions in a wider context. Some overall conclusions are then drawn about how human rights and access to justice points intersect with no-fault comprehensive compensation funds, and suggestions are made for further questions to be analysed.

2. THE FOUR FUNDS' RELATIONSHIP WITH HUMAN RIGHTS LEGISLATION AND CASE LAW

As noted already, two out of the three jurisdictions studied in this book do not possess fundamental human rights law frameworks. The intersection with human rights is not a matter that has been explored in existing scholarly research on these four no-fault comprehensive compensation funds, but it has been identified as an important area for further research and consideration.[6]

In this section, the national and territorial/provincial (where applicable) human rights frameworks of Australia, Canada and New Zealand are each briefly described and then analysed in turn. The analyses are targeted specifically to issues relevant to the no-fault comprehensive compensation funds. A contrasting analysis is then made in the next section with European fundamental human rights frameworks, as they might apply to no-fault comprehensive compensation funds. Clearly, there are no funds in existence in Europe that are on the same scale as the four funds that are the subject of this book or meet the definition of a no-fault comprehensive compensation fund. Therefore the focus is on determining whether Europe's fundamental human rights framework is an

---

5   Justice Albie Sachs, 'Social and Economic Rights: Can They Be Made Justiciable' (2000) 53 *SMU Law Review* 1381.
6   Vansweevelt and others (n 1) 210–211.

Chapter 5. Human Rights, Access to Justice and Dispute Resolution

intrinsic and insurmountable barrier to the creation of a comprehensive no-fault compensation fund.

2.1. AUSTRALIA

The Commonwealth of Australia is a federal parliamentary constitutional democracy. Like the United Kingdom, which can be considered to be one of Australia's legislative 'parents', Australia does not possess a fundamental human rights framework at either the Commonwealth level or the individual state and territory level. Uniquely among common law jurisdictions, Australia does not have a national bill or charter of rights. Human rights protections of Australian citizens and residents are therefore effected through various ordinary statutory instruments and case law precedent. The lack of a detailed description or protection of rights within the Australian Constitution can be seen as providing an impetus for a multi-layered conception of rights.[7]

2.1.1. Historical and Contemporary Context

During the drafting of the Australian Constitution in the late nineteenth century, a Bill of Rights was considered but expressly rejected.[8] One reason for this was the significant influence at the time of British constitutional jurist Albert Venn Dicey.[9] A Dicey-style legal worldview specifically rejected the American constitutional model and its specific identification and protection of individual rights. Rather, trust was placed in 'a system of parliamentary Government with ministerial responsibility.'[10] The Australian Constitution therefore 'contains no unifying theory or vision about rights'.[11] What might be considered to be a fundamental human right in the Australian context is therefore heavily influenced by the history of the common law.[12] Two attempts in the twentieth century to introduce some constitutional rights protections were rejected in public referendums.[13]

---

[7] Matthew Groves, Janina Boughey and Dan Meagher, 'Rights, Rhetoric and Reality: An Overview of Rights Protection in Australia' in Matthew Groves, Janina Boughey and Dan Meagher (eds), *The Legal Protection of Rights in Australia* (Hart Publishing 2019) 1–2.

[8] Michael Taggart, '"Australian Exceptionalism" in Judicial Review' (2008) 36 *Federal Law Review* 1, 4.

[9] Groves, Boughey and Meagher (n 7) 3.

[10] *Attorney-General (Cth); Ex rel Mckinlay v Commonwealth* [1975] HCA 53 [38] (Barwick CJ).

[11] Groves, Boughey and Meagher (n 7) 4.

[12] Spigelman (n 4) 22.

[13] In 1944, there was a popular referendum on the introduction of constitutional restrictions on federal legislative power to restrict freedom of speech and religion. In 1988, there was a popular referendum on a proposal to introduce constitutional protections for a right to trial by jury, religious freedom, and fair terms for the just acquisition of property. See Groves, Boughey and Meagher (n 7) 7–8.

Intersentia

303

A Comparative Law Analysis of No-Fault Comprehensive Compensation Funds

In 2009, a National Human Rights Consultation Committee recommended that a federal human rights statute be adopted, and that a Canadian-style legislative model be adopted.[14] However, that was rejected by the Labor government of the day, due to the likely strong opposition of conservative political parties and possible constitutional problems with the enactment of socio-economic rights.[15]

From the legislative side of things, there is a patchwork of statutory human rights protections at the federal and state/territory levels. In the early 1970s the reformist Whitlam Labor government – the same federal government that attempted to introduce a Woodhouse-style no-fault comprehensive compensation fund – tried to pass a human rights bill.[16] This would have enacted the International Covenant on Civil and Political Rights into Australian law. That bill lapsed when the Labor government fell.[17] Parts of that bill have ultimately been enacted as ordinary federal statutes;[18] however, none of these statutes deal with access to justice issues.

Separately, Victoria has enacted a human rights charter via the Charter of Human Rights and Responsibilities Act 2006 (hereafter 'the Victorian Charter'). This framework sets out some basic human rights, requires public authorities to act and legislatures to legislate in a way that is compatible with the protected rights,[19] and requires courts and tribunals to interpret legislation in a manner

---

[14] 'National Human Rights Consultation Report' (2009) at xxix 'Recommendations' <https://alhr.org.au/wp/wp-content/uploads/2018/02/National-Human-Rights-Consultation-Report-2009-copy.pdf>. See also Rosalind Dixon, 'A Minimalist Charter of Rights for Australia: The UK or Canada as a Model?' (2009) 37 *Federal Law Review* 335.

[15] Groves, Boughey and Meagher (n 7) 9.

[16] The Human Rights Bill 1973 (Cth). For an overview of the scope of that proposed bill, see ibid 8–9.

[17] For contextual reasons, European readers unacquainted with Australian political and legal history may be interested to learn more about the extremely scandalous and spectacular way that the Whitlam government fell. The Whitlam government's huge reform efforts (including the attempt to establish an expansive no-fault comprehensive compensation fund, even wider than New Zealand's ACC) and financial scandals led to an impasse with the Opposition parties, who held control of Australia's upper house. Ultimately, the unelected Governor-General (Queen Elizabeth II's representative in Australia, as Head of State) sacked Gough Whitlam's government and instated the Opposition leader, Malcolm Fraser, as a caretaker prime minister. The impact of the 1975 Australian constitutional crisis continues to cast a long legal and political shadow over Australia, impacting the desire and ability of Australian governments to undertake major constitutional, societal and political reforms. See Anne Twomey, 'Australian Politics Explainer: Gough Whitlam's Dismissal as Prime Minister' (*The Conversation*) <https://theconversation.com/australian-politics-explainer-gough-whitlams-dismissal-as-prime-minister-74148>.

[18] For example the Age Discrimination Act 2004, the Disability Discrimination Act 1992, the Racial Discrimination Act 1975, and the Sex Discrimination Act 1984. An independent human rights supervisory body, the Australian Human Rights Commission, was established by the Australian Human Rights Commission Act 1986.

[19] Charter of Human Rights and Responsibilities Act 2006 (Victoria) s 38.

that is consistent with human rights (so far as practically possible).[20] The rights in the Charter primarily derive from the International Covenant on Civil and Political Rights.[21] The rights protected by the charter may be made subject to 'such reasonable limits as can be demonstrably justified ... based on human dignity, equality and freedom, and taking into account all relevant factors'.[22] In other words, the Victorian legislature retains the power to balance human rights and other public interests, and override human rights within the Charter if necessary.[23] The Charter effectively relies upon the executive to enforce its application, and fits within the broader context of Australian human rights being non-entrenched and in a narrowly libertarian (rather than social democratic) tradition.[24]

From the common law (i.e. non-legislative) side of things, Australian case law precedent has established a number of (rebuttable) presumptions that Parliament did not intend to effect.[25] A seminal Australian High Court decision has established that the courts should not infer an intention in the legislature to 'interfere with fundamental rights. Such an intention must be clearly manifested by unmistakable and unambiguous language.'[26] Access to the courts *may*, according to case law, be one such fundamental right that parliament cannot limit without express wording.[27] However, by European standards, the protection of this right is far from certain.

2.1.2. The Intersection with Issues Relevant to No-Fault Comprehensive Compensation Funds

In Australia (and Victoria specifically), one might raise the question of whether the Transport Accident Commission scheme breaches some of the imprecisely defined fundamental or human rights that are possibly available under Australian statute and case law. With reference to the loosely defined 'common law bill of

---

[20]   ibid s 32.

[21]   Explanatory Memorandum Charter of Human Rights and Responsibilities Bill.

[22]   Charter of Human Rights and Responsibilities Act 2006 (Victoria) s 7.

[23]   George Williams, 'The Victorian Charter of Human Rights and Responsibilities: Origins and Scope' (2006) 30 *Melbourne University Law Review* 880, 899.

[24]   Russell Solomon, 'Reviewing Victoria's Charter of Rights and the Limits to Our Democracy' (2017) 42 *Alternative Law Journal* 195 <http://journals.sagepub.com/altlj>.

[25]   Spigelman (n 4) 23.

[26]   *Coco v The Queen* [1994] HCA 15.

[27]   *Public Service Association of South Australia v Federated Clerks' Union of Australia & others* (1991) 173 CLR 132, 160; Jennifer Corrin, 'Australia: Country Report on Human Rights' (2009) 40 *Victoria University of Wellington Law Review* 37, 42; Chief Justice RS French, 'The Common Law and the Protection of Human Rights' (September 2009) 3 <https://www.hcourt.gov.au/assets/publications/speeches/current-justices/frenchcj/frenchcj4sep09.pd>.

rights' proposed by former New South Wales Chief Justice James J Spigelman AC,[28] the likely intersections that appear are:

a. The rebuttable presumption that Parliament did not intend to restrict access to the courts.[29] In Victoria specifically, this can be linked to the Charter right to a fair hearing.[30] This intersection is based on the TAC scheme's legislative restriction on recovering common law damages associated with a qualifying transport-related personal injury,[31] except in the case of serious injury.[32]

b. The rebuttable presumption that Parliament did not intend to retrospectively change rights and obligations.[33] This intersection is based upon the TAC's limited scope adjustments to the scheme that have had a retrospective effect upon enactment. These include the scheme extension to some kinds of cyclist injuries and the temporary eligibility adjustment to some kinds of third-party mental injury harms.[34]

Another human rights intersection that is relevant to consider (more briefly) is TAC's compliance with the Victorian Charter of Human Rights and Responsibilities in its daily operations and the payment of compensation to claimants. This is broadly relevant to the larger question of whether a large no-fault comprehensive compensation fund can be seen as generally conflicting or existing in harmony with human rights frameworks. Due to the absence of previous research in this area, it is also relevant to consider any human rights and/or access to justice analyses that have been made in relation to other Australian no-fault compensation funds or redress schemes.

Firstly, let us consider the restriction on accessing court and/or the Victorian right to a fair hearing. Section 93(1) of the Transport Accident Act 1986 enshrines the general statutory bar against a person bringing proceedings in relation to transport accident personal injury or death. The rest of section 93 qualifies this bar to carve out the limited exception for serious injury. At the time of the statute's passage through the Victorian legislature, there was no discussion of any potential human rights impact of the proposed severe curtailing of common law access to the courts for transport-related injury. The

---

28   Spigelman (n 4).
29   *Plaintiff S157/2002 v Commonwealth of Australia* [2003] HCA 476; *Magrath v Goldsborough Mort & Co Ltd* (1932) 47 CLR 121.
30   Charter of Human Rights and Responsibilities Act 2006 (Victoria) s 24.
31   Transport Accident Act 1986 (Victoria) s 93(1).
32   ibid s 93(2)(a).
33   *Rodway v R* [1990] HCA 19.
34   Transport Accident Commission, 'TAC Legislation Changes' <http://www.tac.vic.gov.au/providers/for-service-providers/for-legal-professionals/tac-legislation-changes>.

Chapter 5. Human Rights, Access to Justice and Dispute Resolution

scheme was proposed as being a proportionate limitation for the transport accident injury problem:

'The effect of the Transport Accident Bill is to rationalize [the existing] hybrid system and replace it with a system which relies totally on the principle of no-fault. It is the Government's view that this is the appropriate and fair principle to apply to transport accidents.'[35]

This approach seems unsurprising given the explanation above about the severely limited embeddedness of a human rights perspective in Australian law-making generally. However as noted in Chapter 4 section 3, there had been strenuous opposition from the legal profession to the Victorian government's original plan to completely eliminate access to court proceedings and damages (i.e. a New Zealand-style scheme). The phrasing used by the legal profession in one opinion piece framed access to court as being a fundamental right: 'The Government intends to abolish the right of innocent victims to sue for damages at common law, whereas the [legal profession] regards the right to sue as *fundamental* to a proper system of compensation.'[36]

Various interpretations of section 93 by the courts have confirmed that the statutory bar should be seen as a contingent extinguishment of the common law rights to access the courts, within the specific realm of qualifying transport injury. Those rights will only not be extinguished where a claimant qualifies for one of the limited avenues to common law damages set out under section 93 (i.e. serious injury).

In *Wilson v Nattrass* the plaintiff had brought a claim for damages sustained in a motor vehicle accident outside Victoria (but a Victorian-registered vehicle was involved). The defendant argued that the claim was barred by section 93 because the TAC had not determined the plaintiff's degree of impairment (i.e. whether the plaintiff was eligible under the serious injury carve-out). The majority decision of the court agreed stating that 'subject to a condition or contingency being established, the common law right of action previously enjoyed by persons injured in transport accidents in this State is extinguished.'[37]

Primary Health Care Ltd v Giakalis goes even further and states the right to access court proceedings and the potential liability of a third party do not even exist unless and until the gateway of section 93 has been accessed by a

---

[35] Second reading of Transport Accident Bill, Victorian House of Assembly Hansard, 8 May 1986 at 2021.

[36] Law Institute of Victoria, 'Government Faults – Where the Transport Accident Bill Takes Turns for the No-Fault Worse' (1986) 60 *Law Institute Journal* 768 at 768, cited in Ian Malkin, 'Victoria's Transport Accident Reforms – In Perspective' (1987) 16 *Melbourne University Law Review* 254, 261.

[37] *Wilson v Nattrass* [1995] VicSC 233, (1995) 21 MVR 41.

Intersentia

claimant (via a TAC compensation application).[38] This builds from the position in *Swannell v Farmer*, which found that the potential existence of a 'field' of serious injury causes of action could not exist if the section 93 pathway steps had not been taken, and if the relevant claimant died before the serious injury assessment could be made.[39]

However, the extinguishment effected by section 93 does not apply to all causes of action in all fields of law. In *Lavrick v Lease Auto Pty Ltd*,[40] the non-Victorian plaintiff, Mr Lavrick, whose transport injuries were caused by the defendant's faulty rental car, was *not* precluded from suing the rental company under a contractual cause of action. In other words, only Mr Lavrick's *tortious* causes of action were extinguished by section 93. However, the rental company in turn was entitled to enjoy an indemnity (for Mr Lavrick's contractual claim) from the TAC under section 94 (as the rental company had correctly paid the relevant levies for the faulty vehicle).[41]

In the key legislative statements and key case law on the interpretation of section 93, there is therefore no discussion of whether the statutory bar is an impermissible or a disproportionate infringement of (mostly common law) access to court rights in relation to transport personal injury. We can therefore conclude that the clear words and statements made in the TAC's establishing statute are a valid rebuttal of the ordinary presumption that individuals in Victoria (and Australia) have a right to access to the courts. There has been no breach of any fundamental right of access (notwithstanding the language used by the legal professional lobby during political negotiations over the scheme's establishment) because such a right is only 'rebuttable' and not entrenched. Under the framework of common law and constitutional rights in Victoria and Australia, it is acceptable for the government to use clear words and appropriate justifications to legislate away ordinary access to the courts and replace it with a statutory set of entitlements and an administrative scheme.

From a comparative law perspective, it is extremely telling that key Victorian case law centres on statutory interpretation of the TAC statutory bar itself, and is silent on access issues or human rights issues.[42] This means that, in comparison with a jurisdiction that *does* entrench access to the courts, there is no clear structural equivalency for analysis (as well as the obvious differences in context).

---

38   *Primary Health Care Ltd v Giakalis* [2013] VSCA 75 [69].

39   *Swannell & Transport Accident Commission v Farmer* [1998] VSCA 104.

40   *Lavrick v Lease Auto Pty Ltd* [2002] FCA 599.

41   *Transport Accident Commission v Lease Auto Pty Ltd* [2002] FCAFC 430.

42   Apart from issues to do with the extra-territorial application of the TAC scheme to non-Victorian residents or accidents occurring outside Victoria (but involving at least one Victorian-registered vehicle) – see the discussion about the *Sweedman v Transport Accident Commission* case in Chapter 3 section 3.4.

Chapter 5. Human Rights, Access to Justice and Dispute Resolution

In terms of the rebuttable presumption that Parliament did not intend to retrospectively affect rights and obligations, this seems (unsurprisingly) to cause complexity in cases involving a person who is not automatically covered by the broad indemnity in the TAC legislation.

In *Transport Accident Commission v Lanson*,[43] there was a dispute about whether the TAC was entitled to seek reimbursement for fatal injury related payments from a defendant who was not entitled to a TAC statutory indemnity. The facts of the case concerned a mother who was driving home with her children and another minor when their car struck a horse in the dark. The mother was killed in the accident, which occurred in 1995. Legislation to allow TAC to recover death benefit reimbursement from relevant parties (in this case, the horse owner who had allowed it to negligently stray onto the main road) was only passed in 1998. This amendment brought TAC's subrogation powers for death benefits in line with its existing powers for other no-fault TAC benefits. However the lack of any clear wording by Parliament stating that the legislation had retrospective effect – although it would have been very simple for the legislature to include such a phrase – meant that the 1998 amendments could only be interpreted as applying prospectively. The potential common law negligence actions of the minor children in relation to their own injuries and the (financial) impact of the death of their parent were statutorily limited due to the operation of the Transport Accident Act (and section 93 in particular). The horse owner therefore escaped civil responsibility because the TAC could not pursue them, yet any potential avenues of civil action by the victims were also extinguished. This is an 'acceptable' result according to the Australian framework – but one could argue that the result is unjust.

TAC v Lanson is a particularly good example of the limited Australian human rights framework in active intersection with the large no-fault compensation fund. The section 93 bar on accessing court for most transport personal injury claimants is acceptable because the relevant provision is clearly worded (the default presumption has been rebutted by Parliament), but in this case less clear statutory wording about retrospectivity is insufficient to rebut default presumptions. In other words, it is an illustration of the point that there is unlikely to be a *legal* barrier to the establishment of a no-fault comprehensive compensation fund in Australia, so long as there is adequate legislative clarity of intent and application.

From the small amount of relevant available case law it is also possible to identify some other intersections with human rights law that are relevant to no-fault comprehensive compensation funds. These are particularly helpful for a comparative law analysis with jurisdictions that *do* have fundamental rights frameworks.

---

43   *Transport Accident Commission v Lanson* [2001] VSCA 84; [2001] 3 VR 250.

Intersentia

Dawson v Transport Accident Commission[44] concerned a woman who had suffered a transport-related injury prior to having children, and required long-term ongoing therapy as part of her rehabilitation. She requested that the TAC pay for her childcare costs so that she could continue to attend her therapy sessions.[45] TAC declined this request (because her injury did not impact her ability to care for her children on a daily basis) and the plaintiff sought a review of that decision. The plaintiff also claimed that the TAC had failed to take the Victorian Charter into account when making its decision,[46] specifically its protections in relation to families and children (section 17), equality before the law (section 8) and the right to privacy (section 13). The plaintiff alleged that the TAC's interpretation of the statutory entitlements limited her right to the enjoyment of family life.[47] The TAC, meanwhile, argued that the plaintiff was in reality arguing that she had a right to childcare, something that was not actually protected by the Victorian Charter.[48] The plaintiff also relied upon European Court of Human Rights case law to support her argument, specifically precedent relating to article 8 protections of private and family life.[49] However the Tribunal found in favour of the TAC, and disagreed that any relevant human rights were being engaged by the TAC in its interpretation of the relevant statutory provisions.

Most relevantly for present purposes, the Tribunal also took a very cold view towards the comparative relevance and applicability of European human rights law concepts to the Victorian Charter or the scope of the TAC scheme. Specifically that 'care needs to be taken in applying European authorities based on [an] Article of the European Convention to the Victorian Charter'. A specific direct comparison was made with the positive obligations imposed by article 8, compared with the more passive protections of families and children under section 17 of the Victorian Charter. A 'simple failure'[50] to pay a benefit under a no-fault compensation fund would not activate the Victorian Charter in the same

---

[44]   *Dawson v Transport Accident Commission* [2010] VCAT 644.

[45]   The plaintiff relied on section 60 of the Transport Accident Act 1986, which requires the TAC to pay *inter alia* the reasonable associated costs of rehabilitation for a claimant's transport-related injury.

[46]   Section 32(1) of the Victorian Charter requires that statutory provisions be interpreted, so far as possible, in a way that is compatible with human rights. Section 38(1), meanwhile, makes it unlawful for a public authority to not take human rights into account when making a decision. See *Dawson v Transport Accident Commission* (n 44) paras 20–27.

[47]   ibid 48.

[48]   ibid 56.

[49]   Specifically, the plaintiff relied upon *J, R (on the application of) v London Borough of Enfield* [2002] EWHC 432 (Admin) 35 and *R v London Borough of Enfield, Ex Parte Bernard* [2002] EWHC 2282 (Admin). See ibid 82–83.

[50]   ibid 84.

Chapter 5. Human Rights, Access to Justice and Dispute Resolution

way that article 8 of the ECHR would be activated. Further, the socio-economic dimensions of the ECHR were found to be wholly different to the protections of privacy offered by the Victorian Charter, meaning that the denial of a TAC benefit could not activate any human rights breach in a Victorian context.[51]

Rekatsinas v Transport Accident Commission[52] concerned an application on behalf of the deceased plaintiff, who had been killed in a transport accident. As a result of Mr Rekatsinas' death, his family were entitled to a number of TAC benefits. The plaintiff's Greek Orthodox heritage meant that his family arranged for elaborate (and expensive) funeral and headstone arrangements in accordance with cultural tradition, which cost more than the TAC's interpretation of the maximum statutory entitlement.[53] The plaintiff's family argued that the cultural practices of the deceased victim's community should have been taken into account by TAC when determining the amount of a funeral benefit. To this end the plaintiff relied on section 19 of the Victorian Charter, which offers a basic protection of cultural, religious, racial or linguistic rights. The TAC in its defence relied heavily upon the plain wording within the statute, which referred to the 'reasonable costs of burial and cremation' – in TAC's view, the meaning of this phrase did not extend to include a monument. The Tribunal agreed with the TAC's narrower interpretation. Ultimately the Tribunal did not make findings on the intersection with the Victorian Charter, because the impact of the *Dawson* decision meant that counsel did not rely as heavily on the Charter in oral submissions.[54]

However the general findings in this case – that there is no automatic 'activation' of human rights dimensions when the TAC uses its statutory powers and makes discretionary compensation determinations – are instructive. They reveal the potential human rights related difficulties of a no-fault comprehensive compensation fund in managing non-typical costs and effects of an injury. The TAC in this case directly benefited from the narrow focus on ordinary statutory interpretation that is favoured by Victorian and Australian courts generally, and the passive effect of human rights protections. A no-fault comprehensive

---

[51] ibid 85–86. This kind of narrow approach at the Victorian Civil and Administrative Tribunal level seems in tune with the broader Australian legislative and judicial approach to human rights, but there is other VCAT precedent that argues in favour of a broad and generous approach being taken to human rights – see *Kracke v Mental Health Review Board* [2009] VCAT 646.

[52] *Rekatsinas v Transport Accident Commission* [2010] VCAT 967.

[53] Section 60(2A) of the Transport Accident Act 1986 requires the TAC to pay for the 'reasonable costs of burial and cremation'. Section 3 of the statute allows the TAC to exercise a discretion in the determination of what is a 'reasonable' amount. At the time of Mr Rekatsinas' death, A$500 was the TAC's interpretation of a 'reasonable' amount. It should be noted that at the time of writing, this has been revised to a total of A$16,200 for all relevant funeral costs – Transport Accident Commission, 'When a Family Member Dies' <https://www.tac.vic.gov.au/what-to-do-after-an-accident/how-to-claim/when-someone-dies>.

[54] *Rekatsinas v Transport Accident Commission* (n 52) para 15.

Intersentia

311

compensation fund and its tendency towards a homogenised approach to compensation could, in my view, lead to tensions with entrenched protections found in other jurisdictions. This case is a useful illustration of that point.

Shafton v Victoria[55] concerned a disclosure/discussion about the plaintiff claimant's medical information that took place between the plaintiff and TAC's medical specialists, (mistakenly) without obtaining the plaintiff's authority. The TAC claimed that the plaintiff's case lacked substance, because *inter alia* the sharing of information was permitted by the TAC regime or other relevant healthcare legislation. The plaintiff's claims were ultimately dismissed. The most relevant point of this case for current purposes relates to the plaintiff's unsuccessful claim that his right to privacy was interfered with 'arbitrarily' (and thus breached section 13 of the Victorian Charter) by the sharing of information. The Tribunal found that any kind of collection of information by TAC for the purpose of assessing its claim – i.e. carrying out its statutory purpose – could not be categorised as 'arbitrary'. In this case, the implied need for the TAC to access information was found to be of greater importance than the plaintiff's right to privacy. It was adequate that the TAC did not collect information in an 'arbitrary' way. What is relevant for present purposes is not any prediction of whether, for example, a court referring to a different human rights framework would have made a different assessment on the same set of facts. Rather, the balancing of the different elements in this case shows that, once again, a clearly described statutory framework will have greater weight or strength before a court than the protections provided under a basic and vaguely worded human rights architecture.

What is useful to observe here is the lack of any real balancing of the Victorian Charter obligations against the TAC legislative framework, in the context of important principles about the handling of a patient's confidential information. The clear and comprehensively described no-fault compensation fund statutory provisions (and Victoria's relevant health practitioner guidelines) once again prevailed over the passive and broad human rights protections of the Victorian Charter. The specifically expressed intent of the Victorian Parliament to enact a comprehensive no-fault compensation fund had a greater weight than vaguely phrased human rights protections.

The case law identified here indicates the significant analytical and structural gulf of differences between an entrenched and Australian non-entrenched vision of protected rights, as applied to the specific context of a no-fault comprehensive compensation fund. The Australian perspective is that the interaction between the claimant and the TAC – specifically, a denial of entitlement to some types of compensation – is unlikely to create friction with human rights, if the

---

[55]   *Shafton v Victoria* [2016] VCAT 971.

interpretation was made in accordance with the plain meaning of the TAC legislation. The Australian perspective reveals a much more limited sphere of potential engagement for a no-fault comprehensive compensation fund with human rights, in comparison with jurisdictions that are underpinned by fundamental human rights protections. The likely result of this in practice is, as we can see from the *Dawson* case, reduced constraints on the operation and scope of a large no-fault compensation fund. *Rekatsinas* illustrates that quantum of compensation can be legitimately tempered by the TAC when exercising a statutory discretion, even where this possibly infringes religious and cultural expression.

The TAC was asked, for this research project, if it had undertaken an assessment of whether the statutory entitlements to compensation and the relevant litigation prohibitions are consistent with the Australian Human Rights Commission Act or the Victorian Charter. The TAC simply responded that its 'legislation is compliant with the Charter'.[56]

The case law discussed here shows a general trend of deference towards to the power of a clearly worded statutory framework, especially when put into direct opposition with common law and Victorian Charter human rights protections. This is illustrated by *Wilson*, *Primary Healthcare* and *Swannell*, where the clear wording of the section 93 statutory bar on tort law claims is accepted to amount to an extinguishment of liability in most cases. It is only where there is statutory silence, as in *Lavrick*, that other alternatives will be possible. *Lanson*, meanwhile, reveals that despite the comprehensiveness of the statutory framework, the courts will not 'read in' provisions that may infringe rights, especially on core common law rights issues like retrospectivity. Ultimately, the Victorian case law reveals a lack of direct interaction between human rights concepts and no-fault comprehensive compensation funds, mostly because of the passivity of the former. It also reveals a situation where, despite the Victorian Charter's requirement that the interpretation of statutory instruments and the actions of public authorities comply with a human rights-based approach, in reality this will only occur in the absence of clear legislative statements to the contrary. These points appear to apply to both substantive (compensation entitlement) and procedural (claims handling) issues.

There is clearly a dearth of relevant legislative and judicial statements from a human rights perspective, specific to the TAC, that are useful for a comparative law analysis. This means that it can be helpful to look at relevant human rights analyses that have been undertaken into other large Australian no-fault compensation funds or redress schemes.

---

[56] Response to questionnaire, received 5 October 2020.

2.1.3. *The Intersection with Other Compensation Funds*

The Australian Redress Scheme for Victims of Sexual Abuse (the Australian Redress Scheme) was assessed for compatibility with human rights at the time of its establishment. The scheme was identified as engaging with a number of different human rights that are enshrined in different international conventions.[57] Among these, the following can be identified as most applicable to a no-fault comprehensive compensation fund:

a. the right to a fair hearing (article 14 of the International Covenant on Civil and Political Rights – 'the ICCPR');
b. the right to health (article 12 of the International Covenant on Economic, Social and Cultural Rights – 'the ICESCR'); and
c. the right to an effective remedy (article 3 of the ICCPR).

The article 14 ICCPR right to a fair hearing requires that in the determination of a person's rights and obligations under the law, everyone shall be entitled to a fair and public hearing by a competent, independent and impartial tribunal. Although the Australian Redress Scheme allows victims to file a separate civil damages claim against a relevant defendant until a scheme award has been accepted, some permanent limitations were placed on victims accessing a Federal Court judicial review of redress scheme decisions.[58] These were identified as potentially infringing article 14 ICCPR. However, this limitation was concluded to be consistent with the 'non-legalistic nature of redress schemes'. Specifically:

> 'The Scheme provides survivors with access to an internal review process, but no rights to external merits review, as this would be overly legalistic, time consuming, expensive (adding considerable costs to administration) and would risk further harm

---

[57] Explanatory Memorandum: National Redress Scheme for Institutional Child Sexual Abuse 2018. The rights that were identified are: the right to state-supported recovery for child victims of abuse (article 39 of the Convention on the Rights of the Child – the 'CRC'); the right to protection from sexual abuse (articles 19 and 34 of the CRC); the freedom from discrimination in upholding the rights of the child (article 2 of the CRC); the right to social security (article 9 of the International Covenant on Economic, Social and Cultural Rights – 'the ICESCR'); the right to maternity leave with adequate social security benefits – article 10 of the ICESCR; the right to health (article 12 of the ICESCR); the right to an effective remedy (article 3 of the International Covenant on Civil and Political Rights – 'the ICCPR'); the freedom from unlawful attack on honour and reputation (article 17 of the ICCPR); the right to freedom of expression (article 19 of the ICCPR); the right to protection against arbitrary or unlawful interferences with privacy (article 17 of the ICCPR) and the right to a fair hearing (article 14 of the ICCPR).

[58] Section 3(zg), Schedule 1 of the Administrative Decisions (Judicial Review) Act 1977 states that decisions made under the National Redress Scheme for Institutional Child Sexual Abuse Act 2018 do not fall with the scope of the judicial review legislation.

Chapter 5. Human Rights, Access to Justice and Dispute Resolution

to survivors. Furthermore, if these avenues were available, many survivors may have unrealistic expectations of what could be achieved given the low evidentiary barrier to entry to the Scheme.'[59]

The different skill-set of the Australian Redress Scheme decision-makers compared to that of a judge was also noted – and the imposition of a 'legalistic lens on a non-legalistic decision making process' was concluded to be inappropriate.[60] The bar on victims seeking civil damages after the acceptance of a redress scheme award was not identified as conflicting with any human rights protections.

The right to health enshrined by article 12 of the International Covenant on Economic, Social and Cultural Rights (the ICESCR) was found to be proactively promoted by the Australian Redress Scheme. Article 12 guarantees the right of everyone to the highest attainable standard of physical and mental health. The redress scheme has a core focus on facilitating victims' access to counselling and psychological care via a financial lump sum or access to services. This was found to be a practical manifestation of the article 12 right.[61] In the four no-fault comprehensive compensation funds studied in this project, their common central focus on comprehensive rehabilitation and prevention of injury also appears to proactively promote this ICESCR right to health.

In the context of the Australian Redress Scheme, the right to an effective remedy under article 3 of the ICCPR primarily relates to a remedy for an infringement of article 24 ICCPR (the right of every child to protection by society). Regardless, some useful general comments on remedies were made in the parliamentary human rights assessment, which are applicable to a no-fault comprehensive compensation fund. The requirement of successful claimants (in order to receive an award) to release potential defendant institutions from all liability relevant to the scope of the redress scheme was flagged as potentially problematic. However, this was balanced with the non-legalistic nature of the redress scheme, the greater degree of accessibility to compensation for a wide group of abuse survivors, and the provision of access to free specialised legal support services.[62] Less convincing are the arguments that the extinguishment of liability was necessary to ensure defendant institution participation in the scheme[63] – this is not something that is relevant to ensuring access to an effective remedy for individual victims.

---

[59] Explanatory Memorandum: National Redress Scheme for Institutional Child Sexual Abuse 2018 126.
[60] ibid 127.
[61] ibid 126.
[62] ibid 122.
[63] ibid 122–123.

Intersentia

The conclusion of the Parliamentary Joint Committee on Human Rights was directly cited in the Australian Redress Scheme human rights assessment, and it is worthwhile to restate it here:[64]

> 'The bar on future civil liability of participating institutions may engage and limit the right to an effective remedy. However, the proposed rules governing the provision of legal services under the redress scheme may operate as a sufficient safeguard so as to support the human rights compatibility of the measure.'

For this comparative analysis, the balancing of the effect of the limitations on access to court with the overall enhancement of victims' access to justice is most salient.

Separately, recent reforms to the Australian Capital Territory's (ACT) no-fault motor injury compensation scheme have created a limitation on access to common law damages. The legislature actively considered the human rights implications of the reforms, and specifically the restriction on access to the common law. The proposed scheme was identified as possibly trespassing 'on rights previously established by law and trespass on personal rights and liberties including recognition and equality before the law; and engage the right to privacy and reputation ... The right to fair trial ... may also be engaged'.[65] There was an identification of engagement with the ACT's human rights legislation, which is broadly equivalent to the Victorian Charter.

It found that limiting access to the common law was, on balance, reasonable for the whole community because it would allow the courts 'to focus on the most seriously injured, children and the family of the person who has died as a result of a motor accident'.[66] As part of this balancing process, consideration was made of whether any 'less restrictive means' were available to pursue the desired aims of the statute.[67] Specific reference was made to research on the direct correlation between a person's recovery and the role of compensation processes, lawyers and adversarialism in producing or perpetuating ill-health in victim claimants.[68] A description was given of the intended safeguarding of victims' access to justice rights by way of a prescribed dispute resolution regime for claim disputes, with the ultimate focus being always on victim recovery.[69]

The ACT approach is an excellent example of an active legislative engagement with the intersection between human rights and a no-fault compensation fund.

---

[64] ibid 123.

[65] Motor Accident Injuries Bill 2019 (ACT) – Explanatory Statement 10.

[66] ibid 10–18.

[67] ibid 10.

[68] Genevieve Grant and David M Studdert, 'Poisoned Chalice? A Critical Analysis of the Evidence Linking Personal Injury Compensation Processes with Adverse Health Outcomes' (2009) <http://papers.ssrn.com/sol3/papers.cfm?abstract_id=1484340>.

[69] Motor Accident Injuries Bill 2019 (ACT) – Explanatory Statement 12.

Chapter 5. Human Rights, Access to Justice and Dispute Resolution

There is direct consideration of issues that were not considered or thought of during the establishment of the TAC scheme, in the language that is now commonly used across multiple legal systems to deal with human rights and access to justice intersections with legislation. After undertaking a balancing exercise, a conclusion was drawn that the 'limits on the identified rights are reasonable and justifiable in a free and democratic society' because, *inter alia*:

a.   where there is some degree of discrimination between certain categories of victims, the least restrictive means have been adopted;[70]
b.   the scheme supports the prevention of motor accidents and the safe use of motor vehicles;
c.   the use of defined benefits under the scheme, which can be classified as personal injury insurance, limits the possibility of discrimination and unequal treatment; and
d.   the scheme supports social benefits to the community by providing compensation as quickly as possible.

The key point that can be drawn from the Australian Redress Scheme and new ACT no-fault compensation fund analyses is that a limitation on access to courts will be acceptable where the compensation fund has the clear legislative and social purpose to transplant the resolution process for the relevant category of injuries *outside of the ordinary legal system*. A wider and more flexible approach to access to justice for these victims is seen as an acceptable trade-off for limitations on access to ordinary legal avenues. This aligns with the statements of a former Australian federal Attorney General, who has argued that Australia would benefit from a broad socio-economic definition of access to justice with 'court [as a] last resort ... while justice should be the norm in our society, experienced by all Australians as a part of our way of life'.[71]

The Australian Redress Scheme and new ACT no-fault compensation fund comparisons also illustrate that it is possible to substantively and successfully grapple with the human rights intersections of redress and liability-averting schemes in an acceptable way. It shows that there needs to be a focus on the social and non-legal nature of these schemes, and the balanced benefits they provide. It is not sufficient to gloss over or ignore the restrictions on ordinary routes to court, but to deal with them directly and justify the restrictions. These examples help to fill the silence left by older schemes which have not had to address human rights intersections in a substantive way.

---

[70]   This relates to issues such as foreigner claimants, the intersection with superannuation/pension payments, criminal acts and offences leading to injury – see ibid 13–15.
[71]   Chris Merritt, 'Access to Justice Redefined', *The Australian* (24 May 2013).

Intersentia

2.2. NEW ZEALAND

New Zealand is a unicameral parliamentary constitutional democracy. Like Australia, the United Kingdom is its main legislative 'parent'. However the New Zealand legislative and parliamentary system is even closer to its ancestor, possessing a very close replica of the British Westminster system.[72] This also means that there is no written constitution or codification of constitutional rights in New Zealand. Unlike Australia, there is a national statutory affirmation of human rights in the form of the Bill of Rights Act 1990 and the Human Rights Act 1993. The Privacy Act 1993 also provides some fortification of human rights protections.

2.2.1. Historical and Contemporary Context

The Dicey-type influences on Australia that were discussed in section 2.1.1 were also present in New Zealand in the late nineteenth century.[73] The legislative power of the New Zealand government was essentially derived from legislative actions in the Westminster parliament – it was only in 1852 that a local representative government was established in New Zealand (by way of a Westminster statute).[74] A confirmation of the power of the New Zealand government to fully make its own laws in respect of that jurisdiction was only passed in 1973.[75] The basic structure of a New Zealand constitutional framework was described for the first time – in ordinary legislation – in 1986.[76] Human rights protections or the protection of fundamental rights were not described in any of these simple legislative actions. Commentators have pointed out that this is a reflection of New Zealand's English heritage, where the protection of individual rights was seen as residing in the representative and responsible government, which could be changed by way of periodic elections.[77]

As in Australia, there was general resistance in New Zealand for most of the twentieth century to the introduction of any sort of bill of rights. It was only after a series of political and economic upheavals of the 1970s that the value of limits on the executive branch's power and dominance of the legislature was

---

[72] Kim Watts, 'New Zealand' in Thierry Vansweevelt and Britt Weyts (eds), *Compensation Funds in Comparative Perspective* (Intersentia 2020) 93.

[73] The only exception from this era to this eschewing of individual- or citizen-focused rights and protections is the Treaty of Waitangi 1840 that was signed between the British Crown and Maori *rangatira* (chiefs). However, the interpretation of what rights were afforded under this treaty has been the subject of considerable debate and conflict between Maori and the Crown.

[74] New Zealand Constitution Act 1862 (UK).

[75] New Zealand Constitution Amendment Act 1973 (NZ). The New Zealand Constitution (Amendment) Act 1947 (UK) granted powers to the New Zealand Parliament to repeat the provisions of the original 1852 constitutional legislation.

[76] The Constitution Act 1986.

[77] Paul Rishworth and others, *The New Zealand Bill of Rights* (Oxford University Press 2003) 5.

identified.[78] The development of a bill of rights in New Zealand began in the late 1980s, around the time of the enactment of the Canadian Charter of Rights and Freedoms. There was significant opposition to a New Zealand human rights statute having a supreme status, because of a perception that it would elevate judicial power over parliamentary power and therefore be anti-democratic.[79] Ultimately, the bill of rights was enacted in 1990, but only as an ordinary statute and with social and economic rights specifically excluded from its scope.[80]

The Bill of Rights Act 1990 offers a general scope of protection of civil and political rights. This includes a right to justice, but this is mainly centred on a requirement for public authorities and tribunals to comply with principles of natural justice when making determinations about a person's rights, obligations or interests.[81] An important handbrake on the power of the bill of rights is the inability of any court to declare any other piece of legislation invalid because of its inconsistency with the bill of rights,[82] and the permissibility of 'reasonable limits' on the bill of rights protections where they 'can be demonstrably justified in a free and democratic society.'[83]

Despite this resistance to the notion of judicial supremacy via a human rights legislative framework, the protection of many human rights in New Zealand is (as in Australia and the United Kingdom) derived from the common law anyway.[84] New Zealand's Court of Appeal has taken the view that 'it is arguable that some common law rights may go so deep that even Parliament cannot be accepted by the Courts to have destroyed them.'[85] In specific relation to the right of individuals to access the courts, case law precedent has also been the source of the clearest statement of rights: '[W]e have reservations as to the extent to which in New Zealand even an Act of Parliament can take away the rights of citizens to resort to the ordinary Courts of law for the determination of their rights.'[86]

Other general protections against discrimination can be found in the Human Rights Act 1993 and the Privacy Act 1993. The former is effectively a mechanism for establishing the Human Rights Commission, and the latter provides protections for information privacy and establishes the office of the Privacy Commissioner.

As we begin to consider the intersection between human rights and no-fault comprehensive compensation funds in a New Zealand context, we can therefore

---

[78]   ibid 6–7.

[79]   ibid 7.

[80]   ibid 8.

[81]   Bill of Rights Act 1990 (BORA) s 27.

[82]   BORA s 4.

[83]   BORA s 5.

[84]   Paul Rishworth, 'Writing Things Unwritten: Common Law in New Zealand's Constitution' (2016) 14 *International Journal of Constitutional Law* 137, 144.

[85]   *Fraser v State Services Commission* [1984] 1 NZLR 116 at 121.

[86]   *New Zealand Drivers Association v New Zealand Road Carriers* [1982] 1 NZLR 374 at 390.

Intersentia

319

identify an overall approach that is slightly different to that of Australia. There is a broad basic protection of civil and political rights, and persuasive case law on the power of rights derived from the common law. However this is severely tempered by the ability of the legislature to impose justified limitations on individual rights where necessary, and the acceptance that there can be inconsistency between the Bill of Rights Act and other pieces of legislation.

2.2.2. The Intersection with Issues Relevant to No-Fault Comprehensive Compensation Funds

The lack of fundamental human rights legislation in New Zealand means that there was never a question or direct consideration of human rights concerns at the time that the ACC Scheme was established. Nor has there been any significant consideration of human rights issues by the government since then. There is no general consideration of human rights issues under the Accident Compensation Act 2001. The only small point of intersection is a carve-out in the statutory bar provision, allowing civil complaints about human rights breaches to be brought before the Human Rights Review Tribunal.[87] There is a basic Code of Claimants' Rights set out within the legislation itself, and this imposes some basic fairness, respect and privacy protection responsibilities on ACC.[88] The meatiest human rights intersections with the ACC Scheme have emerged in case law, and in some important analyses spurred into motion by disability advocates.

In recent years, there have been two key intersections between the ACC Scheme and human rights issues. The first has been the exclusion of certain categories of disabled persons from the scheme, as well as the significant distinction between the support available under the ACC Scheme for (accidental) personal injury, and the ordinary social welfare support available to long-term disabled persons. The second type of intersection has been the human rights implications of personal data mishandling by ACC.

Turning to the first issue, the exclusion of certain categories of disabled persons was directly addressed in the Court of Appeal decision in *Trevethick v Ministry of Health*.[89] That case, which was originally brought before the New Zealand Human Rights Review Tribunal, was brought by a woman who suffered from multiple sclerosis. As her misfortune was caused by a degenerative illness, and not by an accident, she was unable to receive extensive ACC Scheme supports. Ms Trevethick sought leave to appeal to the Court of Appeal on the single point of whether the cause of her disability is included in the definition of 'disability' as a prohibited ground of discrimination in section 21(1)(h) of the Human Rights Act. In other words, did the exclusion of her kind of misfortune

---

[87]   Accident Compensation Act 2001 s 317(4)(b).
[88]   Part 3: Code of ACC Claimants' Rights, and claims ibid.
[89]   *Trevethick v Ministry of Health* [2008] NZCA 397.

320

Chapter 5. Human Rights, Access to Justice and Dispute Resolution

from the scope of the ACC Scheme amount to unlawful discrimination? The Court of Appeal concluded that there was *prima facie* discrimination, but this was a justified limitation (in accordance with the relevant provision of the Bill of Rights Act 1990[90]). The policy choice whereby accidental injury gave rise to entitlement to no-fault statutory compensation, but the costs of illness were to be provided by the State's health system and/or private insurance, led to anomalies but was nevertheless justified.[91] Therefore, the handbrake provided by the Bill of Rights Act against judicial declarations on human rights breaches (in the form of 'justified limitations') neutralised the possibility of a human rights infringement being activated in the *Trevethick* case. It is obvious that this case may have had a different result if a human rights-based approach were part of the New Zealand social policy framework,[92] or if human rights legislation gave more power to judges to declare inconsistency or infringement and require a remedy.

When considering the *Trevethick* decision and the intersection of human rights issues with the ACC Scheme, it is important to bear in mind that issues about the inconsistency of treatment between different classes of victims of misfortune are quite widespread in New Zealand. Recent research suggests that a long-standing policy bias against non-working recipients of social welfare benefits (in contrast to the income-linked benefits of the ACC Scheme) amount to discrimination against the human rights of New Zealand's poorest individuals.[93] Therefore, the 'inconsistent treatment of victims' is a problem is not limited to the ACC Scheme – and should also not be seen as a fundamental fatal flaw of the ACC Scheme alone. Any (much-needed) attempts to correct the inconsistent treatment of individuals' income across different frameworks would naturally have to include a reassessment of the benefits available under the ACC Scheme.[94]

Trevethick confirmed that the ACC Scheme is permissibly out of bounds for individuals whose disability or ailment is not caused by personal injury, regardless of the moral and equitable consequences of that disparity. Since then, a series of socio-legal research reports have revealed possible human rights breaches against individuals whose cases are on the borderline of eligibility and/or who have appealed ACC decisions on eligibility and entitlements. Some of this research has resulted in direct changes to ACC dispute resolution processes, whereas other issues remain outstanding.

---

[90]   New Zealand Bill of Rights Act 1990 s 5.

[91]   *Trevethick v Ministry of Health* (n 89) para 18.

[92]   Māmari Stephens, 'The Right to Social Security' in Margaret Bedggood and Kris Gledhill (eds), *Law into Action Economic, Social and Cultural Rights in Aotearoa New Zealand* (Thomson Reuters 2011) 151.

[93]   Jonathan Barrett and Lisa Marriott, 'Discrimination by Definition: Are Definitions of "Income" Used in New Zealand Statutes Compatible with the State's Duty to Protect Human Rights?' (2020) 26 *Australian Journal of Human Rights* 329.

[94]   This kind of coordination was suggested by the most recent review of New Zealand's social security systems – see Welfare Expert Advisory Group, 'Whakamana Tāngata – Restoring Dignity to Social Security in New Zealand' (2019) 112 <www.weag.govt.nz>.

There is a two-fold reason why disabled claimants would tend to have difficulty accessing their ACC Scheme entitlements, either initially or on an ongoing basis. On the one hand, already disabled complainants may have difficulty showing that the harm they have suffered post-accident is causatively connected with the personal injury they sustained in the accident, rather than their pre-existing disability. On the other hand, personal injury victims who end up disabled are likely to have ongoing interaction with ACC to confirm their continued entitlement to compensation. This is because ACC claimants need to demonstrate their ongoing entitlement, and ACC itself, as a public authority, has rehabilitation targets to move claimants 'off the books' to maintain costs control.[95] This kind of tension and ongoing interaction is likely be more difficult and/or repressive for disabled claimants to have to deal with, compared to non-disabled claimants.

In 2014, ACC Scheme claimant advocacy group, Acclaim Otago, submitted a shadow report to the United Nations Committee on the Rights of Persons with Disabilities (UN disability rights Committee).[96] This took place in the context of the UN's 2014 periodic review of New Zealand's compliance with the Convention on the Rights of Persons with Disabilities (CRPD). In that report, Acclaim Otago detailed a systematic review and survey it had undertaken to assess the ACC Scheme's compliance with the CRPD. The report concluded that the existing ACC Scheme framework and its operation in practice breached a number of CRPD provisions, to the detriment of claimants (particularly disabled ones) who sought or were unable to challenge ACC decisions about eligibility or entitlements.[97] Most relevantly for this research project, it alleged that there was a significant breach of the article 13 CRPD access to justice requirements,[98] and a breach of article 22 CRPD respect for privacy requirements.

In response to the Acclaim Otago shadow report and other submissions, the UN disability rights Committee noted concerns about the lack of a human rights focus to the ACC Scheme legislative machinery. It recommended improvements to legal aid measures and the accessibility of processes, and that all the relevant mechanisms for compensation assessment be given a human rights focus.[99]

---

[95]   Accident Compensation Corporation, 'Annual Report 2019' (2019) 38.

[96]   Acclaim Otago and others, 'The Costs of Paradigm Change: Access to Justice for People with Disabilities Caused by Personal Injury in New Zealand' (2014) <http://www.acclaimotago.org>.

[97]   ibid 2–3.

[98]   Article 13 CRPD requires: '1. States Parties shall ensure effective access to justice for persons with disabilities on an equal basis with others, including through the provision of procedural and age-appropriate accommodations, in order to facilitate their effective role as direct and indirect participants, including as witnesses, in all legal proceedings, including at investigative and other preliminary stages.
2. In order to help to ensure effective access to justice for persons with disabilities, States Parties shall promote appropriate training for those working in the field of administration of justice, including police and prison staff.'

[99]   Committee on the Rights of Persons with Disabilities, 'Concluding Observations on the Initial Report of New Zealand, CRPD/C/NZL/CO/1' (2014) paras 23–24.

Chapter 5. Human Rights, Access to Justice and Dispute Resolution

Acclaim Otago produced a further study in 2015 on the ACC Scheme appeals process and how this hindered access to justice.[100] This included quantitative and qualitative analysis of relevant ACC Scheme appeal court decisions. As discussed previously, in 2016 the New Zealand government commissioned Miriam Dean QC, a senior lawyer, to conduct an independent review of the issues raised by the Acclaim Otago report.[101] Many of the recommendations made by Ms Dean's report were immediately adopted by the New Zealand government.[102] However, human rights issues were specifically excluded from the Dean report's scope.[103] Acclaim Otago produced a further report setting out proposals to improve the ACC Scheme in 2017.[104]

The broad theme of these analyses and reviews, for comparative law purposes, is that the ACC Scheme framework has inadequate legislative structures and consequentially inadequate operational procedures and safeguards to ensure the protection of human rights and the proper facilitation of access to justice for certain disadvantaged categories of claimants.[105] This is in contrast to how well the scheme works for most claims, particularly those involving short-term injury.[106]

In the interests of brevity for an international audience and to facilitate a comparative law analysis, the table below summarises some of the key human rights points (on the themes of access to justice and breach of privacy) that were raised by Acclaim Otago, those picked up by the UN disability rights Committee, those raised by Miriam Dean QC and the issues that have been ultimately implemented by the New Zealand government – and what remains outstanding. Explanations on individual issues are set out in footnotes. In terms of international human rights instruments, reference is only made to the CRPD because that is the only international human rights framework that was referenced by the Acclaim Otago reports. One should assume that identified access to justice issues and breaches of the relevant CRPD principles would likely find broad equivalence in relevant access to justice principles in other rights frameworks.

---

100 Acclaim Otago, 'Understanding the Problem: An Analysis of ACC Appeals Processes to Identify Barriers to Access to Justice for Injured New Zealanders' (2015) <http://www.acclaimotago.org>.

101 Miriam Dean, 'Independent Review of the Acclaim Otago (Inc) July 2015 Report Into Accident Compensation Dispute Resolution Processes' (May 2016) <http://www.mbie.govt.nz/info-services/employment-skills/legislation-reviews/accident-compensation-dispute-resolution/document-and-images-library/independent-review.pdf>.

102 New Zealand Government, 'Further Work to Improve ACC Dispute Resolution' (2016) <https://www.beehive.govt.nz/release/further-work-improve-acc-dispute-resolution>.

103 Dean (n 101) 16–17.

104 Warren Forster, Tom Barraclough and Tiho Mijatov, 'Solving the Problem: Causation, Transparency and Access to Justice in New Zealand's Personal Injury System' ([2017] New Zealand Law Foundation Research Reports p 10).

105 Acclaim Otago (n 100) 2.

106 Acclaim Otago and others (n 96) 1.

Intersentia

323

Table 1. Human rights issues raised concerning the ACC

Issue	Human rights point	Raised by whom?	NZ Government/ACC Scheme response	Current status
Inadequate access to legal advice/funding for claimants seeking to review an ACC Scheme decision on eligibility or entitlements.[107]	Access to justice; breach of article 13 CRPD.	Acclaim Otago 2014 and 2015 reports; UN disability rights Committee 2014 report; Miriam Dean QC 2016 report (but not on the CRPD issue specifically).	Government announced funding increases for community legal advice and guidance services. However efforts to increase the number of lawyers working in the field of personal injury law were seen as going beyond the scope of the government's power.[108] Specifically, the introduction of court procedural mechanisms that would allow judges to appoint counsel to claimants was seen as being fraught with issues, such as undermining claimants' right to self-representation, and the ethical problems associated with third-party litigation funding.	Acclaim Otago 2017 report claimed that there had been no significant change to the originally identified funding problems.[109] However, as of 2020, there are a number of free advice and advocacy services for individuals seeking a review of an ACC decision.[110] Some of these services are independent from ACC but receive funding from ACC under a contract.[111]

---

107 For example, the Acclaim Otago 2014 and 2015 reports both set out respondent data that showed that claimants seeking to challenge ACC Scheme decisions were often in debt (for example, because of their ineligibility for ACC Scheme cover), public legal aid levels were inadequate, and a supply shortage existed of lawyers working in the field of personal injury law. See ibid 14–16; Acclaim Otago (n 100) 49–50.

108 Ministry of Business Innovation and Employment and Accident Compensation Corporation, 'ACC and MBIE Briefing Paper: Update on the Response to the Miriam Dean Review and next Phase of Work to Improve Disputes Performance' (2018) Appendix A.

109 Forster, Barraclough and Mijatov (n 104) 13.

110 'Review an ACC Decision' <https://www.acc.co.nz/contact/get-a-decision-reviewed/#getting-advice-from-a-third-party>.

111 For example the Wayfinders service – see 'Frequently Asked Questions' 'Way Finders ACC Navigation Service' <https://www.wayfinders.org.nz/>.

A lack of procedural fairness: for example inadequate or unbalanced access by claimants to medical evidence;[112] and potential privacy breaches by parties holding claimants' medical evidence.[113]	Access to justice; respect for privacy; breach of article 13 CRPD; breach of article 22 CRPD.	Acclaim 2014 and 2015 reports; Dean 2016 report (but not on the CRPD issue specifically).	NZ Government convened a series of working groups on access to medical evidence, and implemented the resulting recommendations (including the ability for medical experts to confer with one another, rotating the pool of ACC medical experts, and more stringent independence requirements for ACC medical experts).[114] Because existing court procedural rules give judges the discretion to give directions to medical experts (to benefit claimants), it was decided no further work was needed on this issue.	Acclaim Otago 2017 report argues that the existing ACC Scheme centres too much on causation, meaning that in complex cases medical evidence will be required – indicating that the procedural fairness point is possibly unsolvable under the existing framework from the perspective of victims.[115] Specialist ACC lawyers and advocates noted a continuing trend of complex injury claimants being sent frequently for a medical review of their conditions,[116] with limited entitlement to reimbursement for these costs.[117]

(continued)

[112] For example, a sheer lack of access to medical experts because ACC has retained the bulk of the profession, or a reluctance for medical experts to jeopardise their professional relationship with ACC in other matters. See Acclaim Otago and others (n 96) 16–21.

[113] For example, over half of the Acclaim Otago 2014 report survey respondents reported privacy-related problems in their dealings with ACC. Further, an investigation by the Auditor-General revealed an internal failure by ACC to address privacy-related issues. See ibid 14; Acclaim Otago (n 100) 160.

[114] Ministry of Business Innovation and Employment and Accident Compensation Corporation (n 108) Appendices A and C.

[115] Forster, Barraclough and Mijatov (n 104) 21.

[116] Natalie Akoorie, 'ACC Paid Mental Health Specialists $41.9m to Assess Claimants, Then Hundreds Lost Cover', *New Zealand Herald* (23 July 2020) <https://www.nzherald.co.nz/nz/news/article.cfm?c_id=1&objectid=12338340>.

[117] Cate Broughton, 'ACC Tells Minister Justice Issues Have Been Fixed, but Advocates Not so Confident', *Stuff.co.nz* (26 February 2019) <https://www.stuff.co.nz/national/health/110789966/acc-tells-minister-justice-issues-have-been-fixed-but-advocates-not-so-confident>.

Table 1 *continued*

Issue	Human rights point	Raised by whom?	NZ Government/ACC Scheme response	Current status
A lack of procedural fairness: improper and inconsistent approaches being used by non-judicial claims reviewers;[118] lack of independent oversight of the ACC Scheme.[119] This overall contributes to a perception by claimants of not being heard.[120]	Access to justice; breach of article 13 CRPD.	Acclaim 2014 and 2015 reports; Dean 2016 report.	New guidelines for the conduct of FairWay reviews to enable better tracking and triaging; transfer of FairWay to employee ownership to enhance perception of independence.[121]	As of 2020, there are two new providers of dispute resolution services for ACC claim reviews, alongside the existing FairWay: Independent Complaint and Review Authority Ltd, and Talk-Meet-Resolve.[122] The Acclaim Otago 2017 report recommended the introduction of a Personal Injury Commissioner to enhance transparency and increase public trust in ACC processes.[123] At the time of writing, no further proposals for an ACC or Personal Injury commissioner are being advanced.

118 For example, a perception that FairWay reviewers were biased towards the ACC and did not follow the principles of natural justice or take an investigative approach. Acclaim Otago (n 100) 50–52.

119 For example, the lack of a separate statutory commission or personal injury commissioner to oversee the ACC Scheme and its integrity, with reference to international human rights frameworks such as the CRPD. See Acclaim Otago and others (n 96) 23; Acclaim Otago (n 100) 169.

120 This includes the perception that justice is being done, because (for example) the legal issue is being heard by an impartial person and that there has been a fair hearing which will lead to a meaningful remedy. See Acclaim Otago (n 100) 2.

121 Ministry of Business Innovation and Employment and Accident Compensation Corporation (n 108) Appendix A; New Zealand Government, 'FairWay Change Positive for Staff and Customers' (2017) <https://www.beehive.govt.nz/release/fairway-change-positive-staff-and-customers>.

122 ACC, 'We're Changing How We Handle Customer Reviews' (2019) <https://www.acc.co.nz/newsroom/stories/were-changing-how-we-handle-customer-reviews/>. The director of Talk-Meet-Resolve is Warren Forster, a claimant advocate and co-author of the Acclaim Otago reports.

123 Forster, Barraclough and Mijatov (n 104) 48. See also Acclaim Otago, 'New Advocacy Service a Start, but Not the Solution' (2018) <https://www.scoop.co.nz/stories/PO1804/S00309/new-advocacy-service-a-start-but-not-the-solution.htm>.

Chapter 5. Human Rights, Access to Justice and Dispute Resolution

| Inadequate access to necessary legal information.[124] | Access to Justice, breach of article 13 CRPD. | Acclaim Otago 2014 and 2015 reports, Dean 2016 report. | ACC and FairWay produced clearer written and visual information about the how the disputes resolution process works. ACC provides funding to a legal information website to make ACC-related case law more easily accessible. FairWay produces anonymised case summaries. | Steps to increase access to legal information have indeed been completed, as per ACC and Government comments.[125] |

Source: Compiled by the author.

124 For example, access to case law for self-representing litigants. See Acclaim Otago (n 100) 174.
125 Ministry of Business Innovation and Employment and Accident Compensation Corporation (n 108).

From the table above, it is clear that significant efforts have been undertaken by ACC and the New Zealand government to address problematic areas that were infringing access to justice and the human rights of ACC claimants (as identified in Acclaim Otago and UN disability rights Committee reports). However, these efforts have obviously been limited to what was within the discretionary flexibility of the ACC Scheme's existing legislative framework, and can be best seen as an improvement of the status quo. The changes do not substantively engage with some of the larger issues, such as the human rights compliance of the overall scheme. More recent developments support this point. For example, in a 2018 review of their earlier recommendations, the UN disability rights Committee requested information about whether the ACC Scheme framework was taking a human rights-based approach.[126] The New Zealand government's 2019 response to this request did not directly answer whether a human rights approach was being taken. Rather, it placed emphasis on the improved legal navigation service and a general requirement that reviewers act in accordance 'with the principles of natural justice and exercise due diligence in decision-making'.[127]

The New Zealand government's response is very non-committal, as the ACC Scheme framework still lacks a general adherence to or acknowledgement of a human rights-based approach, let alone a specific reference to the issues raised in relation to the CRPD. The scheme changes that have resulted in some general enhancements are not a full satisfaction of the recommendation to explicitly follow a human rights-based approach. It remains to be seen how the UN disability rights Committee will respond on this point in its next periodic reporting cycle.

This non-committal position is unsurprising given the contextual mix of legislative and judicial factors in play. The combination of the comprehensive statutory bar in the ACC legislation (section 317), the limited jurisdiction of the courts in appeals on ACC-related issues (sections 161, 162 and 163) and the 'justified limitations' handbrake in the Bill of Rights Act (section 5) – combine to have a powerful general limitation on the ability to challenge access to justice issues on a human rights footing. This does not mean that it is impossible to enhance and better promote a human rights-based approach – after all, more than minimal efforts have been made by the government and ACC to address the Acclaim Otago and Dean report concerns. However, further legislative clarification is required on how human rights can be enshrined and protected within the scope of the ACC Scheme. For example, broader human rights issues

---

[126] Committee on the Rights of Persons with Disabilities, 'List of Issues Prior to Submission of the Combined Second and Third Periodic Reports of New Zealand, CRPD/C/NZL/QPR/2-3' (2018) para 12a.

[127] Committee on the Rights of Persons with Disabilities, 'Combined Second and Third Periodic Reports Submitted by New Zealand under Article 35 of the Convention Pursuant to the Optional Reporting Procedure, Due in 2019, CRPD/C/NZL/2-3' paras 119–123.

Chapter 5. Human Rights, Access to Justice and Dispute Resolution

will generally not be considered as a valid point of review in a District Court or High Court challenge to an ACC eligibility or quantum of compensation decision. This is because the scope of review that is given under the legislation to the District Court and the High Court is a very narrow one.

Crockett v Accident Compensation Corporation concerned a review of an assessment of ACC Scheme entitlements for the claimant's new hearing aids.[128] The appellant did not seek to challenge the calculation of the award or the assessment under the relevant regulations;[129] rather he challenged the validity of the regulations themselves and alleged that amendments made in 2010 to the main ACC Scheme legislation breached the Bill of Rights Act 1990. Mr Crockett also alleged that the regulations were inconsistent with New Zealand's obligations under the CRPD. Prior to the 2010 amendments, the appellant had simply been provided with new hearing aids by ACC. After the 2010 amendments, there was a minimum work-related threshold of injury required in order for ACC to intervene. The appeal was dismissed on the basis that the District Court was 'not an appropriate forum for such an investigation or debate', because the scope of the court's jurisdiction in ACC-related appeals was limited by the terms of section 161 of the ACC Scheme legislation itself.[130] Even if the court was not limited in this way, the judge said that a declaration that ACC's decision was *ultra vires* would not appear to help the appellant at all, because it would remove 'any statutory basis he has for the Corporation to contribute to the cost of his hearing aids'. The question of whether any particular limitation on the ACC's contribution to hearing aids was discriminatory was a matter for the legislature and the wider community, given 'the importance of the accident compensation system to New Zealand society generally'. This was because the ACC Scheme was 'the product of choices that have been made about what types of medical conditions can be covered or not covered, and if a condition is covered, the extent to which entitlements can be provided by [ACC]'.

Telford v Accident Compensation Corporation concerns an appeal of an ACC decision to decline an application for ongoing weekly compensation and suspend the appellant's ongoing entitlement to treatment.[131] The appellant, aged in his 50s, suffered a back injury at work. He had no history of back injury or pain. ACC declined his claim on the basis of medical evidence that the appellant had asymptomatic age-related pre-existing lumbar degeneration – an

---

[128]   *Crockett v Accident Compensation Corporation* [2018] NZACC 11.

[129]   Accident Compensation (Apportioning Entitlements for Hearing Loss) Regulations 2010. These set out the maximum amounts that ACC will contribute to the cost of hearing aids, including an assessment of how much of the hearing loss comes from ACC-eligible personal injury-related causes.

[130]   Accident Compensation Act 2001 s 161.

[131]   *Telford v Accident Compensation Corporation* [2016] NZACC 25.

Intersentia

329

asymptomatic condition that most people develop as they age.[132] Section 26(4)(a) of the Accident Compensation Act 2001 excludes cover for personal injury caused wholly or substantially by the aging process. There was no dispute about past cover for the income replacement costs and treatment associated with the initial acute injury. Aside from submissions on medico-legal points to do with lumbar injuries, the appellant argued that the ACC Scheme legislation should not be interpreted in a way that is inconsistent with the Human Rights Act 1993 – specifically, its prohibition against age discrimination.[133] The whole appeal was dismissed, but in relation to the human rights points in particular the judge noted that there was 'no evidence of any discrimination in a general sense based on age', but rather an appropriate application of the age-related exclusions within the ACC legislation (i.e., express legislative statements that injuries that were causatively age-related were excluded from cover). There was no scope for the Human Rights Act's general provisions to apply in this case.

In *Hardie v Accident Compensation Corporation*,[134] a woman who suffered serious 'medical misadventure' (now treatment injury) during a complicated caesarean section claimed that a rejection of her ACC Scheme claim for weekly income replacement discriminated against her as a woman on maternity leave. The appellant's injury meant she could not return to work as planned after her maternity leave, so she took voluntary unpaid leave from her employment. When she made a claim to ACC for weekly compensation on the basis of her incapacity, this was declined because she was on unpaid leave at the time of her application and therefore not entitled to earnings-related compensation. The appellant's primary submission was that the relevant ACC Scheme provisions should have been interpreted more generously.[135] Her secondary submission was that the relevant provision was discriminatory to her as a woman on maternity leave and was in conflict with the Bill of Rights Act 1990. The appellant argued that the provision should be interpreted 'so as to give it a non-discriminatory meaning'. The court rejected the appellant's claim. On the Bill of Rights point, His Honour found that the relevant provision in the ACC Scheme legislation was not discriminatory against pregnant women in particular (it would affect all persons on unpaid leave). Even if it were discriminatory, he found that section 4 of the Bill of Rights Act applied. Section 4 states that no court may find another statutory provision ineffective or inapplicable 'by reason only that the provision is inconsistent' with the Bill of Rights Act.

---

[132] Specifically, asymptomatic pre-existing lumbar spondylosis.
[133] Human Rights Act 1993 s 21.
[134] *Hardie v Accident Compensation Corporation* [2002] NZACC 256.
[135] Specifically, that the statutory requirement that a claimant be an earner 'immediately' before the application for weekly earnings compensation be interpreted generously. There was a difference of 21 days between the appellant starting unpaid leave and her compensation application to ACC.

Chapter 5. Human Rights, Access to Justice and Dispute Resolution

In *Freeborn v Accident Rehabilitation and Compensation Insurance Corporation* there was consideration of the relevance and limitation of the Bill of Rights Act protection against self-incrimination in the context of an ACC claim dispute.[136] The appellant was receiving weekly ACC Scheme compensation for an injury, but his payments were stopped after ACC received an anonymous tip-off about the appellant's behaviour and eligibility for compensation, and after the authority conducted further investigations. The appellant was invited to a number of meetings with ACC staff, which he attended with his lawyer and in which he declined to answer any questions. However the appellant did agree to sign statutory declarations for ACC about his situation, which ultimately formed the basis of a criminal prosecution against him. The appellant argued that these statutory declarations were inadmissible evidence because of *inter alia* the section 27 Bill of Rights Act protection against self-incrimination.[137] ACC, for its part, argued that it was entitled, under the relevant statutory provision that was in force at that time, to obtain information from claimants, including statutory declarations. It also argued that it had followed principles of natural justice in its dealings with the appellant. The judge, dismissing the appeal, stated that

> 'the policy of the Act is that only those entitled to compensation receive compensation. The corporation is heavily dependent upon the honesty and integrity of those who claim to be entitled to the payment of taxpayer moneys. The [ACC Scheme statutory processes] are designed to achieve that end. Parliament must be taken to [be] ... fully conscious of the [Bill of Rights Act]'.

His Honour concluded that even if there were a conflict, the ACC legislation was a 'reasonable limitation' on the section 27 protection against self-incrimination in the Bill of Rights Act. This position was recently upheld in another case with a very similar set of facts.[138]

The decisions in *Crockett* and *Telford* are unsurprising and broadly consistent with the general deference given by the judiciary, in Westminster-rooted systems, to the legislature's clearly expressed statutory intent, even on human rights issues. *Freeborn* indicates that the courts will generously presume in the legislature an intention to ensure compliance with the Bill of Rights, even without any express statements supporting that view in the ACC Scheme legislation. *Hardie* confirms

---

[136] *Freeborn v Accident Rehabilitation and Compensation Insurance Corporation* [1998] NZHC 194.
[137] Section 27(1) Bill of Rights Act 1990 states: 'Every person has the right to the observance of the principles of natural justice by any tribunal or other public authority which has the power to make a determination in respect of that person's rights, obligations, or interests protected or recognised by law.'
[138] *Sinclair v Accident Compensation Corporation* [2015] NZACC 231.

Intersentia

331

that the Bill of Rights Act will not be a 'safety valve' against poor or unclear wording of the ACC Scheme that leads to an unfair or discriminatory result.

This interpretation in these cases is logical given the tradition of human rights law application in New Zealand (and other common law jurisdictions like Australia). However, the effect remains that human rights conflicts in particular do not have an obvious location for judicial analysis and consideration as part and parcel of a person's broader request to review a decision about their ACC Scheme entitlements. This conclusion is further reinforced by the way that ACC-related human rights issues – in particular privacy issues – have been handled via the Human Rights Review Tribunal (HRRT) and appeals from that forum. This is the one specific tribunal to which access is still permitted under the section 317 bar, albeit in very limited circumstances.[139] These circumstances include a person with a grievance in relation to a healthcare or disability provider, perhaps brought on their behalf by an independent Health and Disability Commissioner staff member called the Director of Proceedings.[140] They also include civil proceedings arising from complaints to or an inquiry by the Human Rights Commission, in a limited and specified way.[141] The HRRT also has jurisdiction over Privacy Act related complaints, bringing ACC handling of claimant data, and potential human rights breaches associated with that handling,[142] within that tribunal's purview.

Harrild v Director of Proceedings[143] was a tragic but important case before the Court of Appeal concerning a claim originally made to the HRTT in relation to a stillborn baby. The parents made a complaint to the Health and Disability Commissioner in relation to the appellant obstetrician, claiming that he *inter alia* did not communicate properly with them and negatively impacted their dignity. The Director of Proceedings sought pecuniary and non-pecuniary damages on the parents' behalf, via the specific carve-out allowed under section 317(4)(a) of the Accident Compensation Act 2001. The appellant successfully argued that the claim was actually barred by section 317, because it was in fact a claim for a personal injury suffered by the mother because of the foetus' death. The importance of the case for accident compensation law generally centres mainly on the sensitive issue of whether the death of a foetus is a personal injury or not (and an injury to whom), but for our purposes here the

---

[139] Accident Compensation Act 2001 s 317(4).

[140] Health and Disability Commissioner Act 1994 ss 50 and 51; Accident Compensation Act 2001 s 317(4)(a).

[141] Human Rights Act 1993 ss 92B, 92E, 92R, 122, 122A, 122B, 123 and/or 124. Accident Compensation Act 2001 s 317(4)(b).

[142] Privacy as a human right is protected by article 12 of the United Nations Declaration of Human Rights 1948 and article 17 of the International Covenant on Civil and Political Rights 1966.

[143] *Harrild v Director of Proceedings* [2003] 3 NZLR 289.

key interest is the comprehensive power of the statutory bar in a human rights and dignity context. This is the case even where a claim is made out in relation to the specific impact of a defendant's actions on human dignity and breach of patient care rights, within the specific carve-out allowed to the HRTT. If the faintest scent of a claim for personal injury-related compensatory damages can be detected, the claim will be barred. For our purposes, this case shows how limited the bandwidth is for exploring human rights issues in an ACC context, even before a dedicated human rights tribunal.

Vivash v Accident Compensation Corporation is a recent HRRT decision concerning ACC errors and withholding of the claimant's historical claim and medical data dating back to the 1980s. The claimant requested a copy of ACC's file on him from the 1980s, but ACC claimed that it had been destroyed. In relation to one subset of information, this turned out to be false and ACC admitted (late in the proceedings) its error. The claimant alleged that the destruction or unavailability of this data breached relevant privacy laws. ACC acknowledged its error and offered a low amount of damages. The HRRT imposed a much higher level of damages (NZ$50,000) to better compensate the impact and on the feelings, dignity and privacy of the claimant. Given the complexity of the claimant's ongoing injury, the court noted that access to this historical information was essential to both the claimant and ACC.[144]

Williams v Accident Compensation Corporation[145] concerned an erroneous use of medical data by ACC that lead to a claimant's weekly compensation payments being stopped, and an interference with his privacy in a way that caused humiliation, loss of dignity and injury to feelings. ACC staff had misread a medical report about the claimant and concluded that it said he was able to return to his pre-injury employment. The claimant received a letter on Christmas Eve stating that his weekly compensation payments were being immediately stopped. Some months later ACC realised its error, contacted the claimant and backdated the payments. ACC also issued an apology. The claimant sought damages for ACC's actions on the grounds that there had been an unlawful interference with his privacy.[146] ACC had admitted liability and apologised to the claimant, but the issue was the calculation of any damages. ACC argued that it had taken immediate steps to rectify the error when it was discovered,

---

[144]   *Vivash v Accident Compensation Corporation* [2020] NZHRRT 16, [43.1].

[145]   *Williams v Accident Compensation Corporation* [2017] NZHRRT 26.

[146]   Specifically, the claimant alleged a breach of Principle 8 of section 6 of the Privacy Act 1993 which states: 'An agency that holds personal information shall not use that information without taking such steps (if any) as are, in the circumstances, reasonable to ensure that, having regard to the purpose for which the information is proposed to be used, the information is accurate, up to date, complete, relevant, and not misleading.' The broader scope of section 6 is in line with the terms of article 17 of the International Covenant on Civil and Political Rights.

Intersentia

333

and pointed out that ACC was a large organisation that processed significant volumes of data every day. The claimant focused on the intensely negative impact the erroneous decision had had on his daily life, including stress, anxiety and financial problems. The Tribunal focused on the point 'that the apology, on its own or even combined with the declaration of interference, is not sufficient to adequately compensate for what followed as a consequence of the interference with privacy', and made an award of damages that only modestly acknowledged ACC's efforts to remedy the situation. This case showcases the significant power that ACC – as a large public authority – holds in relation to citizens' private medical data, and the severe impact that an even innocent error can have on the life of a claimant. For comparative law purposes, it is worth noting that the damages ultimately awarded in this case – NZ$7,500 – are probably quite low by European standards.

Vivash and *Williams* are two useful decisions that reveal that the HRRT will give serious weight to human rights-associated impacts of ACC's handling of individuals' private medical data. There is recognition in both cases of the essential nature of the private medico-legal data to the claimants for the ongoing management of their health situation and its effect on their wider lives. There is also a clear identification of the power imbalance between ACC and individual claimants that will not be mitigated by an argument of innocent occasional human error in the midst of processing large volumes of individual data. These cases therefore show the power to hold ACC to account, in relation to privacy-related human rights issues at least, in a specific tribunal. However the HRRT's power is not a broad one, and will always be subject to the strict and suppressive limits of the statutory bar. This is illustrated by *Harrild*. The relevant defendant in that case was ultimately the medical practitioner and not ACC – and the inference, however slight, that the claimant parents were seeking to circumvent the statutory bar on compensatory damages was enough for the Court of Appeal to snuff out their claim. These cases show that there is greater potential for individual claimants to hold ACC itself to account in the way that it handles claims and private data rather than pursuing other parties causatively associated with an ACC Scheme covered injury. Although in *Williams* the damages awarded were not compensatory at all (because ACC had backdated the claimant's weekly compensation payments when it rectified its error), the damages awarded in *Vivash* had at least a partial compensatory nature. This scope is consistent with the strict view that New Zealand courts have generally taken towards to the interpretation of the statutory bar in other cases (for example in the *DePuy* litigation) but it indicates a limitation on the possibility for claimants to litigate human rights breaches where the relevant defendant is someone other than ACC.

Two further HRRT cases illustrate the possibility for claimants to request that the tribunal examine human rights-related infringements under the ACC Scheme.

Heads v Attorney-General concerned age discrimination.[147] The question was whether age discrimination occurred because of the ACC Scheme statutory requirement for surviving spouses who are eligible for general superannuation (a pension benefit that is equivalent to a universal basic income) to choose between ACC surviving spouse compensation and superannuation.[148] The claimant's wife had been killed by a truck driver while crossing the road outside her workplace, and the claimant, Mr Heads, was accordingly a recipient of ACC surviving spouse related benefits. The claimant alleged that the requirement to choose between surviving spouse compensation and superannuation was unfair, because had the accident not occurred then the couple would have continued to receive the deceased's work wages *and* the retired claimant's superannuation payments. The claimant sought a declaration that this situation was a breach of section 19 of the Bill of Rights Act 1990[149] that was not permissibly justified (section 5). The Crown argued that the social security legislation underpinning superannuation payments was premised on individuals not receiving two publicly-funded payments for the same purpose, which also explained the connecting restriction under the ACC Scheme legislation. Failing that, the Crown argued that that legislation was permissibly justified legislation under section 5 of the Bill of Rights Act 1990. The HRRT rejected the former argument because it was possible for surviving spouses to claim both superannuation and ACC surviving spouse compensation for 12 months before making the election required by statute. The HRRT also concluded that the claimant was being treated differently than a person in the same situation of a different age, and he had suffered a material disadvantage (the loss of NZ$75,000 worth of superannuation payments) as a result. On the latter point – whether this was justified discrimination – the court found that the Crown could not show that the general requirements and policy intent that the ACC Scheme be sustainable generally had any specific legislative application or purpose in relation to people like Mr Head (a superannuant surviving spouse of a fatal injury victim). In other words, there was no legislative justification for him being discriminated against. This situation was estimated to affect a very small number of claimants (less than 50), so HRRT said the financial sustainability arguments put forward by the Crown were also not plausible. This case directly resulted in the relevant choice requirement clause of the ACC Scheme being repealed by Parliament.[150] The only remedy available to the claimant in this case was a declaration of

---

[147] *Heads v Attorney-General* [2015] NZHRRT 12.
[148] Accident Compensation Act 2001 Sch 1, Part 4, cl 66 (repealed).
[149] Section 19(1) states that 'Everyone has the right to freedom from discrimination on the grounds of discrimination in the Human Rights Act 1993'. The relevant ground of discrimination for this case in the Human Rights Act 1993 is the prohibition against age-related discrimination under s 21(1)(i).
[150] Accident Compensation Amendment Act 2019.

inconsistency between the relevant ACC Scheme provision and section 19 of the Bill of Rights Act 1990.

Alderson v Accident Compensation Corporation[151] concerned a question about whether the unique nature of the ACC Scheme was discriminatory to immigrants who would not expect such a scheme to exist or were disadvantaged compared to New Zealanders in knowing about what kinds of entitlements or options were available. The British immigrant claimant, when moving from ordinary employment to self-employment, had chosen the basic package of ACC weekly earnings compensation for self-employed people. It was only when he suffered an injury that he discovered that he would have received more generous compensation had he chosen one of ACC's add-on packages for self-employed people. Aside from issues to do with the lack of specificity of the grounds of his complaint (the claimant was a self-represented litigant), the HRRT said that it was not clear where the border would lie between an immigrant actually disadvantaged by a lack of information and an immigrant who had lived in New Zealand for a reasonable length of time and who could thus be assumed to have discovered the way in which ACC might apply to himself or herself. Specifically:

> 'We think it is difficult to suggest that the ACC has a human rights-related and statutory obligation – one in respect of which damages for breach can be awarded – to tell the plaintiff when he arrived in New Zealand ... that if ever he was to consider becoming self-employed he really ought also to think about taking out extra cover for personal injury'.

Further, immigration status was not a ground of discrimination under New Zealand human rights law and did not appear to have a logical equivalence with ethnicity. The claim was ultimately struck out for lack of specificity.[152]

Despite their very different facts, *Heads* and *Alderson* illustrate some broad differences between what will be a successful challenge to the ACC Scheme regime on a human rights basis, and what will not. In order to show a breach of human rights law, a plaintiff will need to specifically identify clearly defined discrimination that is not otherwise justified by way of clear and exact policy or legislative expression. The broader and more general the discrimination is alleged to be, the less likely that the plaintiff's claim will be successful. This is because broader claims are more likely to be caught within the general ambit of the legislative choice and purpose of the ACC Scheme. The plaintiff in *Alderson* was arguing discrimination on the basis of the general policy differences between the ACC Scheme and customary insurance and social security structures found

---

[151] *Alderson v Accident Compensation Corporation* [2009] NZHRRT 33.
[152] However, the HRRT gave the plaintiff the option to lodge a more specific and clearly articulated claim.

Chapter 5. Human Rights, Access to Justice and Dispute Resolution

in other jurisdictions. The claimant in *Heads* was arguing that were was a very specific type of discrimination contained in a specific legislative clause, which was not supported by the rest of the ACC Scheme framework. Also important in the *Heads* case was the fact that the plaintiff had suffered a substantial loss compared to other individuals in similar situations. Similarly, specific breaches of privacy law will also lead to unlawful infringement of human rights principles in an ACC context, as evidenced by *Vivash* and *Williams*. However a broader claim, particularly one that is against the causative defendant and not ACC itself, runs the risk of falling into the section 317 statutory bar trap, as in *Harrild*.

ACC was specifically questioned for this research project on whether, since the Miriam Dean QC report, ACC had undertaken an assessment of whether the statutory entitlements to compensation and the relevant litigation prohibitions are consistent with the Human Rights Act 1993 and the Bill of Rights Act 1990. ACC responded as follows:[153]

> 'ACC would not see it as its role to undertake this kind of assessment. ACC is the manager/administrator of the scheme, but it is the Ministry of Business, Innovation and Employment (MBIE) which is responsible for accident compensation legislation and for assessing/dealing with HRA and BORA issues. It's noteworthy that MBIE (and its predecessor the Department of Labour) has managed a number of challenges through both the Human Rights Commission and the Human Rights Review Tribunal. An example is the challenge to age cessation of weekly compensation in Heads v Attorney-General. ... The Crown decided not to appeal this decision'.

The ACC response above and its actions since the Dean report seem to be contextually logical and balanced. Within the context of the wider legal system and its approach to human rights law, the opinion of the fund itself as to its compliance or otherwise with human rights legislation is largely irrelevant: it is subject at all times to parliamentary intent and simply executes the legislative framework that it is tasked with. Although it may be best placed to assess whether its framework is compliant with human rights law and affects access to justice, it has not been directly tasked with this responsibility. Where directed to make improvements for the sake of human rights law compliance and access to justice, the ACC organisation has attempted this as extensively as possible within the legislative possibilities afforded to it.

Overall, it is possible to conclude that the intersections between human rights law and the ACC Scheme will in general be quite generous to the purpose and intent of the no-fault comprehensive compensation fund. This is for a number of reasons, including: the non-fundamental nature of human rights law in New Zealand and in particular the handbrake imposed by section 5 of the

---

[153] Response to questionnaire, received 8 October 2020.

Intersentia

Bill of Rights Act 1990; the reluctance (typical of a common law jurisdiction) of judges to critique express or clearly implied legislative intent; the limited scope and venue for review of ACC decisions and actions on a human rights basis; and, most importantly, the powerful statutory bar on virtually all court proceedings associated with personal injury. There are narrow possibilities for seeking a declaration of inconsistency for a human rights breach via the HRRT. Although ACC itself does not make express reference to human rights principles and processes in its decision-making and activities, it is important to note that it and the New Zealand government are not resistant to improving the Scheme's compliance with human rights. The aftermath of *Heads* shows that the legislature will be responsive and amend the ACC Scheme to avoid unnecessary specific discrimination. The measures undertaken by ACC and the New Zealand government since the Dean 2016 report also show that significant efforts will be made to improve intersections between the ACC Scheme and human rights principles – but only up to a point. Further development is limited by the wider context of the New Zealand human rights environment and traditions (which is at its core, not dissimilar to the Australian standoffishness towards human rights) and the phrasing of the legislation itself. It is also impossible for ACC or the legislature to enshrine further human rights compliance in the scheme without reckoning with the core incoherency of having a comprehensive and humane compensation scheme in place for personal injury, but a sparse and inadequate social welfare scheme in place for other misfortunes (as illustrated by *Trevethick*).

The evidence of its operation and case law shows that the ACC Scheme is not fundamentally irreconcilable with a stronger human rights framework, if the intersections between ACC law and human rights law were more clearly defined by the legislature. However that kind of intersection is a next evolution away from where the ACC Scheme legislation currently stands. Better human rights intersections and more clarity would probably benefit ACC itself and its claimants, but would almost certainly require a significant statutory renewal. Therefore, it can be concluded that any inconsistencies between human rights law and ACC law are primarily to do with broader contextual issues in the application of a human rights framework to New Zealand, rather than the ACC Scheme itself.

2.3. CANADA

Canada is a federal parliamentary constitutional democracy. Like Australia and New Zealand, Canada is a legal descendant of the United Kingdom and therefore shares a common legislative ancestry with those two jurisdictions. However in relation to private law matters, Canada is a mixed civil and common law jurisdiction. Public law, criminal law and federal law matters all

Chapter 5. Human Rights, Access to Justice and Dispute Resolution

follow the dominant common law tradition in all Canadian provinces. In the Québec province however, private law matters follow that province's civil law tradition, which is historically derived from French law.[154] Canada's constitution is a combination of codified statutes,[155] uncodified traditions and conventions (which is similar to New Zealand) and relevant judicial rulings about constitutional topics. The Canadian Supreme Court has ruled that the right of access to justice and to the courts is a constitutional right (at least in the context of court fees),[156] although there is not a clear and precise expression of this right in the relevant legislation. Therefore, although Canada (and Québec specifically) can be said to have fundamental guarantees of human rights (which will be explained and discussed in more detail in the next section), the framework is not as comprehensive as what is available in other jurisdictions with fundamental human rights frameworks. On the specific subject of access to justice or access to the courts, there also remain specific uncertainties about the application of human rights frameworks to no-fault comprehensive compensation funds.

2.3.1. Historical and Contemporary Context

The constitutional timeframes of Canada are very similar to those of New Zealand. A constitution statute was passed in the mid-1800s by the UK Parliament, giving a formal framework to the federal and provincial structure of Canada.[157] That Act specifically delegated power to the provinces over property and civil rights.[158] Diceyan influences were also dominant in Canada at this time, and so the creation of constitutional power in Canada was therefore focused generally on the division of legislative powers between the federal level and the provinces.[159] A number of specific political crises and civil rights movements in the twentieth century motivated public discourse about human rights and

---

[154] The Civil Code of Québec came into force in 1866, and was directly inspired by the French Civil Code of 1804. Codification of French-style civil law was perceived at that time as a necessary protection against Anglo-American legal encroachment in the province, and a protection of the French cultural heritage of the Québécois. See Jean-Louis Baudouin and Allen M Linden, 'Canada' in Britt Weyts (ed), *The International Encyclopaedia for Tort Law* (Wolters Kluwer 2015) 21–23.

[155] The Constitution Act 1982, the Constitution Act 1867, the Canada Act 1982, the Canadian Charter of Rights and Freedoms, and a number of other important historical documents and legislative instruments which are listed in section 52(2) of the Constitution Act 1982.

[156] *Trial Lawyers Association of British Columbia v British Columbia (Attorney General)* 2014 SCC 59.

[157] The Constitution Act 1867, originally known as the British North America Act 1867.

[158] ibid s 92(13).

[159] David Schneiderman, 'A.V. Dicey, Lord Watson, and the Law of the Canadian Constitution in the Late Nineteenth Century' (1998) 16 *Law and History Review* 495.

Intersentia

339

the enactment of numerous provincial human rights statutes to protect citizens from infringements on their civil liberties by the federal state.[160] At the federal level, the Canadian Human Rights Act 1977 enshrined anti-discrimination protections in relation to federally regulated activities.

The 1980s saw the most significant revolution forward in human rights law as applied to the Canadian territory. Confirmation that Canada alone had jurisdiction over its own laws came with the passing of the Constitution Act 1982 by the Westminster Parliament. This statute included the passage of Canadian Charter of Rights and Freedoms (the CCRF). The CCRF guarantees civil and political rights for Canadian citizens and residents, including specific legal rights that are centred on the citizen or resident's interaction with the justice system.[161] The CCRF has relevance to New Zealand, as it formed the basis of what eventually became the (non-fundamental) New Zealand Bill of Rights Act 1990.

Compared with Australia and New Zealand, the Canadian legislature has, in recent years, undertaken extensive work to ensure legislative frameworks are compliant with a human rights-based approach. This has included a litigation strategy review to end appeals and litigation positions not consistent with the CCRF or 'Canadian values' and funding test cases to clarify certain aspects of human rights law.[162] However, the fact remains that there is no clearly defined access to court or access to justice right within the relevant legislation. The best current available definition is that individuals should have 'reasonable and effective access to courts of law and other tribunals and the opportunity to obtain legal services from qualified professionals'.[163] However, this has not translated into either ready access to funded legal advice for potential plaintiffs or easy access to the courts.[164]

Individual Canadian provinces have their own human rights frameworks too. The Québec province was actually the first Canadian province to have some kind of human rights underpinning, culminating in the protection of

---

[160] For example, occurrences of anti-Semitism and other forms of discrimination in employment, property law and commercial freedoms. In the late 1940s, the existence of a suspected communist spy-ring led the federal government to invoke wartime powers to detain, interrogate, and prosecute suspects. The October Crisis in the 1970s involved the federal government suspending citizens' civil liberties via the War Measures Act 1927 in response to Québec nationalist activities. See Dominique Clément, 'Human Rights Law' (*Canada's Human Rights History*) <https://historyofrights.ca/history/human-rights-law/6/>.

[161] Canadian Charter of Rights and Freedoms ss 7–14.

[162] Government of Canada, 'National Report Submitted in Accordance with Paragraph 5 of the Annex to Human Rights Council Resolution 16/21' (2018) paras 7–8 <https://documents-dds-ny.un.org/doc/UNDOC/GEN/G18/081/95/PDF/G1808195.pdf?OpenElement>.

[163] *Christie v British Columbia (Attorney General)*, 2005 BCCA 631 at para 30.

[164] Micah B Rankin, 'Access To Justice and the Institutional Limits of Independent Courts' (2012) 30 *Windsor Yearbook of Access to Justice* 101; Melina Buckley, 'Searching for the Constitutional Core of Access to Justice' (2008) 42 *Supreme Court Law Review* 567.

Chapter 5. Human Rights, Access to Justice and Dispute Resolution

religious freedom for the ethnically French Catholic Québécois in the eighteenth century.[165] In the private law sphere, the Québec legislature closely followed social security developments in France and Germany in the nineteenth and twentieth centuries, specifically the worker insurance and the curtailments of tort law that those legislative developments entailed. The establishment of the SAAQ scheme was a further significant step that preferred a risk-based approach to the allocation of transport injury damages,[166] balancing the community sharing of risk with the individual curtailment of any possible access to court rights that might have existed in the private sphere (even though they are not specifically articulated). Meanwhile, the Québec Charter of Human Rights and Freedoms (Québec Charter) is a fundamental human rights framework in that province for civil and political rights, with the relevant judicial rights centred mainly on the rights of individuals facing criminal charges.[167] It is worth noting, however, that there is not necessarily equivalent protection of rights under the CCRF and the Québec Charter.[168] Manitoba also has a local human rights framework in the form of the Human Rights Code 1987, but it is not expressed as a fundamental piece of legislation. It provides a basic level of protection against discrimination for Manitoba residents, and also enshrines education functions.

2.3.2. The Intersection with Issues Relevant to No-Fault Comprehensive Compensation Funds

As in Australia and New Zealand, human rights issues and compliance were not a prominent feature of discussion during the legislative establishment of either the SAAQ or the MPI. The chair of the Québec investigating commission was an actuary, which may explain an overwhelming focus in that report on the actuarial costs of transport accidents and not on the human rights implications of a choice between a fault-based system and a strict liability or no-fault system. The Kopstein Report that preceded the establishment of the modern MPI scheme said that 'constitutional questions concerning the validity of a pure no-fault plan are open.'[169] This is in spite of the fact that the Québec Charter was in force at the time of the SAAQ being established, and the CCRF and Manitoba Human Rights Code being in force at the time of the MPI being established.

An important case, decided almost immediately after the establishment of the MPI scheme, directly considered whether a no-fault scheme was an

---

[165] Québec Act 1774.

[166] Baudouin and Linden (n 154) paras 32–36.

[167] Chapter I, Fundamental Freedoms and Rights – Charter of human rights and freedoms (c 12).

[168] Mélanie Samson, *Le Droit à l'égalité Dans l'accès Aux Biens et Aux Services : L'originalité Des Garanties Offertes Dans La Charte Québécoise*, vol 38 (2008).

[169] Robert L Kopstein, 'The Report of the Autopac Review Commission – Volume 1' (1988) 30.

Intersentia

341

A Comparative Law Analysis of No-Fault Comprehensive Compensation Funds

intended limitation on the right of access to the courts. *McMillan v Rural Municipality of Thompson*[170] was a case centred on the legal question of whether it was possible for an automobile injury victim (who was covered by and had received compensation from the MPI) to also bring a case in negligence against the defendant municipality. The plaintiffs had suffered serious injuries when their automobile plunged into an unmarked gap in a road caused by the washing out of a bridge (and the municipality's alleged negligence in failing to properly maintain the bridge). The municipality argued that the plaintiffs' negligence claim was extinguished by virtue of the statutory bar within the MPI legislation.[171] The judge at the initial stage allowed this tort claim on the basis that the plaintiffs' injuries were not caused by the use of an automobile. Rather, it 'was, for the purposes of this motion, the negligence of the defendant. The use of the automobile was merely fortuitous.'[172] The Manitoba Court of Appeal, when overturning this decision, said that if the plaintiffs' claim was allowed to proceed it would lead to serious consequences for the MPI Scheme and illogical, unfair results that did not match legislative intent.[173] Helper J.A. noted that

> 'It was not the legislative intent to introduce a cumbersome two-step system which necessitates a trial on the issue of negligence in all accidents involving an automobile and thus perpetuates the uncertainty of the result for a victim. Nor could it have been the legislative intent to provide different remedies for victims depending upon the proximate cause of an accident.'

Although this case does not reference the CCRF or the Manitoban Human Rights Code, it is an express judicial statement confirming the extinguishment of any common law rights to access the courts within the scope of the newly passed MPI legislation.

The more recent decision by the Canadian Supreme Court in *Godbout v Pagé*, that was previously discussed at in Chapter 3 is a logical confirmation of an equivalent kind of extinguishment within the SAAQ Scheme.[174] However, this should be contrasted with a recent class action against the Québec government, the City of Montréal and the SAAQ, concerning whether individuals trapped in their vehicles during a blizzard (due to the alleged failure of the city to properly clear snow) should be entitled to extra compensation.[175] This entitlement was

---

[170] *McMillan v Thompson (Rural Municipality)* (1997) 144 DLR (4th) 53; *McMillan v Rural Municipality of Thompson* [1996] 6 WWR 563.
[171] The Manitoba Public Insurance Corporation Act s 72.
[172] *McMillan v Rural Municipality of Thompson* (n 170) para 51.
[173] Jeffrey Schnoor, 'No-Fault Automobile Insurance in Manitoba : An Overview. Les Cahiers de Droit' (1998) 39 *Les Cahiers de droit* 335, 340–342.
[174] *Godbout v Pagé et al* (2017) SCC 18. See also *Downer v Attorney General of Quebec* 2019 QCCS 1280.
[175] *Beauchamp c Procureure générale du Québec* 2017 QCCS 5184.

342

Intersentia

based on the Québec Charter right to freedom and integrity of the person.[176] The Québec government and SAAQ argued initially that the scope of the SAAQ scheme meant that the class claimants were only entitled to ordinary SAAQ compensation in relation to the incident. However, the government and the SAAQ ultimately agreed to enter into a class action settlement,[177] so a determination of the human rights intersections (as they relate to SAAQ) was not made.[178]

The important decision of *J.A. v SAAQ*,[179] which was discussed earlier, directly concerned a human rights intersection – namely, whether the exclusion of snowmobile accidents from the scope of the SAAQ scheme breached the right to equality enshrined by article 15 of the CCRF. The reader may recall that the appellant plaintiff in *J.A.* was a child who had been catastrophically injured by a snowmobile, in a northern region of Québec where snowmobiles are the default mode of transport for a significant portion of the year. The appellant argued that because

> 'snowmobiles and ATVs are the main means of transportation for the Inuit people of Nunavik and are essential in maintaining their lifestyle and because the [SAAQ statute] aims to compensate road accident victims, it follows that the [SAAQ statute] discriminates against snowmobilers from northern Québec in comparison to drivers from the rest of the province'.[180]

The Québec Court of Appeal found that the relevant SAAQ provision[181] did not breach article 15 CCRF in either purpose or effect because:

a. Nunavik residents were entitled to the same SAAQ cover as all other Québec residents, and there was no entitlement in any Québec resident to cover for snowmobile injuries. No-fault compensation for snowmobile-related injuries was not a benefit required by law.[182] A finding otherwise would require an entire rearrangement of the SAAQ framework.

b. Previous article 15 case law said it was 'not open to the court to rewrite the terms of the legislative program except to the extent the benefit is being made available or the burden is being imposed on a discriminatory basis'.[183]

---

[176] Quebec Charter Art 1.

[177] *Beauchamp c Procureure générale du Québec*, Entente de règlement avec la Procureure générale du Québec, No: 500-06-000853-172, 14 March 2019.

[178] However, the class action against the City of Montréal itself is ongoing – see Trudel Johnston & Lespérance, 'Vehicles Stuck on Highway 13/ Snowstorm of March 14th, 2017' <https://tjl. quebec/en/class-actions/vehicles-stuck-on-highway-13-snowstorm-of-march-14-2017/>.

[179] *J.A. v Société de l'assurance automobile du Québec* 2010 QCCA 1328.

[180] ibid 20.

[181] Automobile Insurance Act (Québec) s 10(3).

[182] *Auton v British Columbia (Attorney General)* [2004] 3 SCR 657.

[183] *Hodge v Canada* [2004] 3 RCS 357, note 18 at [26].

The Court of Appeal said that the appellant's arguments would require such a 're-writing' to change the meaning of automobile as it applied to Nunavik residents. Further, the appellant's isolation and location of residence in Nunavik were not actually prohibited grounds of discrimination under article 15.

From a moral perspective, the decision in *J.A. v SAAQ* is clearly troublesome. Taking an ordinary everyday interpretation of the facts, the use of a snowmobile in Nunavik is for practical purposes equivalent to the use of an automobile in other parts of Québec. However, the decision is logical (although obviously tragic for the appellant) in the context of the Canadian courts' interpretation of how article 15 should be applied. It is also logical within the context of comparison with the other three funds that are the subject of this study: a clear legislative statement of what is a qualifying injury for no-fault compensation will naturally involve the exclusion of other injuries (no matter how similar or different they may be). The possibility of these exclusions was directly grappled with by the legislature at the time of the SAAQ Scheme's creation – which was bound at that time by the Québec Charter and its equivalent protections of equality.[184] The very specific description of what is a qualifying injury (expressly rather than vaguely described in the SAAQ and other funds' establishing legislation) is confirmation of that legislative intent. Now, the court in *J.A. v SAAQ* was of course bound by precedent to not re-write or significantly alter the legislative purpose of the SAAQ Scheme – this is the wider human rights context that applies to all interpretations of article 15 CCRF, not just those involving no-fault comprehensive compensation funds. There is therefore coherency in this judgment, from the perspective of the substantive interpretation of human rights law as it applies to compensation funds. The size of the SAAQ scheme (compared to, for example, a smaller no-fault compensation fund) means that a finding that there had been discrimination – and that the entire SAAQ Scheme should therefore be changed accordingly – could be perceived as actual judicial overreach into legislative power (rather than a check on those powers).

The sense of unfairness that one is left with after reading this decision (that the Québec Court of Appeal shared, noting its sympathy with the appellant) is because of the harsh vagaries of a tort-based default approach being aroused within the context of human rights-based pleadings, where the focus is on equivalent treatment of similar victims. The case presents a direct contrast between a traditional fault-based approach to loss and a no-fault system. We feel that the result is unjust, yet the decision in this case is actually sound on the basis of Canadian human rights legislation, ordinary statutory interpretation and authoritative case law precedent. Is the feeling of unjustness therefore

---

[184] Québec Charter Art 10. The appellant did not rely upon this statute in her pleadings.

Chapter 5. Human Rights, Access to Justice and Dispute Resolution

because the principle *casum sentit dominus* is actually inherently unjust for personal injury victims who face an insolvent tortfeasor? The fact of the matter is that appellant would not have had to bring her case against SAAQ at all, had the owner or driver of the snowmobile been insured (as they were legally required to be, but were not). It is not the responsibility of human rights law to fix the problems associated with the intersection between itself and default tort law principles, or perhaps the failure of the Québec legislature to implement an insurer of last resort fund for snowmobile accidents (as part of the wider insurance and compensation landscape). If we are still left feeling that the result in this case is unjust, then that is an argument in favour of a scheme expansion to cover *all* personal injury (like the scope of the ACC Scheme).

Another direct human rights intersection can be found in *Downer v Attorney General of Québec*.[185] This case was discussed earlier, in Chapter 3. In *Downer*, the plaintiffs alleged negligence by provincial road maintenance staff and sought punitive damages for the infringement of their right to life and security guaranteed and enabled by sections 7 and 24 of the Canadian Charter of Rights and Freedoms. Both the Superior Court and the Court of Appeal found no legal basis for these claims. The plaintiffs' injuries and the late Mrs Downer's death were already covered by the scope of the SAAQ scheme, but the plaintiffs sought extra exemplary or punitive damages of C$4 million. The Superior Court found that the 'tight' scope of the no-fault comprehensive scheme precluded the ability to claim exemplary damages, and this was confirmed by the Court of Appeal. The plaintiffs argued that this exclusionary scope of the civil damages bar was impermissible under the CCRF. The Superior Court and the Court of Appeal found that negligent road signage, which misled the driver of the other vehicle to drive in the wrong direction, resulting in the fatal collision, did not amount to a breach of fundamental justice requiring a remedy. Furthermore, there was nothing constitutionally justifying the limitation of the civil damages bar under the SAAQ legislation (section 83.57). No violation to life or security of the person was caused by section 83.57. The Court of Appeal noted that the plaintiffs were ultimately trying to circumvent the tort bar in the SAAQ legislation by bringing a claim under the CCRF. This case confirms that human rights remedies will not be available as an alternative to compensation under the big no-fault framework, nor will CCRF human rights protections and freedoms defeat the effect of the civil damages bar.

Errors and failures in the management of private data and the impacts of this on an individual can also be the basis of a human rights intersection between an individual and the SAAQ or MPI. In *Roy v Québec (SAAQ)*[186] an

---

[185] *Downer v Procureure générale du Québec et Société de l'assurance automobile du Québec* 2019 QCCS 1280; *Downer v Procureure générale du Québec et SAAQ* 2019 QCCA 1893.

[186] *Roy c Québec (Société de l'assurance automobile)* 2016 QCCS 3920.

Intersentia

345

administrative error led to the suspension of the plaintiff's driver licence and the subsequent impounding of his vehicle. The plaintiff sought compensatory, moral and punitive damages, partially on the grounds that there had been a breach of his Québec Charter rights to freedom, dignity and enjoyment of his property.[187] SAAQ argued that it was covered by the relevant provisions of the legislation governing the SAAQ organisation itself which protected the organisation and its employees from litigation where they were acting in good faith.[188] The Superior Court of Québec found that although the unintentional nature of the error protected SAAQ from punitive damages, it nevertheless had to pay compensatory and moral damages for the error.

The entitlement of individuals to funded support and assistance when seeking a review of an MPI or SAAQ decision may also lead to a human rights intersection. This is similar to the issues raised in New Zealand by the Acclaim Otago reports – a person challenging a comprehensive no-fault compensation fund's decision will be going up against a well-resourced public authority defendant, and there are limitations to what a plaintiff can challenge on a procedural basis in a review case. Certainly, a move away from a court-focused arena for the resolution of personal injury compensation matters runs the risk of an increased number of claimants representing themselves in disputes – there is recent scholarly discussion of the challenges faced by self-representing litigants before bodies such as Québec's SAAQ.[189] However, relevant case law indicates that human rights protections are unlikely to be a fruitful avenue to address these issues, because these kinds of issues are of a more general 'access to justice' nature.

Lejins v. Manitoba Public Insurance Corp[190] related to a dispute about the plaintiff's entitlement to physiotherapy treatment funded by the defendant, that was decided in MPI's favour by Manitoba's Automobile Injury Compensation Appeal Commission. The plaintiff, seeking leave to appeal to the Manitoba Court of Appeal, alleged that he could not afford legal representation to help him before the Commission, and that the defendant's failure to provide him with representation was therefore a breach of various CCRF legal rights. The plaintiff also argued that the Commission's refusal to hear from the plaintiff's chosen expert witness also breached the rules of natural justice. The Manitoba Court

---

[187] Specifically, the plaintiff argued that there had been a breach of article 24.1 of the Québec Charter of Human Rights and Freedoms which states 'No one may be subjected to unreasonable search or seizure.'

[188] Act respecting the Société de l'assurance automobile du Québec art 16.

[189] Emmanuelle Bernheim, Richard-Alexandra Laniel and Louis-Philippe Jannard, 'Les Justiciables Non Représentés Face à La Justice : Une Étude Ethnographique Du Tribunal Administratif Du Québec Les Justiciables Non Représentés Face à La Justice : Une Étude Ethnographique Du Tribunal Administratif Du Québec' (2019) 39 *Windsor Review of Legal and Social Issues* 67.

[190] *Lejins v Manitoba Public Insurance Corp* 2004 MBCA 171.

Chapter 5. Human Rights, Access to Justice and Dispute Resolution

of Appeal found that there was no factual evidence provided to support any breach of CCRF rights. The plaintiff's lack of equal access to legal counsel was based on pure economic circumstance rather than by the law or any MPI action which breached his CCRF rights. The Commission's refusal to hear from the plaintiff's expert witness was a matter of procedure, from which no appeal was possible. This case illustrates that human rights law will not necessarily provide a remedy for general access to justice issues (that exist not purely because of the no-fault comprehensive compensation fund) or provide the basis for a challenge to procedural decisions of the relevant non-court tribunal.

The SAAQ and MPI both have wide functional powers in relation to transport and driver regulation. For example, both organisations have the power to issue or suspend driver licences and authorise the registration of vehicles. This is an important part of these compensation funds' lateral risk management and injury deterrence regulatory functions. Those functions are necessary in the absence of any hypothetical tort deterrence function due to the complete no-fault nature of the schemes and the corresponding statutory bar. This kind of lateral regulation is also the location of a potential human rights intersection for these comprehensive no-fault compensation funds.

In 2015, the Superior Court of Québec authorised a class action against SAAQ and other relevant Québec agencies on behalf of individuals arrested for drink driving between 2011 and 2016 who were subsequently refused driver licences by SAAQ ('*Lepage* class action').[191] The questions to be decided by this class action are entirely human rights-related, specifically that a questionnaire used by SAAQ to evaluate the convicted impaired drivers' risk of re-offending was discriminatory. This was because the questionnaire relied upon factors such as the driver's marital status and level of education. Punitive and other human rights-related damages are sought by the plaintiffs.[192]

The full trial of the class action is yet to proceed, and potential class action members have until September 2022 to join the class/bring their own action.[193] Therefore the questions raised by the *Lepage* class action are beyond the time-limits and the scope of this research project. However, regardless of the outcome, the *Lepage* class action indicates that the human rights intersections of a no-fault comprehensive compensation fund will extend – just like

---

[191] *Lepage c Québec (Société de l'assurance automobile)* 2015 QCCS 1606; *Lepage c Société de l'assurance automobile du Québec* 2019 QCCS 1195; *Lepage c Société de l'assurance automobile du Québec* 2019 QCCA 1981.

[192] Article 49(2) of the Québec Charter states that in the case of unlawful and intentional interference with a protected Charter right, punitive damages may be awarded. Article 24(1) of the CCRF states that the court may award a remedy as it considers appropriate and just in the circumstances.

[193] For further details and copies of the relevant interlocutory and class action court judgments, see 'Daniel Lepage c. SAAQ et al. (200–06-000172-141)' <http://www.stephanemichaudavocat.com/>.

A Comparative Law Analysis of No-Fault Comprehensive Compensation Funds

New Zealand's ACC – to issues beyond the calculation of compensation for personal injury. This is an important contextual factor in the analysis of the application of human rights to such big funds, and a point of distinction from smaller, non-comprehensive no-fault compensation funds.

In *Manitoba Public Insurance Corp. v Paul*[194] the MPI sought reimbursement from the defendant (via its subrogation powers) of compensation it had paid to a third party in relation to a traffic accident involving the defendant. MPI denied indemnity coverage to the defendant because his licence was suspended at the time of the accident – but the defendant had not received papers from MPI informing him of this decision. The legislation at that time deemed such notices as served once they had been sent by mail or registered mail. The Court found that this breached article 7 of the CCRF.[195] This decision relates to the previous MPI framework that was *not* a comprehensive no-fault compensation fund, but this decision has not been overturned and is substantively still relevant to how the indemnity (as the mirror benefit of the tort bar common to MPI and all comprehensive no-fault compensation funds) intersects with human rights law.[196]

In order to seek clarity about these human rights intersections, both the SAAQ and the MPI were surveyed for this book on whether their organisations had recently[197] undertaken an assessment of whether their scheme's statutory entitlements to compensation and the relevant litigation prohibitions are consistent with the Canadian Charter of Rights and Freedoms and/or their provincial equivalent. SAAQ responded that they could not answer this question,[198] which is unsurprising given the ongoing *Lepage* class action.

However, the MPI did give a fuller answer on this point. The MPI's General Counsel responded that:[199]

'There has been no deep dive review of whether the [MPI no-fault] program is consistent with human rights legislation. That said, when legislation is drafted the drafters are aware of human rights issues and ensure that the legislation they are drafting does not violate the human rights of Manitobans. However, human rights law is ever changing and what may have been viewed as valid in 1994 may not be viewed the same in 2020. MPI's legal team is also continually working with the PIPP [Personal Injury Protection Plan] legislation and are cognizant to be on the lookout for potential violations. Finally, most identifications of legislative human

---

[194]   *Manitoba Public Insurance Corp v Paul* [1985] 4 WWR 714.

[195]   Article 7 CCRF states that 'Everyone has the right to life, liberty and security of the person and the right not to be deprived thereof except in accordance with the principles of fundamental justice.'

[196]   Cf *Barker v Manitoba (Registrar of Motor Vehicles)* [1988] 2 WWR 28.

[197]   As in the past 5 to 10 years.

[198]   Email dated 17 September 2020.

[199]   Response to questionnaire, received 18 September 2020.

348

Intersentia

Chapter 5. Human Rights, Access to Justice and Dispute Resolution

rights violations come from complaints from people who believe their human rights have been violated. You and I may look at a particular provision from our individual perspective and not tweak [sic] to how it might negatively impact another individual. The most recent example at MPI relates to the gender x issue of driver licences and identification cards. Not seeing the world from the perspective of a transgender individual you may not realize that having just M or F on a driver licence might violate a person's human rights until they identify it.

The human rights complaint process is probably the best way of identify potential human rights violations. At MPI all such complaints are taken seriously and considered thoroughly.'

The MPI response suggests a simple on-going compliance approach to the management and identification of potential human rights related infringements. However it appears obvious that without legislative overhaul, there is unlikely to be active grappling with the human rights consequences of the scheme. This legislative overhaul might (most realistically) be of either the MPI Scheme legislation or the Manitoba human rights framework – in the case of the latter, to enshrine access to justice provisions or a stronger requirement for human rights compliance. The mention of the driver licence gender issue also shows that the MPI, with its wide functional responsibility for regulation of the whole automobile transport sector, will have to consider human rights issues that emerge in relation to non-compensation issues. For example, the MPI has been a defendant in recent litigation relating to whether, in its automobile regulatory function, its rejection of certain personalised licence plates was an infringement of constitutional freedom of expression rights.[200] Those kinds of intersections are mostly outside the scope of this research project, but it illustrates that the context a no-fault comprehensive compensation fund's human rights intersections is directly affected by the wide functional and structural scope of the fund. This is a potential point of distinction from non-comprehensive no-fault compensation funds. *Comprehensive* no-fault compensation funds will have wider human rights intersections to consider, and this is a contextual backdrop to what may be a justified or unjustified limit on a claimant or customer's human rights.[201] *Comprehensive* funds have wider objectives and social implications than *non-*

---

[200] *Troller v Manitoba Public Insurance Corporation* 2019 MBQB 157. See also Kathleen Martens, 'Constitutional Challenge May Help NDN CAR Ride Again', *APTN News* (10 April 2019) <https://www.aptnnews.ca/national-news/constitutional-challenge-may-help-ndn-car-ride-again/>.

[201] There is currently no research or other scholarly literature directly on this point, but indications of the issue can be identified in other literature across the scientific spectrum. For example, the issue of whether a preference for male or female driving assessors should be accommodated for the benefit of individuals' religious beliefs – mentioned in Howard Adelman, 'Contrasting Commissions on Interculturalism: The Hijāb and the Workings of Interculturalism in Quebec and France' (2011) 32 *Journal of Intercultural Studies* 245 <https://www.tandfonline.com/action/journalInformation?journalCode=cjis20>.

Intersentia

349

comprehensive funds, and this affects how human rights issues and intersections can be analysed in relation to them.

2.3.3. The Intersection with Other Compensation Funds

Given the fundamental protections afforded by the CCRF, it is also useful to look at relevant case law from other Canadian provinces that have no-fault compensation frameworks in place. Remember, Saskatchewan and Ontario both also have automobile injury compensation frameworks underpinned by no-fault. Further, every Canadian province has a no-fault worker injury compensation scheme in place – which although comprehensive, did not fall within the relevant definition for this research project. The structural features of those schemes mean they do not meet the definition of a no-fault comprehensive compensation fund for the purposes of this project, but some case law on human rights intersections from those provinces concerning those other schemes is highly relevant to our analysis here.

Moxham v Canada[202] relates to the Saskatchewan no-fault transport injury framework.[203] The plaintiff was injured in a collision with a Royal Canadian Mounted Police (i.e. federal police) vehicle. The legal question to be resolved was whether the plaintiff could bring a claim in the federal court for general and special damages (i.e. a tort claim) against the Crown defendant. In other words, did the provincial Saskatchewan no-fault scheme apply to the federal police service and therefore absolve it of liability? – what was the constitutionality of these provisions? The Court found that the relevant provisions of the Saskatchewan no-fault scheme only affected the rights of the plaintiff, not the Crown defendant's rights. Further, the legislation could be properly seen as having been approved indirectly by the federal parliament, based on an interpretation of the relevant provision of the Crown liability legislation.[204] The plaintiff then argued that if the Crown's liability was indeed extinguished by virtue of the no-fault legislation (and some other federal legislation that was relevant to this case), then this amounted to a breach of article 15 of the CCRF (equality before the law).[205] However, the Court found that article 15 of the CCRF could not logically be seen as having application in this case –

---

[202]   *Moxham v Canada* [1998] 2 FC 441.

[203]   As a reminder, the key point of difference between that scheme and the four systems studied in this project is the fact that the Saskatchewan scheme is not compulsory. A tort-based system remains a choice. However, in practice, nearly all motorists choose for the no-fault policy (which is also the default choice if the policyholder does not actively choose the tort option).

[204]   Crown Liability and Proceedings Act 1985 s 32.

[205]   Article 15(1) states that 'Every individual is equal before and under the law and has the right to the equal protection and equal benefit of the law without discrimination and, in particular, without discrimination based on race, national or ethnic origin, colour, religion, sex, age or mental or physical disability.'

Chapter 5. Human Rights, Access to Justice and Dispute Resolution

'there is no issue of discrimination "based on race, national or ethnic origin, colour, religion, sex, age or mental or physical disability". All that we are dealing with in this case is a simple automobile accident governed by the laws of the Province of Saskatchewan. Secondly, the plaintiff is not being discriminated against. All persons involved in an automobile accident in Saskatchewan are equally governed by the law of the Province. Bert Moxham is not particularly being singled out.'[206]

In other words, the fact that the plaintiff was prohibited in this province from bringing civil proceedings (but may not have been in other Canadian provinces, for example), was not a violation of the CCRF. Indeed, the scope of the no-fault compensation framework for automobile injury applied equally to everyone in the province. The arguments raised in this case and the judicial conclusions on the scope and effect of a no-fault compensation fund or scheme with a tort bar have parallels with the Australian case of *Sweedman v Transport Accident Commission*.[207]

More recently, *Campisi v Ontario Attorney General*[208] concerned a question of whether the statutory restriction on accessing court to resolve disputes about benefit levels under Ontario's no-fault automobile injury scheme was lawful, or if it breached the CCRF.[209] Following a 2016 statutory amendment, all disputes about that scheme's statutory no-fault compensation benefits could only be resolved by the Licence Appeal Tribunal. Access to court was prohibited except in relation to questions of law or judicial review. Ultimately, the case was struck out because the plaintiff did not have the relevant personal or public interest standing to bring proceedings. The plaintiff was a personal injury lawyer who sought to generally challenge the constitutionality of the restriction on accessing court. There was also no factual evidence provided by the plaintiff of any negative effect that the statutory restriction was having on actual automobile injury claimants. However the judgment from the Ontario Superior Court of Justice also went into more substantive detail about why the plaintiff's claim lacked merit:

a. There was no breach of article 15(1) of the CCRF, because automobile injury victims (who may or may not have been physically disabled by their accident) were not being singled out on the basis of physical injury or disability for different or discriminatory treatment.

b. There was also no breach of article 7 of the CCRF because Canadian case law had already established that neither 'a statutory limitation on tort

---

[206] *Moxham v Canada* (n 202) para 34.

[207] *Sweedman v Transport Accident Commission* [2006] HCA 8.

[208] *Campisi v Ontario (Attorney General)* 2018 ONCA 869; *Campisi v Ontario* 2017 ONSC 2884.

[209] Ontario's no-fault scheme is administered by private insurers, which is effectively what make it ineligible for study under this research project.

Intersentia

351

A Comparative Law Analysis of No-Fault Comprehensive Compensation Funds

damages nor the elimination of a court option deprives an accident victim of his or her right to life, liberty or security of the person'.[210]

c. Further, unwritten constitutional principles about the rule of law 'may help in interpreting the text of the written constitution, but they do not provide an independent basis for striking down statutes'.[211]

The Ontario court's decision was approved on appeal, and the Canadian Supreme Court ultimately rejected leave to appeal the decision.[212]

Medwid v Ontario[213] is a slightly older decision concerning the scope of the statutory bar against civil proceedings that forms a core part of the worker accident compensation framework in Ontario (and all other Canadian provinces). The legislation in question allowed the right to sue in some specific limited circumstances. The plaintiff alleged that this was discrimination that breached article 15 of the CCRF. The court in this case said that (unlike in the United States), the civil right to bring an action in the courts for damages in respect of personal injury was not a constitutional right protected by the CCRF.[214] Further, in the context of this legislation, any disadvantage created by the different circumstances where the statutory bar applied was balanced out by the availability of no-fault compensation for those affected by the bar. Although the differing application of the statutory bar might be called unequal, it was not discriminatory – 'The loss of a right to sue has been balanced with no fault coverage'.[215]

The subsequent decision of *Hernandez v Palmer*,[216] also relating to the Ontario no-fault automobile injury compensation framework, confirmed the point in *Medwid* that the right to bring private law proceedings for personal injury is not a protected right under the CCRF.[217] It also established that the enhanced access to justice benefits provided by a no-fault compensation fund more than adequately compensate for any disadvantage created by a statutory bar on tort proceedings. The judge in *Hernandez* found that 'the right to sue in tort for damages does not form part of the "basic tenets of our legal system", nor

---

[210] *Campisi v Ontario (Attorney General)* (n 208) para 31. The relevant case law here (which was not decided in specific relation to a no-fault compensation scheme for transport injury) is *Whitbread v Walley* [1988] BCJ No. 733 (CA), *Filip v Waterloo (City)* (1992) 98 DLR (4th) 534 and *Rogers v Faught* (2002) 212 DLR (4th) 366.

[211] ibid 55. See also *British Columbia v Imperial Tobacco Canada Ltd* [2005] SCC 49 and *Daley v Economical Mutual Insurance Company* (2005) 206 OAC 33 (CA) [40].

[212] *Campisi v Ontario (Attorney-General)* [2019] SCCA No. 52.

[213] *Medwid v Ontario (Minister of Labour)* (1988) CarswellOnt 937.

[214] ibid 39.

[215] ibid 47.

[216] *Hernandez v Palmer* (1992) CarswellOnt 65.

[217] This position has also been confirmed in relation to limitations on damages and intersections with the CCRF in provinces where automobile-related personal injury compensation is governed by the fault system – see *Morrow v Zhang* 2009 ABCA 215.

Chapter 5. Human Rights, Access to Justice and Dispute Resolution

does it fall within the "inherent dominion of the judiciary as guardian of the justice system", for three key reasons:

a.   The 'right to sue' is not analogous to any of the rights protected by articles 8 to 14 of the CCRF;[218]
b.   'Legislatures have frequently abolished rights of action in the public interest'[219] – for example, worker injury compensation schemes, as confirmed in *Medwid*;
c.   'the common law itself often imposes civil liability on a basis other than fault (e.g. strict liability)'. Further, a no-fault system 'appears to provide prompt and comprehensive compensation to all individuals, thereby furthering the values of liberty and security of the person guaranteed by [article 7 CCRF]'.[220]

F.E.E.S.P. c. Béliveau St-Jacques[221] is a Canadian Supreme Court case concerning the Québec Charter's intersection with that province's no-fault worker compensation system. The appellant in the case had alleged harassment by her employer and a failure to prevent harassment in the workplace. Despite the statutory bar against bringing a damages claim against an employer in these circumstances, the appellant sought civil damages for a breach of article 49 of the Québec Charter (damages resulting from an unlawful interference with a protected right or freedom). The majority judgment found that damages for a breach of human rights were not available if a no-fault compensation fund had already provided compensation for that loss and there was a statutory bar against civil proceedings. The majority found that article 49 damages had equivalence with a civil remedy, because of the civilian law nature of damages in the Québec province (which did not generally recognise the existence of exemplary damages). Article 49 did not have the primacy over other legislation as other provisions in the Québec Charter did. Victims of employment injury were, further, not denied access to any compensatory remedy for their injuries, but were rather subject to a special scheme (which balanced a no-fault basis with limited fixed-rated compensation).

---

218   Articles 7 to 14 of the CCRF concern 'Legal Rights'. Article 8 contains the right to be secure against unreasonable search or seizure; article 9 comprises the right not to be arbitrarily detained or imprisoned; article 10 concerns proper arrest procedures, the right to counsel and *habeas corpus* rights; article 11 contains a number of criminal procedure rights; article 12 deals with the right not to be subjected to any cruel and unusual treatment or punishment; article 13 concerns witness' rights against self-incrimination and article 14 relates to the right the assistance of an interpreter.
219   *Hernandez v Palmer* (n 216) para 140.
220   ibid 141–142.
221   *Fédération des employées et employés de services publics inc v Béliveau St-Jacques* [1996] 2 SCR 345.

Intersentia

353

The cases detailed in this subsection provide a strong and clear statement that the structure (with a complete tort bar) of a no-fault comprehensive compensation fund is *not* inconsistent with Canada's fundamental human rights framework(s). Specifically, the right to sue for personal injury in the private law sphere has been repeatedly held not to be a protected right at either the CCRF level or the provincial human rights level. Even where some inequality or difference in treatment is identified (as it was in *J.A.*, *Medwid* and *F.E.E.S.P*) this is not fatal, because there is a balance achieved by virtue of the benefits of a no-fault compensation framework for victims. *Hernandez's* identification that modifications to court access are relatively commonplace (for example, worker injury compensation, or strict liability) reinforces this conclusion that a complete tort bar is not an intrinsic barrier to the establishment or operation of a no-fault comprehensive compensation fund – so long as there is clear intent expressed by the legislature and framing of the statute. Vague philosophical principles about access to the courts – that are not enshrined in fundamental or non-fundamental human rights and justice-related legislation – are insufficient to attack clear legislative statement. Indeed, this is logical, because a finding otherwise would require an entire rearrangement of the no-fault compensation fund statute and its eligible class of victims. In Canada more broadly, it has become commonplace to provide an alternative tribunal for individuals to litigate or defend their rights, as it is recognised that the ordinary courts system is inaccessible to most individuals.[222] Therefore it is no great stretch of the imagination to see that a no-fault comprehensive compensation fund that allows for immediate compensation for harm, with the possibility of a review on limited points in the case of dispute, is something that is harmonious with the human rights infrastructure of that jurisdiction.

The Canadian approach here is a persuasive argument that a no-fault comprehensive compensation fund is *not* – at least not by default, anyway – incompatible with fundamental access to justice provisions within a human rights framework. This answers the first question of this chapter and this point is a novel conclusion that has not previously been identified in other comparative law research on no-fault compensation funds.

However, there is certainly the possibility for more specific infringements of human rights law by a no-fault comprehensive compensation fund. As with ACC cases in relation to privacy issues, there may be successful challenges on lateral functional regulation responsibilities of the compensation fund, as a public authority with powerful horizontal powers in its functional sector. The judgment(s) in the *Lepage* class action, when eventually determined, will provide an updated and much-needed clarification on this point.

---

[222]   Dominique Clément, 'Renewing Human Rights Law in Canada' (2017) 54 *Osgoode Hall Law Journal* 1311.

2.4. EUROPE: A SIMPLE STRUCTURAL AND ANALYTICAL COMPARISON

An analysis of the human rights intersections with no-fault comprehensive compensation funds has shown a progression from minimal intersection (in Australia), to sporadic interaction (in New Zealand) to a somewhat clearer definition of boundaries (in Canada). As only two out of four of our big no-fault compensation funds are located in jurisdictions with fundamental human rights frameworks in place, it is difficult to thoroughly assess the impact of a fundamental human rights framework on no-fault comprehensive compensation funds. Therefore, it is useful to undertake a basic comparative law exercise with European human rights frameworks.

The relevant fundamental human rights frameworks for comparison here are the European Convention on Human Rights (the ECHR) (as interpreted and applied by the European Court of Human Rights – the ECtHR) and the Charter of Fundamental Rights of the European Union (the EU Charter) (as enforced by the Court of Justice of the European Union). The former is the most relevant framework, given its wider application. The latter framework is less obviously relevant, because it would be more applicable to a hypothetical comprehensive no-fault compensation fund that was established at an EU level. However the two frameworks have relevance to one another[223] and so their provisions and relevant intersections are considered alongside one another where appropriate.

It is methodologically appropriate to choose European human rights frameworks as a simple comparator here, because a functional comparison with certain Belgian, French and Nordic compensation funds was undertaken in Chapter 3. Further, European fundamental human rights frameworks have had a strong influence on the development of the United Kingdom's human rights law and precedent, although the EU Charter obviously no longer applies to a post-Brexit UK. As the United Kingdom is the most important legislative parent of Australia, Canada and New Zealand (and a continuing influence, in terms of persuasive case law) that influence logically filters down to those jurisdictions. The strong recent statements by Canadian courts that there is *no* fundamental right to bring a compensatory damages claim for personal injury under private law before a court also begs direct comparison with the position on this point under a different fundamental human rights framework. Finally, the fact of a comparative exercise also means that the conclusions of this book are more

---

[223] European Union Agency for Fundamental Rights, European Court of Human Rights and Council of Europe, *Handbook on European Law Relating to Access to Justice* (2016) 16 <https://fra.europa.eu/en/publication/2016/handbook-european-law-relating-access-justice>.

relevant and applicable to a European context, where a comprehensive no-fault compensation fund or scheme may be implemented in the future.[224]

Given the references to the ICCPR and other international human rights instruments in earlier subsections of this chapter, it might be queried why there was no consideration of the intersections of no-fault comprehensive compensation funds with principles from international human rights frameworks. Firstly, there is not scope to undertake that exercise in addition to the comparison with European frameworks. Secondly, those instruments need to be translated by ratification and domestic implementation into local legislation. As has been seen already, there can be significant differences between jurisdictions' approach to human rights, based on contextual factors and structural constitutional dynamics.

At the outset, it should be noted that the analysis here in this subsection does not attempt to make a complete assessment of whether a no-fault compensation fund will be, in all circumstances, compatible or not compatible with European human rights law. Similarly, there is no scope to consider intersections between no-fault comprehensive compensation funds and the human rights or constitutional law intersections of specific European jurisdictions. There is currently no compensation fund within Europe that meets the definition of a comprehensive no-fault compensation fund, so it is not actually possible to undertake that kind of analysis within this book with any kind of certainty. Further, because this analysis is limited to very large no-fault compensation funds, there is no consideration of the human rights intersections with *non-comprehensive* no-fault compensation funds – that is a matter best left to researchers considering Europe's various smaller no-fault compensation funds in one or more jurisdictions.

As identified in the previous subsections of this chapter, the lateral extra regulatory powers possessed by a big no-fault compensation fund means that some different kinds of human rights intersections are likely to occur anyway, when compared with smaller no-fault compensation funds. The specific comparative law analysis that is being undertaken here is whether the access to justice provisions within ECHR and other European fundamental rights instruments would in fact be an insurmountable barrier to the creation of a no-fault comprehensive compensation fund. There are many outstanding and compelling questions to answer in relation to no-fault compensation funds and human rights.[225] However, the modest and realistic goal here is – for the specific

---

[224] For example in the context of addressing liability and insurance problems associated with automated vehicles – see Kim Watts, 'Potential of No-Fault Comprehensive Compensation Funds to Deal with Automation and Other 21st Century Transport Developments' (2020) 12 *European Journal of Commercial Contract Law* 1; EFD Engelhard and RW de Bruin, 'EU Common Approach on the Liability Rules and Insurance Related to Connected and Autonomous Vehicles.' (Utrecht Centre for Accountability and Liability Law 2017).

[225] Vansweevelt and others (n 1) 210–211.

category of very large no-fault compensation funds – to identify the broad European human rights intersections that are comparable with the identified human rights intersections in Australia, New Zealand and Canada. This will enable a conclusion to be drawn about whether there are fundamental obstacles at a European level to the creation of a no-fault comprehensive compensation fund. That kind of conclusion is relevant more generally to whether no-fault comprehensive compensation funds are compatible (or not) with fundamental human rights frameworks.

2.4.1. The Intersection between European Human Rights Frameworks and Private Law Generally

There is no specific wording within either European framework about how human rights principles should be seen as applying to a system that replaces tort or non-contractual liability. In other words, what can we determine to be the refined and specific grounds for the relevance of European human rights frameworks to a system that upends private law?

A first point of consideration is how human rights are seen as intersecting with private law generally. There is logical relevance where a compensation fund is a replacement for a public authority's liability in instances of mass harm or where personal injury was caused by a public authority of some kind. However, in practice, questions of human rights infringements tend to run parallel to questions of tort liability, and these might not be solved simultaneously.[226]

In contrast, what can we make of situations where the ordinary non-contractual liability between two parties is affected by the application of a no-fault comprehensive compensation fund – for example, two individuals who have an automobile collision with one another, leading to injury? The traditional view of fundamental rights is that it is limited to vertical relationships, and therefore limited to public law.[227] This is changing, but the normative desirability

---

[226] An example of this parallel treatment is a recent case that was brought before the ECtHR by a woman seeking a damages remedy from the Irish state in relation to sexual abuse she had suffered in the 1970s at the hands of her former primary school principal. Before the domestic Irish courts, the plaintiff had argued that the Irish state was vicariously liable. However, the Irish Supreme Court found that the state had no vicarious liability in relation to public primary schools, because they were actively administered by the Catholic Church. The plaintiff then brought a successful claim before the ECtHR, where the focus of the case shifted from issues of vicarious liability to Ireland's failure to establish adequate child protection frameworks and provide her with an effective remedy. See *O'Keeffe v Ireland* (2014) (Application no. 35810/09); Kim Watts, 'Managing Mass Damages Liability via Tort Law and Tort Alternatives, with Ireland as a Case Study' (2020) 11 *Journal of European Tort Law* 57 <https://www.degruyter.com/view/journals/jetl/11/1/article-p57.xml>.

[227] Verica Trstenjak, 'General Report: The Influence of Human Rights and Basic Rights in Private Law' in Verica Trstenjak and Petra Weingerl (eds), *The Influence of Human Rights and Basic Rights in Private Law* (Springer 2016) 7.

A Comparative Law Analysis of No-Fault Comprehensive Compensation Funds

of this is uncertain.[228] To varying degrees in different European jurisdictions, fundamental rights have influenced judicial interpretation of private law rules – but there has been a more limited influence on legislation. A judicial interpretation of private law rules with reference to fundamental rights has been described as an indirect horizontal effect of human rights law.[229] Ultimately, although fundamental rights can influence the interpretation of private law rules, they may not directly determine their application unless there is a specific legislative statement to that effect.[230] Many European jurisdictions have underlying general principles of full reparation in the tort context, and differing degrees of general entitlement to pecuniary and non-pecuniary damages.[231] Therefore fundamental rights have a role to play in how those principles and entitlements might be specifically applied, whether in individual cases or via enshrinement in local ordinary or supreme legislation.

In summary, there is clearly a degree of dynamic intersection between fundamental rights and private law in Europe that continues to evolve. However the defined scope of application of fundamental rights to private law rules is far from certain at this point. This is a relevant departure point to keep in mind when considering the intersection between European human rights frameworks and comprehensive no-fault compensation funds. There is clearly space here for the human rights intersections from the conclusions drawn in this book about other jurisdictions' approach to big compensation funds to be relevant to the development of this specific niche of jurisprudence.

2.4.2. Access to Justice Rights: The Right to a Fair Trial and an Effective Remedy

The most relevant functional and structural comparison that can be made here, in the context of large no-fault compensation funds, is with European access to justice rights; in other words, the right to access a remedy to one's legal problem or harm, usually by judicial means. Articles 6 and 13 of the ECHR and article 47 of the EU Charter are the core European human rights provisions relating to access to justice.

a. Article 6(1) ECHR states that 'In the determination of his civil rights and obligations or of any criminal charge against him, everyone is entitled to a fair and public hearing within a reasonable time by an independent and

---

[228] Jan Smits, 'Private Law and Fundamental Rights: A Sceptical View in: Constitutionalisation of Private Law', *Constitutionalisation of Private Law* (Brill 2006).

[229] Dorota Leczykiewicz, 'Horizontal Application of the Charter of Fundamental Rights' (2013) 38 *European Law Review* 479, 490.

[230] Trstenjak (n 227) 9.

[231] For an overview of the differences across a selection of different European jurisdictions, see ibid 22–26.

358

Intersentia

Chapter 5. Human Rights, Access to Justice and Dispute Resolution

impartial tribunal established by law.' The scope of article 6 includes 'civil rights and obligations'; however, it must concern a dispute regarding a civil right or obligation recognised in domestic law, irrespective of whether it is protected by the ECHR.[232]

b.   Article 13 ECHR prescribes the right to an effective remedy before a national authority for possible violations of ECHR rights.

c.   Article 47 of the EU Charter enshrines the 'right to an effective remedy before a tribunal in compliance with the conditions laid down in this Article' and then 'a fair and public hearing within a reasonable time by an independent and impartial tribunal previously established by law. Everyone shall have the possibility of being advised, defended and represented.' An entitlement to legal aid is also contained. Although article 47 is substantively wider (because it also applies to violations of rights outside the Charter), it only applies to European Union law, and therefore has a more limited scope of application than articles 6 and 13 of ECHR. However, there is a general correspondence between article 6 ECHR and article 47.[233]

The right to a fair trial has been defined by the relevant ECtHR and CJEU as including the right of access to a court, as courts are important mechanisms for holding up the rule of law. The right of access to courts is not absolute – but any limitations must not 'impair the very essence of the right'. Local legislatures have the freedom and responsibility for designing systems of remedies procedures that are compliant with these access to justice provisions.[234] The ECtHR has specifically noted (in the context of medical injury cases and concerning article 8 ECHR[235]) that Member States can choose *inter alia* a liability based approach or a no-fault approach when organising their legal systems and positive obligations under the Convention.[236] However this discretion does not allow local legislatures to undermine effective judicial protection of access to justice rights.[237] For example, a legislative mechanism that allows no substantive review has been found to be impermissible.[238]

---

[232]   European Union Agency for Fundamental Rights, European Court of Human Rights and Council of Europe (n 223) 27.

[233]   *Trade Agency Ltd v Seramico Investments Ltd* (C-619/10) ECLI:EU:C:2012:531, [24].

[234]   *Unibet (London) Ltd and Unibet (International) Ltd v Justitiekanslern* C-432/05, ECLI:EU:C:2007:163, [37–42].

[235]   Article 8 ECHR.

[236]   *Vasileva v Bulgaria* (2016) (Application no. 23796/10) [67], [70]. See also *Erdinç Kurt and Others v Turkey* (2017) (Application no. 50772/11) [51]; *Jurica v Croatia* (2017) (Application no. 30376/13) [89–90].

[237]   *DEB Deutsche Energiehandels- und Beratungsgesellschaft mbH v Bundesrepublik Deutschland* (Case C-279/09) ECLI:EU:C:2010:811, [59].

[238]   *Boxus v Région wallonne* (C-128/09) ECLI:EU:C:2011:667.

Intersentia

A Comparative Law Analysis of No-Fault Comprehensive Compensation Funds

What is the relevance of these principles and how they can be interpreted in relation to no-fault comprehensive compensation funds? Specifically, we have already identified that a defining characteristic of these large funds is their comprehensive statutory bar against civil proceedings that applies in most or all circumstances. Is this kind of statutory bar intrinsically incompatible with European human rights frameworks, as a type of well-entrenched fundamental human rights framework? We have seen that statutory bars are not an intrinsic barrier in the other studied jurisdictions, including Canada where there is a fundamental human rights framework in place.

Göç v Turkey[239] is a highly relevant ECtHR case concerning the lack of an oral hearing in proceedings concerning the applicant's claim for no-fault compensation under a non-comprehensive scheme. The applicant had spent time in police detention where he was treated badly, and he made an application for compensation under Turkey's relevant statutory no-fault scheme for such claims. The Turkish court, upon reviewing the application, awarded the applicant compensation – albeit at a lower rate. Both the applicant and the government appealed this decision. The chief prosecutor at the Turkish Court of Cassation submitted an opinion on both appeals (recommending that they be rejected), but this opinion was not communicated to the applicant. The Court of Cassation, without holding a hearing, upheld the lower court's judgment. The applicant alleged *inter alia* that the failure to hold an oral hearing was a breach of article 6 ECHR (as was the failure of the prosecutor to send his opinion to the applicant).

The Turkish government claimed that article 6 did not apply in this case as it did not concern a civil right. It alleged that

> 'the award of compensation to a victim of unlawful detention is of a 'statutory and sui generis nature' based on the objective liability of the State. Once the domestic court had confirmed that the detention had been unlawful, compensation automatically followed.'[240]

Further, the claimant had not actually requested an oral hearing at the time. The majority judgment of the ECtHR Grand Chamber rejected this argument, stating that article 6 applied and there was a civil right in the context of a 'statutory compensation scheme ... [if] ... the subject matter of the applicant's action was pecuniary and ... the outcome of the domestic proceedings was decisive for his right to compensation.' On the matter of the lack of an oral hearing, the Turkish government claimed that the point of this was to provide 'a speedy means for dealing with compensation claims without the expense and delay of an oral hearing' and this was equivalent to redress schemes in other

---

[239] *Göç v Turkey* (2002) (Application No. 36590/97) [2002] ECHR 589.
[240] ibid [40].

360

Intersentia

Chapter 5. Human Rights, Access to Justice and Dispute Resolution

jurisdictions.[241] However the Grand Chamber said that an oral hearing before a court was a key aspect of article 6 as it related to proceedings administered in the judicial arena. An oral hearing could only be dispensed within exceptional circumstances (which did not exist in this case), and further matters (such as the personal nature of the applicant's experience) could not be merely addressed in written submissions or applications for compensation. A breach of article 6 was therefore upheld.

It is, however, useful to also take note here of the minority dissenting judgment in this case, which solely disputed the majority's finding that there was a breach of article 6(1) due to the lack of an oral hearing. The comments of the minority are specifically relevant to the analysis here. The minority judgment said ECtHR case law had never required an oral hearing in all circumstances – in fact, there was significant and varied case law in support of that point.[242] For example, there would be no hearing required in cases where there was no public interest issue raising the need for oral submissions. In cases where exceptional circumstances justified the dispensation with an oral hearing, 'there must be no factual or legal issue which requires a hearing; the questions which the court is required to answer must be limited in scope and no public interest must be at stake.'[243] The minority judgment said that the application, as submitted under the relevant compensation fund scheme, appeared to be a simple and straightforward application for 'strict liability' compensation that raised no special issues, and the application had not made any extra submissions on the desirability of an oral hearing. The minority also expressed the general view that the requirement of 'exceptional circumstances' to dispense with an oral hearing was questionable and too simple to be applied to complex legal situations. It would be preferable to speak of different 'types' of procedures, some of which may be capable of being dealt with without an oral hearing:[244]

'It would be more appropriate to say that the circumstances should be *typical* for certain types of procedure, like the specifically regulated compensation procedure which was at issue in the present case, in which a hearing is not *normally* required.

---

[241] ibid [44].

[242] ibid [20]. 'Relevant authorities include *Håkansson and Sturesson v. Sweden* (judgment of 21 February 1990, Series A no. 171-A, pp. 20–21, §67), which concerned a dispute over the lawfulness of a sale; *Schuler-Zgraggen v. Switzerland* (judgment of 24 June 1993, Series A no. 263, pp. 19–20, §58), concerning an appeal to the Federal Insurance Court about an invalidity pension; *Allan Jacobsson v. Sweden (no. 2)* (judgment of 19 February 1998, *Reports of Judgments and Decisions* 1998-I, p. 169, §49), concerning an appeal to the Supreme Administrative Court, ruling at first and last instance, against a refusal of planning permission; and the inadmissibility decision of 25 April 2002 (Third Section) in *Lino Carlos Varela Assalino v. Portugal* (no. 64336/01), concerning an application for a will to be declared null and void and for a declaration of unworthiness to inherit.'

[243] ibid.

[244] ibid p 22.

Intersentia

361

In this typical procedure the balance between individual interests and the public interest has already been taken into account in the establishment of the procedural rules as such. It is only in more exceptional situations that the need for an oral hearing has to be shown. The method of solving legal problems by 'type', that is to say by introducing, on the basis of a careful assessment of the competing interests, a specific procedure which normally does not call for a hearing, is one of the classic methods for the solution of problems of a more or less technical nature.' [Emphasis added]

The nuanced comments of the minority judgment would be directly relevant to a no-fault comprehensive compensation fund which aims to create a 'hearing-free' fast procedure for a comprehensive category or 'type' of claims – the majority of which are simple and involve minor injuries and minor levels of compensation. However, the impact of the majority judgment cannot of course be discounted – there is a civil right being activated or affected here, and caution must be taken to ensure that access to an oral hearing is not unnecessarily being infringed. The emphasised portion of the minority judgment quoted above also implies and requires a clearly enunciated and direct balancing of the public interest versus the private interest in limiting access to an oral hearing via a compensation fund. This is in line with long-established ECtHR precedent on proportionality in limiting article 6 rights – a balance must be struck between the means employed and the aim sought to be achieved.[245] Scheme size and the fact of a statutory scheme being created will not be enough; a direct balancing of interests will be a necessary signposting exercise. Subsequent case law has confirmed that refusal to hold a hearing does not have to be limited to rare cases – in particular, the efficient operation of social security-type schemes that issue benefits on a technical basis and with regard to expert evidence might be negatively impacted by a requirement to always hold an oral hearing.[246, 247] There has been specific application of this point in a case concerning a comprehensive industrial injury scheme (as part of the wider social security framework).[248]

It is useful to contrast these conclusions with comments and findings that have been made in European case law about the dissolution or extinguishment of

---

[245] First established in *Ashingdane v United Kingdom* (Application no. 8225/78) [1985] ECHR 8, [57].

[246] *Miller v Sweden* (Application no. 55853/00) judgment of 8 February 2005, 29. Noteworthy also here are the dissenting comments of Justice Costa at page 16 of the judgment here that the stringent position of *Göç v Turkey* is not necessarily desirable – 'Written proceedings (which the Court itself generally uses) are frequently reconcilable with the proper administration of justice; they do not always result in unfair proceedings.' See also *Schuler-Zgraggen v Switzerland* (1993) (Application no. 14518/89) judgment of 24 June 1993, 19–20; *Fexler v Sweden* (2011) (Application no. 36801/06).

[247] *Salomonsson v Sweden* (2002) (Application no. 38978/97), judgment of 12 November 2002, [38]. See also *Lundevall v Sweden* (2002) (Application no. 38629/97) [34].

[248] *Döry v Sweden* (2002) (Application no. 28394/95) [41].

Chapter 5. Human Rights, Access to Justice and Dispute Resolution

liability. Dissolution of liability or immunity from liability relates to the (legally permissible) extinguishment of the hypothetical plaintiff's cause of action in a large no-fault fund. This extinguishment is a substantive restriction on access to court. The ECtHR has repeatedly held that article 6 has no power to create a right which does not substantively exist in the domestic court – there are no guarantees of specifically what might be contained within local legislation.[249] However, this is balanced with the autonomous meaning of article 6 that exists independently of whatever is found in local statute.[250] States retain a margin of appreciation to make rules that may vary depending on 'the needs and resources of the community and of individuals'.[251]

Two important British ECtHR cases illustrate the still unclear position on whether unavailability of a tort remedy is an infringement of either article 6 or the article 13 right to an effective remedy. These two cases are especially relevant to the tort-excluding funds in this research project, as they consider the English-style approach to tort law. *Osman v United Kingdom* related to a claim that police had not taken adequate steps to investigate or apprehend an individual who ended up killing the first applicant's husband and seriously injuring the other applicant (her son). The applicants had attempted to bring a claim in negligence in the British courts against the Metropolitan Police, but this had failed due to existing binding English case law on police negligence and public policy grounds favouring immunity from suit for the police.[252] The plaintiffs brought a claim before the ECtHR alleging *inter alia* a breach of article 6. The ECtHR found that the immunity on public policy grounds granted to the police was a disproportionate restriction on the plaintiffs' right to access court under article 6 and have a substantive assessment of their claim's merits. In other words, the domestic extinguishment of a possible tort remedy in clear terms (via case law), on public policy grounds, was a breach of article 6(1). It was found there was no need to separately decide whether there was an article 13 breach, given the findings in relation to article 6. The ECtHR judgment in *Osman* provoked significant criticism from British quarters.[253] Specifically, the ECtHR

---

[249]   *Roche v United Kingdom* (2005) (Application no. 32555/96) [119]; *Lithgow & Others v United Kingdom* (1986) (Application no. 9006/80) [192].

[250]   *Ferrazzini v Italy* (2001) (Application no. 44759/98) [24]; *König v Germany* (1978) (Application no. 6232/73) [88–89].

[251]   Case 'relating to certain aspects of the laws on the use of languages in education in Belgium' v Belgium (Application no. 1474/62) (1968) 1 EHRR 252 [5]; *Golder v United Kingdom* (1975) (Application no. 4451/70) [38].

[252]   *Osman v Ferguson* [1992] EWCA Civ 8. The Court of Appeal relied heavily on the precedent of *Hill v Chief Constable of West Yorkshire* [1989] AC 53 – the Court said that as in that case, the matters in issue for the *Osman* plaintiffs were failures in investigation of crime and thus public policy doomed the action to fail. The *Osman* plaintiffs were denied leave to appeal the decision to the House of Lords.

[253]   See for example Mark Lunney, 'A Tort Lawyer's View of Osman v United Kingdom' (1999) 10 *King's Law Journal* 238; Conor A Gearty, 'Unravelling Osman' (2001) 64 *Modern Law*

Intersentia

363

A Comparative Law Analysis of No-Fault Comprehensive Compensation Funds

was accused of overstepping its authority and encroaching on parliamentary sovereignty 'seeking to impose a Voltairean uniformity of values upon all the member States'.[254]

The *Osman* decision was reversed shortly thereafter in *Z v United Kingdom*.[255] That case was brought by five abused children who claimed that the local authority had taken inadequate protective measures to intervene in and protect them from their abusive parents. The plaintiffs had been unsuccessful before the British courts because the relevant social care legislation did not appear to show any intention to create a private law action against the private authorities, and there were strong public policy reasons against imposing liability. The plaintiffs also alleged that they had no access to court or an effective remedy, because a tort remedy was the only possible remedy available to plaintiffs in their situation. In a direct reversal of *Osman*, the Court found that there was no breach of article 6 because, *inter alia*,

> 'the inability of the applicants to sue the local authority flowed not from an immunity but from the applicable principles governing the substantive right of action in domestic law. There was no restriction on access to a court of the kind contemplated in Ashingdane'.

Extreme deference in the decision was given to the local courts' powers to shape the scope of tort liability. A breach of article 13 was found, but the court nevertheless refused to make conclusions under article 13 about whether only court proceedings would count as an effective remedy.

Both *Osman* and *Z* are primarily relevant to the sphere of public authority tort liability (which is significantly weaker in the United Kingdom compared to other European jurisdictions[256]). Yet there is instructive relevance to our topic in the Strasbourg court's fluid and imprecise position on whether it is *impermissible* to have a tort remedy be unavailable, from a human rights perspective. There is certainly outstanding unclarity about the issues of immunity from suit and/or immunity from liability being an impermissible limitation on access to justice rights.[257] A more recent suite of ECtHR litigation found that there was a

---

[ ] *Review* 159. However compare with Claire McIvor, 'Getting Defensive about Police Negligence: The *Hill* Principle, the Human Rights Act 1998 and the House of Lords' (2010) 69 *Cambridge Law Journal* 133.

[254] Rt Hon Lord Hoffman, 'Human Rights and the House of Lords' (1999) 62 *The Modern Law Review* 159.

[255] *Z & Others v United Kingdom* (2001) (Application no. 29392/95).

[256] For further recent comparative scholarly discussion on this point, see Ken Oliphant (ed), *The Liability of Public Authorities in Comparative Perspective* (Intersentia 2016).

[257] Recently, a strident dissenting opinion by Justice Pinto de Albuquerque in *Nagy v Hungary* argued that the distinction between immunity from suit and immunity from liability has not been properly explored by the Court, and the distinction between the two concepts is likely illusory – see *Nagy v Hungary* (2017) (Application no. 56665/09) 45.

breach of article 13 because the relevant domestically available tort remedy was not particularly effective – and an *ex gratia* compensation fund has been the approved solution to that unavailability of a tort solution.[258]

The position is therefore far from settled at the European level, and these limited intersections with the issues of tort liability exclusion and the occasional relevance of redress schemes show that there is not *per se* an insurmountable barrier, but this depends on the overall characteristics of the limitation as well as the contextual relevance of the domestic system. For example, a contrast can be made with the older ECtHR case of *Bellet v France*.[259] This case concerned the entitlement of a dying contaminated blood products victim to sue relevant defendants as well as receive a no-fault payment from the relevant compensation fund (that might need to be reimbursed in the case of a successful court action). In ruling for the plaintiff, the Court relied heavily on the fact that the French legislature expressly foresaw the possibility of such a victim being able to bring a separate damages claim against the relevant defendant, with cumulation rules of the fund ensuring there was not double recovery. A limitation on bringing a tort claim was not contextually logical within the French statutory framework to do with this kind of damage – and such a conclusion did not require an assessment of the merits of the compensation scheme framework.

Macleod and Hodges have made the simple recommendation that, in order to protect article 6 ECHR rights, redress scheme claimants generally *should* be allowed to bring court claims, but only after unsuccessfully progressing though a redress scheme/compensation fund or rejecting an award.[260] This implies that it may not be possible to completely eliminate court reviews or reassessments within a European context. Indeed, there is a clear ECtHR statement that it

> 'would not be consistent with the rule of law in a democratic society or with the basic principle underlying Article 6 §1 – namely that civil claims must be capable of being submitted to a judge for adjudication – if, for example, a State could, *without restraint or control by the Convention enforcement bodies*, remove from the jurisdiction of the courts a whole range of civil claims or confer immunities from civil liability on large groups or categories of persons.'[261] [Emphasis added]

---

[258] *O'Keeffe v Ireland* (n 226); 'Third Submission on Behalf of the Minister for Education and Skills on Behalf of the State to the Independent Assessor' (2019) <https://www.education.ie/en/Learners/Information/Former-Residents-of-Industrial-Schools/ECHR-OKeeffe-v-Ireland/jan-2019-implementation-of-the-ecthr-judgement-in-the-louise-o'keeffe-case.pdf>; Watts, 'Managing Mass Damages Liability via Tort Law and Tort Alternatives, with Ireland as a Case Study' (n 226).

[259] *Bellet v France* (1995) (Application no. 23805/94).

[260] Sonia Macleod and Christopher Hodges, *Redress Schemes for Personal Injuries* (Hart Publishing 2017) 649.

[261] *Fayed v United Kingdom* (1990) (Application no. 17101/90) [65]; *McElhinney v Ireland* (2001) (Application no. 31253/96) [24].

The four large funds analysed in this book all allow a review or some kind of final access by the courts, if only on limited points of law. Tribunal or court supervision of the fund's compliance with human rights requirements also exists for all four funds. This indicates that these four funds would not fall foul of the existing ECtHR interpretations on access to justice. The structural proximity in law of these big funds to large social security schemes (although they have some key differences from social security) means that more leeway can be expected to be given to limitations on hearings.[262] However, it would be necessary for substantive review safeguards to be clearly enshrined in a fund's legislative framework in order for a hypothetical big compensation fund to be compliant with European human rights law. Specific explanation in the establishing legislation that there is a retained possibility of review by relevant tribunals on human rights grounds would be desirable.

Without a specific functional example of a hypothetical big European fund, we cannot fully test whether European rights to a fair trial and an effective remedy are an insurmountable barrier to the existence of such big funds. There is simply inadequate information available to undertake that exercise in a comprehensive way. Further, that kind of exercise would require consideration of additional constitutional law barriers of individual European states that might exist at a local level. For example, a recent comprehensive legal study commissioned by the European Parliament that strongly advocated a no-fault approach to injury and damage caused by autonomous vehicles gave an option to reduce or eliminate the role of civil liability, but was silent on any access to justice and human rights implications that this might raise.[263]

What is possible and useful, however, is to consider the classic *Ashingdane* calculation as applied to a comprehensive no-fault compensation fund. The *Ashingdane* test for a limitation's compliance with article 6 is that:[264]

> 'the limitations applied must not restrict or reduce the access left to the individual in such a way or to such an extent that the very essence of the right is impaired ... a limitation will not be compatible with Article 6 para. 1 (art. 6-1) if it does not pursue a legitimate aim and if there is not a reasonable relationship of proportionality between the means employed and the aim sought to be achieved.'

---

[262]   *Salomonsson v Sweden* (Application no. 38978/97) (n 247); *Lundevall v Sweden* (n 247); *Döry v Sweden* (2002) (Application no. 28394/95) (n 248).

[263]   Engelhard and de Bruin (n 224) 112–113. See further discussion on this specific functional field in Watts, 'Potential of No-Fault Comprehensive Compensation Funds to Deal with Automation and Other 21st Century Transport Developments' (n 224).

[264]   *Ashingdane v. United Kingdom* (1985) (Application no. 8225/78) (n 245) para 57.

Chapter 5. Human Rights, Access to Justice and Dispute Resolution

A very similar approach is taken to proportionality under EU law, with a focus on 'objectives of general interest' and a requirement to use the least restrictive method possible.[265]

Firstly, do no-fault comprehensive compensation funds have a legitimate aim? This can easily be answered in the affirmative: they aim to create a statutorily guaranteed right to compensation for a wide range of losses with a common cause. They seek to severely limit the number of individuals, within a broad category, who would lack access to compensation for loss *but for* the success of a tort law action. Secondly, is there a reasonable relationship of proportionality between the means employed and the aims sought to be achieved? This is the area where there is likely to be the most tension between the approach taken in the jurisdictions with our four large compensation funds, and the European position generally. The position taken in relation to our four funds, by both the legislature and judiciary, is that the creation of a no-fault comprehensive compensation fund is a specific policy choice to change how a whole *broad* class of injuries are resolved. There is a legislative choice to substantively extinguish a field of law and replace it with something different. Those who normatively view the private law right to bring a compensatory damages claim before a judicial body as some kind of fundamental right would, logically, take the view that this kind of big framework is *not* a proportional response in any circumstance. However, it does not appear that the statements of European courts have gone this far. Ultimately, the wide availability of compensation, speed of delivering compensation and low threshold for accessing support are the benefits that counterbalance the restriction on accessing a tort remedy, and could quite reasonably be seen as proportional, so long as a solid supervisory role of some kind was still available to courts. There remains freedom for limitations and modifications to be made to the structural availability of civil law rights, so long as it is done in a proportional and procedurally appropriate way.

The question of whether the 'essence of the right' is impaired also naturally leads to some tension when considered in relation to a no-fault comprehensive compensation fund. This is because the essence of the right – in the sense that the right is the entitlement to seek a court-based remedy for certain kinds of civil harms – is fundamentally changed by a big compensation fund. It is taken out of the sphere of law for everyday purposes, and replaced with a social sphere. It remains unclear, on the basis of existing case law, whether a fundamental replacement on a clear statutory basis with a kind of right to reparation would be interpreted as an impairment. The best solution is for any hypothetical legislative framework to deal directly with the question in terms of both the relevant ECHR (and European Charter, if relevant) and other relevant

---

[265] *Volker und Markus Schecke GbR and Hartmut Eifert v Land Hessen* Joined cases C-92/09 and C-93/09, ECLI:EU:C:2010:662 at [50], [74].

Intersentia

367

fundamental rights frameworks. The reversal of *Osman* by *Z v United Kingdom* shows that there is a sensitivity to specific legislative choices in the sphere of tort or non-contractual obligations that have a strong public policy character. It would be wise to assume that any such big fund in a European context *would* be swiftly challenged, in the absence of strong legislative consideration of the human rights impact of the limitation and replacement of traditional civil access to justice rights and remedies. The kind of judicial deference to parliamentary intent (and all the multitude of legislative sins and oversights that might encompass) that is common to Westminster-based systems should certainly not be expected in a wider European context, but it does mean that the barriers to creation of a big no-fault compensation fund are not insurmountable.

The next question that therefore logically arises is whether the existing allowances in European human rights law for accessing justice through non-judicial means might be applicable to a no-fault comprehensive compensation fund. A broader view of access to justice includes both courts and non-judicial avenues, and this view has been acknowledged and foreseen by various European institutions.[266] A highly novel mechanism for the speedy non-court resolution of a wide range of civil claims across European jurisdictions already exists in the form of the European Online Dispute Resolution (ODR) platform – a framework that is perceived as significantly enhancing access to justice.[267] Nonetheless, a non-judicial body that can issue substantial compensation and make binding decisions is likely to require judicial supervision in order to ensure European human rights compliance.[268] As noted already, this level of supervision is not fundamentally incompatible with a no-fault comprehensive compensation fund, but the supervisory role and scope needs to be clearly foreseen within the relevant establishing legislation in order to avoid claims of inconsistency with access to justice rights.

2.5. CONCLUSIONS OF LEGISLATION AND CASE LAW COMPARATIVE EXERCISE

Our four big no-fault compensation funds were all established without significant consideration or calculation of human rights intersections. However we know

---

[266] European Union Agency for Fundamental Rights, 'Bringing Rights to Life: The Fundamental Rights Landscape of the European Union' (2012) 18–20 <http://publications.europa.eu/others/agents/index_en.htm>.

[267] Pablo Cortes, 'Using Technology and ADR Methods to Enhance Access to Justice'. For critiques of earlier proposals that were derived from a more traditional litigation-type worldview, see Christopher Hodges, 'Collective Redress: The Need for New Technologies' (2018) 42 *Journal of Consumer Policy* 59 <https://doi.org/10.1007/s10603-018-9388-x>.

[268] *Zumtobel v Austria* (1993) (Application no. 12235/86) [29–32]. See also European Union Agency for Fundamental Rights, European Court of Human Rights and Council of Europe (n 223) 48–49.

Chapter 5. Human Rights, Access to Justice and Dispute Resolution

from the background sketched out in Chapter 3 that legal professional bodies at the time all vigorously defended the civil right of individuals to litigate their personal injury claims through the courts. The absence of this conceptualisation of human rights intersections is logical given the constitutional context of Australia, Canada and New Zealand – and also speaks to the age of these funds.

The core issue of a big no-fault compensation fund limiting access to the courts has been deemed to be an acceptable and proportional legislative choice in all three jurisdictions in order to achieve significant social benefits. A prising open of the legislative structure and restrictions in the four funds would lead to legal incoherency and results that go against the grain of legislative intent.

The statements made by Canadian courts that there is no specifically protected right to bring a civil claim for personal injury damages are directly on point but could not be seen as directly equivalent to the ECtHR's more general statements that the right to access a court is not absolute. It may be possible, however, to contextualise the interaction with regard to the (non)existence of substantive rights at the domestic level. This could lead to the conclusion, in the context of a hypothetical no-fault comprehensive compensation fund with a broad statutory bar, that there is no specific right to bring a civil law claim in relation to compensatory damages for a covered harm *except* to the extent that those rights are substantively protected elsewhere – for example by the constitution or other relevant civil codes of a domestic legal system. That will mean, of course, that a different proportionality calculation (and a margin of appreciation assessment) would need to be undertaken for specific local contexts. However, we can reliably conclude that, as a baseline, European human rights law will not be an insurmountable hurdle to this core element of a no-fault comprehensive compensation fund. It goes without saying, however, that the deference to legislative intent seen in relation to our four large funds is unlikely to be replicated in European courts.

The fact that there is discrimination between eligible claimants and other kinds of harm sufferers has not been seen as a core discrimination problem in our four big funds. This is because there was a significant policy choice to establish the scheme and place the compensation of victims of the broad category of harms outside the legal system – and certain kinds of persons were directly excluded by the clear wording of the scheme. The failings of other compensation sources and the wider legal system are not something that can be used to defeat a big no-fault fund – they will simply be relevant to a subjective contextual assessment.

A wider range of human rights intersections is likely to occur with no-fault comprehensive compensation funds than with non-comprehensive funds. This is because these big funds have a significant societal presence, have broad horizontal regulatory responsibilities, and manage and process large amounts of highly sensitive claimant data. The three transport funds that have broad functional responsibility in the transport sector can affect the ability of individuals to access driver and motor vehicle licensing. In the case of long-term seriously injured

Intersentia

claimants, the fund may be a significant presence in the life of the claimant for years or decades. Courts appear to tolerate a high degree of power being wielded by big no-fault compensation funds in their operational sectors, but do require compliance with privacy (data protection) and fairness rules. The narrower and more specific an infringement of human rights rules by a big no-fault fund, the more likely a claim is to be successful before the relevant court or tribunal.

It will be necessary for legislatures to have greater specific cognisance of human rights law principles in the further development and expansion of big no-fault compensation funds. Clear expression of how a legislative framework is intended to affect human rights protections is, in my view, necessary to ensure ongoing compliance. This must be undertaken by the legislature rather than by the fund itself. A clear articulation of the foreseen supervisory power of the relevant human rights court or tribunal would also be ideal.

3. THE NO-FAULT COMPREHENSIVE COMPENSATION FUND AND ACCESS TO JUSTICE

What is the role of the no-fault comprehensive compensation fund as an access to justice tool – and in the alternative, as a mechanism that restricts access to justice? These kinds of big funds are a wholesale replacement of traditional legal mechanisms that also have a foot within the social sphere. Therefore they have the potential to affect access to justice in both positive and negative ways, to a more significant degree than smaller non-comprehensive schemes. We have observed already in this chapter how the existence of these funds has overall good effects, but nevertheless causes problematic human rights intersections for some individuals. Access to justice points are a helpful broader area to explore, that put in context the issues of no-fault comprehensive compensation funds' direct intersections with specific fundamental or received common law human rights principles.

In this section the concept of 'access to justice' will be defined, with specific reference to no-fault compensation funds in general and no-fault comprehensive compensation funds in particular. There will then be an analysis of the no-fault comprehensive compensation fund, firstly as an enhancer, and then as a barrier, to access to justice.

3.1. DEFINING ACCESS TO JUSTICE

It is important to first define what is understood and meant by 'access to justice'. There is no single precise definition of this phrase. Traditionally and primarily, access to justice has been framed as referring to adequate access to traditional

Chapter 5. Human Rights, Access to Justice and Dispute Resolution

court mechanisms using legal aid and ensuring adequate access to legal professionals. In other words, there is no question about fundamental change to the justice system itself, but rather a focus on ensuring as wide access as possible to the traditional players and mechanisms. This topic of securing adequate access to lawyers is still a dominant focus of much access to justice literature, rather than a question of whether individuals' problems are actually best served by focusing on access to lawyers as the solution.[269] However, access to justice can also be regarded as a global reform movement that, alongside trends towards increased use of alternative dispute resolution mechanisms, advocates a whole range of different mechanisms in both private and public spheres of dispute resolution and access to legal information.[270]

A classic description of access to justice following a comprehensive comparative law study was made by Mauro Cappelletti and Bryant Garth in 1978.[271] This envisaged three 'waves' of access to justice: the first being the provision of legal aid for the poor, the second being the provision of legal aid for diffuse interests, and the third being comprehensive reform of the legal system to substantively enhance access to justice.

What comments have been made in access to justice literature about no-fault compensation funds generally? Seminal access to justice scholar Deborah L. Rhode has directly identified 'specialized no-fault compensation systems in areas like medical malpractice and automobile accidents' as being necessary structural innovations to improve the functioning of dispute resolution processes and the delivery of legal services in those functional fields.[272] Although there is a risk of undercompensating victims, such under-compensation also exists in the tort system, as well as the larger problem of entrenched and endemic overcompensation of lawyers,[273] who hold a privileged position of power within the legal system. Indeed, she notes that the vested financial interests of lawyers in maintaining their essential position of access to the legal system is a key barrier to reform, when evidence from the operation of these funds in other jurisdictions indicates that fewer lawyers did not lead to poorer outcomes. Rhode advocated using a yardstick of societal goals concerning efficiency, deterrence, fairness, costs and accessibility to assess the utility of no-fault compensation funds and other ADR schemes within individual legal systems.[274] At the same time, heed needs to be taken of the danger flagged many years ago by Cappelletti

---

[269]   Herbert M Kritzer, 'To Lawyer or Not to Lawyer: Is That the Question?' (2008) 5 *Journal of Empirical Legal Studies* 875 <http://doi.wiley.com/10.1111/j.1740–1461.2008.00144.x>.

[270]   Jacqueline Nolan-Haley, 'SYMPOSIUM : International Dispute Resolution and Access to Justice : Comparative Law Perspectives' [2020] *Journal of Dispute Resolution* 391, 393.

[271]   Mauro Cappelletti and Bryant Garth, 'Access to Justice: The Newest Wave in the Worldwide Movement to Make Rights Effective' (1978) 27 *Buffalo Law Review* 181.

[272]   Deborah Rhode, *Access to Justice* (Oxford University Press 2006) 189–190.

[273]   ibid 34.

[274]   ibid 43–45.

Intersentia

371

and Garth that an abundance of 'streamlined, efficient procedures will abandon the fundamental guarantees of civil procedure'.[275] It is also necessary to balance the reality that gains in access to justice by one group are likely to lead to losses for another in terms of *their* access to justice.[276]

What comments have been made in access to justice literature about no-fault *comprehensive* compensation funds in particular? Cappelletti and Garth referred to the then infant New Zealand ACC Scheme as being a prominent example of a simplified legal remedy with many virtues, within the 'third wave' of access to justice.[277] More recent socio-legal research has pointed to how simplicity and speed within a comprehensive scheme enhance access to justice, but at the same time the challenges of meeting causation requirements (particularly in medical injury schemes) can be a barrier to accessing justice.[278]

A detailed scholarly consideration by Tiho Mijatov, Tom Barraclough and Warren Forster of the concept of access to justice, with specific application to New Zealand's ACC Scheme, identified four dimensions to the theory of access to justice, and that the existing ACC Scheme only fulfilled one very narrow dimension of this theory, thereby limiting access to justice.[279] This analysis will be considered in more detail in later subsections.

3.2. THE NO-FAULT COMPREHENSIVE COMPENSATION FUND AS AN ENHANCER OF ACCESS TO JUSTICE

As noted already, the concept of a no-fault compensation fund is regarded, at its most basic level, as enhancing access to justice. The main ways that a no-fault comprehensive compensation fund can be seen as enhancing access to justice fall mostly under the yardsticks identified by Deborah Rhode: efficiency, fairness, costs and accessibility.

The efficiency of a big no-fault fund relates mostly to the speed of determining eligibility and delivering compensation to victims after the harm event, in comparison with non-comprehensive no-fault compensation funds and other types of legal remedies. All four funds have very fast claims processing speeds for most simple claims. Technology is being increasingly used to further

---

[275] Cappelletti and Garth (n 271) 291.

[276] Lawrence M Friedman, 'Access to Justice: Some Historical Comments' (2010) 37 *Fordham Urban Law Journal* 11 <https://ir.lawnet.fordham.edu/uljAvailableat:https://ir.lawnet.fordham.edu/ulj/vol37/iss1/4>.

[277] Cappelletti and Garth (n 271) 287–288.

[278] Anne-Maree Farrell, Sarah Devaney and Amber Dar, 'No-Fault Compensation Schemes for Medical Injury: A Review' (10 January 2010) 9–10 <http://www.ssrn.com/abstract=2221836>.

[279] Tiho Mijatov, Tom Barraclough and Warren Forster, 'The Idea of Access to Justice: Reflections on New Zealand's Accident Compensation (or Personal Injury) System' (2016) 33 *Windsor Yearbook of Access to Justice* 197.

Chapter 5. Human Rights, Access to Justice and Dispute Resolution

enhance those speed efficiency gains, and all four funds have high levels of social and economic efficiency.[280] The sustainability of the funds and costs control identified already illustrate the funds' economic efficiency. Further, the lateral focus on the prevention of accidents and rehabilitation of victims, present in all four schemes, forms part of that efficiency.

The significantly reduced overall legal costs associated with big no-fault compensation funds can also be seen as enhancing access to justice under Rhode's yardstick. There is no cost or need for legal assistance in order to make an initial claim to our four funds, and most claims can be resolved without legal assistance. Although the overall systems have centralised administration costs, this is balanced against the reduction in legal costs for society overall and the enhanced social benefits that are more difficult to precisely quantify.

Our four funds also satisfy Rhode's accessibility yardstick criterion. The thresholds for initial applications are very low, especially because hospital staff tend to help claimants with their application and are the basic gatekeepers to scheme entry. Client satisfaction and/or increased user-friendliness is a focus of all four schemes – although there is some evidence that certain vulnerable groups may have more difficulty in applying for compensation.[281]

The fairness yardstick is also broadly satisfied by no-fault comprehensive compensation funds, although there is still room for improvement (as will be discussed in the next subsection). So long as a claimant meets the broad statutory threshold of eligibility, then there will be statutorily guaranteed entitlement to compensation and support for as long as it is medically necessary. Macleod and Hodges' research on redress schemes – of much wider definition than the schemes in this text – found that evidence from the operation of all kinds of 'no-blame' schemes reveals that they satisfy the fairness requirements for multiple parties involved or associated with the relevant harm.[282] Indeed, quantitative and qualitative research comparing the perceptions of users of the TAC Scheme with bordering New South Wales' tort-based system revealed significantly higher perceptions of fairness in relation to the former scheme.[283]

It is therefore easy to conclude that, as was intended by their creation, no-fault comprehensive compensation funds do enhance justice in a broad and consistent way. This is in contrast to a pursuit of absolute justice under a traditional tort

---

[280] Alan Clayton, 'Some Reflections on the Woodhouse and ACC Legacy' (2003) 34 *Victoria University of Wellington Law Review* 449, 462.

[281] Acclaim Otago and others (n 96).

[282] Sonia Macleod and Christopher Hodges, 'Part IX: Conclusions' in Sonia Macleod and Christopher Hodges (eds), *Redress Schemes for Personal Injuries* (1st edn, Hart Publishing 2017) 644.

[283] Nieke A Elbers and others, 'Differences in Perceived Fairness and Health Outcomes in Two Injury Compensation Systems: A Comparative Study' (2016) 16 *BMC Public Health* 1 <http://dx.doi.org/10.1186/s12889-016-3331-3>.

Intersentia

system, which seeks only to deliver traditional retributive justice within the circumstances of each individual case. Big no-fault funds seek to establish a consistent and predictable way for a broad class of victims to be compensated for their loss and rehabilitated, with as minimal interaction as possible with legal mechanisms – thereby enhancing access to justice by effectively allowing the recuperation of the victim. 'Access to justice' therefore relates to 'access to a just outcome' that restores the victim, rather than justice in relation to a judgment made against any causatively relevant person. In my view, it is worth considering the parallels between no-fault comprehensive compensation and restorative justice mechanisms, as these have equivalence with one another as contemporary justice mechanisms.[284] Rhode's yardstick for evaluating access to justice is therefore mostly satisfied by these big funds. It is the funds' largeness, economies of scale, speed of dispute resolution and social pervasiveness as legal frameworks that facilitate those access to justice qualities. Smaller no-fault compensation funds that do not have this kind of inherent momentum may not have equivalent access to justice characteristics.[285]

What about the fact that big no-fault compensation funds provide only one compensation and/or justice route for a wide category of claimants? A plethora of different justice mechanisms would provide more opportunities for an individual to exercise his or her rights. But in order to prevent double recovery, comprehensive no-fault compensation funds require the (near) extinguishment of access to court to seek common law damages in relation to the injury or event that is the subject of the compensation fund claim.[286] In contrast, this is not a defining feature of a non-comprehensive fund.[287] An obvious critique of no-fault compensation funds of all kinds (whether comprehensive or more limited), and their associated extinguishment of common law rights, is that they remove choice for claimants and remove their freedom to seek larger amounts of compensation via a common law claim. This reduction in freedom could logically be translated as a barrier to accessing justice. However this is contextual, and the overall

---

[284] Kathleen Daly, 'What Is Restorative Justice? Fresh Answers to a Vexed Question' (2016) 11 *Victims & Offenders* 9 <https://doi.org/10.1080/15564886.2015.1107797>.

[285] Consider, for example, the delays and uncertainty endemic to the Belgian Fund for Medical Accidents – see Thierry Vansweevelt, Steven Lierman and Wannes Buelens, 'No-Fault Law on Medical Accidents in Belgium: An Evaluation after Six Years' (2019) 10 *Journal of European Tort Law* 257.

[286] There has been some recent recognition, however, that low levels of compensation available under a compensation fund lead to opposition by potential claimants and lawyers. In Scotland, where a historical abuse redress scheme is being planned, the government has said that successful claimants will not be barred from bringing a further civil claim. See 'Child Abuse Survivors "Can Still Seek Damages after Redress Payouts"', *The Scotsman* (3 May 2019) <https://www.scotsman.com/news/politics/child-abuse-survivors-can-still-seek-damages-after-redress-payouts-1-4920012>.

[287] Particularly for a compensation fund that takes a submissive role in relation to other compensation mechanisms – see Vansweevelt and others (n 1) 202.

advantages of a widely accessible compensation mechanism (whether a fund or a change to other compensation frameworks) neutralise the negative effects of reduced choice. For example, Australia's Productivity Commission concluded that the high cost of fault-based systems versus the advantages for people's wellbeing under alternative insurance arrangements meant that '[f]reedom of choice per se, is not a sufficient basis for maintaining all common law rights.'[288] A big compensation fund should also not be blamed for access to justice problems that result from contextual difficulties. For example, as discussed earlier in this chapter there is a niche carve-out under the ACC Scheme statutory bar for an appeal on limited grounds to the Human Rights Review Tribunal.[289] However, a case brought before this forum is likely to face significant delays due to a lack of resourcing and funding, at the same time as increased numbers of applications (particularly privacy-related cases, a likely topic of challenge based on the available case law).[290] This correlation in access to justice woes is *not* the same issue as a large no-fault compensation fund actively causing access to justice problems. This is a useful segue to turn towards the ways in which a big no-fault fund might indeed be perceived as blocking access to justice.

3.3. THE NO-FAULT COMPREHENSIVE COMPENSATION FUND AS A BARRIER TO ACCESS TO JUSTICE

Despite their broad access to justice benefits, no-fault comprehensive compensation funds are not perfect. Unintentionally or by design, they can operate as an access to justice barrier in specific ways.

Mijatov, Barraclough and Forster undertook a specific analysis of access to justice issues in relation to the New Zealand ACC Scheme and the CRPD shadow report prepared in 2015 by Acclaim Otago.[291] This analysis isolated four conceptions of access to justice that take the jurisprudence a step further along from the 'third wave' of access to justice reforms, and are specifically related to big no-fault fund funds. These conceptions are:[292]

'(1) access to justice as a synonym for equality or non-discrimination before the law in the manner of earlier human rights conventions; (2) a multi-factorial and wide

---

[288] Productivity Commission, 'Productivity Commission Inquiry Report – Disability Care and Support, Volume 2' (2011) 828 <http://www.pc.gov.au/inquiries/completed/disability-support/report/disability-support-volume2.pdf>.

[289] Accident Compensation Act 2001 s 317(4).

[290] Eleanor Ainge Roy, 'New Zealand's Human Rights Tribunal "breaching Human Rights" Due to Delays', *The Guardian* (11 April 2018) <https://www.theguardian.com/world/2018/apr/11/new-zealands-human-rights-tribunal-breaching-human-rights-due-to-delays>.

[291] Mijatov, Barraclough and Forster (n 279).

[292] ibid 210.

account of access to justice that includes judicial and non-judicial formal institutions as well as informal institutions such as community organizations, disabled peoples' organizations, and even the application of accepted or contested norms of social justice; (3) a version that rejects courts as creators and resolvers of disputes, reflecting their perceived failure to dispense justice and therefore emphasizing non-legal institutions; and (4) a version that takes law as justice and regards access to law as access to justice, therefore regarding the courts as justice institutions essential to the application of legal rules and the dispensation of justice.'

Mijatov and his co-authors argue that the existing implementation of the ACC Scheme falls under the third and fourth conceptions. The traditional tort system falls within the first conception. Mijatov and his co-authors argue that the ACC Scheme should strive to fall also within the second conception of access to justice. The ACC Scheme's embodiment of the third and fourth conceptions was seen as a failure of the full potential of the scheme and of a full vision of access to justice, as originally envisaged by the late Sir Owen Woodhouse. Therefore, the ACC Scheme allegedly contains a barrier to comprehensive access to justice, even if it is an embodiment of a basic conception of access. In my view this is probably a fair interpretation, in access to justice 'jargon', of the fact that the ACC Scheme serves some victims of misfortune very well and not others (for example, people whose disability is caused by disease and not accidental injury). If one insists upon a classic Woodhouse vision of one scheme to cure all forms of misfortune, then that is a valid interpretation that ACC currently comprises a barrier to full access to justice. However, comparative law scholarship tells us that the greatest difficulty currently faced by most no-fault comprehensive compensation funds is poor definition, a lack of streamlining and an absence of proper principled parameters.[293] Therefore, one can certainly conclude that schemes like the ACC are a barrier to a full conception of access to justice from an extra-legal perspective. However, this has to be counterbalanced by what comparative law research tells us about the need for greater certainty and coherency in the use of this kind of legal framework.[294] This inevitably involves some degree of defined scope and ultimate judicial supervision to ensure compliance and coherency with the wider legal landscape that the fund operates in.

As noted in the previous section, the fact that the wider system does not provide adequate compensation options for non-covered claimants is not actually something that is the fault of the big no-fault compensation fund itself. This does not mean that the plight of the child catastrophically injured by a snowmobile in northern Québec, or the psychologically traumatised terrorist attack witness in New Zealand should be viewed unfeelingly or without regard to what they are

---

[293] Vansweevelt and others (n 1) 208; Macleod and Hodges (n 282) 647–648.
[294] Vansweevelt and others (n 1) 207–213.

Chapter 5. Human Rights, Access to Justice and Dispute Resolution

missing out on by virtue of the SAAQ and ACC schemes' respective wording. However these are not problems to be answered by the big no-fault compensation fund – adequate solutions should be designed and facilitated by the legislature if it is perceived as morally unacceptable that these victims are forced to bear their own loss. There is no limit to how far a comprehensive no-fault compensation fund could theoretically be extended, and yet there would always be one victim or another who might miss out. It is the legislature that is responsible for the whole legal compensation framework in society, not a no-fault comprehensive compensation fund (despite its wide functional scope).

Turning to more practical ways that no-fault comprehensive compensation funds act as a barrier to accessing justice, the most obvious way that this manifests is via reduced access to courts and legal information. As discussed already, reduced access to the courts seems to be tempered by the wide entitlements available under the scheme and the ultimate availability under all four schemes of recourse to the courts, if only on points of law. However, reduced access to legal information and guidance is certainly an access to justice barrier faced by claimants under all four schemes. As discussed already, it is only the MPI that makes free substantive legal advice available to all claimants with a dispute (after the initial review stage), with the TAC offering a structured pathway to legal advice that may be subsidised in some cases. Given that we have discovered that (probably complex) causative disputes are the most common form of dispute in all four big funds, providing better access to specific legal advice (not merely navigation or guidance) seems to be essential to reducing this information and guidance barrier.

The lower quantum of compensation available to most claimants is another obvious way that big no-fault compensation funds stop individuals – particularly those who might otherwise be able to prove significant personal injury-related loss, including pain and suffering – from the fullest realisation of justice for their harm. However, as discussed in Chapter 4, the focus within these funds is the social and vocational rehabilitation of the injury victim in a post-accident reality. For some catastrophically injured claimants, potentially unlimited compensation may be available. Further, the Canadian schemes show that it is possible to sustainably include non-pecuniary damages for pain and suffering within a big no-fault compensation fund. Although all four funds use indexing to keep statutorily described compensation levels rising in line with inflation, there is certainly scope for the legislature to review the substantive bands of compensation available from time to time. Although all four schemes are sustainable, there are some significant discrepancies in the amounts and heads of compensation available between the four schemes. An inadequacy in compensation available for a certain class of victims leads to the temptation to use other mechanisms outside the scheme to 'top-up' payments to these victims, without proper legal justification. This is a particular problem within the ACC Scheme and its lack of any non-pecuniary compensation combined with only

Intersentia

limited levels of lump sum compensation. It could therefore be concluded that a failure to regularly rationalise the amount and heads of compensation under big no-fault compensation funds is a way that that these schemes can block access to justice.

However, it should also not be assumed that no-fault comprehensive compensation funds will, by virtue of creating a statutory right to compensation, adequately address compensation issues for marginalised and persistently disadvantaged groups (who are *prima facie* entitled to cover). As one example, a big no-fault compensation fund does not, without specific design, ensure gender neutrality of compensation. Feminist legal scholars have argued that both judicial calculations of court damages *and* statutory compensation schemes are inherently biased in favour of male economic losses.[295] Women, by contrast, tend to suffer injuries in circumstances where there is no head of damage or where statutory schemes do not provide enough compensation.[296] This is particularly relevant to, for example, wrongful birth cases that are covered by the ACC Scheme. The relevant 'injury' that may be compensated for is the pregnancy, childbirth and immediate postnatal period[297] – but the long-term emotional and economic impact of childrearing that disproportionally affects women is not included in this calculation of quantum.

If court-based damages do not adequately compensate for typically 'female' injuries, then this is a type of barrier to accessing justice caused by the non-individualised nature of compensation under big no-fault funds. No-fault comprehensive compensation funds have the potential to more adequately compensate losses in a more gender-neutral way – but only if this need for equality is properly catered for within the compensation fund system design. The New Zealand ACC Scheme, given its universal application to all accidental injuries (including those occurring in the home), is on one hand a system that provides more egalitarian compensation to all classes of injury (both a stay-at-home mother who trips and falls and the male road worker will receive compensation and rehabilitative support). On the other hand, non-earners are not entitled to any income replacement compensation, which has greater adverse effect on a victim whose occupation is an unpaid caring role. Further, even the generous New Zealand compensation fund and court definitions of the statutory entitlements have restricted women from recovering the whole cost of childcare and loss of wages in the case of an unwanted pregnancy after sterilisation failure.[298] This is an illustration of a specific way that a large no-fault compensation fund can actually entrench barriers preventing access

---

[295] Reg Graycar, 'The Gender of Judgments: An Introduction' (2009) 09/73 <http://ssrn.com/abstract=1465171http://ssrn.com/abstract=1465171.>.

[296] Kylie Burns, 'The Gender of Damages and Compensation' (2019) 151 *Precedent* 9.

[297] *J v Accident Compensation Corporation* [2017] NZCA 441.

[298] Anthea Williams, 'Wrongful Birth and Lost Wages: *J v Accident Compensation Corp*' (2018) 2 *New Zealand Women's Law Journal* 295.

Chapter 5. Human Rights, Access to Justice and Dispute Resolution

to justice. Where there is no secondary avenue for legal redress (for example the possibility of a court challenge on the issue of adequate compensation is blocked by way of the fund's relevant statutory bar), then the compensation fund solidifies dominant biases and failures to recognise inequality of chances and outcomes for specific types of harm victims. Further, it may be more difficult to effect recognition of these inequalities by way of legislative amendments than by securing a judgment in a test case or class action on a specific type of loss – although this will of course depend upon the specific facts at hand. The Canadian schemes, which provide an entitlement to compensation for unemployed (but employable) victims with reference to the median industrial wage, do a better job of limiting this barrier to justice.

There are other unintentional negative side-effects in relation to access to justice caused by a no-fault comprehensive compensation fund. The wide exclusion of a particular type of remedy for harm (in this case, the tort action for personal injury for a wide category of victims) will mean that other enforcement or regulatory mechanisms will take on greater importance. The failure of those parallel mechanisms to work as effectively as hoped will result in significant consequences and a specific access to justice 'gap', despite the existence of a broad no-fault compensation fund which in general terms is perceived as a positive access to justice mechanism. When aspects of the civil justice system become imbalanced, society experiences adverse effects.[299] This was identified by New Zealand medico-legal scholar Joanna Manning in relation to the Health and Disability Commissioner complaints process, which is the sole remaining avenue for disgruntled patients to bring a claim in relation to a healthcare professional who has caused harm (the compensatory losses flowing from that harm being covered by ACC).[300] Manning pointed to qualitative and quantitative evidence which showed that no substantive action or investigation was undertaken for a significant number of complaints. This left complainants with no remedy because a medical negligence action was barred and the only other possible avenue, the Ombudsman, had shown reluctance to intervene and only has power to require the Health and Disability Commission to review his decision. These factors all combine to result in significant limitations on access to justice for a severely harmed minor category of victims. Specifically:

'successive governments have been and remain in breach of their side of the social contract underpinning the citizen's loss of the tort action. Access to ACC cover and

---

[299]   Victor E Schwartz and Cary Silverman, 'The Case in Favor of Civil Justice Reform' (2016) 65 *Emory Law Journal Online* 2065, 2085 <http://www.manhattan-institute.org/pdf/TLI-KStreet.pdf>.

[300]   Joanna M Manning, '"Fair, Simple, Speedy and Efficient"? Barriers to Access to Justice in the Health and Disability Commissioner's Complaints Process in New Zealand' (2018) 4 *New Zealand Law Review* 611 <http://www.legislation.govt.nz/act/public/1994/0088/latest/viewpdf.aspx>.

Intersentia

compensation only partly fulfils the state's side of the bargain, as was recognised by the creation of a complaints regime designed to address consumers' non-financial needs after an adverse event. All too often complainants and consumers who utilise the complaints regime, which is the only avenue available to them to address their grievances, are denied access to justice.'

4. CONCLUSION

The analyses in this chapter and the following conclusions further answer the second research question: What is the interaction between comprehensive no-fault compensation funds and human rights law, principles of access to justice and practical dispute resolution issues?

Human rights law was not considered in any detail during the establishment of our four schemes. However, their scope and implementation have been found to be *broadly compliant with the existing human rights frameworks* in each jurisdiction. This is partially for reasons of the contextual constitutional design and human rights framework, and partly due to recognition by courts of the wider *access to justice goals and social contract* intended by these big funds. However, the domestic compliance of the schemes does not guarantee that there will be compliance with international human rights frameworks, particularly civil and political rights frameworks for disabled persons.

The *statutory bar on tort proceedings* within comprehensive no-fault funds has been found to be *human rights compliant* and a *justified limitation* on civil justice rights, because of the wide compensation entitlements and broader access to justice they provide. Courts have found this to be a justified social choice by the legislature. In *relevant Canadian case law, it has been established that there is no fundamental right to bring a civil claim for personal injury damages.* This is a clear statement of compliance, compared to the more nuanced position taken in European human rights case law. This does not mean, however, that the matter of human rights law has been settled for the purposes of large no-fault compensation funds – there is a direct legal and policy gap that has not been adequately addressed by any of the four legislatures that supervise our four funds.

There is a *wider range of possible human rights intersections* created by a comprehensive no-fault compensation fund compared to a non-comprehensive fund. This is because of their broad lateral regulatory function and the sensitive nature of claimant data that the funds process. It seems more likely that a *human rights-based challenge on regulatory scope or privacy issues* will be successful than a challenge to the validity of the whole scheme.

Funds have displayed a practical *willingness to be as compliant as possible* with human rights law, to the extent that is possible under their legislative framework. Further directions on big funds' intersections with human rights

380

Intersentia

law need to be specifically clarified by legislatures. Generally speaking, *it will be necessary in the future for compensation fund legislation to be more specifically cognisant of human rights* and to foresee appropriate oversight.

Comprehensive no-fault compensation funds are part of *the 'third wave' of the global access to justice movement* and continuing developments. Broadly speaking, these big funds enhance access to justice because they meet the requirements of efficiency, fairness, cost-effectiveness and accessibility. However, they may also create or worsen barriers to accessing justice. This manifests mainly in:

a. reduced access to legal information and advice for most claimants;
b. lower compensation quantum or inadequate heads of compensation for persistently disadvantaged groups; and
c. indirect overall reduction of access to justice via the legislature's failure to meaningfully legislate horizontally in parallel regulatory functions.

However, care should be taken to not jump to the likely erroneous conclusion that scheme extension would fix these and other problems.

CHAPTER 6

COMPENSATION FUND GOALS AND PRACTICAL APPLICATIONS

1. INTRODUCTION

This book has so far crystallised and analysed, for the first time, a definition of the largest type of no-fault comprehensive compensation funds that are publicly administered. It has also developed a suitable comparative law methodology for analysing such funds. There was an initial consideration of the core problems associated with the classification of compensation funds generally. This is because there is a lack of agreed definition within existing literature and practice about no-fault compensation funds generally. There has also been no significant scholarly analysis of the largest types of no-fault compensation funds in particular. In Chapters 3 and 4 there was a practically focused crystallisation of the defining and key features of very large and mature no-fault compensation funds, with appropriate functional and structural comparisons. There was also a novel first principles consideration of the intersections between very large no-fault compensation funds and human rights, with a specific focus on access to justice and dispute resolution issues. This crystallisation and analysis approach has added to the existing literature by providing a clear picture, for the first time, of the key legal landmarks of comprehensive no-fault compensation funds, as a subset of the wider no-fault or no-blame[1] compensation funds.

However, in order to be most relevant and useful, this research also needs to look toward the future development of large no-fault compensation funds. There is potential for no-fault frameworks, as a non-liability compensation solution, to be used to address contemporary and future problems. These problems range from issues as diverse as new jurisdictions adopting the comprehensive no-fault model for transport injury, artificial intelligence damages applications, to the implementation of national and global vaccine injury compensation funds to underpin the COVID-19 global vaccination campaign. The analysis undertaken in this book provides more definitional clarity and guidance about the positive

---

[1]   Sonia Macleod and Christopher Hodges, 'Part IX: Conclusions' in Sonia Macleod and Christopher Hodges (eds), *Redress Schemes for Personal Injuries* (1st edn, Hart Publishing 2017) 615.

Intersentia   383

and negative elements of these very big schemes, which enables more informed legislative and policy choices to be made about the future of our four existing funds and the development of new funds.

This is not simply a theoretical exercise. Two Canadian provinces have recently investigated a big no-fault compensation fund model for transport injury (based on MPI and SAAQ). The European Parliament has proposed a resolution on an EU-wide civil liability regime for artificial intelligence applications that would include a compensation fund.[2] Liability associated with COVID-19 vaccine injury is a high-profile topic at the time of writing, and novel new no-fault compensation solutions have been created at the multinational and national levels.[3] No-fault compensation schemes have also been proposed as a tool to sustainably complement insurance frameworks for losses associated with the impacts of climate change and necessary adaptations.[4] It is not possible to answer in this book whether all types of no-fault compensation funds are a useful tool to address these topical problems. However, it is certainly possible to answer whether and how *very large, compulsory/non-subsidiary* and *publicly administered* no-fault compensation funds could be used to address contemporary legal problems common to multiple jurisdictions.

In this chapter, a handful of different but interrelated legal analytical problems will be tackled. There will be an analysis of realistic future legal goals for the four existing big funds that were the subject of this project's comparative analysis. This includes specific consideration of the outstanding and future legal problems associated with large no-fault comprehensive compensation funds. These pieces of analysis will then inform a discussion about the potential suitability of the comprehensive no-fault compensation framework to two contemporary practical applications. The first potential application is a large no-fault compensation fund framework for personal injury losses caused by automated vehicles and by other artificial intelligence applications. The second potential application – which was rapidly evolving and had unexpectedly become a tangible reality at the time of writing – is a large, globally coherent no-fault compensation fund framework for COVID-19 vaccine injuries.

There is a pressing need for greater understanding about the potential usefulness of very big no-fault compensation frameworks to new kinds of

---

[2]   Clause 22 European Parliament resolution of 20 October 2020 with recommendations to the Commission on a civil liability regime for artificial intelligence (2020/2014(INL)).

[3]   Kim Watts and Tina Popa, 'Injecting Fairness into COVID-19 Vaccine Injury Compensation: No-Fault Solutions' (2021) 12 *Journal of European Tort Law* 1.

[4]   The Australia Institute, 'The National Climate Disaster Fund' (2019) <https://www.tai. org.au>; Julie-Anne Richards and Liane Schalatek, 'Not a Silver Bullet: Why the Focus on Insurance to Address Loss and Damage Is a Distraction from Real Solutions' (Heinrich Böll Stiftung North America 2018); Pak-Hang Wong, Tom Douglas and Julian Savulescu, 'Compensation for Geoengineering Harms and No-Fault Climate Change Compensation' <http://geoengineeringgovernanceresearch.org>.

Chapter 6. Compensation Fund Goals and Practical Applications

applications, and inadequate existing literature to properly inform the relevant legal choices that can be made by legislatures and executives. The two applications analysed in this chapter reflect two themes of contemporary applications of big no-fault compensation funds. The first is an unprecedented liability and bodily harm uncertainty, caused by novel artificial intelligence applications. The second is an unprecedented public health crisis and an unprecedentedly fast pharmaceutical response, with the potential for bodily harm. These themes are different to the typical application range of existing big no-fault compensation funds – existing and well-understood bodily harm risks, such as traditional transport injury or general bodily harm risks. There are other potential applications for large no-fault compensation funds – specifically disaster-related physical damage applications associated with climate change – but there is not space or scope within this text to consider this.

There will therefore be an analysis in this chapter about whether the research results relating to existing functional applications and identified key pillars of big no-fault compensation funds are also relevant to these new functional scopes. The research conclusions in this book's previous chapters have demonstrated that no-fault comprehensive compensation funds are most logically relevant when they are established to address a clearly articulated societal risk associated with a wide functional category of harm. This can be described as a hurt or harm where it is more appropriate, or perhaps simply reasonable, to assume community (read: public) responsibility or solidarity for organising compensation for this kind of harm. The establishment of such a large no-fault fund will be closely linked to activities that aim to prevent that kind of widespread harm from occurring in the first place. Personal injury – rather than economic damage – is also the most logical type of harm to be addressed by such large funds. This is also because of the community responsibility or solidarity purposes of the funds – guaranteed compensation and recovery from harm is a social contract enshrined in a statutory framework that excludes private law remedies.

The key learning aims of this chapter are therefore:

a.   The realistic goals for our four existing no-fault comprehensive compensation funds, in terms of matters such as legal coherency and purpose, financial stability and sustainability, compensation quantum, subrogation, planning and legislative reform, and human rights intersections. This includes consideration of the outstanding problems associated with big no-fault compensation funds.

b.   A preliminary analysis of how no-fault comprehensive compensation funds could be used to address liability and compensation problems associated with impending artificial intelligence applications. This includes analysis of both the benefits and drawbacks of using the typical big no-fault compensation fund framework for this application.

c. A preliminary analysis of how no-fault comprehensive compensation funds could or should be used to address injury consequences associated with COVID-19 vaccines. This includes analysis of both the benefits and drawbacks of using the typical big no-fault compensation fund framework for this application.

Matti Urho has concluded – in relation to Nordic drug injury compensation funds – that three essential requirements of a good no-fault compensation fund are: transparency, fairness, and functionality.[5] Sonia Macleod and Christopher Hodges have argued that the following (rather similar) parameters should govern the design of a compensation scheme (especially one in a contemporary European democracy): objectivity and a lack of bias; clear identification; adequate expertise and authority; efficiency; transparency; fairness; and maintenance and improvements in performance. These principles are an appropriate reference point against which to explore the legal goals, problems, redefinitions and potential applications set out in this chapter. However, these principles are arguably common to many legal frameworks. Looking more widely at emerging trends in the field of legal design theory, one can see that the criteria of usability, procedural justice, engagement, legal capability, achievement of resolution and the weight of administrative burden are also relevant.[6]

It is therefore also appropriate to add some extra criteria that are specific to no-fault compensation funds but incorporate the principles articulated by other scholars. The analysis undertaken in this book indicates two extra criteria that can be used for the assessment of no-fault compensation funds generally, and very large no-fault funds specifically.

The first new criterion is coherency, both of purpose and context. A recent comparative law assessment of no-fault compensation funds has found that this field of alternative redress systems can achieve 'more coherent development' by way of 'good procedure and decent systems design' that properly matches an individual jurisdiction's perception of appropriate compensation.[7] Therefore, the framework establishing the scheme should be legislatively coherent in terms of its objectives and also maintain that coherency across its different provisions. Coherency of context is also important – for example, one of the failings of the New Zealand ACC Scheme is that it is not coherent with non-injury compensation and protection.

---

[5] Matti Urho, 'Compensation for Drug-Related Injuries' (2018) 4 *European Review of Private Law* 467, para 53.

[6] Margaret Hagan, 'Legal Design as a Thing: A Theory of Change and a Set of Methods to Craft a Human-Centered Legal System' (2020) 36 *Design Issues* 14 <https://doi.org/10.1162/desi_a_00600>.

[7] Thierry Vansweevelt and others, 'Comparative Analysis of Compensation Funds' in Thierry Vansweevelt and Britt Weyts (eds), *Compensation Funds in Comparative Perspective* (Intersentia 2020) 210.

The second new criterion is preciseness about non-eligibility – or in a layperson's terms, being more honest about who is excluded from the fund and why. Cane and Goudkamp have already identified that it is more desirable to accept the reality of distinctions made between different categories of victims, and design a scheme around legislatively justified differences in treatment that reflect appropriate priorities for the use of public funds and other resources.[8] This is something that is perhaps most relevant to very large no-fault compensation funds. We have seen that the exclusion of certain categories of individuals from compensation cover has been deemed by the courts to be acceptable where there is express legislative intent to exclude those persons. This is because of the large, social choice nature of these schemes that offers an alternative structure and legal model. In other jurisdictions, and in relation to smaller no-fault compensation schemes, this point of distinction could well amount to unfair discrimination. The issue about whether excluding certain groups from the scope of a no-fault compensation fund is unfair or discriminatory *per se* is therefore somewhat neutralised in our four large funds. It is not as fundamentally problematic an issue as might be the case in smaller, *ad hoc* schemes. This is because, as discussed in Chapter 5, the legislatures and the judiciary of those jurisdictions have all confirmed repeatedly that it is acceptable, in their legal system, to make such distinctions because of the significant policy and legal philosophical choice that has been made. There is nothing that conflicts with these legislative choices and judicial statements in the supreme laws and human rights laws of the four jurisdictions. Of course, it is still possible to critique these distinctions on normative fairness and justice grounds or from a human rights perspective.

However, regardless of scope and purpose (and legislative and judicial comment), a no-fault compensation fund of any kind should be required to show quite clearly and specifically who is excluded from its scope, and why that decision has been made. This is therefore similar to analyses about discrimination in relation to smaller no-fault compensation funds, but from a slightly different angle. Where a no-fault compensation fund is small in scope and subsidiary in availability, this criterion may end up having a lesser weighting than other assessment criterion. This is because a victim may have multiple possible sources of compensation (even where there are rules against double recovery in place).[9] However, a very large compensation fund may be the only possible compensation option available, and we have seen that exclusion from the scheme may have a significant impact on the victim. The more refined criterion for preciseness is therefore – has there been a precise articulation within legislation and other publicly available information about who falls and does not fall within the scope

---

[8]   ibid 212–213; Peter Cane and James Goudkamp, *Atiyah's Accidents, Compensation and the Law* (9th edn, Cambridge University Press 2018) 446–447.

[9]   Vansweevelt and others (n 7) 201–203.

of the scheme, and why? Has there been adequate justification for any exclusions on the grounds of the wider legal and social frameworks, human rights law and principles of justice?

We can therefore summarise the following principles as core reference points for our assessment of the goals, future development and practical applications of no-fault comprehensive compensation funds:

a. Efficiency. This includes issues like financial sustainability and the speed of making decisions and handling claims.
b. Transparency. This relates to issues such as adequate clarity and consistency about how the scheme is managed and how decisions are made.
c. Fairness. This includes issues like an absence of bias, and adequate compensation.
d. Functionality. This includes periodic revisions of the fund to maintain and improve such functionality.
e. Coherency. This includes a consideration of whether the fund is coherent with its wider legal environment, and is legislatively and practically coherent in terms of its own stated purpose.
f. Preciseness about eligibility. Unlike the issue of fairness (i.e. whether claimants are treated fairly), this criterion asks whether the fund is specific enough about whom it includes and excludes from eligibility, and why. The large scope of comprehensive no-fault compensation funds makes this important to consider.

2. REALISTIC LEGAL GOALS FOR EXISTING NO-FAULT COMPREHENSIVE COMPENSATION FUNDS

We turn first to the development of realistic legal goals for our existing four large no-fault compensation funds. As a reminder, the specific definition of this kind of very large compensation fund is as follows:

a. It is a single-pot fund-based system that provides compensation to real (human) persons, usually of a pecuniary nature.
b. A legal standard of fault is not relevant to an applicant's eligibility for compensation – the scheme is truly no-fault. However, there are specific causation criteria for eligibility.
c. The fund is comprehensive, which means that it covers a broad scope of functionally or thematically-linked events or losses. This is in contrast to the more common kind of non-comprehensive compensation fund which only compensates for injuries that occurred in a very limited and specific way.

Chapter 6. Compensation Fund Goals and Practical Applications

d. The compensation is paid or administered by a single public or quasi-public centralised body, out of a specific single pot. However, the funding of that pot might come from more than one source.

e. The fund is established by statute rather than by executive decree or as a consequence of a judicial proceeding (for example, a class action settlement fund).

f. The purpose of the financial support paid by the scheme is compensation. Mixed purposes are permissible (e.g. pecuniary, non-pecuniary and symbolic), but compensation must be *one* of the purposes of the financial payment or support provided. It is compensation, not an *ex gratia* gift.

g. The compensation provided is a compulsory alternative in (nearly) all circumstances to a tort law compensatory damages action or a public law damages action before the courts. The victim cannot choose a different system – the fund is non-subsidiary in nature.

h. The fund is not a wholesale part of the general social security system.

i. The fund does not compensate for contractual loss, bad conduct or insolvency.

j. The fund is available to all causatively eligible victims, not only those who have paid a levy. In this way, it is different to government-backed or government-underwritten insurance schemes.

What can we discern, based on this study, as the most realistic legal goals for the kind of big no-fault legal frameworks that fit the above definition? It is already clear that a simple expansion of eligibility or scope is not the answer to no-fault compensation fund inadequacies.[10] Nor is an abrupt repeal or reversion back to a traditional liability framework logical or necessary, given these big funds' broad empirical successes, popularity and financial sustainability. However, this does not mean that our four funds are immune from criticism – this study has revealed a number of problematic elements in the operation of this kind of large alternative liability mechanism over many decades. In all four funds, there are a number of areas of possible improvement that should be strived for. These goals should also be seen as part of the best practice for the model of large no-fault compensation funds generally, and elements that may have structural relevance to different types of no-fault schemes. The goals set out here have been drawn from the analyses and conclusions in earlier chapters, and are explored in more specific detail in the subsections below.

The analyses and recommendations that are made within this subsection relate to matters that are either within the control of the funds themselves or within the logical remit of the relevant government minister or legislators. However, sometimes it might be necessary to point generally to issues that are

---

[10] ibid 212–213.

Intersentia

389

outside of the statutory framework of the large no-fault compensation fund. For example, is the fund being blamed or made responsible for something that would actually be more logically relevant to another legal structure or legal inadequacy? Is there a mismatch between the public perception about what this big no-fault solidarity-infused fund is supposed to do, and what it is (or can, realistically be) tasked with via statute? If there is such a mismatch, does that reveal a fundamental theoretical or purposive unsustainability of the scheme?

2.1. IMPROVED COHERENCY OF PURPOSE AND LEGISLATIVE DESIGN

A lack of legal coherency is an issue that has already been identified in relation to the no-fault compensation fund field generally.[11] The field of compensation funds has evolved in a largely piecemeal fashion, especially since the retraction of interest in public no-fault solutions in the 1990s. As we have seen, this was partially due to a normative policy preference for privately managed solutions. Developments in different jurisdictions have generally occurred in reaction to specific insurance crises or mass harm disasters, and not on the basis of a principled development of alternative liability frameworks. This trend is also observable in relation to our four no-fault compensation funds. Some specific recommendations can be made about goals for our four funds, that would improve their coherency of purpose and legislative design. It is also possible to draw conclusions about what kind of *function* large no-fault compensation funds are best suited to.

It is important to state that no conclusions are being made about what kind of (social or legal) purpose is most normatively suitable for a comprehensive no-fault compensation fund. The study undertaken in the book has shown that the big no-fault compensation fund is a socio-legal structure that is heavily influenced by the legal, financial and social context in which it is created. The four funds are functionally all related to personal injury caused by common or everyday harms (three with a transport focus), so it could be said that a purpose that is relevant in some way to the compensation for and reduction of injury is ideal for these kinds of structures to have. However, this would exclude the possibility of this kind of scheme being used for other kinds of harms or for other purposes. If the large no-fault compensation fund is to be seen and critiqued as the legal tool it is – no different to other kinds of legal problem-solving mechanisms – then a definitional analysis should eschew normative assumptions and accept the contextual element of the purpose that is set by the legislature (and perhaps tested by judicial challenge).

---

[11]   ibid 207–210. See also the recommendations for more coherent 'no-blame' scheme design at Macleod and Hodges (n 1) 648–650.

390   Intersentia

As discussed earlier, in Chapter 2, there is a common proactive purpose that can be found in no-fault comprehensive compensation funds. Specifically, these schemes have been established proactively to compensate hypothetical future claimants for harms that have not yet occurred. This is different to the more common simpler type of reactive model, which is a no-fault compensation fund established for a specific known category of claimants that already exist but are ill-served by existing mechanisms.[12] This kind of proactive design and activity has led to either a complete or partial departure from tort law, that creates a new standalone compensation legal mechanism. However, as discussed later, there needs to be a legislative confirmation of this revolution and a renewed definition of scope and purpose for our four funds. As noted already, it is challenging to objectively assess the fairness and limitations of these funds and the revolutions that they embody, without a coherent and updated purpose being articulated by the legislature.

How could an improved coherency of purpose therefore be achieved for our four funds, based on the findings of this comparative law study? Each fund and its potential purpose goals will be considered separately – this is because of that core socio-legal and contextual uniqueness of each fund. However conclusions can also be drawn about purpose-setting for the large no-fault compensation fund model more generally.

2.1.1. New Zealand's ACC

The ACC has the most obviously urgent need, out of all four funds, to revise and redefine its purpose. It has maintained the same broadly coherent definition of its purpose since its establishment – namely of community responsibility for personal injury. However, there is no precision or recent restatement about the goals of the scheme, and how it should achieve contextual balance with other New Zealand legal frameworks. This has been most succinctly described by Simon Connell, who points out that the ACC remains successful because of its ability to be ambiguous about whether it is community insurance or compulsory insurance, thus appealing to a broad political consensus.[13] The courts and the New Zealand Treasury have enforced strictness about the current statutory framework and range of entitlements, arguing correctly that it would be inappropriate and incoherent to make *ad hoc* extensions for certain categories of victims.

As analysed in this study, there is no coherency and logic to the exclusion of certain forms of harm from compensation under this extremely broad

---

[12]   Vansweevelt and others (n 7) 197–198.
[13]   Simon Connell, 'Community Insurance versus Compulsory Insurance: Competing Paradigms of No-Fault Accident Compensation in New Zealand' (2019) 39(3) *Legal Studies* 499 <https://www.cambridge.org/core/product/identifier/S0261387518000508/type/journal_article>.

A Comparative Law Analysis of No-Fault Comprehensive Compensation Funds

no-fault scheme, simply because they do not fit the strict statutory criteria. Nor in contrast (such as the *DePuy*[14] case) is there any coherency or logic to restrictions on seeking extra pecuniary compensation from a defendant that does not enjoy the benefit of the scheme or contribute to it. The very wide scope of the scheme makes these kinds of exclusions more problematic, because there is not one simple functional theme of the injuries that are covered (as with the other three schemes, which are focused on transport injury). The ACC Scheme claims to be a 'fair and sustainable scheme for managing personal injury', but it does not actually fairly cover all types of loss that could logically be called personal injury or harm. The original plan for the scheme to be extended to cover sickness and disability – never realised – also hangs like a dark cloud over the scheme whenever the topic of reform is raised. Many vocal advocates argue that the scheme should revert back to Woodhouse's original vision, with its original social security-style funding structure.[15] Others have recognised that reform with different functional categories of injury in mind would be a better approach.[16] Voices that argue for a full Woodhouse vision ignore the structural reality of the scheme as it exists today – and others like it – and the success of the status quo for the structural stability of these schemes.

As mentioned already, one problem that the ACC Scheme faces is a societal (i.e. contextual) one – the other New Zealand social security and healthcare frameworks are inadequate to address gaping inequality and human development problems in that country.[17] The design of the ACC Scheme, as a comprehensive no-fault compensation fund, simply does not match the Beveridge style mid-twentieth-century nature of other social protection structures in New Zealand. This has some significant consequences. The ACC Scheme is being expected to step up to address failings that are not logically its responsibility, and in a sense is being held hostage by its own success. One topical example is the lack of income and health support for mental health victims of a terrorist attack.[18] ACC and the

---

[14] *McGougan v DePuy International Limited* [2018] NZCA 91.

[15] Susan St John, 'Reflections on the Woodhouse Legacy for the 21st Century' (2020) 51 *Victoria University of Wellington Law Review* 295 <https://ojs.victoria.ac.nz/vuwlr/article/view/6572/5734>.

[16] For a recent analysis that advocates a different purposive approach being taken for workplace-related injuries under ACC, see Dawn Duncan, 'Beyond Accident: A Model for the Compensation of Work-Related Harm in New Zealand' (Victoria University of Wellington 2019).

[17] 2019 reporting on a survey by the Organization for Economic Cooperation and Development noted that New Zealand has worse inequality and skewed social development outcomes than most advanced economies – see 'New Zealand Economic Snapshot' <https://www.oecd.org/economy/new-zealand-economic-snapshot/>.

[18] Veronica Schmidt, 'Why ACC Is Turning Away Traumatised Mosque Survivors', *Radio New Zealand News* (14 May 2019) <https://www.rnz.co.nz/news/in-depth/389140/why-acc-is-turning-away-traumatised-mosque-survivors>; Ministry of Business Innovation and Employment, 'Extended Mental Health Support for Those Affected by the 15 March 2019 Terrorist Attack'; Cabinet Business Committee, 'Minute of Decision CBC-19-MIN-0014'.

Chapter 6. Compensation Fund Goals and Practical Applications

relevant Minister argued for an *ad hoc* extension to cover these victims, because there was no other government body capable of delivering help to these victims effectively. However, this was rebuffed by Treasury accurately pointing out that this would create inconsistencies in the scheme. Another example recently in the public eye is the decision by ACC to withdraw cover for virtually all perinatal birth injuries, unless they fall squarely within the definition of treatment injury.[19] The treatment of perineal tears is something that would logically fall within the spectrum of general postnatal healthcare. However, the lack of treatment availability and income-replacement payments during recovery under the public health and social security system has made affected women desperate to regain ACC cover, because there is effectively nothing else available to them.

This problem extends to long-tail issues too – specifically, the increased impact of chronic health and demographic issues like obesity, diabetes and ageing, which are being caught by ACC only when they translate into personal injury. Further, this range of risk groups may not be accurately levied, based on current financial design of the scheme, to cover the associated compensation and rehabilitation costs. ACC's parallel prevention investments cannot and should not possibly capture all of the public health costs and dimensions of these kinds of chronic health and demographic issues.

The existence of the ACC Scheme and its blurry edges of wide cover, combined with the inferior nature of the wider health and social security protections, also puts the ACC Scheme into a risky 'too big to fail' position. It is now extremely difficult to undertake any meaningful reform of this large no-fault compensation fund for the better in terms of coherency, because a sharpening of purpose will likely have significant impacts on other publicly funded services and will be highly politically sensitive.

It is not within the scope of this book to make recommendations about the wider health and social policy settings that New Zealand should aim for. It seems likely that some coordinated revision is likely within the near term.[20] This will hopefully help to resolve a variety of coherency and contextual issues, including

---

[19]   Accident Compensation Corporation, 'Perineal Tear Treatment Injury' (2020) <www.acc. co.nz/lodgementguide>; 'Midwives Urge ACC to Rethink "inequities" around Perineal Tear Cover', *Radio New Zealand News* (1 April 2021) <https://www.rnz.co.nz/news/ national/439631/midwives-urge-acc-to-rethink-inequities-around-perineal-tear-cover>; Anusha Bradley, 'Lawyers Question ACC's New Policy on Perineal Tears', *Radio New Zealand News* (31 March 2021) <https://www.rnz.co.nz/news/national/439591/lawyers-question-acc-s-new-policy-on-perineal-tears>.

[20]   At the time of writing, the sixth Labour Government of New Zealand had announced that it would investigate the creation of social insurance structures in other parts of the welfare system. This indicates that co-ordinated reform, that will have some intersection with ACC, is likely in the medium term. See 'Finance Minister's Budget 2021 Speech' <https:// www.beehive.govt.nz/speech/finance-ministers-budget-2021-speech>. See also *Health and Disability System Review: Final Report / Pūrongo Whakamutunga* (2020) <www.systemreview. health.govt.nz/final-report>.

Intersentia

393

the problematic treatment injury test that still ends up relying on fault-based principles. However, some specific recommendations about legal coherency goals can be made.

a. Firstly, there should be a clear choice made between whether the ACC Scheme can be defined as a type of community solidarity programme, or a type of compulsory insurance. Based on the observations of the scheme's structural and functional operation, it seems logical to conclude that it is indeed a compulsory insurer in line with social insurance programmes in other jurisdictions (including its three big no-fault cousins in Australia and Canada). However the *contextual* problems of the wider New Zealand social structure landscape have meant that it is subject to the political turbulence of a community solidarity programme. By specifically articulating that the ACC is a compulsory insurer, that exists to fulfil a specific social choice, the scheme would be freer to more accurately levy risk and stand more independently from political influence. This would significantly improve the coherency and transparency of the scheme.

b. Secondly, there should be a clearer legislative statement made about which kinds of harms are selected for cover, and why. This is a restatement of the point made already by Cane and Goudkamp.[21] If sickness and disability (i.e., non-injury harms) remain excluded from the scope, this should be stated along with a clear justification of why personal injury is being treated differently to other kinds of harms. Potential reasons could perhaps include: the suitability of a risk-based model for accidental injury, because wider public health structures are perceived as being better suited to handle chronic and disease-caused illness, or because of a desire to maintain public underwriting and control of the costs of personal injury. If there is improved precision about eligibility and its justifications within the legislation itself, then this provides a less vague reference point for civic discourse and possibly even judicial challenges to unfairness. Many of the current political and public sphere disputes about ACC centre on what it does *not* cover and why it should cover *more* types of harm. As discussed already, some of the arguments in favour of an increased ACC scope of cover are inappropriate and incoherent with the mature and stable version of the scheme as it exists today. Although these kinds of changes would undoubtedly help the extra victims covered, they would undermine functionality and coherency. The principled and coherent development of the ACC Scheme would be most successful if purist Woodhouse visions of the future of ACC – a fully expanded scheme that includes sickness and disability – were recognised

---

[21] Cane and Goudkamp (n 8) 446–447.

Chapter 6. Compensation Fund Goals and Practical Applications

for what they are. Namely, something that may not be entirely suitable to create more than 50 years after they were first suggested – because society, the economy, and ACC itself are now quite different beasts to what they were then.[22]

2.1.2. Victoria's TAC

Turning next to the TAC, we see a much clearer purpose and legislative design than the ACC scheme. It began with much less clarity of purpose than the ACC Scheme – in terms of the concepts of a revolution away from tort law – but over time it has developed a sharp focus on managing the social risks associated with road transport. The fund itself has developed a goal for itself to be the 'world's best social insurer', with an aggressive focus on improving safety and eliminating road accident deaths. However, it is still possible to set some coherency goals for the TAC, based on the comparative law analysis undertaken in this study.

a. The main goal for improved coherency of purpose in the TAC scheme relates to the scope of the common law carve-out for serious injury. This has already been identified in this study as an element of the scheme that is legally incoherent with the rest of the scheme, amounting to only a partial departure from tort. The wide territorial coverage of the liability exemption within the TAC legislation means that in nearly all cases, the costs of serious injury claims will be covered by the TAC itself (i.e. by road users). On the other hand, despite the incoherency, the common law carve-out appears to be well-managed procedurally and generally financially sustainable (because it is available to only a very limited number of road accident victims). Therefore, in order to improve coherency the applicable test for 'serious' should be better defined in the legislation, specifically to reduce the complexity associated with the relevant legal tests. As discussed in Chapter 3, when the TAC makes its assessment of serious injury it does so with reference to the American Medical Association's Guides to the Evaluation of Permanent Impairment.[23] However, if the claimant disagrees with this assessment and brings it before a court for a review, then a different and highly complex legal test is used.[24] It would be better if the legislation specified the relevant test to be used by both the TAC and a judge upon

---

[22] For an interesting discussion hinting at similar themes more than 15 years ago, see Ken Oliphant, 'Beyond Woodhouse: Devising New Principles for Determining ACC Boundary Issues' (2004) 35 *Victoria University of Wellington Law Review* 915.

[23] Transport Accident Act 1986 (Victoria) s 46A.

[24] See *Transport Accident Commission v Katanas* [2017] HCA 32; Judicial College of Victoria, *Serious Injury Manual* (2019) <http://www.judicialcollege.vic.edu.au/eManuals/SIM/index.htm#53962.htm>.

Intersentia

395

review for the same standardised determination of personal injury in accordance with medical standards. It is not coherent to have the TAC and the court use different tests for the determination of serious injury – or for a pure no-fault framework to allow a speculative and highly subjective method of calculation of compensation for limited numbers of claimants. Consistency in the tests applied by the TAC and the courts in serious injury cases would be a realistic coherency goal.

b.   Secondly, there should be coherency about the application of the TAC to other forms of road users, particularly given the growing importance of multimodal transport and micro-mobility devices. As noted in Chapter 3, there is only limited coverage for bicycle users under the TAC scheme (although coverage was expanded in 2018),[25] and there is no coverage as yet for new types of transport devices like e-scooters. This approach is not coherent with the current global shifts in individual mobility that are currently underway, and which show no sign of slowing down.[26] As an increasing amount of public space and urban planning is allocated to different modes of transport, it will be necessary to adapt the relevant regulatory frameworks. The City of Melbourne's Transport Plan 2030 envisages widespread use of micromobility devices – but says 'The City of Melbourne's Transport Strategy 2030 envisages extensive use of micromobility devices, but a regulatory framework is needed for dockless transport to manage large numbers of vehicles, risks and maximise benefits'.[27] Meanwhile, the Victorian Government plans to carry out a trial of e-scooters. Therefore, it seems likely that some kind of revision to the TAC's scope will be considered in the near future. However, that revision will require consideration of whether micromobility devices should be treated like bicycles and public transport (only activating TAC cover in limited circumstances) or like the traditional automobile (activating TAC cover in most circumstances). In my view, a review of scheme coherency on this point should anticipate that the automobile may not be the dominant transport device in the future, at least not in metropolitan Melbourne. This would mean giving equivalent treatment to multiple different transport modes. A well thought out reassessment of these issues would improve coherency, functionality and fairness.

---

[25]   Treasury and Finance Legislation Amendment Act 2018; Transport Accident Commission, 'TAC Legislation Changes' <http://www.tac.vic.gov.au/providers/for-service-providers/for-legal-professionals/tac-legislation-changes>.

[26]   Kim Watts, 'Potential of No-Fault Comprehensive Compensation Funds to Deal with Automation and Other 21st Century Transport Developments' (2020) 12 *European Journal of Commercial Contract Law* 1.

[27]   City of Melbourne, 'Transport Strategy 2030' (2019) 92 <https://www.melbourne.vic.gov.au/SiteCollectionDocuments/transport-strategy-2030-city-of-melbourne.pdf>.

2.1.3. Québec's SAAQ

Moving to Canada, similar issues of scheme coherency inform suitable goals for the SAAQ. The scheme overall has fairly good clarity of purpose, given its singular focus on transport injury and global coverage for Québec residents. However, there can still be improvements made to scheme coherency that could improve fairness and preciseness about eligibility. These centre on the results of the case *J.A. v SAAQ*, which declined SAAQ coverage for a child severely injured by an uninsured snowmobile. This was in Nunavik, a sparsely populated part of the province that is north of the 55th parallel of latitude. The appellant had argued that north of the 49th parallel of latitude (72 per cent of the Québec province falls within this category), snowmobiles are used for much of the year in the same way as automobiles. Police and municipal authorities policed these vehicles practically in the same way as ordinary automobiles. Thus, the argument was posed that snowmobiles should fall within the SAAQ legislation's definition of automobiles in those regions where snowmobiles are used as automobiles. The practical result of the current legislative framework, the applicant alleged, is that Québec residents in more remote regions are treated differently to others. As discussed already in Chapter 3, the clear existing definitions of 'automobile' and its purpose within the legislation meant that the claim failed. However the appeals court judge noted that 'The debate brought before us by the appellant is basically political. She is arguing in favour [of] widening the [SAAQ legislation's] scope. This objective is not merely defensible but certainly praiseworthy.'[28]

As noted in Chapter 3, it is possible to argue that an expansion of the SAAQ scheme to include snowmobiles could in effect make the scheme a kind of universal risks coverage scheme like the ACC. However, that does not justify continued incoherence and unfairness on this point. It would be appropriate to have a legislative revision of the scheme to determine whether it is still appropriate to exclude snowmobiles from the scope of the scheme. This could be undertaken at the same time as a review of how to best include new types of transport devices (such as micromobility devices and automated vehicles). It might be concluded that alternative insurance frameworks or a guarantee fund would be preferable to ensure victim coverage in snowmobile accidents (and other harms) if there is no legislative desire to expand the existing SAAQ scheme beyond the automobile (and perhaps other urban-focused transport devices like bicycles and electronic scooters). So long as inequalities, incoherence and lack of precision in eligibility are all better managed, it does not really matter in the end whether these different harms are included in the SAAQ or other legislation

---

[28]   *J.A. v Société de l'assurance automobile du Québec* 2010 QCCA 1328 [40].

designed to operate in parallel. Given the SAAQ's functional control of the transport injury sphere in Québec, it would be most logical from a legal design perspective to simply expand SAAQ coverage. However, there is a significant degree of political bargaining and actuarial calculation in this legislative choice that would need to be reckoned with.

2.1.4. Manitoba's MPI

Turning to the MPI, this fund shows the most legislative coherency out of all four big no-fault schemes. This is because a primary objective of the scheme is, and has always been, maintaining stable automobile insurance costs for Manitoba residents. All elements of the MPI scheme are guided by this principle, and it is the primary justification for the choice of a no-fault scheme. The sole goal for scheme coherency that can be set for the MPI relates to current transport technology and modality shifts. Out of all four schemes, the MPI has grappled least with how it will adapt to transportation shifts that include micromobility. Currently, new transport technologies like e-bikes and e-scooters have no clear place within the MPI framework. It will be necessary to directly grapple with the impact of these devices, whether the MPI scheme should be expanded to include them, and if so what levies should be applied to them. As with the other transport-focused schemes, in my view, it is most logical to extend the scheme to include all types of mobility devices – however, normative choices on this point will be influenced by contextual political factors. If there is a choice to *not* include these devices within the scope of the MPI framework, then a suitably harmonised insurance and liability framework for new transport technologies should be created instead. This will ensure coherency, fairness, and preciseness about eligibility.

In summary then, all three transport-related big no-fault compensation funds need to improve coherency in relation to how they cover different and emerging transport technologies that are not currently included within the scopes of their legislative frameworks. Some schemes, like the TAC, offer partial cover for public transport and cycling already. However all three have not yet coherently handled micromobility and new transport technologies. Where trial programmes are underway (such as in Victoria and Québec), the data from these must inform a legislative scheme review that directly considers scheme purpose and improvements to legal scheme design to make them more forward-thinking. The two Canadian funds studied in this project should also aim to achieve legislative coherency (where feasible) with the new no-fault compensation funds for transport injury that are emerging in the provinces of Alberta and British Columbia. This will ensure the coherent development, at a Canadian level, of comprehensive no-fault legal frameworks for transport injury as a legal system choice and a complete departure from tort law. This kind of coherency has benefits for the jurisprudence of both no-fault and tort more generally.

2.1.5. Conclusions on Improved Coherency and Legislative Design

The ACC Scheme faces the most problems with coherency, by virtue of its aim to be universal in coverage. This problem is only really able to be remedied by a major legislative review of the scheme alongside complementary system frameworks.[29] Given the tenuous political balance of the current scheme,[30] it is likely that a reimagining of the ACC Scheme would be highly politically charged, far more so than at the time it was created. However, such major scheme reassessment is an important goal to set, to improve major issues surrounding coherency, fairness, functionality and precision about eligibility. This shows that one can conclude that a multi-function comprehensive no-fault compensation fund is likely to lead to legal coherency problems down the track, even where it is well managed and stable. It will be necessary to harmonise the wider social security structure to mitigate the effect of gaps created by the no-fault scheme – in essence, taking the Nordic approach to coherency of legal and social systems.[31] There is no doubt that the ACC Scheme has achieved stability and performs efficiently and transparently for minor injuries that require little rehabilitation. However, it is difficult to see where ACC can easily go from here – a mass expansion to include sickness and disability (as advocated by many Woodhouse traditionalists) is not justified on a financial basis (as revealed by this study) and it could lead to even more incoherency. It would also likely significantly affect functionality. From a comparative law perspective we can therefore say that ACC is still a strong example (and a successful one) of doing things a different way and facilitating a complete tort law revolution, but it has some serious coherency difficulties; more than the other three funds that are in its same class. One logical conclusion that can be drawn from this is that a very large no-fault compensation fund legal framework is best suited to a single wide function, rather than multiple functions. Using the example of the schemes studied in this project, it is easier to define a specific purpose for transport-focused schemes, and achieve coherent intersection with other regulatory elements about the transport sector than to try and achieve control over multiple functions and other regulatory intersections.

Perhaps the only way to resolve the ACC Scheme's coherency problems with expansion is a decision that, if one wishes to operate such a big scheme, it must be located more proximately to social security systems. That choice would severely undermine current (financial and stability) successes and be a big change, meaning the Scheme would take on a lot more risk. The results of this comparative law study show that the ACC Scheme's coherency problems can be more easily fixed by legislative action to improve other unsatisfactory legal and

---

[29]   Kim Watts, 'New Zealand' in Thierry Vansweevelt and Britt Weyts (eds), *Compensation Funds in Comparative Perspective* (Intersentia 2020) 134.

[30]   Connell (n 13).

[31]   See Chapter 3 section 8.

social frameworks in New Zealand. Then, ACC's legislative framework should be harmonised with those other improved frameworks to mitigate the relevant gaps between them – or provide clear legislative justification for exclusions. From a legal philosophical perspective, this would give an opportunity to consider whether 'community responsibility' has the same definition as the 'solidarity' that is used as a justification for no-fault compensation funds in civil law systems.[32] For the three transport-focused funds, addressing their coherency goals would also require consideration about whether there is a solidarity-based approach required for different and emerging types of transport injuries.

2.2. IMPROVEMENTS TO FINANCIAL MECHANISMS AND SUPERVISION

The comparative law study undertaken in this project has provided conclusions on financial mechanisms and supervision that can be the basis of realistic goals for our four funds. All no-fault comprehensive compensation funds manage very large amounts of funding, and all four schemes have statutory compensation for significant long-tail financial risks. All four schemes operate on a fully-funded basis like a private insurer, but they are all publicly underwritten and make limited (or no) use of reinsurance for their long-tail risks. A common purpose to their financial structures is a goal of balancing intergenerational fairness (today's levy-payers not paying over the odds for tomorrow's injuries, in short) with the scheme having enough capitalisation or solvency to cover their liabilities, including unpredictable long-tail costs of lifetime care and/or catastrophic injuries. Investment income forms an important part of paying for those long-tail risks, but it is also sometimes used to cover immediate or near-term compensation costs (for example, the importance of investment income to the 'treatment injury' and non-earner compensation costs under the New Zealand ACC Scheme).

The financial choices that have been made by the four funds are logical given the existing nature of their legislative designs, and the fact of their publicly underwritten nature. However, the consequence of these legislative choices about financial structures means that all four funds have much lower levels of solvency than other types of insurance organisations. This is part of the social contract of solidarity element of the schemes – the government has agreed to underwrite the costs of certain types of risks. However it is also political – the guaranteed first-party cover of a no-fault scheme means that if private levels of solvency had to be met, then levies would probably have to rise and the policy justification for the scheme's existence could be challenged. There is an implicit assumption – not

---

[32]   See Chapter 3 section 7.6.

400   Intersentia

Chapter 6. Compensation Fund Goals and Practical Applications

firmly articulated in any of the four schemes' legislative frameworks – that the taxpayer would have to step in if there were major solvency problems with the compensation fund. The danger of this risk materialising has been minimised in recent decades by good returns on investment income. However, fluctuations in that income in recent years now present more obviously the risk to the public purse. Of course, the functional coverage of these schemes – and the caps on possible compensation entitlements – means that large-scale financial disasters might not materialise. One might, for example, make a contrasting comparison on this point with the potential liabilities of a no-fault scheme that covers high-value property damage associated with natural disasters.[33] The fully-funded nature of all four schemes and the indexing of levies have short-circuited any repetition of the financial problems faced by the ACC Scheme in the late 1980s and early 1990s, and by the SAAQ by the early 2000s.[34] However, there remains a clear and present danger of unmanageable financial risks materialising that could de-stabilise all four schemes and require significant taxpayer injections of funding. It is appropriate to set financial goals that address these risks and improve the stability and sustainability of these four funds.

Firstly, there should be greater legislative clarity about the extent and applicability of the need for the scheme to call on taxpayer support. Currently, all four funds rely on levies and investment income to fund their activities (except for the ACC Scheme, which relies on taxpayer funding for limited categories of claimants). The four funds all present comprehensive annual statements, and within these corporate documents make statements about how they balance their different financial pressures to achieve financial stability and sustainability. However, more clarity in the actual legislation is needed about how this balance between fairness and solvency is going to be achieved. There is presently no specific statement about what ratio of solvency needs to be achieved, and what steps should be followed if there are unexpected strains on scheme finances that necessitate taxpayer funding injections.[35] Provisions to handle these kinds of situations should be included within the main legislation. Should, for example, certain activities of the fund be curtailed in order to ensure that compensation payments can continue? The SAAQ provides an example of how such an issue can be handled legislatively – as mentioned earlier, the fund underpinning the SAAQ is required to put the financial stability of the scheme before accident prevention and highway safety activities.[36] The two Canadian schemes also give

---

[33] See Chapter 3 section 2.5.

[34] See Chapter 4 section 6.

[35] There are merely general statements about the reserves that need to be held and how monies received should be handled. For example, see ss 166 to 166C of the Accident Compensation Act 2001; ss 27 to 33 of the Transport Accident Act 1986 (Vic); Division III of the Act respecting the Société de l'assurance automobile du Québec; ss 15 to 18 of the Manitoba Public Insurance Corporation Act.

[36] Act respecting the Société de l'assurance automobile du Québec s 23.0.3.

Intersentia

401

an example of how external monitoring of solvency issues can be incorporated directly into the legislation – in both schemes, levy changes are required to be approved by an independent body.[37] More extensive legislative statements on these points should be incorporated into the frameworks of all four funds.

Secondly, more formal external and independent prudential and financial supervision should be imposed as a requirement of all four funds. As all our big no-fault comprehensive compensation funds ultimately report back to the relevant minister, there is no non-executive or non-legislative oversight to ensure that the financial direction of these large schemes is not unduly influenced by political preferences or even political mismanagement. This is a major concern, because these funds handle significant financial reserves for the compensation of individual citizens who are barred from bringing a private law action to seek reimbursement for their losses. Although of course all state-managed financial matters are susceptible to such a problem, comprehensive no-fault compensation funds remove the private law remedy choices of citizens by statute. In a system that uses a liability-based approach to compensation for broad categories of harms, it is nearly always the case that the actual costs of damage are paid by the insurer that covers the relevant party.[38] That insurer will be subject to legally mandated solvency requirements to ensure it can pay its liabilities. If the liable party is not insured, a guarantee fund might exist to support the victim. That guarantee fund might be paid for by insurers or taxpayers, but that mechanism will only be covering the liabilities of a very small number of claims. In contrast, our four big funds are covering hundreds of thousands or millions of claims per year.

This solvency risk justifies greater independent financial and prudential supervision of the direction of the funds, rather than assuming political good management or that the supervision provided by public authority auditing processes will be sufficient. This is not impossible to achieve. The two goals set out below may have some efficiency and functionality trade-offs (in that more bodies are involved in the supervision of the system), but these would be no greater than the burdens faced by private insurers. The goals would improve the transparency and fairness of the schemes, and better guarantee long-term financial stability.

a.   The schemes should be made subject to the same prudential supervision as private insurers, and this should be formalised within the legislation

---

[37]   An independent panel of experts in the case of the SAAQ, and the Public Utilities Board in the case of the PUB. See ibid ss 17.6 and 17.7; The Manitoba Public Insurance Corporation Act s 6.4.

[38]   PS Atiyah, *The Damages Lottery* (Hart Publishing 1997) 156.

Chapter 6. Compensation Fund Goals and Practical Applications

of each scheme. The reason for this formalisation is not to add extra complexity; rather it is a legal mechanism to support the stability of these large outstanding liabilities. If there is internal mismanagement, higher level political error or investment losses that lead to significant failure of the scheme, the taxpayer will need to step in and the stability of compensation for victims would be at risk. This is a potentially dangerous outcome for the taxpayer and the fund. Actuarial comment has indicated that it is not clear (at least in the case of the ACC Scheme) whether the private insurance sector could step in to cover risks immediately (without speculative pricing)[39] if a scheme change was urgently needed due to political or organisational mismanagement of the scheme, or catastrophic investment income losses. This is a mirror risk of the 'insurance crisis' situation that often prompts the creation of no-fault compensation funds.

b.   Compulsory independent actuarial supervision of levy-setting is the second arm of extra external supervision that is required in all four funds. The two Canadian schemes require this already, and that should be replicated by the TAC and the ACC. There is too much risk of political interference in levy-setting if there is no independent actuarial guidance provided on a regular basis on the setting of levies – and upon which activities there should be levies. This kind of interference has already manifested itself in the ACC Scheme in terms of, for example, the removal of vehicle risk ratings on socio-economic fairness grounds (rather than actuarial grounds),[40] and the reluctance to levy healthcare professionals and organisations for the Treatment Injury Account.[41]

2.3.   BETTER COMPENSATION FOR SPECIFIC CATEGORIES OF CLAIMANTS

Another goal that can be set for comprehensive no-fault compensation funds is the improvement of quantum of compensation for specific categories of claimants. Addressing this matter goes to the heart of some of the classic

---

[39]   Jamie Reid and Andrew Mackessack, 'New Zealand Accident Compensation: What's Happening?', *Institute of Actuaries of Australia Accident Compensation Seminar* (Brisbane November 2011) 17–18.

[40]   'Vehicle Risk Rating (VRR) Removed from ACC Motor Vehicle Levy' <https://www.acc.co.nz/newsroom/stories/vehicle-risk-rating-vrr-removed-from-acc-motor-vehicle-levy/>.

[41]   Grant Duncan, 'New Zealand's Universal No-Fault Accident Compensation Scheme: Embedding Community Responsibility' in Joannah Luetjens, Michael Mintrom and Paul 't Hart (eds), *Successful Public Policy Lessons from Australia and New Zealand* (ANU Press 2019) 341 <http://press-files.anu.edu.au/downloads/press/n5314/pdf/ch14.pdf>.

private law critiques of no-fault compensation. For example, when critiquing the New Zealand scheme, Koziol argues that

> 'the limits on the amount of compensation for personal injury and thus the incomplete protection afforded to the highest-ranking good must be considered a major fault of this system. It does not seem plausible that the notion of community should end up meaning that the innocent victim must bear a substantial part of the harm her or himself when there is serious damage'.[42]

In truth, there is no real answer or complete rebuttal to the general critique that where a no-fault compensation fund caps the amount of damages that could be received, this is unfair. The bargain that is struck between quick procedure and statutory entitlements delivers a mixed purpose type of compensation, but it is not always such a good deal for every victim who falls within the scheme's scope. That is a normative compensation choice issue that informs legislative choices about the use and application of no-fault. However, there is a very valid point to be made about quantum of compensation as it relates to certain categories of victims. Many claimants – particularly those with minor or moderate injuries – receive guaranteed no-fault compensation that will often be more than adequate for their rehabilitative needs. However, other claimants – seriously or catastrophically injured claimants, who may never truly recover from their injuries – may receive very inadequate compensation compared to a tort-based calculation. It will never be possible under a comprehensive scheme for all claimants to receive full tort-like compensation for their injuries – the impact of the serious injury carve-out on the TAC scheme's costs discussed in Chapter 3 is clear evidence of this. As noted already, there is a mixed purpose of compensation under a no-fault scheme – compensatory and symbolic compensation aims are mixed. However, the mixed purpose does not mean we can evade the issue of compensation quantum.

The following goals can therefore be set for compensation quantum that would improve the fairness of our four schemes. Given the generally good financial positions of the funds, these are certainly realistic goals to aim for.

a. Firstly, the scheme should ensure that there is adequate access for victims to non-pecuniary compensation, especially in cases of permanent impairment and loss of life. New Zealand's ACC Scheme, which chose to effectively eliminate non-pecuniary compensation in its 1992 reforms, does the worst on this point out of all four schemes by some margin. Permanent impairment injury compensation under that scheme is up to a maximum of around NZ$133,000 and that includes only a small element of non-pecuniary loss.

---

[42] Helmut Koziol, 'Compensation for Personal Injury: Comparative Incentives for the Interplay of Tort Law and Insurance Law' (2017) 8 *Journal of European Tort Law* 41, 46.

The survivor's grants that are available to the partner and children of a fatal accident victim are shockingly low – less than NZ$7,500 for a partner and less than NZ$3,500 per dependent child. This cannot possibly be described as real compensation – to use Sir Owen Woodhouse's words – for the loss of human life.[43] Lump sum compensation payments for non-pecuniary losses were intended under the original Woodhouse framework as a direct substitute for the right to sue for general damages at common law in respect of such losses.[44]

Guaranteed compensation for medical costs aside, the ACC Scheme certainly represents a 'bad bargain' for permanently impaired claimants and the families of fatal injury victims. For these types of victims, they would be better served by either the negotiated serious injury carve-out within the TAC scheme or its generous permanent impairment benefits.[45] In Canada, there is the possibility of quite generous non-pecuniary compensation under both the SAAQ and MPI schemes – the MPI in particular offering very generous potential compensation.[46] This disparity – and remedying it – may also indicate whether a multi-functional no-fault framework can actually ever compensate for non-pecuniary injury adequately. Unlike its Australian and Canadian cousins, the ACC Scheme would need to cover non-pecuniary compensation in *all* its functional categories. The cost blow-outs of the TAC indicate that this is potentially a financially risky proposition indeed for a multi-function comprehensive fund. On the other hand, less than 0.01 per cent of ACC claims each year are new serious injury claims, and just 0.06 per cent of all claims are fatal injury claims.[47] If generous non-pecuniary compensation were limited to just serious injury claims and fatal injury dependants, then it could be possible to provide much fairer compensation

---

[43] The blow is slightly softened in cases of workplace-related injury, where reparations might be possible following a criminal prosecution under the parallel work safety legislation. See Worksafe, 'Prosecution Policy' <https://www.worksafe.govt.nz/laws-and-regulations/operational-policy-framework/operational-policies/prosecution-policy/>.

[44] Stephen Todd and others, *The Law of Torts in New Zealand*, Stephen Todd (ed) (8th edn, Thomson Reuters 2019) 84.

[45] As noted at Chapter 4 section 4.2, the TAC offers a permanent impairment benefit (mixed pecuniary and non-pecuniary) of A$366,900. For the common law damages that may be available for serious injuries, there is a minimum amount of common law damages of A$56,960. The maximum amount of common law damages available is A$1,282,520 for pecuniary losses, and up to A$569,970 for non-pecuniary compensation.

[46] As noted at Chapter 4 section 4.2, the SAAQ offers a maximum death benefit to survivors of C$392,500, while the MPI offers C$505,000. These figures are annually indexed. For permanent impairment, the SAAQ offers dedicated non-pecuniary compensation up to a maximum of C$256,383. The MPI offers a maximum of C$164,187. Catastrophically injured MPI victims may be able to access further compensation up to a maximum of C$259,245. The MPI has discretion to award further non-pecuniary compensation up to a lifetime maximum for any one individual of C$1,205,794.

[47] Accident Compensation Corporation, 'Annual Report 2020' 123 <https://www.acc.co.nz/assets/corporate-documents/annual-report-2020-acc8234.pdf>.

for these claimants without destabilising the whole scheme. Further quantitative analysis – beyond the scope of this legal study, which should be done with the co-operation of ACC itself to access its data – is needed to identify suitable levels of non-pecuniary compensation. It is submitted that the MPI model is an ideal reference point, as it specifically categorises catastrophically injured claimants for special attention and allows the MPI to exercise discretion to issue further compensation in special circumstances.

b.   Secondly, the purpose of compensation more generally under the four funds should better reflect what the claimant has lost, and not solely focus on the new reality of the claimant's post-injured life. This kind of loss may not be fully captured in non-pecuniary losses. As noted in Chapter 3, compensation is calculated with reference to what is necessary to restore the claimant to his or her best achievable social and vocational participation in a post-accident reality. This is certainly logical, given the rehabilitation focus of all four schemes. However, for certain types of claimants (depending on their pre-injury employment in particular), they may only be employable in a role that earns much less than their previous position or have much less favourable working conditions holistically (including long-term prospects for promotion, extra-legal benefits and pension plan payments). For claimants who suffer from significant disparity, there should be better recognition and compensation for this change in socio-economic status. This would improve fairness for claimants who, by chance of the accidental personal injury that they have suffered and the work that they happened to do beforehand, now face a much more unstable economic future. The legislative frameworks could specifically give the fund discretion to make a special payment to the claimant that recognises instances of specific and significant disparity of outcome post-accident.

2.4.   EFFECTIVE USE OF SUBROGATION

As a publicly underwritten legal structure that provides guaranteed statutory entitlements to a large group of claimants, the comprehensive no-fault compensation fund has significant financial liabilities. This is underlined by the immunity from civil liability/statutory tort bar that is also enshrined in these schemes. Subrogation is a means by which the fund can recover monies from parties not entitled to the liability shelter of its framework. However, use of subrogation in theory and practice as analysed in this project shows significant variations across all four funds, and it cannot be said that there is a coherent common approach. It is therefore appropriate to set some goals on the use of subrogation.

Firstly, it is not clear from the comparative law analysis of publicly available material and limited qualitative research undertaken in this study whether

Chapter 6. Compensation Fund Goals and Practical Applications

subrogation is financially justified for the three funds that actively use their subrogation rights. The use of subrogation is either not methodically tracked, or is outsourced to another agency (in the case of the TAC). The SAAQ, with a dedicated in-house subrogation team, appears to have the best picture of the costs and utility of subrogation in the context of a large no-fault fund. Therefore, a goal should be set for each fund to undertake further quantitative and qualitative research on the practice, costs and (actual and perceived) effectiveness of subrogation. The findings of this research should be made publicly available and reported back to the supervising government minister, the legislature and any other relevant supervisory body. This would facilitate a clearer picture of how subrogation can be used within these large schemes, and allow comparisons to be made with subrogation frameworks in non-comprehensive no-fault funds and private insurers. The data results of such a study would then help to inform normative choices – that should be matched with improved coherency of purpose goals that were mentioned under section 2.1 of this chapter – in legislative reform about subrogation. This would significantly enhance the transparency of large funds' use of subrogation, its functionality and efficiency.

As a means of controlling the costs of subrogation and ensuring it is a tool carried out with reference to the overall purpose of the no-fault fund, a further goal can be set about where subrogation activities are located. The SAAQ shows that the most clarity and coherency are achieved when the relevant subrogation staff are retained in-house. Where another parallel agency is responsible for a larger quantity of subrogation claims (such as Victoria's parallel WorkSafe agency, handling most of the TAC's subrogation activities), then it may be appropriate to consolidate or outsource some practical elements of subrogation. However, this should not be at the expense of control over the data and strategy of subrogation activities. This would improve the coherency and functionality of subrogation efforts.

Another goal that can be set is a clarification of the normative litigation approach of the fund. What broad direction should be set in the legislation for the fund about how it acts as a litigant? We see in the SAAQ a normative choice for the fund to avoid court proceedings wherever possible. In contrast, the TAC uses a highly adversarial approach, except where recovery is likely to be fiscally impossible. It is probable that a SAAQ-type approach is more suitable for a scheme that aims to be a complete departure from traditional liability approaches – and that certainly would be more coherent and achieve efficient outcomes (given the cost and complexity of litigation). However this is ultimately a normative choice for the legislature. Further, the elimination of tort actions for the individual claimant means that the subrogation power given to the fund does not have to completely line up with the ordinary private law rights that were withdrawn from the victim. So long as there is adequate justification within the legislative framework that is coherent with the purpose of the fund, it

Intersentia

407

A Comparative Law Analysis of No-Fault Comprehensive Compensation Funds

is possible to design subrogation powers that look quite different from a classic assignment of rights and obligations.

Finally, it is unequivocal that the ACC Scheme should be empowered with a general entitlement to pursue a subrogated action. As the outcomes of the *DePuy* litigation and the arguments set out by O'Sullivan and Tokeley[48] illustrate, there is no logical or coherent reason why ACC should not be able to pursue redress actions against individuals and organisations who effectively free-ride on the liability immunity provided by ACC, even where gross negligence is present. Unless parallel legal frameworks – such as workplace injury prosecution frameworks – provide a suitable avenue for another legal outcome, severely or permanently injured victims and society itself lose out. A Menyawi-style public tort liability approach[49] would be the best choice for the ACC, because it would not conflict with the framework of statutory entitlements and the extinguishment of tort private law rights. The subrogation or public tort liability power could be reasonably limited to situations of 'serious injury' or 'where it is in the public interest'. If preferred by the legislature, the ACC subrogation power could be made subsidiary to prosecution or regulatory enforcement frameworks under other statutory regimes, in order to avoid a 'double jeopardy' situation for the defendant. Naturally, the design of the subrogation power should reflect the revised purpose of the fund.

A recent real-life case study involving mass loss of life illustrates neatly the distortion caused by a lack of subrogation powers being available to the ACC. This case study underlines the urgent goal stated here of establishing a subrogation power for the fund.

Case Study: The CTV Building

The February Christchurch 2011 earthquake led to the collapse of the CTV Building, resulting in 115 deaths. Although it was a relatively new building (built around 1986), its deficient design was probably not compliant with building codes and 'resulted in the floor slabs pancaking [during the earthquake, leaving most of those inside the building with no chance of survival]'.[50] The surviving family members of those victims have only been entitled to basic ACC survivor compensation – as little as NZ$70 per week

---

[48]   Trish O'Sullivan and Kate Tokeley, 'Consumer Product Failure Causing Personal Injury Under the No-Fault Accident Compensation Scheme in New Zealand-a Let-off for Manufacturers?', *Product Safety, Consumers' Health and Liability Law Conference* (Springer 2017) <https://doi.org/10.1007/s10603-018-9383-2>.

[49]   Hassan El Menyawi, 'Public Tort Liability: An Alternative to Tort Liability and No-Fault Compensation' (2002) 9 *Murdoch University Electronic Journal of Law* <http://www.bepress.com/gj/advances/vol3/iss1/art1>.

[50]   Vol 6, section 9.15 'Royal Commission of Inquiry into Building Failure Caused by the Canterbury Earthquakes' (2012) <https://canterbury.royalcommission.govt.nz/Final-Report-Volume-Six-Contents>.

Chapter 6. Compensation Fund Goals and Practical Applications

for a spouse and NZ$30 a week for each child.[51] A Royal Commission of Inquiry found that the design and construction of the building were deficient.[52]

However, no criminal charges for negligent manslaughter were brought against the two engineers who designed the building because of (1) police perception that there was inadequate evidence to meet the *criminal* standard of proof (beyond reasonable doubt) and therefore there was no reasonable prospect of conviction and (2) the existence of a time bar within the criminal legislation requiring charges to be laid within a year and a day of the relevant act. The statutory bar within the ACC legislation barred the possibility of any civil claim being brought by family members of the victims, or ACC itself. As noted earlier in Chapter 3, even though there is an exemplary damages carve-out within the no-fault framework, in practice it is extremely difficult for victims to use. Although it is far from certain that a civil claim (if available) would be successful, the standard for meeting the burden of proof would only have been the civil standard rather than criminal standard.

There are no grounds within the normative choices that underpin the ACC scheme that justify the result in this case. The ACC framework has directly enabled the engineers (and other possible relevant defendants) to escape any possibility of legal accountability at all for their actions, because of inadequate evidence to meet a much higher criminal standard of proof. In addition to the inadequate non-pecuniary compensation available to victims' family members under the ACC scheme, this lack of any civil recourse at all undermines the solidarity or community responsibility philosophy behind the scheme. If the ACC were empowered to bring a subrogated or 'public tort liability' action to recover compensation costs or even seek exemplary damages, then this would improve the fairness and functional impact of the no-fault framework. It would also enhance public confidence in the 'bargain' that underpins the ACC scheme.

2.5. COMPULSORY LEGISLATIVE REVIEWS AND PLANNING MECHANISMS

Like any legal framework, a no-fault comprehensive compensation fund is a product of the time when it was created, with adaptations to circumstance over time. We have seen that the context of these large schemes' establishment continues to cast a long shadow over their modern operation. What is significant about this point, for the purposes of a no-fault comprehensive compensation

---

[51] Kurt Bayer, 'Petition Launched to Get Compensation for February 22, 2011 Christchurch Earthquake Victims', *New Zealand Herald* (5 February 2019) <https://www.nzherald.co.nz/nz/petition-launched-to-get-compensation-for-february-22-2011-christchurch-earthquake-victims/F6SW6V3JFIDOOL5YSDAONGYGA4/>.

[52] Vol 6, section 9.15 'Royal Commission of Inquiry into Building Failure Caused by the Canterbury Earthquakes' (n 50).

fund, is that the sheer size of these frameworks makes the issue of legislative review and reform potentially problematic. These funds stand outside normal dispute resolution and liability-based frameworks for the resolution of human interactions. The results are not as personalised as they would be under ordinary private law approaches. In that way, this is where our big funds are a lot like social security frameworks. They are created with a particular social bargain in mind, at a particular time. There may be additions or tweaks over time (which could be politically influenced). If the framework becomes too clunky or leads to too much incoherency or imprecision (as we see with the New Zealand ACC scheme), it then requires massive legislative reform that is as politically challenging to contemplate as the establishment of the scheme itself was. It is therefore appropriate to set goals on this subject for our four funds, as this will improve the efficiency, transparency, fairness, functionality, coherency and precision of the schemes – all the identified criteria for the assessment of big no-fault funds. Such a goal would also be in step with the long-term evaluation elements of emerging legal design theory, which is a movement to make the legal system work better for humans.[53] Empirically-informed human-centred design that strikes a balance with legal coherency and fairness is a realistic goal for large no-fault comprehensive compensation funds.

One of the main conclusions of this book's analysis is that comprehensive no-fault compensation should be subject to regular legislative reviews. This can be set as a goal for all four schemes. The time horizon for such reviews could be longer than the time-periods for levy-setting and internal strategic planning, which occur roughly every five years. Therefore, a specific legislative requirement of a full scheme review once every 10 years would seem to be appropriate. This could be handled by law reform bodies in conjunction with independent supervisory bodies that were recommended earlier in this chapter to be more closely involved in the scheme (for example, the financial and prudential regulator). Alternatively, a private consultancy could be hired to ensure complete independence of the review, as was done for the ACC Scheme's 2008 review that was carried out by independent researchers at PriceWaterhouseCoopers.[54]

The analyses and conclusions in this study indicate that the following issues will be the most relevant reference points during such a legislative review of big no-fault compensation funds.

a. Is the no-fault scheme meeting its original objectives, as described in legislation and other key foundational documents?

---

[53] Hagan (n 6).
[54] Disclosure Statement PriceWaterhouseCoopers, 'Accident Compensation Corporation New Zealand Scheme Review' (2008) v.

Chapter 6. Compensation Fund Goals and Practical Applications

b. Have any major contextual circumstances changed that mean that the fund's original objectives may need to change or be achieved differently? This can include legislative and socio-economic changes.

c. Is the scheme financially sustainable and stable, according to an assessment by the scheme itself *and* independent financial analysis?

d. Is the quantum of compensation received by claimants adequate to offer real compensation for their losses? Are there any particular categories of claimants who ought to receive more (or less) compensation?

e. Is the scheme compliant with human rights obligations? Further goals on this subject will be set in the next subsection.

f. What future risks and issues should the scheme be aware of, and reassess at the next scheme review?

It is also worth noting here that a difficult balancing act is required to protect a no-fault comprehensive compensation fund from ever-changing political influence, whilst also allowing for proper reform and development when necessary. A suitable basic goal for all comprehensive no-fault funds is a requirement within the compensation fund's legislation to hold a public referendum before major changes to the scheme, such as the introduction of privatisation measures. This is a requirement that is embedded within the MPI's statutory framework.[55] This would help to ensure predictability of a big no-fault fund's strategies and programmes, and would complement the purpose and legislative design goals. In New Zealand, stakeholders have critiqued the ACC Scheme as being a 'constantly changing organisation that does not maintain commitments to [injury prevention] programmes'.[56] Improved purpose and protection from political interference would limit such fluctuations. To go even further, a goal could be set about the selection process for the fund's governing body and executives. In Québec, the appointment by the government of the members of the SAAQ's governing board must be done following consultation with relevant stakeholder groups (from sectors including insurance, law, health and road accident victims).[57] Enshrining such stakeholder consultation within the legislation itself is a useful way to ensure that board members are representing the collective interests of those who are involved or affected by the compensation fund.

---

[55] Section 14.1(1) of the Manitoba Public Insurance Corporation Act requires any government attempts to privatise the corporation, its 'insurance undertaking' or other parts of its operation to be subject to the approval of a public referendum.

[56] Julie Chambers, 'Swings and Roundabouts ... The Making of Child Injury Prevention Policy in Aotearoa New Zealand: An Exploration' (Thesis, University of Waikato 2019) 83 <https://researchcommons.waikato.ac.nz/bitstream/handle/10289/12424/thesis.pdf?sequence=4>.

[57] Automobile Insurance Act (Québec) s 7.

2.6. DIRECT LEGISLATIVE CONSIDERATION OF HUMAN RIGHTS LAW INTERSECTIONS AND BETTER ACCESS TO LEGAL INFORMATION

In Chapter 5 there was extensive analysis, for the first time, of the human rights intersections of large no-fault compensation funds. This identified a number of problems. Although our big no-fault funds are broadly compliant with their contextual frameworks, this is more likely to be to do with the lack of constitutional controls for human rights issues (particularly in Australia and New Zealand) than with them actually being compliant with broad, internationally agreed human rights principles. The practical reality is that human rights intersections in a statutory refinement of a private law field were not an identified topic of concern at the time our four funds were established. It is only in recent years in Canada that courts have directly grappled with the constitutionality of the tort bar, concluding that the right to bring private law proceedings for personal injury is not a protected right under the Canadian Charter of Rights and Freedoms.[58] This allows us to come to the basic conclusion that a no-fault comprehensive compensation fund with a tort bar may not be wholly incompatible with fundamental human rights frameworks. However, this does not mean that our four big funds are in fact human rights compliant. Certainly, the picture internationally is far from clear on whether no-fault frameworks are compliant with human rights standards, particularly in relation to how they discriminate between different categories of claimants.[59] Therefore, it is essential to set specific goals on this topic. These goals, if achieved, would improve the fairness, functionality, coherency and preciseness of eligibility of our four large funds.

How should these goals be designed? Firstly, examination of the human rights law intersections of each big no-fault compensation fund should take place as a core part of a review of scheme purpose and/or compulsory legislative review that were already proposed as a goal. That is the logical venue for these issues to be considered, because such review will have regard to the wider context of the scheme's operation as a revolutionary private law mechanism, and not solely be located within a human rights law arena. A review of human rights issues as a standalone matter may not properly balance the private law trade-offs and may suggest outcomes that are not coherent with the wider legal framework. As noted earlier, although fundamental rights can (and should) influence the interpretation of private law rules, they might not directly determine the application of those rules unless there is a specific legislative statement to that effect.[60]

---

[58] See Chapter 4 section 2.3.3.
[59] Vansweevelt and others (n 7) 211.
[60] Verica Trstenjak, 'General Report: The Influence of Human Rights and Basic Rights in Private Law' in Verica Trstenjak and Petra Weingerl (eds), *The Influence of Human Rights and Basic Rights in Private Law* (Springer 2016) 9.

Secondly, we can take guidance from other no-fault compensation funds and redress schemes that have touched on human rights intersections. It is clear from the analysis in Chapter 3 that our big no-fault compensation funds do not trigger fatal conflicts with existing human rights frameworks. Therefore, it is necessary to see if other no-fault compensation funds have identified relevant trigger points. In particular, the Australian Redress Scheme for Victims of Sexual Abuse and the Australian Capital Territory's no-fault motor injury compensation scheme show some direction for what matters should be considered.[61] These schemes have considered the influence of both domestic and international frameworks on a no-fault or no-blame compensation choice. We can therefore set the following international human rights framework elements as suitable basic reference points for a human rights review in all our four funds:

a. the right to a fair hearing under article 14 of the International Covenant on Civil and Political Rights (ICCPR);
b. the right to access to justice under article 13 of the Convention on the Rights of Persons with Disabilities (CRPD). This has been raised previously in relation to the ACC Scheme[62] but is relevant to all four funds because of their coverage for individuals with long-term injuries;
c. the right to health under article 12 of the International Covenant on Economic, Social and Cultural Rights (ICESCR); and
d. the right to an effective remedy under article 3 of the ICCPR.

It may also be relevant to refer to the right to social security (including social insurance) under article 9 of the ICESCR. However, this may not be applicable all four funds because of how the schemes operate purposively (again, improved coherency of purpose and legal design will inform this) and their own perception of their function. The MPI and SAAQ may not be sufficiently proximate to social security to merit an article 9 intersection. However, the TAC – which has set a goal for itself of being the world's best social insurer – would fall within the ICESCR scope. The ACC Scheme, with its multi-function universal coverage, would certainly fall within the scope of article 9 ICESCR.

There are also wider human rights intersections to consider, beyond the tort bar. Unlike a non-comprehensive no-fault fund, our large funds have a much broader lateral regulatory function, and handle large amounts of sensitive claimant data. It was identified already that a human rights-based challenge on regulatory scope or privacy/data protection issues would be more realistic than a challenge to the validity of the whole scheme.[63] This justifies specific goals to

---

[61]   See Chapter 5 section 2.1.3.
[62]   Chapter 5 section 2.2.2.
[63]   Chapter 5 section 4.

be set for the improved handling of claimant data, and supervision of privacy issues. An appropriate goal to set here would be the creation of a dedicated Ombudsman or independent supervisory commission for broader human rights and privacy concerns of comprehensive no-fault compensation funds. This is something that was recommended by disability advocates for the New Zealand ACC Scheme, but has not been implemented.[64] For the transport-focused funds, this could take the shape of a dedicated transport commissioner, tasked with ensuring equity, fairness and human rights compliance in transport-related matters. Where there is an existing human rights agency or supervisory body in existence, that body could certainly be given the task of regulatory oversight of this subject. However, caution should be exercised in terms of capacity – the wide scope of our four funds could generate excessive workload for existing bodies. This kind of victim-focused oversight could be a third pillar of regular legislative supervision of the scheme – complementing the proposals set out already in this chapter for increased financial supervision (via the existing regulator) and regular legislative reviews.

As discussed earlier,[65] there is also inconsistent access to basic legal information for claimants across all four schemes. This represents a barrier to accessing justice and is a failing of this legal model. Although the model of big no-fault compensation funds aims to facilitate the achievement of compensation for harm in a speedy and non-legal way, that does not mean claimants never require legal advice. The funds all provide the dominant, non-subsidiary form of compensation for harm in their functions, and the type and level of entitlements that an individual can access will significantly impact their life and rehabilitation. Adequate access for claimants to legal information enhances big no-fault schemes' transparency, fairness, functionality and their precision about eligibility. Therefore, it is appropriate to set goals for the improvement of this issue.

The MPI and the TAC show two different models for enabling free or low-cost legal information for claimants. The Manitoba approach is the simplest, where the government established a free legal advice service funded by the MPI for claimants from the internal review appeal stage. The establishment and funding of the advice service is set out in the MPI legislation.[66] The TAC's negotiated protocol arrangement with legal practitioner bodies is a good second choice. The TAC approach is logical for a fund that gives a dedicated role for lawyers to engage with the no-fault framework – by way of the serious injury carve-out. It is less clear how the legal profession would be motivated to engage

---

[64] Warren Forster, Tom Barraclough and Tiho Mijatov, 'Solving the Problem: Causation, Transparency and Access to Justice in New Zealand's Personal Injury System' (2017) 52–63.

[65] Chapter 3 section 5.3 and Chapter 5 section 3.3.

[66] The Manitoba Public Insurance Corporation Act s 174.

Chapter 6. Compensation Fund Goals and Practical Applications

with providing discounted legal advice in a fund that has a complete tort bar (as we see in the other three funds) – lawyers have no logical intersection with the fund. Therefore, we can make the distinction that a fully funded legal service is ideal for a no-fault fund with no carve-out to its statutory tort bar, whereas a collaborative approach with the legal profession is more suited to a no-fault fund that does have a carve-out.

In contrast, there is less justification for the blanket guidance and mediation-based approach currently favoured by the ACC under the Talk–Meet–Resolve service. Time will tell whether this model delivers positive impacts for claimants, but it is unclear why a mediation-based approach would be of assistance when most ACC cover disputes factually relate to causation issues.[67] This point is also justification for the establishment of compulsory legislative reviews of the scheme, which was the goal set in the previous sub-section.

3. NEW APPLICATIONS OF BIG NO-FAULT COMPENSATION FUNDS

The third question of this book is: How can no-fault comprehensive compensation funds be used to address contemporary legal problems common to multiple jurisdictions? This has been partially answered already through the analysis on how our four big no-fault funds address modern risks and losses such as new forms of transport technology and mobility,[68] and increasing public social risks like terrorism.[69] There has also been direct analysis for the first time of whether the legal scholarship and practice of large no-fault compensation funds has relevance (as a legal problem solving tool for compensation) to difficult societal harms like large-scale historic child abuse, which involves a restorative justice element.[70] The analysis in this project of the advantages and drawbacks of the very large, publicly underwritten and managed style of no-fault compensation funds can inform analysis about further applications. Specifically, is our big no-fault model helpful for solving liability and insurance problems associated with, firstly, technically novel harms and new types of risk, and secondly, emergency large-scale liability problems?

In this section, I analyse the suitability of the large no-fault model to:

a. broad artificial intelligence applications; and
b. emergency public health liability applications, such as compensation for injury from COVID-19 vaccines.

---

[67] See Chapter 4 section 5.2
[68] See Chapter 3 section 6.1.
[69] See Chapter 3 section 6.4.
[70] See Chapter 2 section 5.

Intersentia   415

These two topics are the next boundaries to be crossed in the use of no-fault generally to address a problematic legal risk. They are also the next logical step on from the modern analysis and re-framing of comprehensive no-fault compensation funds that has been undertaken in this book. No-fault generally may (and as will be discussed in the next two subsections, is quite likely to) be a useful theoretical tool to address emerging types of broad societal risk. However, it is not clear *what shape* of no-fault solution is going to be best suited to these problems, and whether a different shape of no-fault (or a different solution entirely) might be more appropriate.

As this and other studies have shown, no-fault compensation funds are not a homogenous group of frameworks. Different types of no-fault scheme are suited to different contexts, risks and normative outcomes. The applied analysis in the next two subsections will consider whether the very large no-fault model is suitable for two kinds of contemporary and future applications. These potential applied uses of big no-fault compensation funds will be assessed against the yardsticks of efficiency, transparency, fairness, functionality, coherency and preciseness about eligibility.

It is important to note that there is not space and scope here to consider whether *any* type of no-fault is suitable for these harms. It is also worth exercising caution, given that both applications are highly time sensitive, and a dizzying number of developments specific to no-fault solutions for novel applications were emerging at the time of writing. Therefore, the treatment here is focused solely on a high-level analysis of the relevance of the large no-fault model, which incorporates relevant developments at the time of writing. This analysis can then be used to guide and inform further applied research. By taking this measured approach, this study will make a novel contribution to the scholarship about liability systems alternative to compensation that (hopefully) continues to be relevant beyond the immediate time of publication of this book.

3.1. ARTIFICIAL INTELLIGENCE APPLICATIONS

Artificial intelligence can be defined as the 'science and engineering of making intelligent machines, especially intelligent computer programs'.[71] These machines 'display human-like capabilities such as reasoning, learning, planning and creativity'.[72] Artificial intelligence poses important questions

---

[71] John McCarthy, 'What Is Artificial Intelligence?' (2004) <http://www-formal.stanford.edu/jmc/>.

[72] 'What Is Artificial Intelligence and How Is It Used?', *European Parliament* (29 March 2021) <https://www.europarl.europa.eu/news/en/headlines/society/20200827STO85804/what-is-artificial-intelligence-and-how-is-it-used>.

Chapter 6. Compensation Fund Goals and Practical Applications

about the interaction of technology, property and civil rights.[73] Machine learning is the most common type of artificial intelligence used in systems that currently impacts society; examples include automated vehicles, predictive analytics, fraud detection, and automated medicine applications.[74] Machine learning refers to computer programs that learn rules from existing data, can adapt to new situations and changes, and can improve their performance with experience.[75]

There is currently no clearly agreed way to address how to compensate individuals for loss caused by AI-based goods and services. This is because it is unclear whether traditional concepts of (strict) liability – shaped in an analogue world for human actors – are adaptable to artificial intelligence applications. Further, insurance companies rely on clear liability rules in order to calculate risk and claim reimbursement from liable parties.[76] When individual claimants must prove liability to access compensation, opaqueness about the allocation of liability for artificial intelligence-related harm adds a complexity hurdle and a risk of unexpected coverage gaps. As humans rapidly relinquish more and more decision-making control to automated and artificial intelligence technologies, there remain these unresolved questions of law and ethics about who is responsible for those injuries, whether liability can be apportioned in the normal way, and how much compensation should be paid for those injuries.[77] This subsection considers broadly whether our model of big no-fault compensation funds is relevant to two types of artificial intelligence applications: automated vehicles and medical technologies. These two applications have been chosen because the relevant harms fall within the remit of our funds, and (as machine-learning applications) they are the already in use (to varying degrees). Of course, only automated vehicles will fall under the scope of all four funds, and ACC is the only one of our four large schemes scheme that would regularly cover medical applications.[78]

---

[73]   Sonia K Katyal, 'Private Accountability in the Age of Artificial Intelligence' (2019) 66 *UCLA Law Review* 54.

[74]   Harry Surden, 'Artificial Intelligence and Law: An Overview' (2019) 35 *Georgia State University Law Review* 1306, 1315.

[75]   Avrim Blum, 'Machine Learning Theory' (2007) 1.

[76]   European Commission, 'Report on the Safety and Liability Implications of Artificial Intelligence, the Internet of Things and Robotics' (2020) 13 <https://ec.europa.eu/info/sites/info/files/report-safety-liability-artificial-intelligence-feb2020_en_1.pdf>.

[77]   Iria Giuffrida, 'Liability for AI Decision-Making: Some Legal and Ethical Considerations' (2019) 88 *Fordham Law Review* 439 <https://ir.lawnet.fordham.edu/flr/vol88/iss2/3>.

[78]   Although as noted at Chapter 3 section 6.2, the SAAQ, following *Godbout v Pagé* will cover all the medical injury incidents flowing from a covered transport injury. Therefore compensation for artificial intelligence healthcare applications could fall under the scope of that scheme (and likely also the MPI and TAC) in a limited way.

3.1.1. Automated Vehicle Applications: Possibilities and Problems

The AI harm application most relevant to the kinds of compensation funds analysed here is of course automated motor vehicle injury. The potential for no-fault compensation schemes to address this problem has already been identified by several legal scholars, as part of an urgent need for a rethinking of remedies that is relevant to artificial intelligence technology.[79] This was a subject that was discussed in more detail in Chapter 3.[80] It was shown that all four of our existing no-fault comprehensive compensation funds are capable of covering automated vehicles, with no adjustment to scheme scope or legislative framework. Therefore, it would seem that our model of comprehensive no-fault compensation funds is *prima facie* well suited to this application. These big funds also have the benefit that they may cover losses associated with co-existing new transport technologies (like e-scooters), as well as multimodal trends in transport that aim to balance automobiles, public transport, cyclists/micro-mobility users and pedestrians. This lines up with conclusions reached by recent expert European analysis that a no-fault insurance framework solution of some kind is probably the best choice for handling damages resulting from automated vehicles.[81] Partially analogous strict liability solutions have also been advocated in the United States.[82] Meanwhile, the European Green Deal's new mobility strategy asserts that 'Europe must seize the opportunities presented by connected, cooperative, and automated mobility (CCAM)' with a single, function-specific public agency tasked with harmonising regulatory frameworks.[83] All of these developments point, from a comparative law basis, to the suitability and transferability of the comprehensive no-fault compensation funds' model to contemporary transport applications in different jurisdictions.

---

[79] Watts (n 26); Maurice Schellekens, 'Law, Innovation and Technology No-Fault Compensation Schemes for Self-Driving Vehicles No-Fault Compensation Schemes for Self-Driving Vehicles' <http://www.tandfonline.com/action/journalInformation?journalCode=rlit20>; Mark A Lemley and Bryan Casey, 'Remedies for Robots' (2019) 86 *University of Chicago Law Review* 1311, 1315; Giuffrida (n 77).

[80] See also the more detailed discussion in Watts (n 26).

[81] EFD Engelhard and RW de Bruin, 'EU Common Approach on the Liability Rules and Insurance Related to Connected and Autonomous Vehicles.' (Utrecht Centre for Accountability and Liability Law 2017) 6.

[82] Kenneth S Abraham and Robert L Rabin, 'Automated Vehicles and Manufacturer Responsibility for Accidents: A New Legal Regime for a New Era' (2019) 105 *Virginia Law Review* 127 <http://www.virginialawreview.org/sites/virginialawreview.org/files/A%26R_Book_0.pdf>; Ryan Calo, 'Commuting to Mars: A Response to Professors Abraham and Rabin' (2019) 105 *Virginia Law Review Online* 84 <http://www.virginialawreview.org/sites/virginialawreview.org/files/Calo_Book.pdf>.

[83] European Commission, 'Sustainable and Smart Mobility Strategy – Putting European Transport on Track for the Future' (2020) <https://transport.ec.europa.eu/system/files/2021-04/2021-mobility-strategy-and-action-plan.pdf>.

However, we also have to take into account our core reference principles and the goals that were set earlier in this chapter for our large no-fault compensation funds. It is also important to take account of problems identified with the existing schemes. Do any of these affect the applicability of our big no-fault fund model to automated vehicle injury? In the following paragraphs some likely flash points are discussed.

Firstly, there is currently no scope within any of the four schemes for the manufacturer or distributor to pay a levy into the scheme. This is highly relevant to automated vehicles because, with increasing degrees of automation, the device or technology involved with the automobile device becomes the causative element of the risk. However, it is difficult to apportion the risk because of the 'black box' effect, which can make it impossible for humans to understand the processes or workings of an artificial intelligence system – even if the inputs and outputs of the system are known. It would be most fair and coherent (given the new technology effects) for all parties involved in the automated vehicle (user, manufacturer, software manager, distributor or support body, etc) to pay a levy. The levy could be imposed at the point of sale of products or services, or at the time of licensing. However, this kind of levy design is not foreseen within the framework of the existing funds, where transport registration, licensing and/or fuel levies are paid by the user alone. A workaround can be a requirement for the manufacturer to reimburse the cost of no-fault compensation paid in accidents involving an automated vehicle, as proposed in Québec.[84] Whether this is a realistic proposal for large-scale roll-out of automated vehicles depends on the data that emerges about the injuries and loss associated with these new types of vehicles. For coherency with other types of road users (e.g. non-automated vehicles), a per-sale or lease levy could be more appropriate. Therefore, considerations of precision of eligibility (and eligibility for levies) are needed before the existing funds can be used in relation to automated vehicles.

Secondly, in all four large schemes, there are limited opportunities for subrogation – and in the case of the New Zealand ACC Scheme, effectively no opportunity for subrogation. Effective subrogation powers need to be designed with specific reference to artificial intelligence applications in all four funds. Consider, for example, the situation of an automated vehicle user failing to install a necessary software update for their vehicle that indirectly leads to an accident. Would this be treated similarly to a situation (under the MPI, as one example) of a driver breaking road rules and no longer being entitled to the full protection of the scheme? Some parallels can be seen in the United Kingdom's new legislative framework for self-driving vehicles, which allows insurers to exclude coverage

---

[84] Watts (n 26) 12.

under the strict liability scheme if a user does not install relevant software updates.[85] What about a situation where an owner/driver installed third-party software that is either open-source in nature or supplied by an organisation that does not pay a levy into the scheme – and this directly or indirectly causes an accident? These are unanswered questions that are best answered by a coherent and purposive review of the no-fault compensation fund legislation *at the same time* as road safety regulations and applicable product liability legislation. This includes consideration of appropriate coverage limitations, substantial fines for non-compliance with safety rules,[86] and/or subrogation possibilities. What is the risk to the financial stability of the fund in the case of a cyberattack that leads to large-scale harm?[87] These problems demonstrate that although there is *prima facie* coverage of the automated vehicle risk, it is not sufficiently coherent or functional, nor does it have adequate precision about eligibility without further legislative revision and planning.

Thirdly, it is widely anticipated that one of the key benefits of the widespread roll-out of automated vehicles will be a significant reduction in the number of serious and fatal road accidents.[88] These devices will also potentially improve social equity outcomes, by bringing mobility to persons who cannot drive (like the elderly or disabled) and are under-served by other transport modes.[89] Will this require adjustment to the purpose of the no-fault fund and how it treats different forms of risk activity? For example, if it indeed turns out that automated vehicles deliver vast safety improvements and reductions in harm, this might objectively justify a significant increase in levies on traditional vehicles. That would certainly be perceived as unfair by traditional vehicle owners who could not afford or did not want to buy an automated vehicle. It is not clear how such a disruptive change would impact the traditional balance in the existing four

---

[85]   Ken Oliphant, 'Liability for Road Accidents Caused by Driverless Cars' [2019] *Singapore Comparative Law Review* 190, 195.

[86]   This was one of the recommendations of the comparative analysis in Dasom Lee and David J Hess, 'Regulations for On-Road Testing of Connected and Automated Vehicles: Assessing the Potential for Global Safety Harmonization' (2020) 136 *Transportation Research Part A: Policy and Practice* 85 <https://doi.org/10.1016/j.tra.2020.03.026>.

[87]   One technical analysis of potential risks identified that all of the following automated vehicle systems would be at risk of a cyberattack: infrastructure sign, machine vision, GPS, in-vehicle devices, acoustic sensors, radar, lidar, odometrical sensors and maps. External on-road systems such as smart lane LEDs could also be attacked. The types of attacks that would have the highest risk of injury or fatality to drivers, passengers and other road users would be the injection of fake safety messages and map database poisoning. See Jonathan Petit and Steven E Shladover, 'Potential Cyberattacks on Automated Vehicles' (2015) 16 *IEEE Transactions on Intelligent Transportation Systems* 546.

[88]   This is because it is estimated that around 90% of road accidents involve human error of some kind. See European Commission, 'Report on the Safety and Liability Implications of Artificial Intelligence, the Internet of Things and Robotics' (n 76) 2; European Commission, 'Saving Lives: Boosting Car Safety in the EU' (COM(2016) 787 Final) 4.

[89]   Lee and Hess (n 86).

Chapter 6. Compensation Fund Goals and Practical Applications

funds between their cost stability, prevention, rehabilitation and compensation goals. A redesign of purpose is likely to be necessary as automated vehicles begin to appear on roads in greater numbers, which could be addressed in the proposed compulsory legislative reviews. However, it remains unclear whether the disruption of the schemes would lead to increased unfairness among certain categories of potential claimants.

Fourthly, if there are indeed overwhelming safety benefits delivered by automated vehicles, then this might render the existential purpose of a very large no-fault comprehensive compensation fund void. On the one hand, it has been identified that automated vehicle-associated disruption could prove to be a disruptive and destabilising event to the private insurance sector. This is because changes to the fundamental shape of the market may mean that insurers might no longer be in a dominant position in relation to information about behaviour and risk calculation, which could significantly affect the dynamics of the transportation insurance market.[90] On the other hand, if fatalities and serious injuries from transport accidents were made a rare occurrence thanks to artificial intelligence, then there would be little need for a very large scheme dedicated to transport injury prevention, compensation and rehabilitation. Operator-passengers might have the most practical need for non-physical damage insurance, which our four funds have all successfully left to the private insurance market to manage. In that hypothetical future, a much more limited role for no-fault would exist, possibly as a damage or guarantee fund, with levies to support this fund being placed on individual insurance policies.

Finally, it is unclear whether there will be coverage for harms flowing from new types of autonomous devices that operate in spaces that are not currently used for personal mobility. One example here is the use of automated drones for delivery services.[91] These devices, and their fast-moving propellers, could foreseeably cause injury to a child.[92] Normally these kinds of devices would be regulated by airspace authorities. However, drones' direct interaction with individuals at their home or workplace could justify a transport-focused no-fault comprehensive compensation fund to have oversight of their operation

---

[90] This is because software as a service (SaaS) companies like Uber or Google 'gather more information on drivers and the mobility ecosystem than incumbent insurance companies' – Iva Bojic, Roman Braendli and Carlo Ratti, 'What Will Autonomous Cars Do to the Insurance Companies?' in *Autonomous Vehicles and Future Mobility* (Elsevier 2019) 69. See also Watts (n 26) 7.

[91] For example, Amazon plans to offer a 'Prime Air' drone delivery service once it has regulatory approval. This would deliver packages of up to 2.5kg in 30 minutes or less to customers. See 'Amazon.Com: Prime Air' <https://www.amazon.com/Amazon-Prime-Air/b?ie=UTF8&node=8037720011>.

[92] Shiva Ram Reddy Singireddy and Tugrul U Daim, 'Technology Roadmap: Drone Delivery – Amazon Prime Air' in Tugrul Daim, Leong Chan, and Judith Estep (eds), *Infrastructure and Technology Management* (Springer 2018) 387 <https://link.springer.com/chapter/10.1007/978-3-319-68987-6_13>.

Intersentia

and the compensation costs flowing from their use. In this, we see a parallel with the tensions experienced by the three road transport injury funds and their present exclusion of off-road vehicles (such as snowmobiles in the Canadian schemes). If drone-related injuries are covered under a universal scheme (like in New Zealand), then choices about levies and/or operator contributions to the fund must be made. If drone-related injuries are *not* covered (i.e., they are outside the scheme as they are not on a public road or involving an automobile, as in the three transport-focused funds), then the results of this project show that incoherent and unequal results will emerge unless the legislature implements mandatory insurance coverage for those devices, possibly supported by a non-comprehensive guarantee fund.

We can therefore conclude that large comprehensive no-fault schemes are in a broad sense very well suited to the novel problem of liability for harm caused by automated vehicles. However, automated vehicles are a phenomenon that was not anticipated at the time of scheme design, and there are elements of their operation and potential risk that do not match the existing frameworks. Significant scheme adaption would be necessary to ensure fair and coherent outcomes. The next evolution of compensation for losses associated with transportation might look different to what can be provided by our four funds as they currently operate.

3.1.2. Healthcare Applications: Possibilities and Problems

We can turn next to healthcare applications of artificial intelligence. Does the large no-fault compensation fund model have relevance to this topical application of AI technology? Artificial intelligence devices in healthcare have been in development for many decades, but a recent renaissance has been drive by the successful application of deep learning to large sources of labelled (healthcare) data.[93] AI, as applied to image-based diagnoses, is currently one of the most successful healthcare applications, and there is great potential in other areas such as clinical outcome prediction and monitoring, and autonomous robotic surgery.[94] AI systems are most likely to be introduced when they make fewer errors than healthcare professionals, rather than being perfect systems.[95] Reasonably extensive use of AI systems in clinical practice has been predicted to occur within 10 years.[96]

---

[93] Kun Hsing Yu, Andrew L Beam and Isaac S Kohane, 'Artificial Intelligence in Healthcare' (2018) 2 *Nature Biomedical Engineering* 719, 720 <http://dx.doi.org/10.1038/s41551-018-0305-z>.

[94] Yu, Beam and Kohane (n 93).

[95] Søren Holm, Catherine Stanton and Benjamin Bartlett, 'A New Argument for No-Fault Compensation in Health Care: The Introduction of Artificial Intelligence Systems' (2021) 29 *Health Care Analysis* 171, 175 <https://doi.org/10.1007/s10728-021-00430-4>.

[96] Thomas Davenport and Ravi Kalakota, 'The Potential for Artificial Intelligence in Healthcare' (2019) 6 *Future Healthcare Journal* 94, 97.

Chapter 6. Compensation Fund Goals and Practical Applications

There are two main problems that are likely to emerge from the use of AI healthcare applications from a damage perspective. The first are AI systems errors related to data.[97] The second are AI system errors related to deep learning reasoning that are too mathematically complex to be given a humanly comprehensible representation (the so-called 'black box' problem).[98] The first problem might not be so problematic in a liability-based system, if the manufacturer clearly used an inadequate training set for the system. However the second problem is extremely difficult – if it is not possible to explain why or how the error happened, how can liability be apportioned?[99] Holm et al have recently argued, with specific reference to the New Zealand ACC Scheme, that no-fault compensation systems can 'handle the issues created by [healthcare] AI systems in a much more straightforward way'.[100] This is because it would not be necessary to consider why the AI malfunctioned, why the healthcare provider followed its advice, whether other healthcare providers would have followed that advice, or whether another AI system would have done better.[101]

An identifiable benefit of a big no-fault compensation fund model is that it overcomes the first issue by default – the data sharing problems that are a current barrier to the further implementation of AI healthcare technologies. Once an AI system is deployed with initial training from historical data, a continued stream of data is necessary for the system's continued development and improvement.[102] Liability-based models may not adequately incentivise the sharing of data to ensure that an AI system is adequately 'fed'. A comprehensive no-fault compensation fund that has responsibility for processing all compensation claims – and has a prevention mandate to minimise the incidence of harm – would arguably create an environment for healthcare system operators that encourages (or at least, does not discourage) adequate input of information into an AI system.

Holm et al refrained from postulating a design for a potential fund, but did make some specific recommendations for its structure. They argued that it should be funded by a mix of state and/or stakeholders, and it should have subrogation or public tort liability-type powers to pursue a designer or manufacturer (where appropriate). The analyses in this book mean it is possible to add to Holm and his co-authors' arguments by making a direct comparison with what we know about very big no-fault compensation funds.

---

[97] Holm, Stanton and Bartlett (n 95) 177–178. This means inadequate or poor-quality information being inputted to the artificial intelligence algorithm – commonly known as 'Garbage In Garbage Out'.

[98] Brent Mittelstadt and others, 'The Ethics of Algorithms: Mapping the Debate' (2014) 3 *Big Data & Society* 23.

[99] Holm, Stanton and Bartlett (n 95) 179.

[100] ibid 172.

[101] ibid 14.

[102] Fei Jiang and others, 'Artificial Intelligence in Healthcare: Past, Present and Future' (2017) 2 *Stroke and Vascular Neurology* 241 <http://svn.bmj.com/>.

As a reminder, the treatment injury provisions of the ACC Scheme require a person to have suffered a personal injury that was caused by a treatment provided by (or at the direction of) a registered healthcare professional.[103] There will not be cover for effects that are a necessary part or ordinary consequence of the treatment, taking into account all the circumstances of the case (including the claimant's underlying health conditions and the state of clinical knowledge at the time of the treatment). There will not be cover for cases where the treatment simply did not achieve the desired result, where the injury was solely attributable to a resource allocation decision, or because of the claimant unreasonably withholding or delaying consent to treatment. The definition of treatment includes giving treatment; diagnosis; a decision about the treatment to be provided; a failure to provide treatment (including a failure to treat in a timely manner); a failure to obtain consent; a failure of any equipment, device or tool; and the application of any support system.[104] Based on the scheme as it exists today, there would therefore be *prima facie* coverage for artificial intelligence applications that are used in a healthcare setting, under the operation or supervision of a registered healthcare professional.

However, there are a number of likely flashpoints between healthcare applications of artificial intelligence and treatment injury under the ACC Scheme. These reveal some of the precise challenges that would have to be overcome if a legislature wished to use the big no-fault model for healthcare artificial intelligence applications. In many respects, some of the problems associated with healthcare artificial intelligence applications under a comprehensive no-fault compensation fund are manifestations of existing problems that were described in Chapter 3.

Firstly, the failure to provide treatment[105] and failure of any equipment, tool or device[106] are the most obvious problematic elements in the current ACC legislature framework. If the alleged failure relates to internal decision-making on the part of an AI application, how can failure be ascertained? Although the intention of treatment injury category reforms in the mid-2000s intended to remove fault-based concepts from decisions, the reality is that they still persist. The ACC itself, and the courts in resolving questions of law, still persist in using phrasing that is suggestive of a fault-based standard when ascertaining 'failures'.[107] This approach will be extremely difficult, if not impossible, to apply to an AI system's reasoning if that reasoning is not possible to penetrate. Even using

---

[103] Accident Compensation Act 2001 s 32(1).
[104] ibid s 33.
[105] ibid s 33(1)(d).
[106] ibid s 33(1)(g).
[107] Joanna M Manning, 'Plus ça change, plus c'est la même chose: Negligence and treatment injury in New Zealand's accident compensation scheme' (2014) 14 *Medical Law International* 22, 35–37.

a generous Nordic-style 'avoidability' standard, as advocated by Manning,[108] it is difficult to understand what the relevant comparator would be. Should the reasoning of the AI system be compared with what a competitor product would have done? A specialist medical doctor? One might also foresee problems where an error is made by a human doctor (in a decision about treatment based on diagnostic imaging, for example) that would *not* have been made by an artificial intelligence system, had that system been available or used. There is currently inadequate precision of eligibility and cover under the ACC Scheme in relation to AI healthcare applications. It is necessary for the legislature to specifically define what 'failure' within the ACC legislative framework means when it refers to an AI system. Given the continued infusion of fault-based reasoning in the calculation of the 'failure' test,[109] a wider threshold might be appropriate for artificial intelligence that simply allows cover if an AI system was used and consequences occurred that were not an ordinary consequence of the treatment, with no detailed comparisons with other systems or attempts to ascertain the AI system's reasoning. This would ensure functionality, although it would unhelpfully create different tests for a human healthcare professional compared to an AI healthcare application.

Secondly, if a simpler and more open standard of causation and result is applied, as suggested, then it would also be vitally necessary for the ACC Scheme to have a suitable subrogation or public tort liability framework in place. This matches Holm et al's recommendations.[110] This would ensure that claimants could access compensation speedily for their injuries, but enable ACC to pursue a manufacturer or distributor if it perceived that there were in fact system errors in the AI application. The original New Zealand scheme was not designed with technical advances like artificial intelligence in mind, and it does not seem fair or coherent to allow an international software manufacturer or distributor (who may pay nothing in the way of ACC levies) to free-ride on the no-fault system. This is in line with goals already set in this chapter for the ACC Scheme generally.

Thirdly, the funding structures of the ACC Scheme's Treatment Injury Account are currently not adapted to the new risks (and benefits) of artificial intelligence. As discussed already, the levy design of the Treatment Injury Account for the ACC Scheme is already currently inadequate. Not all participants in the healthcare system are levied, and there has been a political reluctance to impose levies on healthcare providers (who already pay levies to the Earner Account). From that starting point, it is not clear how manufacturers, distributors, software services and healthcare professional users of healthcare artificial intelligence applications would or could be levied. As with automated

---

[108]   Manning (n 107).
[109]   ibid 34–36.
[110]   Holm, Stanton and Bartlett (n 95) 184.

A Comparative Law Analysis of No-Fault Comprehensive Compensation Funds

vehicles, it could be possible to require manufacturers and/or distributors to pay for any compensation consequences factually caused by their product that are covered by the ACC Scheme. As New Zealand's medical device regulations do not currently require pre-market authorisation, it would also be necessary to adjust the wider regulatory framework. A levy or notification of a compensation reimbursement requirement could be applied at the time of market entry. There therefore need to be coherency improvements to funding and parallel regulatory frameworks before the ACC Scheme can be said to be applicable to and functional for AI healthcare applications.

3.2. A COMPREHENSIVE NO-FAULT COMPENSATION FUND FOR COVID-19 VACCINE DAMAGE

The COVID-19 pandemic is a global phenomenon that emerged part-way through this research study, and has had a pervasive impact on all human societies. It had some substantive impacts on this research project (such as curtailing the possibility of extensive in-person qualitative interviews), but it also has created new categories of large-scale harm and an emergency contextual situation that is very relevant to the study of comprehensive no-fault compensation funds. The impact of the COVID-19 virus spurred an unprecedented scientific endeavour to research, develop, test and deliver numerous novel vaccines – in record time – to protect the global population from death and severe illness.[111]

Vaccines injury is thankfully rare, and the various COVID-19 vaccines that are available to the public have proven to be generally very safe and effective. However, the various COVID-19 vaccines were developed and trialled at high speed and there is a lack of longitudinal studies about their long-term side effects.[112] Some instances of severe harm have already resulted from COVID-19 vaccinations. Specifically, there have already been blood clot adverse reactions

---

[111] As of April 2021, the following COVID-19 vaccines had met the World Health Organization's necessary criteria for safety and efficacy: AstraZeneca, Johnson & Johnson, Moderna and Pfizer BioNTech – see 'COVID-19 Vaccines Advice' <https://www.who.int/emergencies/diseases/novel-coronavirus-2019/covid-19-vaccines/advice>. As of May 2021 there are currently 101 COVID-19 vaccine products in clinical development, and 183 vaccine products in pre-clinical development. See 'Draft Landscape and Tracker of COVID-19 Candidate Vaccines' <https://www.who.int/publications/m/item/draft-landscape-of-covid-19-candidate-vaccines>.

[112] 'The use of new "first-in-human" vaccine technologies, and the limited sample size and duration of follow-up in phase III clinical trials, make it possible that rare, but serious, vaccine-related adverse effects will not be identified before widespread population use is needed in the context of the current devastating pandemic.' Nicholas Wood and others, 'Australia Needs a Vaccine Injury Compensation Scheme – Upcoming COVID-19 Vaccines Make Its Introduction Urgent' (2020) 49 *Australian Journal of General Practice*.

Chapter 6. Compensation Fund Goals and Practical Applications

associated with the AstraZeneca vaccine,[113] as well as the Janssen (Johnson & Johnson) vaccine.[114] Given the global necessity of achieving herd immunity in order to bring the pandemic under control,[115] and the difficulty of predicting who will suffer an adverse reaction to a vaccine, this makes COVID-19 vaccine injury a type of 'unavoidable risk'.[116]

The damage and compensation landscape associated with COVID-19 vaccines is rapidly evolving as cases of vaccine injury occur. This makes it a difficult topic to analyse in the context of a book, which is relatively fixed in time as a research output.[117] However, these developments cannot be ignored because COVID-19 vaccine injury has spurred some major milestones in large-scale no-fault compensation fund frameworks. Pre-COVID, there had already been arguments made by some scholars in favour of a global compensation fund to address vaccine-related injury.[118] These developments show the potential for further developments in the scholarship and practice surrounding large no-fault compensation funds, and the issue of whether other COVID-19 medical products of all kinds (i.e. vaccines and other drugs) should be covered.[119] A renewed interest in the potential of no-fault, as applied to COVID-19, has

---

[113] Elisabeth Mahase, 'AstraZeneca Vaccine: Blood Clots Are "Extremely Rare" and Benefits Outweigh Risks, Regulators Conclude' (2021) 373 *British Medical Journal* n931 <http://dx.doi.org/10.1136/bmj.n931>; Jacqui Wise, 'Covid-19: European Countries Suspend Use of Oxford-AstraZeneca Vaccine after Reports of Blood Clots' (2021) 372 *British Medical Journal* (Clinical research ed.) n699 <http://dx.doi.org/10.1136/bmj.n699>; 'Brussels warns that AstraZeneca will miss already reduced targets' *Financial Times* <https://www.ft.com/content/f9e5b8d8-8153-474a-bd57-97f5adbeb638>.

[114] Elisabeth Mahase, 'Covid-19: US Suspends Johnson and Johnson Vaccine Rollout over Blood Clots' (2021) 373 *British Medical Journal* n970 <http://dx.doi.org/10.1136/bmj.n970>; David K Shay and others, 'Safety Monitoring of the Janssen (Johnson & Johnson) COVID-19 Vaccine – United States, March–April 2021' (2021) 70 *MMWR. Morbidity and Mortality Weekly Report* <http://www.cdc.gov/mmwr/volumes/70/wr/mm7018e2.htm?s_cid=mm7018e2_w>.

[115] The threshold for COVID-19 herd immunity (through a combination of vaccination and infection) may be as high as 82% of the population – see Steven Sanche and others, 'High Contagiousness and Rapid Spread of Severe Acute Respiratory Syndrome Coronavirus 2' (2020) 26 *Emerging Infectious Diseases* 1470, 1475.

[116] Vera Lúcia Raposo, 'Pigs Don't Fly and You Cannot Expect Absolutely Safe COVID-19 Vaccines (But You Should Expect a Fair Compensation)' (2021) 28 *European Journal of Health Law* 1, 18 <http://www.ncbi.nlm.nih.gov/pubmed/33878713>.

[117] For a more time-sensitive analysis, see Watts and Popa (n 3); Duncan Fairgrieve and others, 'In Favour of a Bespoke COVID-19 Vaccines Compensation Scheme' (2021) 21(4) *The Lancet Infectious Diseases* 448 <https://doi.org/10.1016/S1473-3099>; Duncan Fairgrieve and others, 'Products in a Pandemic: Liability for Medical Products and the Fight against COVID-19' (2020) 11(3) *European Journal of Risk Regulation* 565 <https://doi.org/10.1017/err.2020.54>.

[118] Sam F Halabi and Saad B Omer, 'A Global Vaccine Injury Compensation System' (2017) 317 *JAMA: The Journal of the American Medical Association* 471 <http://dx.doi.org/10.1001/jama.2016.19492>; John D Winter, Cassye Cole and Jonah Wacholder, 'Toward a Global Solution on Vaccine Liability and Compensation' (2019) 74 *Food and Drug Law Journal* 1 <http://www.who.int/csr/don/7-september-2018-ebola-drc/en/>.

[119] Yasuhiro Fujiwara, Yutaka Onda and Shuichiro Hayashi, 'No-Fault Compensation Schemes for COVID-19 Medical Products' (2021) 397 *The Lancet* 1707 <https://www.hrsa.gov/cicp/>.

merged because of liability difficulties associated with a novel vaccine. Firstly, it is not empirically certain whether or not there is a definitive causative link between COVID-19 vaccines and the reported injuries.[120] This poses a significant hurdle for claimants trying to establish liability under either a fault-based or strict liability system. Secondly, a high level of herd immunity globally will be necessary to get the pandemic under control.[121] From an ethics perspective, this suggests that the responsibility to compensate victims of vaccine injuries falls on society at large.[122] Thirdly, vaccine manufacturers may not be able to obtain commercial insurance to mitigate their commercial risk associated with novel vaccines.[123] This is one of the factors that have spurred manufacturers to insist upon a liability exemption or no-fault compensation framework of some kind as a condition of supply.[124]

These are some of the most important developments that have occurred since late 2020:

a. The world's largest ever no-fault compensation fund has been created to address COVID-19 vaccine injury. The COVAX scheme is an equitable vaccine access programme[125] that aims to deliver vaccine access to people living in 92 low- and middle-income countries. In February 2021, a no-fault compensation fund to underpin the COVAX scheme was announced. This will provide all COVAX scheme COVID-19 vaccine recipients who have suffered a serious adverse event from the vaccine with access to 'a fast, fair, robust and transparent process to receive … a no-fault lump-sum compensation in full and final settlement of any claims'.[126] This will 'significantly reduce the need for recourse to the law courts'.[127] Although

---

[120]   Mahase (n 114); Medicines and Healthcare products Regulatory Agency, 'MHRA Issues New Advice, Concluding a Possible Link between COVID-19 Vaccine AstraZeneca and Extremely Rare, Unlikely to Occur Blood Clots' (7 April 2021) <https://www.gov.uk/government/news/mhra-issues-new-advice-concluding-a-possible-link-between-covid-19-vaccine-astrazeneca-and-extremely-rare-unlikely-to-occur-blood-clots>.

[121]   Sanche and others (n 115).

[122]   Alberto Giubilini and others, 'Nudging Immunity: The Case for Vaccinating Children in School and Day Care by Default' (2019) 31 *HEC Forum* 325, 14 <https://doi.org/10.1007/s10730-019-09383-7>.

[123]   Christopher Hodges, 'Covid-19 Vaccines: Injury Compensation Issues' (2020) 7 <https://papers.ssrn.com/sol3/papers.cfm?abstract_id=3647042>.

[124]   Sam Halabi and others, 'No-Fault Compensation for Vaccine Injury – The Other Side of Equitable Access to Covid-19 Vaccines' (2020) 383(23) *New England Journal of Medicine* e125, 1.

[125]   The COVAX Scheme is coordinated by the Coalition for Epidemic Preparedness Innovations (CEPI), GAVI The Vaccine Alliance, UNICEF and the World Health Organization.

[126]   'No-Fault Compensation Programme for COVID-19 Vaccines Is a World First' <https://www.who.int/news/item/22-02-2021-no-fault-compensation-programme-for-covid-19-vaccines-is-a-world-first>.

[127]   ibid.

Chapter 6. Compensation Fund Goals and Practical Applications

(as of 2019) 25 countries had some kind of no-fault compensation fund for vaccine injury in place,[128] the COVAX no-fault scheme is the 'first and only global vaccine injury compensation mechanism'.[129]

b. In December 2020, the Canadian federal government announced that it would create a pan-Canadian no-fault Vaccine Injury Support Program (VISP). This will cover serious and permanent injuries suffered by Canadian residents in relation to any authorised vaccine, including authorised COVID-19 vaccines.[130] This no-fault compensation fund builds directly on the model of the existing Québec no-fault compensation fund for vaccine injury.

c. Existing no-fault compensation funds and alternative liability frameworks have included COVID-19 vaccines within their scope – examples here include the United Kingdom's Vaccine Damage Payments Scheme[131] and France's ONIAM.[132] Other jurisdictions such as South Africa have also decided to create no-fault compensation funds for COVID-19 vaccine injuries,[133] often as a condition of being able to access vaccine supply from manufacturers.[134] This is in contrast to the approach taken by the European Commission (on behalf of EU Member States) and the Australian government, which is the grant of a liability exemption to manufacturers, but with no corresponding compensation framework being set up for victims.[135]

These developments give rise to two key questions. Firstly, do any of the new COVID-19 vaccine-related injury compensation funds fall within our definition of a comprehensive no-fault compensation fund? Both the COVAX and the Canadian VISP cover a broad scope of functionally or thematically-linked events

---

[128] Randy G Mungwira and others, 'Global Landscape Analysis of No-Fault Compensation Programmes for Vaccine Injuries: A Review and Survey of Implementing Countries' (2020) 15(5) *PLoS ONE* e0233334, p 5 <https://doi.org/10.1371/journal.pone.0233334.g001>.

[129] 'No-Fault Compensation Programme for COVID-19 Vaccines Is a World First' (n 126).

[130] 'Call for Applications: Vaccine Injury Support Program – Canada.Ca' <https://www.canada.ca/en/public-health/services/funding-opportunities/grant-contribution-funding-opportunities/call-applications-vaccine-injury-support-program.html>.

[131] 'Government to Add COVID-19 to Vaccine Damage Payments Scheme' (3 December 2020) <https://www.gov.uk/government/news/government-to-add-covid-19-to-vaccine-damage-payments-scheme>.

[132] 'Vaccination Contre La COVID-19' <https://www.oniam.fr/accidents-medicaux-indemnisés/vaccination-contre-la-covid-19>.

[133] 'Draft Amendments to Regulations Issued in Terms of Section 27(2) of the Disaster Management Act 2002'.

[134] 'South Africa's Vaccine Compensation Fund Could Cost $17.5 Mln in First Year', *Reuters* (20 April 2021) <https://www.reuters.com/world/africa/south-africas-vaccine-compensation-fund-could-cost-175-mln-first-year-2021-04-20/>.

[135] For discussion of the justice and fairness problems associated with a liability exemption approach, see Watts and Popa (n 3). A lack of transparency in the European Commission's

Intersentia

or losses. The unique global and universal impact of the COVID-19 virus and the humanitarian urgency of a global vaccination programme being successful make the functional theme of these two new funds remarkably broad in scope. The COVAX scheme in particular, with its coverage of victims in 92 countries, can certainly be described as comprehensive in its scope of victims, even though it is functionally limited to COVID-19 vaccine injury harms. However, the public and international bodies administering both schemes have chosen to tender for private insurer and claims manager operations, rather than using a public authority to administer them. This means that the two schemes would not fall neatly under the definition of a comprehensive no-fault compensation fund that was used in this book. However, as will be discussed in later paragraphs, this choice of a public-private methodology is indicative of whether a publicly operated no-fault scheme is appropriate in an emergency public health context.

This leads neatly, then, to a second key question – what is relevant, from this study's analysis and conclusions about comprehensive no-fault compensation funds, to big new funds used for COVID-19 vaccine injury applications? What do the legal design choices about these new funds reveal about the suitability of the classic big no-fault model studied here for emergency public health or humanitarian applications? The answer to this question will advance the law. Specifically, it will add to the scholarship of Matti Urho, who concluded in 2018 from his study of Nordic no-fault compensation funds that vaccine injuries should be treated separately from injuries arising from other pharmaceutical products in a scheme that is established by legislation and administered by the state.[136] The suitability of comprehensive no-fault compensation funds for emergency public health applications like COVID-19 will be assessed with reference to the identified principles of efficiency, transparency, fairness, functionality, coherency and preciseness. In terms of practical comparisons, obviously only the New Zealand ACC Scheme is directly comparable. At the time of writing the Canadian VISP scheme was still in the establishment stages,

---

negotiation process has been critiqued by the European Parliament and others. A Member of the European Parliament recently asked the European Commission whether there was a plan to co-ordinate fragmented existing compensation efforts at Member State level; the Commission responded that 'communication about compensation procedures for side effects should take place at national level.' See 'Liability for Side Effects of COVID-19 Vaccine – Parliamentary Questions' (22 February 2021) <https://www.europarl.europa.eu/doceo/document/P-9-2021-001043_EN.html>; 'COVID-19: MEPs Want Safe Vaccines, Full Transparency and Liability for Companies' (*European Parliament*) <https://www.europarl.europa.eu/news/en/press-room/20200904IPR86419/covid-19-meps-want-safe-vaccines-full-transparency-and-liability-for-companies>; 'Covid-19 Vaccinations: More Solidarity and Transparency Needed' *European Parliament* (19 January 2021) <https://www.europarl.europa.eu/news/en/headlines/society/20210114STO95642/covid-19-vaccinations-more-solidarity-and-transparency-needed>.

[136] Urho (n 5) 486.

Chapter 6. Compensation Fund Goals and Practical Applications

and there was no comprehensive information available about the scope and design of the scheme or the application and eligibility processes.[137] The COVAX scheme is already in operation, with claims administration being provided by two insurance and claims processing heavyweights,[138] and detailed eligibility and application information available online.[139]

What are the elements from the big no-fault model that can be identified as being suitable for this problem?

Firstly, the solidarity or community responsibility approach to an unavoidable community risk is obviously most relevant in terms of a theoretical underpinning. This is an element that underpins all four big funds, regardless of their functional scope. It is also relevant to a large vaccination-focused fund. As discussed already, there is a strong ethical and practical justification to a no-fault compensation choice – if everyone[140] must be vaccinated in order for human society to move out of an emergency situation, this places a moral obligation on society as a whole to make compensation readily and proactively available to those who are injured through vaccination. This displays fairness and precision about eligibility and cover.

Secondly, the public underwriting aspect of large no-fault compensation funds is clearly also appropriate to COVID-19 (and other emergency public health) applications. The social necessity and benefit of vaccination justifies a publicly funded response to support injured victims, from both an ethical standpoint and as a way of fostering public support of vaccination. As Matti Urho has noted, it is 'only fair that the majority of the population benefitting from vaccination takes the main responsibility for the damages caused to a small minority of population by contributing to tax revenues.'[141] This means that the taxpayer and investment income funding of the New Zealand ACC Scheme's Treatment Injury Account is not as problematic when it comes to vaccine injury, compared to other harms covered by that account. This is coherent and functional.

Thirdly, the eschewing of a liability-based approach to eligibility for compensation is, as already discussed, desirable in the context of a novel vaccine product. Unless a flexible (and perhaps even unscientific) legal approach to

---

[137] 'Call for Applications: Vaccine Injury Support Program – Canada.Ca' (n 130).
[138] 'Chubb and Marsh Collaborate to Secure Insurance Coverage for the COVAX No-Fault Compensation Program for 92 Low- and Middle-Income Countries' (2021) <https://news.chubb.com/2021-04-29-Chubb-and-Marsh-Collaborate-to-Secure-Insurance-Coverage-for-the-COVAX-No-Fault-Compensation-Program-for-92-Low-and-Middle-Income-Countries>.
[139] 'Program Protocol' (*COVAX AMC*) <https://covaxclaims.com/program-protocol/>.
[140] Aside from those who cannot be vaccinated, for example, due to allergies or another health conditions.
[141] Urho (n 5) 486.

Intersentia

causation is favoured by courts,[142] then there will be a very challenging barrier for victims to access compensation. A simple factual causation link and test, as commonly used by large no-fault compensation funds, is a more desirable. Halabi et al had proposed that a temporal link between vaccination and injury could be the foundation of eligibility, a test based on the balance of probabilities, or a compelling relationship between the vaccine and the alleged harm.[143] The treatment injury threshold under the ACC Scheme means that there will not be cover for ordinary consequences (like a sore arm), but there will be cover for injuries that are not an ordinary consequence (like anaphylaxis or a cellulitis infection).[144] ACC data on accepted claims reveals that infections and adverse reactions are by some distance the highest category of accepted claims, while thrombocytopenia (the rare condition associated in some cases with the AstraZeneca vaccine) makes up only a handful of accepted claims for non-COVID vaccines.[145] The COVAX scheme also excludes ordinary consequences, but sets a specifically defined threshold of hospitalisation, permanent impairment or death in order to access compensation.[146] Impairment is defined specifically within the COVAX scheme protocol, and permanent impairments of all levels are eligible for some kind compensation.[147] This indicates that the general 'out of the ordinary' approach seen in the ACC Scheme is appropriate, but more precision can be used about the actual thresholds of harm when the scheme is being used specifically for an emergency vaccine injury application. Either of the ACC Scheme or COVAX tests is, on balance, fair, and both display adequate precision about eligibility.

Fourthly, the speed of processing claims that is a common focus under a comprehensive no-fault compensation fund is well-suited to COVID-19 vaccine injury. Particularly in a pandemic context, undue delays and an overly legalistic approach to compensation are likely to undermine public

---

[142] As seen in the non-scientific causation test applied in the CJEU case *N.W, L.W and C.W. v Sanofi Pasteur MSD SNC, Caisse primaire d'assurance maladie des Hauts-de-Seine & Carpimko* (C-621/15), 21 June 2017, ECLI:EU:C:2017:484. See further the critiques in Marco Rizzi, 'A Dangerous Method: Correlations and Proof of Causation in Vaccine Related Injuries' (2018) 9 *Journal of European Tort Law* 289.

[143] Halabi and others (n 124) 3.

[144] 'Will ACC Provide Cover for COVID-19 Vaccination Injuries?' <https://covid.immune.org.nz/faq/will-acc-provide-cover-covid-19-vaccination-injuries>.

[145] 'Vaccine Injury Compensation – Types of Injuries' (*data.govt.nz*, 2020) <https://catalogue.data.govt.nz/dataset/vaccine-injury-compensation/resource/ec6f460d-e672-4693-8233-4fa46cf9dc4c>. As of March 2021, only one treatment injury claim associated with a COVID-19 vaccine had been processed by ACC, and this related to an allergic reaction. See 'Treatment Injury Claims Related to the COVID-19 Vaccines' (*data.govt.nz*) <https://catalogue.data.govt.nz/dataset/vaccine-injury-compensation/resource/fc4ea73b-5393-4645-a978-36a0c8350a16>.

[146] 'Program Protocol' (n 139).

[147] ibid.

Chapter 6. Compensation Fund Goals and Practical Applications

confidence in both vaccines and the compensation process. A 'simple, swift and accessible procedure'[148] is necessary, and this is a point upon which big no-fault compensation funds have been shown to excel. The ACC Scheme considers treatment injury claims to be the most complex type of cases and allows up to nine months for processing.[149] The COVAX scheme, meanwhile, imposes much shorter claims processing times, with an initial review of the technical elements of an application to take place within seven days.[150] The ACC Scheme is accessed (for all injuries) by way of a healthcare professional submitting a claim on behalf of the patient, usually online.[151] Meanwhile, applications to the COVAX Scheme can be made online, by email, or by post.[152] Both procedures can be said to be efficient and functional. In the case of the COVAX Scheme, the sole critique would be that it may be challenging for an individual victim to complete the application process with all the requisite information without the assistance of their healthcare provider. The advantage of the ACC model is that all applications are submitted by treatment providers who are familiar with the no-fault compensation framework. More scope for healthcare provider input would have been preferable within the COVAX scheme, as a way of assisting the claimant with their application and achieving clarity about the causative link between the vaccine and injury.

It is also possible to identify a number of points that illustrate ways in which our comprehensive and publicly administered no-fault compensation fund model is *not* suited to an emergency pandemic situation.

Firstly, better compensation for specific categories of claimants has already been identified as a point of concern for big no-fault funds generally. This is particularly relevant in the context of a fund targeted to COVID-19 vaccine injury. The unavailability of non-pecuniary compensation, and low lump sum compensation for permanent impairment and death are all concerns. In order to underline public confidence in a no-fault compensation framework for COVID-19 vaccine injury, Fairgrieve et al have rightly argued that compensation should be 'based on need, and the sums available should be sufficiently high ... there should be no arbitrary cap on damages.'[153] An injured claimant applying to the

---

[148]   Fairgrieve and others, 'In Favour of a Bespoke COVID-19 Vaccines Compensation Scheme' (n 117).

[149]   Accident Compensation Corporation, 'Treatment Injury Claim Lodgement Guide' <https://www.acc.co.nz/assets/provider/405074f420/treatment-injury-claim-lodgement-guide.pdf> 9.

[150]   'Frequently Asked Questions (FAQs) Relating To The COVAX No-Fault Compensation Program For AMC Eligible Economies' <https://covaxclaims.com/faqs/>.

[151]   'Lodging a Claim for a Patient' <https://www.acc.co.nz/for-providers/lodging-claims/lodging-a-claim-for-a-patient/#how-to-lodge-a-claim>.

[152]   'Online Application Instructions' <https://covaxclaims.com/online-application-instructions/>; 'Help' <https://covaxclaims.com/help/#instructions>.

[153]   Fairgrieve and others, 'In Favour of a Bespoke COVID-19 Vaccines Compensation Scheme' (n 117).

Intersentia

A Comparative Law Analysis of No-Fault Comprehensive Compensation Funds

ACC Scheme would have their claim processed quickly, but will most likely only have cover for their medical treatment costs. A lump sum payment may be available, depending on the level of impairment and the judgement of an assessor. Meanwhile, the COVAX Scheme calculates compensation with reference to a formula that incorporates the GDP *per capita* of the country in question and the degree of impairment suffered, as well as a hospitalisation *per diem* payment.[154] This also does not appear to take non-pecuniary harm into account, and the maximum level of compensation will depend on factors outside of matters specific to the claimant's circumstances (i.e. the GDP *per capita* reference). In my view, unless there is scope for non-pecuniary compensation, generous compensation for severely injured claimants and some level of discretion available to the fund (as is seen with the Canadian big no-fault schemes' non-pecuniary compensation levels and the discretion available to the funds themselves), then the no-fault comprehensive style of compensation is unlikely to be adequate given the relative rarity of harm, the unavoidable nature of the risk and the potential for long-term harm or even death. In layman's terms, this kind of framework could very well leave compensation claimants feeling 'short-changed', especially when combined with a bar on tort proceedings. The serious injury carve-out seen in the TAC Scheme is another possible path to ensuring generous compensation and some recourse to full or at least greater compensation for the most severely injured claimants – however, as we have seen already, this carve-out is fraught with complexity (although it is financially sustainable, if the number of eligible claimants is limited).

Therefore, the ACC style of compensation for treatment injury is unlikely to be fair in the context of a pandemic application, and there is also a lack of transparency about how compensation is calculated (compared to the COVAX model's precise formula, for example). The persistence of vaccine hesitancy in New Zealand in relation to the COVID-19 vaccine – despite the entrenched and accepted nature of the ACC framework and a successful public health campaign to control COVID-19's spread in that country – indicates that the existing level of compensation available for vaccine injury via ACC may not be adequate to support the vaccination campaign.[155] A more desirable model of no-fault compensation for COVID-19 vaccine claims would be France's ONIAM scheme, which has elected to provide a free single-window claims processing model for all COVID-19 vaccine injury victims.[156] Claims will be processed

---

[154] 'Program Protocol' (n 139) cl 9.

[155] 26% of participants in a recent survey of New Zealanders said they do not intend to be vaccinated against COVID-19 – see Jagadish Thaker, 'The Persistence of Vaccine Hesitancy: COVID-19 Vaccination Intention in New Zealand' (2021) 26(2) *Journal of Health Communication* 1.

[156] Watts and Popa (n 3) 36–37. See also 'Vaccination Contre La COVID-19' (n 132).

Chapter 6. Compensation Fund Goals and Practical Applications

within six months, and victims will (as with all ONIAM claims) not be restricted from bringing a claim before the courts.[157] This model guarantees a no-fault compensation process to victims, but does not withdraw options from claimants. This is especially important for severely injured claimants and to encourage public support for the vaccination programme.

Secondly, the future-focused, mixed doctrine[158] and long-tail nature of comprehensive no-fault schemes might not be suitable for COVID-19 vaccine injury. At some point in the future, COVID-19 will likely (and hopefully) be either eliminated or under control as an endemic disease.[159] Unless COVID-19 vaccine injury compensation is co-located with general vaccine compensation (as Canada has elected to do), pharmaceutical or all-risks no-fault compensation, there is no need for a long-term framework to be established. The recurring levy and long-term investment full-funding approach to financing for long-term harms is also unlikely to be a precise fit, due to the temporal need (and ethical justification) for a COVID-19 vaccine injury scheme to be publicly funded and immediately available.[160] The COVAX scheme is being funded by a 10 cent (US$0.10) levy on each dose of a supplied vaccine,[161] although it is unclear how this is being co-ordinated in the case of donated vaccines. The COVAX scheme is also being supported by Chubb as lead insurer, and 10 other insurers that were brokered by Marsh.[162] This shows that a public-private partnership framework for insurance may offer more financing flexibility in an emergency short-term context.

Further, a large no-fault compensation framework may be wildly out of step with a jurisdiction's wider liability and insurance frameworks. As we have seen, these big no-fault schemes require extensive and careful initial legislative planning, may have unintended consequences for lateral legal and social frameworks, and require ongoing legislative planning (as recommended in this book) to manage all elements of their publicly managed operations to be most

---

[157] As per the terms of the European Commission's negotiated liability exemptions – what little is publicly available about them – Member States will indemnify manufacturers against any claims. See Watts and Popa (n 3) 7–10.

[158] Vansweevelt and others (n 7) 197.

[159] Ingrid Torjesen, 'Covid-19 Will Become Endemic but with Decreased Potency over Time, Scientists Believe' (2021) 372 *British Medical Journal* 494 <http://dx.doi.org/10.1136/bmj. n494>.

[160] As well as taxpayer funding, it would be ideal for a COVID-19 vaccine injury compensation fund to be funded by a per-dose levy on vaccines, a tax based on a percentage of manufacturers' and distributors' commercial activities or market authorisation fees, or direct scheme funding from manufacturers. See Watts and Popa (n 3) 28–30.

[161] David Meyer, 'If a COVID-19 Vaccine Does Turn out to Be Dangerous, Who's on the Hook?' *Fortune* (7 April 2021) <https://fortune.com/2021/04/07/covid-vaccine-safety-is-astrazeneca-safe-coronavirus-vaccination-liability/>.

[162] 'Chubb and Marsh Collaborate to Secure Insurance Coverage for the COVAX No-Fault Compensation Program for 92 Low- and Middle-Income Countries' (n 138).

Intersentia

coherent, functional and fair. These are factors that may be impossible to achieve politically in an emergency context.

Finally, there is no escaping the fact that the publicly administered model of a no-fault comprehensive compensation fund requires significant organisation and staffing. Urho recommended that a no-fault vaccine compensation fund should ideally be managed by an administrative public panel. However, this seems difficult to set up effectively within pandemic timeframes unless, as per the previous point, COVID-19 vaccine injury compensation is to be co-located with compensation for other harms that will continue to be provided on a long-term basis. It is notable that both the COVAX scheme and the Canadian VISP have chosen a kind of public-private partnership model. Under this model, a public authority designs and supervises the scheme, and a contracted private insurer with claims administration expertise operates the scheme and handles claims. This is a way of quickly establishing a fully-operational no-fault compensation scheme for COVID-19 vaccine injury, especially where there may not be adequate existing processes and resourcing within the public sector. However, this is a different model to the approach used by our four very large no-fault compensation funds. The public-private partnership choice in the context of a pandemic is a logical one, and indicates that the publicly administered model is not suitable for an emergency context. A public-private model may better achieve efficiency and functionality within the timeframes of an emergency situation.

It can certainly be said that a no-fault model in general is ideal for handling COVID-19 vaccine-related injury, for reasons of fairness and because of difficulties of applying a liability-based model to vaccine injuries.[163] However, the comprehensive and publicly entrenched no-fault compensation model studied in this project is not the ideal vehicle for no-fault compensation in a pandemic. A more flexible public-private model involving different stakeholders appears, so far, to be better suited to short- to medium-term emergency compensation needs in the context of a pandemic.

4. CONCLUSIONS ON GOALS AND PRACTICAL APPLICATIONS

This chapter has taken a future-focused approach to identify and analyse suitable goals for no-fault comprehensive compensation funds. This analysis strikes a balance between identified problems in the existing comprehensive no-fault frameworks, good points about their current operations, and legal-political realities that the funds have to face. The four comprehensive no-fault

---

[163] Watts and Popa (n 3) 11–15.

compensation funds studied in this book range from 30 to 50 years of age. They cannot be said to be novel or unusual developments that might be rolled back or significantly modified. They have deep-set roots in the societies that they exist in, and have become an everyday feature of life in the handling of compensation flowing from unavoidable and everyday risks. This means that the goals set in this chapter aim to be cognisant of what is realistically feasible from a contextual comparative law perspective – as well as identifying what legislative reform work is urgently needed.

The potential applications studied in this chapter highlighted two contrasting functional scopes of no-fault compensation – an ordinary but unavoidable risk facilitated by new technology developments (new transport modes and healthcare applications) and an emergency public health issue that also poses an unavoidable risk (the COVID-19 pandemic and the novel vaccines associated with it). Both functional scopes pose everyday unavoidable risks to the general public – which are the kind of functional risks that all big no-fault compensation funds cover. The risk posed by both functions also creates complexities, potential gaps and unfairness when ordinary liability frameworks are applied. An analysis of these two different functional applications therefore provides useful novel scholarship that is relevant to the future development of large no-fault compensation funds. It is also relevant more generally to the use of no-fault as a liability alternative in legal design and theory.

The analyses in this chapter and the following conclusions further answer the first, second and third research questions (see Chapter 4, section 8).

All four funds need to *improve their coherency of purpose and legislative design*, to varying degrees, in order to meet new societal developments and fix legal precision and coherency problems that have emerged during their existence.

a. The ACC Scheme has displayed the most incoherencies due to its wide scope, and needs to make a precise decision about whether it is closer to a social security framework or a social insurer. It is submitted that a social insurer choice is the best in the context of that scheme's current design and operation.

b. The Victorian legislature needs to address the legal incoherency in the TAC-related case law created by the serious injury carve-out. This could be achieved by providing a clear legal test in the legislation that refers to the same medical criteria for serious injury that the TAC itself uses when determining if a claimant has suffered a serious injury.

c. The TAC, SAAQ and MPI schemes all need to proactively consider whether there should be an extension of cover to new types of mobility devices and trends, and to existing types of mobility that are excluded from the current schemes. This needs to be done in order to improve precision about eligibility, fairness and coherency. It would appear logical for the schemes to be adjusted to reflect new transportation trends. However, this may conflict with the original purpose of the schemes. If there is a decision to exclude cover for certain transport types, the legislature should adjust parallel insurance and liability frameworks to ensure victims do not unnecessarily 'fall through gaps' and suffer unfair results.

All four big funds are publicly underwritten and are broadly financially stable and sustainable. However, there is inadequate clarity about *the extent of public underwriting risk* that the taxpayer may be exposed to. This could be remedied with *greater clarity within the legislative frameworks about the extent and applicability of the need for the scheme to call on taxpayer support*. Additionally, these big funds should be *made subject to the same prudential supervision as private insurers*, and this should be formalised within the legislation of each scheme. This formalisation is not intended to add extra complexity, but rather as a legal mechanism to better support the stability of the funds' large outstanding liabilities. Aligned with this, big funds should have compulsory independent actuarial supervision of their levy-setting. This will ensure adequate oversight of levy-setting and protect against political interference in the design and operation of the schemes.

Certain categories of claimants do not receive adequate compensation under a no-fault comprehensive compensation fund. Therefore, *big funds should ensure that there is adequate access for victims to non-pecuniary compensation, especially in cases of permanent impairment and loss of life.* The ACC Scheme currently offers the worst compensation outcomes to seriously injured claimants and the victims of fatal accidents, which could not be said to strike a fair bargain with the loss of access to tort law damages. The two Canadian funds offer good examples of how non-pecuniary compensation can be best provided for under a large no-fault framework. Additionally, *the purpose of compensation more generally under the four funds should better reflect what the claimant has lost, and not solely focus on the new reality of the claimant's post-injury life.* Victims whose income and prospects post-accident have most disparity with their pre-injury circumstances could be targeted in particular. This would maintain the mostly pecuniary and mixed purpose nature of compensation in big no-fault funds, but it would produce fairer results for certain categories of victims who are currently poorly served by the schemes.

Based on information that is publicly available and the qualitative research results of this book, it is still *unclear whether subrogation is financially justified for the three funds that actively use their subrogation rights.* Therefore, each of these three funds should undertake further quantitative and qualitative research on the practice, costs and (actual and perceived) effectiveness of subrogation. The findings of this research should be made publicly available and reported back to the supervising government minister, the legislature and any other relevant supervisory body. The normative litigation approach of the fund should also be clarified within the legislation, to ensure that it matches the purpose and

Chapter 6. Compensation Fund Goals and Practical Applications

legal design of the fund. It is also unequivocal that the ACC Scheme should be empowered with a general entitlement to pursue a subrogated action, because unfair results for victims and society have flowed from the lack of any subrogation possibilities. A Menyawi-style public tort liability approach would be the best choice for the ACC, because it would not conflict with the framework of existing statutory entitlements and the extinguishment of tort private law rights generally.

Comprehensive no-fault compensation funds *should be subject to compulsory legislative reviews every 5–10 years.* This is to address the inconsistencies that emerge over time and new developments, before they become too politically toxic to address. This would be best handled by law reform bodies in conjunction with the independent supervisory bodies that were recommended earlier. Stakeholder participation in these legislation reviews should be guaranteed. Relevant reference points during such a review include the scheme's original objectives; changes in contextual circumstances (both legislative and socio-political); independently assessed financial sustainability and stability; the adequacy of compensation for different categories of claimants; human rights law compliance; and future risks.

To date, *no comprehensive no-fault compensation fund has adequately considered human rights* intersections. These intersections should form a core part of the already-proposed major and ongoing legislative reviews of the schemes, but *should be cognisant of the schemes' operation as a revolutionary private law mechanism.* Articles 3 and 14 of the International Covenant on Civil and Political Rights, articles 9 and 12 of the International Covenant on Economic, Social and Cultural Rights and article 13 of the Convention on the Rights of Persons with Disabilities are the most relevant international human rights protections to consider in relation to a comprehensive no-fault compensation fund. A dedicated Ombudsman or independent supervisory commission for broader human rights and privacy concerns should be created for each fund, which would form a third supervisory pillar of these large schemes' operations.

In order to ensure that all claimants have better access to legal information (thus facilitating better access to justice in these extra-legal big schemes), *better provision for legal guidance* should be specifically made in the legislative framework. Basic guidance or navigation services are inadequate. A *fully-funded legal service is ideal for a no-fault fund with no carve-out from its statutory tort bar*, whereas a collaborative approach with the legal profession is more suited to a no-fault fund that *does* have a carve-out (like the TAC).

At a *general level, big no-fault compensation funds appear to cover harms associated with artificial intelligence automatically,* without any need for significant change. This puts these frameworks at a big advantage, as a starting point, over liability-based systems. However, upon digging deeper, one sees that there are *significant legislative adjustments that have to be made before a big no-fault model can be used to cover these risks in a way that meets the requirements of efficiency, transparency, fairness, functionality, coherency and precision.*

Intersentia

439

In relation to automated vehicles, it is necessary to make adjustment to the *design and application of levies* so that it includes more parties than just the owner/driver. It will be necessary for the big no-fault fund to have *good subrogation powers*, and there will need to be *clear legislative statements on who is excluded from the scheme's liability exemptions* (e.g. the driver who forgets to install a software update vs a third-party software provider). If automated vehicles significantly improve *transport safety* to the point that serious injury and death becomes uncommon, this *could disrupt the purpose and undermine the need* of a comprehensive no-fault compensation fund. There will also need to be legislative decisions made about transport devices that use *spaces not currently used for personal and consumer-related mobility (for example, drones)*. Overall, the liability challenges associated with automated vehicles appear to be a *good match* with the solutions offered by big no-fault compensation funds, if necessary adjustments to legislative frameworks can be made.

Comprehensive no-fault compensation funds can also be a good match for *artificial intelligence applications in healthcare, but there are more fundamental hurdles to be overcome* before this kind of framework is truly suitable. With reference to the ACC Scheme in particular (the only one of our four funds that covers treatment injury), there are current *definitional problems in the application of the 'failure to treat' and failure of equipment tests*. Specifically, a *continued reliance on fault-derived principles* means that specific legislative consideration is needed for how artificial intelligence fits within the ACC treatment injury landscape. As discussed already, *public tort liability-style subrogation powers* need to be given for ACC to exercise in the public interest, to ensure public safety and avoid free-riding by artificial intelligence manufacturers and service providers. Also, the *levy design of the current Treatment Injury Account is inadequate* and does not show how artificial intelligence manufacturers and distributors could contribute to the scheme.

Large no-fault compensation fund frameworks have already been established in relation to *COVID-19 vaccine-related injury*. No-fault in general is the best method of handling the liability problems associated with COVID-19 vaccine injury. However, the *comprehensive no-fault compensation fund model is not the best vehicle* for resolving this broad category of harm. This is because of firstly, *inadequate levels of compensation* (given the need to buttress support for global vaccination efforts); secondly, *the long-tail nature* of comprehensive no-fault funds' structures versus the short- to medium-term nature of COVID-19 vaccine injury risk; and thirdly, the time-sensitive nature of a pandemic situation, which *justifies a public-private partnership approach on organisational structure and funding*, which can be more flexible and quickly arranged than a public authority run scheme.

CHAPTER 7

CONCLUSIONS

1. INTRODUCTION

This book has contributed to the comparative law landscape of compensation funds in general, by identifying the key characteristics and principles of the world's most comprehensive no-fault compensation funds. The field of no-fault compensation has been broad and ill-defined until now, despite many differing shapes of alternative liability schemes existing for decades in multiple jurisdictions. It is only in this century that legal scholars have attempted to more precisely classify these liability frameworks, better understand their function and nature, and apply scholarly rigour to their unruly growth. Very big no-fault compensation funds, which are publicly managed and publicly underwritten, are the purest and most expansive forms of no-fault or no-blame redress structures.

The four schemes analysed in this book are the largest and most expansive of their type, covering around 21.6 million people in total,[1] with automatic entitlement to compensation for certain types of injuries, but severely restricting access to ordinary court remedies. This book is the first scholarly analysis of this category of *comprehensive* no-fault compensation funds. The key learnings of this book are relevant to the existing funds themselves, new funds that are coming into existence, and smaller less comprehensive funds which can define themselves in similarity or contrast with the largest exemplars of no-fault.

Three research questions were posed in the research that underpinned this text. The choice of these research questions was motivated by an observation of knowledge gaps in the current scope and practice of big no-fault compensation funds. The research questions were also motivated by the goal of evolving the understanding of the law surrounding big compensation funds a step further from Peter Cane's bipolar abolitionist and incrementalist camps of tort law reform.[2] The definition of a no-fault comprehensive compensation fund can be

---

[1] The populations of New Zealand, the State of Victoria, the province of Manitoba and the province of Québec.

[2] Peter Cane, *The Political Economy of Personal Injury Law* (University of Queensland Press 2007).

Intersentia

441

summarised as follows. It is a fund that compensates individuals for a statutorily defined comprehensive range of harms, on a no-fault basis (i.e. showing liability is not necessary to access compensation). The scheme is administered by a single public or quasi-public centralised body. The purpose of the payments made by the fund is broadly compensatory, but mixed purposes are possible. Importantly, the compensation fund is dominant in nature – it is a compulsory alternative in (nearly) all circumstances to a damages action before the courts. The scheme displays similarities to both social security and insurance, but does not fit tidily into either camp. It is not necessary for a claimant to have paid a premium or levy in order to access compensation. The four funds that meet this definition are New Zealand's Accident Compensation Corporation scheme, the Transport Accident Commission Scheme in the Australian state of Victoria, the Société de l'assurance automobile du Québec in the Canadian province of Québec, and the compulsory no-fault personal injury compensation elements of the Manitoba Public Insurance framework in the Canadian province of Manitoba.

This concluding chapter distils the answers to the three research questions, and identifies goals for future research.

2. RESEARCH QUESTION 1

Research question 1 is: '*What are the key characteristics of no-fault comprehensive compensation funds and the key pillars, common to multiple jurisdictions, for the successful establishment, administration, operation and further development of no-fault comprehensive compensation funds?*'

From a theoretical perspective, there was no strong legal philosophical underpinning to the choice of no-fault in any of the four funds. This was partly because of the socio-legal and political influences in play at the time of their establishment. These schemes were (like any legislative instrument) an alchemy of justice goals and political bargaining. This book has proposed *a novel new definition of no-fault*:

> the rejection of a legal definition of fault or liability as being relevant to the determination of legal or factual compensation responsibility for an adverse event. In a no-fault compensation fund this means the rejection of fault or liability as being relevant to the victim's eligibility for and/or entitlement to categories of financial compensation for pecuniary and non-pecuniary losses. The rejection of the utility or relevance of a legal definition of fault or liability does not, however, mean that liability or responsibility is extinguished in all senses. However, in the case of a very broad no-fault compensation fund, there may be very few practically remaining avenues for alternative liability possibilities.

Chapter 7. Conclusions

The core reference principles for assessment of comprehensive no-fault compensation funds are *efficiency, transparency, fairness, functionality, coherency and precision about eligibility*. These principles are derived from scholarship on other types of no-fault or no-blame compensation, and the results of this research project. In their current state, the four funds, to varying degrees, do not fully achieve these six requirements.

These schemes are neither purely social security frameworks nor insurance, but they have a foot in both camps. However, their operational function and financial design put them closer to an insurance framework in nature.

Big no-fault compensation funds are underpinned by a social and community responsibility element that goes to the heart of their structure. This has broad equivalence to the French concept of solidarity. However, all four funds currently require a philosophical restatement in legislation that is specific to this kind of very big scheme, in order for them to be more coherent and better tackle existing needs and future risks. This need for restatement is because the element of solidarity, to the extent that it can be defined, is intrinsically antithetical to the notion of insurance. As noted already, big no-fault compensation funds are closer in nature to insurance than social security. A clear legislative framing of solidarity – or at least a statement of a social compromise approach – is urgently needed for all four funds.

From a functional perspective, these big funds appear to be best suited to personal injury losses, rather than property or economic damages. This is because the core focus of all four schemes is compensation for (and prevention of and rehabilitation from) broad types of personal injury. None of the funds try to cover economic loss, and these kinds of losses have been left happily to the respective competitive private insurance markets. This potentially limits the functional relevance of the big no-fault scheme model to other types of losses such as natural disaster-related damage.

Also from a functional perspective, big no-fault funds have an interest in preventing harm and rehabilitating victims from harm. The number of functional categories of coverage affects the ability of the fund to manage the landscape of risk creation and loss. For a fund with multiple functions of coverage (like ACC), it will be difficult to manage the causes of loss and the behaviour of risk-takers. In contrast, funds with a single wide function (e.g. the transport injury function of the other three schemes) can have strong regulatory control over all the elements of risk creation. Schemes with multi-function scopes also have a much greater risk of creating inconsistencies and imprecision about coverage with even minor extensions in scope.

The establishment of a big no-fault scheme is best done by a single large legislative action, in one fell swoop. The evidence from the four big funds is that an incremental attempt to move from non-comprehensive to fully comprehensive is unlikely to be successful. Once the big legislative social choice

Intersentia

443

A Comparative Law Analysis of No-Fault Comprehensive Compensation Funds

has been made, the framework is easier to maintain in the long run. However, periodic scheme reviews (say, once every five to 10 years) are necessary to ensure that the scheme remains fit for purpose. It is imperative that clear legislative foresight and description of the fund's intersections with other legal frameworks is made. This applies for practical issues, such as the border between similar non-covered categories of injury.[3] However, it is also to ensure that fault-based tests do not creep into the scheme unintentionally, thereby undermining the coherency of the scheme. This is especially relevant to qualifying thresholds that are set regarding eligibility and issues of causation. Careful legal design with a cognisance of the surrounding legal context is extremely important to avoid the creation and festering of such gaps. In this regard, the four big no-fault compensation funds do a worse job than the purposive legal system design found in Nordic countries' different categories of no-fault compensation funds.

No-fault comprehensive schemes are ultimately a new form of hybrid socio-legal structure. Where there is no carve-out for tort-style damages, it can be considered to be a complete revolution in tort or private law. Where there is a limited carve-out for tort-style damages (such as in the TAC scheme), it can be considered to be a partial revolution in tort or private law. The fact of big no-fault funds genuinely representing a complete or partial revolution in tort law is evidenced and supported by the stability and longevity of the four funds. They are proof of a modern form of compensation structure that stands outside the ordinary legal frameworks of private law. The socio-legal nature of funds means that empirical knowledge about injury and rehabilitation are key to the structure and operation of the funds. The funds are not a purely legal structure, they are a socio-legal structure.

Where a very big scheme does allow a carve-out for tort damages actions (such as in the TAC scheme), this is legally incoherent and technically incompatible with the context of fund as an alternative liability system. Nevertheless, the legislature may have normative justifications for that creation, and the availability of the carve-out may be popular with the public. It appears from data about the operation of the TAC Scheme that this incoherency is not actually financially unsustainable – but it does create a significant cost burden on the fund. The availability of an incoherent carve-out must be strictly controlled and justified, otherwise it risks destabilising the fund financially.

Claims are processed very quickly under a comprehensive no-fault compensation fund – often in a matter of hours or days. In the ACC and TAC Schemes, fast processing times are prized as an example of the system's efficiency.

---

[3]   Such as the border between transport injury and workplace injury in the three transport-focused funds.

444

Intersentia

Claims are generally processed by human staff who do not have any specific legal training, or (increasingly) by automated claims processing tools. There is not generally strict attention paid to causative elements, unless it is a complex case. This approach means that, in general, very little attention is paid to potential legal issues at the time of claims processing, unless it is one of those complex cases (for example, a treatment injury case in the New Zealand ACC Scheme). This cements the reality of big no-fault compensation funds' status as socio-legal entities. It can also be observed that the wider the scope of the fund, the less opportunity there is for legal analysis of most cases – compare, for example, the new automated processing approach of the ACC Scheme for most cases to enhance efficiency, with the manual processing approach of the MPI to ensure scheme coherency.

The quantum of compensation under a comprehensive no-fault compensation fund is generally capped and limited. Compensation mostly takes the form of pecuniary income replacement and medical expenses. However, there is overall a mixed pecuniary, non-pecuniary and symbolic character to compensation under these statutory schemes. The symbolic elements are linked to the social purpose of the schemes. The goal of the compensation paid and services provided is to support the claimant to achieve social and vocational rehabilitation according to their post-injury status, *not* their pre-injury self. In terms of non-pecuniary compensation, this will generally only be available to seriously injured or permanently impaired claimants. Only the Canadian schemes have prescribed in the statute a reasonably generous amount of non-pecuniary compensation for certain claimants. The TAC's carve-out for serious injury also allows some access to non-pecuniary compensation, although, as noted already, the carve-out is technically incoherent with the rest of the scheme. The ACC Scheme does not provide any non-pecuniary compensation at all, and offers only token compensation to family members of fatal injury victims. This is a significant failing of that scheme and grossly unfair.

Insurance-style full-funding is the core method of funding for all four schemes. The schemes' operational costs and long-term obligations are covered by levies and investment income. It is only in the case of a multi-function fund (the ACC Scheme) that there is a direct taxpayer contribution. This means that the schemes are broadly sustainable and in a good financial position. However a heavy reliance on investment income poses potential risks in the event of unpredictable market fluctuations or poor investment choices. Independent actuarial design and supervision of levies is common, but not universal to all four schemes. In a multi-function fund (the ACC Scheme) not all risks are currently being levied for, and this is problematic.

There is currently inadequate formal financial and prudential supervision of no-fault comprehensive compensation funds. This is in comparison with the level of supervision required of private insurers. The reason for this light-touch regulation is because all four funds are publicly underwritten, and can call upon a taxpayer funding injection if required. However, there is inadequate legislative clarity about when that taxpayer funding may be called upon. More compulsory pillars of supervision is a good idea for all four schemes. This is not intended to add complexity, but rather to ensure the stability of the schemes. Also, all four funds do not currently use reinsurance to adequately protect their long-term risks, and this option should be further explored.

Subrogation is used in a limited way in three out of the four funds to recover monies from individuals not within the ambit of the scheme. The New Zealand ACC Scheme does not use subrogation at all, mostly as a consequence of the complete tort bar on personal injury compensatory damages claims. However, there is a lack of clarity on how subrogation is best used within a big no-fault compensation fund. There is no precise data gathered on the costs of subrogation and the financial returns on these activities. This is especially the case where the subrogation activities are delegated to an external body or authority. It is only where all subrogation activities are handled in-house (such as in the SAAQ) that there is a clearer picture of the costs of subrogation. Differing litigation and negotiation strategies are used by the schemes, and this appears to be linked to their self-perception of their social character. More qualitative reporting by the funds themselves and quantitative research is urgently needed on this point. The use of a public tort liability approach appears very suitable for the likes of the ACC Scheme, and would mean that the subrogation power given to the fund would not need to line up directly with the tort bar.

All four funds need to improve their coherency of purpose and legislative design, to varying degrees. This is to meet the challenge of new societal and technological developments, and to fix existing legal precision and coherency problems. The ACC Scheme displays the most incoherencies in purpose and design. The legislature needs to completely reassess the scheme and make precise decisions about its scope. It should be clearly classified as being a type of mandatory or social insurer, rather than a part of the social security system. In respect of the TAC, the Victorian legislature needs to address the legal incoherency problems presented by the serious injury carve-out. It is also necessary for the legislature to directly tackle new transport technologies and trends, and plan how the TAC scheme should (or should not) cover these changes. Turning to Canada, the SAAQ and MPI show more legal coherency than their Antipodean cousins, but the relevant legislatures also need to directly tackle new (and existing) transport technologies and trends, to ensure that the schemes and their surrounding legal landscapes provide coherent cover for harm.

As noted already, all four funds should be subject to compulsory scheme reviews. This would ensure that necessary reforms are not left so long that they become too politically toxic to action. Scheme reviews should be managed by law reform bodies in conjunction with independent supervisory bodies (such as the financial and prudential regulator, an independent actuarial supervisor and an Ombudsman or injury commissioner), before going to the legislature. The relevant reference criteria to be considered during such a review should be:

a. the scheme's original objectives;
b. changes in contextual circumstances (both legislative and socio-political);
c. independent assessment of financial sustainability and stability;
d. the adequacy of compensation quantum for different categories of claimants;
e. human rights law compliance; and
f. future risks.

These criteria are compliant with current trends in legal design theory.

3. RESEARCH QUESTION 2

Research question 2 is: '*What is the interaction between comprehensive no-fault compensation funds and human rights law, principles of access to justice and practical dispute resolution issues?*'

Human rights law and principles were never dealt with in any detail during the establishment of our four schemes. This was mainly for legal contextual reasons, rather than the legislature deliberately choosing to ignore or override human rights principles. The tradition of primacy of parliamentary authority in Westminster/Dicey-derived systems means that there were no fundamental or constitutional law handbrakes on the choices that could be made by the legislature in relation to the creation of a big no-fault compensation fund. The creation of a scheme that facilitated guaranteed access to compensation for large numbers of victims was perceived as balanced and not overriding unwritten common law rights to access the courts. The recognition of wider access to justice goals inherent in the schemes and the fact of a social contract were deemed sufficient. All four funds are broadly compliant with the human rights frameworks in their jurisdictions.

Therefore, it can be said that the statutory bar on tort proceedings within very large no-fault compensation funds is *contextually* and *domestically* compliant with human rights law, and a justified limitation on civil justice rights. Specifically, Canadian case law has affirmed that there is no fundamental right in that jurisdiction to bring a civil claim for personal injury damages. However this conclusion does not mean that human rights law issues are settled for the purposes of comprehensive no-fault compensation funds.

As noted under the first research question, a comprehensive no-fault compensation fund is a stand-alone legal structure that constitutes a complete or partial revolution in tort law. However, it still needs to be subject to human rights monitoring and compliance. It is not enough for the legislature to state

Intersentia

447

that the scheme constitutes a social choice to establish a new alternative liability framework. These frameworks have significant practical and civil justice impacts on the millions of people within their scope, and they therefore need adequate oversight on human rights points. All four schemes have shown great willingness to be as compliant as possible with human rights law, to the extent that is possible under their existing legislative framework.

The core intersection with human rights issues is the fact that there is no default access to a court permitted under a comprehensive no-fault compensation fund. The method of accessing compensation for covered harms is via the regime set out in the statute, and this statute also sets out procedures for dispute resolution. In terms of dispute resolution, the first option under all four schemes is an internal review, which may be appealed (on points of law only) to an administrative court or tribunal or a general court. Therefore, recourse to the courts is possible – but only in limited circumstances and as a last resort. Alternative dispute resolution services and concepts feature prominently in all four schemes. However, it is not clear whether this is actually appropriate, given the fact that most disputes relate to causation issues – i.e. which turn on statutory interpretation and medical evidence points.

In terms of access to legal information, a guidance or navigation service for claimants (as seen in the ACC Scheme) is helpful, but a fully-funded legal advice service that is foreseen within the legislation (as seen in the MPI) is a better choice to ensure adequate access to justice and legal support. As an alternative, a partnership with the legal profession that allows subsidised legal advice and support to be available to certain claimants may also be a good choice. However, partnership with the legal profession will only be logical and practical where there is a carve-out to the tort bar in the scheme. As it stands, direct legal information and legal advice is only available to claimants who have a dispute about their claim. Aside from the possibility of legally-informed guidance (which is provided by an independent agency) under the ACC Scheme, there is no free legal advice or information available to all claimants under the four funds.

This lack of legal advice is particularly pertinent when one considers that the scheme design, where it is imprecise or uneven about eligibility for compensation, enables problematically different treatment of similar classes of victims. This impacts access to justice and is a human rights flashpoint. This different treatment is deemed acceptable under the human rights frameworks of Australia, Canada and New Zealand (because of the social choice made by the legislature), but in a jurisdiction with more comprehensive human rights protections (such as European jurisdictions) this different treatment is likely to be problematic.

Comprehensive no-fault compensation funds also have more and different kinds of potential human rights intersections than a more limited no-fault scheme. This is because of their broad regulatory role, especially in funds that relate to a single large function like transport injury. For example, in Québec there is an ongoing class action about whether a questionnaire used by SAAQ to evaluate drivers' risk of re-offending (where those drivers had been previously convicted for impaired driving) was discriminatory. These big funds also process large amounts of highly sensitive data about claimants, and their comprehensive compulsory nature means that they wield a significant amount of influence over the lives of claimants. In New Zealand, claimant challenges against ACC on specific human rights and privacy grounds have been more successful than attempts to get around the strict tort bar.

Big no-fault compensation funds are part of the third wave of the global access to justice movement. They broadly meet the third-wave criteria of efficiency, fairness, cost-effectiveness and accessibility. Big no-fault schemes with a very wide scope can be a way of facilitating access to justice for harms that are difficult to litigate in tort – for example, historic abuse and human rights infringements. This because these schemes can compensate, in a mixed compensatory and symbolic way, for the harm suffered for infringement of fundamental personal integrity rights (e.g. institutional child abuse).

However, this study has shown that big no-fault compensation funds also create or worsen some barriers to justice. Specifically, they reduce access to legal information, may offer severely inadequate compensation to certain categories of claimants, and indirectly affect overall access to justice. The Canadian schemes and the TAC perform better on these points than the ACC Scheme, which facilitates the most barriers to justice overall. It is therefore possible to conclude that a very big no-fault compensation fund, despite facilitating access to justice generally, will also increase barriers to justice in other ways unless there is careful legal design of the framework. Scheme extension is not a solution to these problems. Careful legislative redesign is the actual solution to this problem, with cognisance of best practices in other similar schemes.

Under research question 1 it was argued that all four schemes should be subject to periodic compulsory scheme reviews, as well as an urgent overhaul in the short-term to improve the coherency and purpose of the schemes. It is submitted that human rights issues should be a core part of these legislative reviews. Those reviews should consider each jurisdiction's own human rights framework, but it would also be appropriate to directly consider: articles 3 and 14 of the International Covenant on Civil and Political Rights, articles 9 and 12 of the International Covenant on Economic, Social and Cultural Rights and article 13 of the Convention on the Rights of Persons with Disabilities.

4. RESEARCH QUESTION 3

Research question 3 is: 'How can no-fault comprehensive compensation funds be used to address contemporary legal problems common to multiple jurisdictions?'

Big no-fault compensation schemes continue to be relevant to contemporary legal problems, as evidenced by efforts relating to two new big schemes for transport injury in the Canadian provinces of British Columbia and Alberta. The schemes are directly and indirectly inspired by the SAAQ and MPI. Therefore, the big no-fault compensation fund model shows continuing suitability for the transport function in particular.

Further, the model of comprehensive no-fault compensation fund has also shown itself to be very suited to new kinds of unavoidable risks. It is possible for these schemes to be used for all kinds of artificial intelligence applications, because they avoid the need to solve problematic liability issues associated with AI. The large no-fault model can also be relevant to public health applications, such as injury associated with COVID-19 vaccines. However, specific adjustments would need to be made to the existing schemes and model to meet the requirements (identified under research question 1) of efficiency, transparency, fairness, functionality, coherency and precision of eligibility.

In relation to automated vehicles, it is necessary to make adjustments to the design and application of levies so that levies are paid by more parties than just the owner/driver of the vehicle. It will also be necessary for the fund to have strong subrogation powers, combined with a clear legislative statement on who is exempt from the scheme's coverage. If automated vehicles significantly improve transport safety in the future to the point that serious injury and death become uncommon, this could disrupt the purpose and undermine the existential necessity of a comprehensive no-fault compensation fund. There will also need to be legislative decisions made about transport devices that use spaces not currently used for personal mobility, like drones. Overall, the liability challenges associated with automated vehicles and multimodality appear to be a good match with the solutions offered by big no-fault compensation funds, if necessary adjustments to legislative frameworks can be made.

Big no-fault compensation funds can also be a good match for artificial intelligence applications in healthcare, but there are more fundamental hurdles to be overcome (compared with transport) before this kind of framework can be said to be truly appropriate. With reference to the ACC Scheme in particular (the only one of our four funds that covers treatment injury), there are current definitional problems in the application of the failure to treat and failure of equipment statutory tests. Specifically, a continued reliance on fault-derived principles during assessment means that specific legislative consideration is needed of how artificial intelligence fits within the ACC treatment injury landscape. As discussed already, public tort liability-style subrogation powers also need to be given to ACC for it to exercise in the public interest. This is to ensure public safety and avoid free-riding on the scheme by artificial intelligence manufacturers and service providers based in other jurisdictions. Also, the current levy design of the Treatment Injury Account is inadequate and does not

Chapter 7. Conclusions

show how artificial intelligence manufacturers and distributors could contribute to the scheme.

Turning next to public health or emergency applications, large no-fault compensation fund frameworks have been established in relation to COVID-19 vaccine-related injury. These were novel and unexpected developments that occurred during the course of this research project. No-fault can be said in general to be the best and fairest method (for victims) of handling the liability problems associated with COVID-19 vaccine injury. However, the comprehensive no-fault compensation fund model is not the best no-fault vehicle for resolving this broad category of harm. This is because of, firstly, inadequate levels of compensation (given the need to buttress support for global vaccination efforts); secondly, the long-tail nature of comprehensive no-fault funds' structures is not well-matched to the short- to medium-term nature of COVID-19 vaccine injury risk and thirdly, the time-sensitive nature of a pandemic situation justifies a public-private partnership approach on organisational structure and funding, which can be more flexible and quickly arranged than a scheme operated by a public authority.

5. GOALS FOR FURTHER RESEARCH

The large research gaps in existing scholarship about no-fault compensation funds, and the imprecise definition of the field, justified a strictly definitional approach being taken in this project. The advantage of this approach is that it has facilitated more precision in the field of no-fault compensation. It has also facilitated the first comparative law study of the world's largest examples of no-fault compensation funds. This advances the law and scholarship, and provides useful information for scholars, legislatures and the funds themselves. However, this strictly definitional approach also has its disadvantages. The most obvious disadvantage is that is has excluded the possibility of a comparison with less comprehensive schemes, or those that are managed by private insurers. Those kinds of comparison are therefore a logical goal for further research. The public-private partnership choices displayed in the new Canadian and COVAX vaccine injury compensation schemes also point to a need for further comparative work on this point. It is hoped that the clarity provided by the conclusions of this study will be a helpful starting point for further comparative studies.

The qualitative and quantitative data gaps revealed by this study also point to suitable directions for further multidisciplinary research. The conclusions of this study show that no-fault comprehensive compensation funds are socio-legal constructs, whose creation and operation are shaped by knowledge from many different scientific disciplines. Within the field of health research, it has

Intersentia

451

already been identified that there should be more meaningful involvement of end-users in research, in order to improve research outcomes.[4] Future broad studies of no-fault comprehensive compensation funds should therefore ideally incorporate knowledge and empirical methods from other scientific disciplines. Specifically, collaboration is required with scholars in actuarial studies, economics, sociology, medicine, and rehabilitation.

Finally, there should be specific research that considers the relevance of comprehensive no-fault compensation funds to other types of increasingly unavoidable risks like climate change impacts. There needs to be analysis of whether this kind of big no-fault framework could be useful and relevant to long-term universal risks that pose potential bodily *and* property harm impacts, or whether another model is more suitable.

---

[4] Peter Slattery, Alexander K Saeri and Peter Bragge, 'Research Co-Design in Health: A Rapid Overview of Reviews' (2020) 18 *Health Research Policy and Systems* n17 <https://doi.org/10.1186/s12961-020-0528-9>.

BIBLIOGRAPHY

'About the PUB' <http://www.pubmanitoba.ca/v1/about-pub/index.html>

Abraham KS and Rabin RL, 'Automated Vehicles and Manufacturer Responsibility for Accidents: A New Legal Regime for a New Era' (2019) 105 Virginia Law Review 127 <http://www.virginialawreview.org/sites/virginialawreview.org/files/A%26R_Book_0. pdf>

——, 'The Future Is Almost Here: Inaction Is Actually Mistaken Action' (2019) 105 Virginia Law Review Online 91 <http://www.virginialawreview.org/sites/virginialaw review.org/files/Abraham%26Rabin_Book.pdf>

'ACC Earners' Levy Rates' <https://www.ird.govt.nz/income-tax/income-tax-for-individuals/ acc-clients-and-carers/acc-earners-levy-rates>

'ACC Levy Guidebook 2020/21' <https://www.acc.co.nz/assets/business/acc7686-levy-guidebook-2020-2021.pdf>

Accident Compensation Corporation, 'Impairment Assessment Lump Sum/Independence Allowance Operational Guidelines' (2014) <https://www.acc.co.nz/assets/contracts/ imp-og.pdf>

——, 'Statement of Intent 2015–2019' (2015) <https://www.acc.co.nz/assets/corporate-documents/ACC6969-Statement-of-intent-2015-2019.pdf>

——, 'Annual Report 2017' (2017) <https://www.parliament.nz/resource/en-NZ/ PAP_75085/cd5473578a0a648b7c15d0d819d2f36d8ba477c2>

——, 'Briefing to the Incoming Minister' (2017) <https://www.acc.co.nz/assets/ corporate-documents/minister-briefing-2017.pdf>

——, 'Financial Condition Report' (2017) <https://www.acc.co.nz/assets/corporate-documents/acc7847-financial-condition-report-2017.pdf>

——, 'Service Agreement 2017/18' (2017) <https://www.parliament.nz/resource/en-NZ/ PAP_75186/92e34677ae6c78c38354d975e2ad5eb774ab2c66>

——, 'What to Do If You're Injured' (2017) <https://www.acc.co.nz/im-injured/what-to-do/>

——, 'Privacy Impact Assessment: Statistical Models Used to Improve the Claim Registration and Approval Process' (2018)

——, 'Statistical Models to Improve ACC Claims Approval and Registration Process Statistical Modelling to Support the ACC Automation Cover Decisions and Accident Description' (2018)

——, 'Annual Report 2019' (2019)

——, 'We're Changing How We Handle Customer Reviews' (2019) <https://www.acc. co.nz/newsroom/stories/were-changing-how-we-handle-customer-reviews/>

——, 'Annual Report 2020' (2020)

——, 'Client Reviews – Heartbeat Survey May 2020' (2020)

——, 'Financial Condition Report 2020' (2020) <www.acc.co.nz/about-us/corporate>

——, 'Perineal Tear Treatment Injury' (2020) <www.acc.co.nz/lodgementguide>

——, 'E-Scooters: Wellington City, It's Your Turn' <https://www.acc.co.nz/newsroom/stories/e-scooters-wellington-city-its-your-turn/>

——, 'New Campaign to Tackle Low Awareness of ACC's Role' <https://www.scoop.co.nz/stories/PO2001/S00017/new-campaign-to-tackle-low-awareness-of-accs-role.htm>

——, 'Paying for Patient Treatment' <https://www.acc.co.nz/for-providers/invoicing-us/paying-patient-treatment/>

——, 'Treatment Injury Claim Lodgement Guide' <https://www.acc.co.nz/assets/provider/405074f420/treatment-injury-claim-lodgement-guide.pdf>

——, 'What We Do' <https://www.acc.co.nz/about-us/who-we-are/what-we-do/>

——, 'What Your Levies Pay For' <https://www.acc.co.nz/about-us/how-levies-work/what-your-levies-pay/>

Accident Compensation Corporation and Department of Labour, 'Review of Medical Misadventure' (2003)

'Accident Services: A Guide for DHB and ACC Staff' (2018) <https://forms.acc.co.nz/ACC32>

Acclaim Otago, 'Understanding the Problem: An Analysis of ACC Appeals Processes to Identify Barriers to Access to Justice for Injured New Zealanders' (2015) <http://www.acclaimotago.org>

——, 'New Advocacy Service a Start, but Not the Solution' (2018) <https://www.scoop.co.nz/stories/PO1804/S00309/new-advocacy-service-a-start-but-not-the-solution.htm>

——, 'The Costs of Paradigm Change: Access to Justice for People with Disabilities Caused by Personal Injury in New Zealand' (2014) <http://www.acclaimotago.org>

'Additional Extension Products' <https://www.mpi.mb.ca/Pages/other-extensions.aspx>

Adelman H, 'Contrasting Commissions on Interculturalism: The Hijāb and the Workings of Interculturalism in Quebec and France' (2011) 32 Journal of Intercultural Studies 245 <https://www.tandfonline.com/action/journalInformation?journalCode=cjis20>

Agarwal R, Gupta A and Gupta S, 'The Impact of Tort Reform on Defensive Medicine, Quality of Care, and Physician Supply: A Systematic Review' [2019] Health Services Research 1475 <https://onlinelibrary.wiley.com/doi/abs/10.1111/1475-6773.13157>

Ainge Roy E, 'New Zealand's Human Rights Tribunal "Breaching Human Rights" Due to Delays' *The Guardian* (11 April 2018) <https://www.theguardian.com/world/2018/apr/11/new-zealands-human-rights-tribunal-breaching-human-rights-due-to-delays>

Akoorie N, 'ACC Paid Mental Health Specialists $41.9m to Assess Claimants, Then Hundreds Lost Cover' *New Zealand Herald* (23 July 2020) <https://www.nzherald.co.nz/nz/news/article.cfm?c_id=1&objectid=12338340>

'Alpine Fault: Probability of Damaging Quake Higher than Previously Thought' *Radio New Zealand News* (20 April 2021) <https://www.rnz.co.nz/news/national/440834/alpine-fault-probability-of-damaging-quake-higher-than-previously-thought>

'Amazon.Com: Prime Air' <https://www.amazon.com/Amazon-Prime-Air/b?ie=UTF8&node=8037720011>

Anderson M, 'Surprise! 2020 Is Not the Year for Self-Driving Cars' *IEEE Spectrum* (22 April 2020) <https://spectrum.ieee.org/transportation/self-driving/surprise-2020-is-not-the-year-for-selfdriving-cars>

Andersson H, 'The Tort Law Culture(s) of Scandinavia' (2012) 3 Journal of European Tort Law 210

'Appealing an Injury Claim' <https://www.mpi.mb.ca/Pages/injury-claim-appeals.aspx>

Armstrong K and Tess D, 'Fault versus No Fault – Reviewing the International Evidence', *Institute of Actuaries of Australia 16th General Insurance Seminar* (Coolum Qld, November 2008) <https://actuaries.asn.au/Library/Events/GIS/2008/GIS08_3d_Paper_Tess,Armstrong_Fault versus No Fault – reviewing the international evidence.pdf>

'Arrêté Numéro 2018-18 Du Ministre Des Transports, de La Mobilité Durable et de l'Électrification Des Transports' *Gazette officielle du Québec* (29 August 2018)

Askeland B, 'Basic Questions of Tort Law from a Norweigan Perspective' in Helmut Koziol (ed), *Basic Questions of Tort Law from a Comparative Perspective* (1st edn, Jan Sramek Verlag 2015)

Association of Workers' Compensation Boards of Canada, 'Canadian Workers' Compensation System – Year at a Glance' <http://awcbc.org/?page_id=11803>

——, 'Scope of Coverage – Industries/Occupations' (2016) <http://www.statcan.gc.ca/tables-tableaux/sum-som/l01/cst01/demo31a-eng.htm>

Atiyah PS, *The Damages Lottery* (Hart Publishing 1997)

Attwell K and Navin MC, 'Childhood Vaccination Mandates: Scope, Sanctions, Severity, Selectivity, and Salience' (2019) 97 The Milbank Quarterly

'Audi Quits Bid to Give A8 Level 3 Autonomy' <https://europe.autonews.com/automakers/audi-quits-bid-give-a8-level-3-autonomy>

Australian Government, 'Medical Treatment Injury Discussion Paper' (2017) <https://static.treasury.gov.au/uploads/sites/1/2017/06/Medical_treatment_injury_discussion_paper-1.pdf>

——, 'The National Redress Guide (v1.02)' (2019) <http://guides.dss.gov.au/national-redress-guide>

Australian Lawyers Alliance, Transport Accident Commission and Law Institute Victoria, 'No Fault Dispute Resolution Protocols' (2016)

Australian Treasury, 'National Injury Insurance Scheme' <https://treasury.gov.au/programs-initiatives-consumers-community/niis/>

Austroads, 'Trials' <https://austroads.com.au/drivers-and-vehicles/future-vehicles-and-technology/trials>

Automobile Insurance Advisory Committee, 'Report on Fundamental Reform of the Alberta Automobile Insurance Compensation System' (2020)

Avraham R, 'The Law and Economics of Insurance Law – A Primer' (2012) University of Texas Law, Law & Economics Research Paper No 224 <http://ssrn.com/abstract=1822330>

Badeau A and others, 'Emergency Department Visits for Electric Scooter-Related Injuries after Introduction of an Urban Rental Program' (2019) 37 American Journal of Emergency Medicine 1531

Baker T and Siegelman P, 'The Law and Economics of Liability Insurance: A Theoretical and Empirical Review' (2011) <http://scholarship.law.upenn.edu/faculty_scholarshiphttp://scholarship.law.upenn.edu/faculty_scholarship/350>

Balakrishnan R and Curtis J, 'Advancing Human Rights through Economics', *Series on Economics and Law in Conversation* (Laboratory for Advanced Research on the Global

Economy, Centre for the Study of Human Rights, London School of Economics 2016) <http://www.lse.ac.uk/sociology/assets/documents/human-rights/HR-SO-5.pdf>

Balasubramanian R, Libarikian A and McElhaney D, 'Insurance 2030: The Impact of AI on the Future of Insurance' (2018, updated March 2021) <https://www.mckinsey.com/industries/financial-services/our-insights/insurance-2030-the-impact-of-ai-on-the-future-of-insurance>

Barbot J, Parizot I and Winance M, '"No-Fault" Compensation for Victims of Medical Injuries. Ten Years of Implementing the French Model' (2014) 114 Health Policy 236

Barrett J and Marriott L, 'Discrimination by Definition: Are Definitions of "Income" Used in New Zealand Statutes Compatible with the State's Duty to Protect Human Rights?' (2020) 26 Australian Journal of Human Rights 329

Baudouin J-L, 'La Nouvelle Législation Québécoise Sur Les Accidents de La Circulation' (1979) 31 Revue internationale de droit comparé 381

Baudouin J-L and Linden AM, 'Canada' in Britt Weyts (ed), *The International Encyclopaedia for Tort Law* (Wolters Kluwer 2015)

Bayer K, 'Petition Launched to Get Compensation for February 22, 2011 Christchurch Earthquake Victims' *New Zealand Herald* (5 February 2019) <https://www.nzherald.co.nz/nz/petition-launched-to-get-compensation-for-february-22-2011-christchurch-earthquake-victims/F6SW6V3JFIDOOL5YSDAONGYGA4/>

Beever A, 'Justice and Punishment in Tort: A Comparative Theoretical Analysis', *Obligations III* (2006)

Bekhit MNZ, Le Fevre J and Bergin CJ, 'Regional Healthcare Costs and Burden of Injury Associated with Electric Scooters' (2020) 51 Injury 271 <https://linkinghub.elsevier.com/retrieve/pii/S0020138319306084>

Bellefontaine M, 'No-Fault Auto Insurance Should Be No-Go in Alberta, Lawyers Say' *CBC News* (30 October 2020) <https://www.cbc.ca/news/canada/edmonton/no-fault-auto-insurance-should-be-no-go-in-alberta-lawyers-say-1.5784807>

Bernheim E, Laniel R-A and Jannard L-P, 'Les Justiciables Non Représentés Face à La Justice : Une Étude Ethnographique Du Tribunal Administratif Du Québec Les Justiciables Non Représentés Face à La Justice : Une Étude Ethnographique Du Tribunal Administratif Du Québec' (2019) 39 Windsor Review of Legal and Social Issues 67

Besson S, 'Comparative Law and Human Rights' in Mathias Reimann and Reinhard Zimmermann (eds), *The Oxford Handbook of Comparative Law* (2nd edn, Oxford University Press 2019)

Beulens W, 'Fonds Medische Ongevallen – Quo Vadis?' *De Specialist* (2019) <https://www.despecialist.eu/nl/nieuws/beroepsnieuws/fonds-medische-ongevallen-ndash-quo-vadis-nbsp-wannes-buelens.html>

Beveridge W, 'Beveridge Report' Social Insurance and Alllied Services (1942) HMSO Cmd 6404 <https://www.sochealth.co.uk/national-health-service/public-health-and-wellbeing/beveridge-report/>

Birch B, *Accident Compensation: A Fairer Scheme* (Office of the Minister of Labour 1991)

Blaikie D, 'Manitoba History: The Origins of Autopac: An Essay on the Possibility of Social Democratic Government in Manitoba' (2008) <http://www.mhs.mb.ca/docs/mb_history/59/autopac.shtml>

Blum A, 'Machine Learning Theory' (2007)

Blunt M, 'Highway to a Headache: Is Tort-Based Automotive Insurance on a Collision Course with Autonomous Vehicles' (2017) 53 Williamette Law Revew 107

Boisvert Y, 'Un Système Injuste, à Jeter' *La Presse* (13 September 2019) <https://www.lapresse.ca/actualites/201909/12/01-5241027-un-systeme-injuste-a-jeter.php>

Bojic I, Braendli R and Ratti C, 'What Will Autonomous Cars Do to the Insurance Companies?', in *Autonomous Vehicles and Future Mobility* (Elsevier 2019)

Borges G, 'New Liability Concepts: The Potential of Insurance and Compensation Funds' in Sebastian Lohsse, Reiner Schulze and Dirk Staudenmayer (eds), *Liability for Artificial Intelligence and the Internet of Things* (Hart Publishing 2019)

Bradley A, 'Lawyers Question ACC's New Policy on Perineal Tears' *Radio New Zealand News* (31 March 2021) <https://www.rnz.co.nz/news/national/439591/lawyers-question-acc-s-new-policy-on-perineal-tears>

Brady M and others, 'Automated Vehicles and Australian Personal Injury Compensation Schemes' (2017) 24 Torts Law Journal 32

Brodie J, 'Citizenship and Solidarity: Reflections on the Canadian Way' (2002) 6 Citizenship Studies 377 <https://www.tandfonline.com/action/journalInformation?journalCode=ccst20>

Broughton C, 'ACC Tells Minister Justice Issues Have Been Fixed, but Advocates Not so Confident' *Stuff.co.nz* (26 February 2019) <https://www.stuff.co.nz/national/health/110789966/acc-tells-minister-justice-issues-have-been-fixed-but-advocates-not-so-confident>

Brown C, *No Fault Automobile Insurance In Canada* (Carswell 1988)

Brown C and Mercer A, *Introduction to Canadian Insurance Law* (4th edn, LexisNexis Canada 2018)

Bruggeman V and Faure M, 'Compensation for Victims of Disasters in Belgium, France, Germany and the Netherlands' (WRR 2018) <https://www.wrr.nl/binaries/wrr/documenten/working-papers/2018/10/10/wp30-compensation-for-victims-of-disasters-in-belgium-france-germany-and-the-netherlands/WRR+WP+30+Compensation+for+victims+of+disasters.pdf>

Brüggemann P and others, 'Claims in the Digital Age: How Insurers Can Get Started' (2018) <https://www.mckinsey.com/industries/financial-services/our-insights/claims-in-the-digital-age>

'Brussels warns that AstraZeneca will miss already reduced targets' *Financial Times* (11 March 2021) <https://www.ft.com/content/f9e5b8d8-8153-474a-bd57-97f5adbeb638>

Buckley M, 'Searching for the Constitutional Core of Access to Justice' (2008) 42 Supreme Court Law Review 567

Buckmaster L, 'The National Disability Insurance Scheme: A Quick Guide' (2017) <http://parlinfo.aph.gov.au/parlInfo/download/library/prspub/4790922/upload_binary/4790922.pdf>

Buelens W, *Het Medisch Ongeval Zonder Aansprakelijkheid* (Intersentia 2019)

'Building Stronger Support for Workers Post COVID' (Beehive.govt.nz) <https://www.beehive.govt.nz/release/building-stronger-support-workers-post-covid>

Burgess K, 'Workers Injured on Roads Will Have to Choose between Insurance Schemes' *The Canberra Times* (12 November 2018) <https://www.canberratimes.com.au/

story/6000552/workers-injured-on-roads-will-have-to-choose-between-insurance-schemes/>

Burns K, 'The Gender of Damages and Compensation' (2019) 151 Precedent 9

Cabinet Business Committee, 'Minute of Decision CBC-19-MIN-0014'

'Call for Applications: Vaccine Injury Support Program – Canada.Ca' <https://www.canada.ca/en/public-health/services/funding-opportunities/grant-contribution-funding-opportunities/call-applications-vaccine-injury-support-program.html>

Callander M and Page SJ, 'Managing Risk in Adventure Tourism Operations in New Zealand: A Review of the Legal Case History and Potential for Litigation' (2003) 24 Tourism Management 13

Calo R, 'Commuting to Mars: A Response to Professors Abraham and Rabin' (2019) 105 Virginia Law Review Online 84 <http://www.virginialawreview.org/sites/virginialawreview.org/files/Calo_Book.pdf>

Cameron M, *Realising the Potential of Driverless Vehicles: Recommendations for Law Reform* (The Law Foundation New Zealand 2018) <https://www.lawfoundation.org.nz/wp-content/uploads/2018/04/Cameron_DriverlessVehicles_complete-publication.pdf>

Canadian Hemophilia Society, 'Compensation Programs for Individuals with HIV or Hepatitis C' (2014) <https://www.hemophilia.ca/files/EN Compensation Programs-HIV, HepC-English – final14-11-2014.pdf>

Cane P, *The Political Economy of Personal Injury Law* (University of Queensland Press 2007)

Cane P and Goudkamp J, *Atiyah's Accidents, Compensation and the Law* (9th edn, Cambridge University Press 2018)

Cappelletti M and Garth B, 'Access to Justice: The Newest Wave in the Worldwide Movement to Make Rights Effective' (1978) 27 Buffalo Law Review 181

'Challenging an ACC Decision' (*Community Law Manual: Accident Compensation*) <https://communitylaw.org.nz/community-law-manual/chapter-19-accident-compensation-acc/challenging-an-acc-decision/mediation-and-other-alternative-ways-of-resolving-disputes/>

Chambers J, 'Swings and Roundabouts … The Making of Child Injury Prevention Policy in Aotearoa New Zealand: An Exploration' (Thesis, University of Waikato 2019) <https://researchcommons.waikato.ac.nz/bitstream/handle/10289/12424/thesis.pdf?sequence=4>

'Child Abuse Survivors "Can Still Seek Damages after Redress Payouts"' *The Scotsman* (3 May 2019) <https://www.scotsman.com/news/politics/child-abuse-survivors-can-still-seek-damages-after-redress-payouts-1-4920012>

Chinen M, *Law and Autonomous Machines: The Co-Evolution of Legal Responsibility and Technology* (Edward Elgar Publishing 2019)

'Chubb and Marsh Collaborate to Secure Insurance Coverage for the COVAX No-Fault Compensation Program for 92 Low- and Middle-Income Countries' (2021) <https://news.chubb.com/2021-04-29-Chubb-and-Marsh-Collaborate-to-Secure-Insurance-Coverage-for-the-COVAX-No-Fault-Compensation-Program-for-92-Low-and-Middle-Income-Countries>

City of Melbourne, 'Transport Strategy 2030' (2019) <https://www.melbourne.vic.gov.au/SiteCollectionDocuments/transport-strategy-2030-city-of-melbourne.pdf>

Claims Conference, 'Learn More About Compensation Programs' <http://www.claimscon.org/what-we-do/compensation/background/>

Clayton A, 'Some Reflections on the Woodhouse and ACC Legacy' (2003) 34 Victoria University of Wellington Law Review 449

Clayton R, 'Calls for E-Scooter Laws to Change as People Flout the Rules and Police Turn a Blind Eye' *ABC News* (14 December 2019) <https://www.abc.net.au/news/2019-12-14/calls-for-escooter-laws-to-be-relaxed-across-australia/11800280>

Clément D, 'Human Rights Law' (*Canada's Human Rights History*) <https://historyofrights.ca/history/human-rights-law/6/>

——, 'Renewing Human Rights Law in Canada' (2017) 54 Osgoode Hall Law Journal 1311

Clun R, 'Coronavirus Australia: Johnson & Johnson Vaccine Not Purchased as Sector Calls for Compensation Scheme' *Sydney Morning Herald* (12 April 2021) <https://www.smh.com.au/politics/federal/no-johnson-and-johnson-covid-19-vaccine-for-australia-as-sector-calls-for-compensation-scheme-20210412-p57ih9.html>

Cockfield S, 'Road Safety – the Experience of the Transport Accident Commission in Victoria, Australia' (2011) 2011–24

Committee on the Rights of Persons with Disabilities, 'Combined Second and Third Periodic Reports Submitted by New Zealand under Article 35 of the Convention Pursuant to the Optional Reporting Procedure, Due in 2019, CRPD/C/NZL/2-3'

——, 'Concluding Observations on the Initial Report of New Zealand, CRPD/C/NZL/CO/1' (2014)

——, 'List of Issues Prior to Submission of the Combined Second and Third Periodic Reports of New Zealand, CRPD/C/NZL/QPR/2-3' (2018)

'Common Law Protocols' (2016)

'Compensation' <https://www.cnesst.gouv.qc.ca/en/procedures-and-forms/workers/compensation-and-reimbursements/compensation>

—— (*Oxford Dictionary*) <https://www.lexico.com/definition/compensation>

'Compensation Table for 2020' (2020)

Connell JO and Brown C, 'A Canadian Proposal for No-Fault Benefits Financed by Assignments of Tort Rights' (1983) 33 University of Toronto Law Journal 434

Connell S, 'Justice for Victims of Injury: The Influence of New Zealand's Accident Compensation Scheme on the Civil and Criminal Law' (2012) 25 New Zealand Universities Law Review 181

——, 'Community Insurance versus Compulsory Insurance: Competing Paradigms of No-Fault Accident Compensation in New Zealand' (2019) 39(3) Legal Studies 1 <https://www.cambridge.org/core/product/identifier/S0261387518000508/type/journal_article>

Conseil d'experts sur les contributions d'assurance automobile, 'Avis Du Conseil d'experts' (2019)

—— <http://conseilexpert.aauto.ca/index_en.htm>

Contant J, 'The Story behind ICBC's Bold Change to Auto Insurance' *Canadian Underwriter* (12 February 2020) <https://www.canadianunderwriter.ca/insurance/the-story-behind-icbcs-drastic-change-to-auto-insurance-1004173792/>

'Contesting a Decision by the SAAQ' <https://saaq.gouv.qc.ca/en/traffic-accident/contesting-decision/>

Bibliography

Controller and Auditor-General, 'Accident Compensation Corporation Case Management: Progress on Recommendations Made in 2014' (2020)

Corrin J, 'Australia: Country Report on Human Rights' (2009) 40 Victoria University of Wellington Law Review 37

Cortes P, 'Using Technology and ADR Methods to Enhance Access to Justice'

Council of Australian Governments, 'COAG Meeting Communiqué, 9 June 2017' (2017) <https://www.coag.gov.au/meeting-outcomes/coag-meeting-communique-9-june-2017>

Council of Australian Governments Senior Officials' Working Group, 'ATTACHMENT A – Interactions between the National Injury Insurance Scheme (NIIS) and the National Disability Insurance Scheme (NDIS)' <https://treasury.gov.au/sites/default/files/2019-03/Document-7-7.pdf>

'COVID-19: MEPs Want Safe Vaccines, Full Transparency and Liability for Companies' (*European Parliament*) <https://www.europarl.europa.eu/news/en/press-room/20200904IPR86419/covid-19-meps-want-safe-vaccines-full-transparency-and-liability-for-companies>

'Covid-19 and Sovereign Wealth Funds: What Does the Future Hold?' (*Oxford Business Group*) <https://oxfordbusinessgroup.com/news/covid-19-and-sovereign-wealth-funds-what-does-future-hold>

'COVID-19 Insurer & Reinsurer Loss Reports' *Reinsurance News* <https://www.reinsurancene.ws/covid-19-insurer-reinsurer-loss-reports/>

'Covid-19 Vaccinations: More Solidarity and Transparency Needed' *European Parliament* (19 January 2021) <https://www.europarl.europa.eu/news/en/headlines/society/20210114STO95642/covid-19-vaccinations-more-solidarity-and-transparency-needed>

'COVID-19 Vaccines Advice' <https://www.who.int/emergencies/diseases/novel-coronavirus-2019/covid-19-vaccines/advice>

Daly K, 'What Is Restorative Justice? Fresh Answers to a Vexed Question' (2016) 11 Victims & Offenders 9 <https://doi.org/10.1080/15564886.2015.1107797>

'Daniel Lepage c. SAAQ et Al. (200-06-000172-141)' <http://www.stephanemichaudavocat.com/>

Davenport T and Kalakota R, 'The Potential for Artificial Intelligence in Healthcare', (2019) 6 Future Healthcare Journal 94

Davison I, 'Farmers Could Be Asked to Contribute to New EQC-like Fund for Biosecurity Threats' *New Zealand Herald* (20 May 2018) <https://www.nzherald.co.nz/nz/news/article.cfm?c_id=1&objectid=12055129>

Dean M, 'Independent Review of the Acclaim Otago (Inc) July 2015 Report Into Accident Compensation Dispute Resolution Processes' (May 2016) <http://www.mbie.govt.nz/info-services/employment-skills/legislation-reviews/accident-compensation-dispute-resolution/document-and-images-library/independent-review.pdf>

'Definition of Legal Liability' (*Cambridge English Dictionary*, 2020) <https://dictionary.cambridge.org/dictionary/english/legal-liability>

Department of Health and Social Care, 'Payment Scheme for Former British Child Migrants' (*Gov.UK*, 2019) <https://www.gov.uk/government/news/payment-scheme-for-former-british-child-migrants>

Department of Labour, 'Regulatory Impact Statement: Response to the Recommendations of the ACC Stocktake' (2010)

'Determining Your Rates' <https://www.mpi.mb.ca/Pages/your-rates.aspx>

Devlin RA, 'A Comparison of Automobile Insurance Regimes in Canada' (2019) 86 Assurances et gestion des risques 55

Dickson K and others, 'No-Fault Compensation Schemes: A Rapid Realist Review to Develop a Context, Mechanism, Outcomes Framework' (2016) <https://eppi.ioe.ac.uk/ CMS/Portals/0/PDF reviews and summaries/No Fault Comp Schemes 2016 Dickson.pdf>

Dima FC, 'Fully Autonomous Vehicles in the EU: Opportunity or Threat?' (University of Twente 2019) <https://essay.utwente.nl/72945/2/DIMA_MA_PA.pdf>

Dixon R, 'A Minimalist Charter of Rights for Australia: The UK or Canada as a Model?' (2009) 37 Federal Law Review 335

'Draft Amendments to Regulations Issued in Terms of Section 27(2) of the Disaster Management Act 2002'

'Draft Landscape and Tracker of COVID-19 Candidate Vaccines' <https://www.who.int/ publications/m/item/draft-landscape-of-covid-19-candidate-vaccines>

Draper P, 'Atheism and Agnosticism' in Edward N Zalta (ed), *The Stanford Encyclopedia of Philosophy* (August, 2017) <https://plato.stanford.edu/archives/fall2017/entries/ atheism-agnosticism/>

Driesen DM and Malloy RP, 'Critiques of Law and Economics' (2015) <http://ssrn.com/ abstract=2572574>

Dubé E and others, 'Vaccine Injury Compensation Programs: Rationale and an Overview of the Québec Program' (2020) 46 Canada Communicable Disease Report 305

Duncan D, 'Beyond Accident: A Model for the Compensation of Work-Related Harm in New Zealand' (Victoria University of Wellington 2019)

Duncan G, 'New Zealand's Universal No-Fault Accident Compensation Scheme: Embedding Community Responsibility' in Joannah Luetjens, Michael Mintrom and Paul 't Hart (eds), *Successful Public Policy Lessons from Australia and New Zealand* (ANU Press 2019) <http://press-files.anu.edu.au/downloads/press/n5314/pdf/ch14.pdf>

'E-Scooter Injuries – Datasets' (data.govt.nz, 2020) <https://catalogue.data.govt.nz/ dataset/e-scooter-injuries#dataset-resources>

'E–Scooters (Declaration Not to Be Motor Vehicles) Notice 2018' *New Zealand Gazette* <https://gazette.govt.nz/notice/id/2018-au4674>

Earthquake Commission, 'The Natural Disaster Fund' <https://www.eqc.govt.nz/about-eqc/our-role/ndf>

Easton BH, *In Stormy Seas: The Post-War New Zealand Economy* (1st edn, University of Otago Press 1997)

——, 'The Historical Context of the Woodhouse Commission' (2003) 34 Victoria University of Wellington Law Review 207

El Menyawi H, 'Public Tort Liability: An Alternative to Tort Liability and No-Fault Compensation' (2002) 9(4) Murdoch University Electronic Journal of Law <http:// www.bepress.com/gj/advances/vol3/iss1/art1>

Elbers NA and others, 'Differences in Perceived Fairness and Health Outcomes in Two Injury Compensation Systems: A Comparative Study' (2016) 16 BMC Public Health 1 <http://dx.doi.org/10.1186/s12889-016-3331-3>

Engelhard EFD and de Bruin RW, 'EU Common Approach on the Liability Rules and Insurance Related to Connected and Autonomous Vehicles.' (Utrecht Centre for Accountability and Liability Law 2017)

Bibliography

EQC Earthquake Commission, 'EQC Insurance' <https://www.eqc.govt.nz/what-we-do/eqc-insurance>

Erdélyi OJ and Erdélyi G, 'The AI Liability Puzzle and A Fund-Based Work-Around' (2019)

European Commission, 'Saving Lives: Boosting Car Safety in the EU (COM(2016) 787 Final)' (2016)

——, 'Report on the Safety and Liability Implications of Artificial Intelligence, the Internet of Things and Robotics' (2020) <https://ec.europa.eu/info/sites/info/files/report-safety-liability-artificial-intelligence-feb2020_en_1.pdf>

——, 'Sustainable and Smart Mobility Strategy – Putting European Transport on Track for the Future' (2020) <https://transport.ec.europa.eu/system/files/2021-04/2021-mobility-strategy-and-action-plan.pdf>

European Union Agency for Fundamental Rights, 'Bringing Rights to Life: The Fundamental Rights Landscape of the European Union' (2012) <http://publications.europa.eu/others/agents/index_en.htm>

European Union Agency for Fundamental Rights, European Court of Human Rights and Council of Europe, *Handbook on European Law Relating to Access to Justice* (2016) <https://fra.europa.eu/en/publication/2016/handbook-european-law-relating-access-justice>

Fairgrieve D and others, 'Products in a Pandemic: Liability for Medical Products and the Fight against COVID-19' (2020) 11(3) European Journal of Risk Regulation 565 <https://doi.org/10.1017/err.2020.54>

——, 'In Favour of a Bespoke COVID-19 Vaccines Compensation Scheme' (2021) 21(4) The Lancet Infectious Diseases 448 <https://doi.org/10.1016/S1473-3099>

Farrell A-M, Devaney S and Dar A, 'No-Fault Compensation Schemes for Medical Injury: A Review' (10 January 2010) <http://www.ssrn.com/abstract=2221836>

Farris M, 'Compensating Climate Change Victims: The Climate Compensation Fund as an Alternative to Tort Litigation' (2009) 2 Sea Grant Law and Policy Journal 49

Faure M, Hartlief T and van Maanen G, 'Compensation Funds in the Netherlands' in Thierry Vansweevelt and Britt Weyts (eds), *Compensation Funds in Comparative Perspective* (Intersentia 2020)

Faure M and van Boom WH, 'Concluding Remarks' in *Shifts in Compensation between Private and Public Systems (Tort and Insurance Law Vol. 22)* (Springer 2007)

Faust F, 'Comparative Law and Economic Analysis of Law' in Mathias Reimann and Reinhard Zimmermann (eds), *The Oxford Handbook of Comparative Law* (2nd edn, Oxford University Press 2019)

Field A, 'There Must Be a Better Way: Personal Injuries Compensation Since the Crisis in Insurance' (2008) 13 Deakin Law Review 67

'Finance Minister's Budget 2021 Speech' <https://www.beehive.govt.nz/speech/finance-ministers-budget-2021-speech>

Financial Services Commission of Ontario, 'Motor Vehicle Accident Claims Fund' <https://www.fsco.gov.on.ca/en/auto/mvacf/pages/default.aspx>

'Financial Support If Someone Has Died from an Injury' <https://www.acc.co.nz/im-injured/financial-support/financial-support-after-death/>

Fitt H and Curl A, 'E-Scooter Use in New Zealand: Insights around Some Frequently Asked Questions' (2019) <https://ir.canterbury.ac.nz/handle/10092/16336>

Fleming Z, 'Tourist's ACC Refund Offer Rejected' *Radio New Zealand News* (8 June 2017) <https://www.rnz.co.nz/national/programmes/checkpoint/audio/201846823/tourists-acc-refund-offer-rejected>

Fletcher M, 'Towards Wellbeing? Developments in Social Legislation and Policy in New Zealand' (Max Planck Institute for Social Law and Social Policy 2018) <http://www.mpisoc.mpg.de>

Flood CM and Thomas B, 'Canadian Medical Malpractice Law in 2011: Missing the Mark on Patient Safety' (2011) 86 Chicago-Kent Law Review 1053

Fonds de Garantie, 'The Guarantee Fund Corporate Project – Cap 2020 : L'excellence Au Service Des Victimes' <https://www.fondsdegarantie.fr/en/guarantee-fund/the-guarantee-fund-corporate-project/>

——, 'The History of FGAO' <https://www.fondsdegarantie.fr/en/fgao-2/the-history-of-fgao/>

——, 'The History of FGTI' <https://www.fondsdegarantie.fr/en/fgti-2/the-history/>

——, 'Chiffres Financiers – Rapport Annuel' (2017) <https://rapportdactivite.fondsdegarantie.fr/chiffres-financiers>

Fookes Z, 'Navigating the Law Reform Route for Driverless Cars in New Zealand' (2016)

'Ford Delays Commercial Automated Vehicle Launch To 2022' <https://www.forbes.com/sites/samabuelsamid/2020/04/28/ford-delays-commercial-automated-vehicle-launch-to-2022/#74c49447083c>

Forster & Associates, 'Expansion of ACC' <https://www.forster.co.nz/beyond-injury/expansion>

Forster W, Barraclough T and Mijatov T, 'Solving the Problem: Causation, Transparency and Access to Justice in New Zealand's Personal Injury System' (New Zealand Law Foundation Research Reports 2017)

Forwood MR, 'Whither No-Fault Schemes in Australia: Have We Closed the Care and Compensation Gap?' (2018) 43 Alternative Law Journal 166

French CJR, 'The Common Law and the Protection of Human Rights' (September 2009) <https://www.hcourt.gov.au/assets/publications/speeches/current-justices/frenchcj/frenchcj4sep09.pd>

'Frequently Asked Questions (FAQs) Relating To The COVAX No-Fault Compensation Program For AMC Eligible Economies' <https://covaxclaims.com/faqs/>

Friedman LM, 'Access to Justice: Some Historical Comments' (2010) 37 Fordham Urban Law Journal <https://ir.lawnet.fordham.edu/uljAvailableat:https://ir.lawnet.fordham.edu/ulj/vol37/iss1/4>

Fronsko A and Woodroffe A, 'Public vs. Private Underwriting and Administration of Personal Injury Statutory Insurance Schemes', *Actuaries Institute Injury & Disability Schemes Seminar* (Brisbane, November 2017)

Fujiwara Y, Onda Y and Hayashi S, 'No-Fault Compensation Schemes for COVID-19 Medical Products' (2021) 397 The Lancet 1707 <https://www.hrsa.gov/cicp/>

Fukuyama F, *The End of History and the Last Man* (Free Press 1992)

'Funding Policy Statement in Relation to the Funding of ACC's Levied Accounts' *New Zealand Gazette* (8 July 2020)

'Further Work to Improve ACC Dispute Resolution' <https://www.beehive.govt.nz/release/further-work-improve-acc-dispute-resolution>

Gambrill D, 'David Marshall on Why Quebec's Auto Insurance System Works – and Ontario's Doesn't Canadian Underwriter' *Canadian Underwriter* (25 September 2019) <https://www.canadianunderwriter.ca/insurance/david-marshall-on-why-quebecs-auto-insurance-system-works-and-ontarios-doesnt-1004168833/>

Gammon R, 'Family Violence: New Zealand's Dirty Little Secret' (*Massey University*) <https://www.massey.ac.nz/massey/about-massey/news/article.cfm?mnarticle_uuid=C61AEFE4-B1D7-0794-48A1-CFA90FEDDEFF>

Gardner D, 'Automobile No-Fault in Québec as Compared to Victoria' (2000) 8 Torts Law Journal 89

——, 'Quelques Points de Comparaison Entre Les Deux plus Anciens Régimes Intégrés d'indeminisation Des Victimes d'accidents d'automobile: Québec et Nouvelle-Zélande' (2004) 71 Assurances et Gestion des Risques 591

Gaskins R, 'Reading Woodhouse for the Twenty-First Century' [2008] New Zealand Law Review 11

——, "Regulating Private Law: Socio-Legal Perspectives on the New Zealand Accident Compensation Scheme' (2009) 17 Torts Law Journal 24

——, 'Accounting for Accidents: Social Costs of Personal Injuries' (2010) 41 Victoria University of Wellington Law Review 37

——, 'The Enigma of Community Responsibility: Ethical Reflections on Accident Compensation' (2015) 46 Victoria University of Wellington Law Review 789

Gearty CA, 'Unravelling Osman' (2001) 64 Modern Law Review 159

'German Fund Ends Payments to Nazi-Era Forced Laborers' *DW.com* (11 June 2011) <https://www.dw.com/en/german-fund-ends-payments-to-nazi-era-forced-laborers/a-2584879>

Gibson E, 'Is It Time to Adopt a No-Fault Scheme to Compensate Injured Patients?' (2016) 47 Ottawa Law Review 303 <https://commonlaw.uottawa.ca/ottawa-law-review/sites/commonlaw.uottawa.ca.ottawa-law-review/files/olr_47-2_02_gibson_final.pdf>

Giubilini A and others, 'Nudging Immunity: The Case for Vaccinating Children in School and Day Care by Default' (2019) 31 HEC Forum 325 <https://doi.org/10.1007/s10730-019-09383-7>

Giuffrida I, 'Liability for AI Decision-Making: Some Legal and Ethical Considerations' (2019) 88 Fordham Law Review 439 <https://ir.lawnet.fordham.edu/flr/vol88/iss2/3>

'Going up against the SAAQ? You'll Probably Lose' *CBC News* (28 March 2019) <https://www.cbc.ca/news/canada/montreal/going-up-against-the-saaq-you-ll-probably-lose-1.5074039>

Gössling S, 'Integrating E-Scooters in Urban Transportation: Problems, Policies, and the Prospect of System Change' (2020) 79 Transportation Research Part D: Transport and Environment 9 <https://doi.org/10.1016/j.trd.2020.102230>

Goudkamp J, 'Reforming English Tort Law: Lessons from Australia' in Eoin Quill and Raymond Friel (eds), *Damages and Compensation Culture: Comparative Perspectives* (Bloomsbury Publishing 2016)

Government of Canada, 'Canada-United States Regulatory Cooperation Council (RCC)' <https://www.canada.ca/en/health-canada/corporate/about-health-canada/legislation-guidelines/acts-regulations/canada-united-states-regulatory-cooperation-council.html>

—, 'Extraordinary Assistance Plan – Financial Assistance to Individuals Infected with HIV Through the Canadian Blood System' <https://www.canada.ca/en/public-health/services/infectious-diseases/extraordinary-assistance-plan-financial-assistance-individuals-infected-hiv-through-canadian-blood-system.html>

—, 'National Report Submitted in Accordance with Paragraph 5 of the Annex to Human Rights Council Resolution 16/21' (2018) <https://documents-dds-ny.un.org/doc/UNDOC/GEN/G18/081/95/PDF/G1808195.pdf?OpenElement>

'Government of Canada Announces Pan-Canadian Vaccine Injury Support Program' <https://www.canada.ca/en/public-health/news/2020/12/government-of-canada-announces-pan-canadian-vaccine-injury-support-program.html>

Government of South Australia, 'Lifetime Support Authority of South Australia's 2020 Strategy' <http://lifetimesupport.sa.gov.au/wp-content/uploads/2020-Strategy.pdf>

'Government to Add COVID-19 to Vaccine Damage Payments Scheme' (3 December 2020) <https://www.gov.uk/government/news/government-to-add-covid-19-to-vaccine-damage-payments-scheme>

Grant G and Studdert DM, 'Poisoned Chalice? A Critical Analysis of the Evidence Linking Personal Injury Compensation Processes with Adverse Health Outcomes' (2009) <http://papers.ssrn.com/sol3/papers.cfm?abstract_id=1484340>

Graycar R, 'The Gender of Judgments: An Introduction' (2009) 09/73 <http://ssrn.com/abstract=1465171http://ssrn.com/abstract=1465171.>

Groves M, Boughey J and Meagher D, 'Rights, Rhetoric and Reality: An Overview of Rights Protection in Australia' in Matthew Groves, Janina Boughey and Dan Meagher (eds), *The Legal Protection of Rights in Australia* (Hart Publishing 2019)

Hagan M, 'Legal Design as a Thing: A Theory of Change and a Set of Methods to Craft a Human-Centered Legal System' (2020) 36 Design Issues <https://doi.org/10.1162/desi_a_00600>

Halabi S and others, 'No-Fault Compensation for Vaccine Injury – The Other Side of Equitable Access to Covid-19 Vaccines' (2020) 383(23) New England Journal of Medicine e125

Halabi SF and Omer SB, 'A Global Vaccine Injury Compensation System' (2017) 317 JAMA: The Journal of the American Medical Association 471 <http://dx.doi.org/10.1001/jama.2016.19492>

Harrison M, 'Evidence-Free Policy: The Case of the National Injury Insurance Scheme' (2013) 20 Agenda <http://ro.uow.edu.au/cgi/viewcontent.cgi?article=2384&context=eispapers>

Hayward M, 'EQC Gets Another $45m Top up from the Public Purse' *Stuff.co.nz* (11 June 2019) <https://www.stuff.co.nz/national/politics/113373906/eqc-gets-another-45m-top-up-from-the-public-purse#comments>

Health and Disability System Review: Final Report / Pūrongo Whakamutunga (2020) <www.systemreview.health.govt.nz/final-report>

Heath R, '"Treat Every Victim the Same" Urges Brussels Terrorist Attacks Widow' *Politico Europe* (21 March 2017) <https://www.politico.eu/blogs/playbook-plus/2017/03/treat-every-victim-the-same-urges-brussels-terrorist-attacks-widow-charles-michel-jim-cain-cameron-cain-karen-northshield/>

Heirbaut D, 'The Belgian Legal Tradition: Does It Exist?' in Marc Kruithof and Walter De Bondt (eds), *Introduction to Belgian Law* (Wolters Kluwer 2017)

Helleringer G, 'Medical Malpractice and Compensation in France: Part II: Compensation Based on National Solidarity' (2011) 86 Chicago-Kent Law Review 1125

'Help' <https://covaxclaims.com/help/#instructions>

Henderson JA, 'New Zealand Accident Compensation Reform' (1981) 48 University of Chicago Law Review 781

Herwig A and Simoncini M, *Law and the Management of Disasters: The Challenge of Resilience* (Routledge 2016)

'History of the TAC – Accident Compensation in Victoria' <https://www.tac.vic.gov.au/about-the-tac/our-organisation/what-we-do/history-of-the-tac>

Hodges C, 'Collective Redress: The Need for New Technologies' (2018) 42 Journal of Consumer Policy 59 <https://doi.org/10.1007/s10603-018-9388-x>

——, 'Covid-19 Vaccines: Injury Compensation Issues' (2020) <https://papers.ssrn.com/sol3/papers.cfm?abstract_id=3647042>

Hoecke M Van, 'Law and Method Methodology of Comparative Legal Research' [2015] Law and Method 1 <https://www.bjutijdschriften.nl/tijdschrift/lawandmethod/2015/12/RENM-D-14-00001.pdf>

Hoffman RHL, 'Human Rights and the House of Lords' (1999) 62 The Modern Law Review 159

Holm S, Stanton C and Bartlett B, 'A New Argument for No-Fault Compensation in Health Care: The Introduction of Artificial Intelligence Systems' (2021) 29 Health Care Analysis 171 <https://doi.org/10.1007/s10728-021-00430-4>

House of Representatives Standing Committee on Industry Innovation Science and Resources, 'Social Issues Relating to Land-Based Automated Vehicles in Australia' (2017)

'How to Bird' <https://www.bird.co/how/>

Howarth J and Sutherland R, 'NZ's next Large Alpine Fault Quake Is Likely Coming Sooner than We Thought, Study Shows' *The Conversation* (19 April 2021) <https://theconversation.com/nzs-next-large-alpine-fault-quake-is-likely-coming-sooner-than-we-thought-study-shows-159223>

Hutchinson AC, 'Beyond No-Fault' (1985) 73 California Law Review

'Il y a 40 Ans, Lise Payette Créait l'assurance Automobile Au Québec' *Radio Canada* (2018) <https://ici.radio-canada.ca/nouvelle/1086058/lise-payette-assurance-automobile-quebec-archives>

'Improving the Accredited Employers Programme' <https://www.shapeyouracc.co.nz/enhancing-the-accredited-employer-programme/improving-the-accredited-employers-programme/>

'In the Event of a Death in a Traffic Accident' <https://saaq.gouv.qc.ca/en/traffic-accident/death/?ADMCMD_prev=IGNORE>

Ingber S, 'Rethinking Intangible Injuries: A Focus on Remedy' (1985) 73 California Law Review 772

'Injury Manual – Tort Actions Available to Part VIII Beneficiary: The Ability to Sue' <https://www.sgi.sk.ca/documents/625510/627089/1_Ability_to_Sue.pdf/7557ceba-0271-4283-b100-11a113370358>

'Institutions That Have Joined the Scheme' <https://www.nationalredress.gov.au/institutions/joined-scheme>

'Insurance' (*Reserve Bank of New Zealand*) <https://www.rbnz.govt.nz/financial-stability/overview-of-the-new-zealand-financial-system/insurance>

Insurance Commission of Western Australia, 'Proposal to Add No-Fault Catastrophic Injury Cover to Western Australia's Compulsory Third Party Insurance Scheme' (2015) <https://www.icwa.wa.gov.au/__data/assets/pdf_file/0014/1274/ctp_consultation_report.pdf>

International Transport Forum, 'Safe Micromobility' (2020) <https://www.itf-oecd.org/sites/default/files/docs/safe-micromobility_1.pdf>

Ison T, *The Forensic Lottery: A Critique on Tort Liability as a System of Personal Injury Compensation* (Staples Press 1968)

Jansen C, 'Accidental Harm Under (Roman) Civil Law' in Klaas Landsman and Ellen van Wolde (eds), *The Challenge of Change – A Multidisciplinary Approach from Science and the Humanities* (Springer Open 2016)

Jeram J, 'Embracing a Super Model: The Superannuation Sky Is Not Falling' (4 December 2018) <https://www.nzinitiative.org.nz/reports-and-media/reports/embracing-a-super-model-the-superannuation-sky-is-not-falling/>

Jiang F and others, 'Artificial Intelligence in Healthcare: Past, Present and Future' (2017) 2 Stroke and Vascular Neurology <http://svn.bmj.com/>

Johnston K, 'Privacy and Profiling Fears over Secret ACC Software' *New Zealand Herald* (14 September 2017)

'Joining the Accredited Employers Programme (AEP)' <https://www.acc.co.nz/for-business/understanding-your-cover-options/accredited-employers-programme/>

Judicial College of Victoria, *Serious Injury Manual* (2019) <http://www.judicialcollege.vic.edu.au/eManuals/SIM/index.htm#53962.htm>

Kaner I, 'The Israeli System of Road Accidents Victim Compensation', *HILA-AIDA Summit* (Athens May 2014) <http://ilankaner.co.il/assets/files/Articles/Israeli-System-of-Road-Accidents-Victims-Compensation---Ilan-Kaner-May-2014 (1).pdf>

Katyal SK, 'Private Accountability in the Age of Artificial Intelligence' (2019) 66 UCLA Law Review 54

'Keeping ACC Levies Steady until 2022' *New Zealand Government* (6 July 2020) <https://www.beehive.govt.nz/release/keeping-acc-levies-steady-until-2022>

Kelly F, 'CervicalCheck Compensation Scheme Set to Cost up to €15m' *The Irish Times* (4 January 2019) <https://www.irishtimes.com/news/ireland/irish-news/cervicalcheck-compensation-scheme-set-to-cost-up-to-15m-1.3747226>

Kelly M, Kleffner A and Tomlinson M, 'First-Party versus Third-Party Compensation for Automobile Accidents: Evidence from Canada' (2010) 13 Risk Management and Insurance Review 21

Kent L and Hermant N, 'Catastrophically Injured Australians Still Waiting for National Insurance Scheme Meant to Roll out with NDIS' *Australian Broadcasting Corporation News* (19 February 2020) <https://www.abc.net.au/news/2020-02-20/national-injury-insurance-scheme-injured-australians-waiting/11796928>

Kleeberg JM, 'From Strict Liability to Workers' Compensation: The Prussian Railroad Law, the German Liability Act, and the Introduction of Bismarck's Accident Insurance in Germany, 1838-1884' (2003) 36 NYU Journal of International Law and Politics 53

Knetsch J, *Le droit de la responsabilité et les fonds d'indemnisation: Analyse en droits français et allemand* (LGDJ 2013) <https://docassas.u-paris2.fr/nuxeo/site/esupversions/f60b2840-bda3-453e-8626-788d7c4de001>

——, 'Compensation Funds in France and Germany' in Thierry Vansweevelt and Britt Weyts (eds), *Compensation Funds in Comparative Perspective* (Intersentia 2020)

Knutsen ES, 'Auto Insurance as Social Contract: Solving Automobile Insurance Coverage Disputes Through a Public Regulatory Framework' (2011) 48 Alberta Law Review

——, A Reflexive Approach to Accident Law Reform' in Eoin Quill and Raymond J Friel (eds), *Damages and Compensation Culture: Comparative Perspectives* (Bloomsbury Publishing 2016)

Kopstein RL, 'The Report of the Autopac Review Commission – Volume 1' (Government of Manitoba 1988)

Kós S, 'Disaster & Resilience – The Canterbury Earthquakes and Their Legal Aftermath', *Supreme and Federal Courts Judges Conference* (Brisbane 2016)

Koziol H, *Basic Questions of Tort Law from a Germanic Perspective* (1st edn, Jan Sramek Verlag 2012)

——, 'Comparative Conclusions' in Helmut Koziol (ed), *Basic Questions of Tort Law from a Comparative Perspective* (1st edn, Jan Sramek Verlag 2015)

——, 'Compensation for Personal Injury: Comparative Incentives for the Interplay of Tort Law and Insurance Law' (2017) 8 Journal of European Tort Law 41

Kritzer HM, 'To Lawyer or Not to Lawyer: Is That the Question?' (2008) 5 Journal of Empirical Legal Studies 875 <http://doi.wiley.com/10.1111/j.1740-1461.2008.00144.x>

Kruithof M, 'Belgium' in Britt Weyts (ed), *International Encyclopaedia for Tort Law* (Wolters Kluwer 2017)

——, 'Tort Law' in Marc Kruithof and Walter De Bondt (eds), *Introduction to Belgian Law* (2nd edn, Wolters Kluwer 2017)

Laleng P, 'Redress Schemes for Personal Injuries – Book Review' (2018) 25 European Journal of Health Law 469

Law J (ed), *A Dictionary of Law* (9th edn, Oxford University Press 2018)

Leczykiewicz D, 'Horizontal Application of the Charter of Fundamental Rights' (2013) 38 European Law Review 479

Lee D and Hess DJ, 'Regulations for On-Road Testing of Connected and Automated Vehicles: Assessing the Potential for Global Safety Harmonization' (2020) 136 Transportation Research Part A: Policy and Practice 85 <https://doi.org/10.1016/j.tra.2020.03.026>

Lemley MA and Casey B, 'Remedies for Robots' (2019) 86 University of Chicago Law Review 1311

'Less Legal Costs' (*ICBC 2021*) <https://2021.icbc.com/less-legal-costs>

'Liability for Side Effects of COVID-19 Vaccine – Parliamentary Questions' (22 February 2021) <https://www.europarl.europa.eu/doceo/document/P-9-2021-001043_EN.html>

Liew YK, Wee CPJ and Pek JH, 'New Peril on Our Roads: A Retrospective Study of Electric Scooter-Related Injuries' (2020) 61 Singapore Medical Journal 92 <https://doi.org/10.11622/smedj.2019083>

Lifetime Support Authority, 'Lifetime Support Scheme Rules' (2017) <http://lifetimesupport.sa.gov.au/wp-content/uploads/Final-LSS-Rules.pdf>

'Lime Electric Scooter Rentals' <https://www.li.me/electric-scooter>

Linden AM and others, *Canadian Tort Law* (11th edn, LexisNexis Canada)

Littlewood M, 'Why Does the Accident Compensation Corporation Have a Fund?' (Retirement Policy and Research Centre, University of Auckland 2009) Pension Commentary 18

'Lodging a Claim for a Patient' <https://www.acc.co.nz/for-providers/lodging-claims/lodging-a-claim-for-a-patient/#how-to-lodge-a-claim>

Loth M, 'How Does Tort Law Deal with Historical Injustice?' (2020) 11 Journal of European Tort Law 181

Lowry J, Rawlings P and Merkin R, *Insurance Law: Doctrines and Principles* (3rd edn, Hart Publishing 2011)

Lundy P, 'What Survivors Want From Redress Introduction: The Project and Panel of Experts on Redress' (March 2016) <https://www.amnesty.org.uk/files/what_survivors_ want_from_redress.pdf >s

Lunney M, 'A Tort Lawyer's View of Osman v United Kingdom' (1999) 10 King's Law Journal 238

Macleod S and Chakraborty S, *Pharmaceutical and Medical Device Safety* (Hart Publishing 2019)

Macleod S and Hodges C, 'An Introduction to the Schemes' in Sonia Macleod and Christopher Hodges (eds), *Redress Schemes for Personal Injuries* (1st edn, Hart Publishing 2017)

——, 'Part IX: Conclusions' in Sonia Macleod and Christopher Hodges (eds), *Redress Schemes for Personal Injuries* (1st edn, Hart Publishing 2017)

——, *Redress Schemes for Personal Injuries* (Hart Publishing 2017)

Macleod S, Urho M and Hodges C, 'Part III: Nordic States' in Sonia Macleod and Christopher Hodges (eds), *Redress Schemes for Personal Injuries* (1st edn, Hart Publishing 2017)

'Magdalene Laundry Survivor Awarded Compensation for Unpaid Work' *The Irish Times* (21 August 2019) <https://www.irishtimes.com/news/social-affairs/magdalene-laundry-survivor-awarded-compensation-for-unpaid-work-1.3992743>

Mahase E, 'AstraZeneca Vaccine: Blood Clots Are "Extremely Rare" and Benefits Outweigh Risks, Regulators Conclude' (2021) 373 British Medical Journal n931 <http://dx.doi. org/10.1136/bmj.n931>

——, 'Covid-19: US Suspends Johnson and Johnson Vaccine Rollout over Blood Clots' (2021) 373 British Medical Journal n970 <http://dx.doi.org/10.1136/bmj.n970>

'Making a Claim and Dealing with ACC' (*Communtity Law Manual: Accident Compensation*) <https://communitylaw.org.nz/community-law-manual/chapter-18-accident-compensation-acc/making-a-claim-and-dealing-with-acc/>

Malkin I, 'Victoria's Transport Accident Reforms – In Perspective' (1987) 16 Melbourne University Law Review 254

Manitoba Public Insurance Corporation, 'Annual Report' (2017)

——, 'Annual Report (2018)' (2019)

——, 'Annual Financial Statements 2018/9' (2019)

——, 'Annual Report 2019' (2020)

——, 'Injury Rehabilitation' <https://www.mpi.mb.ca/Pages/injury-rehabilitation.aspx>

——, 'Our History' <https://www.mpi.mb.ca/pages/our-history.aspx>

——, 'Personal Injury Protection Plan' <https://www.mpi.mb.ca/Pages/personal-injury-protection-plan.aspx>

——, 'Personal Injury Protection Plan – Your Guide' <https://www.mpi.mb.ca/Documents/ PIPPGuide.pdf>

——, 'Where Do Your Premium Dollars Go?' <https://www.mpi.mb.ca/Pages/where-do-your-premium-dollars-go.aspx>

——, 'Who We Are' <https://www.mpi.mb.ca/pages/who-we-are.aspx>

Manning JM, 'Plus ça change, plus c'est la même chose: Negligence and treatment injury in New Zealand's accident compensation scheme' (2014) 14 Medical Law International 22

——, 'Does the Law on Compensation for Research-Related Injury in the UK, Australia, and New Zealand Meet Ethical Requirements?' (2017) 25 Medical Law Review 397 <https://academic.oup.com/medlaw/article-abstract/25/3/397/3769302>

——, '"Fair, Simple, Speedy and Efficient"? Barriers to Access to Justice in the Health and Disability Commissioner's Complaints Process in New Zealand' (2018) 4 New Zealand Law Review 611 <http://www.legislation.govt.nz/act/public/1994/0088/latest/viewpdf.aspx>

Marshall D, 'No-Fault Compensation for Medically Caused Injury: A Comment on the Current Proposal' (1991) 21 Western Australia Law Review <http://www.austlii.edu.au/au/journals/UWALawRw/1991/14.pdf>

Martens K, 'Constitutional Challenge May Help NDN CAR Ride Again' *APTN News* (10 April 2019) <https://www.aptnnews.ca/national-news/constitutional-challenge-may-help-ndn-car-ride-again/>

McAllister S and others, 'Do Different Types of Financial Support after Illness or Injury Affect Socio-Economic Outcomes? A Natural Experiment in New Zealand' (2013) 85 Social Science and Medicine 93

McCarthy J, 'What Is Artificial Intelligence?' (2004) <http://www-formal.stanford.edu/jmc/>

McGarry P, 'Government Plans to Broaden Magdalene Redress Scheme Welcomed' *The Irish Times* (18 April 2018) <https://www.irishtimes.com/news/social-affairs/government-plans-to-broaden-magdalene-redress-scheme-welcomed-1.3465533>

McIvor C, 'Getting Defensive about Police Negligence: The Hill Principle, the Human Rights Act 1998 and the House of Lords' (2010) 69 Cambridge Law Journal 133

McKenzie P, 'The Compensation Scheme No One Asked For: The Origins of ACC in New Zealand' (2003) 34 Victoria University of Wellington Law Review 193 <https://www.victoria.ac.nz/law/research/publications/vuwlr/prev-issues/vol-34-2/mckenzie.pdf>

Mead T, 'Government to Pay $12m to Uninsured Christchurch Red Zone Homeowners' *Newshub* (21 August 2018) <https://www.newshub.co.nz/home/new-zealand/2018/08/government-to-pay-12m-to-uninsured-christchurch-red-zone-homeowners.html>

'Medical Services Reimbursement Rates' (*Transport Accident Commission*) <https://www.tac.vic.gov.au/providers/invoicing-and-fees/fee-schedule/medical-practitioners>

Medicines and Healthcare products Regulatory Agency, 'MHRA Issues New Advice, Concluding a Possible Link between COVID-19 Vaccine AstraZeneca and Extremely Rare, Unlikely to Occur Blood Clots' (7 April 2021) <https://www.gov.uk/government/news/mhra-issues-new-advice-concluding-a-possible-link-between-covid-19-vaccine-astrazeneca-and-extremely-rare-unlikely-to-occur-blood-clots>

Meenan J C, 'Report on an Alternative System for Dealing With Claims Arising From CervicalCheck' (Department of Health, Ireland 2018) <https://www.gov.ie/en/collection/4ed476-judge-meenan-report-on-an-alternative-system-for-dealing-with-claims/>

'Mental Health and Wellbeing Services' (*Transport Accident Commission*) <https://www.tac.vic.gov.au/clients/how-we-can-help/treatments-and-services/services/mental-health-and-wellbeing-services>

Mental Health and Work: New Zealand (OECD 2018) <https://www.oecd-ilibrary.org/social-issues-migration-health/mental-health-and-work-new-zealand_9789264307315-en>

Meredith WR, 'The Meredith Report' (1913) <http://awcbc.org/wp-content/uploads/2013/12/meredith_report.pdf>

Merriam-Webster, 'Subrogation' <https://www.merriam-webster.com/dictionary/subrogation#legalDictionary>

Merritt C, 'Access to Justice Redefined' *The Australian* (24 May 2013)

Meyer D, 'If a COVID-19 Vaccine Does Turn out to Be Dangerous, Who's on the Hook? | Fortune' *Fortune* (7 April 2021) <https://fortune.com/2021/04/07/covid-vaccine-safety-is-astrazeneca-safe-coronavirus-vaccination-liability/>

'Midwives Urge ACC to Rethink "inequities" around Perineal Tear Cover' *Radio New Zealand News* (1 April 2021) <https://www.rnz.co.nz/news/national/439631/midwives-urge-acc-to-rethink-inequities-around-perineal-tear-cover>

Miers D, 'Victims, Criminal Justice and State Compensation' (2019) 9 Societies 29 <https://www.mdpi.com/2075-4698/9/2/29>

Mijatov T, Barraclough T and Forster W, 'The Idea of Access to Justice: Reflections on New Zealand's Accident Compensation (or Personal Injury) System' (2016) 33 Windsor Yearbook of Access to Justice 197

Millán L, 'Legal Aid Agreement Reached with Quebec Government' *LexisNexis The Lawyer's Daily* (16 October 2020) <https://www.thelawyersdaily.ca/articles/21654/legal-aid-agreement-reached-with-quebec-government>

Millar A, 'Redress for Survivors of Abuse – Could It Be a Reality across the UK?' (*Leigh Day Blog*, 2018) <https://www.leighday.co.uk/Blog/September-2018/Redress-for-survivors-of-abuse---could-it-be-a-rea>

Milquet J, 'Strengthening Victims' Rights: From Compensation to Reparation' (March 2019) <https://ec.europa.eu/info/sites/info/files/strengthening_victims_rights_-_from_compensation_to_reparation_rev.pdf>

Ministry of Business Innovation and Employment, 'Changes to ACC Funding Settings' (2020) <https://www.mbie.govt.nz/dmsdocument/11596-changes-to-acc-funding-settings-proactiverelease-pdf>

——, 'Extended Mental Health Support for Those Affected by the 15 March 2019 Terrorist Attack' <https://www.mbie.govt.nz/dmsdocument/5890-extended-mental-health-support-for-those-affected-by-the-15-march-2019-terrorist-attack-proactiverelease-pdf>

Ministry of Business Innovation and Employment and Accident Compensation Corporation, 'ACC and MBIE Briefing Paper: Update on the Response to the Miriam Dean Review and next Phase of Work to Improve Disputes Performance' (2018)

Ministry of Transport, 'Ministry of Transport AV Work Programme' <https://www.transport.govt.nz/multi-modal/technology/specific-transport-technologies/road-vehicle/autonomous-vehicles/ministry-of-transport-av-work-programme/>

——, 'Safety Annual Statistics – Motorcyclists' <https://www.transport.govt.nz/statistics-and-insights/safety-annual-statistics/sheet/motorcyclists>

——, 'Overview of Ministry's Autonomous Vehicles Work Programme' (2019)

Mittelstadt B and others, 'The Ethics of Algorithms: Mapping the Debate' (2014) 3 Big Data & Society

Bibliography

'Montreal Pulls the Plug on E-Scooters on Its Territory' *Montreal Gazette* (19 February 2020) <https://montrealgazette.com/news/local-news/montreal-pulls-the-plug-on-e-scooters-on-its-territory>

Moore A, 'ACC for the Cows? Analysing How Best to Deal with the Losses Caused by Biosecurity Breaches' (2019) 26/2019 <https://ssrn.com/abstract=3477020>

Moréteau O, 'Basic Questions of Tort Law from a French Perspective' in Helmut Koziol (ed), *Basic Questions of Tort Law from a Comparative Perspective* (1st edn, Jan Sramek Verlag 2015)

'Motor Accident Injury Insurance and Automated Vehicles: Discussion Paper' (2018) <www.ntc.gov.au>

'Motor Accidents (Compensation) Act (Northern Territory)'

Motor Accidents Insurance Board, 'Annual Report 2017-2018' <http://www.maib.tas.gov.au/wp-content/uploads/2018/10/AnnualReport2018.pdf>

'Motor Vehicle Accidents (Lifetime Support Scheme) Act 2013 (South Australia)' <https://www.legislation.sa.gov.au/lz?path=%2FC%2FA%2FMOTOR%20VEHICLE%20ACCIDENTS%20(LIFETIME%20SUPPORT%20SCHEME)%20ACT%202013>

Muir C, Johnston IR and Howard E, 'Evolution of a Holistic Systems Approach to Planning and Managing Road Safety: The Victorian Case Study, 1970-2015' (2018) 24 Injury Prevention i19 <https://injuryprevention.bmj.com/content/24/Suppl_1/i19>

Mungwira RG and others, 'Global Landscape Analysis of No-Fault Compensation Programmes for Vaccine Injuries: A Review and Survey of Implementing Countries' (2020) 15(5) PLoS ONE e0233334 <https://doi.org/10.1371/journal.pone.0233334.g001>

Namiri NK and others, 'Electric Scooter Injuries and Hospital Admissions in the United States, 2014-2018' (2020) 155 JAMA Surgery 357

'National Human Rights Consultation Report' (2009) <https://alhr.org.au/wp/wp-content/uploads/2018/02/National-Human-Rights-Consultation-Report-2009-copy.pdf>

National Injury Insurance Agency Queensland, 'Annual Report 2017–18' <www.niis.qld.gov.au>

National Transport Commission, 'Barriers to the Safe Use of Innovative Vehicles and Motorised Mobility Devices' (2019) <www.ntc.gov.au>

——, 'Barriers to the Safe Use of Personal Mobility Devices' (2019) <www.ntc.gov.au>

——, 'Motor Accident Injury Insurance and Automated Vehicles' (2019) <www.ntc.gov.au>

New South Wales Law Reform Commission, 'Accident Compensation: A Transport Accidents Scheme for New South Wales', vol 43 (1984)

'New Zealand Economic Snapshot' <https://www.oecd.org/economy/new-zealand-economic-snapshot/>

New Zealand Government, 'A Blueprint for Health & Safety at Work' (2013) <http://www.mbie.govt.nz/info-services/employment-skills/workplace-health-and-safety-reform/document-and-image-library/working-safer-key-documents/safety-first-blueprint.pdf>

——, 'Further Work to Improve ACC Dispute Resolution' (2016) <https://www.beehive.govt.nz/release/further-work-improve-acc-dispute-resolution>

——, 'FairWay Change Positive for Staff and Customers' (2017) <https://www.beehive.govt.nz/release/fairway-change-positive-staff-and-customers>

New Zealand Law Commission, 'Personal Injury: Prevention and Recovery – Report on the Accident Compensation Scheme' (1988) <http://www.lawcom.govt.nz/sites/default/files/projectAvailableFormats/NZLC R4 part 1.pdf>

New Zealand Parliament, *Personal Injury: A Commentary on the Report of the Royal Commission of Inquiry into Compensation for Personal Injury in New Zealand* (Government Printer 1969)

New Zealand Transport Agency, 'Testing Autonomous Vehicles in New Zealand' <https://www.nzta.govt.nz/vehicles/vehicle-types/automated-and-autonomous-vehicles/testing-autonomous-vehicles-in-new-zealand/>

New Zealand Treasury, 'New Zealand's Future Natural Disaster Insurance Scheme: Proposed Changes to the EQC Act 1993' (2015) <http://www.treasury.govt.nz/publications/reviews-consultation/eqc/pdfs/eqc-rev-discussion-doc.pdf>

Nguyen C and Noy I, 'Insuring Earthquakes: How Would the Californian and Japanese Insurance Programs Have Fared after the 2011 New Zealand Earthquake?' (2020) 44(2) Disasters 367

'No-Fault Compensation Programme for COVID-19 Vaccines Is a World First' <https://www.who.int/news/item/22-02-2021-no-fault-compensation-programme-for-covid-19-vaccines-is-a-world-first>

Nolan-Haley J, 'SYMPOSIUM: International Dispute Resolution and Access to Justice: Comparative Law Perspectives' [2020] Journal of Dispute Resolution 391

Northern Territory Motor Accidents (Compensation) Commission, 'Annual Report 2016-17' <https://www.ntmacc.com.au/MACC_Annual_Report_2017.pdf>

'NT Government Confirms $424m TIO Sale after Months of Speculation' *ABC News* (2014) <https://www.abc.net.au/news/2014-11-24/nt-government-confirms-$424m-tio-sale/5912838>

O'Scannlain DF, 'What Role Should Foreign Practice and Precedent Play in the Interpretation of Domestic Law' (2005) 80 Notre Dame Law Review 893

O'Sullivan T and Tokeley K, 'Consumer Product Failure Causing Personal Injury Under the No-Fault Accident Compensation Scheme in New Zealand-a Let-off for Manufacturers?', *Product Safety, Consumers' Health and Liability Law Conference* (Springer 2017) <https://doi.org/10.1007/s10603-018-9383-2>

O Neill I, 'Independent Assessment of Claims for Ex Gratia Payment Arising from the Judgment of the ECtHR in the Louise O'Keeffe v Ireland Case' (2019) <https://www.education.ie/en/Learners/Information/Former-Residents-of-Industrial-Schools/ECHR-OKeeffe-v-Ireland/independent-assessment-process/okeeffe-v-ireland-decision-of-the-independent-assessor.pdf>

OECD, 'Global Insurance Market Trends' (2019) <www.oecd.org/daf/fin/insurance/oecdinsurancestatistics.htm>

Office of the Ombudsman, 'Opportunity Lost: An Investigation by the Ombudsman into the Administration of the Magdalen Restorative Justice Scheme' (November 2017) <https://www.ombudsman.ie/publications/reports/opportunity-lost/>

Oliphant K, 'Beyond Woodhouse: Devising New Principles for Determining ACC Boundary Issues' (2004) 35 Victoria University of Wellington Law Review 915

Bibliography

——, 'Beyond Misadventure: Compensation for Medical Injuries in New Zealand' (2007) 15 Medical Law Review 357

——, 'Landmarks of No-Fault in the Common Law', *Shifts in Compensation between Private and Public Systems (Tort and Insurance Law Vol. 22)* (Springer 2007) <http://link.springer.com/10.1007/978-3-211-71554-3_3>

——, 'Basic Questions of Tort Law from the Perspective of England and the Commonwealth', *Basic Questions of Tort Law from a Comparative Perspective* (Jan Sramek Verlag 2015)

—— (ed), *The Liability of Public Authorities in Comparative Perspective* (Intersentia 2016)

——, 'Liability for Road Accidents Caused by Driverless Cars' [2019] Singapore Comparative Law Review 190

'Online Application Instructions' <https://covaxclaims.com/online-application-instructions/>

Owen S, 'Regressivity in Public Natural Hazard Insurance: A Quantitative Analysis of the New Zealand Case' <https://wzukusers.storage.googleapis.com/user-30969499/documents/5b44142c06e87eKoIwKZ/Owen_Sally.pdf>

Palmer G, 'Sir Owen Woodhouse Memorial Lecture 2018' (Wellington September 2018)

——, *Compensation for Incapacity: A Study of Law and Social Change in New Zealand and Australia* (Oxford University Press 1979)

——, *Reform: A Memoir* (Victoria University Press 2013)

Paterson T, 'Germany Admits Enslaving and Abusing a Generation of Children' *Independent.co.uk* (14 December 2010) <https://www.independent.co.uk/news/world/europe/germany-admits-enslaving-and-abusing-a-generation-of-children-2159589.html>

'Paying Levies If You Own or Drive a Vehicle' <https://www.acc.co.nz/about-us/how-levies-work/paying-levies-if-you-own-or-drive-a-vehicle/>

Pearl T, 'Compensation at the Crossroads: Autonomous Vehicles and Alternative Victim Compensation Schemes' (2018) 60 William & Mary Law Review 1827

Perry A, 'Electric Scooters Work Brilliantly in Europe – So Why Not Here?' *The Age* (14 September 2019) <https://www.theage.com.au/national/victoria/electric-scooters-work-brilliantly-in-europe-so-why-not-here-20190913-p52r1e.html>

Petit J and Shladover SE, 'Potential Cyberattacks on Automated Vehicles' (2015) 16 IEEE Transactions on Intelligent Transportation Systems 546

Peyer S, 'Sonia Macleod and Christopher Hodges, Redress Schemes for Personal Injuries (Book Review)' (2019) 27(3) Medical Law Review 534 <https://academic.oup.com/medlaw/advance-article-abstract/doi/10.1093/medlaw/fwy037/5146517>

Pillath S and European Parliamentary Research Service, 'Briefing: Automated Vehicles in the EU' (2016) <https://www.europarl.europa.eu/RegData/etudes/BRIE/2016/573902/EPRS_BRI(2016)573902_EN.pdf>

Popa T, 'Practitioner Perspectives on Continuing Legal Challenges in Mental Harm and Medical Negligence: Time for a No-Fault Approach?' (2017) 25 Tort Law Review 19

——, 'Don't Look for Fault, Find a Remedy! Exploring Alternative Forms of Compensating Medical Injuries in Australia, New Zealand and Belgium' (2019) 27 Tort Law Review 120

Posner RA, *Economic Analysis of Law* (9th edn, Wolters Kluwer Law & Business 2014)

'Preliminary Findings of the Visit to Belgium' (*United Nations Office of the High Commissioner for Human Rights*, 2018) <https://www.ohchr.org/EN/NewsEvents/Pages/DisplayNews.aspx?NewsID=23164&LangID=E>

PriceWaterhouseCoopers, 'Accident Compensation Corporation New Zealand Scheme Review' (2008)

'Private Health Care Covered by the Public Automobile Insurance Plan' <https://saaq. gouv.qc.ca/en/traffic-accident/public-automobile-insurance-plan/covered-how/ health-care/?ADMCMD_prev=IGNORE&cHash=433a574c7ff36b131fcd8f373a9 5e879>

Productivity Commission, 'Productivity Commission Inquiry Report – Disability Care and Support, Volume 1' (2011) <http://www.pc.gov.au/inquiries/completed/disability-support/report/disability-support-volume1.pdf>

——, 'Productivity Commission Inquiry Report – Disability Care and Support, Volume 2' (2011) <http://www.pc.gov.au/inquiries/completed/disability-support/report/disability-support-volume2.pdf>

——, 'Productivity Commission Inquiry Report – Overview and Recommendations' (2011) <http://www.pc.gov.au/inquiries/completed/disability-support/report/disability-support-overview-booklet.pdf>

——, 'Study Report – National Disability Insurance Scheme (NDIS) Costs' (2017) <http://www.pc.gov.au/inquiries/completed/ndis-costs/report/ndis-costs.pdf>

'Program Protocol' (*COVAX AMC*) <https://covaxclaims.com/program-protocol/>

Province of British Columbia, 'Better Benefits, Lower Rates: Moving to a Care-Based Insurance Model' (February 2020)

Province of Manitoba, 'Manitoba Hepatitis C Compassionate Assistance Program (MHCAP)' <http://www.gov.mb.ca/health/hcv/index.html>

Québec Government, 'Rapport Du Comité d'étude Sur l'assurance-Automobile' (1974)

Quirke J, 'The Magdalen Commission Report' (May 2013) <https://www.justice.ie/en/ JELR/THE%20Quirke%20report.pdf/Files/THE%20Quirke%20report.pdf>

Rankin MB, 'Access To Justice and the Institutional Limits of Independent Courts' (2012) 30 Windsor Yearbook of Access to Justice 101

Raposo VL, 'Pigs Don't Fly and You Cannot Expect Absolutely Safe COVID-19 Vaccines (But You Should Expect a Fair Compensation)' (2021) 28 European Journal of Health Law 1 <http://www.ncbi.nlm.nih.gov/pubmed/33878713>

Reid J and Mackessack A, 'New Zealand Accident Compensation: What's Happening?', *Institute of Actuaries of Australia Accident Compensation Seminar* (Brisbane, November 2011)

Reid TR, *The Healing of America: A Global Quest for Better, Cheaper, and Fairer Health Care* (Penguin 2010)

Rennie D, 'ACC and the Woodhouse Principles: Real Compensation' (*New Zealand Law Society*, 2019) <https://www.lawsociety.org.nz/news/lawtalk/issue-926/acc-and-the-woodhouse-principles-real-compensation/>

Resodihardjo S and others, 'The Reform of Dutch Disability Insurance: A Crisis-Induced Shift of Preferences and Possibilities' in *Reform in Europe* (1st edn, Routledge 2018) 107

'Review an ACC Decision' <https://www.acc.co.nz/contact/get-a-decision-reviewed/ #getting-advice-from-a-third-party>

Rhode D, *Access to Justice* (Oxford University Press 2006)

Richards J-A and Schalatek L, 'Not a Silver Bullet: Why the Focus on Insurance to Address Loss and Damage Is a Distraction from Real Solutions' (Heinrich Böll Stiftung North America 2018)

Rishworth P, 'Writing Things Unwritten: Common Law in New Zealand's Constitution' (2016) 14 International Journal of Constitutional Law 137

——, *The New Zealand Bill of Rights* (Oxford University Press 2003)

Rizzi M, 'A Dangerous Method: Correlations and Proof of Causation in Vaccine Related Injuries' (2018) 9 Journal of European Tort Law 289

'Road Injury Dashboard Shines a Light on Real Cost of Road Trauma – IRAP' *iRAP* (29 March 2021) <https://www.irap.org/2021/03/ausrap-news-road-injury-dashboard-shines-a-light-on-real-cost-of-road-trauma/>

Robinson MA, 'Accident Compensation in Australia – No-Fault Schemes' <http://www.robinson.com.au/Accident Compensation in Australia-No-Fault Schemes-book.pdf>

Rosen K, 'MPI Returning $110M to Provide Financial Relief to Policy Holders' *CTV news* (23 April 2020) <https://winnipeg.ctvnews.ca/mpi-returning-110m-to-provide-financial-relief-to-policy-holders-1.4908417>

Rousseau-Houle T, 'Le Régime Québécois d'assurance Automobile, Vingt Ans Après' (1998) 39 Les Cahiers de droit <https://doi.org/10.7202/043491ar>

Royal Commission into Institutional Responses to Child Sexual Abuse, 'Final Report Recommendations'

——, 'Redress and Civil Litigation' <https://www.childabuseroyalcommission.gov.au/redress-and-civil-litigation>

——, 'Redress and Civil Litigation' (2015) <http://www.childabuseroyalcommission.gov.au/policy-and-research/redress>

——, 'Final Report – Preface and Executive Summary' (2017)

'Royal Commission of Inquiry into Building Failure Caused by the Canterbury Earthquakes' (2012) <https://canterbury.royalcommission.govt.nz/Final-Report-Volume-Six-Contents>

Royal Commission of Inquiry into Historical Abuse in State Care, 'Terms of Reference' (2018) <https://www.dia.govt.nz/diawebsite.nsf/Files/Royal-Commission-of-Inquiry-into-Historical-Abuse-in-State-Care/$file/Royal-Commission-Terms-of-Reference-for-consultation.pdf>

Royal Commission to Inquire into and Report upon Workers Compensation, *Compensation for Personal Injury in New Zealand* (Government Printing Office 1967)

——, 'Part 2 – Introductory Survey' (Government Printing Office 1967)

——, 'Part 9 – Conclusions and Recommendations' (Government Printing Office 1967)

Sachs JA, 'Social and Economic Rights: Can They Be Made Justiciable' (2000) 53 SMU Law Review 1381

SAE International, 'Taxonomy and Definitions for Terms Related to Driving Automation Systems for On-Road Motor Vehicles'

'SAE International Releases Updated Visual Chart for Its "Levels of Driving Automation" Standard for Self-Driving Vehicles' (December 2018) <https://www.sae.org/news/press-room/2018/12/sae-international-releases-updated-visual-chart-for-its-"levels-of-driving-automation"-standard-for-self-driving-vehicles>

Samson M, *Le Droit à l'égalité Dans l'accès Aux Biens et Aux Services: L'originalité Des Garanties Offertes Dans La Charte Québécoise*, vol 38 (2008)

Sanche S and others, 'High Contagiousness and Rapid Spread of Severe Acute Respiratory Syndrome Coronavirus 2' (2020) 26 Emerging Infectious Diseases 1470

Saskatchewan Government Insurance, 'The Ability to Sue'

Scally G, 'Scoping Inquiry into the CervicalCheck Screening Programme Supplementary Report' (June 2019) <http://scallyreview.ie/wp-content/uploads/2019/06/Supplementary-Report-Final-Master-190607.pdf>

Schellekens M, 'Law, Innovation and Technology No-Fault Compensation Schemes for Self-Driving Vehicles No-Fault Compensation Schemes for Self-Driving Vehicles' <http://www.tandfonline.com/action/journalInformation?journalCode=rlit20>

——, 'No-Fault Compensation Schemes for Self-Driving Vehicles' (2018) 10(2) Law, Innovation and Technology 314 <https://www.narcis.nl/publication/RecordID/oai:tilburguniversity.edu:publications%2F5dc6cc56-ce7a-46ff-986b-0b2f8a28010a>

Schmidt V, 'Why ACC Is Turning Away Traumatised Mosque Survivors' *Radio New Zealand News* (14 May 2019) <https://www.rnz.co.nz/news/in-depth/389140/why-acc-is-turning-away-traumatised-mosque-survivors>

Schneiderman D, 'A. V. Dicey, Lord Watson, and the Law of the Canadian Constitution in the Late Nineteenth Century' (1998) 16 Law and History Review 495

Schnoor J, 'No-Fault Automobile Insurance in Manitoba: An Overview' (1998) 39 Les Cahiers de droit 335

Schulz JL, 'Evaluating Manitoba's Automobile Injury Mediation Pilot Project' (2018) 41 Manitoba Law Journal 21 <https://movisa.org.mx/images/NoBS_Report.pdf>

Schwartz VE and Silverman C, 'The Case in Favor of Civil Justice Reform' (2016) 65 Emory Law Journal Online 2065 <http://www.manhattan-institute.org/pdf/TLI-KStreet.pdf>

Select Committee on Compensation for Personal Injury in New Zealand and Gair GF, *Report of Select Committee on Compensation for Personal Injury in New Zealand.* (Government Printer 1970)

Shay DK and others, 'Safety Monitoring of the Janssen (Johnson & Johnson) COVID-19 Vaccine – United States, March–April 2021' (2021) 70 MMWR. Morbidity and Mortality Weekly Report <http://www.cdc.gov/mmwr/volumes/70/wr/mm7018e2.htm?s_cid=mm7018e2_w>

Siems M, 'New Directions in Comparative Law' in Mathias Reimann and Reinhard Zimmermann (eds), *The Oxford Handbook of Comparative Law* (2nd edn, Oxford University Press 2019)

Simpson A, 'Sweedman v Transport Accident Commission: State Residence Discrimination and the High Court's Retreat into Characterisation' (2006) 34 Federal Law Review 363

Singireddy SRR and Daim TU, 'Technology Roadmap: Drone Delivery – Amazon Prime Air' in Tugrul Daim, Leong Chan and Judith Estep (eds), *Infrastructure and Technology Management* (Springer 2018) <https://link.springer.com/chapter/10.1007/978-3-319-68987-6_13>

Slattery P, Saeri AK and Bragge P, 'Research Co-Design in Health: A Rapid Overview of Reviews' (2020) 18 Health Research Policy and Systems <https://doi.org/10.1186/s12961-020-0528-9>

Smits J, 'Private Law and Fundamental Rights: A Sceptical View in: Constitutionalisation of Private Law', *Constitutionalisation of Private Law* (Brill 2006)

Smyth J, 'New Zealand's "Go Hard and Early" Covid Policy Reaps Economic Rewards' *Financial Times* (17 December 2020) <https://www.ft.com/content/b8c4ab58-99db-4af2-9449-5fd70a9235ce>

Société de l'assurance automobile du Québec, 'Proposed Insurance Contributions for 2019–2021' (2017)

——, 'Rapport Annuel de Gestion 2018' (2018) <https://saaq.gouv.qc.ca/fileadmin/documents/publications/rapport-annuel-gestion-2018.pdf>

——, 'Rapport Annuel de Gestion' (2019)

——, *The Insurance Policy for All Quebecers* (2019) <https://saaq.gouv.qc.ca/fileadmin/documents/publications/automobile-insurance-policy-quebec.pdf>

——, 'A Brief History of the SAAQ' <https://saaq.gouv.qc.ca/en/saaq/a-brief-history-of-the-saaq/accessible-version/>

——, 'Automobile and Home Adaptation' <https://saaq.gouv.qc.ca/en/traffic-accident/public-automobile-insurance-plan/covered-how/automobile-home-adaptation/>

——, 'Autonomous Vehicles' <https://saaq.gouv.qc.ca/en/road-safety/modes-transportation/autonomous-vehicles/>

——, 'If You Have an Accident in Québec' <https://saaq.gouv.qc.ca/en/tourists-and-newcomers/accident/>

——, 'Indemnity for Students' <https://saaq.gouv.qc.ca/en/traffic-accident/public-automobile-insurance-plan/covered-how/financial-compensation/students/>

——, 'Insurance Contributions' <https://saaq.gouv.qc.ca/en/traffic-accident/public-automobile-insurance-plan/insurance-contributions/>

——, 'Low-Speed Electric Scooters' <https://saaq.gouv.qc.ca/en/saaq/documents/pilot-projects/low-speed-electric-scooters/>

——, 'Occupational, Educational or Social Reintegration' <https://saaq.gouv.qc.ca/en/traffic-accident/public-automobile-insurance-plan/covered-how/occupational-reintegration/>

——, 'Personal Home Assistance' <https://saaq.gouv.qc.ca/en/traffic-accident/public-automobile-insurance-plan/covered-how/personal-home-assistance/>

——, 'Strategic Plan' <https://saaq.gouv.qc.ca/en/saaq/performance/strategic-plan/>

Solomon R, 'Reviewing Victoria's Charter of Rights and the Limits to Our Democracy' (2017) 42 Alternative Law Journal 195 <http://journals.sagepub.com/altlj>

'South Africa's Vaccine Compensation Fund Could Cost $17.5 Mln in First Year' *Reuters* (20 April 2021) <https://www.reuters.com/world/africa/south-africas-vaccine-compensation-fund-could-cost-175-mln-first-year-2021-04-20/>

Spencer K, 'Unemployment Insurance: What Can It Offer NZ?' Report for the Technology and the Future of Work Inquiry (Productivity Commission July 2019)

Spigelman JJ, 'The Common Law Bill of Rights', *Statutory Interpretation and Human Rights: McPherson Lecture Series* (University of Queensland Press 2008) <http://ssrn.com/abstract=1806775>

St John S, 'Reflections on the Woodhouse Legacy for the 21st Century' (2020) 51 Victoria University of Wellington Law Review 295 <https://ojs.victoria.ac.nz/vuwlr/article/view/6572/5734>

Stephens M, 'The Right to Social Security' in Margaret Bedggood and Kris Gledhill (eds), *Law into Action Economic, Social and Cultural Rights in Aotearoa New Zealand* (Thomson Reuters 2011)

Stewart K and Toy-Cronin B, 'The New Zealand Legal Services Mapping Project: Finding Free and Low-Cost Legal Services' (2020)

'Stiftung Anerkennung Und Hilfe – Wer Kann Sich Anmelden?' <http://www.stiftung-anerkennung-und-hilfe.de/DE/Infos-fuer-Betroffene/Wer-kann-sich-anmelden/wer-kann-sich-anmelden.html>

Strong SI, 'Large-Scale Dispute Resolution in Jurisdictions without Judicial Class Actions: Learning from the Irish Experience' (2016) 22 ILSA Journal of International and Comparative Law 341

Studsrød I and Enoksen E, 'Money as Compensation for Historical Abuse: Redress Programs and Social Exchange Theory' (2020) 13 The Journal of the History of Childhood and Youth 288 <https://doi.org/10.1353/hcy.2020.0039https://muse.jhu.edu/article/754490>

Sugarman SD, 'Quebec's Comprehensive Auto No-Fault Scheme and the Failure of Any of the United States to Follow' (1998) 39 Les Cahiers de droit 303

'Supplementary Common Law Protocols' (2020)

Surden H, 'Artificial Intelligence and Law: An Overview' (2019) 35 Georgia State University Law Review 1306

'TAC IRAP Road Injury Dashboard' (*Transport Accident Commission*) <https://www.tac.vic.gov.au/road-safety/statistics/online-crash-database/irap-road-injury-dashboard>

Taggart M, '"Australian Exceptionalism" in Judicial Review' (2008) 36 Federal Law Review 1

Talk – Meet – Resolve, 'Why Use TMR?' <https://www.talkmeetresolve.co.nz/using-our-process/Why-try-TMR>

Tennent D, *Accident Compensation Law* (LexisNexis New Zealand 2013)

Thaker J, 'The Persistence of Vaccine Hesitancy: COVID-19 Vaccination Intention in New Zealand' (2021) 26(2) Journal of Health Communication 1

The Australia Institute, 'The National Climate Disaster Fund' (2019) <https://www.tai.org.au>

The Law Society of the ACT, 'ACT CTP – Cheaper Premiums Come at a Cost' <https://www.actlawsociety.asn.au/news-media/media-releases-2018/act-ctp-cheaper-premiums-come-at-a-cost>

——, 'ACT CTP – Don't Trade Away a Fair and Stable Scheme for Illusory Savings' <https://www.actlawsociety.asn.au/news-media/media-releases-2018/act-ctp-dont-trade-away-a-fair-and-stable-scheme-for-illusory-savings>

The Scottish Government, 'Child Protection: Justice and Support for Child Abuse Survivors' <https://www.gov.scot/policies/child-protection/supporting-child-abuse-survivors/>

'Third Submission on Behalf of the Minister for Education and Skills on Behalf of the State to the Independent Assessor' (2019) <https://www.education.ie/en/Learners/Information/Former-Residents-of-Industrial-Schools/ECHR-OKeeffe-v-Ireland/jan-2019-implementation-of-the-ecthr-judgement-in-the-louise-o'keeffe-case.pdf>

Thompson J and others, 'The Association between Attributions of Responsibility for Motor Vehicle Accidents and Patient Satisfaction: A Study within a No-Fault Injury Compensation System' (2015) 29 Clinical Rehabilitation 500

Thouvenin D, 'French Medical Malpractice Compensation since the Act of March 4, 2002: Liability Rules Combined with Indemnification Rules and Correlated with Several Kinds of Proceedings' (2011) 4 Drexel Law Review 165

Todd S, 'Treatment Injury in New Zealand' (2011) 86 Chicago-Kent Law Review 1169

——, *The Law of Torts in New Zealand*, Stephen Todd (ed) (8th edn, Thomson Reuters 2019)

Bibliography

Torjesen I, 'Covid-19 Will Become Endemic but with Decreased Potency over Time, Scientists Believe' (2021) 372 British Medical Journal 494 <http://dx.doi.org/10.1136/bmj.n494>

Tourism Industry Aoetearoa, 'Submission to Accident Compensation Corporation' (2018) <www.tia.org.nz>

'Transport Accident Amendment Bill 2015 – Explanatory Memorandum'

'Transport Accident Bill 1986 – Explanatory Memorandum'

'Transport Accident Bill 1986 (No. 2) – Explanatory Memorandum'

'Transport Accident Charges Including GST and Duty' (2020)

Transport Accident Commission, '2017/18 Annual Report' <http://www.tac.vic.gov.au/__data/assets/pdf_file/0009/298629/2017-18-TAC-Annual-Report.pdf>

——, 'Annual Report 2019-2020' <https://www.tac.vic.gov.au/__data/assets/pdf_file/0011/470576/TAC-ANNUAL-REPORT-WEB.pdf>

——, 'Claims Statistics' <https://www.tac.vic.gov.au/about-the-tac/our-organisation/what-we-do/claims-statistics>

——, 'Common Law Compensation' <https://www.tac.vic.gov.au/clients/how-we-can-help/compensation/common-law-compensation>

——, 'Dispute Resolution' <https://www.tac.vic.gov.au/clients/working-together/resolving-your-issues/dispute-resolution>

——, 'Having a TAC Decision Reviewed' <https://www.tac.vic.gov.au/content/content/how-we-manage-your-claim/having-a-tac-decision-reviewed>

——, 'Impairment Benefits – Policy' <http://www.tac.vic.gov.au/clients/compensation/impairment-benefits#tabs-3>

——, 'Income Support for Employees' <https://www.tac.vic.gov.au/clients/how-we-can-help/income-support/income-support#howmuch>

——, 'Income Support for Self-Employed People' <https://www.tac.vic.gov.au/clients/how-we-can-help/income-support/income-support-for-self-employed-people>

——, 'Loss of Earnings Capacity (LOEC) Benefits' <https://www.tac.vic.gov.au/clients/how-we-can-help/treatments-and-services/policies/other/loss-of-earnings-capacity-loec-benefits>

——, 'Making a Claim for Compensation' <https://www.tac.vic.gov.au/clients/what-we-can-pay-for/policies/other/making-a-claim-for-compensation>

——, 'Overpayments and Recoveries' <https://www.tac.vic.gov.au/clients/what-we-can-pay-for/policies/other/recoveries#nontacindem>

——, 'Return to Work Support' <https://www.tac.vic.gov.au/clients/how-we-can-help/return-to-work-support>

——, 'Support for Family Members' <https://www.tac.vic.gov.au/clients/how-we-can-help/support-for-family-members?tab=2>

——, 'TAC 2020 Strategy' <https://www.tac.vic.gov.au/__data/assets/pdf_file/0009/192753/TAC_Strategy2020_UPDATE_WEB.pdf>

——, 'TAC Legislation Changes' <http://www.tac.vic.gov.au/providers/for-service-providers/for-legal-professionals/tac-legislation-changes>

——, 'Transport Accident Charge' <http://www.tac.vic.gov.au/about-the-tac/our-organisation/transport-accident-charge>

——, 'Treatments and Services' <https://www.tac.vic.gov.au/clients/how-we-can-help/treatments-and-services>

——, 'Victoria Leads The Way With Self Driving Vehicles' <http://www.tac.vic.gov.au/about-the-tac/media-room/news-and-events/2016/victoria-leads-the-way-with-self-driving-vehicles>

——, 'What We Do' <https://www.tac.vic.gov.au/about-the-tac/our-organisation/what-we-do>

——, 'When a Family Member Dies' <https://www.tac.vic.gov.au/what-to-do-after-an-accident/how-to-claim/when-someone-dies>

——, 'WorkCover – Transport Accidents and Accidents Arising out of the Use of Vehicle Claims' <http://www.tac.vic.gov.au/clients/what-we-can-pay-for/policies/other/workcover-transport-accidents-and-accidents-arising-out-of-the-use-of-vehicle-claims>

——, 'Towards Zero 2016–2020' (2016)

——, 'Annual Report 2018/19' (2019)

Transports Québec, 'Trottinettes Motorisées' <https://www.transports.gouv.qc.ca/fr/modes-transport-utilises/trotinettes-motorisees/Pages/trotinettes-motorisees.aspx>

'Treatment Injury Claims Related to the COVID-19 Vaccines' (data.govt.nz) <https://catalogue.data.govt.nz/dataset/vaccine-injury-compensation/resource/fc4ea73b-5393-4645-a978-36a0c8350a16>

Trebilcock MJ, 'Incentive Issues in the Design of No-Fault Compensation Systems' (1989) 39 University of Toronto Law Journal 19

Trivedi B and others, 'Craniofacial Injuries Seen With the Introduction of Bicycle-Share Electric Scooters in an Urban Setting' (2019) 77 Journal of Oral and Maxillofacial Surgery 2292

Trivedi TK and others, 'Injuries Associated With Standing Electric Scooter Use' (2019) 2 JAMA network open e187381

Trstenjak V, 'General Report: The Influence of Human Rights and Basic Rights in Private Law' in Verica Trstenjak and Petra Weingerl (eds), *The Influence of Human Rights and Basic Rights in Private Law* (Springer 2016)

Trudel Johnston & Lespérance, 'Vehicles Stuck on Highway 13/ Snowstorm of March 14th, 2017' <https://tjl.quebec/en/class-actions/vehicles-stuck-on-highway-13-snowstorm-of-march-14-2017/>

Twomey A, 'Australian Politics Explainer: Gough Whitlam's Dismissal as Prime Minister' (*The Conversation*) <https://theconversation.com/australian-politics-explainer-gough-whitlams-dismissal-as-prime-minister-74148>

'Types of Cover for Self-Employed' <https://www.acc.co.nz/for-business/understanding-your-cover-options/types-of-cover-for-self-employed/>

'Understanding Levies If You Work or Own a Business' <https://www.acc.co.nz/for-business/understanding-levies-if-you-work-or-own-a-business/>

Urho M, 'Compensation for Drug-Related Injuries' (2018) 4 European Review of Private Law 467

US Department of Transportation and National Highway Traffic Safety Administration, 'Federal Automated Vehicles Policy: Accelerating the Next Revolution In Roadway Safety' (2016)

'Vaccination Contre La COVID-19' <https://www.oniam.fr/accidents-medicaux-indemnisés/vaccination-contre-la-covid-19>

Bibliography

'Vaccine Injury Compensation – Types of Injuries' (data.govt.nz, 2020) <https://catalogue.data.govt.nz/dataset/vaccine-injury-compensation/resource/ec6f460d-e672-4693-8233-4fa46cf9dc4c>

'Vaccine Injury Compensation Program' <http://sante.gouv.qc.ca/en/programmes-et-mesures-daide/programme-d-indemnisation-des-victimes-d-une-vaccination/>

van Boom WH and Faure M (eds), *Shifts in Compensation between Private and Public Systems (Tort and Insurance Law Vol. 22)* (Springer 2007)

van Boom WH and Faure M, 'Introducing "Shifts in Compensation Between Private and Public Systems"' in Willem H van Boom and Michael Faure (eds), *Shifts in Compensation between Private and Public Systems (Tort and Insurance Law Vol. 22)* (Springer 2007)

van Dijck G, 'Victim Oriented Tort Law In Action: An Empirical Examination of Catholic Church Sexual Abuse Cases', *Conference on Empirical Legal Studies* (2018) <https://www.law.ox.ac.uk/sites/files/oxlaw/ssrn-id2738633_3.pdf>

van Doorn J and others, 'An Exploration of Third Parties' Preference for Compensation over Punishment: Six Experimental Demonstrations' (2018) 85 Theory and Decision 333 <https://doi.org/10.1007/s11238-018-9665-9>

Van Horn R, 'Corporations and the Rise of Chicago Law and Economics' (2018) 47 Economy and Society 477

Vandersteegen T and others, 'The Impact of No-Fault Compensation on Health Care Expenditures: An Empirical Study of OECD Countries' (2015) 119 Health Policy 367 <https://www.healthpolicyjrnl.com/article/S0168-8510(14)00240-1/pdf>

Vandersteegen T, Marneffe W and Vandijck D, 'Advantages and Disadvantages of the Belgian Not-Only-Fault System for Medical Incidents' (2017) 72 Acta Clinica Belgica 36 <https://www.tandfonline.com/doi/full/10.1080/17843286.2016.1202371>

Vanhooff L, 'Compensation Funds in Belgium' in Thierry Vansweevelt and Britt Weyts (eds), *Compensation Funds in Comparative Perspective* (Intersentia 2020)

Vanhooff L, Vansweevelt T and Weyts B, 'So Many Funds, so Many Alternatives: Compensation Funds as a Solution for Liability Issues in Belgium, the Netherlands and the United Kingdom' (2016) 8 European Journal of Commercial Contract Law 41

Vansweevelt T and others, 'Comparative Analysis of Compensation Funds' in Thierry Vansweevelt and Britt Weyts (eds), *Compensation Funds in Comparative Perspective* (Intersentia 2020)

Vansweevelt T, Lierman S and Buelens W, 'No-Fault Law on Medical Accidents in Belgium: An Evaluation after Six Years' (2019) 10 Journal of European Tort Law 257

'Vehicle Risk Rating (VRR) Removed from ACC Motor Vehicle Levy' <https://www.acc.co.nz/newsroom/stories/vehicle-risk-rating-vrr-removed-from-acc-motor-vehicle-levy/>

Veitch S, 'The Sense of Obligation' (2017) 8 Jurisprudence 415 <https://www.tandfonline.com/action/journalInformation?journalCode=rjpn20>

VicRoads, 'Scooters & Wheeled Recreational Devices' <https://www.vicroads.vic.gov.au/safety-and-road-rules/road-rules/a-to-z-of-road-rules/scooters-and-wheeled-recreational-devices>

Victoria State Government, 'Transport Accident Commission Patients' <https://www2.health.vic.gov.au/hospitals-and-health-services/patient-fees-charges/admitted-patients/compensable-patients/tac>

Victorian Funds Management Corporation, 'Annual Report 2019-20'

Victorian Law Reform Commission, 'Review of the Victims of Crime Assistance Act 1996' (July 2018) <www.lawreform.vic.gov.au/wp-content/uploads/2021/07/VLRC_Victims-of-Crime-Assistance-Act-Report_Web.pdf>

Vines P, Butt M and Grant G, 'When Lump Sum Compensation Runs Out: Personal Responsibility or Legal System Failure?' (2017) 39 Sydney Law Review 365

Wagner G, '(Un)Insurability and the Choice between Market Insurance and Public Compensation Systems', *Shifts in Compensation between Private and Public Systems (Tort and Insurance Law Vol. 22)* (Springer 2007)

——, 'Tort, Social Security, and No-Fault Schemes: Lessons from Real-World Experiments' (2012) 23 Duke Journal of Comparative & International Law 1 <https://pdfs.semanticscholar.org/0849/1023d1456ce49ab02483101a6b5ddcfa988d.pdf>

——, 'Comparative Tort Law' in Mathias Reimann and Reinhard Zimmermann (eds), *The Oxford Handbook of Comparative Law* (2nd edn, Oxford University Press 2019)

Waldie P and Cheney P, 'Quebec, Manitoba Systems Called the Best' *The Globe and Mail* (14 June 2003) <https://www.theglobeandmail.com/news/national/quebec-manitoba-systems-called-the-best/article1017430/>

Watson K and Kottenhagen R, 'Patients' Rights, Medical Error and Harmonisation of Compensation Mechanisms in Europe' (2018) 25 European Journal of Health Law 1

Watts K, 'New Zealand' in Thierry Vansweevelt and Britt Weyts (eds), *Compensation Funds in Comparative Perspective* (Intersentia 2020)

——, 'Managing Mass Damages Liability via Tort Law and Tort Alternatives, with Ireland as a Case Study' (2020) 11 Journal of European Tort Law 57 <https://www.degruyter.com/view/journals/jetl/11/1/article-p57.xml>

——, 'Potential of No-Fault Comprehensive Compensation Funds to Deal with Automation and Other 21st Century Transport Developments' (2020) 12 European Journal of Commercial Contract Law 1–21

Watts K and Popa T, 'Injecting Fairness into COVID-19 Vaccine Injury Compensation: No-Fault Solutions' (2021) 12 Journal of European Tort Law 1–39

'Way Finders ACC Navigation Service' <https://www.wayfinders.org.nz/>

Welfare Expert Advisory Group, 'Whakamana Tāngata – Restoring Dignity to Social Security in New Zealand' (2019) <www.weag.govt.nz>

Wessels AB, 'Developing the South African Law of Delict: The Creation of a Statutory Compensation Fund for Crime Victims' (Stellenbosch University 2018)

'What Is Artificial Intelligence and How Is It Used?' *European Parliament* (29 March 2021) <https://www.europarl.europa.eu/news/en/headlines/society/20200827STO85804/what-is-artificial-intelligence-and-how-is-it-used>

Whyte BS, 'Jury's in: More People Covered, Lower Premiums in New CTP Scheme' *The Canberra Times* (24 April 2018) <https://www.canberratimes.com.au/story/6021573/jurys-in-more-people-covered-lower-premiums-in-new-ctp-scheme/>

Wiesbrot D and Breen KJ, 'A No-Fault Compensation System for Medical Injury Is Long Overdue' (2012) 197 Medical Journal of Australia 296 <www.mja.com.au>

Wilhelmsen T and Hagland B, 'Norway' in Britt Weyts (ed), *International Encyclopaedia for Tort Law* (Wolters Kluwer 2017)

Wilkinson G, 'Letter to Hon Gordon Rich-Phillips MLC (28/10/2013)'

'Will ACC Provide Cover for COVID-19 Vaccination Injuries?' <https://covid.immune.org.nz/faq/will-acc-provide-cover-covid-19-vaccination-injuries>

Williams A, 'Wrongful Birth and Lost Wages: J v Accident Compensation Corp' (2018) 2 New Zealand Women's Law Journal 295

Williams G, 'The Victorian Charter of Human Rights and Responsibilities: Origins and Scope' (2006) 30 Melbourne University Law Review 880

Winkler K, 'Effects of No-Fault Auto Insurance on Safety Incentives' (February 2015) <https://ssrn.com/abstract=2747006>

Winter JD, Cole C and Wacholder J, 'Toward a Global Solution on Vaccine Liability and Compensation' (2019) 74 Food and Drug Law Journal 1 <http://www.who.int/csr/don/7-september-2018-ebola-drc/en/>

Winter S, 'Australia's Ex Gratia Redress' (2009) 13 Australian Industrial Law Review 49 <http://www.austlii.edu.au/au/journals/AUIndigLawRw/2009/3.pdf>

——, 'Redressing Historic Abuse in New Zealand: A Comparative Critique' (2018) 70 Political Science 1 <https://www.tandfonline.com/action/journalInformation?journalCode=rpnz20>

——, 'Two Models of Monetary Redress: A Structural Analysis' (2018) 13 Victims & Offenders 293

Wise J, 'Covid-19: European Countries Suspend Use of Oxford-AstraZeneca Vaccine after Reports of Blood Clots' (2021) 372 British Medical Journal (Clinical research ed.) n699 <http://dx.doi.org/10.1136/bmj.n699>

Wong P-H, Douglas T and Savulescu J, 'Compensation for Geoengineering Harms and No-Fault Climate Change Compensation' <http://geoengineeringgovernanceresearch.org>

Wood N and others, 'Australia Needs a Vaccine Injury Compensation Scheme – Upcoming COVID-19 Vaccines Make Its Introduction Urgent' (2020) 49 Australian Journal of General Practice

Woodhouse O, 'The ACC Concept' <http://docs.business.auckland.ac.nz/Doc/ACC-Forum-2011-17-Woodhouse-ACC-Concept-Paper-revised.pdf>

WorkSafe, 'Prosecution Policy' <https://www.worksafe.govt.nz/laws-and-regulations/operational-policy-framework/operational-policies/prosecution-policy/>

——, 'Role and Responsibilities' <https://worksafe.govt.nz/about-us/who-we-are/role-and-responsibilities/>

World Bank, 'Strength of Legal Rights Index' <https://data.worldbank.org/indicator/IC.LGL.CRED.XQ?locations=NZ>

World Health Organization, 'Child Maltreatment' (2016) <https://www.who.int/news-room/fact-sheets/detail/child-maltreatment>

Yoshikawa J, 'Sharing the Costs of Artificial Intelligence: Universal No-Fault Social Insurance for Personal Injuries' (2019) 21 Vanderbilt Journal of Entertainment Technology Law 1155

Yu KH, Beam AL and Kohane IS, 'Artificial Intelligence in Healthcare' (2018) 2 Nature Biomedical Engineering 719 <http://dx.doi.org/10.1038/s41551-018-0305-z>

INDEX

A

access to court   48, 73, 177, 216, 294, 301, 307, 314, 341, 366, 447
   statutory bar on tort proceedings   380
access to justice   294, 299–300, 337, 354, 358, 370–372, 375, 381, 414, 439, 447–449
   access to legal information   414, 439, 448
   definition   371, 381
   enhancements of   372, 449
   limitations on   375, 449
Accident Compensation Corporation (ACC) Scheme   11, 16, 45, 50, 53–55, 57, 59–76, 78, 81–82, 128, 134–135, 137, 139, 144, 146, 148–150, 152–153, 157, 159, 170, 173, 175, 181, 190, 192, 195, 201, 210, 212, 216–221, 227, 229–231, 233–236, 239–240, 242–245, 247, 250, 252, 282, 318, 320, 324, 326, 376, 391, 394, 399, 408, 424–426, 432, 437, 438, 440, 450
   access to court   73, 216, 326
   access to justice   376
   administration   72
   background   54
   claims procedure   71, 190, 192, 195
   comparison to liability based system   76, 128, 150, 159
   comparison to other compensation fund structures   78, 170
   dispute resolution   216–221, 229–230, 233–236
   eligibility   59, 63, 146, 150, 153, 320, 394
   evolution   219, 231, 239, 282
   expansion   78
   extension   62–63, 66–67, 135, 137, 144, 152, 175, 391, 399, 408
   funding   59, 240, 247, 250, 425
   historical abuse   45
   human rights   318, 324
   industrial diseases   54, 65, 70
   interaction with other legislation   74–75, 144, 426
   legal profession   55, 57, 75, 220, 227, 235, 324
   legislation   57, 391
   levies   78, 139, 239, 242–245, 252, 394, 425
   purpose   54–55, 62, 64, 73, 75, 81, 128, 149, 181, 391, 399, 437
   purpose of compensation   212
   quantum of compensation   71, 210, 234, 438
   scope   54, 61, 64–65, 68–69, 72, 74, 82, 134, 149, 153, 437

   structure   60–61
   treatment injury   68, 70, 146, 157, 170, 173, 234, 252, 424, 432, 440, 450
   type of compensation   71, 152, 201
   workplace accidents   54, 75, 148
artificial intelligence   49, 135, 140, 145, 191, 415–416, 418, 422, 439–440, 450
   autonomous vehicles   418, 440, 450
   healthcare applications   422, 440, 450
Australia   28, 42, 45, 81, 86, 100, 147, 160, 315, 413
   National Disability Insurance Scheme   28, 81, 100
   National Injury Insurance Scheme   28, 81, 86, 100, 147
   National Redress Scheme for Victims of Sexual Abuse   45, 315, 413
   Northern Territory   18

B

Belgium   147, 149, 153–155, 159–161, 355
   Fedris   29
   Fund for Medical Accidents   29
birth-related injuries   6

C

Canada   120–121, 126, 429, 436
   Alberta   14, 121, 450
   British Columbia   14, 121, 450
   Ontario   18, 121
   Saskatschewan   120
   vaccine injury compensation schemes   126, 429, 436
causation   29, 186, 194, 236, 425, 428
civil law   38, 49, 198
climate change   7, 49, 452
common law   2–3, 11–12, 15–16, 21, 31, 49, 90, 198
compensation   36, 41, 152, 202–209, 211–213, 238, 242, 278–279, 403–404, 406, 434, 438, 440, 445
   levy   242
   non-pecuniary   202–209, 211–213, 404, 438
   pecuniary   152, 202–209, 211–213
   purpose   41, 152, 404, 406
   quantum   36, 41, 238, 278–279, 403, 434, 440, 445
compensation fund   5, 11, 18, 28–29, 33, 44, 47, 50, 129–132, 145, 161, 163, 170–171, 176, 181, 183–184, 186, 188–238, 277–279, 295–296,

Intersentia

485

Index

317, 386, 388, 390, 403, 409, 420, 429–432,
434–437, 439–440, 442–443, 446, 450
claims procedure   189–190, 194–195,
295, 432, 444
comparison with tort   198, 214–215
core principles   388, 430, 442
crime victim compensation fund
37, 39, 47
definition   5, 11, 18, 29, 33, 44, 176, 184, 186,
386, 388, 429, 442
dispute resolution   215–236, 296, 447
eligibility   131, 145, 431
establishment   183, 198–215, 436,
440, 443
evolution   47, 129–130, 132, 197, 278, 409,
420, 450
justification   44, 161, 184, 237
legislative design   390, 437, 439,
444, 446
purpose   50, 129–130, 132, 161, 163,
170–171, 181, 198, 200, 277, 295, 317, 390,
435, 437, 442–443, 446, 450
purpose of compensation   211, 213–215
quantum   198, 200
quantum of compensation   210, 214–215,
238, 278–279, 295, 403, 434, 440, 445
scope   237
type of compensation   188–198, 201–214
criminal injury   6

D
dispute resolution   4

E
economics   31
emergency public health applications   415, 426,
440, 451
empirical evidence   41, 49, 177, 189, 197, 200,
236, 292, 406, 444
Europe   30, 39, 299, 310, 355, 358, 429
European Convention on Human
Rights   299, 310, 355, 358
ex ante   30
ex gratia   33–35, 41–42, 50, 365

F
financial   18, 29, 33, 201, 236–279, 296–297,
400–403, 405, 411, 419, 431, 438, 440,
442–443
actuarial approach   237, 267, 274–276, 400,
402–403, 431, 445
funding   18, 29, 201, 236–279, 296, 400–401,
445
investment income   275, 401, 445
levy   33, 275, 419, 440, 442, 450
prudential supervision   276, 297, 402, 438,
445
sustainability   18, 236–279, 296, 405, 411,
438, 444
France   147, 149, 153–155, 159–161,
355, 429

H
historic abuse   36–37, 51, 150
compensation funds   40, 44, 47–48
historical harms   6
human rights   2–4, 21–22, 26, 47–48, 50, 117,
299, 302, 314, 357, 370, 380, 411–413, 439,
447
interaction with private law   357
socio-economic rights   302, 314,
413, 449

I
insurance   1–10, 12–17, 19–21, 23, 30–33, 50,
102, 105, 107–108, 114, 121, 130–131, 137,
140, 142, 151, 155, 164, 167–168, 170–172,
194, 239, 250, 435, 442–443
international law   7
Ireland   42

L
legislatures failing   187
liability   4, 41, 149, 185, 187, 279–294, 297, 363,
406, 408, 419, 428, 435, 438–440, 450
public tort liability   281, 288, 408, 439,
446, 450
subrogation   279–294, 297, 406, 419, 438,
440, 446

M
Manitoba Public Insurance (MPI)   11, 13,
103–109, 111–116, 118–119, 121, 123, 125,
127–128, 134–135, 138–139, 145, 147–148,
150, 152–153, 182, 190, 193, 195, 206,
210–211, 213, 223–225, 227, 232–236,
268–273, 284–287, 289–290, 341, 348, 350,
353, 369, 437
access to court   112–113, 341, 353, 369
administration   107
background   105
claims procedure   109, 190, 193, 195
comparison to liability based system   119,
127–128, 150
comparison to other compensation fund
structures   103, 119, 121, 123, 125,
127, 350
dispute resolution   223–225, 232–236
eligibility   114–115, 145, 150, 153
extension   135, 138, 152
funding   268–273
human rights   348, 369
interaction with other legislation   112, 114
legal profession   106, 227, 235
legislation   107, 111, 115
levies   139, 268, 272
purpose   106, 108, 112, 115, 118, 128,
182, 437
purpose of compensation   213
quantum of compensation   119, 210, 234
scope   104, 111–113, 115–116, 134,
147, 153
structure   108, 112, 119

Index

subrogation 284–287, 289–290
type of compensation 109, 152, 206, 210
workplace accidents 148
medical treatment injury 5
methodology 48
military invasion 7
moral hazard 187
motor accident 5
multimodal transport 135–136, 396, 398, 421, 437
multi-party actions 36, 342

N

natural disasters 6, 401, 443
Netherlands 30, 154
New Zealand 47, 78
  Natural Disaster Fund 78
  Royal Commission of Inquiry into Historical Abuse in State Care and in the Care of Faith-based Institutions 47
no-fault 4
  definition 442
non-pecuniary 5
Nordic countries 147, 168–171, 178, 355, 430, 444

O

oil pollution 7

P

pecuniary 5, 30
personal injury 5
pharmaceutical injury 6
political 2, 8, 19, 21
privately administered 18
public interest 32, 141, 408, 440
publicly administered 18

R

restorative justice 37, 213

S

social insurance 8, 28–29, 53, 59, 61–62, 67, 72–73, 81–82, 84, 90, 100, 112, 150, 155–156, 164, 166–168, 170, 172, 175, 177, 251
social security 1–3, 5–6, 8–9, 11–12, 16–17, 20–23, 27–30, 50, 150, 251, 392–393, 399, 442–443
Société de l'assurance du Québec (SAAQ) 11, 13, 103–106, 108–109, 111–119, 121, 123, 125, 127–128, 134–135, 138–139, 142, 145, 147–148, 150, 152–153, 167, 182, 190, 193, 195, 199, 206, 210–211, 213, 223–225, 227, 232–236, 263–268, 284–287, 289–290, 338, 343, 347, 350, 353, 369, 397, 437
  access to court 112–113, 117, 353, 369
  administration 106
  background 104–105
  claims procedure 109, 190, 193, 195
  comparison to liability based system 116, 118–119, 127–128, 150
  comparison to other compensation fund structures 103, 119, 121, 123, 125, 127, 350
  dispute resolution 223–225, 232–236
  eligibility 114–115, 145, 150, 153, 343, 397
  extension 135, 138, 142, 152, 397
  funding 263–268
  human rights 338, 369
  interaction with other legislation 112, 114, 148, 347
  legal profession 106, 227, 235
  legislation 106, 111, 115
  levies 139, 263, 266–267
  purpose 106, 108, 112, 115, 117–118, 128, 167, 182, 437
  purpose of compensation 213
  quantum of compensation 119, 199, 210, 234
  scope 104, 111–113, 115–116, 118, 134, 147, 153
  structure 108, 112, 119
  subrogation 284–287, 289–290
  type of compensation 109, 152, 206, 210
  workplace accidents 148
socio-economic rights 2
solidarity 20, 81, 107, 160, 164–165, 177, 394, 400, 431, 443
strict liability 8

T

terrorism 6
tort litigation 14, 444, 447
Transport Accident Commission (TAC) 11–12, 82, 84–93, 98, 100, 102, 128, 132–135, 139, 143, 145, 147–148, 150, 152–153, 182, 186, 190, 193, 195, 201, 205, 210, 212, 221–223, 227, 232–236, 238–263, 284–287, 289–290, 303, 307, 309, 311, 314, 338, 395, 405, 437
  access to court 84, 307
  administration 82
  background 82
  claims procedure 85, 190, 193, 195
  comparison to liability based system 91, 93, 128, 150
  comparison to other compensation fund structures 91–93, 98, 100, 314
  dispute resolution 221–223, 232–236
  eligibility 85, 87, 145, 150, 153, 309
  extension 100, 102, 135, 139, 143, 152
  funding 82, 87, 238–263
  human rights 303, 338
  interaction with other legislation 89
  legal profession 84, 132, 222, 227, 235
  legislation 84
  levies 139, 257–263
  purpose 84, 90, 128, 182, 395, 437
  purpose of compensation 212
  quantum of compensation 85, 88, 201, 210, 234

Index

scope 86, 88, 91, 133–134, 147, 153, 311
serious injury 86, 186, 205, 222, 238, 395, 405, 437, 444
structure 85
subrogation 284–287, 289–290
type of compensation 85, 152, 201
workplace accidents 148

V
vaccine injury 7, 105, 126, 426, 430
   COVAX scheme 7

W
Woodhouse Report 55
workers' dust disease injuries 6

ABOUT THE AUTHOR

Dr Kim Watts is a Postdoctoral Researcher at the University of Antwerp, Belgium. She holds a PhD in Law from the University of Antwerp, an LLM in Commercial Law and a BA/LLB, both from the University of Auckland. She has many years of experience in legal practice (New Zealand), academic research, the non-profit sector (Ireland, Belgium and the United States), regulatory projects and consulting. She was a Doctoral Research Fellow at the University of Antwerp's Faculty of Law and the recipient of a foreign researcher scholarship from Research Foundation Flanders (FWO). Her doctoral thesis was an international study of alternative liability systems and their application to contemporary risk challenges.

Printed in the USA
CPSIA information can be obtained
at www.ICGtesting.com
LVHW060737300524
781359LV00003B/8